PENGUIN BOOKS

MIRACLE AT MIDWAY

The late Gordon W. Prange was born in Pomeroy, Iowa, on July 16, 1910. He was educated at the University of Iowa and the University of Berlin. He taught history at the University of Maryland as an instructor, assistant professor, associate professor, and full professor from 1937 until his death in May 1980. During World War II he served as an officer in the Naval Reserve, and during the occupation of Japan, from December 1945 until July 1951, he joined General Headquarters, Far East Command, Tokyo, as a civilian. From October 1946 to June 1951 he was chief of General Douglas MacArthur's G-2 Historical Section, and from June through July 1951 he was acting director of the Military History Section. Mr. Prange was the author of the celebrated *At Dawn We Slept: The Untold Story of Pearl Harbor*, also published by Penguin Books.

Donald M. Goldstein is Associate Professor of Public and International Affairs at the University of Pittsburgh.

Katherine V. Dillon is a Chief Warrant Officer, USAF (Ret.).

D0112046

MIRACLE AT MIDWAY

Gordon W. Prange

with Donald M. Goldstein and
Katherine V. Dillon

PENGUIN BOOKS

Penguin Books Ltd, Harmondsworth,
Middlesex, England
Penguin Books, 40 West 23rd Street,
New York, New York 10010, U.S.A.
Penguin Books Australia Ltd, Ringwood,
Victoria, Australia
Penguin Books Canada Limited, 2801 John Street,
Markham, Ontario, Canada L3R 1B4
Penguin Books (N.Z.) Ltd, 182–190 Wairau Road,
Auckland 10, New Zealand

First published in the United States of America by
McGraw-Hill Book Company 1982
Published in Penguin Books by arrangement with
McGraw-Hill Book Company 1983

LIBRARY OF CONGRESS CATALOGING IN PUBLICATION DATA
Prange, Gordon William, 1910–1980
    Miracle at Midway.
    Bibliography: p.
    Includes index.
    1. Midway, Battle of, 1942. I. Goldstein, Donald M.
II. Dillon, Katherine V. III. Title.
D774.M5P7   1983   940.54'26   83-9637
ISBN 0 14 00.6814 7

Printed in the United States of America by
R. R. Donnelley and Sons Company, Crawfordsville, Indiana
Set in Linotron Caledonia

CONTENTS

List of Illustrations

INTRODUCTION

When the late Gordon W. Prange, Professor of History at the University of Maryland, passed away in 1980, he left behind several manuscripts in various stages of completion. The first of these, a massive study of the Japanese attack on Pearl Harbor, came to light in a condensed version in November 1981 under the title *At Dawn We Slept: The Untold Story of Pearl Harbor.*

The current volume is the sequel to *At Dawn We Slept.* Readers of that book will recognize many of the personalities here. Indeed, Prange's thirty-seven years of research on Pearl Harbor gave him considerable insight into the Midway conflict even before the *Reader's Digest* requested that he submit a manuscript on that subject—published in condensed form in November 1972. In particular, several of the Japanese friends whom he interviewed in connection with Pearl Harbor were also veterans of Midway, or had studied the subject. Prange's Japanese interviews are especially valuable, for little Japanese documentation on Midway is available. Whatever war plans, orders, working papers, messages and other documents were aboard Nagumo's four carriers were lost forever when those ships went down at Midway.

On the American side, a number of participants, from Admiral Chester W. Nimitz on down, gave him splendid cooperation. American records of the battle are readily available, for units involved submitted detailed reports. Yet one must approach these documents with a skeptical eye and an open mind, remembering that they were written much too close to the event for proper perspective and are understandably tinged with wishful thinking. This is especially true of accounts of air warfare, with its foreshortened vision. If one accepted as gospel all the claimed results at Midway, the Americans sank everything short of the Imperial palace. By the same token, the Japanese press touted the engagement as a resounding victory.

Prange and the two of us have striven for a balanced judgment. Thus, in this volume the Americans and the Japanese receive as near "equal time" as is possible in view of the material available.

Any work of history is necessarily a joint venture. Space does not permit thanking everyone who contributed to the current work. But we wish to pay special and heartfelt tribute to two individuals. The first is Robert E. Barde, a former U.S. Marine Corps officer who was one of Prange's students at the University of Maryland. Under Prange's direction, Barde wrote a doctoral dissertation on the subject "Midway—A Study in Command." Barde very generously turned over to Prange this dissertation as well as the background material upon which it was based. These documents included the records of many interviews which Barde held with survivors of Midway, both in the United States and in Japan. This material has been invaluable in piecing together the current work.

The other individual whom we wish to thank is Masataka Chihaya, formerly an officer of the Imperial Japanese Navy, who for many years was Prange's representative in Japan and a close personal friend. Chihaya conducted a number of interviews on behalf of Prange when the latter was unable to be in Japan to do so for himself; and he collected valuable source material unavailable in the United States.

In view of Prange's drive to bring in all the sheaves meticulously before he began threshing, it is possible that he would not have considered his Midway manuscript ready for publication. But we think otherwise, and we as co-authors have worked diligently to try to meet the standards of our mentor. It is a good story, one in which all Americans can take pride. More than a decade has elapsed since the last book-sized treatment of Midway; we believe that the current generation may be ready for a retelling of what military historians consider among the most decisive battles of history.

This volume complements, rather than supplants, other fine works in this area. *Midway: The Battle That Doomed Japan*, by Mitsuo Fuchida and Masatake Okumiya, edited by Clarke H. Kawakami and Roger Pineau, remains a prime source from the Japanese side, and the writers are much indebted to it. We also wish to give a special salute to Samuel Eliot Morison's naval history, *Coral Sea, Midway and Submarine Actions,* and to Walter Lord's wonderfully human *Incredible Victory.* Other worthy and valuable works are cited in the bibliography.

Because the story of Midway is such a complicated one, with several actions going on at once, the authors have tried to make the reader's task a little easier by compartmentalizing the chapters dealing with the actual battle. Hence, the attack on Midway is treated separately, as are the attacks by land-based bomber, carrier-based torpedo plane, carrier-based dive bomber, etc. Anyone interested in knowing exactly what went on at a given minute is referred to the timetable in the appendices.

The reader will find herein little or nothing of the interplay of politics with the military which was necessary for an understanding of Midway's historical opposite, Pearl Harbor. War was a settled fact; the national course was set. So Midway is the saga of a straightforward naval operation, albeit a very complicated and intricate one, wherein, ironically, surface ships never came in contact with one another.

We would like to bring to the reader's attention a few of the idiosyncrasies of the text:

1. In conformity with the documentation and with naval custom, we have used the military twenty-four-hour clock. This has the great virtue of preventing any confusion between A.M. and P.M.

2. Whenever possible, times given are local. Events taking place in Japan are given in Tokyo time; events at and near Midway in Midway time. Tokyo was twenty-one hours ahead of Midway; i.e., an event taking place at 0700 on June 5 Tokyo time happened at 1000 on June 4, Midway time.

3. For the sake of brevity and "local color," we have used naval abbreviations of the day in many places throughout the text. Most of these are self-explanatory, but for the reader's convenience we have included a glossary of such terms. We have also followed the navy custom of omitting the article "the" when referring to a warship by name.

4. Along with the glossary, we have included a list of key personnel, the composition of forces, and a timetable of major events.

5. The pictures and charts herein represent a selection among the many available in the Prange files.

6. The bibliography is selective rather than comprehensive.

Readers looking for sensational revelations in this book will not find them. The battle took place; certain results were obtained. What remains of controversy is either in the area of speculation—what if the Japanese had won?—wherein the reader may give imagination free rein, or in the tactical, where the wisdom or folly of a given action is endlessly debatable by those who enjoy such debates. We have reached certain conclusions, with which no doubt some may disagree.

Above all, for the reader we wish a few hours of the interest and pleasure of a good story, and a quickening of pride in America's heritage.

DONALD M. GOLDSTEIN, PH.D.
Associate Professor of
Public and International Affairs
University of Pittsburgh
Pittsburgh, Pennsylvania

KATHERINE V. DILLON
CWO, USAF (Ret.)
Arlington, Virginia

PREFACE

No plot pattern is as dear to the American heart as that of the victorious underdog. Because of the power, size, geographical location, and nature of this country, very seldom in the last century has the United States had the luxury of being in that position. The battle of Midway was one of those few occasions when the Americans were underdogs and victorious.

Less than six months after their victory at Pearl Harbor, the Japanese sent forth an enormous, combat-seasoned fleet of eighty-eight surface warships* with the dual mission of capturing Midway atoll and luring the remains of the weakened U.S. Pacific Fleet to their destruction. This was to be the opening salvo of their second phase operations which contemplated the isolation of Australia at one extreme and possible capture of Hawaii at the other.

But events did not conform to the Japanese pattern. Forewarned through superior cryptanalysis and radio intelligence, American naval forces much inferior numerically to the Japanese (twenty-eight surface warships),* but superbly led and manned, sped past Midway and were waiting on the enemy's flank.

The result was by no means a foregone conclusion. The Japanese spearhead held the veteran carriers *Akagi*, *Kaga*, *Hiryu*, and *Soryu*, under the command of Vice Admiral Chuichi Nagumo. This was the admiral and four of the six carriers which had attacked Pearl Harbor on December 7, and since then the Nagumo task force had scored one victory after another in the south Pacific and Indian Oceans.

---

*These figures do not include the ships committed to the concurrent Aleutian campaign but do include the Guard Force which sortied with the Japanese Main Body.

Nagumo, his carrier captains, and his airmen fought skillfully and bravely at Midway as flight after flight of American bombers struck impotently. Then, suddenly, superb command decisions, precision dive bombing and a pinch or two of luck all came together. When the battle ended, Japan had lost her four carriers, a heavy cruiser, and over 300 aircraft. Yet the battle could have gone the other way, and even so, the United States lost one carrier, *Yorktown*, and a destroyer, *Hammann*.

Events at Midway cast serious doubt upon the popular contention that, had the Japanese not achieved surprise at Pearl Harbor, they would have been open to almost certain defeat. This time the U.S. Pacific Fleet knew the Japanese were coming, almost to the minute when they would strike, where and in what strength. American ships were in the open sea, free to maneuver and with the advantage of surprise. Nevertheless, the results were such a narrow squeak that we believe the title *Miracle at Midway* is not so much alliterative as exactly factual. Land-based bombing proved totally ineffectual and carrier-based efforts equally so until the last-minute linking up and successful marksmanship of the dive bombers. In view of the fact that six months of war had passed since Pearl Harbor, with consequent combat seasoning on the part of commanders, ships and crews, one cannot help but suspect that, had the U.S. Pacific Fleet sortied to meet Nagumo's task force on December 7, results might have been just as bad if not worse. This was the opinion of Admiral Nimitz, who frankly considered it "God's mercy" that Admiral Husband E. Kimmel's ships were at their moorings instead of on the deep Pacific.

In some ways, Midway was the reverse image of Pearl Harbor. This time the story was one of Japanese overconfidence, careless planning, slipshod training and contempt for the enemy; of American cool-headedness, ingenuity, and intelligence well acted upon. At the time, the nation rejoiced that Pearl Harbor had been at least partially avenged. Yet Midway was much more than that; it is generally conceded to have been the turning point in the Pacific war. Over three years of hard-fought combat remained but the United States had captured the initiative. Before Midway, Japan had been fighting an aggressive war of conquest, spreading the boundaries of her Greater East Asia Co-Prosperity Sphere ever outward. After Midway, her problem became how to hold what she had; how to defend an ever-shrinking periphery until at the last she had been driven back where she started and beyond.

Midway offers many opportunities and temptations to play with the fascinating "ifs, ands and buts" of history, especially on the American side. Suppose Nimitz had not stuck with his assessment that Midway was the main Japanese target, that their projected simultaneous assault on the Aleutians was primarily a diversion? He was under enormous pressure to reject the validity of the information being fed to him by the Combat Intelligence unit on Hawaii. Some of his own staff found it difficult to credit that Admiral Isoroku Yamamoto, formidable Commander in Chief of the Combined Fleet, would assemble such an armada against Midway, not to mention Kiska and Attu. It was like fishing for minnows with a harpoon. The commanding general of the Hawaiian Department was sure that Yamamoto planned another assault on Oahu, this time in force. And some in the high reaches of the War Department believed that the Japanese were headed for the West Coast, to launch air strikes against the aircraft factories in southern California.

Nimitz was not an obstinate man; he listened courteously and respectfully to all sides of the question. But once he made his decision, he proceeded full speed ahead. For that, the United States owes him a tremendous debt.

The story of any major battle is necessarily complicated. At Midway many events were going on at the same time, so that not even participants—perhaps participants least of all—could see the big picture or know what was going on. Little of genuine controversy remains, although the wisdom of decisions is forever arguable, and some tactical events are blurred in the heat and smoke of battle. So inevitably some readers will disagree with one or another of our findings and conclusions. This is fine with us. Gordon Prange never claimed to possess the all-seeing eye, the all-knowing mind, and still less do we, his literary successors.

If he were here to do so, we believe he would want us to dedicate this book to all those on both sides of the Pacific who made it possible, and who helped bring it to fruition. This we do with our gratitude.

Abe, RADM Hiroaki — Commander, CruDiv 8
Adams, Lt. Samuel — Operations Officer, VS-5
Ady, Lt. Howard P. — USN reconnaissance pilot
Amagai, Capt. Takehisa — Air officer, *Kaga*
Arnold, Cmdr. Murr E. — Air officer, *Yorktown*
Best, Lt. Richard H. — Commander, VB-6
Brockman, Lt. Cmdr. William H., Jr. — Captain, *Nautilus*
Browning, Capt. Miles S. — Chief of staff, Task Force 16
Buckmaster, Capt. Elliott — Captain, *Yorktown*
Burford, Lt. Cmdr. William P. — Captain, *Monaghan*
Chase, Lt. (j.g.) William A. — USN reconnaissance pilot
Chigusa, Lt. Cmdr. Sadao — Gunnery officer, *Jintsu*
Collins, Capt. James F., Jr. — Leader, B-26s at Midway
Davidson, Brig. Gen. Howard C. — CG, 7th Fighter Command
Delany, Lt. Cmdr. John F. — Engineering officer, *Yorktown*
Dobson, Lt. (j.g.) Cleo J. — USN reconnaissance pilot
Doolittle, Lt. Col. James H. — Leader, air raid on Japan
Draemel, RADM Milo F. — Chief of Staff, Pacific Fleet
Eaton, Ens. Charles R. — USN reconnaissance pilot
Emmons, Lt. Gen. Delos C. — Commanding General, Hawaiian Dept.
Fletcher, RADM Frank Jack — Commander, Task Force 17
Ford, Cmdr. John — Movie director
Foster, Lt. Cmdr. J. G., Jr. — Air operations officer, *Hornet*
Fuchida, Cmdr. Mitsuo — Flight leader, *Akagi*
Fujita, Lt. Iyozo — Zero pilot, *Soryu*
Fujita, RADM Ruitaro — Commander, Seaplane Tender Group
Gallaher, Lt. W. Earl — Commander, VS-6
Gay, Ens. George H. — Pilot, VT-8
Genda, Cmdr. Minoru — Air officer, 1st Air Fleet
Gray, Lt. James S. — Commander, VF-6
Hara, Lt. Cmdr. Tameichi — Commander, *Amatsukaze*
Hashiguchi, Cmdr. Takashi — Air officer, *Hiryu*
Hashimoto, Lt. Toshio — Bomber pilot, *Hiryu*
Henderson, Maj. Lofton R. — Commander, VMSB-241
Holmberg, Lt. (j.g.) Paul A. — SBD pilot, *Yorktown*

Hosogaya, VADM Moshīro — Commander in Chief, Northern Force
Johnson, Lt. Cmdr. Robert R. — Commander, VB-8
Kaku, Capt. Tomeo — Captain, *Hiryu*
Kakuta, RADM Kakuji — Commander in Chief, 2d Carrier Striking Force
Katsumi, Capt. Motoi — Captain, *Tanikaze*
Kawaguchi, Sub Lt. Taketoshi — Engineering officer, *Mikuma*
Kiefer, Cmdr. Dixie — Executive officer, *Yorktown*
Kimes, Lt. Col. Ira E. — Commander, MAG-22
King, Admiral Ernest J. — Commander in Chief, U.S. Fleet
Kobayashi, Lt. Michio — Bomber pilot, *Hiryu*
Kondo, VADM Nobutake — Commander in Chief, 2d Fleet
Kurita, RADM Takeo — Commander in Chief, Close Support Group
Kuroshima, Capt. Kameto — Senior staff officer, Combined Fleet
Kusaka, RADM Ryunosuke — Chief of Staff, 1st Air Fleet
Kyuma, Lt. Cmdr. Takeo — Engineering staff officer, *Hiryu*
Layton, Capt. Edwin T. — Intelligence Officer, Pacific Fleet
Leslie, Lt. Cmdr. Maxwell F. — Commander, VB-3
Lindsey, Lt. Cmdr. E. E. — Commander, VT-6
Lindsey, Lt. Robin — Landing signal officer, *Enterprise*
Makajima, Teuchi — Photographer aboard *Akagi*
Massey, Lt. Cmdr. Lance E. — Commander, VT-3
Masuda, Cmdr. Shogo — Air officer, *Akagi*
McCaul, Maj. Verne J. — Executive officer, MAG-22
McClusky, Lt. Cmdr. Clarence Wade — Commander, Air Group, *Enterprise*
Mitchell, Lt. Cmdr. Samuel G. — Commander, VF-8
Mitoya, Lt. Cmdr. Sesu — Communications officer, *Kaga*
Mitscher, RADM Marc A. — Captain, *Hornet*
Miwa, Capt. Yoshitake — Air officer, Combined Fleet
Murata, Lt. Cmdr. Shigeharu — Torpedo leader, *Akagi*
Murray, Capt. George D. — Captain, *Enterprise*
Nagumo, VADM Chuichi — Commander in Chief, 1st Air Fleet
Nakazawa, Capt. Tasuku — Chief of staff, Northern Force
Nimitz, Admiral Chester W. — Commander in Chief, Pacific Fleet
Norris, Maj. Benjamin W. — Commander, VMSB-241
Ohara, Cmdr. Hisashi — Executive officer, *Soryu*
Okada, Capt. Jisaku — Captain, *Kaga*
Okumiya, Lt. Cmdr. Masatake — Air staff officer, 2d Carrier Striking Force
Parks, Maj. Floyd B. — Commander, VMF-221
Pederson, Lt. Cmdr. Oscar — Commander, Air Group, *Yorktown*
Ramsey, Cmdr. Logan C. — Operations Officer, Ford Island NAS
Reid, Ens. Jack — USN reconnaissance pilot
Ring, Cmdr. Stanhope C. — Commander, Air Group, *Hornet*
Rochefort, Cmdr. Joseph — Chief, Op 20-02 (Hypo)
Sakiyama, Capt. Shakao — Captain, *Mikuma*
Saruwatari, Lt. Cmdr. Masayushi — Damage control officer, *Mogami*
Shannon, Col. Harold D. — Commander, 6th Marine Defense Bn.
Short, Lt. Wallace C. — Commander, VS-5
Shumway, Lt. D. W. — Dive bomber pilot, VB-3
Simard, Capt. Cyril T. — Commander, Midway NAS
Soji, Capt. Akira — Captain, *Mogami*

Spruance, RADM Raymond A.   Commander, Task Force 16
Sweeney, Lt. Col. Walter C., Jr.   Leader, B-17s on Midway
Takagi, VADM Takeo   Commander, CruDiv 5
Takasu, VADM Shiro   Commander in Chief, Guard Force
Tanabe, Lt. Cmdr. Yahachi   Commander, *I-168*
Tanaka, RADM Raizo   Commander, Transport Group
Thach, Lt. Cmdr. John S.   Commander, VF-3
Theobald, RADM Robert A.   Commander, Task Force 8
Tinker, Maj. Gen. Clarence L.   Commanding General, 7th Air Force
Tomonaga, Lt. Joichi   Leader, air attack on Midway
True, Cmdr. Arnold E.   Captain, *Hammann*
Ugaki, RADM Matome   Chief of staff, Combined Fleet
Waldron, Lt. Cmdr. John C.   Commander, VT-8
Warner, Major Jo K.   AAF liaison officer, Midway
Watanabe, Capt. Yasuji   Plans officer, Combined Fleet
Yamaguchi, RADM Tamon   Commander in Chief, 2d Carrier Div.
Yamamoto, Admiral Isoroku   Commander in Chief, Combined Fleet
Yanagimoto, Capt. Ryusaku   Captain, *Soryu*

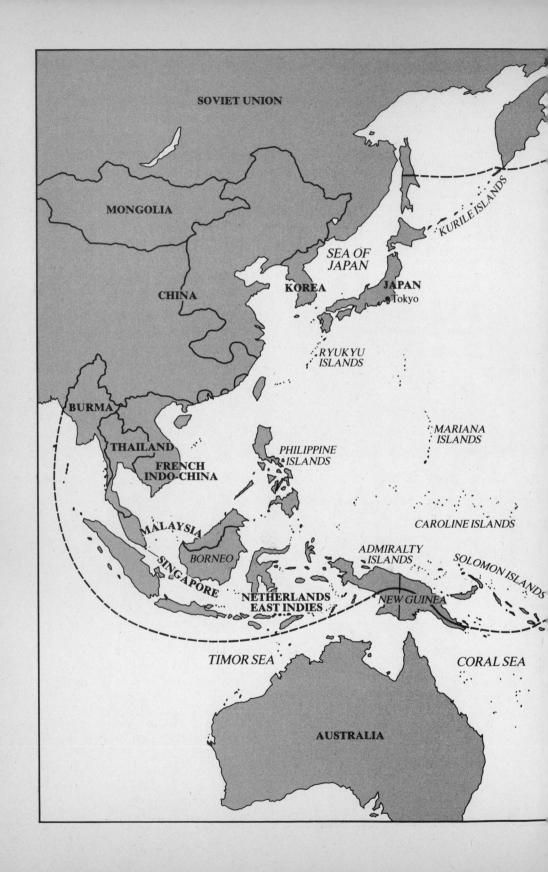

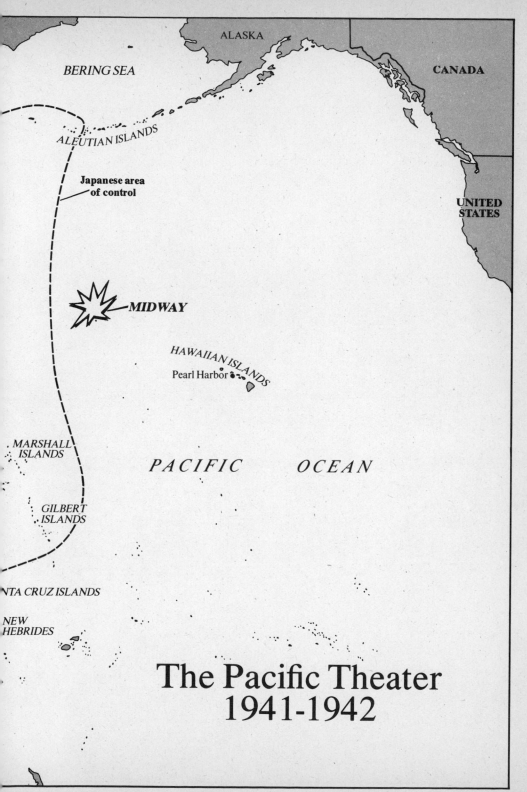

BERING SEA

ALASKA

CANADA

ALEUTIAN ISLANDS

Japanese area
of control

UNITED
STATES

MIDWAY

HAWAIIAN ISLANDS
Pearl Harbor

MARSHALL
ISLANDS

PACIFIC OCEAN

GILBERT
ISLANDS

NTA CRUZ ISLANDS

NEW
HEBRIDES

The Pacific Theater
1941-1942

Paul J. Pugliese

MIRACLE
AT
MIDWAY

CHAPTER 1

"A Breath of Fresh Air"

The success-crowned Japanese carrier task force under Vice Admiral Chuichi Nagumo slashed toward Japan through heavy seas. Their attack upon the U.S. Pacific Fleet at Pearl Harbor and the installations of the Hawaiian Air Force on December 7, 1941, had succeeded beyond all expectations, certainly beyond the expectation of Nagumo himself. He had entertained the liveliest doubts of the operation, and shared the estimate of the planners that he would probably lose one-third of his task force. Instead, he was bringing back to Japan every one of his ships with not so much as a chip in its paint due to enemy action. Seldom can any voyage homeward have been so solidly satisfying, broken only by the detachment of his Second Carrier Division, under Rear Admiral Tamon Yamaguchi, to support the Japanese strike on Wake Island, where the U.S. Marines were giving the invaders some unexpected difficulties.

Early on December 23, the task force sailed through Bungo Channel and soon saw the mountains of Shikoku lift over the horizon. Welcoming aircraft from shore-based units hovered overhead like mechanical *amoretti* in a rococo allegory of victory, and ships of the coastal defense force patrolled proudly on both sides of the returning conquerors.[1] The next morning, Nagumo and some of his officers visited the battleship *Nagato*, flagship of the Combined Fleet, to pay their respects to Admiral Isoroku Yamamoto, Commander in Chief of the Combined Fleet. Chief of the Naval General Staff Admiral Osami Nagano turned up in person to congratulate the victors.

Diminishing all else to insignificance, Nagumo and his two air commanders, Commander Mitsuo Fuchida and Lieutenant Com-

mander Shigekazu Shimazaki, visited the Imperial Palace by command of Emperor Hirohito himself, so that they might brief him
personally on this operation which had shed so much gold dust upon
the Imperial banners.[2]

It was all heady stuff, and contributed in no small measure to a
smug self-confidence in their invincibility, which Nagumo, his subordinate commanders and their staffs took into their next operations,
and for which they would bitterly chastise themselves in the not too
distant future.

In contrast, the Americans had received a salutary but exceedingly
unpalatable dose of enforced humility. Average Americans might
squabble over internal politics and over foreign policy, but they had
shared a belief and pride in the United States' power, solidly based
on its vast natural resources, humming technology, hard-working people, and its military potential. World War I was only a quarter-century
in the rear; memories of the mighty AEF were still green. John Q.
Public was especially proud of his Navy, believing that the U.S. and
British fleets combined formed an unbeatable combination Japan would
never challenge, let alone defeat.

Now, suddenly, that rock of faith had dissolved. "The great shock
of this attack upon the United States is not so much that Japan has
struck at us . . . ," wrote the Birmingham (Alabama) News, "but that
she should have struck so suddenly and so recklessly at a point like
our great naval base at Pearl Harbor . . ." The attack might have
been, in the words of the Los Angeles Times, "the act of a mad dog,"[3]
but a mad dog's bite can kill, and the mad dog must be destroyed.

A small newspaper in Meridian, Mississippi, uninhibited by any
sense of self-important, big-city dignity, fairly foamed at the mouth:
"At last Nippon bares its yellow fangs . . . Let America raze Tokyo
and other Jap 'tinder' towns . . . Blast the 'flowery Kingdom' into
nothingness! Blow the pagan Jap and his treacherous 'Son of Heaven'
to hell!"[4]

Nothing would have pleased the American public more than to
do just that. The question was, how to do it. With what? Thus it came
about that the immediate post-Pearl Harbor period was unique in
the American experience. A brief echo of it sounded in the 1980
hostage crisis with Iran. But in volume and intensity, that incident
cannot truly compare with those few months following Pearl Harbor,
when most of the nation's able-bodied young men were pawns in a

game wherein the enemy seemingly ruled the board. To the explosion of outrage over Pearl Harbor were soon added furious frustration and impatient shame at the apparent impotence of the U.S. armed forces.

It was not the psychology of despair; nowhere in the press, documents, or memories of the day appears the slightest apprehension that the Axis might triumph in the end. Nevertheless, any jaunty prewar conviction which might have existed that when, as and if the Americans entered the conflict, they would clean up in a hurry, perished with a death rattle of reality. Alan Barth, charged with reporting on public opinion to his superiors in the Treasury Department, summed up the situation neatly:

> Press reaction to the Pacific fighting has described a parabola. From a wringing of hands immediately after the attack on Pearl Harbor, sentiment rose sharply to an expectation of easy victory over the Japanese. It was not until the middle of the past week that the newspapers began to realize that further serious reverses were almost certainly in store for the British and American Far Eastern forces. Now, suddenly, the downswing has set in.[5]

Every active front showed the same grim colors of red and black. Britain seemed to have outlasted the threat of direct invasion, but still lived under the shadow of an almost equally deadly menace. In American waters, German U-boats operated virtually at will, sinking an appalling tonnage of the Allied shipping sustaining Britain's island economy. Prime Minister Winston Churchill later admitted that had Hitler concentrated more effort in the Atlantic, he could have prolonged the war indefinitely and seriously upset all Allied war plans.[6] Of much less moment, but highly irritating and humiliating to the United States, Japanese submarines were operating in the waters between Hawaii and the West Coast.

Contrary to many expectations, the Soviet Union had survived the winter. But Germany still held it locked in mortal combat. If the Russians folded—and Stalin had already shifted his diplomatic capital from Moscow to Kuibyshev—the Germans might push the Russian fighting forces beyond the Urals, out of European Russia, then return against England, or move south to advance through the Middle East and link up with Japan, for Field Marshal Erwin Rommel still dominated the North African scene. By midspring the Japanese had captured Singapore, conquered the Netherlands East Indies and Burma, and who knew what designs they had on India, exceedingly restive under British rule? Above all, Australia feared invasion.

In these first months of war, Pearl Harbor was almost neurotically attack conscious. What else could be expected, while there in Battleship Row lay the hideously grim reminders of what the Japanese could do if they got through in a surprise thrust? Since December 7, the U.S. commanders in Hawaii had looked for the Japanese to return. Surely Admiral Isoroku Yamamoto, for whom the American admirals entertained high professional respect, would repent the Japanese sins of omission and send Vice Admiral Chuichi Nagumo's carriers back to blast the docks, the repair shops and, above all, the tank farm! In effect, this would starve the U.S. Navy out of the central Pacific and back to the West Coast. Then what would prevent the Japanese from invading the Hawaiian Islands and establishing their own advance base there?

Rear Admiral Claude C. Bloch, commandant of the Fourteenth Naval District, made frantic if belated efforts to improvise antitorpedo nets for drydocks and ships at anchor:

> We tore down fences, tore down the fence between Hickam Field and Pearl Harbor Navy Yard, took the extruded material that was used for the fence and welded it, lapwelded it to other sections in order to get a sufficient baffle that we could hang in the water at the ends of docks and around ships. And in so doing, of course, we had no knowledge whether that kind of net would be any good at all, but it was the best we had. We also took all of the target rafts we had and hung sections of fence below them and put them in front of the dock caissons and some of the important repair docks.[7]

Morale was low at all levels of the armed forces on Oahu. "Everyone was very apprehensive," recalled Colonel William C. "Cush" Farnum, in charge of supply and engineering at Hickam Field. "The Navy people above all were apprehensive. They were like a defeated football team—really down and out."[8]

The presence on Oahu of, first, Secretary of the Navy Frank Knox and second, Associate Justice of the Supreme Court Owen J. Roberts and his commission appointed to investigate the disaster, did nothing to boost morale.[9] Along with the threat of another Japanese attack, the possibility of professional ruin hung over every man associated in any way with the defense of Pearl Harbor and the ships at moorings there.

On December 16, 1941, the Navy relieved Admiral Husband E. Kimmel as Commander in Chief, U.S. Fleet (CinCUS), and as Commander in Chief, U.S. Pacific Fleet (CinCPAC), temporarily turning the command over to Vice Admiral William S. Pye. During the latter's brief tenure occurred the event which, of all others, seemed to epitomize the ineffectiveness and frustration of the U.S. Pacific Fleet. This was the capture by the Japanese of Wake Island, a saga too long to deal with in detail here.[10]

In brief, had Kimmel remained in command, Wake's story might have been different. The offensive-minded Kimmel hoped to close with the Japanese. He had an excellent plan for the relief of Wake, and dispatched ships for that purpose, but a series of delays held them up. After Pye relieved Kimmel, Washington sent him a message that Wake was "considered a liability . . . ," which, according to the eminent naval historian Rear Admiral Samuel Eliot Morison, gave Pye authority to evacuate Wake at his discretion instead of reinforcing its defenders. While Pye hesitated, on December 20 the Japanese commenced landing.

However, task forces centering around the carriers *Saratoga*, under Rear Admiral Frank Jack Fletcher, and *Lexington*, under Vice Admiral Wilson Brown, were hastening toward the scene and could have engaged the enemy, even if too late to save Wake. Moreover, Task Force Eight, with Vice Admiral William F. Halsey flying his flag from the carrier *Enterprise*, was steaming near Midway and Pye could have ordered him to assist.[11] Halsey's cruiser commander, Rear Admiral Raymond A. Spruance, for one, would have welcomed a definite assignment. His orders were "to operate in the northern area." These vague directions disgusted the clear-minded Spruance. "Operate, operate!" he said disdainfully in retrospect. "I wish you could tell me what it meant. We had no specific orders. We were out there as bait for the Japanese subs."[12]

But, like so many others, Pye feared for Hawaii's safety and called off the Wake operation. He reached this decision without benefit of pressure from Washington. "While believing in the principle of the offensive and suffering with those at Wake," he explained, "I could not but decide that the general situation overbalanced the special tactical situation, and that under the conditions the risk of even one task force to damage the enemy at Wake was unjustifiable . . ."[13]

Pye would have had a hard time selling that line of reasoning to

Saratoga's personnel, some of whom actually wept in their fury and disappointment.[14]

The top brass in Washington were also much disgruntled. Captain Frank E. Beatty, Knox's aide, who had been in the secretary's office when the recall message arrived, went to ask Chief of Naval Operations Harold R. Stark if he would so notify the President. The admiral jibbed at the melancholy assignment. "No, Frank, I wouldn't have the heart, please ask Secretary Knox to do it." When Knox returned from his distasteful errand to the White House, "he said that the President considered this recall a worse blow than Pearl Harbor."[15]

This may seem like an over-reaction, but psychologically it was sound. Morison wrote later, "God knows, America needed a victory before Christmas, 1941."[16] The need was more basic than that; the nation wanted a show of fight. The American people would forgive—even honor—one who lost after putting up a good scrap. "Alamo" conjures up fires which "San Jacinto" does not; Robert E. Lee is more beloved than Ulysses S. Grant. On December 22, 1941, the unofficial log of *Enterprise's* Fighter Squadron Six (VF-6) summed up the national frustration in two devastating sentences: "Everyone seems to feel that it's the war between the two yellow races. Wake was attacked this morning and probably surrendered with the SARATOGA but 200 miles away and us steaming around in circles east of the 180th." (Capitals in original.)[17]

It would be difficult to imagine a less propitious moment to take over command of the U.S. Pacific Fleet. "I'm the new Commander in Chief." Thus baldly did Rear Admiral Chester W. Nimitz break the news to his wife, Catherine. He was in such obvious distress that she reminded him, "You've wanted this all your life."

"But sweetheart," protested the admiral, "all the ships are at the bottom."[18] Under the circumstances, this was an understandable bit of exaggeration.

The difficult, technical and ultimately amazingly successful task of raising ships from the bottom of Pearl Harbor Nimitz must leave to others. But there was something he could and must salvage—the careers and psyches of the staff officers at Pearl Harbor. Having just left duty as chief, Bureau of Navigation, which at that time handled personnel matters, Nimitz knew well that both Kimmel's staff and Pye's interim one contained able, well-trained and dedicated professional seamen. He blamed neither them nor Kimmel for the disaster at Pearl Harbor, believing that, granted the same conditions, "The same thing could have happened to anybody."[19] Arbitrary replacement of these staffs would be not only an injustice but such a blow to each man's self-confidence that it could mean serious psychological injury to a valuable public servant. "Now all of these staffs," explained Nimitz in retrospect, "were in a state of shellshock, and my biggest problem at the moment was morale. These officers had to be salvaged."

Nimitz assumed command, with the rank of admiral, at 1000 on December 31, 1941, aboard the submarine *Grayling*—an appropriate setting in view of his long background as a submariner. That same day, he called together the staffs of Kimmel, Pye, and Rear Admiral Milo F. Draemel, the commander of destroyers, whom Nimitz selected as his chief of staff. He assured them of his faith and confidence in their abilities and his intention of keeping them on. He wanted the right officer in the right job, not just a body in a slot. If some officers did not work out in their posts, he would not hesitate to make needed adjustments. However, in that event, he would do whatever he could to assist displaced officers to find jobs suitable to their abilities.[20]

There can be no doubt that by this action Nimitz raised spirits "several hundred per cent," to quote Morison.[21] Commanders at sea also experienced that uplift of the heart. "It was like being in a stuffy room and having someone open a window and let in a breath of fresh air," said Spruance.[22] But Nimitz did not delude himself that the job was done. He stated later that it was about six months before morale at Pearl Harbor returned to normal.[23]

That went for Nimitz himself, who impressed the fleet aviation officer, Commander Arthur C. Davis, as being "scared and cautious" before the Midway crisis.[24] And indeed, results which the U.S. Pacific Fleet produced early in 1942 were so unimpressive that Nimitz wrote to his wife, "I will be lucky to last six months. The public may demand action and results faster than I can produce."[25]

The record was sad enough—heavy losses punctuated by victories which in their very insignificance were almost more humiliating than the defeats. By Christmas of 1941 the Japanese had completed their landings in the Philippines and the tiny Asiatic Fleet could do nothing to stop or even delay them. At noon that day, Admiral Thomas C. Hart turned over the remaining forces of the Asiatic Fleet in the area to Rear Admiral F. W. Rockwell, and with his staff escaped in the submarine *Shark*.[26]

Five U.S. submarines, on patrol as far as the coast of Japan, between January 5 and 8 managed to sink only three freighters. On January 11, the carrier *Saratoga* was torpedoed 500 miles southwest of Oahu. Although she made it safely to Oahu and thence to Bremerton for repairs, she was out of the battle just when most needed. From January 6 to 23, the *Enterprise* and *Yorktown* forces successfully covered Marine reinforcements to Samoa, but more than balancing that was the landing of Japanese forces at Rabaul, under the air umbrella of Nagumo's carriers. This brought the Coral Sea within range of Japanese bombers. And that same day, a U.S. strike on Wake was aborted when a Japanese submarine sank Brown's oiler *Neches*.[27]

Morale received a boost with the battle of Balikpapan, in which four U.S. destroyers penetrated a convoy. But, thanks to many torpedo misses, their kill was not as large as it should have been. However, they sank four transports and one patrol craft, all of which had no effect whatsoever upon the strategic situation but made pleasant reading for a change.[28]

February brought a few more exploits, gallant but of questionable value. Extravagant claims were made for Halsey's air strikes against Wotje, Maloelap, and Kwajalein on February 1, but in fact his men shot down only a few Zeros and suffered a hit on the USS *Chester*. Fletcher was to hit Jaluit at this time, but he encountered bad weather. Six of his planes were shot down, and he retired. Halsey sailed northward and raided Wake Island. But his score was one small patrol boat, a bag not worth the loss of one U.S. plane and its crew.[29]

Ill luck struck again on February 27, at the disastrous battle of the Java Sea, in which the Allies were badly defeated, and the Japanese lost no ships to compensate. Neither did the U.S. component involved, but the Americans proved of little use in this engagement. And that same day, the old USS *Langley*, ferrying planes and crews from Australia to Bombay, was so badly damaged by land-based naval aircraft of Japan's Eleventh Air Fleet that she had to be scuttled.[30]

The United States lost the cruiser *Houston* at Sunda Strait in a fight running from February 28 to March 1, and three days later Halsey struck Marcus Island. This was quite a daring attempt, for the island was less than 1,000 miles from Tokyo. However, he encountered no enemy planes and lost a bomber to heavy antiaircraft fire.[31]

All of these actions were like mosquito bites on a mastodon compared with such major Japanese victories as the capture of Guam, the sinking of the British battleship *Prince of Wales* and battle cruiser *Repulse*, the loss of the Philippines, the surrender of Singapore, and Nagumo's damaging air raids on Darwin in northern Australia.

So Nimitz could count very few blessings. But he knew what a close thing Pearl Harbor had been. He was also aware that in spite of the terrible damage, U.S. forces had been fortunate. In the first place, the Japanese had hit and run. The next time, he believed, they would follow through and complete the job. That meant they would leave no targets like the submarine base and the fuel storage tanks free of their bombs, as they did in their initial air strike. "Had the Japanese destroyed the oil supply," he said of their blitz, "it would have prolonged the war another two years."

As for the ships—"It was God's mercy that our fleet was in Pearl Harbor on December 7, 1941," he said. Elaborating on this point, he added, "Had Kimmel had advance notice that the Japanese were coming, he most probably would have tried to intercept them. With the difference in speed between Kimmel's battleships and the faster Japanese carriers, the former could not have come within rifle range of the enemy's flattops. As a result, we would have lost many ships in deep water and also thousands more in lives."[32]

A very genuine fear that the Japanese would return to strike Hawaii and possibly go even further generated some manifestations which are peculiar, to say the least, from the vantage of hindsight. Newspapers displayed a strange ambivalence, as Barth reported: "Editors are busily warning readers to beware of headline writers." A number of commentators, too, urged the public "to be on guard against overconfidence or the expectation of an easy victory.

"But the cable editors . . . continue to treat each successful American bombing raid as an important victory."

Barth cited an editorial by the New York *Daily News* Syndicate as a possible indication of a resurgent isolationism. This editorial claimed that fall of the Philippines was "only a question of time," with that of Singapore and the Dutch East Indies inevitably to follow. Therefore, it urged concentration of U.S. strength on Hawaii:

> If we don't hold Hawaii, one guess is as good as another what will happen to us. Our guess is that Jap bomber raids or battleship raids

or both will take to harrying our West Coast shortly after Hawaii goes down, and that we will then be on a bad spot indeed . . . The defense of Hawaii—implacable, last-ditch defense kept supplied remorselessly from the mainland—is, we believe, war job No. 1 for the American people.[33]

Secretary of War Henry L. Stimson, a lawyer and a fair-minded man, worried over the problems inherent in evacuating all Japanese— whether Japanese by race or nationality—from the West Coast, as Lieutenant General John DeWitt, commander of the Western Defense Command, was urging. And well might Stimson worry, for this ill-advised, inhumane action was to prove a hair shirt on the national conscience. Stimson feared that this policy would

> . . . make a tremendous hole in our constitutional system to apply it. It is a terrific problem, particularly as I think it is quite within the bounds of possibility that if the Japanese should get naval dominance in the Pacific they would try an invasion of this country; and, if they did, we would have a tough job meeting them. The people of the United States have made an enormous mistake in underestimating the Japanese. They are now beginning to learn their mistake.[34]

When public servants of the stature and experience of Stimson seriously considered the possibility of a Japanese invasion of the West Coast, Nimitz obviously had inherited a strategical and psychological task of awesome proportions.

Among the assets the United States could count was one which Nimitz would never dream of listing—the man himself. Neither President Franklin D. Roosevelt nor Secretary Knox ever served his country better than when they passed over an impressive seniority list to select this gentle, courtly and highly respected Texan to command the U.S. Pacific Fleet in a desperate hour. Nimitz became a rear admiral in 1938, and had served as chief of the Bureau of Navigation in Navy Headquarters since June 15, 1939. There he gained a reputation for hard work, rigorous attention to detail, efficient organization, strict conformity to official form, as well as mature and ethical judgments. He had hoped for a sea command, but perforce accepted another desk job with no complaint.[35]

He graduated seventh—that mystic, lucky number—in the Annapolis class of 1905. Already his classmates had him fairly well pegged.

"Possesses that calm and steady-going Dutch way that gets to the bottom of things," read the Naval Academy's class book, *Lucky Bag*. He brought to his new command in Hawaii a solid if unspectacular background in submarines, battleships, cruisers, and Navy head-quarters positions. Infinitely more important, he brought a mind, heart and spirit equal to the task. The thundering challenges, the crushing responsibilities of the Pacific command were to prove over the years that here was one of America's great men in the tradition of Robert E. Lee, whom he resembled in temperament, character, and ability.

Superficially Nimitz promised little in the way of picturesque "copy," for he was no exhibitionist and never raised his voice. If he had an eccentricity, it was a mild addiction to the homely pastime of pitching horseshoes.[36] Nor did he look in the least like the popular conception of a gruff old sea dog. In fact, he appeared startlingly youthful, although his once incredibly blond hair had turned so white that some, behind his back, nicknamed him "Cottontail."[37] He had a fresh, fine-textured complexion, and only the lines which experience and humor had etched at his nostrils and candid, steel-blue eyes, gave any hint of his fifty-seven years.

Admiral Ernest J. King, the CinCUS*—the position was sepa-rated from that of CinCPAC at the time of Nimitz's appointment—had given Nimitz a two-fold primary mission—to hold the Midway-Johnston-Hawaii line and maintain the Samoa and Fiji line of com-munications between the United States, Australia and New Zealand.[38] Appearing nowhere on paper, but absolutely basic, was the task of restoring morale shattered first by Pearl Harbor, then by the recall of the Wake relief expedition.

That he accomplished this mission is the supreme tribute to his leadership, tact and understanding, for, as we have seen, he could point to precious few concrete accomplishments of a morale-building nature in the pre-Midway period. At the same time, he had to dodge the sniping of public opinion, which demanded that the United States Navy go somewhere and do something. But Nimitz had endless pa-tience and no time for empty gestures. He could await the hour, and in the meantime work like a king beaver to be ready when it came.

*On March 12, 1942, King changed the abbreviation to Cominch. (Say CinCUS aloud and you will see why.)

"Nimitz combined so many fine qualities that you could not put your finger on any one of them and say, 'Here is the key to the man,' " recalled Spruance. "The one big thing about him was that he was always ready to fight . . . And he wanted officers who would push the fight with the Japanese. If they would not do so, they were sent elsewhere."[39]

CHAPTER 2

"We Should Occupy Midway"

On a day in late December 1941, a man in the uniform of a full admiral stood beside his desk aboard the battleship *Nagato* at anchor near the western end of Japan's Inland Sea. The man was short, broad-shouldered and deep-chested. Alert, intelligent eyes reflected a personality candid yet reserved, aggressive yet sensitive. A prominent nose topped mobile lips and powerfully angled lines from jaw to chin. It might have been the face of one of the great Elizabeth's sea captains—sailor and poet, buccaneer and politician, patriot and man of affairs.

This officer was Isoroku Yamamoto, Commander in Chief of Japan's Combined Fleet. As he stood there, his eyes devoured a damage report of the bombing of Pearl Harbor. Based upon American sources, it pulled no punches. Yamamoto turned toward Commander Takayasu Arima, his submarine officer and the youngest member of his staff. Smashing his fist down on his desk, he shouted, "*Kore wa taihen des!* [This is terrific!]." An enemy with the moral courage to tell the truth, however bitter it might be, would require a lot of licking.[1]

No one knew better than Yamamoto that he faced a strong, resourceful foe. He had studied at Harvard University and had served as naval attaché in Washington. He had traveled broadly and knew the American scene as well as any officer in the Japanese Navy. Because of that knowledge, he had long resisted war with the United States. Nonetheless, he was a Japanese nationalist from the top of his closely cropped head to the polished toes of his Navy shoes. So when it became obvious that Japan's leaders were determined to fight the United States, Yamamoto broke with the Japanese naval tradition of a defensive war in home waters and planned the bold trans-ocean air strike against Pearl Harbor. And now that his country was at war, he would fight with total commitment.

So, during December 1941, Yamamoto pondered the next step in naval strategy. The Pearl Harbor attack had exceeded all expectations, and elements of the Combined Fleet roamed the Western Pacific with impunity. Nevertheless, Uncle Sam's fighting forces based on Oahu were still potentially strong and burning to avenge the humiliating defeat. With this thought in mind, Yamamoto ordered his chief of staff, Rear Admiral Matome Ugaki, and his staff "to plan second term strategy at once."[2]

This "at once" was the first of many "too late's" in the Midway story. In collaboration with the Plans Division of the Naval General Staff, Yamamoto should have had the second stage of grand naval strategy already worked out and ready to implement as soon as Nagumo's task force steamed home from Pearl Harbor.

Ugaki was a handsome man, tall for a Japanese, very brainy, and an eloquent speaker. He was forceful and aggressive, and his slightly bald head teemed with temperament and ideas. He recorded his own thoughts and the day's events every night at about 2100, thus providing posterity with a most valuable war diary.

Ugaki enjoyed the reputation of being one of Japan's best officers and an authority on Japanese naval strategy. He came to the Combined Fleet in late August 1941 because Yamamoto wanted at his right hand a solid, able professional with a thorough knowledge of the top-level naval establishment in Tokyo. Once aboard *Nagato*, Ugaki served Yamamoto efficiently and faithfully.

Now he set to work with his usual enthusiasm and thoroughness. Following preliminary investigation, from January 11 through 14 he wrote up his ideas for future operations, and in his diary at the time jotted a hasty sketch: "After June of this year we should occupy Midway, Johnston, and Palmyra, send our air force forward to these islands and dispatch the Combined Fleet with an occupying force to occupy Hawaii and at the same time bring the enemy fleet into decisive battle."[4] The Japanese considered these islands of such importance to the United States that inevitably the latter would either react to the attacks or attempt to recapture the islands. This would bring about the long-sought decisive engagement between the Japanese and American fleets.[5]

On January 25, Ugaki turned his study over to Captain Kameto Kuroshima, the senior staff officer, to thrash out with the staff. Ugaki fumed while Kuroshima, an intellectual but eccentric operator who would not hurry even for Yamamoto, slept late in his cabin, made heavy forays into the ship's liquor stores, and offered innumerable cigarettes to the war gods while waiting for inspiration to dawn.[6] "One day's delay makes one hundred days' regret," Ugaki impatiently dashed into his diary.[7]

Kuroshima had his reasons for dragging his feet. He believed that Nimitz would not send forth his ships to defend Midway, Johnston, and Palmyra, and that Japan would be left stuck with three islands difficult to maintain.[8] So he recommended instead that Japan's naval strategy be oriented westward toward India and Burma, a concept which Ugaki accepted for the time being.[9]

While these planning sessions went on, Yamamoto transferred his flag from *Nagato* to the superbattleship *Yamato,* launched from Kure just that December. *Yamato* was planned as the first of four such monsters designed to circumvent the 5-5-3 ratio of capital ships established by the Washington Naval Conference of 1921. By this means the Japanese hoped to substitute striking power per ship for number of vessels. Construction started as soon as Japan served notice at the London Naval Conference of 1935 that she would not renew existing treaties. Work on *Yamato* and her sister ship *Musashi,* still under construction at Nagasaki, entailed enormous technological, financial, and security difficulties, but at last the new flagship slid down the ways.

Yamato displaced roughly 70,000 tons at full load, was 863 feet long with side armor sixteen inches thick. She mounted nine 18.1-inch guns capable of firing a projectile weighing more than 3,000 pounds. Each gun turret was about the size of a destroyer.[10] Intended to usher in a new era of superbattleships, the vessel was actually the swan song of an already bygone age, a seagoing dinosaur somehow born into the age of mammals.

While Yamamoto, with his new floating headquarters and other ships of the Main Body which gave him overwhelming superiority in conventional craft, remained at anchor in the Inland Sea, Nagumo's carrier force ranged through the South Pacific almost at will. However, it was never again the full six carriers which struck Pearl Harbor; sometimes Nagumo had the Second Carrier Division under his flag, sometimes the Fifth. But always his nucleus was the flagship *Akagi* and her companion *Kaga.* On January 20 and 21 he hit Rabaul, Kavieng, and New Guinea; on February 19 Port Darwin. Nagumo's fliers wisecracked somewhat bitterly about the "Hashirajima Fleet" back home. To such fervid airmen as Commander Mitsuo Fuchida, who had led the air attack on Pearl Harbor, Yamamoto appeared to be actually waiting for the United States to repair the ships his men had clobbered at Oahu.[11]

At the same time as Nagumo steamed away from Port Darwin toward Java, Captain Yasuji Watanabe studied the feasibility of an Indian Ocean operation. Watanabe's duties were staff officer for logistics, with additional responsibility for gunnery and Marine Corps matters, but he frequently worked in tandem with Kuroshima, who rather favored the Indian project. On February 20–22, table maneuvers were held aboard *Yamato,* attended by a number of Army General Staff officers. Ultimately Premier Hideki Tojo, who acted as his own War Minister, turned down the project, more for political than military reasons. Elections were due in March and he wanted to keep down the cost of the war effort.

Next the Combined Fleet suggested an all-out effort against China, to culminate in the capture of Chungking. Once more Tojo vetoed the idea; in his opinion, this was entirely too large an undertaking for Japan.

Since there seemed no possibility of the Army and Navy agreeing upon a joint venture, Yamamoto's men decided that they must come up with a plan within the scope of the Navy alone. By mid-March they had almost made a full circle back to Ugaki's suggestion of January, and thoughtful dark eyes settled upon the two tiny pinpricks of land comprising Midway. As the plan developed, the operation had a two-fold aim: First, to occupy the atoll and convert it into a Japanese air base and jumping-off point for an invasion of Hawaii; second, to lure the U.S. Pacific Fleet into the Midway area for a knock-down, drag-out fight which would finish it off. While Japan exploited the resources of Greater East Asia and dug in for the duration, this project would secure the eastern sea frontier.[12]

The Combined Fleet staff thus bent major efforts toward deciding the next major naval operation against the United States. At Pearl Harbor, Nimitz and his associates were equally diligent in attempting to predict the target of that operation and thus circumvent it. No one worked harder toward that end than Commander Joseph Rochefort, chief of the Combat Intelligence Office (Op 20 02), familiarly known as "Hypo."* A slender man just under six feet in height, with direct, friendly eyes and an unusually fair complexion, Rochefort was a veteran in that line of work.

Technically, Op 20 02 was not in Nimitz's command at all. Operationally it was under Commander Laurence F. Safford, chief of Security Intelligence of Naval Communications in Washington. For administration it was attached to the Fourteenth Naval District with headquarters at Pearl Harbor.

Safford was a long-time associate and old friend of Rochefort's.[13] A mathematical genius and chess fancier, a code-and-cipher demon and a man of unshakable personal rectitude, Safford had originally set up the cryptanalysis section of naval intelligence. He also understood the vulnerability of ciphers and codes, and worked tirelessly to protect the American ones with increasingly sophisticated means.[14]

The American Army or Navy cryptanalyst was a rare bird, in the service but not fully of it. No one knew exactly where he fitted in the scheme of things, for his was a shadow land south of Intelligence and north of Communications.[15] To excel in this work required a particular type of mentality, combining a well-above-average IQ, verging on the genius in mathematics, with an infinite capacity for painstaking detail. He should have genuine enthusiasm for the work, yet maintain a scholarly detachment. He must be without ambition as the world generally understands the term, for his chances of pinning a star on his shoulder were roughly those of being elected President of the United States. Awards or decorations very rarely came his way.

The cryptanalyst spent his days in a super-security chamber where the sunlight never penetrated, poring over letters and numbers in endless permutations. More often than not, a visitor to his home would find him occupied during his free time with a chess problem or cryptogram, like a postman taking a long walk on his day off. The cryptanalyst never moved out of his specialty, so over the years these unique, dedicated men of similar aims and tastes came to know each other well. Each service developed a compact group of experts working together with mellow, anonymous perfection.

---

*"Hypo" was H in the current British alphabet, and H stood for Hawaii.

Such a cell worked for Rochefort in Hypo in the basement of the old Administration Building, not far from Pearl Harbor's Dock 1010. Chief cryptanalyst was Lieutenant Commander Thomas H. Dyer, whom Rochefort called "the best the Navy ever had. With a couple of pills he could work for three or four days at a shot without sleep." Dyer had at his call such men as Lieutenant Commander Joseph Finnegan, the translator. "He was fantastic," said Rochefort. "He could look at a blank sheet of paper and translate it. He was a regular magician who could pull them right out of the air." Among others in this underground powerhouse was Professor of Mathematics Jasper Holmes, on loan from the University of Hawaii. Holmes's task was to make plots on Japanese fleet units and keep them up to date.[16]

From this office came the bulk of the data concerning the Japanese Navy, which Captain Edwin T. Layton, the Fleet Intelligence Officer, passed to Nimitz. Rochefort issued a daily intelligence bulletin and an estimate of the situation, sending a copy of each of these publications to Layton and to Navy headquarters in Washington. Hypo's principal day-to-day activity was reading Japanese fleet call signals, and Rochefort tried to keep all of these covered.

Over a period of eighteen years, the U.S. Navy had developed a highly skilled group of radio operators—chief petty officers and enlisted men—who were the backbone of this exceedingly complicated operation, just how complicated one can visualize by realizing that each navy command involved had between ten and twenty circuits, each with its own group of call signals. One circuit, for example, involved traffic from the Japanese Naval General Staff to Combined Fleet Headquarters. Separate circuits ran from Yamamoto to each of his subordinate commands, then from each headquarters to its units, and so on down to the last destroyer and most remote shore station.

Sorting out and interpreting this multitude of call signals demanded long experience, deep knowledge, and acute sensitivity. Rochefort's team had all these qualities, and by spring of 1942 had refined their work to the point of being able to recognize individual Japanese operators by their transmission habits—rapid, slow or medium, sending with light, heavy or in-between touch. For instance, *Akagi*'s thump was unmistakable—the operator seemed to sit on the key and bounce.

By March 1, 1942, Rochefort knew within three to four hundred miles where most Japanese ships were located. He kept Layton posted through his daily bulletins and by personal contact if he gleaned anything particularly interesting, as he did Admiral Bloch. Layton sometimes exasperated Rochefort by upgrading his estimates—if Rochefort spoke of four Japanese carriers, Layton changed it to six.[17]

But Layton knew from bitter experience how the operational officers tended to regard the intelligence types as alarmists. The words of a luncheon partner the day before Pearl Harbor rang in his ears: "Here comes Layton with his usual Saturday crisis!"[18] So if Rochefort estimated four Japanese carriers were on the prowl, Layton would report six. Then, if the staff charged up about one-third to intelligence calamity-howling, they would be back at the original figure.

Of course, Layton knew what the U.S. Pacific Fleet planned to do about the information Rochefort provided, but the latter did not. And he preferred to remain in the dark about United States operations, lest such knowledge color his thinking and interfere with his objective analysis of the information about the Japanese which his men pulled out of the air.[19]

The Japanese Navy's operational code, JN25, was the system under special attack at Hypo. It included some 45,000 five-digit numbers, representing words and phrases. An even larger pool of random numbers was available to the sender, which he could toss into a message to—hopefully—baffle analysis. A special group signaled where this smoke screen would begin. And, of course, new random number books came out from time to time.[20]

Thus when one speaks glibly of breaking the Japanese naval code, one should not visualize a process such as translating a passage of Russian into English—first transposing the Cyrillic letters into their Roman equivalent, then translating the words thus revealed. It was much more like the initial attacks on the Rosetta stone—a comparison here, an assumption there, a small breakthrough with many large blanks.

Before and during World War II, machines had already entered the code-breaking field, and indeed the computer has since sent the code to join the spear and siege-engine.[21] But Rochefort had no decoding machine, nor did he have a Japanese code book. Yet by March and April of 1942, Hypo could read approximately every fourth or fifth grouping in each message. No one man was responsible for the breakthrough; it was the result of efficient teamwork and dogged persistence. And each group decoded made the next one a little bit easier. These bits and pieces were fitted into the gleanings from radio analysis in the attempt to make a meaningful pattern. Not the least asset at Hypo was Rochefort's phenomenal memory of something seen or heard days or even weeks before. Rochefort admitted to being "a lousy organizer. I didn't keep very good files; I carried it all in my head."[22]

In his early days at Pearl Harbor, Nimitz had not been too much impressed with Hypo and was quite skeptical of its value. If radio intelligence was all that efficient, how had the attack of December 7, 1941, been possible? Layton later explained that, if the Japanese confided anything about Pearl Harbor to radio, they had used no code the Americans had broken. And the Nagumo force had kept complete radio silence.[23]

Once convinced, Nimitz became "very cooperative and under-standing." Rochefort could use a little cooperation and understanding, for certain desks in Navy headquarters in Washington were somewhat cool toward his efforts. But Nimitz was "a thinking leader, a real intellectual," who comprehended the intelligence mentality. Having come to appreciate the value of the work, he insisted that Rochefort have complete freedom to carry on his essential if off-beat activity. "You are supposed to tell us what the Japanese are going to do," he told Rochefort, "and I will then decide whether it is good or bad and act accordingly."[24]

CHAPTER 3

"A Shiver over Japan"

On March 28, Kuroshima rounded up his staff officers to begin studying the Midway scheme in earnest.[1] Before they could proceed too far, however, a formality remained to be surmounted. The Combined Fleet was one of three major divisions of the Imperial Navy, the others being the Navy Ministry and the Naval General Staff. Responsibilities might be summarized very roughly as operations, housekeeping and planning, respectively. Specifically, formulating war plans was the duty of the Plans Division of the Naval General Staff, a collection of up-and-coming young officers under intelligent, cool-headed Captain Baron Sadatoshi Tomioka.

At this time the Naval General Staff visualized three possible avenues of approach that the United States might take to counter Japan: the Aleutians, the Marshalls, and Australia. The latter they considered the most dangerous threat.[2] So Tomioka's Plans Division favored striking Samoa and the Fiji Islands, in the belief that such a move would smoke out the American fleet to save the line of communication with Australia. But Yamamoto disagreed with this premise, and dispatched two representatives to Tokyo to fight it out with Tomioka and his staff.[3]

Anyone who knew Yamamoto could have predicted that his emissaries would be Kuroshima and Watanabe, for both were fanatically loyal to the admiral and would fight for any plan of his to the last ditch.

The senior staff officer, Kuroshima, consumed amazing quantities of food and drink, and continued to look like an El Greco monk during Lent. He was individual to the point of weirdness in a nation and at

21

a time when the nonconformist aroused dislike and suspicion. But his taut-skinned head contained a brilliant if erratic, tortuous mind, and Yamamoto valued him highly.

Watanabe was Kuroshima's best friend on the staff and a prime favorite with Yamamoto. Tall, raw-boned, with big white teeth which frequently split his oblong face in an amiable grin, Watanabe was an excellent plans officer and a man of simple, homely goodness of character.[4]

At a series of meetings from April 2 through April 5, these two officers—sometimes in tandem, sometimes individually—presented Yamamoto's case fluently and plausibly. In the first place, they argued, Fiji and Samoa were so remote from the United States mainland that their loss might not stir up American opinion sufficiently to coax out the Pacific Fleet. In the second place, Japanese ship-building sacrificed distance for speed, so operating this far from Japan would not be practical. Third, the United States naval air force was still strong.[5]

This inter-staff battle was no pushover. The Combined Fleet emissaries encountered opposition of varying intensity at every level. Tomioka's immediate superior, Vice Admiral Shigeru Fukudome, chief of the First Bureau, disliked the Midway plan but interposed no strong objections. Tomioka was much more opposed. He argued that Midway would be difficult to maintain and supply, and would be in constant danger of raids by U.S. long-range planes. The atoll had no strategic value to Japan, and what is more, Tomioka questioned whether the United States would consider it worth the risk of its fleet.[6]

To the suggestion that Midway could be a staging point for an attack on the Hawaiian Islands, both Tomioka and his air expert, Commander Tatsukichi Miyo, turned deaf ears. Even if Japan had the necessary troops and ships for such a grandiose operation, which it did not, Midway was not big enough to handle them.[7]

Miyo was the most violently opposed to the Midway proposition. He preferred a strategy of striking New Caledonia, to cut the allied lines of communication and force a decisive battle in an area near Japanese bases and a long way from the United States. As the only airman in Tomioka's divison, he had a number of technical objections to Midway. The air patrols which Yamamoto wanted to establish there could not cover the entire area between Midway and the Aleutians; they could go 750 miles in a pinch, but 600 would be more realistic.

Even at the 600-mile limit, they could spend very little time in that ultimate position. This fact, plus bad weather, meant that American ships might well escape detection. "It is nonsense to have a patrol base of this type," he said. He pointed out that the scheme might look good on paper, but the base would be indefensible, exposed alike to submarine gunfire and B-17 bombs.

The upshot was that Watanabe phoned Combined Fleet head-quarters to report. When he returned to Tomioka's office he brought the word from on high: Yamamoto had declared that "if his plan was not adopted he *might* resign." In view of Yamamoto's position and prestige, the Naval General Staff withdrew its objections, although reluctantly. It was Pearl Harbor all over again—Yamamoto arrogating unto himself responsibilities which were none of his business, threatening to resign if he did not get his way, and the Naval General Staff yielding to his polite blackmail.*

Miyo was so sick at heart that he "dropped tears." Fukudome instructed him to "tone down" his objections, to study the Combined Fleet's plan and recommend a shift of forces to the Midway plan.[8] By way of an olive branch, Kuroshima and Watanabe promised that the Combined Fleet would tackle Fiji and Samoa after the battle of Midway had been won—and who could doubt that it would be won?[9] Who could question the prowess of the Combined Fleet, especially Nagumo's carrier force, which that very day—April 5—inflicted heavy damage on cargo vessels in the harbor at Colombo, Ceylon, and shortly thereafter sunk two British cruisers, *Dorsetshire* and *Cornwall*?[10]

The Naval General Staff asked for, and the Combined Fleet agreed to, a variation of the plan. Yamamoto's original idea called for massing full strength against Midway. The Naval General Staff wanted to add a strike against the Aleutians, too. This would not only be a diversionary operation—and Watanabe rather liked the idea of dispersion—but it would be a Navy contribution to the Greater East Asia CoProsperity Sphere. The Tokyo planners realized that the foul weather prevalent in the Aleutians would make them difficult to use as effective bases, but the area would be the anchor of a protective arc passing very near Midway and expanding to the Torres Strait between New Guinea and Australia. Besides, Japanese control of the Aleutians would preclude the Americans' running a bombing shuttle from Dutch Har-

*For a full discussion, see *At Dawn We Slept*, Chapter 37.

bor to Vladivostok in the event Russia came into the war against
Japan.[11]

So for a little while everyone was reasonably happy. The Combined Fleet had the Naval General Staff's approval for the Midway
plan; the Naval General Staff had Combined Fleet assurance that it
would incorporate a strike against the Aleutians into that plan. Hap-
piest of all, perhaps, was the Nagumo force, which on April 9 bombed
aircraft and installations at the British base of Trincomalee, Ceylon,
and later that same day sank the British carrier *Hermes* and her escort
destroyer *Vampire*.[12]

If Yamamoto needed any convincing that he was on the right track
in insisting upon Midway, he received it on April 18, 1942, at the
hands of Lieutenant Colonel James H. Doolittle, who with sixteen
B-25s bombed Tokyo, Yokohama and other Japanese cities in a quick
raid. Japanese naval authorities had long faced the possibility of such
an event. "It is almost certain that the U.S., after reorganizing their
forces, will come against us in retaliation . . . ," Ugaki had confided
to his diary on December 26, 1941. "Tokyo should be protected from
air raids; this is the most important thing to be borne in mind."

As early as February 8, 1942, Captain Yoshitake Miwa, the Combined Fleet's air officer, considered the prospect of "an enemy air
raid on Tokyo . . ." He did not think it posed "a big problem"; still,
". . . Tokyo is our capital and the center of our divine country, so in
this sense an enemy air raid on these cannot be allowed to take place
under any circumstances."[13]

This handsome, intelligent airman was no alarmist. Forty-three
at the time, he had come to Yamamoto's staff from the important post
of executive officer at Kasumigaura—Japan's Pensacola—scarcely a
month before the outbreak of war in 1941, because Yamamoto needed
his excellent background in naval aviation and his swift, sure professional judgments. Not only a well-trained pilot, Miwa had been associated with every branch of Japan's naval air arm for almost twenty
years, had studied and understood air tactics and strategy. As a graduate of the Naval Staff College in Tokyo, he was well on his way
toward flag rank.

Nagumo and his staff were not too surprised when they received
the news of the Doolittle raid aboard *Akagi* en route to Japan from
the Indian Ocean, at a point about midway between Formosa and
the Philippines. They had anticipated that sooner or later the Amer-

icans would attempt something of the sort. But they had expected the attack to come from Navy planes aboard a carrier which would have to sail within 300 miles of the homeland to launch. By using Army bombers and launching from some 700 miles, Doolittle threw the Japanese defense plans out of whack, for, although the American task force was sighted and reported, the defenders expected the enemy planes to appear the next day.[14] "Therefore," recorded Miwa, "when a telephone call came in from Tokyo saying that Tokyo and the Yokohama area had been bombed, it seemed entirely unbelievable."[15]

Furthermore, the aircraft flew much lower than anticipated, thus evading the Army fighter aircraft. Fuchida and his airmen considered the raid excellent strategy, and when they discovered that the attack had been one-way, they accorded the enemy sincere admiration.[16]

Despite its low return in actual damage, the Doolittle raid, as Kuroshima put it, "passed like a shiver over Japan."[17] The newspaper *Nichi Nichi* reacted with a sober editorial:

> It is common sense in modern warfare that it is impossible to keep the country absolutely free from hostile air raids. The enemy's air raid on Saturday on the Keihin district and other places simply means that what was unavoidable did happen. In the War of Greater East Asia, Japan is fighting formidable enemies with a mighty air force, and consequently the Japanese nation was fully prepared for such events . . .
>
> The Imperial Household was absolutely safe . . .
>
> Although this was Japan's first experience of a hostile air raid, the nation must be prepared for a frequent recurrence of similar incidents hereafter. On the assumption that future raids will be more violent and on a larger scale, the nation must form a firmer determination to meet them with calm and confidence.[18]

This remarkably objective, practical attitude did not prevail long. The Army promptly announced that it had shot down nine enemy aircraft. "In fact," Miwa confided to his diary, "not even one enemy plane was shot down. What for, I wonder, did the Army make such a false announcement?"[19] The "what for" became obvious, for the press soon instituted a campaign to play down the event. On Wednesday, April 22, the *Japan Times and Advertiser*, the government's English-language newspaper, observed:

> The affair itself proved to be such a small and inconspicuous incident

that most of the population of Tokyo failed to realize that the alarm signal was for anything more than the usual periodical rehearsal . . .

How successful the Japanese defense was can be seen from the fact that only about ten enemy planes actually succeeded about noon in penetrating the Japanese protective cordon . . . This is a most remarkable record of a nearly air-tight defense when it is realized that a single American aircraft carrier is capable of launching nearly one hundred planes in the air.

. . . the fact that the raid was attempted proves most conclusively in what pitifully desperate condition the United States now finds herself . . . It was meant purely as a sop to the American public to quiet their cries of criticism . . .

Despite this dose of soothing syrup, many Japanese were somewhat disillusioned with their Navy for permitting the Americans to sail so close to the sacred shores, and Yamamoto had to dodge a few brickbats in his mail along with the literary bouquets to which he was more accustomed.[20] The raid flicked the admiral's pride, and he was in a dither of anxiety for the safety of the Emperor and the Imperial family. Some measure of his commitment to the offensive drained away, never to be quite restored. He was more than ever wedded to the idea of establishing a picket line between the Aleutians and Midway.[21] Miwa's diary entry for April 20 summed up Yamamoto's reasoning in a nutshell:

According to a statement made by those captured at Nanchao, they seemed to have been launched from carriers. If so, their action, enemy though they were, should be regarded as a good one. If this kind of enemy attempt is to be neutralized, there would be no other way but to make a landing on Hawaii. This makes landing on Midway a prerequisite. That is the very reason why the Combined Fleet urges a Midway operation.

What is more, the Army, which initially had refused to participate in the Midway project, after the Doolittle raid insisted upon becoming a part of it.[22]

Secretary of War Stimson found it "quite interesting to see their [the Japanese] conduct under such conditions. It has not been at all well self-controlled." He had been "a little bit doubtful" about this "pet project of the President's," for he feared it would "only result in sharp reprisals from the Japanese without doing them very much harm." But he admitted the psychological effect has been "very good . . ."[23]

Nevertheless, on April 21 he called in Chief of Staff General George C. Marshall and General H. H. "Hap" Arnold, chief of the Army Air Forces, for "a few earnest words . . . about the danger of a Japanese attack on the West Coast . . ." He explained to his diary,

> . . . I am very much impressed with the danger that the Japanese, having terribly lost face by this recent attack on them in Tokio [sic] and Yokohama, will make a counter attack on us with carriers; and the west coast is still very badly undermanned, and the trouble is that it has been very hard to get any bombers to help in that.[24]

An American analysis of the Battle of the Coral Sea listed as one of the lessons learned the unexpected result of the Doolittle raid:

> This whole operation stresses the strategic principle that a raid may have strategic consequences far above those originally contemplated. This raid was too small to do substantial physical damage, yet its political effect, caused by the fear of additional raids, was great and, in this case, appears to have caused Japan to change military time schedule for other theaters. Apparently, . . . her decision to go ahead with the broad strategic plan, including the capture of MIDWAY, was firmed.[25] (Capitals in original.)

It being geographically unfeasible for the Nagumo carrier force to chase Doolittle's carrier, the Japanese flattops proceeded homeward for rest, repairs, and training, reaching Japan on April 22. As soon as possible, Nagumo and his staff proceeded to *Yamato*, where in the flagship's staff room they heard for the first time about the proposed Midway operation. In general, the carrier men favored it, especially swashbuckling Rear Admiral Tamon Yamaguchi, Commander in Chief of the Second Carrier Division. He was always game for a good fight and yearned to clear the Pacific of the American fleet.[26]

Nagumo's brilliant air officer, Commander Minoru Genda, saw in this new operation the chance to clear up some unfinished business from the Pearl Harbor attack. "I favored the plan because I expected that we could have a chance of forcing a decisive battle with the American main force by launching this Midway operation." As he learned also that the Combined Fleet planned a future attempt to invade Hawaii, he believed Midway atoll would be significant as a first step. But he was much more interested in "Operation MI," as the project was called, as a fleet action than as a landing exercise.

Nagumo's attitude, Genda observed, was "not so definite." Most of his colleagues had little reaction one way or the other at this stage.[27] When Fuchida heard of the idea of a barrier running between the Aleutians and Midway to protect the homeland, he mentally labeled it "grammar school strategy."[28] According to Rear Admiral Ryunōsuke Kusaka, Nagumo's chief of staff, the majority of the First Air Fleet staff "were against the plan, and they fiercely expressed their opposing views to the Combined Fleet headquarters." Kusaka himself spearheaded the opposition:

> I was against the plan on the ground that the task force, though it had accomplished brilliant successes in various theaters since the Pearl Harbor operation, was considerably exhausted, especially in its force of fliers, and its ships and equipment needed repairs. My idea was that its fliers should be transferred to shore-based air bases to train new fliers to cope with the subsequent operation, while the task force should replace its old fliers with new ones and have its ships and weapons repaired and reinforced, so that the task force would be able to meet the next operation with its air force newly trained and replenished. Furthermore, I entertained a good deal of doubt about the wisdom of invading Midway Island.[29]

It soon became evident, however, that the First Air Fleet staff had been invited to *Yamato* to listen, not to argue. As Kusaka observed, "The fact was that the plan had already been decided by the Combined Fleet headquarters and we were forced to accept it as it had been planned." Nevertheless, fair-minded as always, Kusaka admitted that Yamamoto did not have to twist their arms very hard. "We Japanese slighted the strength of the Americans and got self-conceited because of easy successes in the first stage of operations," he wrote bluntly. "In other words, we thought that the enemy could be easily destroyed even if it did come out to meet our force." Certainly Nagumo, although he shared Kusaka's views, had no doubt that his fleet could carry out successfully any task Yamamoto gave them.[30]

On April 28, Yamamoto held a conference aboard *Yamato* to review the lessons learned in the first part of the war. As Miwa rather cynically noted, ". . . the studying conference of so-far-successful operations was pleasant, but did not bring in much fruits."[31]

Yamaguchi urged that the Combined Fleet be reorganized into three great task forces with carriers at their hearts. This was in line with Genda's thinking. Japan had more than enough support vessels—battleships, cruisers, destroyers, etc.—for the screening units, and enough carriers to put two of these super air fleets out to sea. According to schedule, by the end of the year sufficient additional carriers would be available to float the third task force. The airmen gained the impression that Combined Fleet headquarters agreed with their suggestions, but day after day passed and nothing was done to implement them.[32]

At 1800 on April 29 Yamamoto, somewhat irritated by the general atmosphere of self-congratulation, ended the review session with a short speech of warning: "Unless more efforts based upon long-range planning are put into military preparations and operations, it will be very hard to win the final victory," he stated emphatically. "It is like a disease to think that an invincible status has been achieved after being satisfied with the past successful operations."[33]

One wonders what Yamamoto would have said to this gathering of his devoted if somewhat smug officers had he been able to read the message which Nimitz dispatched that same date, April 29, to Admiral Ernest J. King, Commander in Chief, U.S. Fleet:

DEFENSES MIDWAY . . . X CONSIDER ISLAND AT PRESENT ABLE TO WITHSTAND MODERATE ATTACK BUT WOULD REQUIRE FLEET ASSISTANCE FORWARD AGAINST MAJOR ATTACK X AM AM MAKING INSPECTION ABOUT TWO MAY X WILL GIVE FULL CONSIDERATION TO SUCH STRENGTHENING AND DEVELOPMENT AS MAY BE PRACTICABLE.[34]

CHAPTER 4

"One Touch of an Armored Sleeve"

While the discussions were going on between the Combined Fleet and First Air Fleet staffs, Vice Admiral Nobutake Kondo brought his Second Fleet back to the Inland Sea. He had been leading his battleships in a fruitless crisscrossing of the Pacific near Japan, seeking whatever carriers had launched the Doolittle raiders. On May 1, he arrived aboard *Yamato* to attend preliminary war games for Operation MI, and promptly expressed doubts about the forthcoming plan. He pointed out to Yamamoto that the American carrier force had been no more than dented, and that the Midway garrison could bring land-based air power into the picture, which the Japanese could not. In view of this, he wished to forget Midway and concentrate on cutting the lines between the United States and Australia.

But Yamamoto refused to alter the Midway operation. He told Kondo that if surprise was achieved, there was no reason why the Japanese could not be victorious again. To this Kondo posed a formidable question: Granted that Midway could be captured and garrisoned, how did the Combined Fleet propose to keep it supplied? Rather lamely, Ugaki replied that if this proved impossible, they could always evacuate after destroying everything left behind.[1] In short, the Combined Fleet staff had not carried its thinking one step ahead into the mundane but vital area of logistics.

Following Kondo's unsuccessful protest, table maneuvers got under way that same day. Midway was but the starting point of a four-stage scheme which covered operations for the remainder of the spring and summer of 1942:

First, the Main Body of the Combined Fleet would capture Midway and a task force would capture the western Aleutians. This would smoke out the U.S. Pacific Fleet for the Japanese to defeat decisively and rule out as a major force for months to come.

Second, upon completion of the Midway-Aleutians stage, most of the battleships would return to Japan and stand by, while the rest of the Midway force assembled at Truk to prepare for the early July campaign against New Caledonia and the Fiji Islands.

Third, Nagumo's carrier force would launch air attacks against Sydney and other key points of southeast Australia.

Fourth, the Nagumo fleet would rendezvous at Truk with the New Caledonia-Fiji force to replenish supplies. In early August, the full strength of the Combined Fleet would strike Johnston Island and Hawaii.[2]

Ugaki presided with a firm hand, and carried through this grandiose scheme on tabletop with a sunny lack of realism. As he sincerely believed that no situation could exist in which the Japanese would not be in complete control, he allowed nothing to happen which would seriously inconvenience the smooth development of the war games to their predestined conclusion. He did not scruple to override unfavorable rulings of other umpires.[3]

Yamamoto had earmarked over 200 vessels for the massive operation, with June 7 established as N-Day. This date would give sufficient time for overhaul of the Nagumo and Kondo fleets, and at the same time it was the last chance for more than a month to take advantage of full moonlight for night operations.[4] According to plan, on N-Day minus 5, i.e., June 2, Vice Admiral Teruhisa Komatsu's Advance Submarine Force would establish a three-section cordon east of Midway to detect any enemy fleet movements. SubRon 3 (I-168, I-169, I-171, I-174 and I-175) would deploy between latitudes 19°30′N and 23°30′N on longitude 167°W. SubRon 5 (I-156, I-157, I-158, I-159, I-162, I-165 and I-166) would be posted between latitude 29°30′N, longitude 164°30′W, and latitude 26°10′N, longitude 167°W. Finally, SubDiv 13 (I-121, I-122, I-123) would act as a supply train, bringing gas and oil to Lisianski Island and French Frigate Shoals.[5]

According to a plan worked out by Miyo of the Naval General Staff, these submarines would also refuel two Type 2 Kawanishi flying boats, 31-ton monsters with a 4,000-mile range. These would take off from Wotje, refuel from the submarines at French Frigate Shoals, and scout enemy strength and movements, for the Japanese sorely

missed their excellent prewar espionage setup on Oahu. Two of these
seaplanes had already made a dry run over Pearl Harbor on March
4, dropping a few bombs strictly for terrorist purposes.[6]

Despite the vital importance of the advance undersea mission,
the submarine commander, Komatsu, did not attend the war games
in person. But his staff was there in full force. Yet the submarine
sweep never appeared in the official orders for Operation MI. Writing
up the submarine portion of such orders was a normal responsibility
of Commander Takayasa Arima, Yamamoto's submarine officer. For
some reason Kuroshima told Arima that he need not do so.[7]

The next force on station would be Vice Admiral Moshiro Hosogaya's Northern Force, which would strike the Aleutians on N-3, i.e.,
June 4. This was a formidable fleet in itself, consisting of three heavy
cruisers, three light cruisers, one auxiliary cruiser, twelve destroyers,
three minesweepers, one minelayer, three troop transports carrying
an Army landing force of 1,200 troops and a Navy landing party of
1,250, six submarines, and two carriers—*Ryujo* with sixteen fighters
and twenty-one torpedo bombers and *Junyo* with twenty-four fighters
and twenty-one dive bombers.[8]

The main thrust would be against Midway. Nagumo's First Carrier
Striking Force would initiate the action on N-2 (June 5), from approximately 250 miles northwest of the atoll. His mission would be
to clear out any enemy surface and air forces within range and knock
out shore installations. As originally planned, Nagumo would have
his six Pearl Harbor carriers—*Akagi, Kaga, Hiryu, Soryu, Zuikaku*,
and *Shokaku*. The latter two, however, were still committed in the
South Pacific and their availability remained a question mark. But he
could count on the first four carriers. *Akagi* and *Kaga* would supply
forty-two fighters, forty-two dive bombers and fifty-one torpedo
bombers. *Soryu* and *Hiryu* boasted a like number of fighters and dive
bombers, and forty-two torpedo bombers. For support, Nagumo would
have the battleships *Haruna* and *Kirishima*, the heavy cruisers *Tone*
and *Chikuma*, and the light cruiser *Nagara*, with eleven destroyers.[9]

The plan called for Rear Admiral Ruitaro Fujita's Seaplane Tender
Group, consisting of the seaplane carriers *Chitose* and *Kamikawa
Maru*, one destroyer and one patrol boat, to occupy Kure Island,
some sixty miles northwest of Midway, the next day. Kure would
become a base for the twenty-four fleet fighters and eight scout planes
to support the main landings.

According to the war games schedule, that same day, Rear Admiral Raizo Tanaka's Transport Group of twelve transports and three destroyer-transports, moving up from Saipan, would rendezvous with the main body of Kondo's Midway Invasion Force, moving east and slightly south from Japan.[10] To fool the Americans into thinking that the main Japanese force was coming from the south, Tanaka's ships would allow themselves to be seen at this time.[11] This imposed a delicate question of timing: The occupation force wanted to be seen, but not too soon.

At dawn on N-Day, Tanaka would land his 5,000 troops, while Vice Admiral Takeo Kurita's heavy cruisers *Kumano*, *Suzuya*, *Mikuma*, and *Mogami*, plus two destroyers, swinging up from Guam, provided close-in support. Kondo's main body—the battleships *Kongo* and *Hiei*, heavy cruisers *Atago*, *Chokai*, *Myoko*, *Naguro*, light cruiser *Yura*, eight destroyers, and the light carrier *Zuiho* with twelve fighters and twelve torpedo bombers—would remain slightly south and southwest of Midway to cover the flank.[12]

And what of Yamamoto's Main Body? The Guard Force under Vice Admiral Shiro Takasu, with his battleships *Hyuga*, *Ise*, *Fuso* and *Yamashiro*, two light cruisers and twelve destroyers, was scheduled to screen the Aleutians strike. Yamamoto would be aboard *Yamato*, which would be backed up by the battlewagons *Nagato* and *Mutsu*. The light cruiser *Sendai*, nine destroyers, the light carrier *Hosho* with eight bombers, and the seaplane carriers *Chiyoda* and *Nisshin*, carrying midget submarines designed to harry the American ships during the surface engagement, would serve as support.[13]

Thus Yamamoto's vigil would be 600 miles northwest of Midway, far from the potential scene of action, with Takasu's Guard Force 500 miles further north. And Nagumo, the spearhead of the entire plan, would be 300 miles east of Yamamoto. Last, the Second Carrier Striking Force under Rear Admiral Kakuji Kakuta, who by this time would have returned from Alaskan waters, would be at a point 300 miles east of the Guard Force.[14]

If all went according to plan, this tremendous armada would be scattered over 1,000 miles across the north central Pacific. And each of its elements would be waiting for the U.S. Pacific Fleet to poke its bows over the horizon sometime after N-Day.

This spread of forces could move together to concentrate against the enemy's strength in an unforeseen emergency. But no one really

believed in the possibility of such a development. "Practically everyone thought that the battle was already won," said Watanabe. "The
greater part of the U.S. Fleet was in the Atlantic, and under the
circumstances we believed that we had a preponderance of naval
power in the Pacific. We could not help but win if our forces were
properly handled."[15] That in itself was quite an "if." And, of course,
the plan depended upon the Americans acting in a predictable manner.

Painfully obvious to the airmen was the fact that there would be
no reorganization of the Combined Fleet along the lines Yamaguchi
had proposed at the late April conference.[16] The very title "Main
Body" was significant. For all his lip service to the principle of the
offensive and to naval air power, Yamamoto still, perhaps subcon-
sciously, visualized the battleship as the queen of the fleet. And where
would these battlewagons be while Nagumo's carriers bore the full
brunt if by any chance the Americans emerged ahead of schedule?
Yamamoto would be 300 miles to the west, and Takasu almost 1,000
miles north. In any real emergency, for all the good they could do,
they might as well stay at Hashirajima and save fuel. Such screening
and support as Nagumo needed would have to come from his own
resources. Two battleships, two heavy cruisers, and a light cruiser
were slim cover for four—perhaps six—carriers.

Yet such was their self-confidence that the First Air Fleet officers,
bronzed and fit from their months in the southern sun and sea air,
reacted to these considerations with irritation, with disgust, with
disappointment, with sardonic amusement, according to their na-
tures—not with alarm or foreboding. They felt quite capable of taking
on Operation MI all by themselves.

During the course of these complicated table maneuvers, some
of the operational officers observed that the Combined Fleet staff was
seriously underestimating enemy capabilities. Moreover, if any no-
table difficulties arose, Ugaki arbitrarily juggled them in favor of the
Japanese team. But no one felt like complaining and thus bringing
down Ugaki's wrath. Nor did they believe it made any real difference.
The headquarters staff and the tactical officers vied with each other
in self-assurance.[17]

At one point in the war games, both Ugaki and Kuroshima asked
how the First Air Fleet proposed to protect the carriers from enemy
bombers while their own fighter aircraft were escorting the bombers

over Midway. By tacit consent all looked to Genda, rather than to Nagumo, for a reply.[18]

Since the start of the war, every time Genda dealt the cards, Nagumo had come up with a full house, and he was not the man to knock success. Convinced that he had captured the bluebird of happiness, Nagumo leaned more and more on his scintillating air officer. What is more, Genda "was respected with some kind of awfulness by other staff officers." And outspoken men openly referred to the Task Force as "Genda's fleet."[19]

A less gifted man than Genda would have basked in this unquestioning acceptance, but being the fine officer he was, he found the situation uncomfortable and at times downright frightening. For one thing, he had no opportunity to refine and clarify his concepts against a countercharge of shrewd questions and healthy skepticism arising from Nagumo's priceless years of experience. It was like trying to strop his razor on chiffon instead of leather. Even more important, Nagumo's attitude indicated that he was not really thinking, was not truly absorbing the theories and practices of naval air power; he was simply taking Genda's staff work on blind faith. Genda had his full share of self-confidence, but he knew very well that no one is immune to error. When he reflected that a tentative suggestion of his might sway the future of his country, he broke out in gooseflesh.[20]

On this occasion, caution in abeyance and drunk with victory, he flashed back: "*Gaishu Isshoku* [one touch of an armored sleeve]!"[21] He was not being cryptic; this was a poetic Japanese equivalent of the contemporary American "We'll mow 'em down!"

At Genda's reply Ugaki, who had long thought the First Air Fleet's younger officers were too big for their boots, cautioned Nagumo that the possibility of an enemy breakthrough must be taken into consideration. Yet Ugaki himself promptly nullified any good his warning might have done. For during the table maneuvers, the theoretical American forces broke through and bombed Nagumo's carriers while their aircraft were away from their mother ships attacking Midway— the very situation which had concerned Ugaki. Lieutenant Commander Masatake Okumiya, the umpire, ruled that the enemy had scored nine hits, sinking both *Akagi* and *Kaga*. But Ugaki would not suffer such *lèse majesté*, and immediately overruled Okumiya, allowing only three hits, with *Kaga* sunk and *Akagi* slightly damaged. And later, when conducting the second phase practice, he blandly res-

urrected *Kaga* from her watery grave to participate in the New Caledonia and Fiji invasions.[22]

Furthermore, during these war games the "American" fleet did
not sortie for a decisive battle, although this was a possibility. Captain
Chiaki Matsuda commanded the imaginary enemy, and in retrospect
Genda thought "that his (non-American) conduct of the war games
might have given us the wrong impression of American thinking."[23]

Before leaving the Midway phase of the table maneuvers, Yamamoto instructed Nagumo to do his best to reconnoiter the U.S.
Pacific Fleet, particularly the American carriers, and be prepared to
counterattack with torpedoes. For this reason, he requested that one-
half of the Nagumo Force's attacking planes be equipped with torpedoes.

Captain Akira Sasaki, Yamamoto's air staff officer, was responsible
for drafting Combined Fleet orders concerning the First Air Fleet.
However, Kuroshima orally informed Sasaki that it was not necessary
to write Yamamoto's instructions concerning the torpedo bombers
into the orders.[24] Watanabe, who was responsible for reading and
correcting any orders Sasaki might write and discussing their contents
with the air staff officer, offered no *post-facto* excuses for either himself or Kuroshima. Yet one can readily see excellent reasons for Kuroshima's action. Nagumo and his staff had heard the instructions; it
should not be necessary to confirm every tactical detail in writing,
especially as Japan's training and war experience had clearly indicated
that Yamamoto's advice as to the proportion of torpedo bombers was
sound.

So both Kuroshima and Watanabe coordinated the Combined Fleet
order draft, although it contained no express confirmation concerning
either the submarine sweep or the First Air Fleet's torpedo attacks.
"This," reminisced Watanabe grimly, "was our mistake."[25] Nevertheless, the submarine problem proved to be one of timing rather
than of explicit orders, and one could argue reasonably that strapping
the tactical commander into a straitjacket a good month before a
scheduled operation is not the wisest way to run a war.

Genda was worried because the forces were so far-flung that the
Navy seemed to be losing sight of the objective and to be violating
the military principle of mass. During the critique following the war
games, he crossed swords with Kuroshima over this question. "The
main emphasis of the operational plan should be placed on destruction

of the American fleet," he affirmed. "To that end, the Aleutian attack force should be re-employed at Midway and all available strength should be directed to Midway, even to waiting for the Fifth Carrier Division."

"The Commander in Chief of the Combined Fleet can hardly stand to see the capital disturbed," Kuroshima replied, referring obliquely to the Doolittle raid. "The primary mission of the task force is to support the Midway invasion."

So Midway had first priority with the Combined Fleet staff, the U.S. Pacific Fleet second. Genda nodded to himself. He had made his point. There was no use batting his head against a stone wall.[26]

After the *Yamato* conference, which ended on May 4, Lieutenant Commander Shigeharu Murata, who had led the torpedo attack on Pearl Harbor, sounded off loudly: "What a nonsensical operation! The *Yamato* and others are coming 300 miles behind our task force! What the hell do they think they can do with those useless guns to the rear of our carrier force?"

Fuchida added, "If those damned battleships were ahead of our force, those big guns would be of some use and also helpful for the operation of the task force. But, otherwise, I can't help asking myself if they hardly have enough will to fight."

Hearing this exchange, Teuchi Makajima, a photographer who had come aboard *Akagi* in the south Pacific, "thought that the coming operation involved some grave defect."

"Our C-in-C is no good at all, as he is a torpedo man," grumbled Murata.

"Be that as it may," shrugged navigator Commander Gishiro Miura, "we are going to win this time, too."

His habitual good nature restored, Murata grinned. "It won't be much fun this time, as we can't expect the enemy to come out." And with characteristic impishness he offered Makajima a hop in his torpedo plane.[27]

In view of all this light-hearted self-confidence, one wonders just how much if at all the Japanese would have altered their attitude and plans if they knew how close on top of them Nimitz was at this time. The American admiral had not rushed to buy the whole package as Layton and Rochefort saw it. The entire thing could be a trap, Japanese Intelligence feeding the Americans false information. "I had to do a bit of hard thinking," he said, "but I believed that I had the

truth of the problem."[28] Having thus made his decision, Nimitz wasted
no time in doubts or waverings. On May 2, while Yamamoto, Nagumo
and their staffs were bent over their planning tables aboard *Yamato*,
Nimitz flew to Midway and spent the entire day with Lieutenant
Colonel Harold D. Shannon, commander of the Sixth Marine Battalion, and Commander Cyril T. Simard, the naval air station commander. The two islands of the atoll, Sand and Eastern, were self-
sufficient, but the seaplane hangars were on Sand Island and all other
aviation facilities on Eastern. At this time Nimitz did not take the
two officers into his confidence, but asked Shannon what the outpost
would require to hold off a major amphibious attack by the Japanese.[29]

Back at his headquarters, the admiral wrote a joint personal letter
to the two Midway commanders. He praised their fine work at Midway and advised that he had just given them spot promotions to
colonel and captain respectively. He went on to say that the Japanese
were planning an all-out attack on Midway, scheduled for May 28,
the closest approximate date Combat Intelligence had reached. He
outlined the proposed enemy strategy and forces, and promised Midway all possible aid. Naturally, this missive struck Shannon and Simard forcibly, but no one hit the panic button. Midway was already
on the alert. Patrol planes screened to the west at dawn each morning;
the Marines carried rifles and helmets at all times, even to eat and
swim.[30]

Not everyone on the American side accepted Nimitz's evaluation.
Many at high levels were reluctant to believe that the actual target
was not Oahu, or perhaps the west coast of the United States.[31] Among
those fearful for Oahu, not unnaturally, was Lieutenant General Delos
C. Emmons, commander of the Hawaiian Department and military
governor of the Territory of Hawaii. He had replaced Lieutenant
General Walter C. Short about the same time Nimitz arrived on Oahu
to assume his command. In general, he conveyed an impression of
austerity, but he could be charming when he chose.[32] And he so chose
when dealing with Nimitz, for both officers were devoted to the
principle of interservice cooperation. The two leaders got along well
from the start. With the new Japanese threat hovering over the horizon, Emmons had almost daily conferences with Nimitz in CinCPAC
Headquarters.[33] He was an airman and understood both the capabilities and limitations of war in the air.

"The strategic location and importance of the Islands indicate that they may be bombed again, and in strength. The civilian here must assume a duty along with the soldier," he told some 5,000 air raid wardens and spectators on Sunday morning, May 3, at the Honolulu Stadium.

"We must not be complacent or assume that we are immune to attack," he warned. "Our defensive forces are well trained and constantly on the alert. They will inflict damage on the enemy, but it is too much to expect that we will escape damage."[34]

In view of the Pearl Harbor experience, Emmons would have been foolish indeed not to keep immediate danger to his own command in the forefront of his thinking. But this time Oahu was in no immediate danger. "Commander in Chief Combined Fleet will, in cooperation with the Army, invade and occupy strategic points in the Western Aleutians and Midway Island." So Admiral Osami Nagano, Chief of the Naval General Staff, directed Yamamoto on May 5, 1942.[35] And Yamamoto always obeyed the orders of the Naval General Staff—provided he had assured beforehand that such orders marched with his own will.

CHAPTER 5

"The Expected and Constant Threat"

Planning either for or against Operation MI did not occupy the full attention of either Nimitz or Yamamoto in early May. On the 6th, just one day after Nagano issued his order, American fortunes hit bottom with the surrender of General Jonathan Wainwright's gallant but doomed holding forces in Corregidor. From this point, there was nowhere to go but up, and immediately, almost imperceptibly, the upswing began.

While the Midway table maneuvers were in progress, preliminaries for the battle of the Coral Sea took place. Contact was first made on May 7. The Japanese were fully confident that they would win this engagement and occupy Port Moresby in the southeastern part of New Guinea. Even Miwa, who usually expressed himself with sensible moderation in the privacy of his diary, recorded "wild joy ran among us" when the news came to Combined Fleet headquarters that the enemy had been sighted.

Later in the same entry, however, he had to record, "Our Fifth Carrier Division first attacked an enemy force in the south, which actually consisted of an oiler and destroyer, thus making its first attack a failure." Miwa hoped for bigger game than the destroyer *Sims* or the oiler *Neosho*, the latter so miraculously spared at Pearl Harbor,* now settling on the sea bed. "In the meantime," Miwa continued, "the enemy force south of Deboyne Island launched its attack upon our invasion force, with the result that our light carrier *Shoho* was sunk at around 0930 A.M. The battle then came to a stalemate for a while."[1]

---

*See *At Dawn We Slept*, p. 518.

40

"Stalemate" was a good single-word summing up of this clash. This is not the place to go into details of that engagement. The concern of this study with the battle of the Coral Sea is how it affected the forthcoming Midway operation. And it did have important effects. On the morning of May 8, Admiral Fletcher's Task Force Seventeen and Rear Admiral Chuichi "King Kong" Hara's Fifth Carrier Division finally sighted one another. The two forces were remarkably well matched. If Hara had the edge in fighter and torpedo planes, Fletcher had radar and more sophisticated homing devices. If *Yorktown* and *Lexington* had more antiaircraft guns, *Shokaku* and *Zuikaku* had the advantage of months of operating together as a unit. The weather favored the Fifth Carrier Division, which was operating under overcast skies, while in Fletcher's area the sun shone brightly.[2]

". . . The distance between our force and the enemy force is 200 miles," Miwa recorded back on *Yamato,* where every thought strained toward the south. "In such a short distance, both sides seem to have a chance. A fierce fight must be expected. (Although without specific reason, I had confidence of winning the battle and did not have any fear, but Kuroshima seemed to worry about the outcome a little bit.)" Thus Miwa added parenthetically, possibly at a later date. Then he continued:

> Long and hard training is our vantage point. A victorious report could be expected.
>
> At around 0930 A.M. a code signal of "charge" came in, and in ten minutes it was followed by another report of "*Saratoga* sunk." The staff officer room was filled with a wild cry of joy.
>
> Shortly after noon, a brief battle report came in: "The *Saratoga* was hit by nine torpedoes and more than seven bombs and a *Yorktown* type carrier by three torpedoes and more than eight bombs, with the result that both ships were believed surely to be sunk. Our *Shokaku* was hit by several bombs but she could still navigate by her power." A great victory indeed![3]

But *Saratoga* was not at the bottom of the Coral Sea; she was in Puget Sound winding up repairs. For the second time the Japanese were confusing her with *Lexington,* having reported the latter sunk earlier in the year when in fact a submarine had damaged *Saratoga.*[4]

At this stage, the Fifth Carrier Division's report was highly optimistic. *Yorktown* received a number of near misses but only one direct hit. An 800-pounder from a dive bomber plummeted through her flight deck down to the fourth level, killing or seriously injuring sixty-six men. Quick action brought her fires under control, and under the expert maneuvering of Captain Elliott Buckmaster she was able to continue air operations.[5]

Far from the "nine torpedoes and more than seven bombs" of Hara's report, *Lexington* took two torpedoes on her port side, a bomb in a ready service locker and another on the smokestack structure, while near misses sprung several plates. Ironically, the actual battle damage was relatively minor, and the big carrier, like *Yorktown*, still carried on normal flight operations. It appears that American carelessness was more responsible than Japanese marksmanship for the loss of *Lexington.* Someone had left a motor generator running, and about an hour after the carrier battle was over, which was 1140 on May 8, the heat ignited gasoline vapors which a torpedo had released deep in the great ship. This triggered a series of explosions, but so staunch was "Lady Lex" that not until shortly after 1700 did Captain Frederick C. "Ted" Sherman reluctantly order the ship abandoned.[6]

Some vessels are jinx ships, unlucky and unhappy from the laying of the keel. Others are happy ships where everything seems to go right. *Lexington* was one of the latter, cherished by her crew, some of whom had been with her since her commissioning in 1927. To these men, her loss was more than a naval setback; it was a heart-blow. Carefully, gently, as a family might move from a beloved but outgrown furnished apartment, crewmen dusted their equipment and filed papers adrift on their desks while medical personnel prepared the wounded for removal. The sorrowful evacuation was orderly, almost ceremonious. No living soul perished; even Sherman's dog went over the side.[7]

Neither Fletcher nor Sherman had the slightest desire to go down with *Lexington,* dear as she was to them. The United States needed trained officers; costly, empty gestures it could do without. The captain was the last man down the ropes, after a final, thorough search to ensure that only the bodies of her 216 dead remained. As the destroyer *Phelps* loosed the torpedoes that plunged the carrier into the deep, her tough, sea-bronzed sailors "were crying and weeping like young girls."[8]

Hara's Fifth Carrier Division did not escape unscathed. *Shokaku* limped home to Japan, almost capsizing on the way, suffering from three bomb hits which cost her 148 men killed or wounded. One bomb struck her forward bow, setting fire to gasoline and damaging the flight deck so that she no longer could launch her aircraft. Another knocked out her airplane motor repair compartment. *Zuikaku* suffered no hits, but due to personnel and aircraft losses had to follow *Shokaku* back to Japan for remanning.[9]

Aboard *Yamato*, between optimistic reports and wishful thinking, the Japanese believed they had sunk not only *Lexington, Sims* and *Neosho*, but the cruiser *Chicago*, a battleship of the *California* class—presumably HMAS *Australia*, the only battlewagon in the entire Allied force—and possibly *Warspite*, which was not among those present, along with a large bag of sundries.[10]

Taking all this into consideration, Miwa could not understand why Vice Admiral Shigeyoshi Inouye, Commander in Chief of the Fourth Fleet and supreme Japanese commander for the Port Moresby-Coral Sea action, ordered the task force to withdraw north and to suspend the attack. Nor could Ugaki, who immediately sent off a message that "under the prevailing circumstances we see the need to press the enemy more and more. Request you inform us of the reason why it cannot be done." Despite this tart communication, the Fourth Fleet issued still another order postponing the invasion of Port Moresby and "switching its disposition for the invasion of Mauru and the Ocean Islands."[11]

Miwa was furious. "This kind of concept is tantamount to defeatism," he exploded in his diary.

> . . . To do nothing about this Fourth Fleet order might lead to denying the fighting spirit of our Imperial Japanese Navy. Now, we cannot help feeling that we don't need to pay much attention to the respectable authority of the C-in-C of the Fourth Fleet.
>
> It might be possible to succeed in a day attack tomorrow instead of a night attack tonight, but such, if done, will be nothing but luck. At this moment, we must chase the retreating enemy by all means. It is time to press the enemy by throwing anything inflammable into the boilers if fuel runs short . . .

Evidently Yamamoto agreed, for he personally issued "the unprecedented order": "Efforts should be made to chase the remaining enemy and destroy it." But Yamamoto was no more successful than Ugaki. "The Fourth Fleet has so far been 'chicken,' " observed Miwa bitterly. ". . . Now we must conclude that they lack the long-cherished traditional spirit of the Imperial Japanese Navy . . ." He was so angry that he would not even read Inouye's cable which arrived following the action of May 8.[12] Actually, the U.S. Army Air Force's land-based aircraft were making things hot off Papua, and with no air cover, Inouye had little chance of success. So he postponed the Port Moresby landing until July, and it never did take place.[13]

In the Battle of the Coral Sea viewed purely as a sea engagement, the Japanese had the edge, losing one light carrier, one destroyer and several minecraft, with a heavy carrier badly damaged, against the American loss of a heavy carrier, a destroyer, an oiler, and another carrier well mauled. But strategically speaking, any battle which fails of its purpose cannot be considered a victory, and the Japanese failed to achieve their objective—capture and occupation of Port Moresby. So, considered objectively, it was a draw—a tactical Japanese victory versus a strategic American one.

With an estimated attack day of May 28 for Midway hanging over his head, Nimitz did not dawdle in pulling Fletcher back. Barely waiting for the carrier action in the Coral Sea to break off, he summoned Fletcher without, however, indicating any particular urgency. His message read: "When in all respects ready, proceed Pearl Harbor at best sustained speed." The phrase "best sustained speed" does not mean "all possible speed"; it means a good, steady clip, wasting no time but on the other hand wasting no fuel. So Fletcher's Task Force Seventeen had no hint that another major battle was in the offing.[14]

As he plowed toward Oahu, the official Japanese press, never inclined to spoil a good war story by overly modest use of either claims or adjectives, proclaimed a resounding victory. On May 9, the *Japan Times and Advertiser* quoted an *Asahi* interview with Vice Admiral Kiyoshi Nagamura, in which the "noted authority on aircraft carriers" expressed the opinion that "the American losses suffered in the latest battle have shattered the American dream of counteroffensives on Japan and that their wounded pride at the loss of the aircraft carriers suggests the doomed collapse of the United States."

The English-language newspaper's own editorial writer waxed grandiloquent:

> Army or Navy, the incomparable armed might of Japan, consecrated by the August Virtues of His Majesty the Emperor and inspired by the prayers of one hundred million supporters, continues to win astonishing victory after astonishing victory . . .

> The tremendous significance of this Japanese victory can hardly
> be exaggerated. It strikes a deadly blow at the most vulnerable point
> in the Allies' strength, i.e., loss of battleships and carriers . . .[15]

To do the Japanese newsmen justice, they did not invent these stories; they were duly reporting what they received from Navy headquarters. Participants in any military action have difficulty in evaluating the engagement objectively, and throughout the war naval aviators of both sides showed an exuberant tendency to claim near-misses as hits, and damaged ships as destroyed.

Hitler himself sent congratulations to Premier Tojo: "After this new defeat, the United States warships will hardly dare to face the Japanese Fleet again, since any United States warship which accepts action with the Japanese naval forces is as good as lost."[16]

This journalistic euphoria played its deadly part in brewing the "Mickey Finn" fate was preparing for the Japanese Navy. Never doubting that both *Yorktown* and *Saratoga* (as the Japanese still reported *Lexington*) were deep in the Coral Sea, Nagumo took in stride the temporary loss of *Shokaku* and *Zuikaku*. He had lost one-third of his anticipated carrier strength before the battle of Midway was off the planning boards, but the enemy had also scratched two carriers. Nor did his staff officers lose any sleep over this development. "As we were convinced that the First and Second Carrier Divisions were far superior to the Fifth Carrier Division, our confidence in our superiority was not shaken at all in spite of the fact that the Fifth Carrier Division was damaged in the Coral Sea Battle," explained Commander Takashi Hashiguchi, horizontal bombing veteran of the Hawaiian skies and now air officer of *Hiryu*.[17]

The Japanese Navy took its time about repairing *Shokaku* and replenishing *Zuikaku*, with the result that these two great carriers, less than a year old, could not join their comrades where their presence might have turned the tide of battle.

Little shadows of doubt continued to send an occasional chill over the planners on Oahu. Rochefort was almost as sure as man can be of anything that Midway was the prime Japanese target, and, as we have seen, Nimitz was so convinced that he had actually gone to Midway for a personal inspection. Japanese intercepts occasionally referred to some place designated as "AF," and from the context Rochefort had a very strong hunch that it meant Midway. So, on or about May 10, with the permission of Layton and Nimitz, he set a little trap for the Japanese. At his suggestion, Midway dispatched a message in the clear to Oahu, advising that their distillation plant had broken down, and they were having a water shortage. The Japanese snapped at this fly. Within forty-eight hours, Combat Intelligence intercepted a Japanese message advising all commanders concerned that AF was short of water.[18]

While this clinched it so far as Rochefort was concerned, he still had problems with the Navy Department, which kept arguing back and forth with him about such minor matters as the name of a certain Japanese carrier. At last, goaded, he told them, "Give the carrier any name you like." He would know what he meant, anyway.[19]

It was a time of sober triumph for Rochefort's good colleague, Layton, too. "At the time of Pearl Harbor, they didn't want to listen to me," he said later. "But at the time of Midway they did."[20]

But no one yet had succeeded in dragging Emmons into the Amen corner. On May 15, he issued another warning, explaining the martial law that had recently been established in Hawaii:

> Actual invasion and the horrors of warfare have been visited upon us and we are now living under the expected and constant threat of repetition.
>
> All civilian and military effort has been directed to the end that this theater of operation will be prepared to meet any eventuality visited upon it.[21]

What roused Emmons to something like protest was Nimitz's action in ordering a condition of "Fleet-opposed Invasion," which enabled him to place the Seventh Air Force's bombers under CinCPAC. Around mid-May, he sent Nimitz an Army Intelligence critique, with his own favorable endorsement, pointing out that the Navy's planning was predicated upon estimated enemy intentions rather than estimated enemy capabilities. And those capabilities included another attack on Oahu.

The point was well taken; Pearl Harbor had provided a painful object lesson in what could happen when Americans spent too much time deciding what the Japanese might do instead of what they could do. The trouble was that under the circumstances Nimitz had little choice. He did not have the ships or the aircraft to cover all Yamamoto's options. But he could and did appoint one of his staff officers,

Captain James M. Steele, to present counterarguments to every point that Layton, Rochefort and their colleagues brought forward.[22]

Many of Emmons's superiors in Washington were even more skeptical. There is a saying, "If it sounds too good to be true, it probably is." And some of this intelligence seemed excessive. As Chief of Staff George C. Marshall testified to the Congressional Committee investigating Pearl Harbor,

> . . . we were very much disturbed because one Japanese unit gave Midway as its post office address, and that seemed a little bit too thick, so when the ships actually appeared it was a great relief, because if we had been deceived, and our limited number of vessels were there, and the Japanese approached at some other point, they would have had no opposition whatsoever.

Either because Marshall never knew the whole story, or because he had forgotten some of it over the years, he attributed the knowledge of Japan's plans to "Magic"—the breaking of Japan's top diplomatic code, known to the Americans as Purple. But he emphasized that one could not accept everything from Intelligence sources as gospel:

> . . . we always had to be very careful to check, because you never could tell at what moment that would boomerang. It would be the inevitable procedure of the other government, if they knew their business, and they suddenly discovered we had cracked their code and were picking up their information, to endeavor to capitalize on that, to lead us into a ruinous situation.[23]

Of course Nimitz knew what was at stake if he happened to guess wrong, but to make just such excruciating, far-reaching decisions— and to bear the blame for them if they resulted in fiascos—was precisely why the Navy had pinned four stars on his shoulders and given him the title of CinCPAC. So he continued to draw in his lines. Halsey's Task Force Sixteen had been operating about 1,000 miles from the scene of action in the Coral Sea. After depositing a squadron of Marine fighters at Noumea, Halsey continued to scout in the area with his two carriers, four heavy cruisers, eight destroyers and two tankers. He felt hamstrung, and he bristled over Cominch's directive to stay within shore-based air cover. He was thus occupied when he received Nimitz's order on May 15 to return to Pearl Harbor.[24]

As American forces, aboard ship and on shore, focused ever more

sharply upon their target, the Japanese Navy began to realize the
true cost of their so-called victory at the Coral Sea. "Casualty list of
the Fifth Carrier Division came in," Miwa recorded in his diary on
May 14.

> *Zuikaku* lost about forty per cent of her flying crews and *Shokaku*
> approximately thirty per cent. It was a fierce battle, according to
> the casualty list.
>
> Lt. Cmdr. Kakuichi Takahashi was killed in battle . . . Alas!
>
> But we must remember that this spirit is the very one to save
> our country—that is, the burning spirit of the air fighters. This spirit
> should prevail in the Imperial Japanese Navy more and more.

The loss of Takahashi, the phlegmatic, dependable leader of the
Pearl Harbor dive bombers, was a cruel blow. Every one of Japan's
early naval air victories whittled away at the real keystone of her
power—her stockpile of veteran airmen. The new men, no matter
how eager and brave, could not adequately replace such skillful,
seasoned airmen as Takahashi.

CHAPTER 6

"Required to Aim at Two Hares"

The change in quality of personnel was painfully evident to Nagumo as he watched the training being conducted before, during and after the Coral Sea engagement in preparation for Midway. Any knowledgeable observer of these erratic, slipshod exercises would have difficulty in believing that this was the same naval air force which had trained so meticulously and persistently for the Pearl Harbor strike. And in many respects it was not.

Of Nagumo's four carriers, only *Kaga*, a tough old girl reputed to be a lucky ship, was in shape to use for landing and takeoff practice. The others required extensive refurbishing and replenishing after their months at sea. Immediately following the early May war games, therefore, Nagumo transferred his flag to *Kaga* until *Akagi* returned to the Inland Sea in mid-month.[1]

In general, those who felt themselves most responsible for operational training were displeased with the program, and with considerable cause. Each saw the problem from his own particular viewpoint, but all agreed that the result was unsatisfactory.

To Genda, the time factor was a straitjacket. "We did not have ample time to train our fliers," he said, "with the result that our training was not as thorough as in the Pearl Harbor operation. The only exception was the newly acquired 'Suisei' carrier-borne search plane. A small number though they were, they were exclusively trained with emphasis on shadowing enemy carriers." He admitted, however, "Nothing special was done, as I believed that the hitherto-applied training measures and operational procedures could do as well in the incoming Midway operation. But in view of the experiences in the

Coral Sea battle, the torpedo-releasing altitude of the torpedo bombers was made as low as possible."[2]

Hashiguchi observed the sharp difference between the pre-Pearl
Harbor and pre-Midway preparations:

> In the case of Pearl Harbor, attack training was made thoroughly.
> Using Pearl Harbor models, fliers were trained to familiarize them-
> selves with the island's topography to memorize their attack targets,
> attack routes, attack methods, and the like. In the case of Midway,
> however, the training period was short and emphasis was apparently
> placed more in completing preparations and supply than on training.

Hashiguchi added, "Another reason for this might be the fact that
the fleet fliers had been well trained already."[3] No doubt the veteran
airmen, with six months of uninterrupted success behind them, did
not take their routine brush-up for Midway too seriously.

Nagumo fretted over both the shortage of time and the high personnel turnover. Because of these, ". . . practically no one got beyond
the point of basic training," as he reported following the Midway
battle. Indeed, one cannot help wondering how much of his lamen-
tation was an accurate and honest recollection, and how much was
post-facto explanation and exculpation.

> Inexperienced fliers barely got to the point where they could make
> daytime landings on carriers . . . even some of the more seasoned
> fliers had lost some of their skill. No opportunity was available to
> carry out joint training, which, of course, made impossible any co-
> ordinated action between contact units, illumination units, and attack
> units. The likelihood of obtaining any satisfactory results from night
> attacks, therefore, was practically nil.[4]

The horizontal bombing leaders practiced at Iwakuni, using the
target battleship *Settsu,* and reached "a fair degree of skill, but they
had no opportunity to participate in any formation bombing drills."
The dive bombers wasted valuable time coming and going between
their bases and the western Inland Sea, for *Settsu* could not come to
them. Moreover, the men "could not participate in more than one
dive bombing drill a day without seriously interfering with their basic
training." Nor was air combat practice more promising, for the men
got "no further than to actual firing and basic training for lone air
combat operations. The more experienced were employed in for-

mation air combat tactics, but even they were limited to about a three-plane formation."[5]

Torpedo bombing, Japan's specialty, in which she scored heavily at Pearl Harbor, was in the worst shape of all. The mock attacks held in mid-May, with officers from Yokosuka Air Corps as referees, gave no cause for optimism. In fact, "the records of these tests were so disappointing that some were moved to comment that it was almost a mystery how men with such poor ability could have obtained such brilliant results as they had in the Coral Sea."[6]

Evidently no one pointed out that these were not the same airmen who had participated in the Coral Sea battle. Nor did their wonder cause them to inquire whether the Coral Sea results really had been as "brilliant" as claimed. Throughout May, following that engagement, Japan was awash in a sea of self-adulation.

On May 13, the *Japan Times and Advertiser* really blew the trumpet. The writer of an unsigned article declared optimistically, "These [U.S.]naval defeats suffered since the beginning of the War of Greater East Asia practically eliminates [sic] all possibility of a major future naval engagement in the Pacific between Japan and the United States. The main fleet of the American Navy is resting at the bottom of the Pacific and it is doubtful whether the United States can send another fleet over to the Pacific."

Such cool assumption of superiority is not the healthiest attitude to encourage in a navy preparing for "a major future naval engagement." A little less of it, and the Japanese might have rushed the repairs and replenishing of *Shokaku* and *Zuikaku* to the point of participation at Midway. And even considering their low opinion of American efficiency and fighting spirit, the Japanese should have remembered an old Chinese proverb: "A lion uses all its might in attacking a rabbit."[7]

It was a Japanese saying, however, which preyed on Kusaka's mind: "He who pursues two hares catches neither." He feared that it might become applicable to the First Air Fleet's rather ambiguous mission in the coming operation. As Kusaka explained,

> The Combined Fleet's plan envisioned two objectives: one being to serve as a spearhead for a major objective of invading Midway and another being to destroy the enemy task force when it came out to meet our force. Among them, the former should be given more priority in the light of the overall operational plan. Furthermore,

an enemy air attack from a land base should be taken into consideration . . . This was a point about which I was most concerned, as this meant that the First Air Fleet was required to aim at two hares.[8]

Instead of lending Nagumo advice and counsel in this crucial prebattle period, Kusaka was in Tokyo needling the upper brass for posthumous double promotions for the Japanese fliers who had died at Pearl Harbor, as the Navy had done for the midget submariners. This was a delicate subject with Genda, Fuchida, and their airmen, who were thoroughly disgusted with the blatant favoritism displayed toward the brave, self-sacrificing, yet pathetic and ineffectual midget submarine men. They had been willing to die for country and Emperor and deserved honor accordingly; but so had the airmen, and in dying they had accomplished their mission. So the whole First Air Fleet earnestly wanted the same recognition accorded their own heroes. But at this time, it was all in the past. Genda and Fuchida would much rather have seen Kusaka, that human tranquilizer, working toward the next battle instead of fussing over old quarrels.[9]

Nagumo's training troubles continued apace. *Kaga* was on the jump "from early morning to nightfall" with takeoff and landing drills, "but even at that the seasoned fliers were given about one chance each to make dusk landings." Weather permitting, the men trained daily in night flying, but because of the maintenance program and limited time, "only the very fundamentals were learned by the inexperienced fliers." All in all, Nagumo could not ignore the fact that "because of the need for replacements and transfers of personnel, the combat efficiency of each ship had been greatly lowered."[10]

Operational security was far from airtight. As Kusaka said, "We could not help but sense that minute consideration for keeping security of the operational plan seemed to be lacking compared with the case of the Pearl Harbor operation."[11] Indeed, copies of the plan were distributed early and widely, some going even to forces not scheduled to take part in the battle. It appeared to be an open secret around the anchorage that the Combined Fleet was preparing for something big.[12]

The same atmosphere prevailed in the Naval General Staff. Vice Admiral Mitsumi Shimizu, who had commanded the Sixth Fleet (submarines) during the Pearl Harbor operation, had been wounded when a piece of shrapnel slashed into his neck during Halsey's raid against the Marshall Islands in February 1942. But he recovered sufficiently for a temporary post in the Naval General Staff. There he dropped into the office of his close friend, Vice Admiral Seiichi Ito, vice chief of the Naval General Staff, "about every other day." And there in Tokyo Shimizu observed the preparations for Midway. "I felt some apprehension about Midway before it was fought, because people in the Naval General Staff and elsewhere talked too openly about Midway," he observed in retrospect. "This was so much in contrast to the Pearl Harbor operation and it worried me."[13]

Yet such was Japanese confidence that all of these considerations seemed important only in the perspective of time. Genda did not have quite as much faith in the Midway operation as he had had in the Pearl Harbor and the Indian Ocean campaigns. However, he experienced no premonition of disaster—just a rather nebulous sense of being fenced in, of a lack of flexibility. "Freedom of the task force's movement was restricted in terms of the time factor, because the date of commencing an invasion of the island was fixed," he explained. "This resulted in restricting the attack-commencing time of the task force and the selection of its position."[14]

Miwa was one of the few to feel, or at least to admit to feeling, any pre-battle qualms. Although he expressed no doubt of victory, he did have an uneasy impression that matters could be better. On May 14, the same day he lamented the loss of Takahashi, Miwa made another entry in his diary: "The U.S. Navy is reportedly changing its policy of building battleships to building carriers instead. It can be said that they have finally caught on, but if they are going to make an overall change at this time, they are more progressive than we are." An acute and honest observation!

The following day, Japanese scouts reported sighting two American carriers in the south Pacific and correctly identified them as *Enterprise* and *Hornet*. Somewhat bewildered as to what Halsey was doing in those waters, Miwa wrote, "We cannot understand why this enemy force is going down there. This kind of enemy movement makes us feel that their tactics are poor. If and when they employ a tactic of launching a drive from the south with a concentrated carrier force, they could easily destroy even our Truk base. Since they are employing carriers in dispersion, they are being beaten at a corner."[15] Fortunately for the Americans, the Japanese could recognize a violation of the military principle of mass more readily in the enemy than in themselves. Actually, as we have seen, Halsey's two carriers were already on their way back to Pearl Harbor.

At 1700 on May 17, *Shokaku* limped into Kure. "Her damage is not as serious as thought," Miwa recorded. "However, her repair seems to require three months. It must be said that she was indeed in luck, as she sustained damages only to that extent in spite of being attacked by nearly 100 enemy planes. Or, we may assume that the skill of the enemy air force is considerably poor."[16]

Miwa was much more correct than he knew in claiming that *Shokaku* was lucky, for she had a narrow squeak the day before docking. The United States submarine *Triton*, one of a number in Japanese waters, spotted *Shokaku* and her two escort destroyers south of Shikoku. But the submarine was unable to catch up with the swift vessels.[17]

Miwa rather played down *Shokaku*'s injuries. According to Fuchida, the carrier was the most heavily damaged ship to put in for repair since the start of the war.[18] However, in the context of the time, Miwa was justified in thinking that American marksmanship left something to be desired. But most of the American misses were attributable to the miserable quality of their torpedoes. Airmen and submariners alike railed at them bitterly, for the torpedoes frequently failed to explode even upon direct hit, or dropped so far that they sailed harmlessly under the target ship.[19]

Nevertheless, the United States submarine record was far from despicable, and it was improving rapidly. On the 17th, the same day *Shokaku* docked, Lieutenant Commander Charles C. Kirkpatrick, *Triton*'s skipper, was able to console himself somewhat for losing the carrier. Slipping along underwater off Kyushu, his craft sighted the Japanese submarine *I-164*, steaming on the surface. Taking careful aim at the flag painted on the target's conning tower, Kirkpatrick blasted the unsuspecting sub with a single torpedo, sending a large chunk of the hull hurtling skyward.[20] This action might be considered the first blood of the Midway engagement, for *I-164* was part of SubRon 5, which was scheduled to form an important part of the Japanese submarine screen.

Admiral Komatsu, who had replaced the injured Shimizu as head of the Sixth Fleet, needed all the submarines he could muster to fulfill the vital role which Yamamoto had given him—that of spying on U.S. fleet movements. Located aboard the old training cruiser

Katori at Kwajalein in the Marshall Islands, he had already sent SubDiv 13, comprising *I-121*, *I-122* and *I-123*, under Captain Takeharu Miyazaki, hissing through the Pacific to French Frigate Shoals, about 500 miles northwest of Hawaii. As we have already indicated, they were to stand by and refuel two long-range Type-22 flying boats.[21]

Japanese attention on May 17 was also focused on the battered *Shokaku*, which received an inspection from Yamamoto, Ugaki and other staff officers. Like Miwa, Ugaki expressed thankfulness for *Shokaku*'s luck in receiving no further damage. "Mourned over about 100 dead sailors who lost their lives in the engagement—of whom forty were flying crews," the chief of staff noted in his diary. "Paid a visit to the wounded men. Pitied those who were burned."[22]

Miwa, who was one of the inspection party, recorded sententiously that "this is a good experience in war. The fact that Lieutenant Commander Takahashi and forty others were killed in the battle should be called a great sacrifice, but those could be consoled in learning that two enemy carriers were sunk at their sacrifice."[23]

Evaluating the day's results of training maneuvers, Nagumo was less philosophical. His airmen performed actual tests against CruDiv 8, which, although traveling at thirty knots, a relatively high speed, made only 45-degree turns. In spite of this fairly easy setup, "the records made by the fliers were again exceedingly poor," the admiral noted. "With water depth at forty to fifty meters, about a third of the torpedoes were lost."[24]

Following the visit to *Shokaku*, Ugaki had a discussion with Rear Admiral Giichi Nakahara,* chief of the First Section (Personnel) of the Naval General Staff, concerning the prickly subject of the posthumous two-ranks promotions for those killed in the Pearl Harbor operation.

> As an application of this posthumous two-ranks promotion system, either to all the dead men in the operation as the First Air Fleet requested, or to none of them, would bring a great influence upon not only the naval circle but outside circles, we reached the agreement that this system would be applied to selected men as had been decided before.[25]

Thus Ugaki summarized the day's decision. Obviously, he feared

---

*Ugaki's diary indicated that he spoke with "Captain Nakazawa," but his naming the individual in question as chief of the First Section enables us to identify him correctly.

the creation of a precedent which could become exceedingly awkward. In a major war, it would not be possible to bestow double posthumous promotions upon all of the dead. This would rob the honor of all distinction. On the other hand, the Navy had already so rewarded the midget submariners, and could not take back those promotions without scandalizing the entire Empire. The only way to keep the Navy from looking foolish was to coax the First Air Fleet to go along with double promotions for a selected few.

According to Ugaki, Yamamoto informally agreed with the decision, and ordered the First Air Fleet to submit to the Navy Ministry a list of those for whom they desired such promotions.[26] Both of them should have known that Kusaka was much too fairminded to thus pick and choose among his heroic dead. At 1300 on May 19, while *Yamato* lay at mooring buoy in Hashirajima, Nagumo and Kusaka came aboard, and the latter again discussed the problem, "but it was settled to adhere to the decided policy," as Ugaki noted. And there the matter rested.[27]

This little intra-service squabble would not be worth recording had it not contained rather disturbing overtones. The immediate honoring of the submariners, the relative ignoring of the fliers, indicated unmistakably that the Combined Fleet still had not quite accepted the airmen into the full brotherhood of the sea.

That same day, Miwa tangled with Kuroshima over the Second Battleship Division. He preferred to take it out of the Combined Fleet and use it for training purposes, whereas Kuroshima insisted that it participate in the Midway operation. Miwa had a nagging fear that the U.S. Pacific Fleet would not show up as anticipated, and thus what to him was the main point of the massive foray would be lost.[28]

Nevertheless, the next day Yamamoto issued an official order for the fleet tactical forces to participate—as predicated in the war games. It included an estimate of enemy forces at Midway, Hawaii, and the Aleutians, shrugging off the latter as possessing no substantial United States installations or strength except at Dutch Harbor. In the Hawaiian area the Japanese deduced the following units, which probably would sortie in the event of an attack on Midway: two to three aircraft carriers; two to three special carriers; two battleships; four or five Type A cruisers; three to four Type B cruisers; four light cruisers; approximately thirty destroyers; and twenty-five submarines.[29]

As of that date, this was correct as to large carriers, cruisers of all types, destroyers and submarines. But the Americans had no special carriers or battleships in the central Pacific, and, by the time battle was joined, only eight cruisers and fourteen destroyers remained in the Midway area, the rest having been sent to the Aleutians.[30]

The estimate of two or three carriers was based upon the possibility that one of the craft reported sunk in the Coral Sea might have been only damaged, and that *Wasp*, whose whereabouts remained a profound mystery to the Japanese, might be in the Pacific. The estimate also took into consideration possible American aircraft in the Hawaiian area, for these could be sent to Midway immediately in an emergency. This air power was considered to be around sixty flying boats, 100 bombers, and 200 fighters. This was not a bad estimate, although not absolutely accurate.[31]

According to the best information available to Yamamoto, the Midway garrison comprised two squadrons of flying boats, i.e., twenty-four craft; one squadron (twelve) of Army bombers and one fighter squadron of twenty planes. This strength could be doubled in an emergency, according to the intelligence report. In addition, Midway was conducting day and night air patrol to a distance of some 600 miles westward, and at least three fighters covered the atoll at all times. These air patrols were reinforced by surface craft and a few submarines. The report also indicated that "large numbers of various types of level and high angle large caliber guns as well as high angle machine guns have been installed." Marines had been landed "and all in all, the island was very strongly defended." All of which was reasonably correct.[32]

These estimates provided further arguments for knocking Midway down to size with a powerful air attack or two before sending in the landing force. In a way, the two islets hypnotized Yamamoto and his command more and more as the planning, training and preparations for the coming operations unfolded.

CHAPTER 7

"There Was No Rest"

For the CinCPAC and his staff, the next few weeks were to prove among the most nerve-racking of the entire Pacific war. "I got very little sleep before and during Midway," Nimitz reminisced, "because I had so much on my mind."[1] Nimitz was not a nervous man, but his responsibilities were enough to generate insomnia in *Alice in Wonderland*'s dormouse.

Speculation was rife in the press as to where the Japanese would strike next. In an article by Julius Edelstein, datelined Washington, May 15, the Honolulu *Advertiser* remarked:

> Expert observers here today anticipate a Japanese "spring offensive" against Alaska and Hawaii.
>
> Alaska is the military keystone to the North Pacific and prime objective for an attack which was believed to have been deterred by winter, but an attack has been expected in some quarters since Pearl Harbor.
>
> Lt. Gen. Delos C. Emmons, military governor of Hawaii, has warned the public that assaults are expected against Hawaii . . .

Nimitz was quite sure that he could rule out Hawaii as a Japanese objective in the upcoming campaign, but he had to determine what to do about the threat to Alaska. He could not simply ignore it, even though he was sure this was basically a Japanese feint. On May 17, he decided upon a North Pacific Force under the command of Rear Admiral Robert A. Theobald, consisting of the heavy cruisers *Indianapolis* and *Louisville*, the light cruisers *Honolulu*, *St. Louis*, and *Nashville*, and ten destroyers.

Then, too, there was his responsibility to hold the lifeline between the United States and Australia. His choice indicated breadth of vision: He would continue the normal convoy movement, even though it meant sparing an appreciable number of destroyers from the Midway defense.[2]

He had a strong battleship force under his command which he could have committed to Midway had he so desired. Task Force One, composed of *Pennsylvania, Maryland, Colorado, Idaho, Tennessee, New Mexico*, and *Mississippi*, with eight destroyers and the escort carrier *Long Island*, were stationed at San Francisco, under the command of Admiral Pye, whom Nimitz had succeeded as CinCPAC.[3] "Full consideration was given to employment of Task Force One in the defense of Midway," Nimitz reported to King after the battle. "It was not moved out because of the undesirability of diverting to its screen any units which could add to our long range striking power against the enemy carriers."

Undoubtedly other considerations entered the picture, for he diverted to the Aleutian theater screening units which he certainly could have used at Midway. Both he and King estimated that "the enemy's plans included an attempt to trap a large part of our Fleet."[4] The battleship force was too slow to operate with the swift carrier forces and Nimitz could spare no air cover to augment *Long Island*, which carried only twenty planes.[5]

Perhaps a less tangible element entered his calculations. An officer who knew both admirals indicated that Nimitz did not have complete faith in Pye—"the great brain but no guts"—and hesitated to trust him against the Japanese beyond a certain point.[6]

Be that as it may, Nimitz's decision was both farsighted and daring in the context of the time. Here was a clean break with tradition. For years the United States Navy had clung to the concept of the battleship as queen of the seas, yet within six months after Pearl Harbor, a seriously outnumbered CinCPAC could deliberately set aside his battlewagons. Nimitz was not an airman, while Yamamoto was the titular champion of naval air power, but it was the American who resolved to take no dead wood to Midway.

What he did want at the ready was air power and plenty of it. On May 18, the Seventh Air Force*, under the command of Major Gen-

---

*On February 5, 1942, the Hawaiian Air Force was redesignated the Seventh Air Force.

eral Clarence L. Tinker, "was placed on a special alert in preparation for meeting a threatened enemy attack." Tinker's best combat weapon at the time was the four-engined B-17 bomber, the legendary Flying Fortress, which could carry a heavy bomb load over long distances. But Tinker and his bomber commander, Brigadier General H. C. Davidson, had only twenty-seven B-17s suitable to strike Yamamoto's vast sea forces when and if they poked their prows over the horizon. Heretofore the Seventh Air Force had used the Flying Fortress both for search and strike purposes. After the "special alert" of May 18, however, Davidson used no B-17s on a search mission for about ten days. Instead, they "were held loaded with 500- and 600-pound demolition bombs as a striking force."

From May 18 on, new B-17s arrived from the mainland in increasing numbers. Usually they landed on Oahu in the morning, and at once were hustled over to the shops of the Air Depot. There maintenance crews removed their extra fuel tanks used on the long flight from the west coast. Then the crews installed auxiliary tanks in the radio compartment and checked their equipment and armament. These new planes generally were turned over to the tactical units within twenty-four hours, to be used either on Oahu or flown post-haste to Midway.[7]

These preparations began none too soon, for Japanese fleet units had already begun to sortie. On May 20, Tanaka's Midway Transport Group left Japan's large naval bases of Yokosuka and Kure, and headed for Saipan, the assembly point some 750 miles from Japan. There this tough, experienced admiral would await further orders, and sail on to Midway at the appointed time. His convoy included, among others, eleven troop transports, several cargo vessels and oilers, auxiliary craft and escorts—more than forty ships in all. These transports carried the Midway Landing Force of approximately 5,000 troops, almost equally divided between soldiers and sailors, under the overall command of Navy Captain Minoru Ota. It comprised the Second Combined Special Naval Landing Force, directly under Ota, as well as the Army's Ichiki Detachment under Colonel Kiyonao Ichiki.[8] Japanese Navy units usually bore numerical designations, while those of the Army were known by the name of their commander. By knowing the rank of the commander, a clever intelligence agent could make a fairly accurate guess as to the unit's strength.

A Seaplane Tender Group under Admiral Fujita moved out with

Tanaka's convoy. It was composed of the seaplane carrier *Chitose*, which held sixteen fighter seaplanes and four scout seaplanes, and the *Kamikawa Maru*, an auxiliary carrier with eight fighter seaplanes and four scout planes. The destroyer *Hayashio* provided protection and Patrol Boat No. 35 carried troops for its special mission. This group was to occupy Kure Island and set up a seaplane base there.[9] These ships were all a part of a single, complex plan for taking and holding Midway.

It was a big enterprise, for Midway lay in the central Pacific some 2,250 miles from Japan's home bases, and only about half that distance from Oahu. With a core area in her four main islands not much larger than California, Japan was already fighting over vast areas of the Pacific and Asia. Yet she was embarking on yet another expansionist venture.

Consider the manpower, resources, ships, and organization necessary to equip, transport, supply, and maintain Japanese forces of all types in these multiple areas! For they were in the home islands, in the Kuriles, on Sakhalin, in Korea, Manchuria, China, Formosa, French Indo-China, the Philippines, Malaya, the Netherlands East Indies, Wake, Guam, Saipan, Tinian, New Britain, the Solomons, the Carolines, the Marshalls, New Guinea, and elsewhere. One need only think in general terms concerning the components of such an effort to have some kind of picture of the immensity of the problem the Japanese had tackled when they made their reckless plunge to glory on December 7, 1941, and what they were up to at Midway.

Because U.S. submarines were on the prowl, Tanaka had an escort of ten of Japan's best destroyers with their incongruously poetic names. Some of them were Pearl Harbor veterans like *Shiranuhi* (Phosphorescent Foam), *Kasumi* (Mist of Flowers), *Arare* (Hail) and *Kagero* (Gossamer). These were swift, powerful ships displacing roughly 2,000 tons, bearing eight 24-inch torpedo tubes and six 5-inch .50 caliber guns mounted in covered pairs.[10]

According to plan, the destroyer skippers would not know their ultimate destination until they reached Saipan, but at least one of them was in on the scheme, thanks to Tanaka himself. On May 20, at Kure, he confided the news to Lieutenant Commander Tameichi Hara, commanding *Amatsukaze*. Hara had been caught up in a wholesale whirl of personnel changes at Kure, and by mid-May had lost nearly all his experienced officers and a good half of his crew. He estimated that at least two months would be necessary to bring *Amat-*

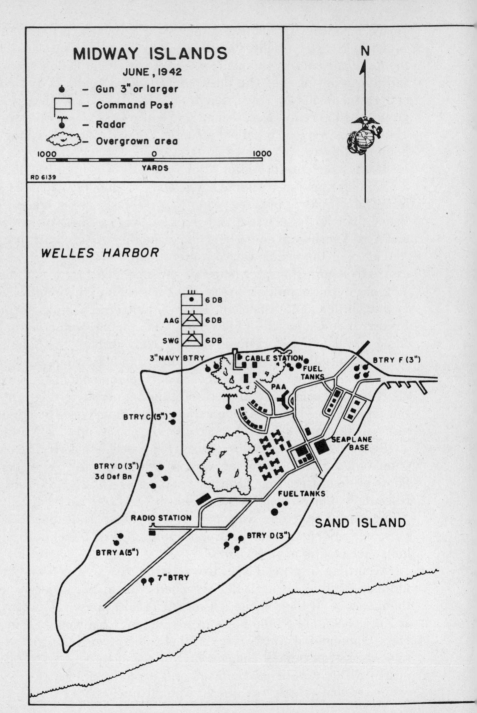

MIDWAY ISLANDS
JUNE, 1942
- Gun 3" or larger
- Command Post
- Radar
- Overgrown area

1000   0   1000
YARDS

RD 6139

N

WELLES HARBOR

6 DB
AAG   6 DB
SWG   6 DB
3" NAVY BTRY
CABLE STATION
FUEL TANKS
BTRY F (3")
PAA
BTRY C (5")
SEAPLANE BASE
BTRY D (3")
3d Def Bn
FUEL TANKS
RADIO STATION
BTRY D (3")
SAND ISLAND
BTRY A (5")
7" BTRY

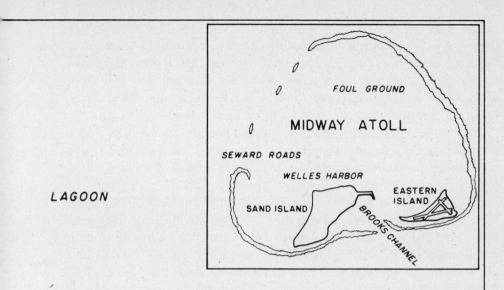

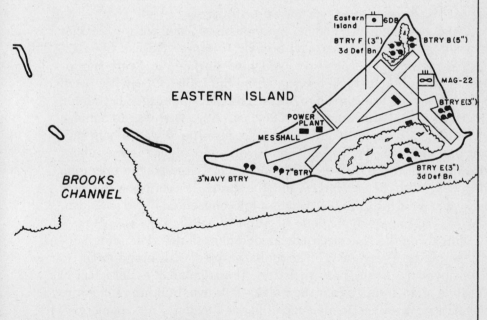

sukaze back to her fighting form, and most of his fellow destroyer skippers were in the same situation. Hara's immediate reaction to Tanaka's information was indicative of the man. He looked at Tanaka as though the high command had lost its individual and collective mind. Then he yammered excitedly, "What? What does this mean, Admiral? Are we going to conduct it with this crew?"

Tanaka shushed his outspoken subordinate and admitted, "As a matter of fact I am not sure about it. I hope it's untrue." But it was true enough, so at least one of Tanaka's escort commanders was sailing for Saipan in a mood considerably short of ecstatic.[11]

Lieutenant Commander Sadao Chigusa, the gunnery officer of the light cruiser *Jintsu*, remembered this voyage vividly, thanks in part to his detailed war diary. "The cruise to Saipan was calm and smooth with loads of sunshine, bright blue skies and soft breezes," he recalled. "It was enough to raise anyone's spirits." But he remembered, too, being tired physically and mentally. "There was no rest, there was no rest," he repeated. "I was a human being like all the others, and we were tired before we left for the battle area. We never doubted our success for a minute, yet we were so tired."

Chigusa was an intelligent, medium-sized man with a pleasant disposition, twinkling eyes, and a modest nature. He had been executive officer of the destroyer *Akigumo* during the Pearl Harbor operation, and he had just returned from the Indian Ocean campaign in April when he transferred to *Jintsu*. The cruiser engaged in training for Midway in Hiroshima Bay. The main objective was to achieve accurate gunfire against land targets, because *Jintsu* was to help support the landing forces by shore bombardment. Chigusa learned about Midway toward the end of April, and he had studied the operation in detail. With Pearl Harbor and the Indian Ocean victories as a background for his thinking, Chigusa told himself en route to Saipan, *War is very simple. We can do it. Midway will be very easy.*[12]

Nobody on the American side kidded himself that defending Midway would be "very easy." The atoll swarmed with preparations to repel invasion. Little Eastern Island, the triangular eastern half of the atoll, almost sunk under the weight of its own buildup. The entire installation was a hectic mélange of harried leaders, new personnel, mixed aircraft, ever-thirsty gasoline tanks, and "gooney birds," a local type of albatross.

In the words of Lieutenant Colonel Ira E. Kimes, commander of the Marine Air Group (MAG-22), "When we got information of what we were up against it seemed that we had a million things to do and no time to do them in. The result was that we worked night and day, just short of the point where people would be too exhausted to take part in the defense."[13]

May 21 saw the beginning of the Midway operation's alert phase. Before that date, MAG-22, consisting of Scout-Bombing Squadron 241, Fighter Squadron 221, and a modest Headquarters and Service Squadron, was the only air unit on Eastern Island. The Group comprised forty-seven officers and 335 men, with twenty-one F2A-3 aircraft and twenty-one SB2-U3s, of which only seventeen were available for use. Even this relatively small population was a strain on the housing and messing facilities, and already some enlisted men lacked dugout bunks. However, enough bunkers were available to hold all the planes.

In the prereconnaissance flight period, normal daily gasoline consumption was around 1,500 gallons. For this, the local stowage system was adequate, consisting of a main unit of 100,000 gallons with a reserve of 51,000 gallons, all in underground tanks, along with an additional emergency supply of about 250 55-gallon drums dispersed at strategic points around the field. A 15,000 gallon barge from which gasoline was pumped into the main system kept the supply current, and in addition two 1,200-gallon tank trucks were available.

Ammunition dumps dotted around the island held approximately thirty-seven 1,000-lb. bombs, 216 of the 500-pounders, and 281 100-lb. bombs, along with twenty-three MK 17-1 depth charges. Also available were 22,000 rounds each of .50 caliber and .30 caliber ammunition. Underground tanks held some 25,000 gallons of fresh water, with another 20,000 gallons stored in exposed tanks. The fresh water was strictly for drinking and cooking, sea water being pumped in for bathing and flushing.[14]

This routine was shortly due for an abrupt change. As Nimitz later wrote, "Midway was meanwhile given all the strengthening that it could take." The awkward fact remained, however, that ". . . Midway itself could support an air force only about the size of a carrier group . . ." Therefore, "despite a heavy inflow of planes from the mainland to Oahu and from there to Midway, the available numbers were never large enough to give a comfortable margin for losses."[15]

That the highest Army levels in Washington were by no means sold on Midway is evident from Stimson's diary:

> For several days we have been getting rather alarming rumors of concentration by the Japs to make a revenge attack upon us for the bombing of Tokyo. They are well authenticated and we are now worried about the place where they may come which may be anywhere from Alaska, the west coast, or Panama. George Marshall is troubled about it and told me this afternoon that he is going to go out to the west coast to look things over.

Later that afternoon, May 21, Stimson found Marshall discussing the subject with representatives of the Air Force and G-2 (Army Intelligence), "with reference to the possible attack by the Japanese upon our plants in San Diego and then a flight by those Japs down into Mexico after they have made their attack." In other words, he feared that the Japanese would follow the pattern of the Doolittle raiders, who had hit Japan, then flown on to China. So Stimson asked State to touch base with their people south of the border. Marshall flew to the West Coast the afternoon of May 22, "because we think there is a very real danger of a Japanese raid very soon on some part of the coast and very likely in the southern part."[16]

Evidently some second thoughts troubled a few minds in Japan. "Although there are considerably strong voices heard suggesting postponement of the coming operation because of the delay in preparations, it was decided to force through the original plan," wrote Miwa. "This decision involves a very delicate point. Too much of a tall order is not good at all, and too much of a soft attitude toward such suggestions is no good either. . . ."[17] Neither *Shokaku* nor *Zuikaku* had progressed far enough in refurbishing to make the original date, and submarine repairs were dragging, yet the Japanese decided to go ahead as planned because, if they upset the schedule, at least a month would elapse before the moonlight would be propitious for a possible night landing on Midway.[18]

At dawn of May 22, Yamamoto's Main Body sailed through Bungo Strait bound for brief sea exercises, passing the Fifth and Sixth Cruiser Divisions returning homeward. *Yamato* courteously signaled congratulations on the Coral Sea victory, but the cruisers did not reply. Miwa wondered if this failure to acknowledge was "out of their consciousness for their poor conduct in the battle."

At 0800 the ten battleships started maneuvering. As these great vessels split the seas in thunderous crashes, who could have believed that this was the last time the Imperial Japanese Navy would engage in major open sea maneuvers? They trained straight through the day until midnight, when they headed for temporary anchorage. "Dead tired," Miwa ended his journal notation for the day.[19]

The same expression could have applied to Major Verne J. McCaul, executive officer of MAG-22, who on May 22 initiated what he termed the "Search and Reconnaissance Phase" on Midway. Eastern Island began to jump. VP-44, consisting of six PBY5As, twenty officers and forty enlisted men, arrived from Pearl Harbor. At once, the defenders commenced work on twelve additional plane bunkers, and stepped up camouflage on important installations. A new radio frequency plan went into effect, and all aircraft were calibrated to the new frequencies. Significantly, the day's routine MAG-22 patrol consumed about 8,000 gallons of gasoline, almost five times the normal daily consumption.

On May 23, the remaining six PBYs of VP-44 flew in with twenty-one officers and forty enlisted men. On this day, too, six PBYs arched out on a search mission to a 600-mile circle, and gasoline use doubled over the previous day.[20]

Yamamoto's Main Body returned to Hashirajima at 1700 on May 23, and the next afternoon Admiral Hara reported to Yamamoto and his staff on the Coral Sea battle. "What he said is quite true," Ugaki admitted.

> On 7 May he was so little favored by the chance of launching an attack that he would have liked to quit the Navy. On the following day he could manage to inflict damage upon the enemy, but his division also received damage. The situation became so complicated that he lacked the boldness to expand his achievement, though he was well aware of the necessity, only obeying instructions issued from above such as "to head north" and "to make attacks."[21]

Ugaki might be appeased, but Miwa was not impressed. "I cannot help feeling that admirals are a little bit spiritless," he confided to his diary. "They seem to forget that a battle is won by those who never give up, and also that war damage sustained appears to be greater than that inflicted upon an enemy. As such, flying officers of Lieutenant Commander and Lieutenant class are more spirited than they. It can't be helped if they are laughed at."[22]

This judgment was rather rough on "King Kong," whose airmen were responsible for the main damage the Japanese inflicted on the Americans in that engagement. Junior officers can afford the luxury of reckless valor: the fate of thousands of men and of great ships does not rest on their actions. Moreover, both Ugaki's excuses and Miwa's scorn clearly reflect that Yamamoto's staff was not quite as overjoyed with the results of the Coral Sea fight as was the Japanese press.

CHAPTER 8

"Can You Hold Midway?"

Before the attacking forces left the homeland, certain questions and problems still remained for the Japanese to resolve. So at 0830 on May 24, the naval clan gathered once more aboard *Yamato* for a second table-top maneuver for Midway and the Aleutians.[1] At the center stood Yamamoto, surrounded by his loyal staff—Ugaki, Kuroshima, Watanabe, Miwa, and others. Each man had full confidence in his beloved chief, the bold Pearl Harbor strategist. How could the plans of this victorious leader go awry?

The maneuvers went off smoothly and according to plan. That afternoon Yamamoto held a critique of the operation, during which this specific question arose: What steps should the Northern Force take in case an enemy fleet came out to meet it? Those present generally agreed that "an air raid upon Dutch Harbor should be carried out as planned unless a powerful enemy comes out."

Kuroshima spoke deliberately yet forcefully: "An invasion operation should be carried out as a main objective. But this principle is not to be applied to a case in which there is a chance of catching and destroying an enemy force including carriers."

Ugaki turned to Captain Tasuku Nakazawa, chief of staff of the Fifth Fleet, the only representative of the Northern Force present. "May the Midway operation be carried out as originally planned, even if the northern operation is found to be impossible?" he asked.

"We don't have any objection to that," replied Nakazawa.

Miwa had been listening attentively, and now spoke up. "In that case," he reasoned, "the invasion operation should be called off for a while, and an engagement with the enemy force should be sought."

At this point Ugaki delivered a little speech stressing the need
for accurate reporting of the enemy situation by reconnaissance aircraft. Then Miwa resumed:

> When enemy forces come out both in the north and south, it may
> be safely assumed that the enemy force in the south is more powerful
> than that in the north. For instance, if two regular carriers and two
> converted carriers with several battleships come out to meet us, it
> may be assumed that the southern force consists of the two regular
> ones, and the northern force of the two converted ones.
>
> In case an enemy force comes out to the south of the island chain,
> our northern force may be ordered to come down to the south to
> join our main forces, depending upon the prevailing circumstances.
>
> In case a powerful enemy force comes out to the north, our
> northern force will try to lure it to the southwest, so that our main
> force may attack it jointly.
>
> On the other hand, in case an enemy force is located east of 160°
> West, submarine attacks will be repeated upon it and the main task
> force will seek an opportunity to attack it. Depending upon weather
> conditions, the invasion operation may be postponed.[2]

Knock out the enemy ships if at all possible! This would be putting
first things first. In solemn reflection, Kuroshima meshed his mental
gears once more: "We must not depend upon the air forces too much,
and the surface forces must be ready to sacrifice themselves when
necessary." This observation he offered as a private opinion.

Ugaki, who often differed from Kuroshima, confirmed him on this
point. "Although air forces are good weapons to hit the enemy at a
weak point, a case may arise where this principle cannot be applied."
He further stressed the vulnerability of carriers, quoting in support
of this Hara's Coral Sea report.[3]

As usual, Ugaki had the last word. "I am pleased, as you are, to
see that we have completed the necessary preparations to launch the
operation at the scheduled time," he purred. Then he scored a note
of caution:

> Since this operation involves a bulk of forces and extends over vast
> areas, we will have to expect that the entirely unexpected could
> happen at any time. So, I must stress the need for maintaining
> coordination among forces, not hesitating to send out messages when
> necessary, and not failing to join other forces when necessary.[4]

Someone should have made an emphatic note of that statement for Nagumo's benefit. During the voyage to Midway, Nagumo broke radio silence for precisely that purpose, and reaped a sour harvest of *post facto* criticism for so doing from all quarters, himself very much included.

Ugaki had not finished. "Enemy submarines have been active of late," he continued seriously. "According to radio interceptions, over twenty new enemy subs have been observed lately, while damages due to their attacks are increasing. The utmost alert must be taken against them."

Then he reflected for a moment upon U.S. intentions. "It is hard to make an accurate judgment of the next enemy move," he said, "but according to newspapers they were reported to be heading for Australia. At present, the whereabouts of two enemy carriers is unknown—either in Australia or Hawaii. Such being the case, we cannot expect to destroy more than half of the enemy force in the coming operation. So it is earnestly hoped to exploit our attacks as much as possible."[5]

Who but Ugaki could thus seriously express disappointment at the prospect of knocking off a mere fifty percent of the enemy?

This portion of the day's business concluded at 1400, and the next hour was devoted to another postmortem of the Coral Sea operation. Vice Admiral Takeo Takagi, the commander of the Fifth Cruiser Division, exasperated Miwa by complaining that fortune was not with the Japanese in that engagement. The airman believed that a man made his own luck.[6]

The next day's headlines were in marked contrast to Miwa's acid but honest comments. The hosannahs of praise resounding in the press mounted to a paean:

Joyous news was reported by the Imperial Headquarters Monday, two days prior to the significant event of Navy Day, which falls on Wednesday . . .

Certain results of the Coral Sea battle were:

Five warships sunk. They are a U.S. *California* type battleship, 33,000 tons, a U.S. *Saratoga* class aircraft carrier, 33,000 tons, a U.S. *Yorktown* class aircraft carrier, 19,900 tons, the American A-class cruiser of the *Portland* class, 9,800 tons, a destroyer.

Two warships severely damaged. They are a *Warspite* class British battleship, 30,600 tons, and an American A-class cruiser of the *Louisville* type, 9,050 tons.

One vessel was more or less severely damaged. It was the American *North Carolina* class battleship, 35,000 tons.
Ninety-eight planes were downed.[7]

That day, Miwa went to Tokyo to visit the Naval General Staff,
where he heard another report on the Coral Sea battle and talked
with the General Staff officers about Midway. He also called at the
Naval Affairs Bureau of the Navy Ministry. The trip was professionally
unprofitable, for Miwa received no concrete guidance and wondered
how much these chairborne officers really understood concerning the
Midway operation.

Personally, he savored to the full this chance to spend two days
with his wife. They were both resigned to the fact that for Miwa "to
leave home in the morning to work might spell the end of married
life." Therefore, he felt no particular excitement on the eve of departing for battle, and Mrs. Miwa, "who of course doesn't know anything, seems to be the same."[8]

For Midway, May 24 saw the continuation of routine patrols and
construction, as well as distribution of emergency rations, which were
either stored in dugouts or buried at various spots across the island.
Then, on the 25th, eighty more men came in for assignment to VP-
44. "Officer's mess now 200% over normal capacity," McCaul noted
worriedly.[9]

In Hypo, Rochefort had spent the night with his men cracking an
unusually long Japanese intercept, and was still hard at work on the
translation when Nimitz summoned him to a staff meeting. Rochefort
was a good half hour late when he showed up, and the admiral was
definitely not happy. But when he saw what Hypo had produced,
any commander would have forgiven the cryptanalyst anything short
of treason or murder. The information amounted to the Japanese order
of battle, plus a few other items. For one thing, *Zuikaku* was still out
of the picture, and the attack would take place around the third of
June at the earliest.[10]

This information allowed Nimitz to come up with an astonishingly
accurate estimate of enemy strength for the Midway phase of two to
four battleships, four or five carriers, eight or nine heavy cruisers,
four or five light cruisers, sixteen to twenty-four destroyers, and a
minimum of twenty-five submarines. He still did not know that Yamamoto's Main Body would be included,[11] which was just as well for

his peace of mind, for even without the Main Body, the Japanese would outnumber the Americans in every department.

Perhaps predictably, the very completeness of the information roused some suspicion, both at CinCPAC Headquarters and in Washington. Were the Japanese feeding the Americans false information? Why was the Combined Fleet committing such highly classified information to the radio waves? Why send such an enormous armada against such modest targets as Midway, Kiska and Attu? But once again, Nimitz stuck with his Intelligence people.[12] Better to base one's strategy upon radio intelligence than upon nebulous "what if's."

Hypo had caught and cracked this vital intercept with not a moment to spare. Having firmed up their plans and broadcast their order of battle, the Japanese changed their JN25 system, and weeks passed before Hypo could make sense of the new one.[13]

That same day, Nimitz wrote to Simard and Shannon that D-Day had been postponed until June 3.[14] This extension gave the two Midway commanders a much-needed few days' grace. Despite the fact that both were in their fifties, they were known as the best tennis doubles partners on the island. They worked to defend Midway with the same teamwork they displayed on the court.

A World War I veteran, Shannon had an unshakable belief in the efficacy of barbed wire as a defense measure. He ordered so much of it strung around that an antiaircraft gunner exploded, "Barbed wire, barbed wire! Cripes, the old Man thinks we can stop planes with barbed wire!"

Along with Shannon's beloved barbed wire, the atoll had so much dynamite on hand that it actually became dangerous to the defenders, and large quantities had to be dumped in the sea.[15]

Shannon shared at least one characteristic with Yamamoto—the gift of instant slumber and equally swift awakening. Although he drank coffee all day, topped off with several cups at midnight, he dropped off promptly. But if anything or anyone awakened him, he was immediately alert.[16]

Under such dynamic leadership, the two little islets bristled with barbed wire entanglements and guns, the beaches and waters were studded with mines. Eleven torpedo boats were made ready to circle the reefs and patrol the lagoon, pick up ditched airmen, and assist the ground forces with antiaircraft fire. A yacht and four converted tuna boats stood by for rescue operations. Nineteen submarines guarded the approaches from 100 to 200 miles northwest to north.[17]

Midway had come a long way since the day in mid-November 1941 when the Pan Am clipper carrying Saburo Kurusu to the United States was held up at the atoll for three days. To give Japan's special envoy an impressive idea of Midway's strength, Shannon and Simard arranged that a trail of Marines plod along the road to the PanAm Hotel. As the car carrying Kurusu and Shannon drove past the men, Shannon explained that this was "a routine training maneuver of a small part of his command." Actually, he had routed out every available warm body, including cooks and messmen, for this "spear-carrier" detail.[18]

When Nimitz inspected the atoll on May 2, he had asked Shannon, "If I get you all these things you say you need, then can you hold Midway against a major amphibious assault?" To which Shannon replied briefly, "Yes, sir." Naval historian Samuel Eliot Morison has agreed with this judgment.[19] Some of the junior officers were eager for the enemy to attack. They had been waiting for the Japanese for six months and were confident that they could not take the island.[20]

Others were not so sanguine. On Sand Island, McCall was as nearly pessimistic as a traditionally cocky Marine ever permits himself to become. He had radar, but it was old, a type SC 270, which could not indicate height of any contact. Also, it showed up many blips which might be Japanese aircraft but might just as easily be low-soaring albatrosses. In an attempt to clear up the situation a trifle, the Marines arranged that friendly aircraft coming in to Midway do so on a certain pattern, and anything in that pattern was assumed to be an American plane.[21] Yet the experience at Pearl Harbor, when the Japanese air armada approached within a few degrees of an anticipated flight of B-17s, had already proved the fallacy of such blanket assumptions.[22]

The Marine dive bombers were SB2U-3s, officially termed "Vindicators" and unofficially nicknamed "Vibrators" or "Wind Indicators." These relics had a habit of ground-looping. During diving tests earlier in the year, the fabric parted company with the wings and had to be mended with adhesive tape.[23]

The fighter aircraft were F2A-3s ("Buffalos"), known grimly as "Flying Coffins."[24] The Buffalo had been a good aircraft in its day, maneuverable and easy to fly. But it had a number of flaws which made it vulnerable to air battle, and events had overtaken it.[25] The Zero could fly faster level than the Buffalo could dive with any degree of safety.[26]

The F4F and SBD had replaced the F2A-3 and SB2U-3 respectively aboard carriers some months before, whereupon the Navy had transferred the older types to the Marines. The Naval War College's analysis of the battle remarked of this arrangement, "This policy of equipping the Marine Corps Air Groups with old types of planes was a contributing factor to the excessive losses sustained in the Midway action by Marine Air Group 22."[27]

To add to everyone's woes, no plan existed for coordinating the Midway air operations, and the crews, although gallant and eager, were a mixture of Army, Navy, and Marines, unused to fighting as a team.[28]

"It looked like a hopeless deal," said McCaul. "A decent battle could not be fought with the material they had. In other words, it was a complete mess." Recognizing Midway's weak position, McCaul believed the only chance any of his men had of coming out alive was to catch the Japanese carriers with their planes on deck. This meant exquisitely precise timing, a monumental dose of luck, or both. Otherwise, Midway would do its best, but could not stand up under a massive Japanese attack.[29]

This was right in line with Nimitz's thinking:

Balsa's* air force must be employed to inflict prompt and early damage to Jap carrier flight decks if recurring attacks are to be stopped. Our objectives will be first—their flight decks rather than attempting to fight off the initial attacks on Balsa. . . . If this is correct, Balsa air force . . . should go all out for the carriers . . . leaving to Balsa's guns the first defense of the field.[30]

Of course, Nimitz understood the situation perfectly and was not depending upon Midway to secure its own fate. His thinking held no provision for passively waiting to be smacked. But his only chance against Yamamoto lay in absolute secrecy, and that secrecy was, if possible, too good. Certain key officers knew that Midway's defenders "would be heavily supported by Naval units including aircraft carriers."[31] But those at operational level did not. In fact, shore-based

*Balsa was the current code name for Midway.

Navy pilots were specifically told that they could not count on carrier assistance—the flattops would be protecting Hawaii.[32]

In view of the circumstances, one can understand that the top brass could not jeopardize security, even to reassure the troops on Midway that they were not expected to perform miracles, and that they were not alone. For these were men of the Navy and its Marine Corps, and knew well enough that the defensibility of any small island depends upon control of the sea around it.

If enough Japanese ships stood offshore out of range of Midway's guns, under a thick fighter cover, the defenders did not have the air strength to drive off the enemy. It is possible that had Yamamoto turned the powerful guns of his Main Body battleships on the atoll, instead of hovering in the background as a floating headquarters, he might have taken the island by sheer weight of steel. Fortunately for the Americans, Yamamoto and Ugaki were obsessed with saving the battleships—for what, the ancestral gods only knew. Ugaki even refused Kusaka the use of *Yamato*'s communications facilities.

"At that time, the Japanese Navy heavily depended upon intercepting enemy radio communications to find out enemy movements," explained Kusaka. "From that point of view, the Combined Fleet headquarters' flagship *Yamato* was more suited to that purpose than *Akagi*, whose masts were far lower than those of *Yamato* . . .

"This view was strongly stressed by me to the Chief of Staff, Combined Fleet, but it was not accepted by him on the ground that such would result in exposing the position of the flagship of the Combined Fleet prematurely . . ."[33]

Yamamoto was also under the influence of Alfred Thayer Mahan, whose doctrines of naval power expounded in his book, *The Influence of Sea Power upon History*, resisted the concept of bombarding shore installations by warship.[34] So Midway was in no danger of this particular type of attack.

Along with Nimitz's revised battle date, May 25 saw the arrival on Midway of a 37-mm antiaircraft battery of the Marine Third Defense Battalion. They promptly emplaced four of these guns on each island. "Since the pointer and trainer seats were high on either side, well above the gun barrel, the result of emplacing the guns high on the dune line for surface firing was that the crews were silhouetted on the sky line like sitting ducks," recalled one eyewitness. "It is fortunate that no landing attempt was made—at least for the 37-mm gunners."[35]

Much more picturesque reinforcements spilled ashore that day—Companies C and D, Second Raider Battalion, under Captain Donald H. Hastie and First Lieutenant John Apergis respectively. This newly formed battalion, commanded by Major Evans F. Carlson, was destined to fame later in the war as "Carlson's Raiders." Their training, attitude, and appearance owed much to Carlson's sojourn as a civilian observer among the Chinese communists, whom he admired extravagantly. His Raiders resembled a conventional Marine battalion as a hard rock festival resembles grand opera. But they could fight if the occasion arose, which was all that concerned the authorities at the moment. Company C disappeared into the underbrush on Sand Island, while Company D went to Eastern.[36]

Carlson, his executive officer Major James Roosevelt, Hastie, and Apergis had received "briefing and instructions" at Pearl Harbor. There they heard "a most amazing story"—the Japanese planned to attack Midway. "How this information was gained is still a mystery," wrote Apergis some years later.

> Rumor had it that "Tokyo Rose" was on our payroll, and through her scheduled radio broadcasts was transmitting information to us; pacifist elements in Japan, because of their desire to bring about a quick end to the war, were supplying us with information; and last, and most probable, the Imperial Japanese code was deciphered by our Navy.[37]

May 26 was a busy day on Midway, with a B-17 bringing Major General Clarence L. Tinker, commander of the Seventh Air Force, and his staff from Oahu for a one-day visit. They brought with them Major Jo K. Warner and two enlisted men, on temporary duty as an Army Liaison Detachment. Nor was this all: The USS *Kitty Hawk* landed twenty-two officers and thirty-five men for MAG-22, nineteen SBD-2 and seven F4F-3 aircraft, which the Marine garrison unloaded throughout the night. "Of the twenty-one new pilots, seventeen were fresh out of flying school," McCaul recorded. "Officer personnel now nearly 300% increased, enlisted 50%."[38] The high percentage of officers over enlisted was due to the large number of pilots. Nor were any of the newly arrived enlisted men maintenance types. Midway could not afford to support more than a bare minimum of non-flying personnel. The air crews would have to perform the routine maintenance of their aircraft.[39]

Of one thing there can be no doubt: At this stage, Midway was rapidly becoming as well manned, well armed, and alert as an island outpost could be, considering the conditions of the day, the state and availability of matériel, and Midway's own geographical limitations. The question was: Would all this be enough?

CHAPTER 9

"An Admiral's Admiral"

Nimitz fully expected to give command of the striking force to Vice Admiral William F. Halsey. Half sailor, half airman, all fighter, Bill Halsey was America's best-known carrier admiral. A graduate of the Naval Academy class of 1904, he was a captain and already had a distinguished career behind him when he decided to switch to naval aviation, and won his wings at Pensacola in 1934. Since that time, he had served as the first commander of Carrier Divisions Two and One, and from June 1940 as commander Aircraft, Battle Force with the rank of vice admiral. His strike into enemy territory against the Marshalls gave the United States the first Navy hero they could cheer about in the Pacific War, and as commander of Task Force Sixteen, which took Jimmy Doolittle and his raiders within bombing range of Tokyo, his reputation was at the top of the mast.[1]

A tall, rather heavyset man, Halsey was almost spectacularly ugly. With his deeply carven features and jutting brows, he bore a startling resemblance to "Tecumseh," the figurehead of the old wooden battleship *Delaware* enshrined at the Naval Academy as a sort of good-luck totem. He was also one of the most likable of men, and his staffs and men swore by him. Whenever two or more American sailors got together, sooner or later they would exchange a Halsey yarn. And the best of them were true.

The two carriers of Task Force Sixteen were due to dock on May 26, and Nimitz awaited them eagerly but with his customary calm patience. *Enterprise* nosed into berth F-2 at Ford Island at 1158 that

day, and *Hornet* moored to Berth F-10-S seven minutes later.[2] While
Halsey sensed that something important was in the wind, he had to
check with the hospital. For he was suffering from a skin eruption
which covered his whole body and drove him wild with ceaseless
irritation. Although he tried every remedy anyone suggested, nothing
gave him any relief, and he had been in this condition since the Tokyo
raid. The doctors diagnosed "general dermatitis," probably brought
on by a combination of nervous tension and tropical sun, and ordered
immediate hospitalization.

Halsey stalled signing in at the Pearl Harbor Naval Hospital until
he conferred with Nimitz. As soon as the latter's eyes lit upon Halsey,
he knew the doctor was right in blowing the whistle on him. The bag
of his uniform revealed at least a twenty-pound loss of weight, and
the dark smudges around his eyes spoke eloquently of sleepless nights.
Six straight months on the bridge, except for very brief dockings, in
physical torment, had taken their toll. Halsey was simply in no condition to lead a fleet into battle.[3]

When Halsey learned that a battle was shaping up for Midway
and that he would have headed the United States striking fleet, he
experienced what he called "the most grievous disappointment in my
career." The loss of the Midway command was the culminating blow
in a series of mischances for Halsey, beginning with the loss of several
of his *Enterprise* pilots to American AA fire at Pearl Harbor and
running through a gauntlet of mishaps climaxed by arriving in the
area too late to participate in the battle of the Coral Sea. Even the
Doolittle raid was not an unalloyed joy, for Army fliers, not Halsey's
men, had had the pleasure of dropping bombs on the Japanese homeland.

It seemed as if Task Force Sixteen's original nomenclature had
worked its baleful jinx. Someone with incredible lack of imagination
had first designated it Task Force Thirteen, giving it for good measure
a sortie date of Friday the 13th for its next venture. Two senior officers
of Halsey's staff promptly formed a delegation to protest to CinCPAC
Headquarters against this rash bid for trouble. There Captain Charles
H. "Soc" McMorris agreed that no sailor in his senses would lift anchor
on Friday the 13th in a Task Force numbered Thirteen. He obligingly
changed the number to Sixteen and upped the sortie date one day.[4]

On that day, May 26, 1942, Nimitz was disappointed that he had
to count Halsey out. As a combat commander, experienced airman,

and morale booster, Halsey was a task force in himself. Yet in the perspective of years, Nimitz would remark, "It was a great day for the Navy when Bill Halsey had to enter the hospital."[5] This seemingly brutal judgment is no reflection upon a great fighting admiral. Halsey played his indispensable role in winning the Pacific war. His day would come, but Midway was not that day. For the circumstances called for qualities of cool, steady judgment which Halsey lacked.

Yet indirectly he contributed to victory at Midway. Before speeding him on his way to the Pearl Harbor hospital, Nimitz asked him to recommend a replacement. Unhesitatingly Halsey replied with the name of his friend and colleague, Rear Admiral Raymond A. Spruance, commander of his cruiser force. Nimitz immediately agreed, for he, like Halsey, held Spruance in high esteem. Spruance was not an airman, but he had served under Halsey since before Pearl Harbor, and could be depended upon to carry on.[6]

So Bill Halsey disappeared from the Midway picture, to watch wistfully from the hospital on the Point as the ships sailed off to battle, then to be shipped, covered with grease like a gun in Cosmoline, back to the mainland for specialist treatment.[7]

Spruance had sailed into Pearl Harbor that same morning with Task Force Sixteen aboard his flagship, the cruiser *Northampton*. After docking, he went over to *Enterprise*, and was waiting there for Halsey at the time the latter was talking with Nimitz. Spruance wanted to present his own report and to ask his chief about plans for the immediate future. Aboard the flagship, Spruance learned that Halsey would probably have to be hospitalized,[8] but had no idea that he would fall heir to the command. "Since I was not an aviator, and there were aviators senior to me at Pearl Harbor," he said, "I thought one of them would take over from Halsey."[9]

While mulling over the news, he received word to report immediately to CinCPAC Headquarters. There Nimitz informed him "that the Japanese planned to attack and capture Midway, with further attacks in the Aleutians; that we would resist these attacks with our available forces," that Halsey had been hospitalized, and he, Spruance, would assume command of Task Force Sixteen and inherit Halsey's staff.[10]

Nimitz further instructed Spruance to sail on May 28. On the 27th, he would have the opportunity to confer with Rear Admiral Frank Jack Fletcher, en route back to Pearl Harbor on the badly damaged *Yorktown*. As Fletcher, commander of Task Force Seventeen, ranked Spruance, he would head the operation.

Nimitz added that after the Midway battle Spruance would return to Pearl Harbor and replace Draemel as the Pacific Fleet's chief of staff. This was not very palatable news for Spruance. "Having had two previous tours of staff duty during my career, I was not too happy about going ashore in the early stages of a big naval war."[11] But he kept his poker face and, having received his orders, listened to an intelligence briefing.

As he left Nimitz's office, Spruance was somewhat surprised but not at all overcome by this "very big responsibility," and naturally was "very pleased at my temporary command of Task Force Sixteen during the operation for the defense of Midway." His appraisal of the situation was realistic but upbeat. "We knew what the Japanese were going to do and I thought we could sock 'em," he said.[12]

Such mild expression of sentiments was characteristic of Spruance. A graduate of the Naval Academy class of 1907, Spruance was fifty-six years old, experienced as a destroyerman, an engineer, and specialist in gunfire control, when this unexpected challenge fell into his lap. He had served as a staff officer at the Naval War College, of which he was destined to become president, as captain of the battleship *Mississippi*, commandant of the Tenth Naval District, and since shortly before the opening of war, as Commander Cruisers of Halsey's Task Force Sixteen.

A slender man with thinning, straight, gray hair, firm facial contours, and eyes as light and clear as sea water beneath a high, thoughtful brow, Spruance fought shy of the ubiquitous war correspondents seeking colorful heroes. He genuinely loathed personal publicity, so he refused interviews and permitted no reporters aboard his flagship, claiming lack of room. Correspondents retaliated by popularizing the picture of a man efficient, but cold and hard.[13]

He was not well known outside the U.S. Navy officer corps, and even some of his fellow officers thought him "a cold fish" with no sense of humor. Actually Spruance had a delightful sense of fun, but being utterly sincere, he smiled only when truly pleased and laughed only when exceedingly amused, so his friends came to recognize a sudden glint in his eye as the equivalent of a less self-controlled man's guffaw.[14] Nimitz had the highest opinion of him. "Spruance, like Grant, was the type who took the war to the enemy," said Nimitz.

"He was bold, but not to the point of being reckless. He had a certain caution and a feeling for the battle. He was a reticent man who, when he said something, made it count, and he had the courage of his convictions."[15]

In many ways Spruance was the antithesis of Halsey, an admiral in the swashbuckling tradition, who tended to head into action first and think about it later. With Spruance, calm and collected thinking preceded action. Halsey appealed to the imagination and the emotions; Spruance spoke to the mind and the intellect. Halsey often wrapped his thoughts in picturesque, exciting words; Spruance expressed himself in economical, pointed language. Halsey loved a good drink and could "knock 'em back" with the best in the Fleet; "I wouldn't punish my stomach with the stuff," said Spruance.[16] Each had his vital, unique place; each made his own tremendous contribution to the naval war in the Pacific. Nimitz, who liked and admired them both, summed up the two men crisply: "Spruance was an admiral's admiral; Halsey was a sailor's admiral."[17]

By the time of Midway, the Japanese Navy was familiar with the name of Halsey. But Halsey's friend was a different matter. "We had never heard of Spruance," said Captain Yasuji Watanabe of Yamamoto's staff.[18] It was a gap in their education soon to be filled.

The day after Spruance's meeting with Nimitz, May 27 Hawaiian time, the U.S. Pacific Fleet base on Oahu fairly crackled with activity. Aboard the warships of Task Force Sixteen, dungaree-clad workers toiled away replenishing oil and gas supplies, loading food, equipment, and ammunition—anything that would contribute to the fighting qualities of these ships. Throughout the earliest hours of the day, *Enterprise* took on fresh water and telephone services from the dock. By 0550 the scene slowly illumined with the soft glow of predawn as the gasoline lighter *YO 24* chugged off from the port side of the carrier, now heavily laden with another 82,405 gallons of aviation gasoline. She had already taken on board 19,080 barrels of fuel oil.

At 0619 the sun officially rose over the eastern horizon, and the hum of activity mounted to a steady purr as the light increased. Just one minute after sunrise, the carrier commenced provisioning, a procedure which continued throughout the day.[19]

Enterprise and her battle mate, *Hornet*, were caught up in the pulsing activity of great warships pausing all too briefly in port between one campaign and another. Daily inspections of the magazines and visual examinations of smokeless powder went off without incident. A steady procession of personnel, both officers and enlisted men, moved on and off the carriers as the many reassignments which go almost unnoticed on shore went into effect in a solid lump.[20]

Over in Battleship Row, acetylene torches flashed brilliantly white, hammers rang, winches squealed, and cables droned as salvage parties labored to reclaim damaged or sunken ships to fight another day. All over and around the huge base patrol planes were on the prowl, lookouts on the *qui vive*, guards on the alert. For many still thought the Japanese might smash through Midway and attack Oahu.

Just two days before, on May 25, powder guns were installed around the yard, two apiece being fixed at "Q" Station and Gate Vessel, with two each movable guns on heavy foundations located at "K" Station and Section Base, each gun provided with sixty-six rounds of ammunition. "These guns are to be manned by personnel now assigned these stations for the primary purpose of defending the harbor against the attack of fast light vessels and destroying them before they can reach the gate." And on May 27, the Yard again "conducted a test 'Alert' consisting of a coordinated drill between Mine and Bomb Observation Stations, Harbor Control Post and Mine and Disposal Unit."[21]

In U.S. Army Air Corps Headquarters on Oahu things were buzzing, too. "It looked awfully bad," said able, affable Colonel James A. Mollison, chief of staff of the Seventh Air Force. "We figured that the Japanese thrust at Midway would come right on and hit Oahu. We knew the Japanese were coming on in strength and that they had troop transports and were going to land. That is why it seemed so dangerous. We figured, too, that it could be either Midway or Oahu."[22]

Not every Air Corps general on Oahu, however, knew about Midway from the beginning. When Rear Admiral Patrick N. L. Bellinger, Commander of PatWing Two, told Brigadier General Howard C. Davidson, the husky Texan who directed the Seventh Fighter Command, about Yamamoto's bold design, Davidson was both surprised and dubious. "What the hell do the Japanese want with Midway?" he asked incredulously. "Distance and logistics alone are too much for them to tackle Midway."

At the time Davidson did not know about the breaking of the Japanese naval code. Bellinger did, so he was sure of his position. Yet he did not reveal the secret to his good colleague. He merely assured Davidson, "I have proof that the Japanese are going to hit Midway." Davidson still shook his head in wonderment. But once in the know, he worked like a demon helping the air forces get ready for battle.[23]

Preparations for sea continued aboard *Enterprise* and *Hornet*. But it was not all work on May 27 aboard the *"Big E."* At 1345 Officers Call sounded and at 1352 the band broke into "Ruffles and Flourishes," the Marine guard presented arms, the bosun's pipe shrilled, and four stars snapped at the truck as Nimitz came aboard. In spite of his urgent problems and numerous anxieties, he found time this busy day to award decorations personally to his officers and men who had "formed up in whites on the flight deck."[24]

First in line stood the *Big E*'s own skipper, Captain George D. Murray, to receive the Navy Cross. His men knew Murray's worth. From the earliest days of the Pacific war, crewmen of *Enterprise* told one another, "The Admiral [Halsey] will get us in, and the Captain will get us out."[25]

As Nimitz worked his way down in order of rank, he came to Lieutenant Commander Clarence Wade McClusky, Jr., a top-notch pilot well worthy of the Distinguished Flying Cross. He would soon add luster to an already impressive record. Next to him stood Lieutenant Commander Roger Mehle to receive the same award. While Nimitz adjusted the medal, he looked into Mehle's alert brown eyes and remarked quietly, "I think you'll have a chance to win yourself another medal in the next several days."[26]

Next to the last man to be decorated was Ensign Cleo J. Dobson, soon to be promoted to Lieutenant Junior Grade. "In the name of the President of the United States, I take great pleasure in presenting to you the Distinguished Flying Cross," Nimitz said as he pinned the medal on what Dobson, whose spelling was highly unorthodox, described as his "heaving busom." This young officer was one of the few Americans to keep a good war diary, to which we are indebted for some personal glimpses of the pre-battle and action phases of Midway. "Thank you, sir," replied Dobson. They shook hands, then Dobson stepped back a pace and saluted his Commander in Chief.[27]

For Dobson that day, the anguish of war far outweighed his moment of glory. On May 20, one of his buddies had crashed and drowned on takeoff. The two had been good friends, and Dobson had to help inventory his effects. "It doesn't seem right for a man whose every

idea & thought was so pure & good should have to go as he did,"
Dobson recorded. Upon arrival at Pearl Harbor, he and another friend
had spent most of the day trying to comfort the lost flier's wife, and
would visit her again that afternoon. Dobson was not only wrung with
sorrow for "little Nancy"; he was furious because the squadron commander so busied himself with personal matters that he had no time
to fulfill this important, traditional duty of a commander.[28]

Last in line aboard *Enterprise* loomed Mess Attendant Doris Miller,
whose huge frame, barrel chest, and enormous hands formed an
incongruous contrast to his softly feminine given name. He stood
rigidly at attention as Nimitz decorated him with the Navy Cross for
valor during the Pearl Harbor attack. Miller was "the first negro to
receive such high tribute in the Pacific Fleet in the present conflict."[29]

Nimitz would have been less than human had he not tingled with
pride as the bosun piped him over the side. He knew, none better,
that Yamamoto's great fleet would far outnumber the force the United
States could send to Midway. But with his Murrays and McCluskys,
Mehles, Dobsons, and Millers, Nimitz could match Yamamoto man
for man without flinching.

CHAPTER 10

"The Moment of Fulfillment"

Slipping in single file at sixteen knots through the sun-dappled waters of the Inland Sea, the Nagumo force presented a gala appearance. Well to the fore sped the light cruiser *Nagara*, the eleven sleek greyhounds of DesRon 10 strung out behind her. Aft of the destroyers followed the heavy cruisers *Tone* and *Chikuma*, comprising CruDiv 8. Then, as if building up to a theatrical peak, the battleships *Haruna* and *Kirishima* surged by. At the last, the climax of the procession, the four aircraft carriers *Akagi* and *Kaga*, *Hiryu* and *Soryu*, steamed majestically seaward.

A few fishing boats bobbed to starboard, and their occupants waved and cheered.[1] As the task force steamed past a number of little islands, several boys on the shores waved small Rising Sun flags. At about 0900, everyone aboard *Akagi* assembled on the quarterdeck for a brief Navy Day ceremony, for this was May 27, anniversary of Admiral Heihachiro Togo's great victory over the Russians at Tsushima. *Akagi's* officers and men bowed deeply in the direction of the Imperial Palace, then Captain Taijiro Aoka, the carrier's skipper, read Togo's farewell address with its message "After a victory, tighten your helmet straps."[2]

The warning was well taken. What a contrast the festive atmosphere of this expedition presented to the stern secrecy which had surrounded the sortie for Pearl Harbor! All the Nagumo force needed to complete the holiday picture was a brass band and a flock of newsmen.

Tokyo could have filled both shortages easily. At 0930 a landing party from the Combined Fleet paraded through the city to martial airs played by the Navy Band, stepping out behind a color guard.

Symbolic of the entire active duty Navy, the men first marched to the plaza before the Imperial Palace to worship the sacred edifice. Then they moved on to Yasukuni Shrine, that holy spot where the nation enshrined the spirits of its honored war dead. Standing rigidly at "Present Arms," the sailors paid homage to the heroes of old as well as to their own fallen comrades.[3]

The morning edition of the Japanese newspapers made sure that the citizens were in the proper frame of mind even before they ventured forth in holiday garb clutching their small Rising Sun banners. Japan's press was never shy about singing the national praises, and this morning it sounded all the trumpets. Those who wished to combine brushing up their English with assimilation of the government line could turn to the *Japan Times and Advertiser*, which caroled,

> This year, Navy Day is not a day of mere remembrance, not a mere reminder; it is a day of fulfillment. The Japanese Navy has not only duplicated the exploits of 37 years ago, but it has repeated it [sic] time and again and on an unbelievably greater scale . . . This is the moment of culmination, the moment of fulfillment.
>
> Today, Britain's control over the seas has vanished, thanks to the work of the German and Italian submarines and more to the work of the Japanese Navy. Britain's auxiliary, the United States, has likewise had her navy practically destroyed by the Japanese Navy. As a result, Japan stands today as the premier naval Power of the world. It may well presage the rise of Japan in the future history of the world to a position comparable to that which Britain has occupied in the past.[4]

The morning press took the occasion to review all the Navy's exploits in the current war, going back to Pearl Harbor and stressing the fighting spirit of the "nine war gods," the midget submariners. In contrast, retired Vice Admiral Ichiro Sato declared, "There is no fighting spirit in the American soldier. If America stages an attack it is just for the purpose of impressing the people at home."[5]

To remind the eager reader how wonderful his Navy actually was, the papers recapitulated the enemy ship casualties in the war to date, real and mythical. Well might the "entire Japanese nation of 100,000,000" be jubilant over these "superhuman accomplishments of the Japanese Navy!" The reader's Axis allies joined in wishing him well. The German nationals in Tokyo and Yokohama took a quarter-page ad in the *Japan Times and Advertiser* to congratulate the Japanese armed forces and the Japanese people—in that order, naturally—on their great successes on all fronts. The smaller Italian colony contented itself with an ad of similar sentiments but half the size, in approximate if unconscious token of Mussolini's status as tail of the Axis kite.[6]

Yamamoto had nothing to say publicly on this auspicious occasion, preferring to let the Combined Fleet speak in deeds rather than words, but his picture adorned the front page of the *Japan Times and Advertiser*, and a story of the Tsushima engagement on page three paid him tribute:

> It was during this historic battle that Naval Cadet Yamamoto lost two of his fingers. Had it been three fingers instead of two, red tape would have prevented his remaining in the naval service. One finger, it can be said, made it possible for this young cadet to assume the same duty as that of the late Fleet Admiral Togo 37 years later. Therefore, one can rightly term this as a manifestation of Heaven's grace for the furtherance of Japan's cause . . .[7]

Captain Hideo Hiraide, Chief of the Navy Headquarters Press Section, extolled the virtues of the Japanese man of arms, leaving the reader to infer that the Imperial soldiers and sailors had no peers in bravery, self-sacrifice, filial devotion, chivalry, and tender consideration for prisoners of war. "I presume this sort of warm treatment for the enemy is accorded only by the Japanese people," purred Hiraide.

The most significant of his remarks, however, slipped by almost unnoticed in his highly fictionalized account of the Battle of the Coral Sea. Claiming the sinking of two American battleships, he emphasized, "Let it be well known in this connection that battleships have an importance incomparable with cruisers or destroyers. The battleship constitutes the nucleus of naval power."[8] Thus spake the official mouthpiece of the Japanese Naval General Staff on the eve of the Battle of Midway, destined to kick the seacocks from the bottom of Japanese naval power without a single battleship firing a shot in anger.

At precisely 1040, the main gate of the Imperial Palace swung open and a big, black Rolls Royce glided slowly out into the street, which was bedecked with flags and alive with jostling crowds. As the spectators caught sight of the slender figure on the back seat, every man, woman and child bowed deeply from the hips, eyes reverently lowered. For this was their Emperor, the Son of Heaven. In honor of Navy Day, His Majesty wore the full dress uniform of a Fleet Admiral, a garb less usual for his public appearances than that of an Army Generalissimo in this nation and age of Army domination.

Behind the Imperial Rolls Royce sailed a fleet of slightly less majestic vehicles bearing officials of the Imperial Household. These rolled in stately procession to the nearby Diet Building, where His Majesty would open the 80th extraordinary session of the Japanese parliament. He did so with a statement which, if not exactly colorful, at least had the virtues of brevity and moderation. After the usual fulsome formal reply, His Majesty took his departure, thereby sparing himself an ordeal by oratory.[9]

The principal business of the two-day session was "to examine the Government's proposal to construct an entire fleet of standard type merchant vessels," according to the press releases, but the reader gathers that the real reason for convoking these statesmen was to provide a captive audience. In fact, the *Japan Times and Advertiser* ingenuously admitted as much when the session ended.

The speech-making began at 1400, when Prime Minister Tojo mounted the rostrum. Tojo was the least gifted and charismatic of the world leaders of his time. Equally far removed from the grandeur of Churchill and the demonic genius of Hitler, he also lacked the deft political touch of Roosevelt and the rabble-rousing ebullience of Mussolini. Indeed, all his life Tojo had made a virtue of necessity and a career of mediocrity. The Japanese Army did not encourage brilliance or individuality in its generals. Promotion and honors went to those who marched strictly by the numbers. The system suited Tojo perfectly, and Tojo suited the system, in such a mutually profitable symbiosis that he was now Premier of Japan, as well as a four-star general on active duty—this last necessary so that he might constitutionally serve as his own War Minister.[10]

Eyes watchful behind horn-rimmed spectacles, ears close-set against his skull like those of an angry cat, large mustache bristling over unusually thin lips, Tojo spoke with all the long-winded pomposity which made him a frequent butt of Yamamoto's ward-room gibes:

> . . . the present favorable situation both at home and abroad means
> but a prelude to an ultimate victory in the prosecution of the war. . . . It
> has been and will remain the inflexible determination of our entire
> nation never to sheathe the sword of righteousness unless and until

the influence of the Anglo-American Powers, with their dream of dominating the world, has been completely uprooted.

The cardinal principle, therefore, of guiding the war prosecution hereafter will be, on the one hand, to demonstrate further the superb coordinated operations of the Army and the Navy, which are now the wonder of the world, and unfailingly crush the enemy by seeking him out . . .

Having shed a few crocodile tears over Australia and China, Tojo turned to the principal enemy: "Suffering defeat after defeat, the United States, hiding the fatal losses from the public, is frantically resorting to false propaganda in order to allay the criticism arising within her borders and to prevent estrangement of neutral countries. I cannot but pity the peoples of the United States and Britain," he continued, with a nasty swipe at General Douglas MacArthur, "who are fighting under such leaders as those who have given a position of trust to a commander who fled, deserting the helpless officers and men, or who are trying to cover up their defeat by loudly exaggerating the guerrilla warfare on the sea, which are [sic] both futile and insignificant."

After a few rather desultory remarks, Premier Tojo drew to a close, but if the Diet thought they had heard the last of the man, they were mistaken. He put on his other hat and treated them to an equally long monologue in his capacity as War Minister. This was merely a detailed recital of Japan's military actions since the last session of the Diet in March, and could have waited for another occasion. But Navy Day or no Navy Day, Tojo was not going to miss the opportunity to blow the Army's bugle loud and clear.[11]

Foreign Minister Shigenori Togo had his hour in the spotlight later that afternoon. He painted with a loving hand the rosy picture of Japan's cordial relations with Germany and Italy. He side-swiped the Soviet Union delicately, hinting that the Russians had nothing to fear as long as they kept their noses clean and abided by the Russo-Japanese Neutrality Pact of the previous year. Then he heaped scorn on the British, whose imminent collapse he predicted, and turned the full force of his vituperation on the Americans:

The United States is withholding from the public all news of her uninterrupted series of military and naval disasters while spreading fictitious reports of victory in an attempt to maintain popular confidence. . . . It is but natural that dissatisfaction is bound to be voiced

among the intellectual classes in the United States over the American
Government which has despotically dragged the nation into an uncertain war with Japan without any chance of success, completely
disregarding the welfare of the masses.

Evidently Togo had picked up a few of the local clichés during
his tour of duty as ambassador to Moscow. Piously he declaimed,
"America and Britain have sinned against God by unscrupulously
spreading the war to various parts of the world through the pursuance
of their traditional policy of victimizing weaker nations. It is clear as
daylight, however, that Britain and America who resort to such out-
rageous policy will eventually come to grief."

Oddly enough, in view of his claims that both enemies were tot-
tering on the brink, Togo soon sounded a brief warning: "It may be
easily imagined that America and Britain will resort to counteroffen-
sive in desperate efforts to retrieve their defeats." But he hastily
added, "However, it is my unshakable belief that there is no room
for doubt that our nation will succeed in prosecuting this great war
to a glorious termination and in constructing a brilliant world, by
bending their efforts tenaciously with the entire nation united like
one man, however long the war may be protracted."[12]

When Navy Minister Admiral Shigetaro Shimada took his place
in the limelight, satisfaction beamed from his round face. An academy
classmate and close friend of Yamamoto's, he knew as he mounted
the rostrum to speak that afternoon that Japanese naval forces had
already begun to move out on a vast scale against the enemy at
Midway. Full of Japan's dazzling achievements, he declared proudly,

> In the naval operations staged up to the middle of March, practically
> all the key strategic points of the enemy in the Southwestern Pacific
> fell into Japanese hands . . .
>
> On the basis of this most advantageous position, the Imperial
> Japanese Navy has, since then, launched and is staging active large-
> scale operations with the firm determination to crush the enemy
> forces . . .

Then Shimada went into a detailed account of the naval war in
the Pacific, including the campaigns in the Indian Ocean and, of
course, the Coral Sea. As the climax of his address, Shimada listed
total war results. According to his amazing recital, the Japanese had
sunk eight battleships, six aircraft carriers, fifteen cruisers, twenty-

four destroyers, fifty submarines, and forty-seven auxiliary ships. They had also heavily damaged five battleships, twelve cruisers, eleven destroyers, twenty-nine submarines, and forty auxiliary craft. And all this had been accomplished at a loss of one small aircraft carrier, one seaplane carrier, one minelayer, six destroyers, six submarines, fourteen small auxiliary ships, seventeen transports, and 248 aircraft.[13]

Here then was Shimada officially stating the erroneous war figures to the Diet itself. His dishonesty was unnecessary. The Japanese Navy's exploits in the war to date had been truly extraordinary, and needed no false claims to bolster the record. The truth held enough honor for a whole generation of sailors. Something of this thought may have touched Shimada's mind, for he sounded a diplomatic warning:

> The enemy who has had to suffer the ignominy of successive defeats is now concentrating his whole energy on rolling back the tide of war and on reinforcing its forces, and it is to be taken for granted that the enemy will resort to all conceivable means to counterattack us, and for this reason we should not, even for a moment, be off our guard.

But Shimada, like his predecessors at the rostrum, ended on an up-beat: "Permit me to assure you that the officers and men of our Imperial Navy are in high spirits and have unflinching faith in our final victory. They are as firmly resolved as ever to achieve the ultimate objective of the war by bringing the enemy to its knees, defying all difficulties and obstacles that may be in store for us . . ."[14]

Just how much of these effusions Suzuki-San, the Japanese man in the street, genuinely believed is impossible to say. No objective— much less anti-administration—newspapers, magazines, books, or commentators offered him the other side of the picture or questioned any statement those in power chose to make. The careful reader could not miss the fact that, buried deeply within the verbosity, every speaker had indicated that a long war was in store. Nevertheless, there is no evidence that Suzuki-San was other than proud of his armed forces, and he had no reason to doubt the veracity of the officially released figures of damage to the enemy and the promises of ultimate victory.

Only with the background of this atmosphere of exultant drive for conquest, of pride and arrogance, can one understand the Midway story. Only in this context of euphoric self-confidence can one appreciate how the meticulous planning, training and security of the Pearl Harbor attack went by the board in less than six months.

The thick shower of journalistic roses buried the unhappy fact that the Nagumo task force was going forth to war "with meager training and without knowing the enemy."[15] Certainly the Japanese planning for Midway shows no evidence of such first-hand, evidential intelligence as had accompanied every step of the planning for the Pearl Harbor attack.

Indeed, the outset of war had abruptly severed the Japanese espionage chain on Oahu. In anticipation of a round-up of Japanese nationals, Naval Intelligence had planted a German in Honolulu as a sort of human delayed action bomb, set to go off in the event of war. But far from becoming the nucleus of a war-time spy ring, Otto Kuehn was tossed into the local clink by the Honolulu branch of the FBI, to whom he sang loud and long.[16]

Furthermore, the Hawaiian press no longer printed the daily chit-chat about the comings and goings of the U.S. Pacific Fleet units which had made espionage a pleasure. Nor had the Japanese succeeded in breaking the top U.S. Navy code. So Yamamoto and his staff had no way of looking into the minds of Nimitz and his planners. It was a disadvantage which Nagumo underscored heavily: ". . . we had practically no intelligence concerning the enemy. We never knew to the end where and how many enemy carriers there were."[17] But what did it matter if Nagumo did not know what the U.S. Pacific Fleet was planning? According to the government and official press, it was virtually kaput!

> . . . Looking at those vast areas which the enemy has to protect and then turning our eyes to the Pacific, we can feel assured that the enemy can allot only a scanty force to the Pacific. We believe that the enemy's remnant forces in the Pacific consists [sic] of only a few battleships with the American aircraft carriers *Hornet* and *Enterprise* as the nucleus. . . .
>
> What movement will be made by the last aircraft carrier group . . . is a point which is worthy of our closest attention at present. But this feeble strength is no match for our invincible navy. With the Battle of the Coral Sea as the turning point the entire sea areas of the Pacific may be said to have fallen into Japanese hands. . . .[18]

No seamen in Japan's long history had added more luster to the Rising Sun than those of the First Air Fleet. In less than six months, from Pearl Harbor to the Indian Ocean, they had branded the ideographs of Nagumo's name deep into American and British hides. Since opening the Pacific war, his men had sunk five battleships, a carrier, two cruisers, seven destroyers, heavily damaged a number of others, and sent any number of tons of minor shipping to the bottom. And he himself had lost not one vessel. No wonder that, in Kusaka's words, "We left Bungo Channel on May 27 with the overconfidence that if the task force takes the van, it will take care of everything."[19]

By noon the striking force had left Bungo Channel behind, and when the cool, salty evening fell over the ships, they were well out to sea. Fuchida crawled into bed early. He had had a busy day and still felt twinges from a pain which had recently sent him to an Army hospital for observation. The Army doctors had diagnosed overindulgence and slammed him on the wagon. At first Dr. Tamai, *Akagi*'s surgeon, did not take Fuchida's ailment seriously and joked that it was probably the result of heavy drinking. This was encouraging, for Tamai was a noted surgeon and crew members kidded among themselves that he was always more than willing to carve up a patient.[20]

But that night Fuchida had barely drifted into sleep when he awoke bent double in agony. His orderly hastily produced Dr. Tamai. "It's acute appendicitis," the doctor informed the sweating airman. "I must operate immediately." He firmly overrode Fuchida's pleas that he be patched up temporarily so that he could carry on for the next week or ten days. In his decision the doctor received reinforcements from Nagumo, Kusaka, and Genda. This trio gathered at Fuchida's bunkside as soon as they heard the bad news. All were unhappy, for Fuchida was an inspirational leader in whom his men reposed every confidence, and they had counted on him to lead Japan's sea hawks into the engagement now on the agenda. But they assured him that they could get along without him, and in any case he would be on tap for advice and counsel.[21]

The dismaying news that Fuchida was out as flight commander spread through the ship. Even Murata plunged into gloom. "I'm afraid that Commander Fuchida's absence may greatly affect the fliers' morale," he fretted.

"We can dismiss any such fear," interjected the executive officer, "because brave, dauntless Butsu-san is going to take his place." At this, Murata, nicknamed Butsu-san (Buddha) in tribute to his good nature, grinned, opened his mouth to its fullest extent, and uttered the single word, "No!"[22]

As if to compound this stroke of bad luck, a few days after Fuchida's appendix came out, a pneumonia bug laid Genda low with a fever.[23] These twin misfortunes, which en route to Pearl Harbor probably would have worried Nagumo no end, seem to have left him professionally unmoved. As for Kusaka, nothing ever disturbed that tranquil Zen Buddhist.

Many Japanese are sensitive to omens, and sailors are traditionally superstitious. But neither admiral saw in the abrupt canceling of two key juniors the figurative passing of a black cat under a ladder. And of course they had no idea that Nimitz was preparing a hot reception for them at and near Midway.

Much more credible to these two fighting admirals would have been the nervousness afflicting the upper reaches of the United States War Department. Marshall had just returned from stirring up the defenses in California in anticipation of a possible Doolittle-type raid on that area. "It is high time," Stimson recorded, "because this afternoon we got word that all lights were out on the Japanese fleet and they have started on their work. The next thing we know will be where they will strike us."[24]

CHAPTER 11

"The Principle of Calculated Risk"

Rear Admiral Frank Jack Fletcher stood on the bridge of *Yorktown* as she slowly moved into Pearl Harbor at 1352 on May 27. The admiral's scant, sandy hair, jutting nose, and straight seam of a mouth over a pugnacious, scarred chin added up to a rugged face. But the brown eyes were keen and merry, and the high, broad brow hid a practical, down-to-earth brain. In another sort of blue uniform, Fletcher might have been the tough but kindly Irish neighborhood policeman in any American town, good-naturedly tapping the saloon door with his nightstick in warning when noise approached the saturation point, but rock firm in real trouble.

Fletcher came to the Navy from Iowa. He graduated from Annapolis in 1906 and picked up years of solid experience with destroyers, battleships and cruisers. He also served in various staff positions, and on January 17, 1942, assumed command of Task Force Seventeen.

Fletcher rated aces high with his Navy colleagues as a man, somewhat less so as an admiral. A member of Nimitz's staff described him as "a big, nice, wonderful guy who didn't know his butt from third base."[1] He had one heavy strike against him: He had commanded Task Force Fourteen, based around *Saratoga*, during the abortive Wake Island mission,* and it is generally conceded that, in Admiral Morison's words, ". . . the failure to relieve Wake resulted from poor seamanship and a want of decisive action, both on Fletcher's part and on Pye's. . . ."[2] His subsequent operations had been workmanlike but not spectacular.

---

*See Chapter 1.

As his carrier inched through the channel, he had "a horrible feeling concerning the damaged *Yorktown*" and he "regretted it very much," but as he said resignedly, "It was just one of those things that happen in battle." Fletcher had "not the least idea what would happen next" or how long he would be tied up in port. The most pessimistic estimate of the time necessary to put *Yorktown* into prime condition was three months. With this Fletcher did not agree, but he believed the job "would take about two weeks or more."

The admiral was looking forward to setting foot on Oahu's hospitable, palm-fringed shore, for he had been away for 102 days. "And that was 102 days without a drink," he pointed out. "I certainly wanted a drink after what we had been through."[3]

While waiting for *Yorktown*, Spruance occupied himself busily all morning. He was glad to be on dry land again for a brief spell, but he itched to get at the Japanese. He considered them a most resourceful, cunning, and brave enemy, and one from whom he could expect absolutely anything. So he began to formulate plans in his own mind on how to deal with the threat.[4]

Yorktown stood into harbor at 1420, and just before she eased into Berth 16, a member of Fletcher's staff informed him that Nimitz wanted to see him. The admiral nodded in acknowledgment, but replied genially, "First I am going to have a drink." The way the subordinate saw it, a wise officer did not keep four stars in suspense while he leisurely sipped a highball. "No, you had better not, Admiral," he urged, "because Admiral Nimitz wants to see you right away."

"No, I'm going to have a drink first," Fletcher maintained firmly. And he did so.[5]

After this brief refueling, he and Rear Admiral William Ward "Poco" Smith,* his good friend and Commander Cruisers of Task Force Seventeen, proceeded to Nimitz's office. There they found the CinCPAC "calm and collected" as usual. Admiral Draemel, his chief of staff, was the only other officer present.[6]

Much to the embarrassment of all concerned, Fletcher had to explain to Nimitz his conduct of the Coral Sea battle. Some question had arisen, apparently unjustifiably, as to his aggressiveness. Fletcher asked for a little time to get his facts together, and the next morning

---

*Smith had been Admiral Kimmel's chief of staff at the time of Pearl Harbor.

defended himself to such good purpose that Nimitz lost whatever doubts he may have entertained about Fletcher's fitness to command Task Force Seventeen.[7]

In the meantime, Nimitz briefed Fletcher on the current situation. To the best of Fletcher's recollection, the conversation went something like this:

"We have to fix you up right away and send you to Midway," declared the CinCPAC.

"Midway?" Fletcher asked blankly, for the idea surprised him.

"Yes, Midway," Nimitz answered briskly. "You have to go to Midway because the Japanese are going to try to take it. In fact," he continued rather dryly, "they are so positive they have already ordered a Captain of the Yard to report there on August 12."[8]

He added that the Japanese would try to occupy Midway on either June 3 or 4. Only a week hence! Not much time to prepare for a major naval engagement! Nimitz did not tell the two admirals from Task Force Seventeen where he got his information, but Fletcher already knew that the United States had broken a top Japanese naval code, and Poco Smith, who had a razor-sharp mind and had served as the Navy's first cryptanalyst back in 1915–1917, "assumed that Washington had broken the enemy cipher."

"The Japanese will have at least four carriers and a strong force to support their landing at Midway," Nimitz continued. Somehow United States forces must hold the island and the Pacific Fleet must beat off the powerful Japanese armada.

Then he told Fletcher and Smith that Halsey was hospitalized, that Spruance would take over Task Force Sixteen and would sortie the next day. Nimitz further informed Fletcher that he wanted him and Spruance to confer with him before the latter sailed in order to study the intelligence picture together and formulate plans.[9]

Nimitz's own operational plan was ready for all task force, squadron, and division commanders: Fletcher and Spruance would position their task forces northeast of Midway, beyond the Japanese search range, whereas U.S. reconnaissance, reaching 700 miles from Midway, would locate the Japanese flattops before their carrier-based aircraft, of much shorter range, could find the Americans.

The CinCPAC had also prepared a special Letter of Instructions for each task force commander: "In carrying out the task assigned . . . you will be governed by the principle of calculated risk, which you shall interpret to mean avoidance of exposure of your force to attack by superior enemy forces without good prospect of inflicting, as a result of such exposure, greater damage on the enemy."[10]

Nimitz instructed Fletcher that he would sail aboard *Yorktown*, catch up with Spruance and then, as senior officer present afloat, assume tactical command of their combined forces. Somehow or other, by luck and God's mercy, *Yorktown* would have to be repaired in time to rendezvous with Spruance before the battle.

This was much easier said than done. Fletcher thought it would take no less than a miracle to get the gallant lady ready in time. Luckily she had survived the Japanese strike at the Coral Sea with no damage to her engines, but otherwise she was not in good shape.[11]

Three bombs hurtling out of the skies on May 8 were responsible for the damage. A direct hit struck the flight deck "slightly forward of frame 108, six feet and six inches to starboard of the centerline." This bomb penetrated the "flight, gallery, main, second, and third decks and exploded in C-402-A, an aviation storeroom, at about frame 107, some feet above the fourth deck." In its passage it caused considerable structural damage, rupturing bulkheads and springing doors. It ripped gaping holes in the ship's innards, hurled splinters and fragments in all directions, started fires, and killed and wounded personnel. Though this strike "did not incapacitate the *Yorktown* to any great extent" it lowered her speed to twenty-five knots. This represented a considerable loss of combat effectiveness and of security, because a carrier, with its thin armor, depends upon speed for protection.[12]

The second bomb had "struck and glanced off the outboard coaming of the forward starboard gallery walkway" and exploded off the bow. This blow pushed in "the lower edge of the armor belt," wrinkled transverse frames and bulkheads inboard, and in a few places tore them from the shell. At the time of impact, the "most serious consequence of this damage was the oil slick formed aft of the ship by oil escaping" from a leaking seam.

The third bomb exploded "on contact with the surface about fifty feet off the starboard bow abreast frame 20." Fragments "pierced the shell in four or five places," and cut a gasoline line at frame 20. But, on the whole, damage from this near miss was relatively slight.[13]

Rear Admiral Aubry W. "Jake" Fitch, a qualified navy pilot who commanded the *Lexington* Carrier Group at the battle of the Coral

Sea, estimated at the time that *Yorktown* would require three months' repair work.[14] Even Fletcher's much more optimistic guess of two weeks would be too late for her to participate in the forthcoming battle. But neither Nimitz nor Furlong's service force was going to write off *Yorktown* without a fight. Without her, the carrier count at Midway would be Japan four, perhaps five, and the United States two—scarcely odds to inspire confidence.

Yorktown needed more than repairs; she also needed a new complement of aircraft and pilots. These were scooped in from Kaneohe Naval Air Station where fighters and dive bombers were waiting for the return of *Saratoga*, anticipated early in June. The very day *Yorktown* berthed, *Saratoga*'s VF-3 squadron merged with *Yorktown*'s VF-5* under Lieutenant Commander John S. "Jimmy" Thach, destined to become a four-star admiral in later days. In the meantime, Fletcher and Smith had a brief respite to catch up with several months' accumulated mail.[15]

The late afternoon sun slanted over Battleship Row and into the windows of Nimitz's office. There five key officers in their khaki uniforms met together, deeply absorbed in the crucial problems of Midway. Behind his desk sat Nimitz, blond as a Swedish baby, courteous, courtly, with his innate ability to make himself felt without histrionics. At this vital moment, his was the directing brain of U.S. naval operations against the Japanese.

Nearby sat his two task force commanders. Fletcher, with his weathered brown face and his air of an alert Irish terrier, came into the picture stone cold that very afternoon. But he was adaptable and willing to fight. Spruance, sparse of speech and figure, was a man secure in the knowledge of his own gifts—a sharp, computer brain, the ability to listen, to absorb the lesson, to think hard on it, and to act with decision.

Two members of Nimitz's staff rounded out the group. Draemel, his right-hand man, tall, lean, graceful of movement, stood ready to take whatever burdens he could off Nimitz's shoulders and to supply

---

*American carriers were numbered in order of commissioning. *Saratoga* was 3, *Yorktown* 5, *Enterprise* 6, and *Hornet* 8. The aircraft squadrons assigned to each carrier bore that ship's number with a letter indicating the type: VB for bomber, VS for scout, VF for fighter, VT for torpedo plane. However, due to the shifting and consolidating necessary to prepare for Midway, squadrons from one carrier could and did operate from another ship, still carrying their original designation.

needed information. Layton, the youngest member present, almost visibly bulged with intelligence data and waited eagerly for Nimitz to tap his storehouse of knowledge. He had already stuck his neck way out. Nimitz had asked him, "When and where do you estimate that we will make contact with the enemy?" And Layton had replied precisely, "I anticipate that first contact will be made by our search planes out of Midway at 0600 Midway time, 4 June, 325 degrees northwest at a distance of 175 miles."*[16]

Nimitz had called these officers together for a final grim stock-taking before plans must be translated into action. In this meeting, no one expressed heady euphoria, fatuous optimism, or smug over-confidence. No one manipulated the awkward facts to fit preconceived notions or fond hopes. On the other hand, these men displayed no dank despair, no bleak pessimism, no enervating self-pity, no mel-odramatics of dying for flag and country.

This was a gathering of dedicated, professional sailors for a cold, sober assessment of cold, sober facts. They knew that the Japanese conquest of Midway would give their bow-shaped homeland a steel-tipped arrow aimed straight at the heart of Hawaii. Moreover, it would be a deadly symbol that Pearl Harbor had been no fluke, that the United States could not protect its own territory even when the element of surprise was absent. Each man realized, too, that the Japanese were tough and resourceful foes who attacked unexpectedly and ruthlessly.

Time crowded against these colleagues. This would be their last chance to go over the latest information, to exchange and compare ideas face to face to size up the enemy and formulate an overall plan of action. For Spruance would be sailing in a matter of hours and Fletcher would follow as soon as possible. Each officer knew that vast consequences would flow from their decisions and actions within the next few days.

Nimitz's soft, level voice was virtually the only one heard that afternoon, for this was his hour to speak, to explain, to direct. Some of his remarks were repetitious, recapitulations of previous briefings, brought up to date by the latest intelligence which Layton provided him.

---

*Layton was exactly five minutes, five degrees, and five miles off. Nagumo's planes were first sighted at 320°, 180 miles from Midway, at 0555.

He informed them that, according to the intelligence picture, the Japanese would be coming into Midway with their carriers from the northwest. For the American admirals, the principal objective was to achieve surprise. They could not afford to place their ships between the enemy and Midway. If humanly possible, they should hit the Japanese on the flank and hit them first.[17]

Not only the achievement of surprise but the iron shackles of logistics demanded this indirection. Fletcher and Spruance would be going out to battle the Japanese with forces so inferior that a knock-down, drag-out slugfest could only end in utter disaster. In a flank attack, dashing in to nip the enemy from the side as a wise old sheepdog harries a wolf threatening his flock, lay the only hope of a United States victory.

Furthermore, Midway was not alone at stake: Admiral Ernest J. King, the Cominch, estimated that the enemy's plans included an attempt to trap a large part of Nimitz's fleet. He had therefore "directed that strong attrition tactics, only, be employed and that our carriers and cruisers not be unduly risked." This directive from Washington was completely in accord with Nimitz's thinking. The American task forces could not go charging out of Oahu right into a Japanese trap. They must sidle up to it, like a mouse bent on nibbling the cheese without tripping the spring.[18]

Spruance would sortie the next day, with Fletcher to follow as soon as he possibly could. They were to rendezvous at 32° north latitude, 173° west longitude, about 325 miles northeast of Midway, a spot which Nimitz had hopefully named "Point Luck."[19]

Fletcher must meet Spruance at Point Luck at the specified time, or the whole American strategy would be thrown off. If he was too late, Spruance would be stymied, or have to go it alone. On the other hand, if he showed up too far ahead of schedule, he would have to lurk in the area waiting for Spruance, which would invite discovery by the Japanese.

But the rendezvous represented only one aspect of the timing problem. Even more exquisitely and sharply cut was the moment for hitting the enemy. They must permit the Japanese to come in far enough, but not too far. They must go as close to the enemy as possible, but not too close. By reconnaissance and by an intuitive feel for the exact moment, Fletcher and Spruance must attempt to catch the Japanese with planes on deck, and themselves avoid being caught with their own planes down. No two aerialists, their lives depending on gripping hands in mid-air, ever needed a more acute sense of split-second precision than these two admirals. As Nimitz later wrote, "The whole situation was a most difficult one, requiring the most delicate timing on the part of our carriers. . . ."[20]

With more time than Fletcher to acclimate himself to the situation, Spruance had already sent his crystalline thought processes ranging ahead. *We must not get between Midway and the Japanese*, he told himself, *because it is possible that the Japanese might change their direction of approach. And we want to know if this happens and be in a position to act accordingly.* Spruance's naval code was basically simple: Seek out the enemy, and when you have found him, hit him at once with everything that isn't nailed down and with everything that is if you can pry it loose. He also tried to put himself inside the enemy's mind. *The Japanese hit Pearl Harbor from the north*, he mused. *Perhaps they might change their approach and hit Midway from the same direction.* In dealing with foes as resourceful as Yamamoto and Nagumo, flexibility must go hand in hand with secrecy.[21]

The information which Layton and Rochefort had assembled indicated that three fleets were converging on Midway—a striking force, a support force and an occupation force. The first of these was under the Commander in Chief of the First Air Fleet, and this fact alone commanded respect. For this was Nagumo of the Japanese victories, Nagumo of the Allied nightmares, Nagumo who had humbled the Americans at Pearl Harbor and the British at Ceylon.

Under his flag would be the carriers *Akagi* and *Kaga*, *Soryu* and *Hiryu*, the light cruiser *Nagara* and twelve destroyers, the battleships *Haruna* and *Kirishima*, the heavy cruisers *Tone* and *Chikuma*. The Support Force Layton estimated as comprising the heavy cruisers *Mogami*, *Mikuma*, *Suzuya*, *Kumano*, a carrier (name unknown), the battleships *Hiei* and *Kongo*, a cruiser of the *Atago* class, and *Jintsu* with ten destroyers. From all indications, the Occupation Force would consist of one *Takao* class cruiser, one or two of the *Myoko* class, Air Squadron Seven (*Chitose*, *Chiyoda*), Air Squadron Eleven (two to four of the *Kamigawa* class), and twelve destroyers, along with troop transports and support craft. And with all this formidable power afloat, sixteen submarines would be prowling deep in the waters throughout the Midway and Hawaii area. The estimate was sobering enough, but at least the Pacific Fleet thought it knew what it was up against.[22]

Actually the estimate, although fantastically accurate concerning the three fleets in question, did not go far enough. For it did not take into consideration Yamamoto's Main Body,[23] with its powerful battleships, steaming behind Nagumo to administer the *coup de grâce* to whatever American ships might have escaped the advanced units when they sailed out of Pearl Harbor to challenge the Japanese occupation of Midway.

Superior intelligence data and surprise were not the only advantages the United States held. She also enjoyed the advantage of interior lines. One look at the map told each officer that Midway was approximately 1,150 miles from Pearl Harbor while Hashirajima, Yamamoto's home base, was a good 2,500 miles astern his fleet.

Another ace up Nimitz's sleeve was the Pacific cable which since 1903 had linked Honolulu to Manila, with Midway as one of its stations. This undersea line carried the bulk of the heavy pre-battle communications exchange between Pearl Harbor and Midway—a line which the Japanese could not tap. Normal radio traffic from shore to ship thus could not give the Japanese a true picture of what the Americans were up to.[24]

Then, too, United States radar was much superior to the Japanese, and the TBS (voice radio telephone) permitted short-range ship-to-ship and ship-to-aircraft communications which the Japanese could not intercept. But no one in this room was kidding himself. This was a shaky hand to hold across the table from the full house Yamamoto could lay down.

They had been together now for an hour or more. With quiet finality Nimitz brought his briefing to a close. Once again he reminded his task force commanders that they must be governed by the principle of calculated risk.[25]

It was typical of Nimitz that, on this day filled with high-level conferences and strategic concerns, he should have thought of the officers and men who must carry out the operation. He sent this message to Task Force Sixteen, scheduled to sortie the next day:

PLEASE PUBLISH AT QUARTERS   ALTHOUGH IN THE CRUISE
JUST ENDED YOU WERE DENIED THE OPPORTUNITY TO MEET THE
ENEMY AND TO REPEAT THE SPLENDID ACHIEVEMENTS OF PAST
OPERATIONS I AM CONFIDENT THAT YOU USED THIS TIME TO INCREASE
YOUR EFFICIENCY FOR FUTURE ACTION   IN THE CRUISE JUST
STARTING YOU WILL HAVE THE OPPORTUNITIES TO DEAL THE ENEMY

HEAVY BLOWS   YOU HAVE DONE THIS BEFORE AND I HAVE
GREAT CONFIDENCE IN YOUR COURAGE SKILL AND ABILITY TO STRIKE
EVEN HARDER BLOWS   GOOD HUNTING AND GOOD LUCK.[26]

The sun had begun to dip beneath the sea on the western horizon
when Nimitz brought the meeting to an end and the officers dispersed. Fletcher and Spruance had much to ponder, for it would be,
as Fletcher described it "nip and tuck—a close business."[27] A tremendous burden had been placed on their shoulders, a burden such
as few men are called upon to bear. But their shoulders were broad
enough to carry the load. As the two admirals walked down the stairs
and out into the soft Hawaiian evening, they faced the forthcoming
trial soberly and realistically, but without fear.

CHAPTER 12

"On a Major Mission"

While Nagumo's First Air Fleet, Nimitz's task forces, and the Marines on Midway prepared for the upcoming confrontation, Admiral Tanaka sortied from Saipan at about 2040 on May 27. He dodged south of Tinian to avoid any enemy submarines that might be lurking around, then headed on course toward the target area.[1]

But the Transport Group saw neither American submarines, aircraft, nor any other manifestation of enemy activity. Sea and skies seemed to demonstrate exactly how the Pacific got its name. "Every day during the long cruise the sea was dead calm," said Chigusa, *Jintsu*'s gunnery officer. "We saw no other ships or planes. Everything was quiet and peaceful, so much so that day by day the crew lost its morale. It was very simple—no enemy."

Chigusa knew that boredom can be as deadly a foe of the sailor as any mortal enemy. A large body of men, virtual prisoners in a confined space, can stagnate all too rapidly unless they have something to occupy their minds. Worse, they can get on each other's nerves, and petty squabbles may arise which erode the team spirit. So Chigusa pondered ways and means to remedy the situation.

True Japanese that he was, he hit upon a combination of group singing and group calisthenics. Each afternoon he rounded up the crew on deck and led them in an hour or so of songs—war songs, navy songs, popular songs, folk songs. He varied the daily program so that the songfest itself would not become just one more boring monotony, and the men responded to this practical psychology, caroling away with gusto. Sometimes they broke impulsively into the

107

national anthem. Then they would swing and bend enthusiastically, limbering their muscles as the vigorous tunes limbered their spirits.

But Chigusa realized that these measures were stopgaps. "If we had only seen one enemy plane, that would have stimulated morale more than all the songs," he said. "Very calm seas, very peaceful atmosphere, very beautiful skies and wonderful weather, not just one day but every day for ten days—things were just too smooth and too good. There seemed no necessity to struggle and work. Everything was just fine. This was not good for us on the eve of such a great battle as Midway." Nevertheless, everyone was fully confident that victory would crown the Rising Sun banner. "All officers aboard *Jintsu* expected only good news concerning Nagumo's air attacks against Midway," recalled Chigusa.[2]

In company with the transports cruised Admiral Fujita's Seaplane Tender Group, consisting of the same units which had accompanied the Tanaka force from the homeland.* According to Yamamoto's plan, this group would occupy Kure Island and establish a seaplane base there.[3]

Admiral Kurita's Close Support Group covered the advance of Tanaka's invasion convoy. Kurita sortied from Guam at about the same time Tanaka's fleet left Saipan, sailing parallel to and about forty miles southwest of the transports. The heart of Kurita's group was CruDiv 7, comprising the four heavy cruisers *Kumano* (his flagship), *Suzuya*, *Mikuma* and *Mogami*. These magnificent vessels averaged 11,200 tons; they bristled with ten 8-inch guns, carried twelve torpedoes in triple mounts above water, and could show a clean wake to any ship in the Imperial Navy. *Mikuma* and *Mogami* were sister ships, never separated since the start of the war. They had sunk two Allied cruisers off Batavia—the United States *Houston* and the Australian *Perth*. Together they had fought through the Andaman Islands, Burma, and Bengal Bay operations, and now they sped toward the greatest adventure of all. With Kurita also sailed the two destroyers of DesDiv 8, *Asahio* and *Arashio*, and the oiler *Nichiei Maru*.[4]

When Nagumo's First Air Fleet was a day at sea, Vice Admiral Hosogaya's northern forces got under way. On May 28 his main body, consisting of the heavy cruiser *Nachi* (flagship), a screen of two destroyers, two oilers, and three cargo vessels, departed the broad bay

*See Chapter 7.

of Ominato in northern Honshu. So did the Attu and Kiska invasion forces. These consisted of several light cruisers, two destroyer divisions, troop transports, minesweepers, and a submarine detachment of four undersea craft commanded by Rear Admiral Shigeaki Yamazaki, a veteran of Pearl Harbor. Hosogaya's mission was to assault and seize the islands of Attu and Kiska and to divert United States naval attention to this northern theater and away from the main thrust at Midway, which would come one day later.[5]

Another of Japan's northern forces had left Ominato Bay at noon on May 26.* This was Rear Admiral Kakuta's Second Carrier Striking Force, the first of Yamamoto's attacking units to leave the homeland. It comprised the light carrier *Ryujo* with sixteen Zero fighters and twenty-one torpedo bombers, plus the escort carrier *Junyo* with twenty-four Zeros and twenty-one dive bombers. A support group of two light cruisers, a screen of three destroyers, and an oiler accompanied the carriers.

The mission of Kakuta's airmen was to soften up Attu and Kiska before Hosogaya's landing forces moved in. They were also to attack and destroy any United States surface units which had the audacity to poke their prows over the horizon. To help do so, several highly capable Pearl Harbor veterans like Lieutenant Yoshio Shiga, leader of the Zeros aboard *Junyo*, and Lieutenant Zenji Abe, leader of the same carrier's dive bombers, stood ready to direct the attacks of Kakuta's airmen.[6]

But this was not all the naval power the Japanese would divert to the northern campaign. The Aleutian Screening Force under Vice Admiral Takasu was a formidable fleet unto itself, consisting of the four battleships *Ryuga*, *Ise*, *Fuso*, and *Yamashiro*, the light cruisers *Oi* and *Kitakami*, and twelve destroyers. Although Takasu's steel monsters were among the oldest of the Japanese battleships, they were still powerful. Takasu's fleet would not sortie until May 29 (Japanese time); then it would go out with Yamamoto's Main Body.[7]

Back in the Inland Sea, Yamamoto's headquarters was busy with preparations for the next day's sortie. Ugaki had his hair cut and teeth fixed, then "put various things in order." Having done so, he felt "calmness in my mind, having nothing to worry about except to await tomorrow's sortie." He had information indicating that at least thir-

---

*See Order of Battle.

teen United States subs were operating near Japan and the Marianas; therefore, he considered that "utmost care should be taken in tomorrow's sortie." Nevertheless, he recorded in his diary, "I firmly believe that the Combined Fleet will surely be blessed by God. We will go on a major mission to the east in high spirits to inflict heavy damage to the enemy."[8]

Miwa, too, was confident of victory, and feared only that the fleet might not encounter enough American ships. "I only pray that God blesses us with a chance of meeting a good enemy force," he noted. "The enemy is suspected of having concentrated its strength in the waters near Australia. In such a case, we shall not be able to launch a major decisive battle, I am afraid."[9]

At Midway on the 27th, the aircraft unloaded from *Kitty Hawk* were placed in commission and tested all day, while the new personnel were assigned to squadrons. Officer living space, like gold, was where you found it. McCaul stashed his officers away in such unorthodox billets as the new command post, the First Sergeant's office, auxiliary sick bay, and the enlisted men's recreation room.

On the credit side of the ledger, McCaul could count completion of fifteen new plane bunkers with wheel tracks installed. From now on until after the battle, the daily gas consumption was written on McCaul's heart. "Pan American gasoline barge placed in commission and gasoline was pumped into the storage system day and night in an effort to fill it to capacity and still keep up with probable daily requirements," he noted.

The 28th was a relatively routine day for McCaul, except that two SB2U-3s groundlooped, as was their habit, and thus were out of commission.[10] Major Warner, the Army Air Corps liaison officer, who had dived into his work promptly and energetically, observed, "Birds are so thick over the Island that at around mid-day they may be dangerous to high speed equipment. The fighters and dive bombers keep the birds falling but damage apparently isn't serious."[11]

By 0645 that morning of May 28, *Yorktown* was under way to change from Berth 16 to Dry Dock No. 1.[12] No sooner had she settled into drydock when she nearly disappeared under a swarm of electricians, fitters, machinists, welders—every type of mechanic that Rear Admiral William Rhea Furlong, commandant of the Pearl Harbor Navy Yard, could turn loose on her. Sparks showered in great arcs from acetylene torches, the incessant rat-tat-tat of riveting guns woke the echoes. No time for blueprints, no time for scale drawings! Wooden templates were made on the carrier, rushed to the repair shops, the parts made on the spot and sped to the ship.[13]

While *Yorktown* was undergoing surgery to her steel innards, Spruance's Task Force Sixteen began to move out. At 0850, tugs commenced removing torpedo nets from the port side of *Enterprise*. At approximately 0900, the seaplane tender *Curtiss* got under way and stood out of harbor. Forty minutes later, the garbage lighter *YG17* nosed up to *Hornet* and at 1015 cast off with its malodorous load. While the carriers tested steering gear, took the draft of the ships, tested the main engines, and energized degaussing coils, the destroyers continued to sortie. The cruisers followed a little later, commencing with *Northampton* at approximately 1040.[14]

At 1110 *Enterprise* cut in boiler No. 2 on the main steam line, all tugs cast off, and the carrier "commenced steaming on various courses and at various speeds conforming to run of channel." The ship went into condition of readiness two, and at 1159 "with black lighted channel entrance buoy No. 1 abeam to starboard and red lighted channel entrance buoy No. 2 abeam to port, stood out of Pearl Harbor channel on course 154° true and pgc., speed 25 knots. . . ."[15]

Hornet got under way at 1134, with a harbor pilot at the controls and the captain and navigator on the bridge. At 1221 the pilot left the ship in Captain Marc A. Mitscher's hands, and "with buoy No. 1 abeam to starboard, distance 40 yards," *Hornet* "took departure and set course 150° true and pgc. Speed 20 knots." During this time, "while passing through dangerous waters," the carrier held torpedo defense.[16]

These carriers were the hard core of Spruance's task force: *Enterprise* under Captain Murray, and *Hornet* commanded by Mitscher, he of the puckered gnome's face and giant's heart. With them sailed the cruiser group (TG 16.2), comprising *New Orleans, Minneapolis, Vincennes, Northampton, Pensacola*, and *Atlanta*, with Rear Admiral Thomas C. Kinkaid in command.

Spruance's destroyer screen (TG 16.4) under Captain Alexander R. Early consisted of DesRon 1 (*Phelps, Worden, Monaghan*, and *Aylwin*), and DesRon 6 (*Balch, Conyngham, Benham, Ellet* and *Maury*). Two of the sleek destroyers were veterans of Pearl Harbor—*Aylwin*, which under the command of an ensign ran the gauntlet into the clear sea, and *Monaghan*, which had rammed and sunk one of the midget

submarines. *Monaghan* still had the same skipper, the indestructible
Lieutenant Commander William P. Burford. He did not have all the
information available to the upper echelon, but he knew enough to
have "a fairly good picture of what was going on." An oiler group,
consisting of *Cimarron* and *Platte*, with their escort destroyers *Dewey*
and *Monssen*, rounded out Spruance's task force.[17]

As straight, flexible, and deadly as a Toledo blade, Spruance watched
the great harbor fall astern. He had already made certain definite
decisions. He would not come within 700 miles of Wake Island, no
matter what the temptation. He knew the Japanese had beefed up
the place, and he did not want to mix with land-based aviation. Nor
did he intend to permit the Japanese to draw him so far west that
they could close in with their superior surface strength and clobber
him.

Spruance wanted to sink as many Japanese ships as possible, but
he had to remember that the United States was painfully short of
both carriers and destroyers, so it was his responsibility to preserve
his ships if at all possible. And a carrier's only use is as a floating
airfield; if too damaged to launch or recover aircraft, it is no asset in
battle. In any case, Spruance's mission did not include hooting after
Japanese ships for their own sake. His job was to keep the enemy
from invading Midway, and this would be quite enough to occupy
his mind in the circumstances. It would be almost miraculous if he
succeeded. Certainly anything accomplished above and beyond that
would be a bonus from fate. Spruance would tack his sails to catch
any wind of chance, but in his ears rang Nimitz's orders: "You will
be governed by the principle of calculated risk. . . ."[18]

That same day (May 28 Hawaiian time, May 29 Japanese time),
at 0500, the Main Body of the Midway Invasion Force, under Admiral
Kondo's overall command, commenced its sortie from Hashirajima.
DesRon 4, comprising the light cruiser *Yura* and seven destroyers,
took the lead out of the Inland Sea and headed for Bungo Channel.
Hard on their sterns plowed the sleek vessels of CruDivs 4 and 5,
whose wide wakes suggested something of their size and power. *Atago*
and *Chokai*, at over 11,000 tons, and *Myoke* and *Haguro*, at over
13,000 tons, resembled pocket battleships. Not only did they boast
formidable armament (ten 8-inch guns each) and a speed of around
thirty-four knots, they were designed to give the greatest possible
protection against submarine attack. Last out sailed the veteran bat-

tleships *Hiei* and *Kongo*, the light carrier *Zuiho* with twelve Zeros and twelve torpedo bombers, and the destroyer *Mikazuki*.[19]

Kondo's flag fluttered from the masthead of *Atago*. Like Nagumo, Kondo had been presented with the Midway plan already gift-wrapped and told in effect to take it or leave it. Although he expressed misgivings, principally based upon a lack of Japanese land-based air support, he perforce accepted the situation.[20]

To look at a portrait of Kondo is to be reminded forcibly of Captain Hara's happy phrase: "Kondo was the British gentleman sort of man." His was the serene, slightly withdrawn face of a man well bred and well educated, calmly confident that he owned the earth but was quite good-natured about letting other people walk on it. According to Hara, who always could be depended upon for an unconventional judgment, Kondo was affable and worthy of great respect, but at the same time Hara considered that one of Yamamoto's weaknesses was a tendency to overrate Kondo's reliability in a scrap. As Hara saw it, "Kondo might have been a great commandant of the Naval Academy, but he was a misfit as commander of a naval fighting unit."[21] On this occasion, however, it so happened that Kondo would not be called upon to do any fighting.

CHAPTER 13

"Constant Vigilance Has to Be Maintained"

Spruance was unaware that on the same day of his own sortie—May 29, 1942 Japanese time—at 0600 Yamamoto's Main Body began to steam out of Hashirajima. By the time Spruance had cleared Pearl Harbor, the Main Body was well on its way to Bungo Channel.

The light cruiser *Sendai*, flagship of DesRon 3, spearheaded the procession, flying the flag of Rear Admiral Shintaro Hashimoto.[1] Like most of Japan's light cruisers, *Sendai* dated from the 1920's, but had been refitted during the 1930's and in 1940. She led an array of no less than twenty destroyers—five divisions of four craft each. Of these divisions two were components of Hashimoto's own DesRon 3, the other three divisions being under the command of Rear Admiral Fukuji Kishi, whose CruDiv 3, the two light cruisers *Kitakami* and *Oi*, followed the destroyers. These two vessels displaced about 5,800 tons each and could carry eighty mines. They had been updated in 1940 and 1941.[2]

But these fine ships, impressive though they were, were merely the hors d'oeuvres. Next Yamamoto served his main course, the battlewagons. Battleship Division One was under the Commander in Chief's direct command—three ships only, but what ships! With a length of over 850 feet, measuring almost 130 feet abeam, and displacing 69,988 tons at full load, *Yamato* was the largest warship in the history of the world to that time. In fact, she would not lose her championship until the launching of the American nuclear carrier

114

Enterprise in 1963. One salvo from her nine triple-turret 18.1-inch guns spewed forth about thirteen tons of explosive. Her 2,500-man crew felt as secure aboard her as they would in their own homes, for no capital ship afloat could approach her near enough to slug it out blow for blow. Yet, with all *Yamato*'s bulk and power, she was surprisingly swift, with a speed of twenty-seven knots.[3]

The combined weight of the sister ships *Nagato* and *Mutsu* was less than that of the flagship, for each weighed 32,700 tons. In spite of this relative lightness, their best speed was about that of the new seagoing mastodon. Both battlewagons were quite old as warships go, *Nagato* having been launched at Kure in November 1920 and *Mutsu* launched at Yokosuka eleven months later. Each mounted eight 16-inch and twenty 5.5-inch guns, as well as a number of antiaircraft and machine guns. Both had been thoroughly refitted in the 1930s, receiving among other improvements new boilers and triple bottoms for increased antisubmarine protection.[4]

Behind Yamamoto's three monsters plowed the four lighter vessels of Battleship Division Two under Vice Admiral Shiro Takasu, who flew his flag from *Ryuga*. All four of Takasu's ships dated from the World War I period. *Ise* and *Ryuga* were sisters, as were *Fuso* and *Yamashiro*, the latter being the oldest battleships in the Japanese Navy, having been commissioned respectively in November 1915 and March 1917. But, if faced with the sort of situation for which they were created—a Jutland-type sea battle*—they could give a very good account of themselves. Their twelve 14-inch guns still packed a terrific wallop and, with their array of lighter supporting guns, comprised extremely heavy armament in relation to their size.[5]

Four modest but necessary oilers joined the party, and the destroyer *Yukaze*, with the light carrier *Hosho*, carrying eight bombers, guarded the rear of this tremendous exhibit of naval power. The little *Hosho*, comparable in size to the USS *Langley*, was something of a celebrity, being the first ship ever conceived and built as an aircraft carrier, although older vessels had been modified for such use. This plucky little pioneer lady was destined to outlive all her mighty sons of Japan's carrier forces, only to surrender at Kure in 1945 and to be scrapped two years later at Osaka.[6]

According to plan, Takasu's battleships, along with Kishi's cruisers

---

*The classic naval confrontation of World War I.

and destroyers, and two of the oilers, would break off on June 3 (June 4 Japanese time) to support the diversionary strike on the Aleutians. Yamamoto would continue toward Midway with his great battlewagons, with DesRon 3, *Hosho* and her escort, and the two remaining oilers. With him also would ply the seaplane tenders *Chiyoda* and *Nisshin*, carrying midget submarines.[7]

While Yamamoto's script called for his big guns to support the Midway invasion, his real mission was to lurk in wait for such pitiful remnants of the U.S. Pacific Fleet as might race to the scene of action. So far, the enemy had refused to come into Japanese home waters for the statutory Great All-Out Battle, so the Japanese Mohammed would go to the American mountain. According to estimates of the Naval General Staff and of the Combined Fleet, it was now safe to move the stage for this classic drama, as stylized and predictable as a *No* play, into the Central Pacific. Japanese naval air power had already chopped the U.S. Pacific Fleet into bite-sized morsels, and Yamamoto's battlewagons would grind them into hamburger.

Surely Clio, the goddess of History, has a sense of humor, if a slightly mordant one. Here were two fleets, each steaming out of its home port on the same day, headed in the other's direction, each ignorant of the other's movement. Neither Nimitz, Fletcher nor Spruance learned until some months after the battle that Yamamoto's Main Body was anywhere near the area, and neither Yamamoto nor any of his staff had the shadow of an idea that any respectable American surface force would show up until the Midway invasion was well along, if not actually completed.

For the United States, this lack of knowledge was not merely irrelevant, it was positively beneficial. Had Nimitz and his fleet commanders known that a Japanese force with a nucleus of seven battleships, including *Yamato*, had been added to the strength against them, it could not have affected their strategy. Midway had to be defended; there was no alternative. Nimitz had already committed to the American plan everything he possibly could. Exact intelligence of just what cards the Japanese had tossed on the table would only have been a heavy psychological burden.

On the other hand, for Yamamoto this ignorance of the enemy movement was disastrous, the difference between an overwhelming Japanese victory and a stunning defeat.

So Yamamoto sortied in all his strength and confidence. "At 2:00

P.M. passed Bungo Strait and bounced in the open sea suspectedly infested by enemy submarines," Miwa recorded. "Since yesterday morning, our antisubmarine force has caught one enemy sub there."[8] Japanese intelligence indicated six American submarines operating near the homeland; therefore, both the Main Body and Kondo's force were very much on the alert for trouble beneath the seas, and ships and planes from Kure scoured the area.

At 1500, about one hour in the open sea, the fleet assumed cruising position. The battleships formed a rough letter H, *Yamato, Nagato,* and *Mutsu* surging along to starboard, Takasu's four to port, with *Hosho* as the crossbar. From this strategic position she could send her aircraft over the battleships in constant antisubmarine patrol. *Sendai* and the twenty destroyers formed the protecting circumference of a circle whose radius was 1,500 meters from the battleship H. The other two cruisers brought up the rear, separated from each other by some 10,000 meters, eyes peeled for stalking submarines. This maneuver completed, the fleet headed southeast at eighteen knots, zigzagging every five or ten minutes.

That night was calm with a beautiful full moon, but its radiance was lost on Ugaki, who wrote in his diary irritably, ". . . the movement of the destroyer squadron in the screen position is very unsatisfactory and constant vigilance has to be maintained. Transferring to night fleet disposition was just like taking kids to bed."[9]

Back in Pearl Harbor, nobody had time to gaze at the moon. Commander Logan C. Ramsey, the husky, black-haired Operations Officer of the Ford Island Naval Air Station, reeled under the impact of a full day's briefing preparatory to flying to Midway. As the island's air strength built up, the need for a capable, experienced officer to take charge of the air operations became increasingly evident. Simard had his hands full with logistics and the overall command of the installation. When the CinCPAC staff decided that Midway needed such an officer, they sought a naval aviator who was a graduate of the Naval War College. This was because, about 1935, one of the War College exercises had been a theoretical Japanese attempt to capture Midway. An officer who had received this instruction would have a built-in, time-saving knowledge of the problem.

As Draemel had been Ramsey's instructor in tactics at the War College, the latter naturally came to mind. Then, too, Ramsey had virtually grown up in the naval air arm and had flown from the old

Langley, Saratoga, Yorktown, and the ill-fated *Lexington*. Having mastered seaplanes, Ramsey then learned to fly land craft, a much different technique. Therefore, he understood both types of planes stationed on Midway. Furthermore, he was the logical choice because, as coordinator of Oahu's air patrol, which included Army planes, he was accustomed to interservice activities and, with his congenial personality, he could work pleasantly and efficiently with Army personnel. This was important, because Nimitz made almost a fetish of Army-Navy cooperation.

Accordingly, Headquarters summoned Ramsey, and there he received a comprehensive briefing on the situation from Draemel and appropriate staff officers, and from Nimitz himself. As Ramsey sat in the Commander in Chief's office absorbing the objectives of his mission, Nimitz gave him broad instructions covering virtually every contingency. Nor did Nimitz flinch from the grim possibility of defeat. If the Japanese took Midway, he would be in bad shape and would need all the air power he could concentrate on Hawaii to meet the new assault the Japanese surely would launch against Oahu when they were ready. So he ordered Ramsey, "If the island should be in danger of falling, be sure to bring out the heavy stuff, the PBYs and B-17s."

Having finished his instructions, Nimitz asked, "Have you any requests?"

"Yes, I do," Ramsey replied promptly. "If this turns out all right, will you bring me back from Midway?"

Nimitz readily promised that he would do so.[10] For if Ramsey conducted a successful patrol search and subsequent air defense of Midway, return to Oahu would be the least reward he would deserve.

Meanwhile, in the navy yard, Furlong's service force men labored on the double repairing *Yorktown* all that afternoon and in shifts through the night. Riveters rapped out a futuristic symphony and welders spilled fiery blossoms throughout the ship. As the workers toiled throughout the night without cease or slackening, *Yorktown* almost visibly sprang back to life under their fiercely determined efforts. Hundreds of workmen still hammered away at the carrier the next morning, May 29 Hawaiian time, when the waters began rising under her. Slowly she inched out of drydock, and cautiously eased into her normal berth, there to refuel and take on aircraft while still under repair.[11]

Much remained to be done, but with the halfway mark passed, it was evident that, if this work pace kept up—and it would, trust Furlong for that!—*Yorktown* would be ready to sortie the next day. Any repairs not actually necessary for operations and safety were ignored. Despite the Navy's devotion to spit and polish, this was no time to worry about appearances. For this reason, "frames and transverse floors between the shell and number one bulkhead were not replaced," although damaged by the near-miss, as "enough material remained to hold the shell in place. The shell was repaired by caulking and welding the leaky seam and rivets . . ."

In the slightly more than forty-eight hours that the carrier was available to the Navy Behind the Navy, "demolished and damaged structure was replaced by material having equivalent weight, strength and section modulus."[12] Let the official Navy report tell the story, for the unemotional, technical language carries its own impact:

49.   On the fourth deck the double door opening in bulkhead 118 was covered by a flat plate welded in place and a standard 26″ × 66″ watertight door installed. The demolished portions of bulkhead 106 were replaced. The heavy stanchions supporting transverse 109 were replaced and the web was replaced where twisted and riddled. The hole in the third deck had been previously covered by the ship's force with a 10 pound plate. Installation of this was completed by the Navy Yard and beams underneath replaced. The holes in the second deck were patched and damaged beams under the deck replaced.

50.   All watertight doors and hatches below the main deck were repaired and tested for water-tightness. Access trunk C-401-T was not replaced and miscellaneous partition and expanded metal bulkheads were not repaired. However, all essential water-tight boundaries on second deck and below were restored.[13]

In the normal course of events, the hidden Navy had to content itself with a generalized consciousness of work well done, but this time they had a ship of their own. For *Yorktown* was as much their ship as it was Fletcher's or Buckmaster's. Whatever came to her in the forthcoming battle, her glory would be their glory, her sorrow would be their sorrow.

Still, it would be a mistake to visualize *Yorktown* as leaving the navy yard's hands in anything like pristine condition. She could move—

at considerably reduced speed; she could launch and recover aircraft. That was about it, but that would prove enough.

On board her, many were upset. They had been through a long, dry pull. By every unwritten law of the service, they were due to return stateside for a long leave. Yet they were to remain on combat duty and, worst of all, the winning team would be broken up. VT-5's airmen would be replaced by *Saratoga*'s VT-3. After undergoing repairs, VB-5 would return, but become temporarily VS-5. Veteran VS-5 would go ashore, replaced by VS-3. Although VT-42 would become VT-3, it would retain many of its experienced pilots and their numbers. Better yet, her fighter planes would be increased to twenty-seven, and they would be the new F4F-4 Wildcats.[14]

VB-5 was the only flight unit not taken off the carrier on arrival at Pearl Harbor, a fact which embittered the fliers. They had suffered heavy casualties in the Coral Sea, and had to assimilate from eight to ten new pilots. Matters were not improved when the group took over the Ford Island Officers' Club for an impromptu party, and were threatened with courts-martial because they came in without neckties. This squall blew over harmlessly, but it did not help pull up the sagging squadron morale.[15]

The morning of the 29th was a sad one aboard *Hornet*, plowing along some 2,000 yards astern *Enterprise*. When she recovered her morning air patrol at 0845, one of her planes was missing. Another pilot reported seeing a splash followed by an oil slick spreading over the water, at 0810. Task Force Sixteen immediately detached the destroyer *Maury* from formation to try to find some trace of the missing pilot, Ensign R. D. Milliman, USNR, and his crewman, RM3c T. R. Pleto. *Maury* combed the area for almost four hours, but unfortunately without result, so the fleet had no choice but to abandon the search and continue on course.[16]

A somewhat similar incident, but one with a happy ending, had taken place on *Enterprise* the previous afternoon, when "plane 6-T-1 struck after end of flight deck and crashed in sea on port quarter." Alert action aboard the destroyer *Monaghan* saved the plane's crew. Lieutenant Commander E. E. Lindsey suffered "several cracked ribs, punctured lung, multiple cuts, and other lacerations." The rest of the crew escaped with "minor injuries."[17]

At 1533 on the 29th *Enterprise* had another flurry of excitement. A lookout reported a four-engine bomber at 356° true, distance 40,000 yards. The watch went on the alert and the carrier commenced zig-zagging. Although the ship challenged the mysterious aircraft, she received no reply. However, nothing alarming occurred and the plane disappeared. This may have been one of Midway's patrols, and indeed the task force had sighted an Army bomber that morning some ten miles away.[18]

Throughout the day, *Enterprise* was handicapped by lack of radar, which had conked out the previous night. "It was out of commission for about twenty-four hours," recalled Spruance. "This was a great disadvantage, and a tremendous relief to us all when it was fixed." By evening the equipment was back in shape, and everyone aboard breathed a little easier.[19]

Logan Ramsey flew out to Midway in a PBY so heavily laden with a torpedo that it was barely able to take off from Ford Island.[20] His was one of twelve PBYs which arrived that day and were promptly put into search service. "New tactical organizations placed in effect and plans for moonlight attacks, and day attacks against enemy surface vessels inaugurated, utilizing VP-44 for torpedo attacks and target location," noted McCaul in his daily report. Midway was also the richer on May 29 for one B-17 and four B-26s with fifteen more officers and twenty men.[21]

Major Warner briefed Kimes on the capabilities of the B-26s, advising him that these aircraft had a radius of 400 nautical miles. The bunkers prepared for the B-26s proved too deep, so four of VF-44s PBYs had to be moved out of their shelters to make way for the bombers. Warner jotted down that they were "unable to load torpedoes at night because of lack of experienced personnel and the B-26s bomb hoists were incomplete. Torpedo specialist is arriving tomorrow morning."

Warner also observed that the day's sector search had spotted two submarines.[22] Friend or foe? One Japanese submarine was in the area, as we shall see, but it is more likely that the Midway scout observed two of the friendly patrol group already deployed between Midway and the approaching danger. "All submarines which could reach the Oahu-Midway area were employed," according to Nimitz's battle report. Twenty-five were available to Rear Admiral Robert H. English, Commander Submarines Pacific Fleet, who from his headquarters at Pearl Harbor was responsible for spotting these craft where they would do the most good. As six of these accompanied the Aleutians Force, a total of nineteen American submarines were prowling the central Pacific. Four lay close together north of Oahu, just in case the Japanese tried another swipe at Pearl Harbor, while three others roamed a line halfway between Midway and Oahu. The remainder "were stationed on the 200 and 150 mile circles covering the western and northern approaches to Midway."[23]

Far to the west, an eighteen-meter-per-second wind tossed up huge waves which set the destroyers of Yamamoto's Main Body reeling and even pounded the cruisers. Around noon, a sullen overcast covered the sky. Later, rain spattered against the towering seas and the battered ships. But the armada struggled steadily eastward, still maintaining antisubmarine guard.[24]

During the day, Yamamoto's radiomen intercepted a long, urgent, coded message to Midway from an American submarine which Ugaki estimated was "either ahead or in the vicinity of our Transport Force." Although the Japanese could not read the American code, the message's length and its "Urgent" classification indicated that it was important. This might well mean that the submarine had discovered evidence of the Japanese naval thrust. But Ugaki was not in the least disturbed. "If the dispatched message were a report of discovering our forces," he told his diary complacently, "it would surely serve to alert the enemy, thus contributing to making our game in battle heavier."[25] In other words, the more American birds were flushed from cover, the bigger the Japanese bag.

The prospect for the northern operation looked fairly tame. "No enemy sighted at Kiska and Attu Islands, while a few enemy ships were seen to be at Adak and Dutch Harbor, according to a reconnaissance report by our submarines," noted Miwa. "A few enemy ships are also in French Frigate Shoals, so the 'K' operation was called off. . . ."[26] Actually, at this time "K" was postponed, and not called off altogether until the next day.

To clear the complicated battle picture of a certain amount of underbrush, let us dispose of "Operation K" here and now. This was the flying boat mission intended to furnish Yamamoto with current intelligence on the U.S. Pacific Fleet position. According to plan, two Type 2 flying boats, the huge craft the Americans called "Emily," were to reach French Frigate Shoals shortly before sunset on the 30th, refuel from the submarines of the Advance Force, and take off for Hawaii immediately, to arrive approximately 0115 May 31, local time. After scouting the American fleet, the planes would fly nonstop to Wotje, arriving shortly after 0900 Tokyo time June 1, with exact data on enemy dispositions to be flashed to Yamamoto.

This scheme, which looked excellent on paper, had a fatal flaw characteristic of all the Japanese planning for Operation MI: Its success demanded that the Americans do exactly what the Japanese intended them to do. So "K" received a severe jolt when *I-123*, one of the fueling submarines, reaching French Frigate Shoals on May 30, found two U.S. ships already there. Probably these were the seaplane tenders *Thornton* and *Ballard*.

I-123 immediately radioed Kwajalein of the presence of enemy ships, advising rather redundantly that under the circumstances prospects for refueling the Emilys were slim. Vice Admiral Eiji Goto, commander of the 24th Air Flotilla, who was responsible for carrying out Operation K, ordered it postponed for twenty-four hours, and instructed *I-123* to keep watch, on the chance the U. S. vessels might pull out in time to reschedule the flight.

But the next day *I-123* had more bad news to report. She had sighted two American flying boats near the entrance, which indicated the enemy was already using the Shoals as a seaplane base, so obviously the Japanese planes could not refuel there. Deeply disappointed, the Japanese abandoned Operation K. Yamamoto's headquarters, however, was still optimistic that the submarine cordon due to be on station between Hawaii and Midway by June 2 would radio concerning any eastward movement of the U.S. Pacific Fleet well before N-Day.[27]

Even if these submarines had been in position at the scheduled time—which they were not, as we shall see—they would still have been too late, for by June 2 Fletcher and Spruance were well over the site of the proposed cordon. Nimitz was a full jump ahead of Yamamoto all through the game.

CHAPTER 14

"Not the Least Doubt About
a Victory"

Everywhere under the Stars and Stripes, Americans paused to honor their war dead on Memorial Day. For the first time in a generation, the traditional small flags fluttered in the soft air of this late spring morning over the sharp oblongs of new graves of young men fallen in battle. ". . . But our honors and our prayers for peaceful repose will be idle if we do not, each according to his individual duty and ability, carry on unflinchingly and unceasingly the task in whose doing they died," observed the Honolulu *Star-Bulletin*.

"Hawaii is, more than ever before in all its history as an American territory since 1898, the nation's outpost of defense in the Pacific . . .

"Never before in all Hawaii's civilized history has there been so formidable a threat from without . . . or so shining an opportunity for magnificent service within."[1]

Elsewhere in its pages, the newspaper offered a few items interesting in the context of the time. It quoted Clarence Buddington Kelland, popular author and Republican national committee publicity director, as saying, "The American people are resentful and humiliated at being kicked around in this war." And Major Alexander P. deSeversky, the aviation expert, warned, "Neither side in this conflict can build warships as fast as aviation can destroy them from the skies."[2]

A fervent hope that the Japanese could not send warships into the Midway area faster than American naval aviation could knock them off animated Nimitz as he came aboard *Yorktown* that morning to wish her and her officers and men Godspeed. Miraculously, the carrier was triumphantly ready for action, all flags flying and, one suspects, all fingers crossed. Like the "old gray mare," she wasn't what

124

she used to be, but she was seaworthy and ready to carry Lieutenant Commander Oscar Pederson's Air Group into battle.

Sensitive as a barometer to the rise and fall of Navy spirits, Nimitz had a special word for the disgruntled airmen. He recognized their problem and dealt with it in typical fashion. He knew that he could depend upon these men to the last inch of endurance once they understood why they were being whisked without respite from one long stretch at sea to another. Nimitz's exact words have not been preserved, but he instructed the captain to inform the crew how sorry he was for having to deny them their well-deserved leave, and to assure them that he would not ask further action of them at this time unless it was absolutely necessary. He had work for them to do—a task and a timing not of his choosing. He promised that when the Midway fight was over, he would send *Yorktown* to the West Coast for liberty.[3]

Task Force Seventeen completed its preliminaries and sortied early, commencing to steam out of Pearl Harbor at 0900 local time, ostensibly "to conduct target practice and then support Task Force Sixteen." *Yorktown*'s escort was rather slender—Poco Smith's two cruisers, *Astoria* and *Portland*, and Captain Gilbert C. Hoover's TG 17.4 Destroyer Screen, comprising *Hammann, Hughes, Morris, Anderson,* and *Russell*.[4]

As *Astoria* slipped down channel, Smith received a message that a replacement for Captain Francis W. Scanland, *Astoria*'s captain and Smith's executive officer, had reported to headquarters. The task force was well under way, so Smith hinted with a grin that if Nimitz wanted Scanland relieved, he would first have to catch him. Therefore the captain fought through Midway with his Annapolis classmate.

Smith spared a moment's sympathy for the heavy cruisers *Indianapolis* and *Louisville*, headed out to sea to join Fuzzy Theobold's Aleutians force. That miserable area was not Smith's idea of a desirable post. The genial Poco was just as ready to fight and die for his country as the sternest of Japanese samurai, but he would prefer to do so in a decent climate.[5]

As Fletcher stood on *Yorktown*'s bridge that Saturday morning, his knowledge of Japanese intentions was by no means perfect. He did not know exactly when, in what strength, and from what angle the Japanese would strike.[6] Nor did any American, whether in Washington, Pearl Harbor, or at sea, know where Yamamoto's Main Body was or where the sea hawk might pounce.[7] Would he stay in the background or be in the battle? American intelligence did not know, and could not be expected to know.

For the Japanese, although they underestimated American capabilities and did not dream that their JN25 code was an open book, were quite discreet in their messages. As Nimitz remarked, "The Japanese should not be played down as Intelligence patsies."[8] So scanty was the information contained in their pre-Midway messages that many Japanese veterans of the battle always believed that the United States could not possibly have learned from that source alone as much as they did about Japanese plans. Kuroshima, for one, believed to the day of his death that "something more went wrong with Japanese plans than just breaking the Japanese code." He was sure that "the United States had previous access to the Japanese plan." The Richard Sorge scandal* convinced him, as well as many others, that Japan was riddled with spies "and that they leaked the news of the Midway plan to the United States." At this time, too, the United States and China were in close communication; could Chinese informers have been working out of Japan for the United States?[9]

Nor were all Americans entirely free of the cloak-and-dagger syndrome. When he saw CinCPAC Operation Plan No. 29-42, setting forth the current U.S. decisions and their bases, Commander Richard W. Ruble, *Enterprise*'s navigator, was so impressed that he reflected, "That man of ours in Tokyo is worth every cent we pay him."[10] Actually, no espionage was involved. Rochefort's Black Chamber broke the Japanese code by hard, patient work; after that, it was a matter of fitting bits and pieces into a meaningful pattern.

After the battle, Miwa noted that the Combined Fleet staff "suspects that our Midway operational plan must have been leaked out to the enemy a great deal." The practical Miwa did not share this opinion—but neither did he think in terms of a code break. In his view, the Americans "could have suspected our intention if they racked their brains a little bit."[11]

Even if the U.S. Pacific Fleet had had absolutely perfect intelligence on the Japanese fleet—that is, if they had known exactly what ships were mustered and under whose command; where those ships

---

*Richard Sorge, posing as a German newspaperman, headed a Soviet spy ring in Tokyo. Its ramifications reached high into Japanese government circles.

would deploy and how their commanders would fight them; the exact day, hour, and minute of every anticipated move—all these things would not have sufficed to secure victory for the Americans at Midway. Intelligence cannot manufacture ships out of blueprints, suitable aircraft from an obsolescent menagerie, experienced airmen from green flying school graduates, nor produce torpedoes that will explode on contact.

If matériel were the only factor involved in a military operation, the Japanese would have won a quick, overwhelming victory at Midway. In checking this modern catalogue of ships and in view of their unbroken series of victories since Pearl Harbor, the officers and men of the Japanese vessels surging eastward had a full excuse for being cocky, as was Miwa, scribbling enthusiastically in his diary:

> The fleet passed north of Chichijima and continued eastward course majestically. This is the greatest expedition the Imperial Japanese Navy ever had. Everybody in the fleet from its head down to the men entertains not the least doubt about a victory. Whence comes such a spirit that overwhelms an enemy before the battle is fought? This is indeed a majestic movement that never fails to impress us to the greatest extent.
>
> Easy is an active operation in which the motive power may be secured. It strikes home deeply that a passive operation should not be made.

Then Miwa broke off his eloquent outburst to return to mundane facts: "Operational radio in the U.S. Pacific area centering at Honolulu is showing extraordinary activities. A number of urgent messages were among them. Whether the enemy has suspected our intention or not, we can't tell at this moment. But we continued the course while strengthening alertness."[12]

Ugaki, too, took note of these things. In the early morning, the fleet changed course to 90°, still proceeding through what Ugaki termed "sub-infested waters." A wind of gale force, driving before it intermittent slashes of rain, grounded the antisubmarine planes at Chichijima base and pinned those with the Main Body to *Hosho*'s flight deck. By 1800, the fleet changed course to 70° and relaxed vigilance, altering the second-degree alert maintained since the sortie to third degree. As *Yamato* drove through the gathering dusk, Ugaki considered the implications of the American radio activity. "Exchanges of urgent messages are very unusual," he informed his diary.

"There are no small signs to make me suspect that they are making counter measures against our suspected movement rather than engaging in operations on their own initiative."

Could sonar have picked up the Japanese sortie? Did the Americans suspect a move to the north through radio intelligence or a report by a Russian vessel? "The worst case would be if our transport force leaving Saipan on the 28th might be discovered by them," Ugaki decided. "Judging from its course and strength, they could suspect that the force was heading toward Midway district.

"Since the said force is not provided with a carrier-borne air cover except for the Eleventh Seaplane Tender Division, it is not without a probability of the force being discovered by enemy subs," he admitted. "Its premature discovery might lead to a showdown with the enemy force, which is rather welcome, but a concentration of enemy subs on the scene is not welcome at all. Be that as it may, however, there is no need to make a change into our plan for the time being."[13]

Yet if the Japanese, too, had had perfect intelligence—never attained in this world—it is highly unlikely that either their plans or their attitude would have altered in any major respect. On paper, the American carrier force racing westward looked like a sea-going David going forth to tangle with a salt-water Goliath. Let us compare the fighting ships under Yamamoto's command with those available to Fletcher, and to be as absolutely objective as possible, let us include a miscellany of United States craft between the Hawaiian Islands and Midway, although these were not actually a part of the task forces. Let us also omit from either side any consideration of the Alaskan operation, which had little or no effect on the main show:

	Japanese	United States
Heavy aircraft carriers	4	3
Light aircraft carriers	2	0
Battleships	11	0
Heavy cruisers	10	6
Light cruisers	6	1
Destroyers	53	17
Total surface fighting ships	86	27

In addition, the Japanese had along forty-three assorted craft including troop transports, oilers, minesweepers, and other support types, while the Americans could summon up twenty-three "cats and dogs" such as PT boats, patrol craft, oilers, and even a converted yacht.[14]

Any admiral thinking in terms of a conventional naval battle would have laughed himself into a permanent state of hiccups at the idea of an engagement on such comparative strengths. Of course, statistics are not decisive. A ship of war is a machine, an asset, liability, or nonentity depending upon who is handling it. Take *Yamato*, for instance. Yamamoto's flagship was structurally the biggest, most heavily armed battlewagon sailing the seas. Yet, in turning her into a floating headquarters, the admiral had trimmed *Yamato*'s claws. For all the good the mightiest battleship in the world did her proud possessors, she might just as well have stayed behind at Hashirajima, and saved Japan the precious fuel she drank to and from the battle.

The day of the sea-going commander in chief was as passé as the battleship itself, a fact which Yamamoto did not realize. The problems of communications alone forbade such gallant but futile gestures as he was making. How to get in touch with his ships without betraying his whereabouts plagued Yamamoto all through the cruise and during the sea fight that followed.

That battle was to be one of aircraft against aircraft, and aircraft against ships. So then, let us look at the Japanese versus American picture of planes available that day:[15]

	Japanese (all carrier-based)	U.S. carrier-based	On Midway	U.S. Total
Torpedo bombers	105	42	6	48
Dive bombers	92	112	27	139
Fighters	96	79	27	106
Fighter seaplanes	24	0	0	0
Scout seaplanes	8	0	32	32
Land bombers	0	0	(B-17) 19	
			(B-26) 4	23
	—	—		
Total aircraft	325	233	115	348

Therefore, in actual numbers of aircraft available, the Americans had the slight edge of twenty-three. Oddly enough, these represented exactly the number of Army bombers stationed on Midway. In view of the results, these Army aircraft might well be ranked as negligible factors, or even as liabilities, because they consumed enormous amounts of space, fuel, and man-hours which could have been used more profitably elsewhere.

Of course, comparing one type of aircraft with another is troublesome and misleading. For example, Japan had overwhelming superiority in torpedo bombers, those slow-moving but deadly craft which had wrought such havoc at Pearl Harbor. And when, as anticipated, the Japanese launched their attack on the American ships, at the head of the torpedomen would fly Lieutenant Commander Murata, the swashbuckling, flippant torpedo ace of the Imperial Navy, who was worth his slim weight in diamonds as a fighting man, leader, and morale-booster. If Yamamoto achieved the expected surprise, and turned loose Murata's torpedomen against an unready enemy, they in themselves could well bring back the victory.

In contrast, in this area the Americans were not only outnumbered but outclassed in men and matériel. The TBD was obsolete, with its slow climb, 100-mile speed, and notoriously poor torpedoes.[16] Improved torpedo planes had reached the area just too late. "The torpedo pilots are damn sore because they get their big chance tomorrow and missed TBFs by a week after waiting three years," recorded the unofficial diary of VF-6.[17]

The Japanese depended heavily upon surprise to pin the Midway-based aircraft to their small atoll, either destroying them outright or keeping them so occupied that they would have no chance to get into the sea battle. Fletcher had twenty more dive bombers than Yamamoto, but the latter had seventeen more fighters, and those were the fabulous Zeros, much superior to anything the United States could boast at the time. And the fighter pilots were superb, such as the leader of *Akagi*'s Zeros, Lieutenant Commander Shigeru Itaya, the intelligent, somewhat aloof spearhead of the Pearl Harbor fighter force.

Surely Yamamoto could depend upon the sleek little Zeros to cancel out the numerical superiority in dive bombers! And surely his own dive-bombing pilots were man for man equal if not superior to the Americans! For Yamamoto had no idea of running into a carrier fight on anything like equal terms. According to the schedule, the American fleet would not show up until after Midway was virtually knocked out. After that, Yamamoto's four battle-seasoned, victory-crowned flattops would block off the enemy carriers with little difficulty. Then, and only then, would his big battleship guns roar forth their thunder and lightning against such remnants of the U.S. Pacific Fleet as dared challenge them.

Toward Midway—two tiny specks almost invisible on a map of the Pacific—raced the sea power of the United States of America and the Empire of Japan—bent upon issues infinitely greater than their material objective. Would the Pacific become for years a Japanese lake? Would Australia and New Zealand be left unguarded, perhaps to suffer the fate of China until the rest of the British Commonwealth was finally free to come to their rescue, and in the meantime to undergo unspeakable agony and despoliation? Would the Philippines' long, patient apprenticeship toward their eagerly awaited independence come to naught? Would they pass from the sometimes bumbling but well-intentioned American hands, only to fall into those of the Japanese and lose forever their hope of freedom? Would war in full fury come to the American west coast? These questions and more rested on the whitecaps around a little Pacific atoll called Midway.

With the ships rode the intangibles. With Yamamoto, along with his superiority in tonnage and firepower, sailed the habit of victory, self-confidence, a warrior tradition, a burning desire to bring "the eight corners of the world" under one roof. With Fletcher sped surprise, flexibility, naval intelligence, and a brisk decision that this nonsense had gone far enough. The U.S. Navy, no less than the American people, were sick and tired "at being kicked around in this war."

Some of this spirit showed itself in the unofficial VF-6 log. "Air and sub contacts show Japs coming as planned," recorded the diarist on May 31. "Hope to really receive them. All the boys anxious to be heroes—and *will* get the chance."

CHAPTER 15

"The Clock Was Running
Ever Faster"

As the two fleets sped toward one another, *Hornet* and *Enterprise*, en route to rendezvous with Task Force Seventeen at "Point Luck," settled back into routine following the previous day's tragedy. On May 30, both carriers conducted gunnery practice and the usual inspections. At 1130 Captain Mitscher held mast* on *Hornet*, and clapped two seamen in the brig for five days each on bread and water, one for "accepting cash for special privilege in laundry," the other for "unauthorized possession of clothing."[1] Life insisted upon mixing the humdrum with its grandeur.

Midway put its air search into effect on this day. Ramsey's plan of procedure was based upon two assumptions, that "ordinarily an area of reduced visibility could be expected about 300 to 400 miles to the northwest," and that as a result "the discovery of enemy carriers approaching Midway from this direction the day prior to any attack could hardly be expected." Therefore, Midway might anticipate an early morning strike any day now. "However, just as the low visibility area to the northwest covered the night run of the enemy, it also prevented a sufficient degree of accuracy in their surface navigation to permit a night launching." From this conclusion Ramsey further deduced that "the enemy would pass out of the bad weather area in the wee small hours but would not launch until he had obtained a navigation fix at morning twilight." In terms of actual times, the air defenders decided that the Japanese would launch their aircraft from 0430 to 0500 local time from about 150 to 200 miles from Midway, which would time their blow on the island at about 0600.

---

*Nonjudicial punishment.

Using these premises as a launching deck, Ramsey's plan called for search to begin as early as possible, the normal time being 0415. The B-17s would take the air fifteen minutes later, with all other aircraft remaining on the ground until the reconnaissance craft had passed the 400-mile mark on their outward legs. This plan of action "definitely increased the logistic problem on Eastern Island as it was not possible to have the B-17s land again until they had been in the air for at least four hours in order to reduce their loading to a point where safe landing was practicable." But the heavy toll in aviation fuel had to be accepted. The only alternative was to keep the Flying Fortresses on the ground, and this hazard Ramsey would not permit.

At this stage, however, Ramsey's greatest concern was the possibility of Japanese land-based planes from Wake Island hitting Midway at night, and in particular of their delivering a night gas attack on Eastern Island.[2] Therefore, Wake was very much in Ramsey's mind when at approximately 0945 one of the PBYs, No. 8V55, flashed a report of "being attacked by enemy aircraft." At 1008 a second PBY, No. 2V55, advised that it, too, had been attacked. Five minutes later, 8V55 sent in his position as 26-55N, 173-20E. By 1035 he advised that he was returning to base. Then, at 1112 came the word that the aircraft attacking this PBY was a Mitsubishi twin-engine bomber, and six minutes later another flash advised of a four-engine bomber strike.[3]

This play-by-play account confused the actual occurrence. Two Catalinas had run into two Japanese land-based bombers, one a twin-engine, one a four-engine aircraft, on routine patrol from Wake, "at the two points where the 500 mile circle from Midway intersected the 600 mile circle from Wake." The Japanese planes badly mauled the slow, vulnerable PBYs, wounding one Navy enlisted man. As a long-range result, the Navy finally agreed with the pilots that the Catalinas were not suitable for combat patrol. Ramsey expressed himself forcibly on this point. "In these two contacts the weakness of the PBY as a search plane was apparent," he reported bitterly. "*Any* type of Japanese plane could, and did, assume the offensive against the PBY." (Ramsey's italics.)[4]

The incident had certain advantages for the Americans. Taking into consideration the point of contact and the estimated speed of the Japanese bombers, Ramsey could make a fairly good guess as to when Wake launched its patrols. He filed away for future reference this conclusion: ". . . if Wake was to be attacked, that the proper time for such an attempt was just at sunset, as only then could these planes be caught on the ground."

For the moment, however, the question was whether or not to use the B-17s on the search arc. Ramsey decided against this, because, first, it would weaken his strike force, and second, he was not eager to let the Japanese know that any four-engine land bombers were stationed on Midway.[5]

Seven more of the big, graceful craft flew in from Oahu that day, bearing Major General Willis P. Hale of the Seventh Army Air Force,* with about twenty-two officers and fifty men. McCaul housed all the officers and enlisted personnel in tents. His MAG-22 combat radio frequency had to be changed, because it had been used during a false air raid alarm, and the aviation radar put on 24-hour duty. The day's activities gulped down around 20,000 gallons of gas, and, as McCaul noted, "transportation facilities strained to the utmost."

McCaul was rapidly reaching a stage of desperation. From the viewpoint of Midway's search and attack mission, he was delighted to welcome an additional nine B-17s, which swooped down on him on Sunday, May 31, but the fact remained that "night taxiing and take-offs" were already "extremely hazardous due to crowded condition of runways." Lieutenant Colonel Walter C. Sweeney, Jr., the B-17 commander, and his thirty officers and sixty men, who flew in with the B-17s, would have to be quartered in tents and more or less take pot luck. "Officers' Mess now feeding approximately 175 officers and working day and night," McCaul wrote in his official diary.[6]

The newly arrived airmen barely had time to modify their Flying Fortresses with a bomb bay tank and take on half a bomb load, performing their own maintenance, when Ramsey sent them aloft. Nimitz had ordered that on May 31 and June 1, if at all possible, B-17s scout the anticipated Japanese rendezvous 700 miles to the west, taking off in time to reach the designated point at about 1500 local time each day. This fine Sunday's search arc offered excellent viewing, except in the area north of 280° beyond 300 miles, where "practically zero-zero weather prevented all search." No contacts developed, but the B-17 force sent to the enemy rendezvous point enlivened the day by losing themselves. Ramsey had to home them in "by a combination of radar and radio direction finder bearings." The last straggler touched

*Hale returned to Oahu on June 2.

down approximately 0350 on June 1, more than four and a half hours late.[7]

This situation did nothing to improve the fuel picture, for the day's activities consumed a staggering 65,000 gallons, ". . . and gasoline situation here and at Sand Island extremely acute," as McCaul recorded in his usual telegraphic style.[8]

McCaul did not confide in his diary the whole distressing truth. As we have seen, the defenders had set up demolition charges at various key points in case they had to blow up some of their facilities to keep them out of Japanese hands if the enemy succeeded in landing. Of course, one of the items marked for destruction was the fuel supply. By an evil chance, on May 22 a work party testing the wiring of these demolition charges touched off the gasoline dump. "They were foolproof," observed a Marine officer acidly, "but not sailor-proof." Thousands of barrels of the precious fuel went up in flames, seriously hamstringing Midway's air mission. Gasoline no longer could be spared for practice flights, however much needed. Worse, all refueling had to be done by hand directly from drums—"a slow and arduous undertaking," as McCaul described it.[9]

When Nimitz heard of the disaster, he became exceedingly worried because, as he said, "the clock was running ever faster and Midway needed that gas." He rounded up a charter freighter, *Nira Luckenbach*, and dispatched her post-haste to Midway with a final cargo of drums of aviation gas.[10] But McCaul's troubles were not over when the vessel pulled up to the dock. The freighter had no sooner dropped anchor than a dispute arose about overtime. Midway's Marines unloaded the drums at night while ship's officers and bosuns operated the winches.[11]

As Spruance's ships plunged and zigzagged their way to rendezvous with Fletcher, they, too, were occupied with the fuel question. For the last time before the battle, *Enterprise* and *Hornet* filled up from the oilers *Cimarron* and *Platte*. *Hornet* received more than fuel this day. Honor, too, came to her when at 1425, to quote the log's unemotional phrasing, "Captain Marc A. Mitscher, U.S. Navy, executed oath of office and accepted appointment as Rear Admiral, U.S. Navy."[12] It was a well-merited advance for the fine officer whose carrier had taken the Doolittle bombers within range of Tokyo.

All of Nagumo's vessels, also, refueled that day (June 1 Tokyo time), without incident.[13] But sick bay finally claimed Genda. The air

officer had not been his usual brisk self since the Nagumo Force
sortied from Hashirajima. A nagging cold, with disquieting indications
of more serious trouble, sapped his energy. At last the doctor, di-
agnosing incipient pneumonia, clapped Genda into bed.

"I think it was caused by tiredness," Genda decided, no doubt
accurately.[14] From the early spring of 1941 he had labored ardently,
almost obsessively, over Yamamoto's scheme to attack the U.S. Pacific
Fleet at Oahu. For if Yamamoto was the father of the Pearl Harbor
plan, Genda might be considered its spiritual and intellectual mother,
coaxing it to life, nourishing it from the wellsprings of his own heart
and mind, defending it against all comers.[15] The morning of December
7 had brought him not only the fierce joy of one who has seen his
hopes and beliefs vindicated against all odds, it had brought him a
whole new load of responsibilities, for thenceforth Nagumo looked
upon him as the man with the answers. Through those incredible,
victory-packed months at sea, Genda stood at Nagumo's left hand,
second in his counsels only to Kusaka. Indeed, Genda in 1941 and
early 1942 could have provided a psychologist or sociologist with a
perfect example of *homo sapiens* under the gun, a classic study in
tension. Now, at last, outraged nature presented her bill of damages.

For the next few days, therefore, Genda was out of touch with
the bridge, because Nagumo and Kusaka were too busy to chat with
him. Of course, friends among the staff and some of the pilots visited
him and kept him posted on important developments.[16] But for three
highly critical days immediately before the battle, Nagumo was without the direct support of the officer best qualified to advise him on
naval aviation matters.

On May 31 (June 1, Tokyo time), Yamamoto's Main Body, scheduled to refuel the following day, sent out a patrol from *Hosho* to find
their tankers which, according to a message from the oiler *Naruto*,
were almost thirty miles behind schedule. But *Hosho*'s planes returned without locating the missing tanker train. So Yamamoto dispatched the Ninth Cruiser Division and two destroyers to hunt for
it also, and to refuel themselves after they found it.

Yamamoto appeared on the bridge with his stocky, high-chested
body glistening in white, for the Imperial Navy went into summer
uniform on June 1, but Ugaki excused the rest of the fleet until further
notice. The weather was still quite cool, and Ugaki decided that "to

put on summer whites prematurely, spending so much time on the bridge, would not be healthful."[17]

At about 1000, a scout plane reported an enemy submarine 8,000 meters port abeam, and the destroyers *Shigure* and *Ayanami* "immediately rushed to the spot to kill the sub. The fleet turned to the right and increased speed to avoid it." Miwa expressed doubts about this alleged contact. *Hosho* signaled a hit, based upon sighting an oil drift twenty by fifty meters, but this might not have been the result of a strike. The slick could have been mistaken for a surface disturbance indicating a submarine. Miwa noted, too, that surfacing whales were sometimes mistaken for submarines.[18]

Nevertheless, there were other submarine sightings that day. A flying boat from Wake spotted them at points 400 to 500 miles north by northeast and northeast of the island. And a plane from Wotje saw a submarine 500 miles north by northeast of that island. So Ugaki was quite sure now that the Americans had some suspicions of Japanese intentions. Of over 180 radio exchanges observed in the Hawaiian district, as many as seventy-two were tagged "urgent."

"It is considered that the enemy are preparing to meet us, after surely having suspected our movement," he wrote. "Especially, it has become almost certain that they have deployed subs in the vicinity of 600 miles bearing southwest of Midway Island and intensified their guard together with planes."[19] In fact, English's cordon was almost directly due west of the atoll.[20]

Another disquieting situation ruffled *Yamato*'s wardroom that evening. "Although radio from Sydney reported that a Japanese attack was made in that harbor, no official report came in from those forces concerned, thus leaving its details in the dark," noted Miwa. "This made me worry a great deal. A good deal of possibility that they failed to return."[21]

The Australian radio referred to a midget submarine operation, a rather silly and quite futile bit of Japanese sleight of hand. The midget submarine program appealed to Ugaki, who had a suicidal turn of mind, and those brave but ineffectual young men were his special pets, at least within the pages of his revealing diary. "As they made attacks, it is supposed that they must have inflicted a considerable damage to the enemy. Pray to God for a safe recovery of their crews."[22]

Alas for Ugaki's convictions of damage and pious prayers for safety! The only damage inflicted was by a torpedo which went under its target, the United States cruiser *Chicago*, and blew the bottom out of an old ferryboat being used as a barracks, killing a number of sailors. *Chicago* sighted and fired on the maurauder, but the midget was too close under the cruiser's guns, which overfired. As a result of this little affair, the Japanese Imperial Headquarters issued a spirited if mistaken communiqué describing the burning and sinking of the British battleship *Warspite* in Sydney harbor.[23]

The *Japan Times and Advertiser* brightened the breakfast tables of its readers that day with an editorial on American naval power:

> The United States is naturally building as frantically as possible, but battleships cannot be built overnight. As for the air arm, as the loss of five of her total of eight aircraft carriers indicates, the United States has suffered the heaviest of all. By the time she succeeds in rebuilding her fleet, Japan will have been able to build an equal number of ships. As for design, the Japanese ships have been proved superior to the American. Moreover, a rebuilt American fleet will not make its appearance all at once, but unit by unit as they are completed. What is there to prevent the superior Japanese Navy from picking off these American ships and disposing of them unit by unit as they appear? Furthermore, the mobility of the American fleet has been almost unbelievably curtailed as the result of the capture of the American bases by Japan . . .
>
> In view of these considerations, what intelligent person is there that can believe that the United States can launch a successful offensive against Japan? What is there in store for the Americans except unending futility?[24]

No thought of "unending futility" disturbed the Americans preparing to counter the Japanese threat. "Praying for contact on Jap surface forces," noted the diarist of VF-6. Then he added a sour note: "Weather very cloudy and calm—good luck, as usual, for the Japs."[25]

Midway, too, continued to work efficiently in its own behalf. The next day, June 1, at a point between 450 and 480 miles west and southwest from Midway, two Catalinas on patrol ran into two Japanese bombers on the same mission. At 0940, one of these PBYs radioed in that it was being attacked by enemy planes at 500 miles, bearing 228. Fifteen minutes later, he amplified this to indicate the striking planes were two bombers, and within six minutes clarified his position: He was 560 miles distant from Midway at 231°. The Midway receiving station heard nothing further until the aircraft reported in and was advised to wait for further instructions. However, five minutes later, the reconnaissance craft snapped back, "Am returning to base. Three men hit." At 1042 came another radio of enemy attack, and this time, without giving details of distance or position, the aircraft crackled off, "Am returning to base," within twelve minutes.[26] When the PBYs returned to Midway, they brought back further confirmation of the vulnerability of the heavy, big-bodied craft, one injured officer and two wounded enlisted men.[27]

When word of this encounter reached Nagumo's flagship, Fuchida did a little figuring as he stretched out on his bed in *Akagi*'s sick bay. The Japanese had estimated that the Americans would be sending out air patrols from Midway to a 500-mile limit. But, according to the description of this incident which the Nagumo force had just received, the contact took place about 500 miles north-northeast of Wotje. This meant that the defenders of Midway had expanded their search arc to 700 miles.

Fuchida did a bit more arithmetic, and scowled at the result. If the Americans were flying that far out of Midway, this meant that the transport invasion force, now proceeding northeast about 1,000 miles west of Midway at the rate of some 240 miles per day, would enter the patrol zone on June 3, two days before the Mobile Force carried out its softening-up strike on Midway. The war games had postulated that Tanaka would permit his ships to be spotted, to deceive the Americans into believing that the main Japanese attack would come in from the south. However, that was supposed to happen on June 6, N-1 Day.* So Tanaka might well be coming along much too rapidly for his own good.[28]

Fuchida was no more worried than Stimson, holding a war council meeting that morning in Washington, where Marshall reported on his trip to the west coast. "We are stripping all the planes we can in order to be sent out there to meet this Japanese threat," recorded the secretary of war. "It is a serious situation for they greatly outclass us in the strength of carrier vessels—aircraft carriers—and our battleships have to hug the shelter of the shore in order to get the protection of land based planes. Nevertheless, if the Navy uses good judgment and doesn't run the risk of getting out from under the air umbrella, we may entice them [the Japanese] into a position where

---

*See Chapter 4.

we may get a chance to do something—some hit and run blows which may even up the situation navally and make it a little more possible."[29]

Stimson's vision of the upcoming battle was interesting, to say the least. It would take place somewhere off the coast of southern California, with the American battleships clinging nervously to shore. If the Navy's mobile forces kept under the protection of the Army's land-based bombers, the former just might get in a few licks which would ease an impossible situation just a little.

Admiral Chuichi Nagumo, Commander in Chief, First Air Fleet.

(*Left*) Commander Mitsuo Fuchida, flight leader of *Akagi* attack on Pearl Harbor. He did not participate in the Battle of Midway because he had appendicitis. (*Below left*) Admiral Yamamoto, Commander in Chief, combined fleet (Japanese Navy). (*Below right*) Admiral Nobutake Kondo, Commander in Chief, Second Fleet.

Japanese submarine.

(*Above*) Chester W. Nimitz presenting Distinguished Flying Cross to Lt. Cmdr. Clarence Wade McClusky, May 27, l942. (*Right*) Admiral Chester W. Nimitz, Commander in Chief, U. S. Pacific Fleet.

Colonel Harold D. Shannon, Base Commander, Sixth Main Defense Battalion.

RADM Raymond A. Spruance, Commander, Task Force Sixteen.

RADM Frank Jack Fletcher, Commander, Task Force Seventeen.

Lt. Howard P. Ady, U. S. Navy reconnaissance pilot, the first to sight Japanese Task Force.

(*Above left*) VADM Tamon Yamaguchi, Commander in Chief, Second Carrier Division. (*Above right*) VADM Ryunosuke Kusaka, Chief of Staff, First Air Fleet. (*Below*) Midway Commanders at Awards Ceremony, June 17, 1942. RADM Frank Jack Fletcher, RADM Thomas C. Kinkaid, RADM William W. Smith, RADM Marc A. Mitscher and RADM Robert H. English.

(*Above*) Yamamoto and the Japanese Combined Fleet Staff. (*Left*) Commander Minoru Genda, Air Officer, First Air Fleet. He planned the attack on Pearl Harbor and helped plan the Battle of Midway, but did not participate because of pneumonia.

(*Above*) An early photo of the *Nautilus*, SS 168. (*Below*) USS *Hornet* CV-8.

CHAPTER 16

"In High Spirits and Full of Confidence"

It might have been the dawn of time, with the great reptiles bellowing to one another through the primeval mists. The melancholy blast of foghorns echoed hollowly. First *Yamato* would sound a long, deep signal, indicating that she was ship No. 1 and suggesting her position. Next *Mutsu*, ship No. 2, would answer in a low, eerie moan. Then *Nagato* would echo in gloomy reply. The shadowy outlines in the distance and the haunting warnings of the foghorns fascinated Watanabe. "It was very impressive," he said, "to see the ships of the Main Body at sea and to hear them answer one another in the fog."[1]

A typical day for Yamamoto on his historic voyage to Midway began no later than 0500.[2] Immediately upon rising, he checked the weather, about which he was very anxious. The nearer the Main Body approached its destination, the thicker grew the fog, and cruising in such weather was not only troublesome but dangerous. As soon as Yamamoto absorbed the daily weather report and donned his spotless white uniform, he took the elevator to the Operations Room, a sizable chamber on the same level as the bridge. In the center of the room stood a large table with a soft bench around it. Charts and diagrams, of which the strategical chart was the most important, littered the table.

After a brief but pleasant "Good morning," the admiral dived into the day's accumulation of messages, which usually numbered about 100. These came from all units of the fleet, comprising such items as the daily operations reports and reconnaissance information. Yamamoto was no skimmer; he read every one carefully, his eyes missing nothing of importance, although he wasted no words in profitless discussion of the contents.

This chore completed, he moved to the bridge at about 0600. There he seated himself on his hard wooden bench, ready for the main business of the day. Ugaki and *Yamato*'s skipper, Captain Gihachi Takayanagi, also had their private benches on the bridge, and spent most of their waking hours there.

Promptly at 0800 Yamamoto returned to the Operations Room, where the table had been set for breakfast. Meals aboard *Yamato* were rather leisurely and combined dining with staff discussions. When the officers had finished eating, the meal was cleared away and they sat around the table chatting about the general situation. Yamamoto made a point of speaking with each member of his staff, who appreciated the fact that the admiral did not latch on to one man and ignore the rest.

In these talkfests Yamamoto was "in high spirits and full of confidence," but when he spoke of the American enemy, he did so with the utmost seriousness. He listened daily to the news broadcasts from Tokyo, and when the newscasters ridiculed the enemy and exalted the Japanese Navy, Yamamoto treated his staff to blistering commentary. The admiral had not an ounce of bombast in his make-up, and these effusions filled him with the irritated embarrassment of a forthright man in the presence of grandiloquence.

Another news subject which awoke Yamamoto's sarcasm was Tojo. The blunt, straightforward admiral considered the premier a pompous windbag who, as a general and his own war minister, produced an inordinate amount of hot air with few concrete results.

Ugaki held down the bridge while the others ate. So that the chief of staff would not miss out on the post-meal chats, which were really semi-official staff meetings, Kuroshima relieved him on the bridge as soon as he had finished his own repast. Thus the senior staff officer did not join these discussions, but this was no sacrifice for him. He was by nature a loner, and many of his fellow officers considered him a weird specimen.

After breakfast and lunch, which came on the stroke of noon, Yamamoto returned to the bridge and remained there all afternoon, concentrating on the movement of his ships, especially their antisubmarine operations, for the admiral was very sensitive about American submarine activities at this time.

The hour of 1800 found him back in the Operations Room for dinner and a repetition of the breakfast and lunch routine of food and discussion, although the evening session lasted somewhat longer. After the dinner-time chat, Yamamoto retired to his cabin for thirty minutes to shower and shave. Whether afloat or ashore, in peace or in war, the admiral performed this ritual in the evening rather than in the morning. The evening clean-up rested and refreshed him and left him free to begin work immediately upon arising in the morning.

Around 2000 he again took the elevator to the bridge, this time to play chess, usually with Watanabe, for whom he felt an avuncular affection. Yamamoto strove for impartiality toward his staff officers, but he would have been less than human had he not been especially drawn to this big, good-humored young man who so obviously considered his admiral to be the greatest man in the world.

Playing chess with his chief was virtually one of Watanabe's official duties, for not only was the ancient game the admiral's hobby, he believed it kept him mentally alert in the performance of his mission. Everyone in the fleet knew where Yamamoto would be found from 2000 until bedtime, but he gave his staff authority to act immediately should an emergency arise during his game. Yamamoto was the type of man who did everything with all his might. When business was in order, he was all business; when he played chess, he played with total concentration. Like many men of active mind, he required much less sleep than the average, finding a change of mental activity more refreshing than the statutory eight hours in bed. He never retired before 2300; more frequently it was midnight or even 0200 before he called it a day.

Even then he could not depend upon uninterrupted slumber, for occasionally an urgent message came in, and Watanabe or the staff duty officer would have to rouse the admiral. At such times Yamamoto read the message, signed for it, courteously thanked whoever brought it, and immediately went back to sleep.

Nimitz was less serene about the whole thing. "I had some anxious and agonizing moments when the Japanese were on their way to Midway," he admitted. Both before and during the battle Nimitz got very little sleep, having so much on his mind that he could not readily dismiss his cares, all the more vivid because he was not on the spot to see for himself how matters were going.[3] Although he did not know the exact forces to be arrayed against him, he was painfully aware that Yamamoto did not play for peanuts and could bring to the fight a much stronger fleet numerically than Nimitz could call forth. He had staked his judgment against powerful voices in Washington when he accepted the Naval Intelligence estimate of the Midway situation, and in so doing he had laid his career on the line. Of far more concern to him was the destiny of the officers, men and ships entrusted to his care, for whom he bore the ultimate responsibility.

Early in the morning of June 2 Japanese time, Yamamoto's air search party sighted the missing oiler *Naruta* twenty miles bearing sixty degrees from the Main Body, so Ugaki ordered the destroyer squadron to refuel. "Because of poor visibility and poor signaling, it took much time to make the order understood," Ugaki recorded. He always spoke of the destroyers with affectionate exasperation, as a parent might refer to an engaging problem child. At 1130 *Toei Maru* and two other tankers were sighted. "Refueling was then made to the hungry kids, the destroyers," wrote Ugaki indulgently. "They are really little children who need much care and attention."[4]

While they refueled, the ships of the Main Body steamed parallel to the tanker train at a reduced speed of twelve knots on a seventy degree course. Drizzle limited visibility to barely a few kilometers. This was a mixed blessing—favorable in that it helped cover the fleet, unfavorable because it pinned the search aircraft to their decks. Toward late afternoon, the fog became so thick that fueling had to be called off, and Ugaki dispatched the light cruiser *Oi* to convey this information to the tanker train.[5]

Despite his fueling problems, Ugaki was preoccupied that day with the fate of his pet midget submariners. He was saddened to learn from an unidentified Australian station that, of the three midgets to enter Sydney Harbor, two were sunk by depth charges and the other one by bomb, having attacked only harbor vessels.

"Unlike in the Hawaii operation, well trained crews took part in the attack this time," he pointed out. "It is regrettable indeed, therefore, to see that even they failed to return safely. Is it due to the fact that the bright moonlight turned out to be in favor of the defending enemy? The moon is equally in favor of the enemy as it is to us . . . This problem requires serious studies and consideration, especially at a time when the use of midget submarines in the future is looked upon with importance."[6] Ugaki was loath to admit even to his diary, which could not talk back, that the entire midget submarine concept was a washout, quite aside from the neutrality of the moon.

Nagumo, too, was in both a literal and figurative fog. He managed to refuel all his ships that day, although visibility steadily decreased from about 1000.[7] The intelligence picture was no clearer than the weather. This was the day the Japanese submarines should have established their advance cordon and commenced sending on-the-spot, up-to-the-minute information concerning the Americans back to Nagumo as well as to Yamamoto. It so happened that the submarines of Squadron Five failed to reach their assigned positions to cover the B cordon line, while those of Squadron Three could not establish A cordon because of the Operation K fiasco.

I-168, however, sent back a few bits of information from the Midway area. This submarine reported observing no craft other than a picket sub south of Sand Island; an intensive air patrol was in force to the southwest about to a 600-mile limit; strict air alert was in force with numerous aircraft on patrol night and day; the presence of many construction cranes on the atoll suggested that the Americans were expanding the installation. This word from *I-168* was the only reconnaissance information of any importance which a Japanese submarine reported before and throughout the engagement, and mighty slim pickings it was.[8]

Akagi, then, although considerably in advance of Yamamoto's Main Body, was no less ignorant of American actions and intentions. Actually, Nagumo was more in the dark than Yamamoto, for the carrier's radio receiver was less powerful than Yamamoto's, a fact which, complicated by radio silence, cut Nagumo off from such messages as Ugaki and Miwa had noted—messages which strongly hinted that the U.S. Pacific Fleet had scented something in the wind.

Such a failure to pool information was exactly what Kusaka had feared from the beginning. Even before the sortie, he had repeatedly urged Yamamoto to relay to *Akagi* any important radio intelligence which Fleet Headquarters might pick up.[9] Inevitably, however, this left open the question of just what was and was not important. Information which meant little or nothing to the surface-minded, battleship-oriented Main Body might convey volumes to the airmen in Nagumo's carrier task force.

Quite aside from any question of interpretation, the very magnitude of the Japanese expedition invited a certain number of snafus.

For example, about this time the Naval General Staff radioed *Yamato* that in the eastern Midway area some U.S. carrier force "could possibly" be moving or perhaps be preparing for an ambush. This radio also bore the First Air Fleet as an addressee. When Yamamoto read this wire, he observed to Kuroshima, "I think we had better send this information to Nagumo in the name of Yamamoto or the Combined Fleet." But Kuroshima replied, "Since this information was also addressed to the First Air Fleet, it will not be necessary to transfer the same thing from the Combined Fleet to Nagumo. As we have radio silence now, we should keep it."[10]

The Americans, too, had their communications troubles. Spruance's radiomen reported that they heard the inshore patrol off Oahu talking with Pearl Harbor, a disquieting hint that TBS was not interception-proof. TBS was a line of sight system, supposedly incapable of passing the horizon. Whatever freak of atmosphere or mechanics which carried it to Task Force Sixteen might not occur again for weeks, or years. But Spruance could take no chances. He visually signaled the entire task force that TBS must not be used at night except in the gravest emergency. During the day visual signals would be used exclusively. Spruance was determined not to lose surprise, nor to give away his position to the Japanese. So, along with his radio clampdown, he informed all of his pilots that during the forthcoming battle they would have to get back to their carriers on their own; they could expect no radio help from the flattops.[11]

On this day, June 1 Hawaii time, *Saratoga*, according to the Japanese press long since sunk, left San Diego with all speed, on the chance that she might reach the Midway area in time to join the fight. This hope proved vain; "Sara" reached Pearl Harbor the day the battle of Midway ended. As for the forces on hand, Fletcher's Task Force Seventeen made its last prebattle refueling from *Cimarron* and *Platte*, while a search mission flew 150 miles out from *Hornet*, but made no contacts with the enemy.[12]

"Cold and wet as hell so the first we'll probably hear of the Japs will be on the Midway radar," observed the VF-6 diarist.[13] The rough seas and heavy clouds which hampered the cruise for both the Americans and the Japanese continued into the next day. Nagumo's ships could not see each other at 600 yards. To avoid collisions and to keep in formation, the admiral authorized the use of searchlights, a risky step, but the wall of fog was so thick that the powerful shafts of light broke against it and dissipated almost before leaving the source. Because the fog prevented launching antisubmarine patrol planes, but would not hamper the American radar-equipped undersea craft, Nagumo kept his force at full alert with double watches at submarine lookout stations.[14]

Nagumo and his staff remained on the starboard side of *Akagi*'s bridge, to keep out of the way of Captain Aoki and his navigation officer, Commander Miura, who from the port side devoted their entire attention to the intricate business of maintaining formation and course with almost zero visibility. The carrier task force was scheduled to change course at 1030, which posed a painful decision. Nagumo had to notify all his ships that the alteration would go through as planned, but signal flags were absolutely useless and the searchlights almost equally so. The only alternative was to use the radio, and this would broadcast the task force's location.[15]

Nagumo did not relish such choices. He was by no means lacking in personal courage, and he was cocky over his long string of victories, but he preferred to operate in a situation where all the i's were neatly dotted and all the t's meticulously crossed. He lacked the flexibility to make a swift decision based upon changing events. At this time, however, he was in a bind not of his own making, for his part in Operation MI was ambiguous. He had two missions, each requiring a basically different approach. He was in the position of a football player expected to run interference and carry the ball at the same time. First, the Carrier Task Force was to precede Kondo's fleet to Midway and work over the atoll to pave the way for the Japanese landing. This mission made it imperative that Nagumo be in a certain place at a certain time, namely, between the goal posts (Midway) and the ball carrier (Kondo). Neither Midway nor Kondo would move for Nagumo's convenience; it was up to him to maintain the planned sailing course. On the other hand, his second mission was independent: to help engage and destroy the U.S. Pacific fleet when and if it sailed out to meet the challenge—a task calling for the utmost operational flexibility and maintenance of secrecy. The two tasks could be reconciled only if Nimitz followed the Japanese plans to the letter, and did not order his ships out until he heard that Midway was under attack.

Nagumo's staff had worried about this dichotomy from the beginning, fearing that the two missions would collide somewhere along the line. Now, in the Biblical phrase, that which they greatly feared had come upon them. Captain Tomatsu Oishi, Nagumo's senior staff officer, summed up the dilemma in some perplexity: "The Combined Fleet operation order gives first priority to the destruction of the enemy forces. . . . But the same order specifically calls for our air attack on Midway on 5 June. . . .

"If we do not neutralize the Midway-based air forces as planned, our landing operations two days later will be strongly opposed and the entire invasion schedule will be upset."

To which Nagumo posed the sixty-four-dollar question: "But where is the enemy fleet?"

Oishi admitted that nobody knew, but added that if it was in Pearl Harbor, the task force would have plenty of time to get in position following its part in the Midway attack. Even if the enemy had already sortied, they could not be far out of anchorage and certainly nowhere near the Japanese carriers. Therefore Oishi cast his vote for giving first priority to the softening up of Midway, taking the necessary risks to keep the ships on scheduled course.[16]

Akagi's intelligence officer could give no clue to possible American ship movements. The carrier's radio had intercepted nothing, and he had received no information from *Yamato*. As the weather situation really left no feasible alternative, the intelligence officer recommended sending the course change by the short-range interfleet radio.[17]

The most powerful argument for this action, however, lay in the instructions which Ugaki had issued at the war games. In postulating just such a position in which Nagumo now found himself, Ugaki's orders were to maintain fleet formation as scheduled, even if necessary to break radio silence to do so.* Nagumo therefore agreed to send the message. As a result, he blamed himself in his post-battle report for this action, which he feared tipped off the Americans to his position. Actually, it is believed that this was one Japanese dispatch the United States interceptors did not pick up, although *Yamato*, 600 miles to the rear, did so. Ironically enough, soon after *Akagi* sent off the controversial message, the fog lifted just sufficiently to permit visual signals.[18]

The weather which generated such worry on the bridge freed the task force's air crews from any flying duties, so they gathered in the

---

*See Chapter 8.

wardrooms to play cards in an atmosphere of laughter and gay conversation.[19]

The Main Body also experienced that slight lessening of the fog, completed refueling the destroyers, then discovered that two ships— *Sendai*, flagship of the Third Submarine Squadron, and one destroyer—were missing. So *Hosho*'s plane took off on another search, and at 1315 discovered the lost sheep some forty-three miles ahead of course. They promptly reversed and before 1600 were back in position.[20]

Ugaki was evidently feeling sentimental that day. His thoughts returned to the midget submariners lost in Australia. "Although they claimed that our attack was unsuccessful, their shock received from our attack must have been tremendous. Even though they failed to inflict heavy damage upon the enemy as planned, their souls could rest free from anxiety for having done so."[21] The loss of those gallant, dedicated if ineffectual young sailors was a heavy price to pay for jolting the strollers on the Sydney waterfront, but where his pets were concerned, Ugaki was determined to see the silver lining.

That afternoon the Main Body resumed zigzagging, but increased speed and changed course when what seemed to be a two-masted, one-funnel merchant ship appeared far to the north. *Hosho* sent out a reconnaissance plane which reported two hours later that they had sighted Japan's No. 7 Patrol Ship, *Nankai Maru*. Ugaki was very disgusted to discover that "what was thought from a distance of 32,000 meters to be a merchant ship of several thousand tons actually turned out to be a patrol ship of only eighty-seven tons. This should be called a typical case of an entirely false report," he wrote severely. Then he softened:

> Be that as it may, their toil with which they came to such a faraway point . . . with such a tiny ship, braving winds and waves to engage in the patrol mission, can hardly be appreciated too much . . . Had we known this, we should have approached her instead of going away from her so that their spirit might be cheered up with the sight of our main force majestically steaming east for the new mission. I regretted our failure very much.[22]

Spruance for one had neither time nor inclination for such gestures. On this day, June 2 Hawaii time, he signaled all ships of his Task Force:

An attack for the purpose of capturing Midway is expected. The attacking force may be composed of all combatant types including four or five carriers, transports and train vessels. If presence of Task Forces 16 and 17 remains unknown to enemy we should be able to make surprise flank attacks on enemy carriers from position northeast of Midway. Further operations will be based on result of these attacks, damage inflicted by Midway forces, and information of enemy movements. The successful conclusion of the operation now commencing will be of great value to our country. Should carriers become separated during attacks by enemy aircraft, they will endeavor to remain within visual touch.[23]

All of Spruance is this dispatch—an unemotional, plain statement of facts unembellished by grandiloquence, a business-like weighing of the possibilities, neither panicky nor overconfident.

He met Fletcher's Task Force Seventeen at 1600 at the rendezvous which Nimitz had designated "Point Luck." The two task forces were now beyond the protective range of Midway's land-based planes and on their own. From this point, Fletcher as senior officer took command, and officially the two task forces became one fighting unit. In actual practice, the two operated independently.[24] Divide a flotilla already hopelessly outnumbered in the face of the enemy? Yes! Having no mass to begin with, Fletcher could not count upon it. He must settle for mobility and, in the homely country phrase, not put all his eggs in one basket.

CHAPTER 17

"Take Off for Attack!"

Lieutenant Commander Masatake Okumiya, staff aviation officer of the Second Carrier Striking Force, stood on the deck of the light carrier *Ryujo*, looking intently into the forbidding arctic sky. Anxiety spread across every feature of his face, scarred from a long-ago aircraft crash. Zero hour was only a few minutes away. The sun would rise officially at 0258 June 3, local time, but because of the long summer day, takeoff was scheduled for 0233. Yet the sky was still dark as *Ryujo* plunged ahead at twenty-two knots, leading the fleet almost due north toward Dutch Harbor—the main target of Japan's diversionary thrust against the lonely Aleutians.[1]

Down on the flight deck, aircraft warmed up in a burst of roaring engines and howling wind. Nearby, the carrier's skipper, Captain Tadao Kato, bear-like in his thick fur coat, had collected the flight unit commanders for a final word. They knew little, if anything, about the enemy and they had never operated under these dreary climatic conditions.

Okumiya felt a tap on his shoulder, and looked around to find his chief, Rear Admiral Kakuji Kakuta, trying to make himself heard above the noise. "Can the attack get off on time?" he asked.

"Please, sir, we will have to wait a little longer," Okumiya bellowed courteously. He glanced at his watch. The hands stood at 0228; only five minutes to go, but the morning was no lighter. Senior Staff Officer Masanori Odagiri squinted up and pointed out that a heavy fog was obscuring the sky, which explained the darkness.[2]

Okumiya clucked impatiently. The sooner this attack was launched, the better. The fliers had enough troubles without unexpected delays. He was not too sure they could even find their target. The map of Unalaska Island from which they were working showed a shoreline

151

liberally broken by dots, indicating unconfirmed guesswork, and their map of Dutch Harbor was based upon a chart more than three decades old. Their only photograph of the American installation was of the same vintage. Japanese cartographers could have produced better maps of Mars than of this Aleutian island. Picking out one strange island of uncertain contour in a sprawling archipelago was no easy task without having to do so in a fog.[3]

Although to Okumiya and to the aggressive Kakuta the wait seemed interminable, within ten minutes other vessels of the striking force began to loom into view like ghost ships. Now, at last, here was the second carrier, *Junyo*, clearly visible at 1,000 meters. This was about the best the Japanese could hope for in these waters, where a fog the color and almost the consistency of New England clam chowder is the rule of weather. So at 0243 Okumiya called out to Kakuta, "Sir, we can launch now." The admiral passed the word to the signal officer who shouted, "Squadrons, take off for attack!"

From the flight decks of the two carriers they rose—eleven torpedo bombers and six Zeros from *Ryujo*, twelve dive bombers and six Zeros from *Junyo*. This was not the entire complement available, for the flagship carried a total of sixteen fighters and twenty-one torpedo bombers, while *Junyo* could muster twenty-four Zeros and twenty-one dive bombers. Lieutenant Yoshio Shiga, commander of *Junyo*'s fighters, led the flight, which was no beautifully disciplined formation. Today it was every man for himself, with a ceiling never higher than 700 feet. Takeoff cost one of *Ryujo*'s bombers, but an escort destroyer swung into immediate action and fished the entire plane crew out of the freezing water quickly enough to save their lives, a remarkable feat in that area.[4]

Such was the beginning of Japan's diversionary strike in the Aleutians, the patter designed to distract the audience while the magician pulled the rabbit out of the hat at Midway. No sooner had the aircraft winged into the mist than several American reconnaissance planes appeared and hovered inquisitively over the Kakuta force. One persistent scout stuck to his quarry closely and dropped several bombs, without result. Then he, too, disappeared. On the flight toward Dutch Harbor, *Junyo*'s aircraft met and shot down an American flying boat, but evading it caused a delay which, coupled with the all-pervasive fog, aborted the mission.

In the meantime, Lieutenant Masayuki Yamagami's group from

Ryujo pressed on through ragged cloud breaks and reaped the reward of their perseverance. Directly over Dutch Harbor the clouds parted for a clear view of the target.

Although American radar spotted the incoming flight and the defenders were ready with heavy antiaircraft fire, in twenty minutes the Japanese shot up the tank farm, radio station and an Army barracks, killing approximately twenty-five soldiers and sailors. They also strafed several PBYs on the water. In exchange, the defending air batteries shot down two bombers and damaged two other aircraft, one a fighter. Considering the size of the raiding party—fourteen bombers and three fighters were all that actually made it to Dutch Harbor—the Japanese had inflicted considerable damage, and provided ammunition for the advocates of air power by proving that even when an attack was expected, enough planes probably would get through to make the effort worth the enemy's while.

However, the Japanese were not too pleased with the morning's work. Okumiya could mull over a whole new batch of good photographs, valuable and surprising, for they showed Dutch Harbor much better equipped than Japanese intelligence had imagined, with modern buildings, tank farm, and an impressive network of roads leading to the installation.[5] Nevertheless, if we may judge by that day's entry in the diary of Captain Tasuku Nakazawa, the Northern Force's chief of staff, no one aboard Vice Admiral Moshiro Hosogaya's flagship, *Nachi*, was overjoyed. After a brief summation of damage suffered and supposedly inflicted, Nakazawa remarked merely, ". . . it is assumed that they launched aerial attacks upon Dutch Harbor as scheduled, but failed to inflict much damage to the enemy due to foul weather."[6]

Actually, according to U.S. records, the weather in the region of Dutch Harbor was not all that bad on June 3, being "average for flying with variable cloudiness."[7] Still, Japanese planes had caught no American shipping of any significance in the harbor, and worst of all, no American fleet had come roaring up to hunt for the invaders. So far there was no indication that the Alaskan sideshow was having any effect on the main event in the center ring.[8]

But neither Okumiya nor anyone else at the time had any way of knowing just how unfortunate for Japan was the diversionary attack on Dutch Harbor. Immediately after the aircraft finished that strike, there occurred what seemed to be just one more tragic, regrettable incident of war. As the bombers and fighters rendezvoused over the eastern end of Unalaska, Flight Petty Officer Tadayoshi Koga of *Ryujo* spotted a thin spume of gasoline blowing back from his Zero. Immediately he informed his flight leader, Lieutenant Minoru Kobayashi, that he could not make it back to the carrier. Then he headed for a small island east of Dutch Harbor previously designated as an emergency landing point. According to plan, a submarine would stop there after the attack to pick up survivors of stranded aircraft.[9]

Kobayashi watched Koga make a perfect approach into a flat clearing, but the instant the wheels touched down, the Zero jerked up and remained standing on its nose. To Kobayashi the plane appeared to be heavily damaged and the pilot undoubtedly dead or seriously injured. Reluctantly he concluded that any attempt to remove the wrecked plane or the pilot over the tundra would be fruitless. Nevertheless, after he made his report to *Ryujo*, the patrol submarine scouted the area closely, but could not find the wreck.[10]

Kobayashi was partly wrong and partly right in his assumptions. Koga was dead, for the Zero's sudden stop and flip-up snapped his head against the instrument panel, breaking his neck. The plane, however, was only slightly damaged and was still in excellent condition when an American search party found it some five weeks later.

This was a terrific break for the United States—capture of a virtually pristine Zero, the terror of the Pacific skies. Sent to the mainland, repaired, studied and put through every possible flight test, the craft soon revealed all its strengths and its weaknesses to the highly interested Americans.[11] And this splendid plane did have weaknesses. To achieve maneuverability, range, and other offensive qualities, the Japanese sacrificed defensive armor and other safety measures. As a result, the Zero was an airborne firetrap, lacking even self-seal fuel tanks, and consistently succumbed to battle damage which even a P-40 or an F4F could take in stride.[12]

With such facts at their disposal, the American aircraft designers rushed to their drawing boards to come up with a fighter which at last could put the Indian sign on the legendary Zero. The answer was the Grumman F6F Hellcat, which outclassed the Zero in almost every department. In retrospect, Okumiya believed that the loss of Koga's single fighter, thus assuring the speedy American conquest of the Zero, was one of the decisive factors in Japan's eventual defeat.[13]

At the moment, of course, the Americans had no time nor thought to spare for one wrecked Japanese on an obscure islet in the Aleutians. As we have seen, Nimitz, although certain that the Japanese feint toward Alaska represented a diversion only, designated Rear Admiral Robert A. "Fuzzy" Theobald,* a brainy and energetic officer of uncertain temper, to command a small task force activated on May 21 to deal with the northern area, just in case the Japanese meant business in that direction. Theobald was no stranger to fog, having been born in San Francisco in 1884. He graduated ninth academically in the Annapolis class of 1907, and his career followed the usual lines of a promising young officer—various sea and shore assignments culminating as Commander Destroyers Pacific Fleet.[14]

Task Force Eight, as Theobald's fleet would be known once it got together, included a main body of two cruisers, three light cruisers, and four destroyers. These ships were scattered all over the Pacific, and in fact the entire group did not meet until some hours after the Japanese strike at Dutch Harbor. In addition, Theobald had an Air Search Group of a few tender-based and land-based aircraft, and a Surface Search Group drawn from Captain Ralph C. Parker's "Alaskan Navy" of converted fishing craft and miscellaneous boats, normally occupied in patrol and escort duty. Task Force Eight also included a Destroyer Striking Group of nine craft, the six "fish" of a Submarine Group, and three tankers.[15]

Then, because he was on Joint Chiefs of Staff orders and in overall area command, Theobald could count on an Army Air Striking Group under Brigadier General William O. Butler. This was a real mixture spread over Anchorage, Cold Bay, Kodiak, and Umnak. Theobald arrived at Kodiak on May 27 to find that Parker and the Army's Alaskan Defense Commander, Brigadier General Simon Bolivar Buckner, had already been alerted for two weeks and were working hard to clear the area of civilian ships and personnel and bring in military ships, planes, and men. So Theobald and his co-workers had just four days to hammer out their organization and an operational plan.[16]

Alaska's defenders had much less detailed knowledge of the Japanese forces and movements than did the Midway task forces. Nimitz had a good idea of what comprised Kakuta's fleet, and he suspected that one or two amphibious units might be along, but not until May

---

*Theobald had acted as Admiral Kimmel's assistant before the Roberts Commission, which investigated the Pearl Harbor disaster. See *At Dawn We Slept*, pp. 597–98.

28 did he have anything really firm to give Theobald. At that time, he advised that his Intelligence sources believed the Japanese had one invasion group scheduled for Attu and another one for Kiska.

Something of an intellectual maverick, Theobald did not swallow the dose without sniffing it suspiciously.[17] Why should any Japanese with his wits about him want to invade either Attu or Kiska? What was so attractive about such dreary jumping-off places, with their few Aleut settlements, where the williwaw howled around the rafters, and underfoot the tundra-covered volcanic ash made impossible the movement of heavy motorized equipment? Imagine several layers of tatami laid on a foundation of gelatine—that was the terrain of the outer Aleutians.

To be sure, water-cooler strategists talked up the Aleutian chain as the logical invasion route between Japan and the United States. And on paper that scimitar of islets swinging so gracefully between the Alaska Peninsula and Kamchatka did indeed appear a formidable weapon. But no map could show the fantastic difficulties of terrain and climate. In the technology of the day, the idea was absurd.

Further in toward the mainland lay something worth the trouble of grabbing, if only to deny them to the Americans—Dutch Harbor itself and, close enough to support the anchorage, a 5,000-foot runway on Umnak Island. True, it was a long, thin trampoline for the fighter craft, whose pilots braced themselves for a thirty-foot bounce when they touched down, and which bent ominously under every bomber, but its very existence was a monument to the skill and persistence of the Army Engineers. Whatever the Japanese purpose—to harass Allied shipping in the event of war with Russia, to strike the American and Canadian west coasts, or just make nuisances of themselves— they could do so much better from Umnak, Unalaska, and the peninsula than from the outer islands.[18] Even if the entire Japanese northern operation was a faked end run, they would not be at all averse to doing the Empire some good at the same time.

Moreover, to plan a diversion within a diversion would be quite in keeping with the intricate Japanese mentality. In other words, Theobald believed that the enemy wanted to lure him out to the far end of nowhere off Attu and Kiska while they swung around him and took Dutch Harbor behind his back.[19] If he moved out beyond the range of his shore-based Army aircraft, there would be Kakuta's carrier-borne aircraft to clobber him, and he did not have enough gunpower to indulge in an old-fashioned slugging match while the Japanese carriers were afloat. Actually, aside from the flattops, the Japanese and American northern forces were amazingly well matched. Japan had one more heavy cruiser—three to the United States's two—while the Americans had one more destroyer—thirteen to the Japanese twelve—and both had three light cruisers. Both sides had the usual miscellany of "cats and dogs," including the three Japanese troop transports, useless in a sea fight.[20]

Taking all these factors into consideration, Theobald made his decision: He would refuse to swallow the Japanese bait; he would stay at Kodiak.[21] Even if the Japanese moves toward Attu and Kiska turned out to be authentic, the only effect on the United States would be a slight nick in the pride at losing a piece of land under the American flag. Strategically and tactically, the islands were worthless.

Theobald's logic was irrefutable; his reasoning sound. There was just one thing wrong with the picture: It was completely false. For the peppery admiral credited the Japanese with being much smarter than they really were. In the first place, they honestly believed that the Americans might try to invade Japan by way of the Aleutians.[22] They even thought that such a project might already be in the preparatory stage, hence dispatched submarines to check on various ports along the presumed invasion route. *I-9* looked over the Western Islands on May 25 and 26; *I-19* reported on its visit of May 28–29 to Dutch Harbor without noting the air strip on Umnak; *I-25* covered Kodiak; and *I-26* even sailed down to Washington state and launched a reconnaissance plane over Seattle, reporting no heavy shipping concentration there.[23]

In the second place, the Japanese almost grotesquely overestimated the American strength in the Aleutians. They estimated Dutch Harbor to house an entire Army division, while they figured Kiska's strength at 200 or 300 Marines. Actually, the entire Kiska complement was ten weathermen with not a gun among them. As for the outermost island, Attu, with a total population of twenty-four adult Aleuts, thirteen children, and one American civilian married couple, this the Japanese figured as housing "a wireless station, observatory, and garrison unit of unknown strength."[24]

So, from their point of view, the Japanese had a reasonable motive for striking Attu and Kiska, quite aside from the tie-in with the Midway operation— to block off a supposed American invasion route.

Unaware of this false enemy intelligence, Theobald arranged with
General Butler to send over half his aircraft to Cold Bay and Otter
Point, to cover the incomplete installations there. So off to Cold Bay
went twenty-one P-40s and fourteen bombers, and twelve P-40s to
Otter Point. These aircraft were all radar-equipped and hence fog-
worthy, but their pilots were not familiar with the terrain, weather,
or techniques of overwater flying.

From these outlying fields and three aircraft tenders, search flights
fanned out for some 400 miles, and 700 miles from Kodiak, beginning
May 28. On June 1, Theobald left the latter point in his flagship, the
light cruiser *Nashville*, headed for rendezvous with his main body,
approximately 400 miles south of Kodiak. So, in the name of cool
logic and calm reasoning, Theobald placed his cruisers where the
action wasn't, and where he himself could command only by breaking
radio silence or by scurrying back to Kodiak. He was en route to the
rendezvous scheduled for 0700 on June 3 when Kakuta's aircraft, not
an invasion party, struck Dutch Harbor.[25]

On the way home to the carriers, one of Yamagami's aircraft radioed Kakuta that he had discovered five United States destroyers at
Makushin Bay on Unalaska's north coast. Kakuta enthusiastically ordered all available aircraft, even the seaplanes from the cruisers *Maya*
and *Takao*, to take off after the destroyers. But the unpredictable
weather again raised a hand. Not one of the twenty-four aircraft sighted
the destroyers and had to return to their carriers in random groups
barely skimming the sea. The last aircraft collected, Kakuta ordered
his force to steam to about 100 miles from the shore.[26]

Two of the reconnaissance seaplanes were lost in a most unexpected manner. Four of these craft, Type 95, from *Takao* and *Maya*,
ran into two U.S. Army P-40s over Umnak. The Japanese had no
inkling of the Fort Glenn airstrip at Otter Point on that island, and
were utterly bewildered when two American land-based fighters ma-
terialized as suddenly as if they had popped out of a djinni's bottle.
In the resulting dogfight, Lieutenants John B. Murphy and Jacob W.
Dixon, piloting the P-40s, shot down two of the Japanese planes and
seriously mauled the other two. By some miracle the latter held
together until their pilots guided them back to the cruisers, but fell
apart as soon as they touched down on the water. Once again, quick
action saved the crewmen.[27]

By noon the day's activity in the Aleutians had ended, and Kakuta began to withdraw to the southwest. That night the destroyers took on oil; then the fleet steamed toward Adak to work it over in accordance with prearranged plan.[28]

News of the attack reached the United States quite rapidly and evoked various reactions. Receiving word from Bremerton that Japanese planes had struck Dutch Harbor, Secretary of War Stimson made arrangements for all messages concerning this attack to be sent to his home. Then he went for a horseback ride with his aide. Stimson took his physical fitness program seriously, and more than a Japanese swipe at the Aleutians would be required to interfere with it. When he returned, he found "that the Japanese were attacking again; the first attack did but little damage though it seems to have caused some casualties and there is a report that the mother ship is somewhere in the neighborhood. We are looking for it."[29]

An editorial in the Honolulu *Star-Bulletin* reflected a sort of nervous bravado:

> News of a Japanese attack on Dutch Harbor concerns but does not dismay the people of Hawaii. . . .
> Dutch Harbor may be an isolated raid or it may be part of a series of attacks all along the Pacific coast and upon Hawaii.[30]

Roosevelt had been almost obsessively concerned about keeping the Soviet Union in the war. "I would rather lose New Zealand, Australia, or anything else than have the Russians collapse," he told Secretary of the Treasury Henry Morgenthau, Jr., on March 11. So now he saw the Japanese move in the light of his preoccupation, declaring, "This attack on the Aleutian Islands, I do not think was directed at the United States or Alaska. I think it is part of their preparatory drive on Siberia." And he added, "However, once we lick the Germans, with the help of England's Fleet we can defeat the Japanese in six weeks."[31]

If Morgenthau quoted the President correctly, this was an astounding assessment, even for Roosevelt, a man not given to dwelling in the shadows of pessimism.

CHAPTER 18

"Extra Luck Riding with Us"

Ensign Jack Reid* kept the nose of his clumsy-looking PBY pointed west-southwest, while his clear, rather quizzical blue eyes scanned the majestic arc of sea and sky. Reid and his crew were on a regular patrol flight out of Midway in the general direction of Wake Island. As the amphibian droned on at 1,000 feet, visibility was unlimited. If anything were to be seen in this sector, these airmen should see it, and if they did not, they could not blame the weather. For this was perfect, and the sunny morning was still young. A glance at his wrist-watch told Reid the time was about 0900.

He and his men had rolled out of their bunks that morning of June 3 at 0300. After the usual breakfast of bacon, eggs, toast and coffee, they attended the early briefing of the twenty-two-plane reconnaissance mission. There they were informed "as to the possibility of an invasion of Midway. . . ."[1]

However, no one had said anything about "the extent of the Japanese forces or the disposition of our task forces." So Reid had no idea of what he might run into, if indeed he might run into anything at all. But he knew that something was going to pop somewhere around Midway soon. "Stay very alert at your stations," he cautioned his crew, of whom he was most proud. "They did this very willingly, even though we had been flying over twelve hours per day for the past several days," he recalled.

Reid's boyishly rounded features and well-shaped lips with a tuck of humor at each corner showed traces of fatigue, as well they might. His Unit, VP-44, had arrived on Midway in increments of two six-plane groups on May 22 and 23, and since that time Reid had flown

---

*Reid's official given names were Jewell Hamon, but he had used "Jack" for years and preferred to be known by that name. (Letter, Reid to Prange, December 10, 1966.)

his PBY5A on daily patrols of at least twelve hours each.[2] But he was in excellent physical condition and as fresh as the morning. Reid's handsome face and air of alert, good-natured intelligence gave him a startling resemblance to the popular movie star Robert Montgomery.

The pilot's eyes swept the sky with particular care, for along with "the possibility of sighting part of the mighty Japanese Navy," he was thinking of "the imminent danger of being spotted by the Japanese patrol planes flying out of Wake Island." The Mitsubishis had already badly mauled four PBYs, and Reid had no intention that his aircraft be the fifth.

Disappointment bit into Ensign Robert Swan as he bent over his charts and instruments. Reid's PBY 8V55, of which he was navigator, was now six hours out of Midway, at the end of its outward search leg, and the crew had not yet spotted a Japanese patrol plane, much less a ship. Reluctantly he prepared to notify Reid that the time had come to turn into the doglcg.[3]

Under normal conditions, no Catalina crewman in his right senses would be disappointed because he did not have to try conclusions with a Mitsubishi 96, but on this particular mission something new had been added. The previous evening, some newly arrived B-17 men had met with Reid's crewmen, and loudly sung the praises of their new .50-caliber explosive cartridges. "If you just hit an enemy plane with one of these blue-tipped shells," the airmen assured their Navy counterparts, "it will blow the plane up."[4]

To the latter, this sounded like just what the doctor had ordered. Their assigned search was pointed toward Wake, so the crew believed the chances were good—or bad, depending on the point of view— of encountering one or two Japanese patrol planes. These wonder shells would go far to even the odds and perhaps give them a chance to avenge their injured buddies. The PBY gunners promptly "traded or borrowed" six of these shells and placed three of them in each waist gun.

"Sir, can't we stretch the sector another ten minutes?" pleaded Chief Radioman Francis Musser. "I'm sure we'll see a Japanese plane." Swan mentally checked the fuel. Yes, they had enough to handle an extra twenty to forty minutes safely. He was just as eager as Musser to try out those blue-nosed shells, so he relayed Musser's request to Reid.[5]

"Bob, you are navigating; just give me the time to turn and I hope we find something before we do turn," Reid replied.[6] He not only liked the idea of dishing out a surprise to the Wake Island patrol; he still hoped for a glimpse of Japanese ships. So he OK'd the first extension of ten minutes, and when that expired fruitlessly, he went on for another ten.[7] Then, deciding that further search was useless, he started to swing into the cross leg to reach the homebound line to Midway.

Just as he did so, Reid spotted some specks on the horizon. At first he thought they were dirty spots on the windshield. He stayed on the original course, then did a quick double-take and shouted to his co-pilot, Ensign Gerald Hardeman, "My God, aren't those ships on the horizon? I believe we have hit the jackpot."

Hardeman snatched up his binoculars for a close look. Yes, those were ships which Reid had sighted. Then, within a few seconds, Ensign John Gammell, the second co-pilot and bow gunner, set up a shout. "I've spotted ships dead ahead approximately twenty-five to thirty miles."[8]

Several minutes later, Reid got off a message: "Sighted Main Body." It reached Midway at 0925. Within two minutes he flashed another signal, "Bearing 262, distance 700."[9]

The news electrified Simard and Ramsey, but they wanted more precise information. So they immediately dispatched orders to amplify.[10] However, Reid was not yet in a position to amplify anything. The ships were at a considerable distance, and he needed a clearer view before he could determine their number and type. So after he had verified the ships' direction—due east—he cut the throttles on the engines and dove to a level almost skimming the whitecaps. Then he turned north on a perpendicular right angle to the movement of the Japanese vessels. After flying on this course for about fifteen minutes, he turned to a westerly heading and flew due west for some twenty-five miles.[11]

In the meantime, Midway was getting impatient. As it stood, Reid's report, though vital, was not detailed enough, and Simard refused to commit the B-17 striking force until he had some idea of how many and what type of vessels were involved.[12] It so happened that 8V55's was not the first contact report of the morning. At 0904, Ensign Charles R. Eaton, piloting plane No. 6V55, radioed, "Two Japanese cargo vessels sighted bearing 247 degrees, distance 470 miles. Fired upon by AA."[13] This was a portion of the Minesweeper

Group under Captain Sadatomo Miyamoto, consisting of four mine-sweepers, three subchasers, a supply ship, and two cargo ships, which by the morning of June 3 had reached the position indicated.[14] But Simard was not fishing for such minnows this morning. At 0953 he dispatched scout No. 7V55 to proceed bearing 261, distance 700, and at 1007 again ordered Reid to amplify his report.[15]

About half an hour elapsed before he could comply. By this time, Reid had gingerly nosed his aircraft to 800 feet and glimpsed some ships about twenty-five miles due south. At roughly that moment, Reid gave Swan another message to encode, advising that the Japanese ships comprised "six large vessels in column." Swan was so scared he "could hardly read."[16] But he got the report off. It reached Midway at 1040, and again exasperated the anxious recipients. Within three minutes they sent out a new order: "Give type, course and speed."[17]

Reid accepted the prodding with good-natured resignation. He knew that he could have made "a more comprehensive report of the Japanese Invasion Force from a higher altitude." But he also wanted to keep from the enemy the fact that they had been sighted, and he was trying to see as much as possible without being seen. He was sure that these Japanese warships carried fighter aircraft for cover. If a keen-eyed watch saw him and sent up a Zero, his heavy-bodied PBY would have no more chance than a turkey against a hawk.

With no cloud cover, his only hope was to play a "cat-and-mouse game," as he called it, changing his altitude frequently, and keeping as close to the surface as possible. Moreover, he wanted to remain astern of the vessels, for not only could he get a better sweep of view from the rear, but the wake of a great ship is often visible before the vessel itself. Then, too, he wisely reasoned, enemies bent on invasion would be more likely to look for a patrol plane in front of them rather than at their stern.

After observing the column of Japanese ships for a few minutes, again Reid dove to within a few feet of the sea and sped westward another twenty-five miles. The plane was now well behind the surface fleet, with an impressive array of hostile steel between it and any possible assistance from Midway in case of trouble.[18] This course of action required an unusual combination of imagination, cool calculation, and physical courage, all of which Reid had in abundance.

Once more the pilot changed his course, switching from west to south, continuing in this direction until he picked up a group of wakes trailing the vessels like long, white tails. This time Reid made a careful count of the main ships,[19] and Swan encoded another report to Midway of "eleven ships, course 090, speed 19," including "one small carrier, one seaplane carrier, two battleships, several cruisers. . . . and several destroyers." In this message, which Midway received at 1125, Reid also requested instructions.[20]

Up to this point, these young men had been much too interested and excited to comprehend exactly what their position was. Now, suddenly, it swept over them in a riptide of reaction. "What do you think of your blue-tipped shells now?" one of the crew asked Musser.

"I just looked at those shells," replied the radioman with a rather shaky grin. "They've turned yellow!"[21]

Reid realized with a jolt that he and his crew actually were "closer to Japan than the Japanese aboard the ships." Furthermore, they were approximately 750 miles west of Midway and had been flying for more than two hours past their scheduled point of return. Barely enough fuel remained to get them back to base, so the Midway radio of 1130, ordering them to return, was exceedingly welcome. Reid asked Swan for a course to Midway which would circumnavigate the Japanese ships.

"I am stating it mildly when I say we were scared, excited, and very happy as we left the Japanese Fleet over the horizon," Reid recalled. "We knew we had been very lucky in sighting the Japanese Fleet and with extra luck riding with us that enabled us to track and observe them for two-and-a-half hours without being sighted."

Once out of range of possible enemy antiaircraft, the men relaxed and ate a bite of lunch. "I am sure everyone said a little prayer of thanks," Reid remarked in retrospect, "I know I did. We also had a job to do to return to Midway safely so we could fly tomorrow during the battle."[22]

Just exactly what had Reid spotted by this historic sighting? From the bearing given and his description of "six large ships in column," it seems clear that he had seen, not Yamamoto's Main Body nor the Nagumo force, but the "Main Body" of the Midway Invasion Force— Kondo's two battleships and four cruisers. Then, after swinging behind and around his quarry, he had seen "one small carrier, one seaplane carrier, two battleships, several cruisers and . . . several destroyers."[23] This indicates that he had made an entirely new sighting, this time of Tanaka's Invasion Force, sailing in company with

Fujita's Seaplane Tender Group, with Kurita's Close Support Group close by.

Of course, this entire fleet contained considerably more than eleven ships, and no battlewagons; however, approaching as Reid did from the stern, at a very low altitude, the perspective would have been shortened, and the forward section of the formation might well have been concealed. The best guess is that Reid saw the four heavy cruisers as well as *Kamikawa Maru* and *Chitose*, respectively on the port and starboard flanks of the transport column, plus a number of the transports themselves and a few escort destroyers. To mistake a heavy cruiser for a battleship from the air is very understandable, and happened more than once during the battle to come.

Meanwhile, Tanaka had dispatched a message to Yamamoto to inform him that an enemy flying boat had discovered his whereabouts, and had clung tenaciously to the transports until heavy antiaircraft fire drove it away.[24] This PBY could not have been Reid's, for he experienced no antiaircraft action whatsoever and remained convinced that the Japanese did not see him. He kept his aircraft between ten to thirty miles away from his quarry at a low altitude, and he argued reasonably that if the Japanese knew an American PBY was watching them, why did they not send up a fighter from one of the vessels to shoot him down?[25]

Yet there is no doubt that the Escort Force did indeed see a United States patrol plane, for important Japanese accounts of the battle mention the incident. According to Commander Hara, whose *Amatsukaze* was the second destroyer to starboard in the spearhead of the Tanaka group, the plane appeared at around 0600 Japanese time, which would be 0900 local time, slightly ahead of the Japanese formation. Hara said nothing about antiaircraft fire, noting only that the plane "went away after a short time."[26]

Despite the discrepancy in reported distance from Midway, it is probable that these advance Japanese ships had seen Eaton's patrol craft 6V55 which, as we have seen, had reported the Minesweeper Force at 0904 and which had encountered antiaircraft fire. On the other hand, plane 7V55 reported at 0923 being "fired upon by AA."[27]

While all this activity was going on to the south, Yamamoto's Main Fleet was primarily occupied with the break-off of Takasu's Aleutians Guard Force. At 35°N and 165°E, Takasu's own Second Battleship Division and Kishi's Ninth Cruiser Division set off northward at 0800.

According to plan, Takasu should be 500 miles south of Kiska by June 6, but would be ready to return to the Yamamoto Main Body in the event of a serious American counterattack. As it happened, however, this large fleet of Takasu's was suspended between the Aleutian diversion and the main Midway operation, and in a position to assist neither in the critical actions of the next day.[28]

The Main Body continued eastward toward Midway, with Yamamoto still expecting every force to move according to plan. "And everyone was in high spirits," said Watanabe, "because the day of battle was not far away."[29] Into this jolly atmosphere plunked Tanaka's message. This was unpleasant news, for Yamamoto and his staff had to assume that the reconnaissance plane had radioed Tanaka's location to Midway and probably also to CinCPAC headquarters in Pearl Harbor. So action should be forthcoming at any minute.

Ugaki was seriously agitated, recording in his diary that ". . . a report came in that the invasion force accompanying twelve transports was sighted by an enemy plane at a point 600 miles from Midway at 0600 this morning and the No. 16 Minesweeper Division was fighting." Doggedly patriotic, Ugaki kept his diary on Japan time. To him the incident occurred at 0600 June 4 and no local nonsense about it. He continued unhappily,

> A premature exposure! If its early close-in is unavoidable because of its slow speed, the first attack of our task force on N-2 day should have been made one day earlier. This problem was brought up in a briefing conference before the sortie, but the date of an aerial attack was not advanced because of the preparation time of the task force.[30]

Ugaki's phraseology was not exactly lucid, but the idea breaks through the fog. In timing their softening-up operation against Midway, the planners had underestimated the speed of the Tanaka force which, as Fuchida had already noted, for some days had been in danger of running ahead of its blockers. Hence, it would have been wiser to schedule the Nagumo strike for one day earlier.

The Japanese were perfectly correct in assuming that action was imminent. Reid's report of eleven ships was followed at 1130 by a radio from plane No. 7V55, pinpointing "two cargo vessels and two small vessels, course 050, bearing 251, distance 270." The distance was obviously in error, the plane at the time being some 500 miles away from Midway,[31] but between the two messages the Midway defenders had enough information to act upon.

While these messages were coming in, the B-17s were refueling from their early morning flight. To keep his precious Flying Fortresses off the airfield in case of an early morning attack, Ramsey sent them up at 0415, first to Pearl and Hermes Reef, about ninety miles east-southeast of Midway, then back, then out on a 265° search for some 200 miles. This reconnaissance being without result, the B-17s returned and touched down on Midway at 0820.[32]

Another B-17 came in from Hawaii that day, piloted by Lieutenant W. A. Smith, who found himself immediately scooped up for search duty. At 1105 he reported his plane ready, received the designation 0V93, and took off at 1158,* a Navy Ensign Kellam along with him as observer and instructor. Smith's mission was to track the enemy and pinpoint its location for the striking force to follow him shortly. The plane carried no bomb, but Ramsey believed that a B-17 would have more chance than a reconnaissance type to beat off Japanese aircraft.[33]

Half an hour later, nine B-17s** under Lieutenant Colonel Walter C. Sweeney, each plane carrying four 600-pound bombs, set out to attack the enemy Main Body. As Ramsey observed in his battle report, this was "the most experienced group of B-17s and its effectiveness, resolution, and communication efficiency and discipline were outstanding."[34]

Throughout their flight, Smith fed them details as to cloud conditions, wind and visibility. Finally, at 1611, about 700 miles out, bearing 261, he discovered and reported two transports and two destroyers. Then Smith climbed to 8,000 feet, watching with interest but unable to do anything about it while the ships maneuvered in circles and fired their AA at him. But the strike force did not show up, and after hovering about two hours, Smith had to leave the scene and return to Midway.[35]

For some time past, the famed movie director Commander John Ford, USNR, heading a field photographic branch of the OSS, and busy making "a pictorial history of Midway," had been somewhat skeptical of the anticipated Japanese intentions toward Midway. "I didn't believe much in the impending action," he reminisced, "if it did come I didn't think it was going to touch us."

---

*According to NAS Diary, he took off at 1240.

**1200, and six B-17s, according to NAS Diary.

Now events made a believer out of him, and when Simard asked him to be prepared to station himself "up on top of the power house . . . ," he readily agreed. That location would be "a good place to take pictures."

"Well, forget the pictures as much as you can," said Simard, "but I want a good accurate account of the bombing. We expect to be attacked tomorrow."[36]

CHAPTER 19

"Even the Midst of the Pacific Is Small"

Sweeney and his B-17s continued winging westward. On the surface, Task Force Sixteen continued its well-planned course. The logs of *Hornet* and *Enterprise* for Wednesday June 3 reflect an almost comically placid picture which could be summed up in the inevitable "Steaming as before," the beginning of virtually every entry. If the determinedly stolid log of *Hornet* reflected the true picture of the day's activities, the most exciting event occurred at 0200 when an unfortunate seaman "while on duty was struck above the right eye by a mess cup." The how and why of this incident remain intriguing mysteries.

At 0859 *Hornet* went to General Quarters because of a radar contact *Yorktown* picked up at 045T, twenty-one miles distant, and at 0905 turned into the wind to launch a combat patrol. Three minutes later, the carrier "received orders not to launch," and at 0930 was advised that the "contact failed to develop." Through the rest of the day, *Hornet*'s log resumed its humdrum continuity.[1]

Evidently *Enterprise* had a similarly uneventful day. She zig-zagged, stopped zigzagging, changed course, and went through routine shipboard inspections which revealed "Conditions normal." At 0715 a seaman "fell off the flight deck onto the catwalk. Diagnosis: contusions and lacerations of face." At 1132 the destroyer *Russell* pulled alongside to deliver the day's mail. The watch sighted "friendly patrol plane bearing 278° distance 10 miles" that afternoon. And at 1600 two seamen were released from the brig where they had been brooding over their misdemeanors in solitary confinement on bread and water. For the rest, "steaming as before."[2]

Yet this was a day of crisis for the American task forces. Midway had relayed to Nimitz and Fletcher the day's sighting reports as they occurred. When Commander Maurice E. "Germany" Curts, the CinCPAC communications officer, hurried the report to Nimitz, the admiral was delighted. This should convince the most die-hard of doubters that his estimate of the situation was correct. Yet the early discovery of the Japanese Invasion Force posed a definite danger to the United States. Had either Nimitz or Fletcher accepted the idea that the ships which Reid had reported as the "Main Body" were actually the enemy's principal striking units, this would have thrown the entire American battle plan out of balance. But having once given his faith, Nimitz did not withdraw it except for overwhelming reasons. He had trusted Layton and Rochefort, whose original Intelligence reports indicated that a carrier force would deliver the main strike, and he continued to trust them now. Therefore he sent out an urgent fleet code message to Fletcher: "That is not repeat not the enemy striking force—stop—That is the landing force. The striking force will hit from the northwest at daylight tomorrow."[3]

Fletcher had already made up his mind that this was the case; however, Nimitz's message was a welcome confirmation. At 1950 he changed *Yorktown*'s course to the southwest, heading for a spot some 200 miles north of Midway which would be his launching position in case the patrols sighted Nagumo's carriers.[4]

In the meantime, the Japanese fleet, quite aside from the Kakuta and Tanaka groups, was having a busy day. The submarines finally positioned A and B cordons, two days behind schedule. Submerging by day and surfacing by night, the submarines exercised the utmost vigilance in screening the area between their cordons and Pearl Harbor, but of course without result, the United States task forces having long since passed this position.[5]

Naturally, the Nagumo ships were in a flurry of pre-attack activity. Shortly after 0600, the five oilers and the destroyer *Akigumo* of Captain Masanao Oto's Supply Group dropped away from the warships on course 130, at a speed of twelve knots. Then, commencing at 0825, signals began to fly between commanders and their ships. At that time Rear Admiral Hiraoki Abe, commander CruDiv 8, sent orders from *Tone* covering the morrow's antisubmarine patrol:

"1. Take-off times: Watch 1, 0130; Watch 2, 0430; Watch 3, 0730.

"2. One plane each from the *Kirishima* and *Chikuma* (3-seat recce's, if needed) will undertake the flights for Watch 2. *Kirishima*'s will be the #1 duty plane, *Chikuma*'s #2 duty plane."[6]

After an uneventful morning, at 1325 Nagumo signaled the entire force the fleet movements to be taken after the attack units had left the carriers:

1. For three hours and thirty minutes following the first wave's take-off, the fleet will proceed on course 135 degrees, speed 24 knots. Thereafter, if the prevailing winds are from the east, course will be 45 degrees, speed 20; if west winds prevail, course will be 270 degrees, speed 20 knots.

2. Change in plans may be necessitated by enemy actions. Bear this in mind in making preparations for assembling and taking aboard the air control units.

3. Unless otherwise specified, the search units will take off at the same time as the attack units.[7]

There, in paragraph two, Nagumo paid at least lip service to the proposition that the enemy represented more than chess pieces to be moved about at Japanese will.

Less than an hour later, he had a further instruction: "Maintain 26 knot momentary stand-by and maximum battle speed 20 minutes standby from 0100, 5th."

At 1830 Abe signaled to all ships of the Cruiser and Battleship Divisions, with information to Nagumo, the changes in the next day's antisubmarine air patrol:

"1. Allocation: For Watches 1 and 3, one plane each from all ships of CruDiv 8. For Watches 2 and 4, one plane each from all ships of BatDiv 3. For Watch 5, one plane each from *Chikuma* and *Kirishima*.

"2. Takeoff times (from Watch 1 through Watch 5 in order): 0130, 0430, 0730, 1030, 1330."[8]

At this time the Nagumo force was steaming at twenty-four knots in a southeasterly direction, the four carriers in the center, with *Haruna* and *Kirishima*, *Tone* and *Chikuma*, *Nagara* and the destroyers forming a rough ring around them for protection.[9] Abruptly *Tone*'s guns commenced firing, and the cruiser hoisted signal that she had sighted enemy planes. Within the minute, three fighters took off from *Akagi* to intercept, but could find nothing. Then at 1940 *Tone* signaled to Nagumo: "Lost enemy planes in direction bearing 260 degrees. About ten planes." Fourteen minutes later, the interceptors returned to *Akagi* with their negative report.[10]

Evidently Nagumo decided that someone on *Tone* had an over-active imagination and therefore he sent no report of the incident to *Yamato*, or else Yamamoto's staff did not take it seriously, for we find no mention of the occurrence in the journals of either Ugaki or Miwa. Instead, both of those conscientious diarists harked back to Nagumo's radio of the previous day. As usual, Miwa took a practical approach: ". . . This made me worry if the radio transmission might lead to our forces being discovered by an enemy. But, nothing can be done now that the cable was actually sent out. Continued advance only hoping God's grace will be upon us."[11]

Uneasy but grimly just, Ugaki recorded the weather conditions—although not his own instructions at the war games—in extenuation of Nagumo's rashness:

> Since fog came in from ahead with the east wind of five meters, there is little prospect about when it will clear up. Yesterday the task force broke radio silence by ordering its new course and speed by radio, and now it is considered that the task force was most likely to have met this same fog and not find another choice under the circumstances to carrying out the subsequent operation as scheduled.

Then a gnawing sense of unrightness took over. "I feel an impression that even the midst of the Pacific is small," he burst out. "All I hope now is that there will not be any trouble in tomorrow's air attack upon Midway Island by the task force."[12]

Certainly the Pacific was not big enough to suit Tanaka, who was kept on the jump that afternoon. Sweeney's B-17s found his force and began their attack at 1640.[13] As soon as the Japanese spotted large American planes coming in from the south, *Jintsu* commenced firing. The bombers zoomed out of range, only to return as soon as *Jintsu* left off. Once more the cruiser's guns barked upward; once more the aircraft disappeared. Hara, who had a ringside seat for this action from his destroyer, found this game of hide-and-seek unnerving, because this portion of the Invasion Force had no air cover.

When dusk was just beginning to settle, the bombers came back, their head-on course revealing the graceful, unmistakable silhouette of the Flying Fortress. All of Tanaka's destroyers opened fire at once,[14] the B-17s dropped their bombs in three high level attacks from 8,000, 10,000, and 12,000 feet. For a few minutes this usually lonesome spot resounded with all the boom of giant guns, whistle and explosion of bombs, clanging of ships' bells, swish of waterspouts, and raucous voices that form the sinister symphony of naval warfare. But when the tumult and the shouting died, nobody was hurt on either side. The Japanese antiaircraft fire, although very heavy, consistently exploded behind the B-17s.[15] A number of American bombs failed to detonate. Captain Cecil L. Faulkner, leader of the Third Element, dropped four bombs from his aircraft, only one of which exploded.[16] His wingman, First Lieutenant Edward A. Steedman, dropped only one bomb, owing to a short in the electric release mechanism.[17]

Although the antiaircraft had been ineffectual throughout the strike, Sweeney did not believe in pressing his luck. He headed his unscathed aircraft back to Midway without lingering to verify the extent of the damage, if any, that he had inflicted.[18] As a result, American claims varied widely. Headquarters Seventh Air Force claimed "five hits, one probable hit, and four near misses . . . on two BBs or CAs and two large transports. One BB and one transport were observed aflame. One waterline hit was made on the other transport."[19] Upon hearing such early reports, Admiral English hopefully ordered out the submarine *Cuttlefish* to finish off the "damaged battleships."[20] Ramsey's official report claimed "a hit on a battleship and one on a transport."[21]

We may be fairly sure that the pilots did not send in deliberately false reports. At such a high level, with perspective distorted and tons of water hurtling skyward, it is an exceedingly gifted observer who can tell the difference between a hit and a miss. Indeed, all on-the-spot records of battle must be liberally sprinkled with salt.

Despite its abortive nature, this incident was the first since the Midway plan originated to send a ripple of genuine concern through Yamamoto's staff. The whole tactical concept relied heavily upon the Tanaka fleet's being undetected until after Nagumo's carriers began their strike at Midway. The appearance of the B-17s canceled any hope the Combined Fleet officers might have entertained that, by some miracle, the American reconnaissance plane did not get word of his contact back to Midway.

"It is now apparent that the enemy came to suspect our intention by this sighting," Ugaki recorded. "Care should be made about it, I believe. In the afternoon came in a report from the CO of the Second

Destroyer Squadron that nine B-17s came to attack our invasion force, but no damage was sustained. Now it is imminent for actions."[22]

Miwa was rather more philosophical about the situation. In recording the discovery and attack, he observed, "This is what is expected. Unless the rarest thing does actually happen, it is impossible to proceed without being sighted. Therefore, the operation continued as planned."[23]

When Reid landed his PBY on Midway that evening after some fourteen hours in the air and with a bare minimum of fuel in his tank, most of Squadron VP-44 was on hand to give him a rousing welcome and congratulations. Then Commander Massie Hughes, head of the reconnaissance group; Reid's Squadron Commander, Lieutenant Commander Robert Brixner; and the squadron operations officer, Lieutenant Don Gumz, bore him off for a debriefing.[24]

Swan was just gathering up his gear and leaving the PBY when one of his squadron officers yelled, "Hey, Swan, hurry over to the flight shack, you're scheduled to go out on a torpedo attack." The navigator was a good and conscientious officer, but enough was enough. He protested vigorously that he had just landed, so the officer checked with flight scheduling and determined that Swan would not have to fly again that night.[25]

Ramsey would not have accepted Swan or any other member of that particular crew for the night attack he was whipping up, because he wanted men in as fresh a physical condition as possible. It so happened that following the unfruitful B-17 strike, Simard and Ramsey came up with a suggestion: Why not equip a few PBYs with torpedoes and send them out against the Japanese transports on a night attack? On its face, the idea came straight out of a comic strip. The slow, vulnerable Catalinas had no torpedo rack, the available crews were untrained in dropping torpedoes, and most of them were dead tired. Moreover, this particular notion had never been put in motion before.

But Simard and Ramsey were willing to try anything once. The latter had no dearth of volunteers, but it is eloquent of the personnel situation on Midway that the four crews he scraped together, picking those who appeared least exhausted, had landed on Midway from Pearl Harbor that very afternoon. The only exception was his flight commander, Lieutenant W. L. "Red" Richards, executive officer of VP-44.

At about 2000, Richards and the three other pilots received a briefing of what to expect in the way of a target, with priorities given as aircraft carriers, battleships, and transports, in that order. Torpedoes secured under their wings by some mechanical witchcraft, the Catalinas lumbered off into the night at 2115. All were radar equipped, essential for this mission in darkness.[26]

They soon ran into bad weather. In Richards's words, "What had begun as a night merely as black as the inside of a coal mine, got really dark."[27] Ensign Allan Rothenburg, piloting one of the PBYs, lost contact with his comrades around midnight. He pluckily continued toward the target on his own, twice running into ineffective antiaircraft fire. However, he could not find the enemy, so when half his gasoline had been consumed, he gave up the hunt and headed back. He jettisoned his torpedoes before landing.[28]

The other Catalinas broke into clear weather as they neared the target, which appeared to be ten or twelve large ships in two columns, "steaming along as unconcerned as geese." Richards signaled for the attack "at precisely one-thirty A.M."[29]

Ensign G. D. "Dagwood" Propst, piloting the Number Three plane, had become separated from the formation. However, by maintaining course and speed he reached the Transport Group. Swinging out in a wide spiral, he approached into the moon path and picked what looked to him like the largest ship in the convoy, the second one from the end of the column, as the best target for his first torpedo. He dropped the missile from fifty feet, claiming a hit on a transport. "As we swung away," he recalled, "the sky began to light up like Coney Island on the Fourth of July. The enemy's antiaircraft fire had opened up." Propst dodged the antiaircraft as well as machine-gun fire, and avoided a single Japanese plane, evidently "a shipboard fighter," and escaped into the clouds.[30]

Richards flew up the moon path, selecting a ship which "presented the largest silhouette and had been reported as possibly being a carrier." Now that he was almost on it, he could see it was "a large transport or cargo ship of about 7,000 tons." Richards launched his torpedo from 100 feet, and later claimed a hit "Right on the button!" As he climbed over the target's stern, two crewmen in the waist of his plane reported "a huge explosion and heavy smoke." Neither antiaircraft nor aircraft challenged Richards as he headed toward the rendezvous point.[31]

Lieutenant (j.g.) Douglas C. Davis was not so fortunate. He made two runs over his intended victim, seeking a perfect launch position, and as he loosed his torpedo every ship in the area sprayed him with machine-gun fire. Davis's port waist gunner strafed the target ship's deck with about sixty rounds from his machine gun. With "several holes in the bow, a damaged bomb sight, and several scattered holes in the hull, wing, and tail surface" of his aircraft, Davis tried to pay the Tanaka Force a return visit to assess damage, but heavy antiaircraft fire drove him off.[32]

Although Richards's torpedo had exploded, in itself rather remarkable for an American torpedo of that period, Propst had scored the only hit. He rang up a strike on *Akebono Maru*, slowing the oiler and killing or wounding twenty-three men. The damage to the ship was superficial and she was able to regain her place in the formation.[33] Nevertheless, the fact that a tired ensign, untrained in dropping torpedoes and flying an aircraft never meant to carry them, was able to hit anything smaller than the Pacific was a fantastic example of skill, or luck, or both.

Abortive as these United States attacks were, they were highly significant as revealing that the Americans knew a Japanese fleet was in the neighborhood and headed for Midway. Battle had been joined. The Mobile Force was the spearhead of the whole massive attack plan, and its Commander in Chief should have received every scrap of information available. Yet just how much Nagumo knew about these developments remains a question. Certainly his own meticulously detailed listing of messages dispatched and received reveals no notice from either Yamamoto's Main Body or the Tanaka Force concerning the B-17 attack or the Catalina torpedo strike. According to Kusaka, Nagumo's staff knew about the PBY sighting. "But we were firmly convinced that the task force had not yet been found by the enemy. We were even so optimistic as to think that the enemy might be rather possessed by the transport ship party."[34] With that attitude, perhaps more information would have made little difference to the Mobile Force.

CHAPTER 20

"This Was to Be the Day of Days"

The blare of loudspeakers waking the air crewmen, the cough of starting engines, and the bellow of motors warming up penetrated *Akagi*'s sick bay and roused Genda at approximately 0245 on June 4.* He was still weak and feverish, but no germ could keep Minoru Genda below decks while the roar of aircraft sang in his ears and the excitement of battle burned in his heart. He scrambled into uniform and made his way to the bridge.

Nagumo's kindly face beamed a welcome and he flung a fatherly arm around Genda's shoulders. "How are you feeling?" he asked.

"I am very sorry, sir, to have been absent so long," replied Genda. "I have a slight temperature but am feeling much better now," he declared, although the glitter of his eyes revealed that he was still more ill than he admitted.

His appearance boosted the already high morale of *Akagi*'s officers and crew, for his place in their regard was unique, and it did their hearts good to see him where he belonged, at Nagumo's side on the flagship's bridge.[1]

Shortly after Genda arose, *Akagi*'s sick bay disgorged another patient. Fuchida found himself unable to lie abed while the men he should have been leading took off for battle. At least, he could see them off and give them his prayerful good wishes in person. So, although a major operation was only a week behind him, and the day before he had left his bed for the first time, Fuchida cautiously levered himself up. He found his door secured, for already *Akagi*'s doors, portholes, and manholes were fastened in preparation for battle. But each door contained a manhole which could be cranked open in emergency.[2]

---

*From this point, all times given are local Midway time.

Fuchida gripped the handle and began to turn it, but *Akagi*'s escape hatches were not exactly flimsy and Fuchida was a very weak man. It required at least a full minute to force the manhole open, and several times faintness swam over him. But finally the cover opened enough to let him squeeze through. Then he had to close the door to maintain the ship's watertight security.

Looking around, Fuchida discovered himself to be in a cul-de-sac, for the gangway, too, was sealed off. He could only ascend to the cabin area by climbing a small ladder and, perched on that insecure foothold, force open another hatch. Along with his precarious base of operations and physical weakness, Fuchida was in a dither of impatience lest his buddies take off before he could reach the flight deck, and it seemed to take him a lifetime before he could crawl through this second manhole. Yet he had only just begun his struggle, for all told, he had to open and close ten escape doors to reach his cabin. His success was a remarkable display of mind over matter. At last, as weak and wet as a newborn kitten, he stumbled into his cabin, where he rested long enough to quiet his quivering muscles. Then he donned his uniform and proceeded to the flight control post.[3]

The sky was still dark, an occasional star winking through high clouds. It gave promise of being a perfect day for the Nagumo force's operations—clear enough for good visibility, yet with sufficient overcast to form a protective cover, and the sea beautifully calm for launching aircraft. But seeing the sturdy Fuchida too feeble to stand and the cool-headed Genda flushed with fever gave Kusaka a momentary sense of a strange isolation.[4]

Fuchida inquired of his friend, Lieutenant Izumi Furukawa, about aerial reconnaissance arrangements. He was slightly uneasy to learn that the search aircraft had not yet taken off, and would not do so until the same time as the launching of the first attack wave.[5] Twice during the Indian Ocean campaign, such single-phase search systems had sighted enemy surface units while the striking force was away from the carriers, causing some worry about the safety of the latter. So Fuchida asked his comrades what the plan was in case the search planes again spotted a hostile fleet while the Japanese attack was under way.

Murata assured him that he need not worry. After the first wave had gone, the second wave, consisting of his own torpedo bombers, Itaya's Zeros, and Lieutenant Commander Takashige Egusa's dive bombers, would be available to tackle any enemy surface force the scouts might discover. Fuchida brightened. This was the Nagumo force's first team which was being held in reserve, and in his opinion nowhere in the entire Japanese Navy could be found their superior in experience or ability. They would have the situation well in hand if any United States ships appeared. His momentary qualms drowned in a surge of his native optimism, and Fuchida expressed his hope "that the enemy fleet does come out so we can destroy it."[6]

Then Furukawa went to the map board and explained to Fuchida exactly what searches were scheduled.[7] If the reader will visualize a Japanese sandalwood fan, made up of seven segments, the connecting ribbon broken so that the pieces fall away from each other instead of overlapping, he will see in essence the chart which Fuchida was watching with such interest.* These imaginary fan spokes radiated from the Mobile Force, and comprised seven individual areas of search, six of which extended for 300 miles over the Pacific, then made a sixty-mile dogleg, and returned to the mother ship.

The Number One segment originated with *Akagi*, which would send a Type 97 ship-based attack plane on a 181° line due south. A similar mission from *Kaga*, flying at 158°, comprised the Number Two section. Numbers Three and Four were Type 0 float reconnaissance craft taking off from *Tone* at 123° and 100° respectively. *Chikuma* would cover Number Five and Six areas, with similar aircraft speeding outward at 77° and 54°, while the final section, covering only 150 miles with a forty-mile dogleg, came from *Haruna*, whose smaller Type 95 float reconnaissance plane was not able to cover a full 300 miles. This aircraft would fly at 31°, which would take the pilot only slightly east of due north, an area where the chances of running into an American surface force obviously were exceedingly slim.[8]

As Fuchida listened to Furakawa's explanation, a little of his first displeasure returned. This type of reconnaissance was simply not sufficient for a truly efficient job, being little more than a token offering to the gods of chance. In the first place, as the term "single-phase" indicates, the reconnaissance would be a one-shot operation. Anything not sighted on the first attempt would remain undiscovered.[9]

Of course, Nagumo had excellent reasons, in the context of the

---

*See illustration on page 180.

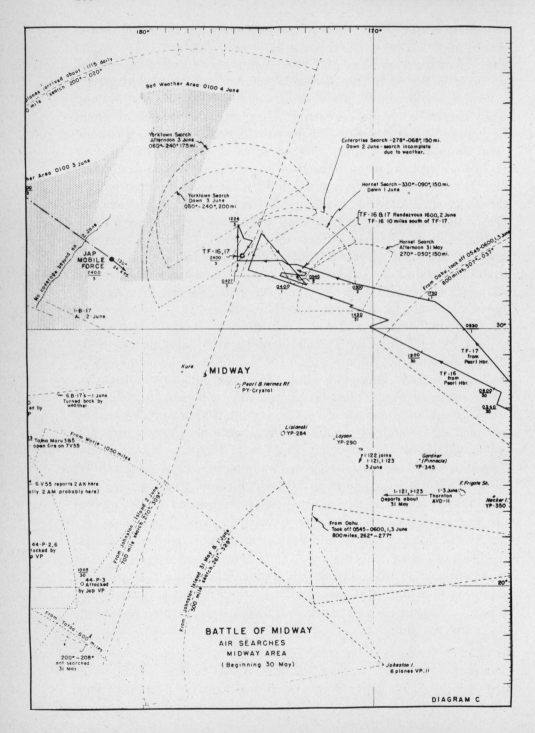

BATTLE OF MIDWAY
AIR SEARCHES
MIDWAY AREA
(Beginning 30 May)

DIAGRAM C

time and his area of knowledge, for establishing this particular search pattern and for starting it off at this precise time. First of all, his aircraft did not yet have radar and had to rely on human vision for their sightings. So Nagumo was caught in a nutcracker, held securely between two immutable factors—the distance capability of his aircraft and the sun itself, which, although the symbolic patroness of Japan, insisted upon rising and setting with distressing neutrality.

A two-phase search, which would secure the greatest possible visibility in the area where an American fleet was most likely to be found, would have to be launched in the wee small hours, so that the first portion of the outward flight—presumably the least dangerous—could be covered in darkness. This first search arc would reach its dogleg as closely as possible to dawn, then return to the carriers. About an hour after the first takeoff, the second reconnaissance flights would be initiated and cover the same area almost entirely in early daylight. Nagumo had enough pilots trained in night flying to establish this system, but obviously twice as many aircraft would have to be committed to reconnaissance.

Before and in the early days of the Pacific war, Japanese naval strategists were obsessed with the offensive. They were most averse to devoting time, thought, training, and matériel to reconnaissance, which they considered fundamentally a defensive concept.[10]

Kusaka planned the air search pattern now being readied for take-off, and in later days blamed himself harshly for failing to institute a double reconnaissance. ". . . I neglected the scouting," he admitted, "trying to save more planes for the offense." This was all the more strange because Kusaka realized the importance of scouting. When he first entered naval aviation in the late 1920s, he had selected for his study the theme, "On detection of the enemy conditions by airplane." And he had been "the originator of various methods of enemy scouting."[11]

Ten percent was the absolute maximum of total strength the Japanese navy would permit to be used for aerial reconnaissance. Naval aviators received no specialized training in search techniques, the subject being presented as a routine course only. Nor did such a thing as a carrier-borne search aircraft exist. When such a mission became necessary, bombers were modified, as in the case of the Number One and Number Two flights from *Akagi* and *Kaga* respectively. This failure to appreciate and utilize aerial reconnaissance handicapped the Nagumo force in every action from Pearl Harbor onward.

An unfortunate experience in the Indian Ocean campaign had also prejudiced Nagumo and his staff against devoting one aircraft more than absolutely necessary to reconnaissance. At that time, the search planes frequently lost their bearings, and the carriers had to break radio silence to bring them home, which tipped off the fleet position to the enemy.[12]

Nagumo might have moved his takeoff time for the search arc back by half an hour, in which case, by 0430, the pilot of *Chikuma's* Number Five aircraft would have had Fletcher's Task Force Seventeen about sixty-five miles ahead of him in a direct flight line, and could hardly have missed it unless the ceiling was opaque. However, an earlier start would have meant that the Mobile Force was just that much farther to the west, away from Midway, and the search arc would barely have reached to the island. It is important to remember that, according to Japanese planning, the United States fleet was supposed to be forming, if at all, well to the east of Midway, as demonstrated by the submarine line lurking hopefully along approximately 165°E. Neither Nagumo nor any of his staff had any real anticipation of finding an enemy force beyond that longitude.[13]

All in all, no doubt the arrangement which Fuchida found inadequate was quite satisfactory to his admiral, for the latter was still aglow with optimism and confidence, as his Estimate of the Situation clearly reveals:

> a. Although the enemy lacks the will to fight, it is likely that he will counter attack if our occupation operations progress satisfactorily.
>
> b. The enemy conducts air reconnaissance mainly to the West and to the South but does not maintain a strict vigil to the Northwest or to the North.
>
> c. The enemy's patrol radius is about 500 miles.
>
> d. The enemy is not aware of our plans. . . .
>
> e. It is not believed that the enemy has any powerful unit, with carriers as its nucleus, in the vicinity.
>
> f. After attacking Midway by air and destroying the enemy's shore based air strength to facilitate our landing operations, we should still be able to destroy any enemy task force which may choose to counter attack.

g. The enemy's attempt to counter attack with use of shore based aircraft could be neutralized by our cover fighters and AA fire.[14]

This estimate, which was almost 100 percent wrong, was no more than a rehash of the staff guesswork upon which the early Midway planning was based. Throughout the battle, and when he wrote his post-operation report, Nagumo believed firmly that the Mobile Force was "not discovered until early in the morning of the 5th [Japan time] at the earliest."[15]

At precisely 0400 *Akagi*'s loudspeakers ordered "Aviators, assemble!" and the pilots crowded to the briefing room for their final instructions.[16] At that exact moment, six Marine F4F fighter aircraft took off from Midway under Captain John F. Carey, to form a cover patrol. As the little planes circled aloft, eleven Catalinas lifted from the lagoon to establish the day's air picket line. They would go only to a radius of 425 miles instead of their usual 700, because Ramsey knew that his reconnaissance capability was limited. Then, too, if the Japanese were still on schedule—and neither Ramsey, Simard, nor Shannon had reason to think otherwise—their vessels should be well within the narrower circle by this time. The PBYs were to concentrate on finding the Japanese carrier force. Hard on the tails of the Catalinas came sixteen B-17s, their crews hopeful of finding and bombing the Japanese troop transports known to be approaching from the west.[17]

About the same time, their briefing over, *Akagi*'s pilots burst back on deck, running toward their waiting aircraft. "All hands to launching stations!" shouted the air officer, Commander Shogo Masuda. "Start engines!" Then he requested Captain Aoki to head the carrier full into the wind and increase speed for a velocity of 19.2 mph.[18]

As the exhausts spurted flame and the engines hummed their war song, Lieutenant Takehiko Chihaya, a much-esteemed officer and a Pearl Harbor veteran, paused to say good-bye to Fuchida, who wished him the best of luck and watched wistfully as Chihaya scrambled down the ladder and into his lead dive bomber near the base of the bridge.[19]

Floodlights sprang up, bathing the flight deck in radiance, as an orderly called out, "All planes ready, sir." Masuda relayed the information to Aoki, who ordered, "Commence launching." Masuda's green signal lamp swung in a large circle, and at 0430 the first Zero rose, sped on by loud cheers, a great brandishing of caps and waving of hands. Eight more Zeros followed, then the dive bombers. Chihaya left his canopy open, and as he led his flight upward he waved goodbye to those left behind.[20]

Some 4,000 meters to port of *Akagi*, flashes of light showed that *Hiryu* was also launching her aircraft. Within fifteen minutes, the entire first attack wave of 108 planes was airborne, circled to gain formation, and headed off toward Midway.[21]

The lead spot which Fuchida had hoped and expected to occupy fell to Lieutenant Joichi Tomonaga, chief of *Hiryu*'s Air Unit. He had joined *Hiryu* just before the sortie from the homeland, and had yet to strike a blow in the Pacific naval war. However, he was a veteran of the China skies, where he had gained a reputation of being, as Genda expressed it, "a brave and capable leader, though he was a little bit passionate."[22] As Tomonaga flew off, personally leading not only the formation but the thirty-six level bombers from *Hiryu* and *Soryu*, no one doubted that the attack unit was in good hands. Behind and to his left came Lieutenant Shoichi Ogawa from *Kaga*, with thirty-six dive bombers. Ogawa had participated in every *Kaga* engagement, including Pearl Harbor, and was famed throughout the Navy for his skill and bravery.

Each carrier contributed nine Zeros as fighter escort, with Lieutenant Masaharu Suganami of *Soryu* in the lead. He was another Pearl Harbor pilot, eager and scrappy. Along with the Zeros shepherding the bombers to the target, another nine took off from *Kaga* as cover for the Nagumo force, and another nine stood by for action on *Akagi*'s flight deck.[23] Eighteen fighter planes to cover twenty-one vessels was shingling the roof with tissue paper, another indication of the cocksureness with which the Japanese approached the battle of Midway, and how little they anticipated an attack on their carrier force.

Among the aircraft soaring aloft were the three reconnaissance planes from *Akagi*, *Kaga*, and *Haruna*, right on the dot of 0430.[24] And as perfectly timed as if the antagonists had synchronized their watches, about 215 miles eastward, Fletcher launched ten SBDs from *Yorktown* to cover an arc to the north reaching 100 miles, just in case the Japanese had scented his task force. The day which broke seven minutes later was a beautiful one, almost too beautiful, with high visibility. The temperature was just right, hovering around 70°, with a soft breeze from the southeast, much too gentle for easy plane launching.[25]

As Fletcher's SBDs roared off, at 0435 *Chikuma* launched her search aircraft to cover the Number Five segment, and three minutes later her Number Six plane. At 0442 *Tone* sent the Number Three aircraft aloft.[26] Delays of five, eight and twelve minutes were bad enough, but *Tone*'s Number Four plane was still nowhere to be seen. The reason for this tardiness remains obscure to this day.

No one was more puzzled than Lieutenant Makoto Kuroda, *Chikuma*'s air officer. At the appointed time, the cruiser's "fliers were ready beside their planes, so that they might leave immediately upon receipt of the departure order. Since the order was not forthcoming after a long wait, I went up to the bridge to urge the skipper to do so." On *Tone*, too, the pilots were awaiting the notice to take off, and "came to the radio room to get reports coming in as soon as possible."[27]

Fuchida understood that *Chikuma*'s Number Six plane had a bit of engine trouble, and that *Tone*'s Number Four aircraft, which did not take the air until 0500, owed its delay to a defective catapult.[28] But Captain Keizo Komura, *Chikuma*'s skipper, disagreed. "I cannot see why the departure of the Eighth Cruiser Division planes was delayed," he testified in connection with an investigation conducted by the New Japanese Navy Defense Agency's Historical Department. "I thought that our planes were dispatched earlier than those of *Tone* as Kuroda urged." This, of course, was true enough. "I don't have the slightest recollection about reasons why their departure was delayed," he added. Nor did Ishikawa, the assistant communications officer of *Tone*, in whose radio room the pilots awaited takeoff signals. "There was no fact that catapults and others had troubles to delay their departures," he insisted. Nor, according to the recollections of Kusaka, Genda and his assistant, Lieutenant Commander Chuichi Yoshioka, did any signals pass from *Akagi* to *Tone*, flagship of the Eighth Cruiser Division, to account for the delay.[29]

Indeed, the whole air search setup was most unsatisfactory. Genda considered the "incomplete search plan" to be "the initial cause for the Midway defeat." As he stated, "It has to be admitted that the planning of the air searching itself was slipshod. It should have been planned more mathematically." He explained further, "This plan was the same one as employed at Pearl Harbor and the Indian Ocean operations, but, in retrospect, it had to be admitted that this plan involved a defect of leaving an uncovered space in the search area, especially when an enemy force moved across or slant-wise the planned search arc. The search plan should have been made more mathematically and precisely."[30]

Whatever the cause, the effect was to prove a serious matter for the Mobile Force. Had the search lines been in place on time, *Chikuma*'s Number Five plane would have flown almost directly over Task Force Seventeen, while *Tone*'s Number Four aircraft would have reached the 300 mile point at 0650, just six minutes before Spruance began to launch his aircraft.[31]

To the north, Yamamoto's Main Fleet staff was up and about almost as early as Nagumo's fliers, for no one wanted to miss any action. Watanabe was on *Yamato*'s bridge, standing the daybreak watch, "full of high spirits and anticipation." He remembered vividly that "all of Yamamoto's staff got up early and gathered in the Operations room of *Yamato*, for this was to be the day of days. Here they eagerly awaited radio reports from Nagumo's force."

Among the heavy spate of messages crackling in came the word of the attack on the Midway Occupation Force, but attention was focused on the carriers. Then, according to Watanabe, "We received a report that Nagumo's attack force accompanied by fighters had begun to launch their attack on Midway."[32]

CHAPTER 21

"Hawks at Angels Twelve"

Tick, tock . . . wait and watch . . . wait and watch . . . tick, tock . . .

Midway waited. Midway watched.

In the air, out of sight but not out of mind, two six-plane fighter groups covered the patrol of the eleven Catalinas, and Sweeney's B-17s sped on toward the Tanaka Force. On the ground, the antiaircraft guns of Shannon's Sixth Marine Defense Battalion were manned and ready for action while eight PT boats poised in their docks, equally eager to rescue survivors or train their machine guns on the attackers. Four Army B-26 bombers and VT-8 Detachment's six Navy TBF torpedo planes awaited the summons to action. The Marine bombing squadron, VMSB-241, stood by with its eleven SB2U-3 Vindicators and sixteen SBD-2 Devastators.[1]

The fighter pilots of VMF-221, on whom would fall the heaviest burden of the Midway defense, shared the general fidgets as the clock ticked off the minutes, indifferent to human hopes and fears. Their new skipper, Major Floyd B. "Red" Parks, formerly their second in command, had conferred in the Command Post the previous night with his predecessor McCaul and their Group Commander, Kimes, working out a plan of action.[2]

The Sand Island Command Post was typical of the dugouts in use all over Midway—a rectangular room of boards covered with paper and tar as a makeshift waterproofing, the whole built in a sand pit some four feet deep. The sand excavated from the pit, plus more if necessary, covered the roof, and over that nested a pile of the brush scraped off when the runways were built. By attack day weeds and grass had started to grow over some of the dugouts, forming a natural camouflage which from the air resembled a sand hummock.[3]

As the three Marines talked together, they bore a rather pathetic
likeness to three earnest German *Hausfrauen* making strudel, bent
on stretching their dough as thin as possible without breaking it. The
MAG-22 plan of battle was already set up. First, as soon as the radar
stations—one each on Sand and Eastern Islands—advised of the Japanese approach, they would clear the field of all aircraft able to fly.
Second, as radar reported the enemy coming closer, radio would
direct VMF-221 to intercept the invaders before they got over the
island. Third, VMSB-241 would rendezvous at a point twenty miles
out of Eastern Island on a 90° bearing and await radio instructions,
either to find and attack the enemy carriers immediately or to stalk
the Japanese aircraft home and then strike.[4]

Kimes, McCaul, and Parks now had to solve the problems of how
best to utilize the twenty-one F2A-3s and seven F4F-3s assigned to
them. One each of the cobby little fighter types must already be ruled
out because of engine trouble. This left Parks with twenty of the
fighters which the Navy called "Buffaloes" and the Marines "Brewsters," and which both unofficially designated "Flying Coffins," plus
six of the newer and better Wildcats.

After a long discussion, the men decided to split their resources
into two groups, in case the Japanese should strike from more than
one direction simultaneously. One section would contain Parks's own
first division of four Brewsters, the fourth division of the same content
under Captain Robert E. Curtin, and the fifth to comprise Carey's
six Wildcats. This gave Parks a total of fourteen aircraft. The other
ten would split into two equal parts—the second division under Captain Daniel J. Hennessy, the squadron executive officer, and the third
led by Captain Kirk Armistead. When the Marines received their
first bearing on the Japanese, these ten Brewsters would orbit at a
designated point until it was certain whether or not all the attackers
were in one group. Then Hennessy and Armistead would receive the
appropriate radio orders. Midnight was almost upon the group when
they reached this decision and threw themselves down for a few hours'
sleep.[5]

As far as possible, pilots whose planes were out of commission
manned the necessary ground positions. Second Lieutenant J. C.
Musselman, Jr., was one of those who found himself grounded, and
took over as VMF-221 Squadron Duty Officer. With him in the Ready
Tent was Second Lieutenant H. Phillips, pilot of the disabled F4F-

3. Phillips stood by the telephone, leaving Musselman free to go where needed.[6] Over at the VMSB-241 Headquarters, planeless Second Lieutenant Elmer P. Thompson relieved the scheduled duty officer so the latter could man his own aircraft.[7]

In the radio shack, the operators still worried lest the Japanese jam the set, although they had done their level best to make this impossible. On the assumption that the Japanese knew the frequency which had been in use for some time, the station had been shifting between frequencies for the past four or five days. They had set up four or five alternates, and if radio silence had to be violated, they immediately shifted to another frequency which had not been used in that area. Nor did they use the so-called "battle frequency" except in grave emergency.

Just to make things more difficult for the Japanese, the radiomen shuffled the logs covering the previous two months. At odd intervals during the day, an operator on duty would read to the airways a random passage or two from the log, so that everything would appear to be running along as usual. These measures seemed to pay off, for throughout the day the Japanese made no attempt to jam the radio. The station was thus free to direct the fighters in the air from an improvised fighter director in the Command Post, relying upon information from radar and the patrol planes.[8]

The radar shack was ready for business, although both the Sand Island and Eastern Island instruments were obsolescent. The plotting device consisted of a table in the Command Post, marked off in 360° to a distance of 150 miles, with an arm marked in nautical miles pivoting from the center. As the radar tracked the distance and bearing of a blip, the plotter swung the arm to the bearing and thus automatically figured the position.[9]

When 0500 came and passed without a sign of the uninvited guests, Midway became restive and a ripple of activity swept across its defenders. Ramsey sent the remaining B-17, one of its engines still out, back to Pearl Harbor. Aircraft engines which had been warming up since about 0430 were ordered shut off and the fuel tanks topped, while the pilots returned to their flight shacks.[10]

A few minutes later Kimes called down the patrol fighters. For some reason, the radios of one division—Captain Francis P. McCarthy and Second Lieutenant Roy A. Corry, Jr.—failed to receive this message, so these two continued to prowl around the sky independently. Then, as the Wildcats of Carey's division taxied to their revetments for refueling, the plane piloted by Carey's wingman, Second Lieutenant Walter W. Swansberger, slid off the wooden tracks and buried its landing gear in the sand. All of a sudden, Carey had three Wildcats instead of six.[11]

Midway subsided into an uneasy calm, scarcely ruffled by a report at 0520 from Catalina Number 4V58 of sighting an unidentified plane. This was destined to be an unforgettable morning for the pilot of this particular aircraft, Lieutenant Howard P. Ady, and his co-pilot, Lieutenant (j.g.) Maurice "Snuffy" Smith. Destiny had given them the patrol arc leading directly to Nagumo's carriers, and the scout had probably spotted one of the Japanese search planes.[12]

Ten minutes later, Midway received another radio from Ady, this time reporting a "carrier bearing 320, distance 180."[13] Now Midway began to crackle with action. The telephone shrilled in Thompson's Scout Ready Room with orders to get all engines started, and the duty officer sent off the squadron truck to round up all pilots.[14] As the same alert and orders reached all aircrews—Army, Navy and Marines—the Sixth Defense Battalion ordered its antiaircraft groups: "Open fire on all planes not identified as friendly."[15]

At 0545, while crews manned their aircraft, radios on and engines warm, what Nimitz termed "the most important contact of the battle" occurred.[16] Lieutenant (j.g.) William A. Chase (Flight 3V58) was scouting in a sector adjacent to Ady's when his observer, Ensign W. C. Corbell, sighted two groups of forty-five planes moving in. Evidently the two scouts were so excited and so sure that in this case speed overrode secrecy that they did not stop to encode. Chase dispatched the word in plain English: "Many planes heading Midway bearing 320 degrees, distance 150."[17]

Meanwhile, weaving in and out of rain squalls in the area, Ady turned his Catalina around. There, through a break in the clouds, he saw an awe-inspiring sight, which gave him the sensation of "watching a curtain rise on the biggest show in our lives."[18] Below him was spread out, not all, but enough of the Nagumo Force to make the eyes of two young fliers pop. At 0552 Chase reported his sighting: "Two carriers and main body ships, carriers in front, course 135, speed 35."[19] Even as he did so, *Tone* spotted what was probably his plane: "One enemy flying boat 45 degrees to port, distance 32 kilometers, at high elevation." Fortunately for Chase and Corbell, the Japanese lost the plane in a squall.[20]

One minute after Chase's transmission, the Sand Island radar tower picked up and relayed to Battalion Headquarters, "Few planes 93 miles, 310 degrees. Altitude 11,000 feet." The planes were not exactly "few," and within minutes the report was changed to "many."[21] In any case, within minutes the air raid alarm was wailing, and at the same time, realizing that the pilots probably could not hear the central alarm over the roar of their turning engines, Kimes sent out the Command Post pick-up truck as a modern Paul Revere, its portable siren shrieking.[22]

Parks's first division shot aloft, Curtin's fourth division right after him. In actual practice, the carefully laid plans of the previous night did not work out. Parks led six Brewsters, not four as planned, while Curtin and his wingman, Second Lieutenant Darrel D. Irwin, operated as a division in themselves. Carey followed with the remains of his Wildcat unit, Captain Marion E. Carl with Second Lieutenant Clayton M. Canfield on his wing. As they began to climb, Carl noticed that he was not gaining altitude as rapidly as he should, and motioned Canfield to move up in support of Carey.[23]

The Wildcats were barely out of sight of Midway when their strays, McCarthy and Corry, rather plaintively radioed that they were short of fuel and could they come in? McCaul told them attack was almost upon them, to land in a hurry, refuel, and get back up on the double.[24]

Meanwhile Armistead had led his group of six F2As skyward to orbit until given his instructions.[25] By this time, the radar pickups, which tracked the Japanese quite well, revealed clearly that, as Kimes recalled, "The enemy's attack was the simplest they could have made for us as far as our radar equipment was concerned. It was well up, around eleven or twelve thousand feet, which gave the large radar on sand [sic] Island . . . an opportunity to pick them up well. They were in one group and they came straight in to the objective."[26] Midway therefore ordered Armistead and Hennessy to vector 320°, which would enable them to support their comrades.[27]

Carey's three Wildcats made the initial contact with the incoming Japanese. Flying high and with a sharp eye out, Carey spied them first. At precisely 0612 he seized his transmitter and sang out: "Tally ho! Hawks at Angels Twelve!" These words told the American fighter pilots as well as the Midway station that he had seen bombers at

12,000 feet.[28] These Japanese planes probably were the high-level bombers from *Hiryu* and *Soryu*. Originally eighteen left the carriers, but one had engine trouble about halfway to Midway and had to return to the mother ship. According to Nagumo, this group was "engaged by enemy F4Fs for 15 minutes about 40 miles short of Midway" at 0616.[29]

Carey saw that the fighters were not preceding the Aichi's in the formation, as might be expected, but were slightly behind and above them. This gave Carey the chance for a quick crack at the bombers before the Zeros could catch up with him. Turning his Wildcat in a smooth roll and screaming down to gain speed, Carey caught a lead plane squarely in his gunsight. A bullet cracked his own windshield, but he pressed his attack and saw his quarry explode in front of him.

Carey swept through the Vee, headed upward and sent his fighter into a tight, skidding turn toward the end of the formation. As he sped back, a rear seat gunner in one of the bombers raked the Wildcat and smashed steel into both of Carey's legs.[30]

Canfield was with Carey all the way, concentrating on the Number Three plane of the Number Two section "until it exploded and went down in flames." In the middle of his run he saw a column of Japanese fighters diving down from the left. To lose the Zeros, Canfield headed for a large cloud about five miles away, flew around the cloud and looked back. A large trail of smoke led his eyes to the Japanese bomber burning on the ocean, but no enemy fighters were in sight, so he rejoined Carey who was now flying in the general direction of Midway "on an unsteady course."[31]

Carey was in severe pain from his wounded legs, which could not work the rudder properly. Taking over the lead, Canfield led his stricken chief homeward, hiding along the way in the cloud cover. Twice Carey nearly passed out with the agony from his shattered legs, but by dogged will power kept on course. Canfield landed first, his gear collapsing as he did so. As soon as the plane stopped sliding, he jumped out of it and into a trench just ahead of the Japanese attack. Carey was right behind him, but as he landed, he felt himself lose control of the plane. Both tires were punctured and his legs had no strength to push the brakes. The Wildcat slithered off the runway and crashed into a revetment. Two men leaped to his aid, pulled him out of the plane and behind the revetment. They had no sooner reached this slight protection than the bombs began to fall.[32]

Meanwhile Carl fired into the Japanese formation. When he looked back to check results, he was astonished to see several Zeros on his tail. He headed straight down at full throttle, and they abandoned the chase at 3,000 feet, evidently fearing that otherwise they could not level off in time to avoid crashing into the sea. Carl climbed back to 20,000 feet, but by this time the battle had passed him by. Therefore he followed the action back to Midway. At about two miles from the base, he saw three Zeros circling at low altitude, so he went into a 45°, full-speed dive to join the party. This brought Carl astern of and inside the circle made by one of the Zeros. He gave the Japanese a burst of fire, the Zero fell off on one wing, and when Carl last saw him, he was dropping almost directly downward trailing smoke.

The two remaining Zeros were closing in on Carl, so he took cloud cover and one gave up the chase. The other kept boring in, sending a shower of bullets thudding against the Wildcat. As the Zero was gaining on him fast, Carl decided to try a little judo and use the enemy's own strength against him. Deliberately and suddenly he cut his speed, throwing the Wildcat into a skid. The Zero overshot wildly, bilked by its own superior speed, Carl blazing away as it went by. Once more Carl tried to bring down the Zero as it slid across his sights, but none of his guns would respond. Discretion now being the better part of valor, Carl escaped into a cloud and saw no more targets. He hovered at 10,000 feet until the battle was over and radio orders to land came through.[33]

Undoubtedly "Red" Parks would have been flattered and amused to know of the Japanese report that *Soryu's* eighteen horizontal bombers ran into "30 to 40 F4F-3s at a point about 20 miles from Midway."[34] VMF-221 never had more than six Wildcats in the air at one time that day. Moreover, for trained Japanese airmen to mistake the antique Brewster for the more up-to-date F4F-3 was a tribute to the skill and daring of Parks's pilots.

But unhappily the gallant major was not destined to survive the battle. Of his own first division, only one, Second Lieutenant Charles S. Hughes, lived through the day, and he never got into action. Hughes's engine began giving him trouble at 5,000 feet. By the time he reached 16,000, it was hacking so badly that he reluctantly concluded that any attempt to join in the fight would be both fruitless and suicidal. Therefore he decided to return to his revetment, hoping to correct the trouble in time to get back into battle later in the day.

He reached Midway at 0625, minutes ahead of the horizontal bombers, and scrambled out of his balky Brewster just as six Japanese
released bombs, uncomfortably close to where Hughes was trying to
disappear into the ground.[35]

Although none of Parks's first division who engaged in combat
returned to tell their story, Darrell Irwin, Curtin's wingman, saw
some of the action. At approximately twenty miles out, Irwin spotted
two divisions of Japanese bombers in a large Vee formation, each
containing seven to nine planes.[36] These were almost certainly *Soryu*'s
level bombers, led by Lieutenant Heijiro Abe.[37] Ahead of Curtin and
Irwin sped Parks's five Brewsters. The lieutenant saw this group make
an overhead approach, then, as he sadly reported later, "never again
saw Captain Curtin or any of the first division." During his own pull-
out, Irwin noted a bomber in flames, presumably bagged by someone
in the first group. With the inevitable Zero at his back, Irwin climbed
to about 16,500 feet and tried to escape his pursuer by diving, but
the Japanese followed him and shot away most of his left aileron.

As he no longer could maneuver well enough for combat, he sped
off toward Midway. The whole trip back, the tenacious Zero, with
another one joining to help him out, continued to make passes at
Irwin, each time going by and then into steep wing-covers for another
run. "Their gunnery was very good," Irwin reported later with com-
mendable objectivity, "and I doubt if on any run that they missed
hitting my plane." His two pursuers kept too close to permit him to
turn on them. He could only hope to shake them or lead them into
antiaircraft fire.

Several times he heard bullets smack against the armor plate on
the back of his seat. Acutely conscious that the armor extended only
shoulder high, he ducked as far down as he could. His head still in
the cockpit, and the two Japanese in hot pursuit, he landed at 0650
in the midst of the dive-bombing attack.[38]

Hennessy spearheaded the six fighters of the second division against
a formation which appeared to Captain Phillip R. White to be three
Vee's of eight planes each. After his first pass, White found a Zero
trailing him, but a violent dive shook it off. Sweeping back to about
1,000 feet, White received a radio transmission that an enemy plane
was leaving the area on a heading of 310°. White spotted him and
closed with a long, swift run. The little Brewster spit bullets, the
Japanese bomber wavered "and made an easy left turn into the water."

Climbing back into the battle, White saw another bomber threading its way in and out of the clouds, evidently returning to its carrier. By forcing every inch of speed from his ancient fighter, White got close enough to loose a blast at the fleeing bomber. He believed he damaged his opponent's engine, for the Aichi slowed down considerably. This loss of speed made the Japanese a sitting duck, but at this moment White discovered he was out of ammunition, so he could not finish off his prey.[39] This may have been Tomonaga himself, for at 0658 Nagumo received a radio from the attack leader: "I have been hit and have ordered each squadron to act separately."[40] White hurried back to Midway, rearmed and took off again, but before he was able to do any more damage to the invaders received the general order to land.[41]

Of the second division, only White and Captain Herbert T. Merrill survived. The latter stayed with his damaged plane so long that he suffered severe burns to his face, neck, and hands, and saved his life only by parachuting into the lagoon.[42] Having seen so many of his friends perish, White was particularly scathing in his comments on the Brewster. "The F2A-3 is *not* a combat aeroplane," he reported. "The Japanese Zero Fighter can run circles around the F2A-3 . . .

"It is my belief that any commander that orders pilots out for combat in a F2A-3 should consider the pilot as lost before leaving the ground . . ."[43]

Armistead's third division had somewhat better luck. As soon as the leader heard Carey's "Tally-ho!" Armistead started to climb, and sighted the enemy droning along at 14,000 feet, about two miles to his right, between five and seven miles out. Hoping to get above and ahead of the Japanese and come down on them out of the sun, Armistead turned to a 70° heading and continued to climb. Unable to reach his objective in time, he started his attack at 17,000 feet on a target of five Vees of from five to nine bombers each. As he saw his five fighters swing in behind him, he noted one Wildcat tagging along. This was Swansberger, his plane back in shape but too late to connect with Carey.

Armistead picked the fourth Japanese division, which consisted of five planes, and made a speedy head-on approach from a steep overhead angle. He could see his incendiary bullets travel from a point in front of the leader back through the left wing of the Vee. Glancing back, he saw two or three planes falling in flames.

As he zoomed up to 14,000 feet, three fighters in column climbed toward him. They were coming up at a very steep angle and with suspicious speed. Sure enough, when the nearest plane was some 500 feet below and behind Armistead, he realized that these were Zeros. He kicked over in a violent split S maneuver, but not before his Brewster received a heavy consignment of Japanese fire, including some twenty rounds of 7.7 ammunition in the left aileron.

Armistead continued to dive at full throttle, the damaged aileron sending him into a leftward spiral. Working frantically, he managed to pull out of it and held the aircraft level at about 500 feet. Then he headed back toward Midway, radioing for permission to land because of the damage. "Roger, wait," the station replied. Circling the area at some fifteen miles out, Armistead saw that Midway was under heavy attack, so he sought a spot up-sun. There he hovered until the strike was over and base radio called upon all fighter aircraft to land, refuel, and re-arm.[44]

Captain William C. Humberd, leader of the third division's second section, followed Armistead in his original approach, and shot down a bomber about thirty to thirty-five miles off Midway. Swinging up to the other side of the Japanese formation in high hopes of bagging a second, he heard a loud noise, and twisted about in his seat to find two Zeros following 200 yards or so astern. He promptly went into a dive, one of the Zeros shadowing him clear down to water level. There Humberd stayed at full speed until he had gained enough distance to turn on his pursuer and give it a long burst. The Zero caught fire, dived out of control and into the water.

By this time Humberd was almost forty miles from his first encounter with the Japanese. Climbing back to 10,000 feet, he found both fuel and ammunition dangerously low, so he radioed Midway for permission to land. As the field was now clear, he received an affirmative reply. Coming in, he found he had lost his hydraulic fluid and neither flaps nor landing gear would lower, so he flopped in with his emergency system. His plane swiftly repaired and replenished, he had just taken off again when the Midway radio ordered the fighters back home.[45]

Second Lieutenant Charles M. Kunz, another of Armistead's pilots, saw two Japanese of the fourth attack Vee go down in flames. He told himself they were very likely shot down by Armistead and Humberd. His own attention was fixed on the fifth Vee, the last in the group. He took a swipe at one of the bombers, saw it blossom into flame and pull out of the formation.

Kunz again swooped up on the starboard side of a bomber, beginning his second strike about 2,000 feet above the formation. He worked his way in from the side, firing frequent short bursts, and had the satisfaction of seeing another target catch fire. He noted that the Japanese pilot on the port outboard side of the Vee pulled out of formation to let the damaged plane through. Kunz had just begun to fire at this plane when a Zero pounced on him. He saw tracers stream by the cockpit and some bullets rip the wings. He tried to shake his pursuer by diving to twenty feet above the water, making sharp turns as he did so, when a glancing bullet struck him in the head.

This was the last straw. The plane was so badly shot up that Kunz knew it could not be used in another attack, so he circled the field until 0750, when he landed, very dizzy from his head wound, and hurried off to the dispensary. He too registered a dim view of his aircraft. "As for the F2A-3 . . . it should be in Miami as a training plane, rather than be used as a first line fighter," he declared.[46]

Second Lieutenant William V. Brooks, Humberd's wingman, had a particularly adventurous morning. As his group left the two Japanese planes burning, Brooks and Second Lieutenant William B. Sandoval, Armistead's wingman, swung down the right side of the bomber formation, one of them striking a plane as they did so. Two Zeros immediately jumped Brooks, who hastened toward the protection of the Sixth Battalion's guns. The antiaircraft fire did indeed drive off the two Japanese fighters, and as his Brewster had taken a hail of bullets which riddled tabs, instruments and cockpit, Brooks intended to land.

At that moment he saw two planes dog-fighting eastward, and hastened to aid a distressed buddy. As he neared the spot, he was dumbfounded when both fighters turned on him. Until that moment, the sun in his eyes blinded him to the true situation: Two Japanese had staged a sham battle to draw an American into their fire. Under the circumstances, Brooks was not at all ashamed to hurry back to Midway as fast as his engine could take him, "collecting a goodly number of bullets on the way." He shook one of his pursuers and blazed away at the other as they passed head-on. This second Zero immediately sped off northward, Brooks hoping and believing that it could not reach its carrier.

Once more Brooks circled for a landing, but as he did so, he saw two Zeros going over a Brewster. This time there was no mistake, and even though three of his guns were jammed, Marine esprit de corps sent Brooks across the island again, firing with his lone gun. But to his great unhappiness, he could not reach the scene in time to save his comrade. As the beset Brewster spun into the water, Brooks sadly returned to the island and this time he landed. Counting up the score, he discovered "72 bullet and cannon holes" in his plane and he had a slight flesh wound in his left leg.

"It is my express desire," wrote Brooks in his action report, "that Lt. Sandoval, deceased, be logged up with the bomber which one of us got in our first run."[47] Truly a knightly gesture by a courageous, loyal, and generous young man.

McCarthy and Corry, the two late-comers from the morning patrol, serviced their Wildcats in ten minutes,[48] but were not able to catch up with the rest of Carey's division. At 8,000 feet, eight Zeros pounced on the two Marines, who promptly broke formation to meet the four-to-one challenge. Corry saw McCarthy shoot down one Japanese almost immediately, only to fall in flames himself. Corry got one of his four tormentors and avoided the other three long enough to knock off a short burst at a bomber leaving the Eastern Island area, its mission already accomplished. The Aichi rolled over and crashed into the sea. By this time, Corry's fuel tanks were leaking badly and the fighters still shooting him up "very effectively," to use his own phrase. Skimming very low on the water, he managed to bring in the remains of his Wildcat safely.

Corry praised the Zero as "by far the most maneuverable plane that exists at the present time. You cannot compare them with our service type ships." He noted, however, that the enemy fighters were not invincible. "The Japanese planes seem to be very vulnerable if you are fortunate enough to bring your guns to bear," he reported.[49] The trick was to catch them.

CHAPTER 22

"There Is Need for a Second Attack"

Midway's defenders braced themselves for the ordeal. "Open fire when targets are within range," Battalion headquarters notified all groups at 0630.[1] By this time, the sky was clear, with good visibility for antiaircraft firing. All gunners on both Sand and Eastern Islands were well protected by sandbags and sand emplacements. Other personnel not manning antiaircraft guns or automatic weapons huddled in dugouts, slit trenches, and the like.[2]

Duty Officer Thompson hoped to get in a few licks himself. He and the squadron timekeeper moved a telephone from the VMSB Ready Room, as well as a gun and ammunition from an incapacitated SB2U-3, and set them up in a nearby machine-gun pit.[3] The PT boats were under way in the lagoon, their machine guns and even rifles and pistols at the alert.[4]

Perched atop the power station on Eastern Island, John Ford marveled at the "very calm," indeed "lackadaisical" air with which the defenders awaited the strike, "as though they had been living through this sort of thing all their lives."[5]

The newly installed radar on Sand Island, one of the very few that could provide height as well as range and bearing, showed that enemy bombers were still bearing down on Midway. The air battle, fierce as it was, had little appreciable effect on the Japanese bombing mission. The Marines noted with professional admiration the skill and discipline with which Tomonaga's pilots maintained formation. As a bomber was shot down, the others in his Vee regrouped and kept their course and speed.[6]

The level bombers reached Midway first, for one of their missions was to neutralize antiaircraft fire, thus clearing the way for the dive bombers and strafing Zeros. Then they would proceed to bomb the airfields and installations. *Hiryu*'s group concentrated on Sand Island. Those of *Soryu* split up, Squadron One assisting the *Hiryu* men over Sand, while Squadron Two blasted Eastern Island. But before either unit could unload its cargo of destruction, two bombers from *Hiryu* fell to "vicious AA fire," to use Nagumo's expression.[7]

To Lieutenant Thompson, the shells appeared to burst slightly behind the planes, but he saw one hit and ignite in mid-air. As Thompson snatched up his field glasses to watch, the bomber broke formation and dove straight down. No one bailed out.[8]

Many observers thought the guns had claimed the Japanese leader. But, although his bomber took a hit in the left wing fuel tank, Tomonaga returned to *Hiryu*. When he did, he told how Lieutenant Rokure Kikuchi, also of that carrier, died valiantly under antiaircraft fire. Realizing that he had drawn the death card, Kikuchi opened the canopy of his bomber, waved in farewell to his comrades, closed the canopy, and fell to his destruction.[9]

No sooner had he struck the earth than a quick-witted black steward streaked for the wreck and heaved out the pilot's body. Ramsey sped right behind him, and was searching the dead enemy's pockets for any items of interest to Intelligence when the first wave zoomed over. With all hell falling from the skies, Ramsey with Simard jumped into their shelter.[10]

The torpedo boats had a good view of the second crash. Eyewitnesses saw the bomber burst into flame and splash into the lagoon, its bomb falling separately nearby, both narrowly missing the PT boats.[11]

The level bombers concentrated heavily on Sand Island. *Hiryu*'s Squadron One scored a direct hit on fuel tanks on the northeast tip of the island, while *Soryu*'s Squadron One silenced an antiaircraft emplacement.[12] From the initial strike, however, horizontal and dive bombers hit together, and it becomes impossible to credit the damage with any degree of accuracy.

As the American fighter craft had gone all out toward the level bombers which led the Japanese formation, and then had to exercise all their ingenuity against the pestiferous Zeros, the dive bombers from *Akagi* and *Kaga* reached Midway unscathed and departed in almost the same enviable condition. Chihaya's airmen, with the mission of attacking the hangars and other air installations on Eastern Island, suffered no losses. Lieutenant Ogawa, leading the *Kaga* group as well as the dive bombers *in toto*, lost one aircraft to antiaircraft fire. Four others were hit but not disabled.[13]

Second Lieutenant Robert W. Vaupell, a pilot of VMCR-241 temporarily grounded because the engineering crew was changing the plugs of his plane at the very time the dive bombers hit Sand Island, saw antiaircraft fire strike one of them. "He continued to fly formation long after he was aflame," reported Vaupell, "and finally went into an uncontrollable spin.[14]

The strike on Eastern Island opened with an incident which no one who saw it ever forgot. "Suddenly the leading Jap plane peeled off. . . . He dove down about 100 feet from the ground, turned over on his back and proceeded leisurely flying upside down over the ramp."[15] Some claim that he thumbed his nose derisively as he sailed by.[16] A deliberate attempt to distract the defenders, a gesture of contempt for an enemy who had not shown the First Air Fleet much, or sheer bravado? Who can say? Whatever it was, for a few seconds it held the watchers too rigid with amazement to fire. Then ". . . suddenly some Marine said, 'What the Hell,' let go at him and then shot him down. He slid off into the sea."[17]

All of the bombs unloaded over Eastern Island fell to the north of Number Two runway. One hit, evidently the work of *Soryu*'s Number Two level bombing squadron, struck near the eastern end of Number One runway, at its center. One of Chihaya's dive bombers blasted a small crater some 500 yards from the eastern end of the same runway. Another dive bomber strike landed squarely in the middle of a VMF-221 rearming pit, exploding eight 100-lb. bombs and 10,000 rounds of .50 caliber ammunition and killing four maintenance men.[18]

With his director's instinct, Ford lined up with his camera on the hangar, which he assumed would be a prime target. Sure enough, a Japanese scored "a very lucky hit, he must have hit some explosives in it, the whole thing went up." Ford was "knocked . . . goofy for a bit . . . ," as shrapnel riddled his elbow and shoulder. But he got the picture, a memorable scene in his subsequent official film, "The Battle of Midway," wherein "one big chunk" of debris blasts straight toward the camera.

A young Marine bandaged Ford's wounds and counseled him earnestly, "Don't go near that Navy doctor; we will take care of you . . ."[19]

Perhaps the most serious damage to Eastern Island came at 0638 when a dive bomber demolished the power house, knocking out the installation's electricity and water distillation plant. Almost equally disruptive was the horizontal bomb which destroyed the fuel lines between the dock area and the main gas stowage. These were already in poor condition before the attack; henceforth American work parties would be busy around the clock refueling aircraft by hand from more than 3,000 drums of gas borrowed from Sand Island.[20] Ford noticed that the Japanese "didn't touch the field itself . . ." He presumed that "their idea was to land there later that day themselves."[21]

A hit on the Marine mess hall sent pots and pans winging skyward and made mincemeat of the entire normal food supply, forcing the Marines on a diet of emergency rations until after the battle.[22] Another direct hit put the Post Exchange out of business, hurtling beer cans far and wide like shrapnel. One can plugged a machine gunner in the solar plexus, knocking him *hors de combat*. "I never could take beer on an empty stomach!" he gasped when consciousness returned. Concussion from the same bomb popped open cigarette cartons and even stripped the individual packs. A white rain of cigarettes fell far and wide, to the satisfaction of the Marines who gathered them up on a finders keepers basis.[23]

Sand Island received the lion's share of Japanese attention. A direct hit, probably from a level bomber of *Hiryu*'s Number One Squadron, completely destroyed three fuel oil storage tanks. These burned for two days, the smoke making the overall damage appear to be much greater than it actually was, and interfering with the efficiency of the antiaircraft batteries.

Another bomb struck squarely on the salt water lines to the Marine area. A *Kaga* dive bomber set ablaze a seaplane hangar. A direct hit also flattened the brig, fortunately unoccupied at the time. Sundry other buildings shook under varying degrees of damage ranging from heavy to superficial, either from hits, near misses, fragments, or concussion.

The Navy dispensary, clearly marked with a large red cross on the roof, was completely demolished as a result of two direct hits and the resultant fires. Another bomb right on target squashed part of the Navy laundry, incinerating, among other things, virtually every article of clothing Ramsey possessed except the uniform on his back. The story is told that when he returned to Pearl Harbor on June 12, still wearing that same outfit, Nimitz summoned him to his office. "I understand you're crawling with—er—eagles," the admiral murmured, "so maybe you'd like these silver ones." Whereupon he showed Ramsey his recommendation for promotion to captain.[24]

Hard on the tails of the bombers swarmed the fighters, strafing everything in sight and engaging in last-minute dog-fights with the remaining Brewsters. Lieutenant Hughes saw the dive bombers coming out of the sun shortly after the level bombers passed. As he watched, two F2Fs tangled with the Japanese fighters, and one of the Americans went down. A withering screen of covering gunfire saved the second. "Both looked like they were tied to a string while the Zeroes made passes at them," Hughes stated bitterly. "I believe that our men with planes even half as good as the Zeroes would have stopped the raid completely."[25]

If the antiaircraft really bothered the Zeros, Lieutenant Irwin, who had tried to lead two of them into the guns, could not notice it. He reported later that "the Japanese had little regard for our ground antiaircraft fire, which almost always burst behind the plane fired upon." As far as Irwin could see, only one Japanese fighter fell to ground gunners. This one was strafing at about 100 feet and almost impossible to miss.[26]

Lieutenant Vaupell also spotted this hit and, according to him, the plane was even lower, at roughly twenty-five feet. This one crashed near the VMF Ready Room.[27] Lieutenant Thompson and his timekeeper, who had been shooting at the dive bombers gallantly but futilely with machine gun and rifle respectively, watched antiaircraft shells strike the Zero's gas tank and the whole plane billow into instant flame.

Thompson cleared his machine gun, which had jammed after he blazed away at about six Japanese planes. He and his good assistant fired at all aircraft which came near their machine-gun pit, "which wasn't many," he reported later, "as they didn't seem interested in any targets near us." It appeared to him that after a few strafes the enemy stayed away from the center of the field.[28]

At this moment, no one on Midway, particularly the survivors of badly stricken VMF-221, were in the mood to spare any sympathy for a Zero pilot. Up to this time, the battle had been a straightforward fight, if a lopsided one, but the manner of Major "Red" Parks's death added an element of personal bitterness. Major Warner, the Army

Air Corps liaison officer, was so choked with fury and grief that his emotions burst out of his official report, brushing aside spelling, grammar, and punctuation. "As soon as his shoot opened the Japs were at him and didn't let up even when he landed on the reef. This enemy is cold blooded in every respect of the word though I disagree with the expression that a Jap will ram his plane into another or take undo chances. Don't let anybody fool you the Jap wants to live every bit as much as we do and this was proven time and again . . ."[29]

The torpedo boat crews saw the Zero strafing Parks's parachute, and two of the little craft tried to reach the scene, but could not get over the reef. They had better luck with Captain Merrill. When he ditched near the reef, Seaman Third Class E. J. Steward dived from his boat and swam to Merrill's rescue, ignoring the heavy surf and jagged coral rocks, and helped the downed flier to safety.[30]

At 0643 Nagumo received a radio from Tomonaga: "We have completed our attack and are homeward bound."[31] Five minutes later, the Midway radar reported to Battalion headquarters, "Many enemy planes leaving on bearing 300 degrees."[32] Not until 0715, however, did Simard sound the all clear, summon home his aircraft and emerge with his staff to count up the score. "Fighters land, refuel by division, Fifth division first," Kimes radioed VMF-221. Receiving no answer, he rebroadcast the message several times, then: "All fighters land and reservice," flashed out repeatedly. "A pitifully few fighters returned in answer to this message, and it was strongly suspected that there were not more to land," Kimes reported.[33] He was all too right. Fourteen out of twenty-six pilots would never answer another roll call, and a number of others were wounded. Only two of the fighter aircraft were fit to fly again.[34]

What had they accomplished in return for this loss? For a long time, the results of the air battle and antiaircraft fire of Midway were anybody's guess, on both sides. Nagumo's official report claimed forty-one American fighters definitely shot down in this engagement with nine probables.[35] Now fifty hits out of twenty-six is pretty good shooting, one must admit. If every Marine fighter in the air looked to the enemy like two, they must have given a very respectable account of themselves. Indeed, in view of the caliber of aircraft they were flying, it is little short of a miracle that any survived, let alone inflicted any damage whatsoever on the Japanese.

As to that score, contemporary American accounts were exceedingly exuberant, running from forty to fifty Japanese planes lost in the air engagement, with ten shot down by ground fire.[36] In his narrative report, Nagumo listed a loss of six—four bombers and two Zeros—and most Japanese accounts go along with these figures. Later, under the heading "Damages Sustained," he admitted a total of eight losses. In the statistical portion of his report, Nagumo broke down his losses by carrier. These total five lost in air battle (three level bombers and two Zeros) with four lost to antiaircraft fire (two level bombers, one dive bomber, and one Zero). The record of planes downed by antiaircraft fire agrees exactly with the recollection of American eyewitnesses. In addition, Nagumo listed sixteen horizontal bombers damaged, four dive bombers, and twelve Zeros, two of the latter being so badly shot up they became inoperational after returning to their carriers.[37] Of course, these figures are not Holy Writ. For example, Nagumo listed no damaged high-level bombers from *Hiryu*, yet we know that Tomonaga was hit because he himself radioed Nagumo accordingly.[38] But Nagumo and his staff had more immediate problems on their minds than reconciling damage claims.

Simard's optimistic estimate of Japanese losses was based upon the extent of damage to Midway versus the size of the attack force as originally spotted, a mistaken count of the Japanese aircraft actually over Midway, and a hopeful assumption that the Americans shot down had done at least as well as those who returned. "Surviving pilots cannot reconcile the small number of bombs dropped with the number of enemy bombers in sight when the initial contact was made," Kimes reported in some bewilderment.[39] Something had been miscounted—aircraft, bombs, or both. Counting only those aircraft which the returning pilots actually saw go down in flames, the score is eight bombers for certain, and one probable; three sure Zeros and one probable. This gives us a much more reasonable total, not too far at variance from the official Japanese figures. While it is understandable that their fellow squadron members wanted to believe that each slain Marine pilot brought down at least one Japanese with him, it is rather more logical to believe that those skillful or lucky enough to tangle with the Zeros and survive were those who made the kills.

In any case, it was all rather futile, and Midway's fate would not have been affected had the defenders left Tomonaga's men entirely to the tender mercies of the Sixth Battalion and sent out the fighters as protection for the land-based bombers seeking Nagumo's carriers even as the Midway defenders emerged from their shelters.

Actually, Midway was in better shape than might be expected. Approximately twenty men had been killed on the ground, a remarkably small casualty list. And the runways were so little damaged that Simard could only assume that the Japanese had deliberately spared them for their own use. Camouflage, too, had been quite effective. Havoc at the installation proved, upon post-attack check-up, to be in large part repairable, and all hands went to work with a will to restore electrical connections, water and sewage lines, put out incidental fires and clear away debris.[40]

As Tomonaga coaxed his mauled bomber back to the rendezvous, he could not know exactly what the score was on Midway. He would not survive the carrier battle, so we cannot know what thoughts were his as he compared what he had seen against his mission. But obviously he was not satisfied. His raid had encountered no bombers or scouts—what Nimitz had called "the heavy stuff"—and the air strips remained in excellent shape to receive such aircraft when they returned to the island. Furthermore, Midway's guns still barked defiance. The Japanese landing party could expect a hot welcome.

Such, in essence, must have been Tomonaga's logic. A machine-gun bullet had knocked out his radio transmitter, so he wrote his recommendation on a small blackboard. This he held up so that his Number Two plane could read it and send it to Nagumo in his name.[41] It went off at 0700: "There is need for a second attack wave."[42]

CHAPTER 23

"A Complete Failure"

Midway's defenders had done their gallant if not very effective best. Now the atoll turned the ball over to the offense, with what hopes and fears who can say? Certainly no scaevola bush on Midway was any greener than Second Lieutenant A. K. Earnest, as he awaited the call to action near his TBF* on its runway at Sand Island. Only six months past his flight training, Earnest had never flown out of sight of land when his detachment of *Hornet*'s VT-8 left Pearl Harbor for Midway on June 1. These aircraft were new, well armed, and carried a 200-knot torpedo inside the body, in contrast to the older 135-knot models slung beneath the plane. Earnest knew that the desired dropping procedure was from a height of 200 feet and at a speed of 200 knots. However, as preparation for torpedoing a swift Japanese carrier, skippered by one of the most experienced, foxy captains in the Imperial Navy, Earnest had dropped a single torpedo on the Quonset Range back on the mainland.[1]

Earnest's Detachment Commander, Lieutenant Langdon K. Fieberling, had briefed his pilots on how to use the torpedoes. If only one flattop was encountered, the detachment's six TBFs would divide in half, one section under Fieberling, the other led by Ensign Oswald J. Gaynier. One section would strike to port of the target's bow, the other to starboard. In this way, no matter how skillfully the carrier might maneuver, it would head into one of them. But if the Japanese fleet held more than one flattop, each pilot would go for the target representing the best possibility, keep alert for radio or hand signals, and hold his torpedo until the last moment.[2]

These torpedo pilots could count on no fighter protection what-

---

*The TBF later became known as the "Avenger," in honor of the torpedo pilots and gunners who died at Midway.

soever. Nimitz had instructed Simard to concentrate on the Japanese carriers, leaving Midway to its own ground defenses.[3] Unfortunately, Simard did not follow these orders literally, but instead assigned all his fighters as a shield for the island. Nor could the TBF crews hope for help from their buddies at sea. According to the briefings they received at Midway, American carriers were in the area, but they were committed to the defense of Hawaii, so the outpost's own aircraft would be its sole aerial protection.[4]

Furthermore, the land-based aircraft scheduled to sally forth against Nagumo comprised an airborne version of the "Baker Street Irregulars"—Fieberling's six TBFs, four B-26s, a batch of Vindicators, and the B-17s. A coordinated attack by such a mixed force was virtually impossible owing to inherent differences in speed and altitude. They would time their strikes at the Japanese as closely as possible, but for all intents and purposes, all units would have to act as if they were nowhere within miles of each other.[5] The prospect before Midway's land-based airmen was dampening, to say the least—an unprotected, catch-as-catch-can air attack on one of the mightiest carrier forces in history, led by a sea hawk with almost as many victories as medals to his name, and each carrier wearing its own halo of the legendary Zeros.

The previous evening, strolling along the edge of the runway, Earnest came across a $2.00 bill. The United States never printed any great quantity of this denomination, so it carried the slightly sinister flavor of the exotic, and inevitably attracted superstition. American public opinion about $2.00 bills was divided roughly along the black cat line: A large majority considered them bad news, while a small but dedicated minority hailed them as good luck charms. Soon Earnest would be able to form his own ideas on the subject.[6]

Fieberling was in the air operations bunker, engaged in a last-minute conference with Kimes and McCall, when they received Chase's message that many enemy planes were headed for Midway. Scooping in his six crews, Fieberling dashed back for the TBFs. The engines were sputtering into life when a Marine orderly leaped onto the wing of Fieberling's plane, shouting, "Attack enemy carriers bearing 320°, distance 180 miles, course 135°, speed twenty-five knots!"

A few minutes after 0600, the detachment was airborne and winging outward. Earnest's turret gunner, Airman Third Class J. D. Manning, spotted the incoming Japanese flight. A passing Zero made a rather tentative swipe at him, but each aircraft passed the other so rapidly that neither had the chance to fire. Fieberling's little group leveled off at 7,000 feet over a perfect cloud coverage—thin enough to hide them but sufficiently broken to see through—with unlimited horizontal visibility.[7]

The dust had scarcely settled from Fieberling's takeoff when Captain James F. Collins, Jr., led his four Army B-26s of the Sixty-ninth Bomb Squadron aloft. For what it was worth to him, Collins could reflect that his was a historic mission, the first time that Army planes would attack with torpedoes. The payload was something less than devastating—one per aircraft fastened to the outside of the bomber's belly.[8]

Collins and Fieberling reached the target area simultaneously at approximately 0710. Earnest was fascinated by the majestic sight "spread all over" beneath him—the first fleet he had ever seen in his life.[9] The Japanese had already spotted their unwelcome visitors. *Akagi* was first, at 0705 reporting "9 enemy planes bearing 150 degrees, distance 25,000 meters . . ." She immediately assumed battle speed and headed straight for the planes, presenting the narrowest possible silhouette to their sights. Evidently the curious mixture flying above them confused the Japanese no end, for *Tone* reported "10 enemy heavy bombers" and *Chikuma* "about 10 PBYs 36 kilometers dead ahead." At 0708 *Akagi* and *Tone* opened fire, and one minute later Nagumo sent up ten fighters to tangle with the Americans. It appeared to the Japanese that at 0710 the U.S. planes "divided into two groups."[10]

Actually, Fieberling and Collins were making their independent attacks. The TBFs had opened their bombbay doors to ensure being able to drop should they have hydraulic failure; however, this cut their speed. They were clay pigeons for the Zeros, but so many Japanese fighters were swarming around by this time that they actually got in each other's way, and by a miracle the vulnerable TBFs pressed on toward the carriers. Manning got off a few bursts with his turret gun.[11]

Seconds later, hearing nothing from the turret, tunnel gunner and radioman, Airman Third Class Harold H. Ferrier glanced back to see why Manning was not firing. There at his gun slumped his friend's lifeless body, victim of a Zero's slugs. Ferrier was just eighteen years old, but he would never be a boy again. Death was no longer a theoretical phenomenon which happened only to peripheral beings in the universe of which he was the center. Death was right there in his own plane.

The next Zero pass shot up the hydraulic system and wounded Ferrier in the wrist. The second sent a bullet through his cap and knocked him unconscious.[12] Thus Earnest found himself temporarily both pilot and crew. A TBF from the second section drew alongside, its pilot gesturing, but before Earnest could figure out what his friend was trying to say, his plane took another hit and he lost control of the elevator. He was almost out of control of himself as well, for a slug struck him in the neck. The wound itself was slight, but like most head cuts, it bled horrendously and Earnest could feel the warm flow trickling down his neck.

With his elevator useless, one gunner dead, the other unconscious, and he himself bleeding like the proverbial stuck pig, Earnest knew he could not possibly hope to attack a carrier. So he headed for a cruiser off to port and dropped his lone torpedo. But he had released it much too high; none of Nagumo's cruisers reported a nearby missile at this time. Instinctively Earnest dropped his hand on the trim tab used for landing, and rolled it back. Surprisingly, it worked, and he felt the plane's nose lift to life. Gingerly he started to gain altitude, two Zeros twisting and turning around him, their bullets streaking into him from all directions. Dodging like a broken-field runner, he managed to spoil some of their runs until, to his surprise and relief, the fighters soared away, probably recalled to their ship or out of ammunition.

Earnest's maneuvers had put him beyond the Japanese fleet, so the entire enemy force lay between him and Midway. He could only pray that he and the plane would hold together until he reached home by a circuitous route. His electrical system was out; the hydraulic system had gone; he could not close the bombbay doors; the compass was in the tail, so he had no compass reading; the air speed indicator and gas gauge were both kaput. In fact, the plane's engine and Earnest himself were all that still ticked. Navigating "by guess and by God" like the sailors of old, he worked his way south, then east until he spotted a column of smoke above the clouds. Breaking through, he found Kure Island. Now he knew where he was. Better yet, Ferrier regained consciousness and moved into position. Earnest had long since given him up for dead. They touched down at Midway at 0940, ignoring a wave-off, went into a ground loop and came to a screeching halt in a billow of dust.[13]

Earnest and Ferrier were the sole survivors of VT-8's Midway Detachment. It was an inauspicious debut for the TBF, but as usual Nimitz put his finger on the problem. The fault lay not in the aircraft itself. "Although the TBF is a well armed plane," reported Nimitz, "it is obvious that it cannot go through fighter opposition without fighter protection."[14]

Meanwhile, Collins's B-26s made for the heart of the Mobile Force. Turning slightly to port, then sharply to starboard to avoid AA fire, and ignoring "several cruisers," they made for a "large carrier in the center of the fleet," obviously *Akagi*. Collins could see the TBFs going into their attack, then had all he could do to look out for himself. All ships were firing, and six Zeros dove at him at about 700 feet. Collins dove to 200, causing most of their fire to pass over him. His Number Two and Three men were not so fortunate, for their chief never saw them again.[15]

Akagi was dodging frantically, making a full turn to starboard and then to port,[16] but Collins was inside the circle and believed that if his torpedo ran true, he could not miss. He released at 800 yards, and saw his surviving teammate, Lieutenant James P. Muri, under and to port of him.[17]

Muri let fly with his torpedo at 450 yards, slightly ahead of *Akagi*; he turned into and over the carrier, thus missing most of its aircraft fire. Nonetheless, his B-26 had taken considerable punishment. "Several hundred rounds hit the ship; many of which penetrated the gas tank," he reported. He sorely regretted the lack of fixed guns. "I had several opportunities to destroy fighter planes with fixed guns," he lamented. And his only defensive fire was the tail gun, which "jammed repeatedly."[18]

One of the Japanese fighter pilots who escaped Muri's faulty tail gun may have been Lieutenant Iyozo Fujita of *Soryu*. A veteran of Pearl Harbor and the Indian Ocean, Fujita had been unhappy with his assignment to protect the carriers; he would have preferred attacking Midway. He perked up when he received a Morse code message from *Soryu* warning of enemy bombers approaching from the northwest. Fujita promptly coralled two of his nine Zeros and headed in that direction. Finding no enemy, he returned to the task force, and there received the word that the Americans were coming in from the northeast. Fujita recognized them as B-26s, and made several runs against them, but had no luck. Like Earnest, he found that the swarming Zeros interfered with each other's aim. Oddly enough, in years to come Fujita and Muri would both work for Japan Air Lines and become good friends.[19]

Collins saw one of the torpedos hit the water cleanly on what looked to him to be a direct run to the carrier.[20] However, *Akagi*'s only damage was from a strafer who severely injured two men manning the No. 3 antiaircraft gun and knocked out the gun's revolving mechanism for half an hour. Observers aboard the carrier saw one torpedo churning along to starboard and two drop to port. One of these crossed astern; the other self-exploded.[21]

The second wave torpedo pilots gathered on *Akagi*'s deck watched this action with particular interest. One of the American planes screamed head-on for *Akagi*, although the carrier was firing all her guns. "It is going to hit the bridge!" someone shouted. But it skimmed by with only a few yards to spare, its white star shining brightly against the dark blue fuselage.[22] Propped up against a parachute near the bridge, Fuchida could easily identify the plane as a B-26.[23] Clearing *Akagi*, it sped on toward *Hiryu*, then suddenly dipped sharply to port and plunged into the sea.

The *Akagi* men literally jumped for joy, but for once Murata had no cocky quip. His good-humored face serious, he stood watching the great waterspout fold downward to mark the spot where the bomber disappeared. Perhaps he sped a prayer toward this unknown enemy who, like himself, was a brave torpedoman willing to die for his country. Perhaps, too, he reflected that such might well be his own fate. The solemn moment burst in a shower of excited laughter. The danger seemed to be over and reaction brought hilarity. "This is fun!" remarked Fuchida.[24]

Collins and Muri limped back to Midway about 0915. Both B-26s would require extensive overhaul before being fit for the air again. Collins was exceedingly bitter about his firepower. Both turret guns hung-up repeatedly, one tail gun balked at the first burst, both tail guns had to be fed by hand because the motors would not pull the ammunition tracks. In fact, all of his guns were unsatisfactory. As Collins truly remarked, ". . . no one bomber is a match for a bunch of fighters and particularly so when the few guns it has won't shoot and the gunners have not had sufficient training to shoot them."[25]

Muri had much the same experience. All three of his gunners were wounded, his hydraulic system destroyed, all propeller blades damaged, his left tire shot off, and the power turret out. Both survivors, however, gave their blessing and approval to the B-26s leak-proof tanks and armor plating.[26]

Earnest did not credit himself with a hit. Collins claimed two certain strikes—one his own and one from "Number Four ship." Muri recorded an estimated result of a carrier damaged.[27] Later the Army claimed the B-26s made three torpedo strikes; the Navy more modestly contented itself with one.[28] Not to be outdone in sea stories, Nagumo claimed to have downed about nineteen American aircraft in this action. *Hiryu* alone credited herself with eight out of nine attacking planes.[29] Modesty was never one of Yamaguchi's more conspicuous characteristics.

Nagumo had scarcely received Tomonaga's message recommending a second attack on Midway when the land-based TBFs and B-26s began their strikes, almost as if underlining its meaning. Ogawa's action report radio of 0707: "Sand Island bombed, and great results obtained (0340),"[30] caused scarcely a ripple. Whatever "great results" had been obtained, United States land-based aircraft were still active, even if, judging from the sample being delivered at that very moment, they were an ineffectual lot.

Squinting upward at the B-26s, Genda observed that "they were not so skillful in the torpedo attack movement. Their attack was a complete failure." Nevertheless, true airman that he was, he believed the first order of business was to destroy these enemy planes and any others which might be aloft when they returned to Midway for a landing.[31]

Then, too, Nagumo could not forget that his principal objective of the day was to soften up Midway preparatory to an amphibious assault. These pesky American aircraft might have much better luck against lumbering troop transports than against speedy, maneuverable carriers, cruisers and destroyers. He also had to consider that "vicious antiaircraft fire" and try to knock out Midway's guns. How many of the actual defenders of Midway Tomonaga's raid had killed off Nagumo had no way of knowing, but the more of them out of the way, the better.

At this time Nagumo had no indication that a United States surface force was anywhere nearer him than Hawaiian waters. The scout planes should have reached the end of their search lines by this time, and as yet they had reported no surface contacts. Of course, they might still see something on their return trip, but this was a rather remote possibility. After all, a reconnaissance pilot was supposed to look ahead to see where he was going, not behind to see where he had been.

Therefore, Nagumo decided to go along with Tomonaga's recommendation. This meant, however, that a lot of action had to be taken care of in a hurry. For, as we have seen, *Akagi*'s and *Kaga*'s second wave planes were equipped with torpedoes against a possible enemy fleet sighting. *Hiryu* and *Soryu* were not involved, because they were to provide the dive bombers for the second group. Their torpedo bombers had gone with Tomonaga as part of his level bombing group, so a precedent had been set. Murata's men on *Akagi* and Lieutenant Ichiro Kitajima's on *Kaga* were on the flight deck, torpedoes in place, ready to go. Nagumo's decision meant that these planes must be lowered to the hangars, torpedoes removed, land bombs affixed, and raised to the flight deck again. This procedure would require almost an hour, and barely enough time remained to complete it if Nagumo wanted to be ready to catch the American planes when they returned to Midway so his pilots could clobber them after they landed.[32]

Hurriedly Genda drafted a message: "Planes in second attack wave stand by to carry out attack today. Re-equip yourselves with bombs." In his capacity as Commander in Chief, First Air Fleet, Nagumo sent this to each carrier at 0715.[33]

This was the action which caused Kuroshima and Watanabe to beat their breasts for not having explicitly included in the Mobile Force's orders that at least one-half of the aircraft were to be loaded with torpedoes at all times.* But Genda challenged the wisdom of such "an inflexible thought." As he observed, "When such was adhered, one-half of the attack force would be kept idle unless a suitable enemy target is located. A decision should be made depending upon the circumstances."[34] Kusaka, too, pointed out,

> . . . Nagumo and his staff well knew that Yamamoto's intention was to have at least one-half of the aircraft of the 1st Air Fleet prepared for attacks upon the expected enemy carrier force. In fact, they had

---

*See Chapter 4.

been kept readied till the limit. Under the circumstances where enemy land-based planes commenced their attacks upon our force and the expected enemy carrier force would not be discovered, however, it was almost intolerable for the commander at the front to keep its half strength in readiness indefinitely only for an enemy force which might not be in the area after all.

Therefore, even though the decision might be questioned in retrospect, Kusaka believed that Nagumo's decisions "were sound under the then prevailing circumstances."[35]

Nagumo has been severely criticized for this action. High in the bleachers of hindsight, the reader may well agree that this was the admiral's big mistake. Yet the authors believe, with Kusaka and Genda, that under the circumstances of the moment, Nagumo took the logical, sensible course. Tomonaga, the man on the spot, recommended a second strike; U.S. Midway-based planes proved the base was still in action; Genda, in whom Nagumo reposed so much faith, and with just cause, agreed with Nagumo's decision; the admiral's own sturdy common sense urged it. And to put the cap on, just the day before he had received a message from Tokyo: "There is no sign that our intention has been suspected by the enemy."[36]

One must see Nagumo's crucial decision in the context of the hour in which he made it on *Akagi*'s bridge. For it was a decision based in part at least on ignorance of the enemy's fleet disposition and capability. As such, it was not a command failure; it was an Intelligence failure. To reverse the old saw, what Nagumo did not know did hurt him.

CHAPTER 24

"There They Are!"

Whatever troubles, if any, may have plagued the mind of a certain Japanese reconnaissance pilot, he could not complain that his morning had been dull. First, his cruiser, *Tone*, had launched him at 0500, an hour behind schedule, in itself a nerve-rasping experience for a precision-conscious Japanese. Then, twenty minutes after he catapulted aloft on his No. 4 search arc, he made his first enemy contact and radioed his mother ship, "Sight two enemy surfaced submarines . . . 80 miles from my take-off point."[1] One of these was almost certainly *Grouper*, the other probably *Gudgeon*, easternmost of English's submarines.[2]

Within the hour, the scout had made another contact and cracked off a second warning, which Nagumo received at 0555: "15 enemy planes are heading toward you." No American attack party had taken off as yet, but he may have spotted *Yorktown*'s ten search planes which launched at 0430. Five minutes later Yamaguchi confirmed a sighting, so Nagumo had sent fighters aloft from all ships, but the U.S. aircraft, real or imaginary, melted into thin air and nothing came of the incident.[3]

Two submarines and "fifteen" enemy planes were surely enough excitement for one day for any scout pilot, but this one was just warming up. He had finished his outward leg and started back when at 0728 he had his big break: "Sight what appears to be 10 enemy surface ships, in position 10 degrees distance 240 miles from Midway. Course 150 degrees, speed over 20 knots."[4]

This message scored a direct hit on *Akagi*'s bridge. *There they are*! thought Kusaka.[5]

"Nagumo and other staff officers felt we were thrown off our guard," recalled Genda. "At the same time, we were at a loss how to make an accurate judgment of the situation."[6]

Certainly the wording "what appears to be 10 enemy surface ships" was not the most lucid of reports. Naturally, any ships in the area covered had to be enemy. Nagumo's own forces comprised the easternmost of the Midway attacking fleet; presumably the ten vessels weren't German and they certainly weren't Italian, so they had to be unfriendly. Lieutenant Commander Kenjiro Ono, the staff intelligence officer, plotted the position and discovered that these ships were just 200 miles away. The big question was whether or not this unit contained any carriers. If it did not, it presented little or no threat to the Japanese. It was well within reach of their own carrier aircraft and could be left to play around to its heart's content until the second attack wave polished off the unfinished business on Midway.

But if the enemy ships did include one or more carriers, this was a much different proposition.[7] Kusaka's first thought was that "there couldn't be an enemy force without carriers in the area reported and there must be carriers somewhere." On the other hand, he did not see how the Japanese could cancel the planned Midway attack because, as he saw it, the sighting of this American force did not alter the considerations which had dictated the earlier decision. Also, Kusaka never forgot the "two hares" hassle and the resulting decree that the attack on Midway was Number One priority.[8]

Therefore, Nagumo made a decision which was in effect a compromise. Although he agreed with retaining the Midway strike on the agenda, he could not ignore the presence in the neighborhood of ten unfriendly vessels nor could he wait twiddling his thumbs while *Tone*'s scout determined the exact type involved. So at 0745 Nagumo signaled his entire force: "Prepare to carry out attacks on enemy fleet units. Leave torpedoes on those attack planes which have not as yet been changed to bombs." Two minutes later he snapped back at *Tone*'s No. 4 aircraft: "Ascertain ship types, and maintain contact."[9]

Nagumo has been subjected to much criticism for the apparent delay of seventeen minutes between the 0728 message and the 0745 orders. His own report indicates that he did not receive the *Tone* scout's radio until about 0800, and with this Kusaka and Genda agree.[10] However, the 0745 and 0747 dispatches indicate that he did in fact get the message before 0745. But there is no reason to assume that he fiddled around indecisively for a quarter of an hour, having the information in hand instantaneously. Previous messages of that morning containing dispatch time reveal delays of from fourteen to twenty-seven minutes between dispatch and receipt. For instance, the submarine sighting radio from the very scout in question, dispatched at 0520, was received at 0545, and Ogawa's "Sand Island" information sent at 0640 reached *Akagi* at 0707;[11] it appears probable that the 0728 message got to *Akagi*'s bridge around 0740, which would give a mere five minutes for plotting the course, staff discussion, Nagumo's decision and the dispatch of orders.

At this point the rearming of the *Akagi* and *Kaga* torpedo bombers was about at the half-way mark. As maintenance crews completed the switch on each aircraft from torpedo to land bomb, the planes were lifted back to the flight deck. At the time Nagumo brought everything to a screeching halt, therefore, the flight decks of these two carriers each held from ten to fifteen bombers all set for a land attack. Of course, they could use these demolition types against ships in a pinch, but torpedoes were much more accurate, and more devastating.[12]

However much the minds of Nagumo and his staff may have been centered on the mysterious enemy ships, Midway had not yet thrown in the sponge. At 0748 *Soryu* signaled, "Sight 6 to 9 enemy planes bearing 320 degrees."[13]

These newcomers were the advance guard of VMSB-241's SBD-2 Dauntless dive bombers, under the personal leadership of Squadron Commander Major Lofton R. "Joe" Henderson. Technically Henderson had eighteen SBD-2s in his control, but engine trouble grounded two of them. Of his pilots, ten had joined the squadron only a week previously. The high percentage of green pilots plus the chronic shortage of gasoline had permitted only one hour of training in that period. Realizing that he did not have time to weld a solid team, he divided them into two units, keeping the more mature, better trained pilots in one and putting the new men in another under experienced sector leaders.

In fact, only three of his pilots had logged any time in the SBD-type aircraft and thus had been forced to practice glide bombing in the SB2U-2s. Henderson had to settle for the less effective gliding instead of the Navy's efficient "hell-diving" technique, because the slower approach permitted the green pilots to drop to 500 feet or less before releasing their bombs. His strike plan for the day was to make a unit approach in a fast power glide from 8,000 to 4,000 feet, maneuver to the best possible position, then let each individual pilot go on his own. Each would retire by hugging the water or seeking cloud cover, and rendezvous twenty miles from whatever enemy surface craft was nearest a course for Midway.

Henderson's men started to take off about 0610. The last one was airborne ten minutes later, a delay caused by "the general scramble of a great number of planes to clear the field." They got away by a whisker minutes ahead of Tomonaga's high-level bombers.

The sixteen aircraft met at "Point Affirm," an imaginary spot twenty miles east of Midway.[14] As they did so, Second Lieutenant Thomas F. Moore, Jr., heard his radio reporting, "Island is now under heavy attack," and looking back, he could see the smoke rising skyward. Then his receiver cracked with MAG-22's instructions, ". . . attack enemy carriers bearing 320 degrees, distance 180 miles, course 135 degrees, speed 25 knots."[15]

Back on Midway, Kimes was very nervous because, although he broadcast this message at intervals for over an hour, he received no replies. Therefore he feared "that the dive bombing attack by VMSB would never materialize." Actually the orders were received and acknowledged, possibly during one of the periods in the course of the attack when the Midway radio was out of commission.[16]

Henderson's SBDs encountered Soryu's fighters just as they caught sight of the Nagumo force. Fleet and interceptors presented a colorful sight. Second Lieutenant Harold G. Schlendering, sneaking quick glances at the fighters, saw they were of two types, some with retractable landing gear, some with fixed. A number of the interceptors flashed silver with red insignia and cowling, others showed a more somber brown with purple insignia and cowl. White smoke from their guns streamed out of their shell's paths, often making smoke rings.[17]

The Americans soon discovered they were up against a clever foe, operating at a double level and with highly effective teamwork. The Japanese fighters seemed to wait until the SBD gunners had used up their 100-round ammunition belts, then dive in for the kill. With unerring instinct they concentrated on Henderson. Captain Elmer G. Glidden, familiarly known as "Iron Man," seeing Henderson's plane catch fire and go out of control, took over, and led his squadron into cloud cover. The bottom of this overcast was much lower than the 4,000 feet Henderson had postulated as the beginning of the individual glides. Glidden broke out at about 2,000 feet, almost directly over a Japanese carrier, all of his planes following him at intervals of about five seconds. A huge rising sun insignia amidships of the flight deck of the flattop made a tempting target, the flight deck itself was a gleaming light yellow, and no attempt had been made to camouflage the carrier.[18]

Back over the task force from his tangle with the B-26s, Fujita made three or four solo attacks on the dive bombers. Two of his colleagues joined him, and together they shot down a number of the slow-moving SBDs. Those remaining went for the carriers, and as soon as they pulled out of their dives, Fujita and his men were right back on their tails. In fact, Fujita flew directly under one of the bombers he had been attacking. As he did so, the SBD banked and plunged into the sea.[19]

Pulling out of his glide, Glidden believed he saw two hits and a miss, the latter "right alongside the bow."[20] Actually, he had neatly boxed *Hiryu*, but the two nearest bombs fell about fifty meters away from the target, one to port and the other off the starboard bow.[21] Small wonder that, in his swift glimpse, Glidden thought he had bagged the carrier, for the men aboard *Akagi*, watching with racing hearts, thought the same thing. Fuchida noticed how bravely the little group held their course although about half had already been shot down, and did not see how they could miss the carrier. *Hiryu* disappeared in a blanket of heavy waterspouts and thick black smoke, but soon she emerged triumphantly, like a grand old trouper taking a curtain call.[22]

Peering down as he peeled off through a thick cloud, First Lieutenant Daniel Iverson, Jr., could see three carriers, "one smoking amidships." He picked out the one which, so far as he could tell, had escaped the attention of his squadron mates. This flattop had two rising suns on the flight deck, fore and aft, appeared shorter than a comparable American carrier but slightly wider, and had no superstructure on the flight deck, not a bad description of *Kaga*. According to his and his gunner's observations, they delivered just astern of the deck "a very close miss" which Iverson hoped might have damaged the screws.[23] *Kaga*'s action diagram shows three near misses centered closely in that very spot, the nearest one twenty meters from the port tip of the stern.[24]

The carrier blazed back with "almost an entire ring of fire from the flight deck," and Iverson soared up with a covey of fighters on his tail. He had the disconcerting experience of feeling a bullet sever his throat microphone. Later he reported that his plane was "hit several times,"[25] a masterpiece of understatement, for after he flopped in for a landing on Sand Island, awed inspectors counted no less than 210 holes in his aircraft.[26]

Lieutenant Moore dropped his bomb at 400 feet, then severe concussion knocked his plane out of control. When he recovered, he was no more than fifty feet from the surface. He looked around to see where his bomb had hit, but instead his eyes fell on three Zeros following him, "and then I was no longer curious about my bomb," he reported. His gunner, Private Charles W. Huber, called out that his gun had jammed, but Moore told him to aim it at the Japanese anyway. Huber went through this pantomime while the Zeros chased them almost to the whitecaps, then he took a bullet wound, not serious in itself but enough to call his bluff. The Zero pilots seemed to sense that something was wrong and screamed in much closer.

Himself slightly wounded, Moore decided to try for cloud cover. As he pulled the plane's nose up, the engine conked out. He reached for the wobble pump, but his plucky gunner beat him to it and got the engine going. Two of the Zeros chose this opportune moment to give up the chase. But the other was made of sterner stuff. Moore fired away at the Japanese with his forward .30 caliber gun; however, every time he turned to face his tormenter, the Zero skipped around to the other side. The two aircraft went through this ballet routine for some time, until the Zero pilot gave up in disgust.

Popping in and out of the clouds to get his bearings, Moore saw Kure Island, but did not try to land, because he wanted to hurry Huber to Midway for medical attention. With his radio out, he could not contact home base, and was seriously alarmed when "after a reasonable length of time" he had not found it. It was the wounded Huber who drew his attention to the black smoke in the distance which marked their goal.[27]

Captain R. L. Blain reached the target area through "very dense" antiaircraft fire and fighters which he estimated outnumbered the Americans at least two to one. He was quite sure that his group "had a direct hit and one close aboard hit along the side" of a good-sized, rather heavy ship. Then Blain's troubles began. Fighters were drilling holes in his wings and fuselage, but he evaded the Zeros in the clouds. However, his fuel pump had failed, and he had to use the wobble

pump until he lost the fighters. Then his gunner, Private First Class
Gordon R. McFeely, took over. Once the engine conked out, but it
caught again about 200 feet above the sea.

A few minutes later their luck ran out, and Blain had to make a
water landing. The SBD remained afloat about three minutes, during
which the men were able to salvage a flare pistol, the first aid kit,
and a parachute to use as a sea anchor. "Upon pulling the valve of
the CO_2 bottle we found, to our disgust, that they had left the emergency inflation valves open," Blain reported. "This meant that the
hand pump came in very handy." When they had inflated the raft,
they discovered a leak which they succeeded in patching "to a certain
extent." Then they had to bail, using a helmet.

After what Blain called a "Helluva" night, they heard an engine
and attracted the attention of a patrol plane. But the pilot could not
land, presumably because he had a full tank of gas. Not until the next
day, and with their last float light, did the men on the raft catch the
alert eye of the gunner in another patrol plane. After "several unsuccessful passes," the rescue plane settled nearby. The pilot turned
out to be a lieutenant whom Blain had known at Pensacola.[28]

Schlendering almost did not make it back. His engine gave up
the ghost about eight miles off Midway, and both pilot and gunner
had to bail out. Schlendering began swimming toward a reef about
five miles away, and turning around, found that his gunner, Private
First Class Edward O. Smith, had disappeared. At about 1000, PT
Boat No. 20, the same which later rescued Merrill after his fighter
went down, fished Schlendering out of the water. They circled the
area as long as possible, but they could find no trace of the missing
man.[29]

The Marines credited themselves with three direct hits and "several close misses" on a Kaga-class carrier.[30] Fujita, who was in the
thick of the action, stated that this group scored no hits,[31] and, as we
have seen, other eyewitnesses and official Japanese records bear him
out. Eight of the sixteen Dauntless crews were lost with no tangible
results to recompense. Of the SBD-2s which did return to Midway,
all "were badly shot up and some were in very unflyable condition."[32]
Once more the Midway garrison had launched a determined, gallant
but futile attack on the Nagumo force.

CHAPTER 25

"The Japanese Were Not As Yet Checked"

Impatiently awaiting advice as to types of ships in the sighting of nearly an hour earlier, and with pestiferous American dive bombers chivvying *Hiryu* and *Kaga*, Nagumo was not in a pleasant mood when at 0758 he received another radio message from *Tone*'s No. 4 scout: "At 0455,* the enemy is on course 80 degrees, speed 20 knots (0458)."[1]

This message revealed a sharp change of course, and should have rung alarm bells in the minds of the men on *Akagi*'s bridge. For the Americans were heading into the wind, an almost certain indication of aircraft launching.[2] How often had Nagumo stood in this spot as *Akagi* turned thus to send up her planes?

Yet nothing in the records or the memories of survivors hints that such a thought occurred to either Nagumo, Kusaka, or Genda. At this stage, evidently Nagumo was less concerned with the enemy's direction than with a positive identification of the ships prowling around to the northeast of him. Fuming, he snapped back to the scout: "Advise ship types (0500)."[3]

To add to the admiral's frustration, he could hardly hear himself think. The dive bombers were whisking around overhead and still more land-based aircraft were droning in. Between their throbbing engines, the scream of fighters on the warpath, the exploding of bombs and the barking of antiaircraft, the officers on the bridge could not hear one another's voices, and even orders over the public address system were barely audible.[4]

---

*The pilot was reporting in Tokyo time, i.e., a twenty-one-hour difference.

Henderson's SBDs had just begun to go into action when *Soryu* had more bad news for Nagumo. "14 enemy twin-engine planes flew over us at 270 degrees, altitude 3,000 meters."[5] Evidently *Soryu*'s lookout could not count past two, for here came Sweeney with his four-engined B-17s.

When Sweeney led his Flying Fortresses out earlier that morning for a possible second try at the Tanaka force, Ramsey had warned him to be on the alert for orders to change his target to a carrier group which the Navy expected to find to the northwest. If these carriers did not show up in time for Sweeney to change his objective, the B-17s were to return to Midway, rearm, refuel, and take off again for another attempt.[6]

When the carrier force sighting report reached Midway, the word sped out to Sweeney in the clear, reaching him when he was about 200 miles from original target. Quick action and smart navigation brought Sweeney within sight of the Mobile Force at 0732, but at that time he could see no carriers. Therefore, he ignored the lesser lights and continued to seek the heart of the enemy fleet.[7] The search took a surprisingly long time, and before he could enter the picture, the Fates had added yet another "eye of newt and toe of frog" to the witches' brew they were stirring up for Nagumo.

At 0806, *Chikuma* reported that enemy planes bearing 25 degrees to port were heading for the fleet concentration. Nagumo's battle chronology noted parenthetically: "(Carrier-based planes. These were the first carrier-based planes noted by this ship.)" The admiral would have been sub- or superhuman had this intelligence not given him a severe belt. Afar off, *Chikuma* may have seen the first elements of Tomonaga's homing flight, or the SB2U-3s which resembled Japanese Aichis and which were about twenty minutes away. But at the moment all Nagumo had to go on was word of "enemy planes" which were "carrier-based" and he must have lived through a nasty three minutes until *Tone*'s Number Four search pilot radioed: "Enemy is composed of 5 cruisers and 5 destroyers."[8]

"At last! Just as I thought," observed Ono smugly as he handed the decoded message to Kusaka. "There are no carriers."[9]

But Kusaka was not thrown off base, although the message admittedly shook his mind momentarily. "This message alone couldn't make it clear that no enemy carriers were there," he explained later.

"Nor could there be an enemy force without carriers in the reported area under the prevailing circumstances."[10]

The nature and extent of the let-up Nagumo and his staff experienced at this information should not be exaggerated. As Genda expressed it, they "felt some kind of relief for a while." Genda himself was neither particularly relieved nor surprised, although in retrospect he declared they all "should have realized that this was an error." No navy would turn loose such a light-weight unit in these waters independently: It must be an escort force. So Nagumo did not immediately toss care to the winds and assume that everything was going his way. He and his staff experienced merely a slight lessening of tension, a feeling of having been granted a breathing spell to concentrate on fighting off the enemy land-based planes and to go on with the plan to bomb Midway the second time.[11] "For one thing," Kusaka related, "I thought at that time that reversing the order of re-equipping attack planes with bombs at such a short interval would only result in adding up much confusion."[12]

Another reason why the Nagumo staff made no change of tactics at this moment was that the experience of the past six months had imbued these men with a bone-deep contempt for American naval aviation, a contempt which the land-based attacks now under way did nothing to dispel.[13] The individual American airman was brave, but seemingly could not hit a Japanese ship from the inside with the hatches closed. Sending these bombers out without fighter cover was unadulterated folly, and the uncoordinated attacks proclaimed a lack of organization and precision well-nigh past belief. If the United States had a carrier in the area, why had it not launched its aircraft to support its land-based comrades?

Once more the gods of sea and air laughed as another batch of American bombers found their targets. Consulting an aircraft recognition chart, Fuchida easily identified them as B-17s.[14] Sweeney's Flying Fortresses could only have reinforced the Japanese sense of security, for no airman in his right mind could mistake these four-engine bombers for carrier-based aircraft.

Sweeney's group had actually flown right across the path of the Nagumo force so far to the northeast that Lieutenant Carl E. Wuerterle, leading the last element of two Flying Fortresses, thought that the preceding four units had missed the carriers. He tried unsuccessfully to attract the attention of either Sweeney or his own section

chief, Lieutenant Colonel Brooke E. Allen, then pulled out of formation and signaled his wingman to hit individually. Cloud conditions
were ideal and he saw no Japanese fighters. His plane dropped three
bombs from 20,000 feet, then observing that these had failed, Wuerterle swung behind a neighboring carrier and released the remaining
five missiles in a direct line across the stern of yet a third flattop.
Believing he had scored at least one hit, he headed homeward.[15]

Wuerterle's wingman, Lieutenant H. S. Grundman, made two
runs on his own particular carrier, but observed no strikes. He could
only console himself by shooting down a Zero.[16]

Allen concentrated the full power of his three-plane element on
what appears to have been *Soryu*.[17] But her luck had not yet run out,
and the entire barrage fell considerably short.[18]

Faulkner, leading the third unit of Sweeney's nine-bomber sector,
believed, like Wuerterle, that Sweeney had not seen the carriers.
Therefore he broke his unit out of formation and "made a run on the
largest of the 4 carriers" he could spot. This flattop, no doubt *Akagi*,
was plunging along beneath a thin cloud cover, but Faulkner had no
trouble in following it. He was sure that the great ship was unaware
of his presence, for it made no attempt to evade. Moreover, Faulkner
had been over the enemy fleet for twenty minutes before he ran into
any antiaircraft fire. When it did begin, however, it was at the correct
level and much closer than the barrage he had met the previous day
from Tanaka's ships.[19] His left wingman, Steedman, took a few shells
in a wing but with no dire results.[20]

The right wingman, Lieutenant Robert B. Andrews, dropped four
bombs but was unsatisfied with the results, so he "broke away from
the element and made an individual run on a large carrier." One of
his bombs broke free prematurely, falling toward a small craft "laying
to just near carrier." On his third attempt he unloaded the last three
near the flattop. Andrews' individual attacks may have been on another carrier entirely, for he noticed no antiaircraft activity and encountered no fighter opposition until he soared off heading back to
Midway. At that time two Zeros pursued him "but by diving and
pouring the coal to it" he left them behind.[21]

In the meantime, Faulkner and Steedman released their full eight-
bomb loads near the original target and turned back toward Kure
Island, believing they had scored one sure hit on the port bow, a
possible one on the starboard, and five near misses. On the way back,

three Zeros streaked after them, one disabling Faulkner's Number Four engine and another wounding his tail gunner in the left index finger. But they did no serious damage and were "easily driven off by turret and tail gun," with one probably shot down.[22]

Sweeney selected as his target a carrier which seems to have been *Kaga*. He bracketed its stern with, he believed, "one bomb hit . . . causing heavy smoke." So far as he could see, no other bombs from his element did any damage. Nor, for that matter, had he or any of his unit's aircraft been struck.[23]

In one respect the B-17 attack had differed sharply from the preceding land-based strikes on the Japanese fleet: The Zeros had barely touched them. Indeed, as Captain Charles E. Gregory reported, "enemy pursuit appeared to have no desire to close on B-17E modified."[24] Fuchida was highly discomfited to observe no fighters take off in pursuit of the American bombers, but reasoned to himself that if the Flying Fortresses were as tough as reported, the Zeros would have had little chance to bring them down anyway.[25]

Naturally, Major Warner was much less charitable, and cited this failure to pursue in support of his claim that the Japanese wanted to live as much as anyone else.[26] Nimitz took the lesson to heart, and commented to Admiral King on "the outstanding value of strongly protected, high speed aircraft like the B-17 in combatting the Japanese Zero Fighter." He urged immediate assignment of this type aircraft to the Navy for scouting, tracking, and bombing.[27]

While the B-17s were unloading their bombs, another menace threatened the Mobile Force. At 0710 the submarine *Nautilus* "sighted smoke of bombing and antiaircraft fire beyond horizon bearing 331°T." Skipper Lieutenant Commander William H. Brockman, Jr., decided that this would bear investigation and headed for the action. An aircraft saw him and strafed at 0755, but five minutes later, sighting a formation of four ships including a battleship or heavy cruiser, Brockman kept boring in until at 0810 *Nautilus* rocked under eleven depth charges exploding from 1,000 to 3,000 yards away. Brockman changed course and cautiously raised periscope for a look. Evidently he had given this portion of the Mobile Force a good scare, for ships were darting about like water bugs and circling to get away from his position. On his port bow, the battleship was thundering at him with her entire starboard battery. Brockman promptly retaliated with a torpedo which the battleship dodged.[28]

Under anything like normal battle conditions, an enemy submarine attack would rouse a certain amount of interest on the flagship's bridge, and it is most difficult to believe that none of the ships notified *Akagi* of this development. Yet Nagumo's exhaustive battle chronology does not mention it even in passing. He had plenty on his mind and can be forgiven if *Nautilus* escaped his attention.

Among other things, destiny selected this moment for Midway's last land-based attack. Major Benjamin W. Norris's twelve SB2U-3 Vindicators had rendezvoused at Point Affirm, some twenty miles on magnetic course 90° from Midway, shortly following Henderson's SBDs.[29] As the unit circled at the meeting place, Second Lieutenant George E. Koutelas noticed a formation of bombers to port. He thought they were SBDs, and not until he returned from the mission did he find out they were Japanese.[30]

At 0710 Kimes radioed Norris to attack "an enemy carrier bearing 325°T, distance 180 miles, on course 135°T, at a speed of twenty-five (25) knots . . ." Climbing to 13,000 feet, the Vindicators were on their way. Just how combat-worthy these planes were is reflected in the names bestowed on them by their own crews: "Vibrators" and "Wind Indicators."[31] Slow and clumsy, they did not reach the outskirts of the Mobile Force until 0820.[32]

By this time Nagumo had sent aloft all of his fighters, including those earmarked to accompany the second attack,[33] so Norris experienced no such shortage of Zeros as did Sweeney. But this fighter attack was not at all of the caliber that cleared the air over Midway or that Fieberling and Collins met over the Mobile Force. Very possibly the fighter pilots were weary and somewhat nervous, with reflexes not quite honed to perfect sharpness. Small blame to them if they were, for they had been on the jump for a full four hours, circling as an air umbrella, fighting off enemy attacks, and also answering a constant stream of false alarms.[34] Second Lieutenant Sumner Whitten, flying Number Eleven aircraft in Captain Leon M. Williamson's Group Two, noted that the Zeros worked in pairs but showed no teamwork, and the American gunners drove them off fairly easily. Of the two fighters which attacked Whitten, one went past "going down on his back," so Whitten assumed they had shot him down.[35]

The same two Zeros pounced on both Whitten and Second Lieutenant Daniel L. Cummings, flying the last aircraft in the formation.

One burst of Zero fire killed Cummings's gunner, a private who "had never before fired a machine gun in the air and could not be expected to be an effective shot much less protect himself."[36]

Nevertheless, the Zero attack was sufficiently determined that Norris, who had no illusions about his "Vibrators," decided not to press on toward the carriers, but to seek a nearby objective. There below him was a fine battleship, which seemed to be the next most desirable target.[37] Norris did not know it, but this was *Haruna*, which, according to early American accounts, Colin Kelly had sunk.[38] If this were its ghost, it was a particularly solid one.

Norris radioed his team, "Attack target below," and led them into a long, high-speed glide. As the Vindicators swung down at close interval, antiaircraft guns opened up with an extremely heavy and troublesome but inaccurate barrage. Williamson released the first 500-pound bomb and hence could not see the results.[39]

Using the battleship's bow as a point of aim, Koutelas released, circled, and "saw the battleship practically ringed with near misses, also one direct hit on the bow." The first part of his statement was a good deal nearer the truth than the last part. As he sped away, the ship was turning to starboard "and smoke was pouring out near the center."[40]

Cummings pulled out of his glide without releasing, because he knew his run was not good and he would only waste a bomb. He looked around for a secondary target, and saw over the horizon about ten ships of various kinds and a squadron of fighters winging in from a carrier some ten miles away. He selected a destroyer as his objective and dropped his bomb, but did not pause to watch the results. For the next fifteen minutes he tried desperately to get away from five Zeros. "In the hit and run, and dog fighting, which was my initiation to real war, my old, obsolete SB2U-3 was almost shot out from under me," he reported. At last he broke away in the clouds. About five miles from Midway his gas gave out and he crash-landed. He had just time to confirm that his gunner was indeed dead when the beat-up aircraft sank from under him. PT Boat No. 20, with Merrill and Schlendering still aboard, picked him up.[41] No. 26 rescued Second Lieutenant Allan H. Ringblom, who ran out of gas about one-and-a-half miles off Sand Island.[42]

Considering the age and decrepitude of the SB2U-3s, they had emerged from the fray not too badly, losing only two aircraft to direct enemy action, with two damaged planes succumbing to shortage of fuel. And the survivors were convinced that they had observed two direct hits on their target and three near misses, leaving "the battleship smoking heavily and listing badly."[43] Yet despite the pilots' positive damage reports, they had not scratched *Haruna*.[44]

Had the battle of Midway ended as the brisk little torpedo boats were fishing Cummings and Ringblom out of the Pacific, the engagement would have been a rousing Japanese victory. Kimes and his staff fully expected the Japanese to play a return engagement. "From the time of the attack and the known position of the enemy carriers, we estimated they would be back in three or four hours," Kimes observed. "Fighting airplanes to repel air attack were practically nil, so there was a pretty anxious time as we waited for the Japs to show up."

As the bombers struggled back, their condition clear evidence of the mauling they had taken, tension on Midway mounted almost to the breaking point. "Of course," said Kimes, "we still had the anti-aircraft artillery of the defense battalion and our smaller stuff and we hoped to do the maximum amount of damage if they did show up." At this time Midway had no communication with Task Force Sixteen or Seventeen,[45] and no matter how brave a face Kimes put on the situation, nothing existed on Midway of more than nuisance value as a defense against a second air raid, a ship-to-shore bombardment, or a landing party of the size Tanaka commanded.

No one knew this better than Nimitz, although at the time he believed various accounts of damage which, even after Intelligence screening, were still absurdly optimistic. He had no reason not to credit what the pilots themselves sincerely believed. Yet despite those inflated summaries before him, he informed King in his clear, characteristic battle report,

> The Midway Forces had struck with full strength, but the Japanese were not as yet checked. About 10 ships had been damaged, of which 1 or 2 AP or AK may have been sunk. But this was hardly an impression on the great force of about 80 ships converging on Midway. Most of Midway's fighters, torpedo planes and dive-bombers— the only types capable of making a high percentage of hits on ships— were gone . . .[46]

CHAPTER 26

"What the Hell Is Headquarters Doing?"

"The enemy is accompanied by what appears to be a carrier in a position to the rear of the others (0520)."[1]

This message from *Tone*'s busy Number Four reconnaissance plane crashed into Japanese consciousness with far greater impact than any bomb thus far dropped that morning.

"I was indeed shocked, though such an eventuality was not entirely outside our consideration," Kusaka recalled.[2] But it is one thing to accept a concept intellectually; it is quite another to believe it. Although Nagumo and his staff knew very well that the *Tone* scout's 0809 message did not preclude the possibility of enemy carriers in the area, hence only took them temporarily off the hook, the actual sighting of a United States flattop caught them by surprise.

Gosh! exclaimed Kusaka silently.

No man can say with any degree of certainty what goes on inside another man's head. But Kusaka understood Nagumo as only a capable, loyal chief of staff knows his commander, which is just about as well as one human being can know another. He saw nothing in Nagumo's manner to indicate that he became either sullen or indecisive in this crisis. "He might have been shocked for a moment," stated Kusaka, "but I think anyone facing such an unexpected eventuality would have been shocked for a moment."[3]

The message reached Nagumo's hands at approximately 0830,[4] and could not have come at a less opportune time. Only minutes before, a large group of planes lifted over the horizon and escort vessels, understandably enough, mistook them for yet another enemy attack group and opened fire.[5] Alert eyes recognized their own returning Midway force before any damage could be done.[6] Tomonaga's returnees were circling and awaiting orders to land even as Nagumo and his staff were absorbing the implications of *Tone*'s latest news.

The simultaneous appearance of Tomonaga's aircraft and the scout's message forced upon Nagumo a decision as difficult as it was crucial. There was no question of whether or not to attack this enemy carrier and its escorting cruisers and destroyers. As Genda remarked, "Our feeling at that time was that we had been ambushed by the enemy force, which made us make up our minds to have a decisive engagement with the enemy force by all means." On this point, Nagumo's duty was clear. The problem was this: Should he immediately send out after the American carrier the aircraft he had available at that precise moment, or should he permit Tomonaga's planes to land, refuel, rearm, and then take care of the menace by a mass attack?[7]

At this moment, Yamaguchi put in his two cents' worth by signal relayed through the destroyer *Nowaki*: "Consider it advisable to launch attack force immediately."[8] The advice was redundant, and had Nagumo wanted it he would have asked for it, but Yamaguchi had been quiet just about as long as his nature would allow. He was of an impatient disposition, eager to rush into battle, and he lost no love on Nagumo. Moreover, he seems to have entertained little doubt that he would have made a much better Commander in Chief of the Mobile Force than his superior.[9]

Nagumo did not need the prod. No one knew the value of surprise and speed better than the victor at Pearl Harbor. But in Nagumo's hands were hundreds of lives for whom he was responsible to Yamamoto, to his Emperor, and to his ancestral gods. At that precise minute, the Mobile Force had available for immediate take-off only the thirty-six dive bombers of *Hiryu* and *Soryu*, as well as those torpedo bombers already re-equipped with the 800 kilogram land bombs, and now resting on the flight decks of *Akagi* and *Kaga*, awaiting the remainder of their fellows.[10]

Three factors militated against sending these off immediately to knock out the American ships. First, horizontal bombing was nowhere nearly as satisfactory and productive as torpedoing, which was the Japanese naval air arm's specialty, and dive bombing was only a little more fruitful. Second, Nagumo had no fighters ready to send along with the bombers. Every one of his interceptors was in the air, either hovering with the Tomonaga force or mopping up the remnants of the Midway land-based attack planes. A number were damaged and all were low on gas.

On this matter Kusaka was firm. "I was not entirely against his [Yamaguchi's] view of launching the attack force without re-equipping, but I couldn't agree with him on the point of letting them go without fighter cover, because I witnessed how enemy planes without fighter cover were almost annihilated by our fighters mercilessly. I wanted most earnestly to provide them with fighters by all means."[11]

Last but far from least, the Midway attackers could not land until the flight decks were clear. A number of these planes were in distress and fuel was dropping by the second. "It was a problem," said Genda, "of whether more than one hundred crack planes of the first wave would be wasted in ditching in the sea or not."

As air officer of the First Air Fleet, Genda "couldn't help hesitating to let some two hundred skilled fliers ditch in the sea, only hoping to be saved by stand-by destroyers." Furthermore, he heartily agreed with Kusaka that "the previous engagement well showed that an attack force without fighter cover could not inflict damage to an enemy force well protected by fighters." For these reasons, Genda advised Nagumo and Kusaka to launch after the first wave planes were recovered.

To bring in the circling, coughing first wave, the flight decks had to be cleared, which in turn gave the opportunity to switch back to torpedoes. With all these considerations in mind, Nagumo indulged in no Hamletian brooding on the bridge. "Decisions were never delayed by indecision," stated Genda firmly.[12] Not more than a minute or two after receipt of the *Tone* scout's radio, Nagumo flashed to his command: "Carrier based bombers will prepare for second attack. Equip yourselves with 250 kilogram bombs [torpedoes]."[13]

"Here we go again!" sang out the invincibly good-tempered Masuda. "This is getting to be like a quick-change contest."[14] Some of the maintenance crewmen, who had to do the actual work of stacking and unstacking, loading and unloading the heavy missiles, were less cheerful. "What the hell is Headquarters doing?" they asked each other.[15]

About five minutes' feverish work cleared the decks, and at 0837 the signal "Commence landing" shot up the yardarm. One *Hiryu* bomber pilot, Lieutenant Hiroharu Kadano, passed out from machine gun wounds the minute his plane landed.[16] As Tomonaga walked away from his plane, he joined Lieutenant Toshio Hashimoto, and observed thoughtfully, "When we were attacked by enemy fighters near the island, I thought I was finally doomed. As I had escaped from death several times since the China Incident, I thought there was nothing to be regretted even if I was killed. But I thought that such a young man as you should not be killed." Hashimoto was touched and gratified that his flight leader, whom he admired from the bottom of his heart, should have thought of him in such a moment.[17]

Chihaya landed on *Akagi* fairly sizzling with indignation. "A gunnery officer who mistakes friendly planes for the enemy should be fired!" he shouted. He and his colleague Lieutenant Yamada reported to the bridge, advising that, contrary to Japanese Intelligence data, there were three air strips on the island.

"Did enemy fighters come out?" asked Fuchida, agog for every detail of the venture he still considered technically his own.

"About ten minutes before we reached the island, Grummans came out to give us a hell of a time," Yamada replied. He added that antiaircraft fire was "fiercer than expected."[18]

The last returning aircraft did not touch down until 0918, and in the meantime *Akagi* fairly jumped with activity. At approximately 0830, the bridge had received another message from the reliable *Tone* scout: "Sight two additional cruisers in position bearing 8 degrees, distance 250 miles from Midway. Course, 150 degrees, speed 20 knots . . ." An almost identical message to *Akagi* came in at 0845.[19]

This radio stirred up little emotion. Kusaka thought this just might indicate the presence of two carrier groups instead of one, in which case the Mobile Force should attack the one sighted first and therefore presumably the nearest their course.[20] But if, as most of the staff seem to have assumed, it meant just two more cruisers added to the group already seen, this did not change the picture one way or another. Nagumo's decision had already been made, and down in the hangars crews sweating in their short-sleeved tropical shirts and shorts were unloading the 800-kilogram bombs, piling them helter-skelter near the hangar instead of taking the time to return the missiles to the magazine.[21]

According to Nagumo's schedule, *Akagi* and *Kaga* should be ready for takeoff, all aircraft refueled and bombers equipped with torpedoes, by 1030, *Soryu* and *Hiryu* not later than 1100. He planned to send up in the first wave three fighters from each of the carriers, eighteen bombers each from *Akagi, Soryu*, and *Hiryu*, and twenty-seven from *Kaga*.[22]

In the meantime, Nagumo ordered *Soryu* to send off one of its swift, experimental-type reconnaissance planes to check on the *Tone* scout's sighting.[23] About the same time, at 0845, Abe instructed *Chikuma* to launch a Type 00 float aircraft on the same mission. Just as he did so, the *Tone* scout advised that he was homeward bound.[24]

Immediately Abe hit him with orders to postpone his homing, and Nagumo directed him: "Go on the air with transmitter for DF purposes." This rather cryptic instruction directed him to act in effect as a beacon to guide the Mobile Force toward the enemy. Abe relayed the same information to the reconnaissance pilot, who must now have been almost overwhelmed with the sudden volume of radio traffic, and further instructed him: "Maintain contact with enemy until the arrival of four *Chikuma* planes."[25]

Yamamoto's Combined Fleet headquarters had kept fairly well abreast of affairs through picking up a number of these messages. The information that a United States carrier was within striking distance of the Mobile Force disturbed them not at all. "At first we were in an optimistic mood, thinking that there was the enemy task force that we had been looking for," Ugaki wrote in his diary, "and how we should wipe out the remaining enemy force after the enemy carrier was first destroyed by our second attack wave to be dispatched immediately."[26]

This irresponsible reaction is almost stupefying in view of the fact that not until then had Yamamoto or his staff received any indication that an American carrier was operating in the vicinity or indeed that any United States craft were west of Midway. It further ignored the unpleasant fact that this sighting was exceedingly premature according to their own timetable.

"Do you think we ought to order Nagumo to attack the United States carrier force at once?" Yamamoto asked Kuroshima. "I think we had better do so."

"Nagumo has prepared half his air force to attack the United States carrier force," Kuroshima reminded Yamamoto, "and maybe Nagumo is already preparing his attack." Therefore Yamamoto dropped the point, for which Kuroshima blamed himself to the end of his days.

Had he answered his chief with a subservient "Yes, sir," a directive over Yamamoto's signature might have spurred Nagumo to an immediate attack. "The fact that Nagumo did not move as the Combined Fleet wanted him to was my responsibility," lamented Kuroshima in retrospect. Actually, the senior staff officer was laboring under a misapprehension. He believed that Nagumo understood that "the aim of the Midway campaign was to attack the U.S. carrier force, so therefore Nagumo should have sense enough to do it."[27]

Yet Kuroshima himself had specifically given the capture of Midway as the Number One priority.* The Mobile Force was thinking and acting accordingly in making the original decision to switch from torpedoes to bombs. Nagumo's delay in attacking was not the result of any intent not to hit the American carrier force. On the contrary, he wanted to do so with a respectable show of strength and the best possible chance of success.

Ironically enough, Nagumo had followed in "Fuzzy" Theobald's footsteps. He had made a theoretically impeccable command decision which happened to be the wrong one. Nagumo did not know that he had lost the initiative, and there is no good reason why he should have suspected this fact on the basis of the information available to him. Certainly he had no cause to go into a panic and lash out half-cocked at an enemy fleet so far inferior to his own.

With the die cast, at 0835 Nagumo blinked out to all his ships: "After completing homing operations, proceed northward. We plan to contact and destroy the enemy task force." Then he officially notified Yamamoto: "Enemy composed of 1 carrier, 5 cruisers, and 5 destroyers sighted at 5 A.M. in position bearing 10 degrees, distance 240 miles from AF. We are heading for it."[28]

He had pared a lot of meat off the situation to reach such bare bones. He did not mention the second sighting of two additional cruisers; he did not explain why he was just setting out for an enemy sighted almost an hour previously; he did not inform Yamamoto that he could not change course until he completed recovery of the Midway attack force. If Yamamoto had had to rely on this information to

---

*See Chapter 4.

give him the picture, he would have been a sorely puzzled admiral.

The last of Tomonaga's bombers touched down at 0859. Only a few fighters remained to complete their homing. At exactly 0901 Nagumo scanned the latest report from the indefatigable *Tone* scout: "Orders received," the pilot had radioed in acknowledgment of the admiral's directive of 0854. To this he added, as if by way of afterthought, "10 enemy torpedo planes are heading toward you . . ."[29]

CHAPTER 27

"At Last They Have Come"

As the soft glow of dawn flushed the Pacific sky that beautiful morning of June 4, Spruance waited eagerly for comparable light to break over the tactical situation. So far the Task Force had no word concerning the position of Nagumo's flattops, which were Spruance's particular pigeons. "That was my mission: to get those Japanese carriers and then protect and preserve Midway from the enemy," he said.[1]

Spruance received the first confirmation that enemy carriers had been sighted when *Enterprise* picked up one of Ady's transmissions at 0534. While this radio was enough to alert the Midway defenders, it was not sufficiently detailed to be of much concrete use to either Fletcher or Spruance as they cruised along with about ten miles separating them, Task Force Seventeen to the northeast of Task Force Sixteen.[2] Then at 0553 *Enterprise* intercepted Ady's famous "many planes" warning. "This report told me and Fletcher that that particular part of the Japanese plan was now in effect," explained Spruance.[3]

This message gave no clue as to the number of carriers and their exact location, but it did give the bearing—320°—and distance—150 miles from Midway—of the incoming aircraft. Armed with this information, Spruance instructed his chief of staff, Captain Miles S. Browning, "Launch everything you have at the earliest possible moment and strike the enemy carriers."

In reaching this vital command decision to withhold no part of his air power, Spruance was just doing what came naturally. He never seriously entertained any idea of less than all-out attack. "I figured that if I were going to hit the Japanese, I should hit them with everything I had," he declared.[4]

Fletcher had already reached the same conclusion the previous night. "There was only one thing to do to the Japanese: attack them and hit them as hard as we could," he said. "We couldn't afford to wait. We had to strike first, strike swiftly, and strike in great force."[5]

Spruance had no sooner given the word to Browning than at 0603 the Task Force radios again picked up one of Midway's reports. This one contained the information the two admirals had been waiting for: "Two carriers and battleships bearing 320°, distance 180, course 135, speed 25." This located the Japanese about 200 miles west-southwest of the American ships.[6]

Fletcher had to do some fast and furious thinking. Like an alert basketball player who sees a teammate nearer the basket than he is, Fletcher passed the ball to Spruance. At 0607 he flashed to his colleague: "Proceed southwesterly and attack enemy carriers when definitely located." He had two excellent reasons for holding *Yorktown* in reserve. In the first place, he wanted to recover his SBDs still fanning out northward on patrol. In the second, the intercepted information spoke of only two Japanese carriers, whereas Naval Intelligence believed four and possibly five were participating in the massive movement toward Midway. Fletcher had been stung in the Coral Sea when he went all-out against *Shoho*, only to find himself wide open to attacks from *Shokaku* and *Zuikaku*. The canny Frank Jack was not the man to be caught twice in the same trap.[7]

Spruance originally planned to launch at 0900, at which time he figured less than 100 miles would separate him from his quarry. But within the next half hour, as reports reached him of the Midway attack progress, it became evident that he did not have another two hours at his disposal if he wanted to inflict maximum damage on the enemy carriers.[8]

He turned to Browning in the attempt to outguess Nagumo. Spruance inherited his chief of staff from Halsey, who "thought he was wonderful." Browning had the disposition of a snapping turtle and Spruance admitted freely that "during the war in the Pacific people hated his guts." But "Browning was smart and quick," and Spruance was not running a charm school. Browning had the aviation knowhow that Spruance needed, which was all that concerned the imperturbable admiral.[9]

Browning estimated that the Japanese attack planes would complete their strike and return to the carriers about 0900. Almost certainly, Nagumo would maintain course until that time. If Spruance wanted to catch the enemy carriers with all planes aboard, he should begin to launch as soon as possible. "We felt that we had to hit him before he could launch his second attack, both to prevent further damage to Midway and to ensure our own safety."[10]

The decision to launch immediately was one of the most difficult he would ever have to make, for the longer range imposed great difficulties on all of his aircraft and practically assured that the slow, low-flying TBD Devastator torpedo bombers, with a combat range of only 175 miles, would not make it back to their carriers.[11] Behind his impassive countenance, Spruance was no less fond and proud of his men than was the demonstrative Halsey, but he faced without flinching the most heart-rending necessity a good commander ever knows: To risk sacrifice of a few that many may live.

The same grim possibility obviously had preyed on the mind of Lieutenant Commander John C. Waldron, the big, aggressive South Dakotan who commanded *Hornet's* VT-8. The previous evening, as his torpedomen awaited a possible call to action in Ready Room Number Four, he had distributed mimeographed copies of a message. He made no comment; none was necessary:

JUST A WORD TO LET YOU KNOW I FEEL WE ARE ALL READY. WE HAVE HAD A VERY SHORT TIME TO TRAIN, AND WE HAVE WORKED UNDER THE MOST SEVERE DIFFICULTIES. BUT WE HAVE TRULY DONE THE BEST HUMANLY POSSIBLE. I ACTUALLY BELIEVE THAT UNDER THESE CONDITIONS, WE ARE THE BEST IN THE WORLD. MY GREATEST HOPE IS THAT WE ENCOUNTER A FAVORABLE TACTICAL SITUATION, BUT IF WE DON'T AND WORST COMES TO WORST, I WANT EACH ONE OF US TO DO HIS UTMOST TO DESTROY OUR ENE-MIES. IF THERE IS ONLY ONE PLANE LEFT TO MAKE A FINAL RUN-IN, I WANT THAT MAN TO GO IN AND GET A HIT. MAY GOD BE WITH US ALL. GOOD LUCK, HAPPY LANDINGS, AND GIVE 'EM HELL![12]

Waldron proudly claimed to be one-eighth Sioux. Whenever he solved a problem by a flash of intuition, he attributed it to his Indian blood.[13] One of the few Naval Academy graduates in VT-8, he devoted a great deal of time and study to naval air tactics in general and those of the Japanese in particular. He held school for his men every day, instructing them in both Japanese and American tactics with black-board demonstrations and lectures. Even off duty, during bull sessions in the Ready Room, while everyone else talked and cracked jokes, "he'd be sitting there looking up at the ceiling thinking about tactics and Japanese . . ." Then after a while he would call the room to order and deliver an impromptu talk lasting well over an hour.

Now, in his final briefing, Waldron told his men that he doubted the Japanese would continue toward Midway. He believed that as soon as they got word that the American Navy was around, they would regroup and retire just far enough to recover their planes. So he instructed them "not to worry about their navigation; just follow him, for he knew where he was going."[14]

On *Enterprise*, Lieutenant James S. Gray, commanding VF-6, had only ten fighters to try to protect thirty-three dive bombers and fourteen torpedo planes. As the former flew high and the latter low, this posed a problem of being in two places at once. Therefore, he got together with Lieutenant Arthur V. Ely, operations officer of VT-6, to arrange a signal. Gray would try to fly high enough to cover both flights, and if Zeros jumped the torpedo planes, the squadron commander, Lieutenant Commander Eugene E. Lindsey, would radio Gray, "Come on down, Jim!" This seemed a sensible arrangement, for Gray's F4F-4s could dive down to torpedo plane level much more readily than they could climb up to the dive bombers.[15]

Lindsey himself was not present at the briefing, and indeed Air Group Commander Clarence Wade McClusky* saw no reason why Lindsey should participate in the engagement. As we have seen, in landing on *Enterprise* as the carrier sortied from Pearl Harbor, Lindsey's Devastator rolled off the deck. Lindsey suffered quite severe injuries and was still so bruised about the face that he could not put on his flight goggles. But when asked whether he could fly that morning, he replied quietly, "This is what I have been trained to do."[16]

Task Force Sixteen's two flattops turned into the wind and began to launch, *Hornet* at 0700 and *Enterprise* six minutes later. At 0720 Spruance split his command in two groups several thousand yards apart, and for the remainder of the day they operated independently. With *Enterprise* were the cruisers *Northampton*, *Vincennes*, and *Pensacola* and the destroyers *Balch*, *Benham*, *Aylwin*, *Monaghan*, and *Phelps*. Mitscher's supporting group comprised the cruisers *Minneapolis*, *New Orleans*, and *Atlanta*, and the destroyers *Ellet*, *Worden* and *Conyngham*.[17]

---

*The same officer whom Nimitz had decorated on May 27, 1942.

Hornet completed launching at 0755 and returned to course to close with the *Enterprise* group. She had no sooner completed the maneuver than at 0815 *Northampton* reported: "Bandit bearing 185°, distance 30 miles. Bandit is single engined twin float seaplane."[18] Radar picked him up, and lookouts confirmed the snooper's presence, but combat patrol could not find it.

Undoubtedly this was our old friend from *Tone*. Exactly what ships this scout spotted at the time of each report is still a mystery. Visibility was excellent, and he could have seen either group of Task Force Sixteen or even Task Force Seventeen. This was Spruance's first indication that the enemy had seen his fleet, and he worried lest he had lost his great advantage of surprise. But his planes were already on the way. There was nothing to do but let the attack go forward as planned and hope for the best.[19]

Spruance envisioned a coordinated strike of torpedo and dive bombers with fighter escort, and had sent up a formidable group of 116 aircraft. From *Enterprise*, McClusky led thirty-three SBD dive bombers of VB-6 and VS-6, for his scouts were also equipped with bombs for the occasion, along with Lindsey's fourteen torpedo planes (VB-8) and Gray's ten fighters (VS-8). *Hornet* contributed thirty-four dive bombers and bomb-laden scouts, Waldron's fifteen torpedo aircraft, and ten fighters of Lieutenant Commander Samuel G. Mitchell's VF-8, all under the overall lead of the Air Group Commander, Commander Stanhope C. Ring.[20] But Lady Luck had not yet quite jilted Nagumo.

At 0917, with only one minute to go for full recovery of attack planes, *Akagi* swung away from her Midway heading and set course 70°,[21] to close with the American task force. Incredibly, Spruance had no news of this change of course. In fact, he had no word of the enemy's whereabouts from receipt of the 0603 interception until his aircraft actually found the Japanese carriers, although they had been under American eyes almost constantly, either patrol scouts or Midway's bombers.

The United States paid dearly at Midway for lack of communication and coordination, which not only exacted a heavy toll of American blood, but may have saved the Japanese from even worse punishment than they finally absorbed. The problem was not that old bugaboo, inter-service noncooperation; it was a Navy-to-Navy one. "This failure to receive adequate information from our land-based forces raises the question as to whether or not full dependence can be placed in units other than our own," Lieutenant Commander J. G. Foster, Jr., *Hornet's* air operations officer, reported in understandable bitterness.[22] Captain Murray of *Enterprise* was equally unhappy about this situation. "The absence of amplifying reports . . . might have been disastrous to our forces. Lack of amplification of contacts and failure of Midway based planes to provide continuous tactical scouting on June 4 and June 5 probably prevented complete destruction of enemy forces."[23]

But the fault was by no means all Midway's. For example, the submarine *Nautilus* had been stalking the Nagumo force since 0710. Emerging again to periscope depth after her attempt on the enemy battleship, *Nautilus* sighted at 0900 a carrier "bearing 083° true" and continued to close on it. The submarine's log reported, "0910 attacked by cruiser. Fired torpedo at cruiser and missed, target maneuvering to avoid. Target returned to attack with six depth charges." Brockman's target was not a cruiser but the destroyer *Arashi*. Brockman took *Nautilus* down at 0918, exactly one minute after Nagumo changed course. But no word of all this action reached the American task forces.[24]

Had Nagumo altered his direction ten or fifteen minutes earlier, he might have avoided any encounter with Spruance's airmen at this time. Even so, he was not where he was supposed to be when *Hornet's* dive bombers and fighters arrived at the anticipated spot.

Hornet planned a coordinated attack of dive bombers and torpedo planes, but during the hour necessary to launch and form, the sky grew so overcast that Waldron's VT-8 and Ring's Dauntless soon lost sight of one another.[25] Ring formed his aircraft in a scouting line with him in the middle setting course and speed. It was an acceptable formation of the day but not the wisest choice under the circumstances. Maintaining a smart line necessitated constant throttle adjustment, and every change in throttle ate up a little more gas[26]—and gas consumption could make all the difference between success and failure, life and death.

When Ring reached the anticipated point of interception, he did not adopt the standard "expanding square" tactic—flying along the sides of a gradually increasing hollow square, which could have resulted in visibility of about fifty miles under the conditions prevailing that day. Instead, he continued on his original course for another fifty miles. This led his group closer to Midway and headed back toward *Hornet*.

By this time, the fuel gauges had dropped alarmingly low. The attack group split up and headed for a possible refueling point. Ring, seventeen planes of VS-8 and three Dauntlesses of VB-8 made it to *Hornet* and landed with gas to spare.[27]

No doubt Ring had good reasons for his course of action, although to the best of our knowledge he never made a public explanation. Perhaps, as Walter Lord has suggested, he estimated that the Japanese had already sailed to a point between Midway and *Hornet*'s aircraft.[28] Whatever his rationale, many in his bitterly disappointed air group blamed him for the failure to find the enemy task force.[29]

The remaining thirteen dive bombers under Lieutenant Commander Robert R. Johnson headed for Midway. Unsure of the proper recognition signals, Johnson jettisoned his bombs as a friendly gesture. But jittery gunners did not take it in that spirit and Johnson's planes had to dodge flak for some time.[30]

Ensign Troy Guillory landed many miles at sea. Seven and a half hours later, a PBY picked up Guillory and his gunner, none the worse for their experience.[31] Another bomber came down within ten miles of Midway, one in the lagoon.[32]

"*Hornet* dive bombers failed to locate the target and did not participate in this attack," Spruance reported to Nimitz. "Had they done so, the fourth carrier could have been attacked and later attack made on *Yorktown* by the carrier prevented."[33] Spruance was not the type to indulge in fruitless might-have-beens, so for him to commit to paper even this much is a strong indication of just how deeply this failure rankled.

Hornet's action report contains a distressing hint that this mixup could have been avoided: "About one hour after the planes had departed the enemy reversed his course and started his retirement. We did not break radio silence to report this to the planes."[34] The implication is inescapable that Task Force Sixteen, or at any rate *Hornet*, knew that the Japanese had changed direction and withheld this information from the attack groups, thereby jeopardizing the entire operation to appease the great god Radio Silence. Such action would have been inexcusable, because, as we have just seen, a Japanese scout had already spotted a part of the U.S. forces, and with the launching of the American air groups, destruction of the enemy would seem to have become the Number One consideration.

Almost certainly the above quotation is the statement which Samuel Eliot Morison mentioned in his account of the battle of Midway, and of which he added, ". . . the officer who wrote this report has explained to me that he did not intend to convey that impression."[35] It would be interesting to know just what impression the officer in question did intend to convey.

VF-8 had even worse luck than *Hornet*'s bombers. All had to ditch for lack of fuel. Mitchell, his operations officer, and Lieutenant (j.g.) Richard Gray landed close enough to share two lifeboats and one set of emergency rations. Four days and twenty hours later, hungry, blistered, and badly scared by a shark, the three men climbed aboard a PBY.[36]

In contrast to Ring, Waldron led his torpedomen along the prescribed course just so far. Then, at exactly the right moment, with an amazing intuitive understanding of the enemy, he turned off and swung in a shallow arc west-northwest. "We went just as straight to the Jap Fleet as if he'd had a string tied to them," recalled Lieutenant George H. Gay.[37]

VT-8 comprised as representative a cross-section of American manhood as ever delighted the heart of a pollster: a former college track star from Sheridan, Oregon; an insurance man from New York State; a Kansas City meat packer; a Harvard law student; the son of a Los Angeles lumber dealer; a former Navy enlisted man who had received a direct appointment to Annapolis; a few regular Academy men.[38]

Gay had gone to Navy flight training at Pensacola from Texas A&M. When he lifted off *Hornet* that morning, it was the first time he had ever carried a torpedo in a plane, let alone taken one off a ship. What is more he "had never seen it done." Nor had any of the other ensigns in the squadron. But as Gay soared aloft with his comrades, no doubts troubled his twenty-five-year-old mind. Waldron had trained and lectured and exercised them within an inch of their young lives, and Gay along with his squadron buddies repaid him with perfect trust and honor. "We could almost look at the back of Commander Waldron's head and know what he was thinking," Gay told an interviewer some time later, "because he had told us so many times over and over just what we should do under all conditions."[39]

Chikuma caught sight of VT-8 at 0918, the exact minute the last of the Tomonaga planes touched down on deck, and also the split second that *Nautilus* dived to avoid *Arashi*'s depth charges. *Chikuma* laid two smoke screens and opened fire, a destroyer set up another smoke screen to port of *Tone*, then *Akagi* spotted the intruders and began to evade.[40] To Genda they appeared "like waterfowl flying over a lake far away."

At last they have come! he told himself, for throughout the time of decision and recovery since the last land-based attack, the Japanese airmen had wondered what was keeping the enemy carrier-based planes. *What a funny approach they are making!* Genda thought. He could not understand why they were flying so low.[41]

Gay waited impatiently for the word to attack, but Waldron took a few precious seconds to try to radio the enemy position and composition to Spruance. Unfortunately distance and low altitude conspired to keep this message from ever reaching the admiral or anyone else. Evidently Waldron planned to strike *Akagi*, but ran into such a withering hail of Zero fire that he turned to the center carrier of the three below him. Gay estimated about thirty-five Zeros jumped them and antiaircraft guns were in action. However, Gay was firm in his belief that, despite Japanese claims, no antiaircraft slug touched any of the bombers. He was the only one who got near enough to the target to be within range. Most of the unfortunate group dropped to the swarming Zeros before they could release their torpedoes.[42]

One torpedo plane closed in on *Akagi* and seemingly tried to make a crash hit with its still torpedo-loaded body on *Akagi*'s bridge. "For a moment I thought we were doomed," recalled Kusaka. But it just missed the bridge and plunged into the sea. Kusaka sent up a quick prayer for the pilot "for his gallant fighting."[43]

Pitifully little is known of the last minutes of this tragic squadron. Gay, the sole survivor, was much too busy to see what happened to each of his teammates.[44] ARM 3/C Leroy Quillen, of VB-8, on the way to Midway, heard over his radio a voice which he was sure was Waldron's, having heard him on the air a number of times. The voice came through with crisp, disjointed phrases: "Attack immediately! . . . Watch those fighters! . . . See that splash! . . . How am I doing? . . . I'd give a million to know who done [sic] that . . . There's two fighters in the water . . . My two wing men are going in the water . . ."[45]

Gay saw his commander's plane burst into flames from the left gas tank. As the stricken plane passed over, he could see Waldron stand up and struggle to get out of the flaming cockpit. Of the remaining three TBDs, two whirled out of sight, and then the number of Gay's own gunner-radioman came up. The young Texan was the sole survivor of VT-8.

He pulled up over a destroyer, then turned back over the carrier below him, evidently *Soryu*, for the other two carriers in view were larger than his target. The electrical torpedo release did not work, so he pulled the manual mechanism, and did not see how he could have missed if he wanted to, for the carrier turned hard starboard right into him. Contemptuous of the erratic antiaircraft fire, he "flew right down the gun barrel of one of those big pom poms up forward." He tried to get a shot at it, but his gun jammed, so he did a flipper turn at the fantail. The carrier was rearming and regassing the planes, and "gas hoses were scattered all over the place." Gay yearned, as he often had, for forward guns on his TBD. He soared up by the bridge where he "could see the little Jap captain up there jumping up and down raising Hell."[46]

From his Zero, Fujita witnessed an action which must have been Gay's attempt. To the best of Fujita's knowledge, only one of the torpedo planes he and his comrades had been blasting was able to release a missile. Fujita saw it and went through some frantic gyrations to attract *Soryu*'s attention—banking his plane and flying over the steel fish's traces. At last *Soryu* turned and the torpedo sped by. Out of ammunition and low on fuel, Fujita landed aboard *Soryu* where he discovered, much to his surprise, that his carrier had not seen the torpedo. Evidently *Soryu*'s escape had been a piece of sheer luck.[47]

Gay had no sooner cleared the ship than five Zeros came down on him in a line. The second or third of them shot out his rudder control and ailerons. One wing snapped off, the TBD sank like a rock, but Gay managed to work his way clear just in time. He grabbed a bag holding the rubber life raft and also a black rubber seat cushion. He did not know exactly what he would do with the latter, but Waldron had told his men that in case they ever got into a spot like this, never to throw away anything. Gay soon discovered that by hiding under the seat he was effectively concealed from enemy view until the battle passed north of him and he could safely inflate his life raft.

There he floated, slightly wounded in both arm and leg, until a PBY came to his rescue the next day.[48]

Mitscher recommended the entire squadron for the Medal of Honor. Although too much could not be said in praise of VT-8's bravery, whoever wrote the justification for the Medal of Honor gave a melodramatic and exaggerated picture of the action's results: "Those who were left dropped their torpedoes at point blank range, saw them run true and explode with blinding flashes against the sides of the enemy carriers. They had made certain for the Task Force, and for the Navy, that Japanese air power was crippled at the start."[49]

After Pearl Harbor, the Japanese press seized upon the midget submariners, lost except for one man, and made of them the heroes of the attack, although they contributed nothing to Japan's victory of December 7, 1941. A similar phenomenon occurred in the United States after Midway in connection with VT-8, somewhat to the resentment of survivors of other units which had performed just as gallantly and suffered equally grievous losses.[50]

One suspects that an unwitting reason for the concentration upon VT-8 was Ensign Gay. Handsome, articulate, with considerable charm and humor, of proven courage and resourcefulness, he was a public relations officer's dream come true.

Decades after the event, it takes nothing from the reputation of *Hornet*'s torpedomen to acknowledge that others, too, fought and died with "conspicuous gallantry" at Midway.

CHAPTER 28

"They Were Almost Wiped Out"

Although Waldron did not know it, he had a fighter escort, quite by accident. Gray's Wildcats of *Enterprise*'s VF-6 were so much faster than the TBDs that they had to swing back and forth in "S" turns to keep the torpedo planes in view. About halfway to his tactical height of 22,000 feet, Gray became confused. He followed VT-8, the advance squadron, mistaking it for Lindsey's VT-6. At approximately the spot where Waldron turned off toward Nagumo's carriers, Gray momentarily lost sight of the TBDs. When he picked them up again, several dozen fighters had already jumped his charges. Gray was in an unfortunate spot. He had lost VT-6 and it was too late to do anything for VT-8. McClusky's dive bombers were not yet in sight. For all Gray knew, he might have lost the entire attacking force.

Evidently Gray decided that the best service he could render was to use his ten fighters as scouting planes, and he continued to fly over the area until he was dangerously low on gas. Then he radioed the task force at approximately 0952 that he was over the target, running short of fuel and would have to return to base soon. About ten minutes later he tried again: "There is no combat patrol over the enemy fleet. We have been flying over the enemy fleet for the past half hour. They are 8 DDs, 2 BB and 2 carriers." Another report indicates that he included, "Course of enemy north." To this *Enterprise* fighter base shot off an uncompromising, "Attack immediately!"[1] According to both Morison and Lord, the voice urging attack was that of Miles Browning, and McClusky, leading the dive bombers, assumed that the message was meant for him.[2] It would have been quite in character for Browning to thus exhort any and every aircraft within reach of voice radio.

This exchange may be the origin of the famous incident which naval expert Fletcher Pratt recounted—that VT-8, having found the Japanese fleet but being low on fuel and lacking fighter cover, requested permission to withdraw and refuel. Spruance is supposed to have flashed back, "Attack at once!"[3] Such a request would have made no sense in view of VT-8's mission and Waldron's character, but it was logical for Gray under the circumstances. Either because he failed to receive this transmission, or because he could not comply, Gray ushered his fighters safely home to *Enterprise* for refueling.[4] Irony piled on irony as, in scouting the Japanese, Gray missed the unit he was supposed to escort. It so happened that the agreed-upon signal, "Come on down, Jim!" would never have been sent in any case, for Lindsey was one of the first shot down.

VT-6 was a much more experienced unit than VT-8, consisting of veterans of the Marshalls, Wake, and Marcus campaigns. Its newest member had racked up more than 2,500 hours of flight time, most of it in torpedo planes. The loss of Lindsey's aircraft just outside Pearl Harbor had decreased the available TBDs to fourteen. Lindsey's attack plan was to divide these aircraft into two equal parts, one under his personal lead, the other under Ely, each to strike at a different carrier.[5]

At 0949, *Chikuma* informed *Akagi* that she had sighted fourteen enemy planes fifty kilometers to port.[6] Lindsey and Ely split their forces and headed for the carrier across the broad protective circle of destroyers, cruisers and battleships.[7] Nagumo's battle timetable notes at 0958, "14 enemy planes divided in two groups are heading for us, particularly for CarDiv 1 . . . ."[8] From his position on *Akagi*'s bridge, Genda had an excellent view and sped a prayer in the direction of Captain Jisaku Okada, whose *Kaga* seemed to be the immediate target.[9]

At 1000, with *Kaga* under fire, Nagumo sent Yamamoto and the Midway attack force fleet commanders a truly astonishing message:

> Carried out air attack on AF at 0330. Many enemy shore-based planes attacked us subsequent to 0415. We have suffered no damages. At 0428, enemy composed 1 carrier, 7 cruisers and 5 destroyers sighted in position TO SHI RI 34, on course southwest, speed 20 knots. After destroying this, we plan to resume our AF attack. Our position at 0700 is HE E A 00, course 30 degrees, speed 24 knots.[10]

Thus Nagumo corrected his previous reporting of the number of enemy carriers sighted, but he did not inform his chief that the Mobile Force was under attack by United States carrier-based torpedo planes, or that an American submarine was snapping at his heels. For at 0930 *Arashi* got around to radioing *Akagi* of *Nautilus*'s attack, adding, "Countered immediately with depth charges, but results unknown."[11] Two of these "ashcans" came much too close for Brockman's peace of mind, and he did not lift his periscope again until 0955.[12] All in all, Nagumo's summary could not have given Yamamoto a true picture and no doubt contributed to the complacency aboard *Yamato*.

Genda continued to gaze at *Kaga*. Either his prayers were efficacious or Okada did not need them, for the carrier skipper was doing fine, maneuvering the big flattop as skillfully as a cowboy reining his pony. "*Kaga* seems to be fighting pretty well," Genda observed. And Nagumo replied confidently, "She is all right."

Fairly sure that it was all over but the shouting, Genda left the bridge and dropped in on the flight command post to question some of the Midway attack pilots. "How about the skill of enemy fliers over Midway?" he asked.

"Enemy fighters are lousy indeed," replied one pilot. "I think they were almost wiped out."

On the unfavorable side, Genda learned that they had caught no enemy planes on the ground and that antiaircraft fire was fierce. On the other hand, he confirmed that Japanese fighter aircraft were far superior to the American.

Lieutenant Okajima, designated to command the Sixth Air Group to be stationed on Midway after the Japanese takeover, observed, "Staff Officer, today's engagement is tough." Since early morning he and his men had been engaged in beating off the series of attacks.

"Yes, it is," answered Genda easily, "but nothing to worry about." With that he hurried back to the bridge. He found that evidently *Kaga*'s attackers had joined other Americans around *Hiryu*. Orange tracer bullets were streaming in all directions and with black bursts of antiaircraft fire and dark spirals of smoke from burning enemy planes, made a sinister pattern of Hallowe'en colors across the sky. The lookouts reported one Devastator after another knocked out of action. Genda was in high feather. If this kept up, they would eliminate the entire American carrier-based torpedo plane force and be in a position to launch an all-out, prompt attack on the United States flattop, unopposed except for a handful of "lousy indeed" fighters.

Excitement swept over Nagumo, Kusaka and all those gathered with them on *Akagi*'s bridge. Lookouts shouted the battle's progress in voices blazing with exultation: "Five planes left!" "Three left, two left, one left!" Then a final cry, "All shot down!"

We don't need to be afraid of enemy planes no matter how many they are! The thought sang through Genda's brain. *Originally I had some doubt about the defensibility of the task force against an enemy air raid, but now I see how great it is,* he told himself.

This is a winning battle! he exulted. *So, we had better first destroy the enemy planes and then destroy the enemy carriers before we launch a devastating attack upon Midway from this midnight to to-morrow morning.*[13]

The ordeal of VT-6 was very little less deadly than that of VT-8. Of the fourteen aircraft which began the attack, ten were shot down. Of those which made it back to *Enterprise*, one was so far gone it had to be pushed over the side.[14] Although many Japanese eyewitnesses spoke admiringly of the enemy's courageous persistence in boring in despite the Zeros and antiaircraft fire,[15] Genda got the impression that "some of them apparently hesitated to make a daring dash in the face of fierce attacks from both the air and the sea."[16]

Genda had no idea just how slow those Devastators really were, especially when weighed down with a heavy torpedo. It was like trying "to make a daring dash" on a tired mule. That any of them escaped was little short of miraculous. At the same time, there is little doubt that the Zero pilots were beginning to feel the strain. One after another returned to their carriers for ammunition, although few ran out of fuel. As soon as the plane was refitted, the same pilot, after an encouraging pat on the back from the maintenance crew, climbed back into his cockpit and took off again—over and over and over.[17]

Lieutenant (j.g.) Robert E. Laub had little opposition as he released his torpedo 800 yards from the target. As he squirmed out of the area, a single Zero made one pass at him, its fire scarcely touching the Devastator.[18] Machinist Albert W. Winchell saw one torpedo explode in a single flash as a freak hit struck squarely on its warhead. He dropped his own torpedo at what he knew was too great a range, but he could not break off his run in time for a second try. Zeros made after him for only a short distance, nothing like the determined pursuit they had made against the Midway planes.

Winchell and his gunner, ARM 3/c Douglas M. Cossett, flew out of the conflict into a private war of their own—one with the sea. They had scarcely cleared the battle zone when fuel pouring out of the tanks and steady engine failure necessitated an emergency landing. Winchell made a beautiful job of it, and his men were able to salvage their life raft, emergency rations, first aid kits, and parachutes. Both were painfully but not seriously wounded, and they settled down to await rescue, using their parachutes as awnings, sails, or sea anchors, depending on the wind and weather. For days they floated on, dipping in the cooling sea when the presence of small fish told them no sharks were around. The latter closed in repeatedly, Winchell and Cossett beating them off with the aluminum oars and a Bowie knife.

Occasionally a plane droned by in the distance, but none close enough to see the raft. Winchell shook his fist at each receding dot and shouted, "All right, you bastards, see if I ever buy you a drink at the O Club!" When emergency rations were gone, the men plotted an assault on an albatross which followed them inquisitively. Braving ominous memories of "The Rime of the Ancient Mariner," Winchell pounced on the bird and slit its throat. But raw albatross was not exactly gourmet fare. Despite its huge wing spread, the body was no larger than a chicken, reeked of fish, and was too tough to chew.

About their twelfth day of drifting, they saw and signaled a submarine. To their despair, it proved to be Japanese. The sub circled them while a number of crewmen and an officer emerged on deck to look them over. But evidently the Japanese decided the refugees were too weak to question and not worth shooting, for the craft turned away and sped off. Not until June 21 did a PBY find the two fliers and whisk them off to the hospital at Midway. They had drifted for seventeen days, had lost about sixty pounds each, and were the last survivors to be rescued.[19]

The story of another plane s crew had no such happy ending. At about 1630 on June 4, *Nagara* spotted a life raft and ordered *Makigumo* to investigate. If the survivors were Americans, the rescuers were to "interrogate the prisoners to ascertain the enemy's situation and then dispose of them suitably."[20]

The men proved to be an ensign and an aviation machinist mate second class of VS-6 from *Enterprise*. At first the Japanese did not abuse them; the surgeon treated their wounds and the crew shared cigarettes with them.[21] Still, their interrogator, Lieutenant Ryuhichi Katsumata, threatened them with a dagger when they refused to answer questions.[22] Whatever the reason, the prisoners gave their captors some surprisingly accurate information about Midway's defenses, although, apparently, little or nothing about the task forces.

A few days later, with *Makigumo* headed toward the Aleutians, Commander Isamu Fujita decided the prisoners had outlived their usefulness. Even the promise of the Americans' personal effects— including the ensign's lighter inscribed with the affectionate little pun, "To my Matchless Husband"—elicited no volunteer executioners.[23] But late that night, the unfortunate men were taken on deck, blindfolded, weighed down with five-gallon kerosene cans filled with water, and thrown overboard.[24] According to Captain Shigeo Hirayama, then *Makigumo*'s navigation officer, the two Americans accepted their fate quietly, with no sign of fear.[25]

Meanwhile, *Yorktown* delayed launching her planes until 0838 on June 4. The air officer, Commander M. E. Arnold, did not believe that Nagumo would keep a steady course to Midway which, if he maintained it, would put him no more than eighty or ninety miles away from the atoll at the time *Yorktown*'s fliers reached the area. Therefore Arnold ordered his squadron commanders to keep to the east of the last reported enemy position. If they did not find the carriers, they should turn starboard and pursue a reverse course.[26] These instructions, in addition to the delayed launching, proved most fortunate for the American cause.

First to take off was Lieutenant Commander Lance E. "Lem" Massey's VT-3, followed in short order by Lieutenant Commander John S. Thach's six Wildcats. Fletcher could spare no more fighters, for he had to keep some aboard to cover VS-3 which he retained in case any more Japanese carriers poked their bows over the horizon.[27]

Lem Massey was one of the most combat-experienced torpedo pilots in the United States Navy, having served with VT-6 on all their early strikes, until on April 17, 1942, he assumed command of VT-3. Under the impact of his drive and know-how, long hours of schooling and flight at Kaneohe Naval Air Station on Oahu, VT-3 entered the battle of Midway as combat-ready as a unit could be.[28]

Moreover, Massey had worked closely with Jimmy Thach, another sharp-as-tacks air officer, concerning protective fighter tactics. The

Wildcats had to fly high to pick up enough diving speed to be of any use against the Zeros. Thach assigned two of his F4F-4s to remain at 2,500 feet, just under the clouds, to warn the others by fighter-to-fighter radio when the Japanese interceptors jumped the Wildcats. Thach with the other three fighter pilots would stay over 5,000 feet and dive when needed. The thinness of the cover would have been laughable had it not been tragic. No amount of skill or will to fight can make a bedspread out of a handkerchief. Thach hoped to lower the odds by a technique he devised and which later became known as the "Thach weave." Two Wildcats would work together, and when a Zero got on one's tail—the customary Japanese tactic—the fighter under attack would swing around and bring the enemy into his gunsights.[29]

Akagi lookouts saw "enemy torpedo plane group of 12" at 45,000 meters to port at 1015.[30] Zero pilot Fujita had hoped for time to snatch a bite of lunch, for he had overslept that morning, hence scrambled into his plane without breakfast. But the alarm sounded before he could eat. Fujita and two of his comrades—in the only planes aboard *Soryu* available for immediate operations—took off again.*[31]

A number of other Zeros jumped the two low-level Wildcats, Thach and his men dived into the fray, and an old-style dogfight claimed the entire attention of the American fighters. Thach and his wingman, Ensign R. A. M. Dibb, operated the Thach weave with smooth perfection, as if they had done it for years. Viewed strictly as a dogfight, Thach came out rather well. He lost one plane early in the fight when Ensign Edward Basset went down in flames. Another had to be scratched when Ensign Daniel C. Sheedy brought his badly shot-up Wildcat back to the task force, but being unable to reach *Yorktown*, crash-landed on *Hornet*. The remaining four had to break off the fight for lack of fuel.[32] But as far as their prime mission, that of protecting VT-3, was concerned, the fighters might as well have stayed out of it.

Fujita decided to ignore the fighters and attack the bombers. His two companions had disappeared. Hungry, exhausted, and, he thought, alone, he headed for the formation. He hit its edge, two of the enemy

---

*Fujita's statement that fighters accompanied this group of torpedo planes helps identify it as VT-3.

fell, and as he repeated the maneuver, about ten Japanese fighters joined him to press the attack.

But Fujita's luck had run out. On his way back to *Soryu,* Japanese antiaircraft fire struck his plane, which began to burn. He had no choice but to hit the silk—an unpleasant option, for his Zero had dropped to about 200 meters above the sea. His parachute opened just as he struck the water. He surfaced promptly, thanks to his life jacket, but he was tangled in the strings of his chute like a fish in a net, and had a long struggle to free himself.[33]

Meanwhile, eighteen or twenty Zeros snarled down on Massey's Devastators, concentrating their fire on the lead plane. Before he overflew the outer destroyer screen, Massey had fought his last fight. The last glimpse his wingman had of him, Massey was standing on the wing stub of his plane, having crawled out of the flaming cockpit at too low an altitude to use a parachute.[34]

Fuchida and his fliers down on the flight deck cheered and whistled encouragement and congratulations as the Zeros shot down one torpedo plane after another. Then a group of Devastators aimed straight for *Akagi,* but much to Fuchida's amazement, just at the perfect release moment, they zipped up over *Akagi* and sped on toward *Hiryu.* Yamaguchi's flagship was almost surrounded by torpedo tracks, but none of the missiles struck home.[35]

Chief Aviation Pilot Wilhelm G. Esders, a highly experienced and competent torpedo pilot, moved up and led his five-plane division against *Hiryu.* The other six pilots, like Massey, never came within launching distance. All five of Esders's section released their torpedoes, but Captain Tameo Kaku swung *Hiryu* hard to starboard. Three missiles passed ahead of the carrier, the other two astern. Esders could clearly see aircraft grouped ready to launch on the after end of the flight deck. He could not pause to see what results, if any, he obtained, for the ubiquitous Zeros were pursuing him out of the area. Although his plane was seriously damaged, the fighters let him get away. He had to make an emergency sea landing just in sight of *Yorktown.* The destroyer *Hammann* picked him up later in the day, but not before his gunner had died of wounds.[36]

The destroyer *Arashi* scooped in one of the pilots who crashed near the Mobile Force, a twenty-three-year-old ensign from Chicago. Kiyosumi Tanikawa, *Arashi's* torpedo officer, the only Japanese aboard with any knowledge of English, interrogated the prisoner. Tanikawa could not speak the language, only read and write it after a fashion. So the session was a slow process of written questions and answers. At least some duress was involved, for Tanikawa loomed over the prisoner, sword in hand, throughout the questioning.

Perhaps the American was too shocked and exhausted to realize the import of what he was saying; perhaps he thought the battle had progressed too far for his information to be of any use to his captors. Or perhaps he talked out of a very human if unheroic and somewhat naïve hope that he could thus save his own life. Whatever his motivation, he parted with some valuable data. At 1300, Captain Kosaku Ariga, commander of DesDiv 4, sent a message to Nagumo, Kondo, and Yamamoto, with which we shall deal at the proper time. The young man's cooperation availed him nothing. The Japanese killed him and his body either fell or was thrown overboard.[37]

Of the forty-one Devastators launched on June 4, only four bedraggled survivors reached their home carriers. No one wasted any tears over the actual aircraft. The ancient, lumbering TBDs had proved totally unsuitable for modern warfare, and the sooner they were replaced by TBFs the better. But the loss of such men as Waldron, Lindsey, Massey, and their young comrades was a cruel blow.

What, if anything, the sacrifice of VT-8, VT-6, and VT-3 contributed to the United States victory at Midway is a matter of speculation. The usual view is that they performed a valuable and heroic, if unplanned, role in distracting Japanese attention from the incoming American dive bombers.[38] Others have stated that full credit for this service should go to VT-3 and Thach's Wildcats, because enough time elapsed after VT-8 and VT-6 made their ill-fated attempts to allow the Zeros to climb to higher altitude.[39] A check of the Japanese chronology indicates that this school of thought has a point.[40]

But other factors must be considered. An element of Japanese choice was involved, for the dive bombers did not sneak in unobserved. Nagumo's timetable clearly reflects warnings from escort vessels of enemy aircraft coming in from the moment they penetrated the outer ring.[41] The Japanese carriers could have diverted a number of Zeros from going over the torpedo planes to deal with this new menace, which could only be dive bombers. To a certain extent, the Japanese were obsessed with the torpedo technique, at which they excelled. Therefore, they concentrated on the TBDs, although American skill at torpedoing was notoriously low, and American torpedoes of such poor quality that when one did hit and explode it was an event to write home about.

What is more, all the American strikes, land- or carrier-based, however abortive, had kept Nagumo's task force on the jump 'all morning. In particular, his fighter pilots had been under relentless pressure. To that extent, at least, every American who participated contributed something to the sum total of victory.

CHAPTER 29

"A Burning Hell"

From his height of 20,000 feet, Wade McClusky had a clear view from horizon to horizon, but however far he craned his neck, all he could see was the Pacific Ocean stretching for limitless miles. The time was 0920, and he had reached the anticipated point of interception, 142 miles from *Enterprise*.[1] Far off to port, a subtle change in the texture of the sea hinted that Midway's shoals lay just over the horizon. Some of his pilots on the formation's far left could see smoke rolling up from the stricken base.[2] But where was the Japanese Mobile Force?

Built rather like his own SBD Dauntless dive bomber—short and stocky—McClusky was almost a stranger to it, being a fighter pilot by training and experience. He had joined *Enterprise* in June 1940 as commander of VF-6 and became Air Group Commander, in charge of all the carrier's airmen, on March 15, 1942. Since that date, he had familiarized himself with the Dauntless as best he could, snatching an hour here, a few minutes there, from his busy schedule. Now, leading thirty-two dive bombers into battle, he knew the plane fairly well, could take off from the carrier and land back on the flight deck, but he had never dropped a bomb from an SBD.[3] So no one, McClusky least of all, would have termed him an experienced dive bomber pilot. What he brought to his job was a gift for command, composed in equal parts of personal fearlessness and the ability to feed unexpected data into his brain cells and click out a prompt, intelligent answer. Spruance, who never tossed adjectives around recklessly, called McClusky "terrific."[4]

Here was a situation which challenged him to the full. Should he assume that he had beaten the Japanese to the location, and circle the area until Nagumo's fleet steamed into view? Conversely, should he continue toward Midway, in case he was behind the Japanese? His planes had eaten up too much fuel for him to send them winging out on an expanding square—the conventional air search tactic—to seek out the missing enemy. Should he get his men home to *Enterprise* while the getting was good? Whatever he decided, he must do so in a hurry, for he could only spare fifteen minutes to search before fuel consumption would force him to take his flight back to the carrier.

After a quick consultation with his plotting board, McClusky decided to go on for an extra thirty-five miles on course 240°, then turn northwest parallel to the anticipated Japanese route.[5] Captain Murray, skipper of *Enterprise*, termed this resolution "the most important decision of the entire action," and Nimitz agreed that it was "one of the most important decisions of the battle and one that had decisive results."[6]

At 0955, about seven minutes after the SBDs swung northwest, McClusky spotted the long, white brush-stroke of a ship's wake across the sparkling blue surface. Following the line through his binoculars, he saw what he took to be a cruiser speeding northward. McClusky rightly deduced that if the "cruiser" captain was in that big a hurry, he must be trying to catch up with the rest of the Japanese fleet. Therefore McClusky changed course from northwest to north and followed the speeding ship.[7] His unwitting guide was the destroyer *Arashi*, which had become separated from the Mobile Force, being engaged in depth-charging *Nautilus* when Nagumo changed his course.[8]

While trailing *Arashi*, McClusky lost one of his aircraft, that of Ensign Eugene A. Greene. The reason for this dropout remains a mystery. Greene and his gunner were reported to have climbed into their lifeboat about forty miles from the U.S. fleet, but after that all trace of them was lost.[9]

The *Enterprise* dive bombers had been following McClusky about ten minutes in his stalking of the Japanese destroyer when the enemy fleet broke into view. But his troubles were by no means over. Just as Ensign Tony F. Schneider's group moved into the outer ring of Japanese screening vessels, his plane ran out of fuel, forcing him to turn south and land in the sea. He and his gunner spent three days in their life raft before a PBY fished them out and took them to Midway.[10]

At almost the same moment that Schneider turned away, Lieutenant Richard H. Best, the blue-eyed, youthful-looking, and combat-seasoned commander of VB-6, caught a signal from Lieutenant (j.g.) Edwin J. Kroeger, one of his wingmen. Kroeger had run out of oxygen. Best could have instructed his wingman to break off and return to *Enterprise* at a lower altitude, but he had a good reason for reluctance to do so. Best knew that his fellow squadron commander, Lieutenant W. Earl Gallaher of VS-6, had to equip his unit with 500-pound bombs because, being the first dive bombers to take off, they did not have the deck space necessary for a run long enough to launch with 1,000-pound bombs. As a result, only Best's men packed the heavy wallop. Rather than lose the extra punch of Kroeger's 1,000 pounder, Best led his squadron down to 15,000 feet. There he removed his own face mask, indicating to his men that they could safely do the same. This movement brought Best below and ahead of McClusky, so that he could not observe any visual signal from his group commander[11]

McClusky broke radio silence to instruct Best to hit the carrier to port, and at the same moment he ordered Gallaher to attack the target to starboard. Deciding to head the starboard strike himself, McClusky added, "Earl, follow me."[12]

Somehow, Best missed McClusky's radioed instructions and assumed his target to be the "left hand" carrier. He so radioed McClusky.[13]

At this time, Nagumo's carriers were lined up in no orderly formation. Two successive ship-by-ship turns to the northeast had left *Akagi* and *Kaga* to the southwest, *Kaga* "positioned in the direction of *Akagi*'s starboard bow," with *Soryu* somewhat to the northeast, *Hiryu* in the same direction but far enough away that she escaped immediate attention. As VB-6 and VS-6 approached from the southwest, there seems little doubt that the carrier to starboard was *Kaga*, and to port *Akagi*.[14]

As Best made for *Kaga*, he split his division in three parts, one to hit straight in, the second to port, and the third to starboard. This would catch the carrier in a squeeze and prevent concentration of her antiaircraft guns. Just as he began his run, McClusky plunged past him like a kingfisher. Best broke off his dive and took off toward *Akagi*, thus unavoidably delaying his strike by a few moments.[15]

All during the torpedo bombing attacks, the Japanese had rushed preparations for their own strike on the enemy task force, prodded along by a message from *Akagi*: "Hurry up preparations for the second wave."[16] Reports reached the flagship's bridge of more American planes coming in, but thus far the clouds concealed them. At 1020, lookouts spotted a dive bomber over *Kaga*, and *Akagi* went into a maximum turn.*[17]

At first Genda was not too concerned, stating in retrospect,

> I thought dive bombers might be troublesome, but, from my own experience of seeing just a while ago that enemy skill was not so good, concluded that they, too, might not be so good. But, I had a concern in that our fighters were flying at low altitude following the previous engagement and they needed some time to climb up again to intercept enemy dive bombers.

Perhaps antiaircraft fire could drive them off, or the carriers maneuver out of their way.[18]

But within the instant a *Kaga* lookout shouted, "Dive bombers!" Captain Takahisa Amagai, *Kaga*'s air officer, felt a moment's professional admiration. "Splendid was their tactic," he observed, "of diving upon our force from the direction of the sun, taking advantage of intermittent clouds."[19]

Communications Officer Lieutenant Commander Sesu Mitoya, standing on the flight deck near the tower, dove flat as the scream from the dive bombers rose to a banshee-like wail.[20] The time was 1022. The first three bombs missed the target.[21] Then Gallaher, roaring down to 2,500 feet to release, dropped his bomb starboard aft squarely amidst the planes massed for takeoff.[22] Instantly the flight deck was a holocaust. As the aircraft tilted over on a wing or forward on the nose, the fuselage formed a chimney flue spouting flame and smoke.[23]

The next two missiles failed to strike, and in this slight relief Lieutenant Fiyuma, the fire control officer, raced to the bridge, where Captain Okada stood staring into space as if he could not take in what was happening. Fiyuma reported all passages below were afire and most of the crew trapped. All power was cut off. Fiyuma urged Okada to leave the bridge and go with his staff to the anchor deck to escape,

---

*Considerable controversy exists over which unit struck which carrier first. It is most natural that the *Enterprise* and *Yorktown* groups should each want credit for drawing first blood. The authors have followed the chronology of Japanese records and eyewitness accounts. Actually, hits were so nearly simultaneous as to make the point of little interest to anyone but a unit historian. All concerned were Americans and there is plenty of credit to go around.

for the carrier was already starting to list. But Okada only shook his head dreamily. "I will remain with my ship," he said. Mitoya left the bridge to try to contact the Engine Room crews through the Ready Room, and when he came back, there was no bridge, no Okada, no Fiyuma.[24]

In his absence, the seventh and eighth bombs had struck near each other in the vicinity of the forward elevator.[25] One of these crashed through the elevator and exploded among the planes on the hangar deck. These aircraft had been armed, fueled and were ready to be lifted for the second wave, destined never to take off. Amagai saw the second hit explode directly over the head of the carrier's maintenance officer, and curiously enough the sight steadied his nerves and engendered a certain objectivity. All men must die, and this was the way he would like to go—in one instantaneous flash. *Let a bomb come upon my head, if it comes,* he thought.[26]

What did fall on his head was command of *Kaga*, for the third direct hit struck a small gasoline truck near the island, and flaming debris killed everyone on the bridge.[27] That left Amagai senior officer aboard, and he devoted all his energies to directing the fire fighting, in the hope that the ship might yet be saved. That hope was to prove vain.[28] The ninth American bomb delivered the fourth and last hit, landing almost directly amidships far to port,[29] and was almost redundant, for without light or power Amagai's efforts were doomed to failure.

Fuchida was so intensely interested in the preparations to launch *Akagi's* second wave that he did not consciously note the attack on *Kaga* immediately. At 1022, the bridge ordered the fighters to take off as soon as readied. Masuda swung his white flag and the first Zero sped down the flight deck. Then a lookout screamed, "Hell divers!" Fuchida glanced up in time to see three planes plummeting down, seemingly aimed straight for the spot near the command post where he sat. He just had time to recognize the stubby silhouette of the Dauntless when three black dots dropped from the aircraft and seemed to float almost leisurely toward *Akagi*. Fuchida prudently crawled behind a mantelet.[30]

According to American records, Best's unit of five dive bombers attacked *Akagi*. To the best of the authors' knowledge, Japanese eyewitness accounts and records were unanimous that only three were involved. Rushing down in a nearly vertical dive, Best saw a plane taking off as he peered through his gunsight. He released his missile at 2,500 feet, fused to ensure a four-foot penetration of a carrier flight deck. He was perfectly sure that he had secured a hit "just forward and on center line."[31] In his book, Fuchida also stated that the first bomb struck.[32] Yet in a personal interview he informed Prange that the first bomb missed. "It dropped on starboard side into sea, *brrrr*," he said in his flavorful English, "and in sea explode. Big water splash."[33] *Akagi's* damage chart shows that the first bomb was a near miss about ten meters off the port bow,[34] and Genda remembered the waterspout which it sent over the bridge, drenching everyone and turning their faces black. According to Genda, Nagumo and his staff "were surprised but not scared."[35]

The second bomb struck near the amidship elevator, twisting it like a piece of futuristic sculpture and dropping into the hangar.[36] Certain that the third bomb would be even more accurate and devastating, Fuchida rolled over on his stomach, pressed his face to the deck and crossed his arms over his head for protection. The actual sound of impact was not quite as strong as the first hit, but it struck near the edge of the port flight deck,[37] and *Akagi's* damage chart notes, "Fatal hit. Several holes."[38] Then followed a moment of uncanny silence.[39]

Genda was surprised to feel so little shock from the two direct hits. This fact, plus his naturally forward-looking disposition, lulled him into a momentary calm. Akagi *has been hit, too,* he thought. *What a pity! We must not be downed,* he added to himself, *as we still have the Second Carrier Division.*[40]

Genda's optimism was not entirely misplaced, for normally the two strikes would not have been fatal. But the dive bombers had caught the First Carrier Division with flight decks full of armed and fueled aircraft, with others in the same condition in the hangar decks waiting to be lifted. Moreover, there had been no time to return the 800-kilogram land bombs to the arsenal. It was induced explosions from this stacked-up destruction and a chain reaction of flaming planes which would shortly turn *Akagi* into what Kusaka called "a burning hell."[41]

Even as Genda reminded himself of Yamaguchi's carriers, he looked toward *Soryu.* She, too, was sending up a billow of white smoke. Genda "was really shocked for the first time"; for once in his life both ideas and speech were knocked out of him.[42]

About 200 men had been flung over *Akagi*'s side.[43] Masuda was frantically trying to corral everyone below deck under cover. Fuchida went to the briefing room, which was rapidly becoming an emergency hospital. He asked a rescue worker why they did not take the wounded to sick bay, and learned that the entire lower levels were afire. On hearing this, Fuchida tried to reach his cabin to salvage what he could, but fire and smoke turned him back.[44] Had he and Genda been content to relax in the comfort of their hospital beds, they would have shared the fate of the other patients, every one of whom perished.

Fuchida wandered back to the bridge, as if instinctively seeking his Eta Jima classmate with whom he had shared so much joy and now must share sorrow. By now Genda realized all too well the full measure of Japan's loss, but he was not the type to weep on anyone's shoulder. He looked at Fuchida briefly and remarked laconically, "*Shimatta* [We goofed]," which seemed to sum up the situation in a nutshell.[45]

Meanwhile, Kusaka had been adding up the score in his usual practical fashion. The radio room and antenna had been destroyed, making any communication impossible. Despite prompt flooding of forward ammunition and bomb storage rooms and activating carbon dioxide fire-fighting apparatus, matters were rapidly getting out of hand.[46] By 1042, the steering apparatus was out of commission, the engines stopped and all hands were ordered to fire-fighting stations. Only two machine guns and one antiaircraft gun remained able to fire.[47]

With all these factors in mind, Kusaka decided the time had come to let Rear Admiral Hiroaki Abe, Commander of CruDiv 8 and next senior officer to Nagumo, assume temporary command of the Mobile Force while Nagumo transferred his flag elsewhere. With the brain trust of the Mobile Force still intact, they could continue the fight with *Hiryu* as the nucleus, preferably in a night attack, the Japanese specialty. Therefore, Kusaka urged Nagumo to leave *Akagi* and reestablish his headquarters on another ship.

"But Nagumo, having a feeling heart, refused to listen to me," recalled Kusaka. "I urged him two or three times, but in vain. He firmly continued to stand by the side of a compass on the bridge." At this point Captain Aoki, an Eta Jima classmate of Kusaka's, moved close to him and said softly, "Chief of Staff, as the ship's captain I am going to take care of this ship with all responsibility, so I urge you, the Commander in Chief, and all other staff officers to leave this vessel as soon as possible, so that the command of the force may be continued."[48]

Thus reinforced, Kusaka raised his voice and scolded Nagumo for letting his heart rule his head in such an important matter. Finally, Nagumo bowed to the dictates of reason and consented to be rescued.[49] His decision almost came too late, for already the stairways from the bridge were blocked by fire,[50] and the staff had to evacuate by shimmying down a rope. Being chunky, Kusaka nearly stuck in the window, but squeezed through with the aid of a few hearty shoves, only to fall from the middle of the rope to the flight deck, twisting both ankles and burning his hands and one leg.[51]

Fuchida was the last man down the rope, which had already begun to smolder. One of the thundering explosions which continually rocked *Akagi* hurled him high in the air and smashed him onto the flight deck with a force that broke both legs in the ankle, arch, and heel region. He thought that this was the end of the line for him, and between pain, grief, and physical weakness, he faced the prospect with few emotions beyond an intense weariness. Little tongues of flame were licking in his direction and his uniform had actually begun to smolder when two enlisted men ran out of the smoke, picked him up and swung him in a net aboard a lifeboat filled with Nagumo and his staff headed for the light cruiser *Nagara*. Fuchida was not officially a member of the staff, hence was not scheduled to evacuate until the rest of the flying officers did so, but he could not be left behind in that condition.[52]

As Genda was about to enter the boat, a petty officer, noting that Genda had burned one hand, pulled off his glove and handed it over, saying, "Air Staff Officer, please use this." At almost the same moment, a sailor, Genda's "boy," rushed up and gave him a *han* (seal) and his bank deposit book. Somehow the boy had braved the flames below deck to salvage what he could of his chief's possessions. Genda was by no means certain he would live to use either item, and in any case his savings were far from princely, but the kindness of both these men, who could think of another at such a moment, touched him deeply.[53]

CHAPTER 30

"A Calamity Like This"

But what of the other carriers? If contemporary American reports of the battle of Midway could be accepted as gospel, nothing happened to *Soryu* at the hands of the dive bombers. Nobody sank her; nobody even tried to sink her. The problem seems to have been, as Walter Lord has observed, a misunderstanding of how big *Soryu* really was.[1] Yet sink she did, so some group must have attacked her. And the preponderance of evidence points to *Yorktown*.

During the hour's delay between launch of Task Force Sixteen's dive bombers and *Yorktown*'s, Fletcher received no amplifying reports. But Task Force Seventeen's staff put the time to good use, studying the initial Japanese plot, course and speed. These calculations indicated that if Nagumo proceeded along these lines, he would be only ninety miles from Midway. This appeared a much closer approach than necessary, so squadron commanders were warned not to overfly the course line—to turn right, because the Japanese probably would reverse course.[2]

Commander Murr E. Arnold, *Yorktown*'s air officer, planned that Massey's VT-3 and Lieutenant Commander Maxwell F. Leslie's seventeen SBDs of VB-3 should strike the enemy in unison. So he directed Leslie to orbit *Yorktown* to give the slower torpedo planes a fifteen-minute head start.[3]

At a few minutes after 0900, Leslie lifted off and began his climb to 15,000 feet. Weather conditions could not have been more favorable: "The visibility was excellent, ceiling unlimited with scattered clouds at 3,000 ft. The sea was calm with little or no wind."[4]

Lieutenant (j.g.) Paul A. "Lefty" Holmberg worried lest the battle be over before VB-3 could get into it. He himself almost missed the action. At takeoff, his aircraft, 3-B-2, was caught in Leslie's slip stream and his left wing brushed the gutter on the forward catwalk. Holmberg greatly feared that he would crash and fail to accomplish this, his first combat mission, for which he had trained so long. But he gained altitude and swung into position as Leslie's wingman.[5]

Leslie was having his own troubles, thanks to a "bug" in the electrical bomb arming mechanism. Shortly after reaching 20,000-foot cruising level, Leslie signaled his men to arm their bombs, pushing his own newly installed electric arm switch as he did so. Instead of activating the bomb, it dropped the missile into the sea. When the same thing happened to three other planes, Leslie had to break radio silence to warn the others to use the manual switch. Holmberg could see Leslie berating himself.[6]

Although the accident was no fault of Leslie's, it would be difficult to imagine a more frustrating experience for an officer as conscientious as Leslie. Not only must he lead his men with his own fangs drawn, but his firepower had dropped from seventeen to thirteen before the group had so much as sighted the enemy. But he could still direct his men and perhaps get in some good licks with his guns.

At around 0945, Leslie flew directly over VT-3 and six of VF-3's fighters. He "continued to 'S' turn and follow VT-3." About fifteen minutes later, he asked Massey, in code, if he had spotted the enemy. According to Lieutenant D. W. Shumway, leader of the Third Division, Massey "replied in the affirmative," but Leslie did not receive it.[7]

At 1005 Leslie's gunner, ARM 1/c W. E. Gallagher, spotted the Mobile Force almost dead ahead about thirty-five miles away. In a few minutes, Leslie heard "considerable discussion over the radio regarding VT-3 being attacked by fighters."[8]

Leslie had no difficulty in choosing his target:

> The carrier was a large one with a full deck painted dark red, a forward elevator, a relatively small superstructure located about $1/3$ of the length of the ship aft from the bow on the starboard side, vertical smoke stacks which were inboard from the starboard side and adjoining the superstructure. It could fit the description of the KAGA except for the vertical smoke stacks. The latest model I have seen of the KAGA shows its smoke stacks encased as one protruding horizontally from the starboard side and aft of the superstructure.[9] (Capitals in original.)

A comparison of overhead line drawings of *Kaga* and *Soryu* shows what Leslie was talking about. Neither carrier had vertical smoke stacks, but the drawing of *Soryu* shows two separate stacks so close to the superstructure that they might be called "adjoining." These projected horizontally, then bent downward. *Kaga*'s stacks were indeed "encased as one and protruded outboard . . ." and were farther aft of the superstructure.[10]

To the westward, Leslie saw another carrier with its superstructure on the port side. Later he deduced that this was *Akagi*.[11] Another flattop was indeed somewhat to the westward, and she carried her bridge to port.[12] But she was *Hiryu*, still busily dodging VT-3's torpedo attacks. Under the impression that Lieutenant Wallace C. Short's VS-5 was nearby, Leslie radioed Short to hit the carrier to westward. Not until much later did he learn that VS-5 had been held back.

By now, Leslie's radioman warned that his target was launching planes. Leslie made one final, unsuccessful attempt to contact VT-3 and VF-3. Then he realized that the coordinated attack so carefully crafted had come apart. It was up to him.[13] He did not know that his group was about to become the third prong of a triple attack which could not have been better coordinated had all concerned rehearsed it for weeks.

At "about 1225" (1025 Midway time) Leslie led his men down, firing at the bridge with his fixed guns. Then further frustration—his guns jammed, so he "retired for $4^1/_2$ minutes at high speed to the SE . . ."[14]

Thus Holmberg had the honor and responsibility of leading the actual bombing attack. Heading slightly stern to bow, he caught the large red circle on the deck in his telescopic sight. He held his dive a bit longer than usual, pulling out around 200 feet. Flames were coming from both sides of the carrier as its antiaircraft opened fire. He felt what he assumed was shrapnel hit his plane, but it did not upset his dive, which was almost schoolbook perfect. As he cleared the ship, he saw his target burst into a mass of colors—red, blue, green, and yellow—as it exploded into flame. A plane was taking off just as the bomb detonated, and it blew the aircraft off the deck and into the water. So reported Ensign R. M. Elder, following in plane 3-B-14.[15]

"Five direct hits and three very near misses were scored immediately thereafter," according to Shumway.[16] A bit on the exuberant side, but the results were quite enough to satisfy all but the most dedicated nitpicker. Of the three carriers struck in the attack, *Soryu* suffered the most prompt, intensified damage.

Commencing at 1025, three direct hits in as many minutes, neatly lined up along the port side, triggered ferocious deck fires as well as induced explosions in the bomb-storage, torpedo-storage, and ammunition rooms, plus gas tanks.[17]

There exists the usual conflicting testimony about hits, but Holmberg believed that he had caught the carrier amidships between elevators,[18] and *Soryu*'s executive officer, Commander Hisashi Ohara, agreed. The second hit crashed through the flight deck just in front of the forward elevator, exploding in the hangar deck. The third struck either forward of the Number Three elevator, or among the armed and fueled aircraft awaiting takeoff.[19]

In any case, "Fires enveloped the whole ship in no time," Nagumo reported.[20] As the flames roared and crackled, Captain Ryusaku Yanagimoto placed himself on the signal tower to starboard of the bridge, shouting commands, and ordering and begging his men to save themselves.[21] Obviously no living thing could last much longer on *Soryu*. Below decks, heat so infernal that it melted and warped the hangar deck doors drove survivors topside. The anchor deck became an impromptu hospital where doctors and medical corpsmen worked like robots, ignoring the choking smoke, to give pain-relieving shots to those badly injured, bandaging and stopping bleeding where they could. Those beyond hope had to be left untended to save those who had a chance for life. A large group of sailors were massed on the forward deck with a number of officers, including Ohara, when a terrific induced explosion shot many of them, Ohara among them, into the sea.[22]

Exactly half an hour passed from the first hit on *Soryu* at 1025 until Yanagimoto ordered "Abandon ship." The main engines were stopped, the steering system inoperable, and the fire mains gone. Thirty short minutes had transformed *Soryu* from a smart, proud carrier to a burned-out crematorium. *Hamakaze* and *Isokaze* hovered nearby to pick up survivors, rescuing some from the water while others were fortunate enough to go over the side in good order.

During the process, someone noticed that Yanagimoto was not with them, and looking up, the men could see their captain still on the tower, shouting words of encouragement to the survivors and crying out "Banzai!"[23] Consternation swept the crewmen when they realized that he meant to go down with the ship. Yanagimoto was one of the best loved and most respected skippers in the Japanese or any other Navy, and the men resolved to rescue him in spite of himself. They deputized Chief Petty Officer Abe, a Navy wrestling champ, to bring him to safety, by force if necessary. Abe did his best. He climbed back up the tower, saluted his captain and said, "Captain, I have come on behalf of all your men to take you to safety. They are waiting for you. Please come with me to the destroyer, sir."

Yanagimoto kept on staring straight ahead as if he had not heard. Doggedly Abe advanced on him to pick the captain up bodily in his great wrestler's arms when Yanagimoto turned slowly. He did not utter a word, but his eyes stopped Abe dead in his tracks. The sailor saluted and left his captain. As he moved away, tears smarting in his eyes, he could hear Yanagimoto softly singing *Kimigayo*, the national anthem.[24]

Seeing that their comrades had dealt effectively with *Soryu*, two pilots, Elder and Ensign Bunyan R. "Randy" Cooner, tried their luck with "the light cruiser plane guard," claiming "a near miss and a hit on the fantail."[25] For neither the first nor the last time, the Americans had mistaken a destroyer for a light cruiser. Nor had they scored a hit. One of *Soryu*'s escorts, *Isokaze*, experienced no worse than a near miss off her stern.[26] Lieutenant O. B. Wiseman and Ensign J. C. Butler went after bigger game—a battleship—crediting themselves with "a direct hit on the stern and a near miss."[27] Later an unidentified officer suggested this might have been "a super-heavy cruiser."[28] Exactly what ship was involved is questionable, but Nagumo's records show no hint of a hit on either of his battleships or heavy cruisers at that time.

The dive bombers had accomplished in three minutes what the preceding attack waves had failed to do in three hours. Yet they were no more and no less trained, determined, and brave than the torpedo bombers who had failed to dent a single ship. The United States owed this amazing success in the main to three factors—McClusky's decision to continue his search with an unconventional pattern, the uncoordinated coordination which brought the *Enterprise* and *Yorktown* pilots on the spot within seconds of each other, and the preoccupation of the Zeros with the torpedo attacks.

The dive bombers did not escape unscathed. The *Yorktown* group was the most fortunate—no one was lost in this action. Holmberg led the way home. As he streaked off, he noticed that he, his instrument panel, and the entire forward part of the cockpit were covered with oil. He asked his gunner, AMM 2/c G. A. La Plant, who was a mechanic, what was causing this. "Check the dials and if they are all right, you have lost hydraulic pressure," La Plant replied. This proved to be correct.

In accordance with radio instructions, Holmberg slowed his pace. First Lieutenant Harold S. Bottomley, Jr., the operations officer, and later Leslie joined him. Eventually the entire squadron formed up to return to *Yorktown* in triumph. But instead of a royal welcome, he received a waveoff. *Yorktown* was under attack, a circumstance which will be discussed shortly. After that action, Leslie and Holmberg ditched near *Astoria* and were promptly rescued.[29]

Enterprise was not so lucky. She had lost fourteen dive bombers, of which a number had to ditch for lack of gas.[30] Two Zeros chased McClusky out of the area, but when his ARM 1/c gunner, W. G. Chocholousek, downed one, the other broke off the hunt. McClusky reached the designated Point Option, and once more found himself gazing at empty sea where a fleet should be. He broke radio silence to ask Lieutenant Leonard "Ham" Dow if Point Option had been changed. Dow replied that this was indeed the case; the new rendezvous point was some sixty miles farther. With only five gallons of gas remaining at the end of the sixty-mile hop, McClusky started to let down on a nearby carrier, but recognizing *Yorktown* and wishing to report to Spruance as soon as possible, he continued toward *Enterprise*. He ignored a waveoff, and landed with barely enough gasoline to clean a necktie. As he was heading for the bridge, one of the staff noticed blood running down McClusky's left hand, and dripping onto the deck. "My God, Mac," he cried out, "you've been shot!" So McClusky was hustled off to sick bay, given two shots of brandy, and had his wound treated. It was not serious, but it was enough to ground him for the rest of the action.[31]

One officer who flew home filled with grim pleasure was Lieutenant Clarence E. Dickinson, leader of Gallaher's second division. He had taken a personal satisfaction in the day's work, as he was one of the morning flight off *Enterprise* which ran into the Japanese attack on Pearl Harbor. Hitting the silk over Oahu that day had been no picnic, and Dickinson was happy with the opportunity to even the score. His missile was one of those which struck *Kaga*. Weaving in and out of antiaircraft fire on his way home, Dickinson could not imagine what was taking him so long. He might have been glued to the area, and his speed indicator registered only ninety-five knots instead of the 250 he should be getting out of his Dauntless. Suddenly he realized that instead of closing his dive brakes, he had lowered his landing gear. He immediately rectified the error and resumed proper speed.[32]

A mistake in his fuel gauge sent Dickinson into the Pacific about twenty miles from *Enterprise*. He landed near a destroyer, and was delighted to see that the ship slicing down on him was *Phelps*, on which he had served for over two years before going to flight training. His old shipmates were just as excited as he when they hauled him out, gave him dry clothes, plied him with a stiff drink, and assaulted him with a barrage of questions.[33]

Lieutenant Joe R. Penland, operations officer of VB-6, had much less luck. His engine gave up the ghost when he was about twenty-five miles away from his target and over 100 miles from Point Option. He and his gunner, ARM 2/c H. F. Heard, took to the life raft and had an unexpected cruise until the next afternoon when *Phelps*, with Dickinson leaning at the rail, picked them up.[34]

Ensign Thomas W. Ramsey and his gunner, AMM 2/c Sherman L. Duncan, had a similar but more protracted experience. They drifted for six days before a PBY rescued them. Then came one of those coincidences in which only history indulges—fiction would never dare. When Ramsey climbed up to the cockpit to thank the pilot, he found himself looking at Lieutenant (j.g.) August A. Barthes, a high school friend from Biloxi, Mississippi, whom he had not seen since they attended classes together.[35]

As Best headed home to *Enterprise*, he saw a third carrier located to his east, exploding and smoking. He also saw a group of torpedo planes coming in. Undoubtedly this was Massey's VT-3, harassing *Hiryu* at this time. Four Zeros passed under Best, heading for the torpedo planes. A float aircraft made a weak pass at him, but his gunner shot at it, and drove it off.

Best made his home carrier with thirty or so gallons of fuel to spare. But Midway cost the U.S. Navy the services of this fine airman. That morning, he had tested an oxygen bottle to be sure it was not leaking caustic soda. His first inhalation was loaded with gas fumes.

He snorted it out, seemingly with no ill effects. But the next day he coughed up blood repeatedly. Thinking that he might have ruptured a blood vessel, he went to the flight surgeon and explained about the faulty oxygen canister. Actually, he had activated latent tuberculosis, although he knew no trace of that disease in his family. He saw no more action, and after long hospitalization was retired from the Navy for physical disability.[36]

Aboard Ensign William R. Pittman's aircraft of VS-6, AMM 2/c Floyd D. Adkins struggled with the twin mount free-gun he was holding in his lap. The 175-pound gun had broken loose from its mount during the dive. Immediately after Pittman pulled out of it, "a Messerschmitt type fighter" attacked. Normally it took three men to handle the heavy, awkwardly shaped weapon, and Adkins was a rather slightly built young man. But in this emergency there came to him that surge of superhuman strength which sometimes animates the brave under stress. Bracing the gun against the fuselage, he fired it so effectively that he shot down the fighter. Challenged to lift the weapon back aboard *Enterprise,* Adkins could not budge it from the deck.[37]

Off near the scene of destruction, Fujita finally freed himself from the parachute, which had threatened to engulf him, and scanned the horizon. There he saw a heart-stopping sight—three columns of black smoke, obviously from burning Japanese ships. The distance was much beyond Fujita's swimming range. "And at this moment I left my fate or destiny in the hands of the gods," he reminisced.

Nevertheless, he would do his part. He stripped off shoes, gloves, and flying cap, then began to swim cautiously. At one time a Japanese seaplane passed low overhead, but did not notice Fujita's urgent signals. Discouraged, the flier allowed himself to drift with the sea and wondered how he would die—by drowning or in the teeth of a man-eating shark.[38]

Meanwhile, Nagumo's lifeboat lurched through the water, the oars scattering liquid diamonds, glittering like the tears some of the rowers could not help shedding. The officers denied themselves this relief, in the stoic tradition of their training. Genda sat down beside Makajima, who had lost his camera, film, and everything else but his life. The photographer was inexpressibly shocked to hear Genda mutter softly, "If *Shokaku* and *Zuikaku* had been here, there wouldn't have been a calamity like this." Makajima looked around apprehensively, to see if Nagumo or Kusaka had heard that word "calamity" coming from such a one as Genda, "who had been regarded as a hope of the Japanese Navy."

Captain Chisato Morita looked at Genda and observed without visible emotion, "The outcome will surely decide the fate of Japan." Every head in the boat flew up, but no word was spoken.

Nagumo lifted his close-cropped gray head, gazed unblinkingly at the bridge where he had commanded in glory, and lowered his head again. Makajima thought the lines in the admiral's face had already deepened, and he appeared to be praying for the souls of his dead.

Fuchida, whom Makajima privately nicknamed "Hitler," because of his little smudge of a mustache and intent eyes, propped himself up and stared back at the burning carrier. Makajima felt sorry for him. "The most capable leader of the Japanese Navy's carrier-borne air force was lying in the boat with his wings clipped and entirely separated from his loved men."

"Sotaicho, you must lie down," Akagi's doctor cautioned him. Fuchida nodded wordlessly and lowered himself.

Kusaka seemed the most composed of the lot. His long devotion to Zen Buddhism and his aristocratic tradition of self-discipline paid off in this terrible hour. But he could not control the twitching of a muscle near his mouth.

The little boat bobbed against Nagara, flagship of Rear Admiral Susumu Kimura, commanding DesRon 10. Nagumo and his staff climbed aboard and hurried to the bridge. Kimura's flag, hastily altered to that of a vice admiral, shot up the mast. Nagara was now flagship of the First Air Fleet.[39]

CHAPTER 31

"We, with *Hiryu* Alone"

"**A**ttack the enemy carriers." Thus briskly at 1050 Abe gave Yamaguchi his orders. And Yamaguchi blinked right back: "All our planes are taking off now for the purpose of destroying the enemy carriers."[1]

The situation was tailor-made for the swashbuckling admiral's self-image. To turn defeat into victory, send his aircraft dashing off to smear the American task force which had dared to lay impious hands on the First Air Fleet, single-handedly rescue Operation MI and return to Japan with Nagumo tagging along behind, an inglorious tail to the Yamaguchi kite—this melodramatic vision suited Yamaguchi right down to the ground.[2]

The disaster to *Akagi*, *Kaga*, and *Soryu* stunned the Second Carrier Division staff officers, but left Yamaguchi composed. "Well," he proclaimed, "we, with *Hiryu* alone, are going to sacrifice ourselves to kill the damned enemy force." To the sailors who had to remain below at their stations and hence saw nothing of the surface action, the intercom announced that the other three carriers had been damaged and that *Soryu*, in particular, was burning badly. It was "now up to the *Hiryu* to carry on the fight for the glory of greater Japan," boomed the loudspeaker.[3]

On the bridge, Yamaguchi and Captain Tomeo Kaku shook hands with each pilot of this strike, and Kaku spoke a few words. Lieutenant Commander Takeo Kyuma, the engineering staff officer, could not hear exactly what he said, but believed the sentiment was this: "I am not going to let you die alone." Lieutenant Michio Kobayashi was shaking so hard his teeth rattled. Kyuma was certain this was not from fear, but from Kobayashi's "firm determination" to fulfill his mission. "I had never seen such an impressive scene before," Kyuma recalled.[4]

Eighteen dive bombers and six fighters, under the overall command of Kobayashi, completed takeoff at 1058. The dive bombers were divided into two equal squadrons, Kobayashi leading the first, Lieutenant Michiji Yamashita the second, while Lieutenant Yasuhiro Shigematsu spearheaded the fighters. This force was top-heavy with bombers and represented what Yamaguchi could round up in a hurry. Respotting the planes of Tomonaga's first wave severely limited the number of aircraft immediately available to him. To leave the runway clear for the planes returning from Midway, *Hiryu* had to remove the second-wave planes either far forward on the flight deck or lower them into the hangar. Refueling and repair work were still in progress when the American carrier-based aircraft struck. When Abe ordered him to attack, Yamaguchi had no torpedo planes ready to join the dive bombers in a well-balanced striking force. Rather than delay the attack, he launched what was available at the time.[5]

Abe radioed *Chikuma*'s Number Four and Five reconnaissance planes at 1100: "Advise position of enemy carriers. Lead the attack unit to it." Ten minutes later *Chikuma*'s Number Five scout advised, "The enemy is in position bearing 70 degrees, distance 90 miles from our fleet's position." Having heard nothing further by 1130, Yamaguchi impatiently flashed to Abe, "Effect measures to maintain contact with the enemy carrier by employment of float recco planes."[6]

This message is most interesting for two reasons. First, the mention of "carrier" in the singular contradicts the "carriers" indicated in the original exchange between the two admirals, and is typical of the confusion which at the time reigned supreme in the Mobile Force. In the second place, this is the phraseology of a man giving orders. Seniority or not, Yamaguchi was taking over. Inside his sausage-shaped body with its face of an amiable bloodhound burned a volcano of impatience and ambition. Actually, for the rest of the day, command of the Mobile Force, for all intents and purposes, was divided. Abe was titular chief for only forty minutes, and at 1130 Nagumo took back the reins aboard *Nagara*.[7] But he was fully occupied with planning, and Yamaguchi commanded the air operation in fact if not in name.

Nagumo and his staff were by no means ready to throw in the sponge. So they decided "to protect *Hiryu* by the entire force and attempt another and final battle." The enemy was not too far off, and

Hiryu's remaining planes might be able to turn the tide and lure the Americans into a night engagement.[8]

By 1140 the *Hiryu* attack unit had sighted its target and dispatched a radio which, if immediately received and decoded, would have given Nagumo the best picture he had yet obtained of exactly what he was up against. "Enemy air force has as its nucleus 3 carriers. These are accompanied by 22 destroyers . . ." Although the observer had lumped cruisers and destroyers together, in total figures he hit it right on the nose. This vital information was fifty minutes late in reaching Nagumo.[9]

By the time Kobayashi's flight sighted the United States fleet, *Yorktown*'s radar picked up a group of enemy planes forty-five miles out, coming toward Task Force Seventeen on bearing 250°. The flagship immediately signaled its support vessels to assume Victor formation against air attack. *Astoria* and *Portland* pushed their speed up to thirty knots, and took their positions respectively off *Yorktown*'s port and starboard bow, while the destroyers churned up the outer screen.[10]

Machinist Oscar W. Myers, the air fuel officer, sprang to the task of clearing the gasoline lines of high octane fuel and replacing it with CO_2. This was a fire prevention technique of his own devising. Before Kobayashi's planes came in sight, the fuel lines were harmless, the gas siphoned back into the storage tanks had been blanketed with a layer of CO_2 to contain the highly inflammable vapor, and an auxiliary tank containing "about 800 gallons of clear aviation gasoline" had been dropped over the side.[11]

Lieutenant Commander Oscar Pederson, acting as fighter director, sent up his twelve Wildcats and radioed his opposite of Task Force Sixteen for reinforcements. Spruance sent him over six of his own sixteen combat patrol planes.[12] The American fighters pounced on the Japanese formation while it was about fifteen miles out. The ensuing dogfight was epic while it lasted—superior Zeros versus more Wildcats—and it rolled rather than flew toward *Yorktown*. By the time the ball of smoke, flashes, wings and noise reached the carrier, approximately ten of the enemy had been shot down.[13]

The remaining bombers split into sections for their run on the carrier. One group of three fell afoul of Lieutenant (j.g.) Arthur J. Brassfield. In peacetime a Missouri high school teacher, Brassfield had bagged three Japanese aircraft in the Coral Sea battle—a fighter, a bomber, and a four-engine patrol plane.[14] As he launched from the carrier that morning of June 4, he led a six-plane division, but as a result of the tangle with Shigematsu's Zeros, he found himself alone near *Yorktown*.

Facing three Japanese bombers, he fixed the leader in his sights and pressed the trigger at 300-yard range. Six slugs found their target, which spiraled down in flames. Flipping over to the left, Brassfield gave the second bomber a short rat-tat-tat at a mere 150 yards. The enemy blew up almost under Brassfield's nose with a concussion which bounced his little Wildcat. The third Japanese hurried off toward a cloud, but Brassfield got him before he could reach safety.[15]

Evidently Kobayashi's was one of the bombers which reached *Yorktown*, because Nagumo's log records a radio from *Hiryu*'s command plane: "We are attacking the enemy carrier. 0900." One minute later, the same source sent: "Fires break out on carrier. 0901." Once more, an amazing time lag of approximately fifty minutes ensued before this exceedingly important information reached Nagumo.[16]

Yorktown's gunners now took over the defense. The dive bombers came in on a curving path individually, which baffled the gunners until the planes actually started their dive. Fire from all automatic guns on the starboard side opened up on the first bomber to scream down, chopping it into at least three large pieces which fell close to the carrier's starboard quarter. But the bomb dropped as well, tumbling onto the flight deck some fifteen feet inboard and within twenty feet of Mount Number Four, killing seventeen men and wounding eighteen. Uninjured sailors hastened to replace the casualties and the guns continued firing without pause, although much reduced in volume.

Punching a hole ten feet square in the center of the flight deck, the bomb dropped into the hangar deck. There it started fires in three planes, two of which were damaged aircraft from *Enterprise* and one a *Yorktown* plane fully fueled and loaded with a 1,000-pound bomb. Lieutenant A. C. Emerson, the hangar deck officer, immediately turned on the sprinkler system, which quickly extinguished the blaze.[17]

Expert gunnery shredded the second plane to dive just as the pilot released his bomb. It whistled down for a near miss close astern, exploding on contact, while pieces of the plane fell into the churning wake of the carrier. Splinters from the missile killed or wounded a number of crewmen manning after port guns and started several small fires on the fantail. The battery officer and his remaining men quickly got them under control.[18]

A group of Japanese planes came in from port, but only one released its bomb before crashing near the carrier's port side. Fortunately for *Yorktown,* the bomb carried a delayed action fuse. Before it detonated, the missile hurtled through the flight deck, the executive officer's office, and the VS-5 Ready Room, where Lieutenant (j.g.) Charlie N. Conaster was busy with his duties as flight scheduling officer. The unexploded bomb hit the big coffee percolator, that oasis and powerhouse of every American office, leaving the room awash in the brown liquid. Then it thudded through on its path of destruction and finally exploded in the stack, the great, burning heart of a ship. The concussion snuffed out the fires in the boilers and ruptured the uptakes from Boilers One, Two, and Three. The carrier's speed immediately dropped to about six knots, and within twenty minutes *Yorktown* was at a dead standstill.[19]

Meanwhile, the third and last strike went through the Number One elevator and exploded on the fourth deck, starting a fire in a rag storage room next to the forward gasoline stowage and the magazines. Damage control officer Commander Clarence E. Aldrich led his fire fighters in battling this blaze, which would have sent *Yorktown* up in a ball of flame had it reached the nearby inflammables. Sprinklers flooded the magazine, while hard work with hose and axe squelched the blaze in the rag area.[20]

These three hits on *Yorktown* were not particularly serious, thanks to the prompt action of the damage control personnel. By a repair miracle as amazing in its way as the major effort at Pearl Harbor which had sent this fighting lady off to Midway, *Yorktown* was back in commission in slightly over two hours.

Captain Buckmaster always kept his crews busy during their interminable days at sea with drills covering every conceivable emergency, and now they knew just what to do. Carpenters rushed to the flight deck with heavy timbers, and twenty-five minutes of their knowhow and determination put it back in business.[21]

Under the direction of engineering officer Lieutenant Commander John F. Delany, the engineers and boiler-room men worked wonders. WT 1/c Charles Kleinsmith and his crew of Boiler Number One, ignoring the stifling heat, choking fumes, and constant danger of being blown to bits, soon worked up sufficient steam to swing the auxiliary power system into operation. One hour and ten minutes after the bomb exploded in the stack, *Yorktown* lowered the breakdown flag and hoisted the signal: "My speed five." A spontaneous cheer rang out from every ship in the carrier's screen, encircling her in a golden ring of joy and affection which warmed the cockles of Buckmaster's heart. As steam pressure built up and repairs continued, *Yorktown* steadily increased speed, and by 1437 was chugging along at a respectable if not breathtaking nineteen knots.[22]

In the meantime, Fletcher decided to remove his flag to *Astoria.* *Yorktown* was no longer practical as a flagship, although in no immediate danger. The decision was sensible and unsentimental, in true Fletcher style. It was better for all concerned that he and his staff part company with Buckmaster and his crew, each to pursue his own business unencumbered. Fletcher chose *Astoria* rather than any other screening ship because it was nearby, and because his chief of staff and close crony, Poco Smith, was aboard her commanding the cruiser group.[23]

At 1313 Fletcher's staff began to swarm down manila lines over the carrier's starboard side into *Astoria*'s Number Two motor whale boat. With one leg over the side, the admiral paused and remarked to the bosun in charge: "I'm too damn old for this sort of thing; better lower me." So two seamen played him out like a large fish at the end of a bowline.[24]

Fletcher and part of his official family climbed aboard *Astoria* eleven minutes later, and the whale boat set off to bring over the remainder. Just as the last passenger was climbing the cruiser's ladder at the end of the second round trip, two SBDs ditched almost adjacent to the gangway. These were Leslie and Holmberg, back from their strike on *Soryu* and out of gas. Pilots and gunners stepped deftly from rubber lifeboat to whale boat to ladder as if the whole timing and maneuver had been rehearsed for weeks.[25]

Every Dauntless of VB-3 had safely escaped after their attack on *Soryu,* and about halfway back to *Yorktown* they had joined forces and proceeded homeward in precise squadron formation, as if returning from target practice. They found *Yorktown* just in time to be waved off to escape the anticipated attack. Fifteen of the SBDs orbited until the last Japanese plane vanished, then headed for *Enterprise,* dodging a few bursts of fire before the carrier recognized them as friends. Leslie and Holmberg, however, had circled the area seeking downed aircraft and hence ran out of gas.[26]

Enterprise began recovery of VB-3's aircraft at 1237, just two minutes after Spruance, seeing a pillar of smoke over the horizon, detached the heavy cruisers *Pensacola* and *Vincennes,* and the destroyers *Benham* and *Balch,* to Fletcher's assistance. *Enterprise,* along with *Hornet,* also refueled and rearmed VF-3, while *Yorktown* herself, becoming more self-sufficient by the minute, rearmed ten more Wildcats and made ready to fuel them.[27]

Hornet had experienced a tragic, frustrating day. She had lost all her torpedo bombers; her dive bombers had missed the action entirely; her fighters ditched for lack of fuel. Now, in playing Good Samaritan to refugees from *Yorktown,* she took another blow. A wounded pilot crash-landed his Wildcat without cutting off his machine guns. As the fighter struck, the impact sprayed slugs toward the island, penetrating one-inch hardened plate and a steel I-beam. The wild shots killed five men and wounded twenty others. Among the dead was the brilliant, promising Lieutenant Royal R. Ingersoll II, son of the Commander in Chief of the U.S. Atlantic Fleet.[28]

Admiral Ingersoll was "a giant of a man, though not in physical stature . . . , always putting what was best for the Navy ahead of any personal feeling or desire he may have had." Shortly after Pearl Harbor, an associate overheard Ingersoll "telling his son that, now that war had been declared, no regular officer could possibly consider a shore assignment; he must ask for a job at sea." So, when it came, his son's death struck with a special impact. In public, Ingersoll took the blow stoically, but late one night, when only he and his associate were in the office, he informed his sympathetic friend "how torn up inside he had been when his advice to his son led to his death."[29] The victory at Midway did not come cheaply, to the high or the low.

(*Above*) USS *Enterprise.* (*Below*) USS *Yorktown* CV-5.

(*Above*) U. S. Marines landing at Midway. (*Below*) Marine Pfc Stanley G. Benson, of Minneapolis, Minn., watches the inimitable antics of Midway's "gooney birds" (Laycan Albatross). After standing watching their dance for five minutes, Benson walked away shaking his head.

(*Above*) General view of burning oil tanks on Midway Island after they were hit by Japanese bombs. Note the gooney birds in the foreground. (*Below*) Damaged F4F at Midway.

Midway Island, 1942. Interior of one hangar on Midway Island, damaged during the raid.

A Japanese torpedo scores on *Yorktown*.

USS *Yorktown* sinking.

The end draws near for USS *Yorktown*.

Douglas SBD dive-bombing.

Japanese ship *Mikuma* damaged.

CA Mogami class damaged.

USS *Hammann* survivors aboard the USS *Bentham*.

CHAPTER 32

"Determined to Sink an Enemy Ship"

On *Enterprise*, Spruance and his staff studied the implications of the attack on *Yorktown* and what to do about it. Browning came to the obvious and correct conclusion that the planes striking the carrier originated from the undamaged Japanese flattop Mc-Clusky's pilots had reported. The peppery chief of staff urged an immediate retaliation. Spruance refused to go off half-cocked. In the first place, his bombers were not yet ready for takeoff. In the second, he wanted a definite position report on the enemy carrier from scouts at that very minute approaching the anticipated location. Inability to find the enemy had already dissipated quite enough American strength for one battle.[1]

Yamaguchi would have despised Spruance's caution, but once more the American admiral had made the correct decision. *Nagara* in the lead, with *Hiryu* at the center of a protecting frame of battleships, cruisers, and destroyers, the carrier and its escorts had moved north until 1320. Then Yamaguchi launched his second attack against *Yorktown*, and cut off northeast.[2] In all probability, an American attack at that time would have missed the carrier altogether, and could not have saved *Yorktown*.

On *Hiryu*'s bridge, Yamaguchi and Kaku gave last-minute instructions to Tomonaga, Hashimoto, and Lieutenant Shigeru Mori, who would lead the second wave: "Launch an attack upon other carriers than the one Kobayashi's group hit and set on fire. If no other carriers are found in the area, direct attack upon the same one." The admiral shook hands with the three leaders, and for years after Hashimoto could feel in memory the impression of Yamaguchi's broad, soft palm.[3]

Then Yamaguchi and Kaku gave the second wave a personal send-off, this time on the flight deck. The admiral shook hands with each

283

pilot, saying, "*Shikkari yatte koi* (hope for a good fight)." Trying to
read the captain's mind, curiously enough Hashiguchi received almost
word-for-word the same impression that Kyuma had sensed earlier:
"I am not going to let you die alone, as I am going to follow you
soon."[4]

When they were about to take off, an orderly from the air officer
displayed a small blackboard showing the latest position of the enemy
forces. Hashimoto marked the position on his air chart. It flashed
through his mind that he should be sure Tomonaga had this information, but had no time to do so in the rush of takeoff.[5]

According to Hashiguchi, everyone knew this sortie had little
chance of returning, but the pilots climbed into their cockpits smiling.
What a different force followed Tomonaga from the mighty air armada
of that morning! Ten torpedo bombers divided into two squadrons,
one under Tomonaga, the other under Hashimoto. Six fighters under
Mori accompanied the bombers—four Zeros from *Hiryu* and two
fugitives from the burning *Kaga*.[6]

There had been no time to repair the punctured tank in Tomonaga's bomber, and with only half a load of fuel he had little chance
of returning to the carrier. However, he insisted upon leading the
sortie, and refused all offers of another aircraft. Tomonaga was something of a loner and did not confide his thoughts and sensations to
anyone. But Hashiguchi, who admired him tremendously and understood him fairly well, gained the impression that Tomonaga felt responsible for the disaster which resulted indirectly from his
recommendation for a second attack on Midway. Hashiguchi felt a
pang of pity for the members of Tomonaga's crew who had no such
qualms but who would have to die with their pilot. "But at that time,"
Hashiguchi remarked, "the whole crew of *Hiryu,* including the fliers,
had resolved to die for the Emperor and the motherland so we didn't
pay much attention to that. Not only the fliers but the ship's crew
actually did not concern themselves much with death," he added, "as
we had determined to sink an enemy ship even if we had to ram into
her."[7]

Hashiguchi's estimate of Tomonaga's motivation may have been
overly romantic, for Hashimoto had no such impression. He believed
that Tomonaga's decision was based on such practical factors as these:
Only *Hiryu* remained operational; so few aircraft were available "that
a reduction of even one plane would have a grave significance to an

expected outcome of an attack," and with the reported enemy position about 100 miles away, even with a damaged plane he should be able to make it back. In fact, Tomonaga said as much to Hashimoto. When the latter urged Tomonaga to use his, Hashimoto's, plane, Tomonaga refused, saying, "The enemy is so close that it is possible to return after the attack."[8]

As his instructions to his flight leaders indicated, Yamaguchi had no idea of a second attack on the same carrier, unless no other was available. Despite a flood of confusing reports from various scout planes, apparently the admiral pinned his faith to the reports of his own aircraft. He had received the *Hiryu* bombers' earlier message advising of three carriers and "22 destroyers" in plenty of time to brief the Tomonaga force. In fact, he informed Nagumo at 1400: "According to reports from our carrier-based bombers, there are three enemy carriers along a north-south line approximately ten miles long."[9]

But with three flattops to choose from, Tomonaga's flight made straight for *Yorktown*. Noting that Tomonaga "was heading for the old enemy position," Hashimoto realized he had not received the new location. He tried to close with Tomonaga's plane to pass on the word, but in vain. He gave up the attempt, for the difference in reported positions was not too large, and they probably would see the target "in the right direction . . ."[10]

Yorktown's radar picked them up at a thirty-three mile range. The carrier immediately ceased refueling the fighters, once more drained the gasoline system and secured it with CO_2, and vectored the six fighters of VF-3 out on combat air patrol toward the enemy. Eight of the ten fighters on board had as much as twenty-three gallons of gasoline in their tanks—enough for local action—and were launched to join their comrades, along with some additional fighters from Task Force Sixteen.

The Wildcats intercepted slightly less than fifteen miles out, and virtually a replay of the midday dogfight ensued, three of the six Zeros falling to the more numerous F4F-4s.[11] One torpedo plane went down to twenty-two-year-old Ensign Milton Tootle, IV, son of a bank president of St. Joseph, Missouri. We suspect that Tootle sneaked into the fight, for his Wildcat had not been refueled from his morning flight when the young man, who had only been aboard *Yorktown* five days, jumped into his cockpit. He had barely cleared the flight deck when he swung onto the tail of a bomber and clung there until about

1,000 yards from the carrier. He caught the plane in a burst of fire before it could drop its torpedo. As Tootle turned his fighter's nose upward, American gunfire brought him down, fortunately uninjured and near the screening vessels, where the destroyer *Anderson* soon found him.[12]

The antiaircraft experienced more difficulty in catching the low-flying Japanese than they had in winging Tootle, and the heavy cruisers resorted to a novel tactic of Poco Smith's devising: They fired their main battery guns into the sea ahead of the torpedo planes, sending up a reverse waterfall.[13] Either the Wildcats or the waterfall kept all but five torpedo planes from reaching the target area. At 1432 Tomonaga radioed his unit: "Take positions in preparation for attack formation," then, two minutes later, "Entire force attack!"[14] Thereupon the attackers split into two groups, Tomonaga to the right, Hashimoto to the left.[15]

An unidentified Japanese plane, either one of *Hiryu's* or a nearby scout, radioed the Mobile Force: "Friendly attack units are attacking the enemy carriers. There are three carriers." This message was dispatched at the same moment that Tomonaga ordered the attack.[16]

Hashimoto released his torpedo almost abeam of the enemy carrier at a distance of about 500 meters and at an altitude of fifteen meters. He flew right over *Yorktown's* bow at the level of her flight deck, and saw "no sign that she had been hit or set on fire." However, as he sped away, he noticed waterspouts followed by brown smoke.[17]

Despite her slow speed of nineteen knots, *Yorktown* had evaded two torpedoes, but two struck home. At 1443 the first crashed into the carrier's port side just about amidships, the second almost simultaneously, slightly forward of the first. The explosions pierced the port fuel tanks, flooded three firerooms and the forward generator room, cutting off all electrical power. A short in the control board blocked off the emergency generator. Her rudder jammed, for the second time that afternoon *Yorktown* stopped in her tracks and tilted to a 17° list to port.[18]

The carrier continued to list until, about ten minutes after the first torpedo strike, she was leaning 26°. At this angle even standing up was a problem, and the port edge of the flight deck was almost touching the surface of the sea which, fortunately, was unusually calm. Aldrich and Delany agreed that nothing could be done to correct the list. Loss of power knocked out lighting and intercom, so loss of communication between one part of the ship and another was almost total. The ruptured fuel tanks were spreading a deadly oil film around the heeling ship, a film which the smallest spark would turn into a sheet of flame. Only six planes remained aboard. In short, *Yorktown* was a dead loss as an aircraft carrier. Her only remaining assets were the men aboard her.[19]

Yet no matter what the circumstances, the decision to abandon ship must remain the most difficult, cruel one a captain ever reaches. Buckmaster discussed the question with Arnold and with Commander Dixie Kiefer, his executive officer, and reluctantly reached the conclusion that he must leave *Yorktown* to her fate. He was responsible for nearly 3,000 men who must be clear of the ship before she listed past the balance point. At 1455 he ordered hoisted the blue and white signal, "Abandoning ship."[20]

Balch, Benham, Russell, and *Anderson* closed in to pick up the evacuees, while others established an antisubmarine screen.[21] It was a deliberate, orderly evacuation, almost too much so to suit Fletcher, watching the operation from *Astoria*'s bridge in a fever of apprehension. "I was biting my nails thinking that Captain Buckmaster made his decision to abandon ship too late," he said. Fletcher was never to have any patience with the chairborne tacticians who in the future would claim that Buckmaster's decision was hasty and ill-advised. "Personally, I was God damn anxious at the time to get the boys off that ship," Fletcher insisted in retrospect. "The saving of the lives of the officers and all of those fine young American boys was highly important to me."[22]

Removal of *Yorktown*'s wounded was "very difficult because, due to the slippery decks and heavy list, it was impossible to carry stretchers across the deck. In some cases stretchers were dragged across, and in other cases patients were carried bodily." By various means, the wounded were lowered gently, and many crewmen from the rescue ships dived overboard to help those unable to swim. Cargo nets, life rafts, and motorboats all played their part.[23]

Kiefer was one of the last off the ship. In charge of the evacuation, he remained until all reports and a personal examination convinced him that he had fully discharged his duty. He tried to lower a man who was afraid to trust himself to the knotted ropes, but in doing so the rope sped through his hands so rapidly that it burned him severely. As a result, he could not get a grip when his own turn came to leave the ship. He fell heavily, striking the carrier's side like the clapper of a bell, breaking both his ankles.[24]

Buckmaster watched the evacuation until certain that everything was under control, then he went off by himself for his last inspection. No doubt he welcomed the opportunity to commune with the ship's spirit and bid her a silent farewell. He struggled along the canting starboard side, moved across the flight deck, down through the dressing station, forward through the flag and captain's quarters, around to port and down to the hangar deck. By this time, the port side of the latter was under water. Satisfied that he was the last living person on board, Buckmaster climbed up to the stern and went overside hand-over-hand. As he hit the water, he heard a mess attendant calling for help. The captain swam over to him and lifted the thrashing man onto a raft, then he climbed aboard too, eventually to be picked up by the destroyer *Hammann* and thence transferred to *Astoria*.[25]

The word which Fletcher and Spruance so eagerly awaited from the scout planes reached them at 1445 in the shape of a message from Lieutenant Samuel Adams, operations officer of VS-5. First by voice transmission, then repeating in dots and dashes, Adams sent in an amazingly accurate report: "1 CV, 2 BB, 3 CA, 4 DD, 31°15′N, 179° 05′W, course 000, speed 15." This located *Hiryu* with Nagumo's support vessels 110 miles from *Yorktown*'s position as of 1150, the search group's point of departure. Actually, the enemy position was 281°, distance 72 miles, an error of 38 miles. As luck would have it, *Hiryu*'s course took her directly toward the attack group.[26]

Spruance immediately ordered aloft the remaining airworthy dive bombers. This time McClusky could not participate because of a wounded arm sustained in his attack on *Kaga*, so command of the composite group fell to Gallaher of VS-6 as next in line of seniority. He led a total of twenty-four aircraft, eleven loaded with 1,000-pound bombs, the remainder with 500 pounders. In addition to Gallaher's, the planes comprised five others from his VS-6, four from VB-6, and the remaining fourteen from *Yorktown*'s VB-3 under Lieutenant De-witt W. Shumway, its executive officer. By 1550 they had all cleared *Enterprise* and were on their way. No fighter accompanied them, defense of the task forces taking priority.[27]

As the attack group sped off, Spruance signaled Fletcher: "TF 16 air groups are now striking the carrier which your search plane reported. . . . Have you any instructions for me?" The courteous inquiry brought Fletcher to a crossroads. He could not exercise tactical command of a carrier battle by remote control. Time was too precious for the rigamarole of signals, blinkers, and radios. He should either transfer with his staff to *Hornet*, a time-consuming process involving, in effect, complete reorganization of the Task Force, or give the power to Spruance. For Fletcher the choice was really no choice at all. With instant selflessness he signaled back, "None. Will conform to your movements."[28]

In the meantime, Yamaguchi was in his element. He had lost all five bombers of Tomonaga's group, including the leader, and all but three of the Zeros, including that of Mori. Still, the admiral was delighted with the results of his two air attacks, planning wholesale death and destruction for the remaining Americans, busily reporting to Nagumo and preparing for yet a third strike.[29] *Hiryu* plunged back and forth, leaving a boiling wake. As the carrier swept past *Nagara* with planes making ready to launch, crewmen and refugees aboard the cruiser shouted, *"Hiryu*, pay off the score!"[30]

At 1531 Yamaguchi advised Nagumo, "After definitely establishing contact with our type 13 Experimental shipbased bomber, we plan to direct our entire remaining power (5 bombers, 5 torpedo planes, and 10 fighters) to attack and destroy the remaining enemy forces in a dusk engagement." His optimism was not quite as zany as it appears, for he firmly believed that his men had sunk or severely damaged two American carriers. The mistake was natural enough. His first wave had reported a carrier afire, while the second had found a flattop which, from the air, appeared undamaged. Yamaguchi made his point clear in a signal to Nagumo at 1600: "Results obtained by second attack wave: Two certain torpedo hits on an *Enterprise* class carrier (not the same one as reported bombed)."[31]

Yamaguchi had approximately another hour to enjoy himself. At 1645 Gallaher's flight caught sight of *Hiryu* and her escort some thirty miles away, with three columns of smoke lifting over the southern horizon.[32] At precisely 1701 *Chikuma* sighted enemy planes to port, directly over *Hiryu*.[33] But a few of Yamaguchi's Zeros were already rushing to the attack. In a swift decision, Gallaher ordered his *Enterprise* men to follow him against *Hiryu* and sent Shumway with his fourteen *Yorktown* planes to work over a nearby battleship.[34] This decision to divert more than half his force from the primary target, as yet untouched, was most unwise, and Gallaher was much more fortunate than he deserved to be.

On *Nagara*, Makajima closed his eyes. He just could not bear to look.[35] Gallaher made straight for the scarlet circle on *Hiryu*'s pale yellow deck. In number one position on the flight deck was the special experimental plane from *Soryu*, returned from her first reconnaissance mission and poised to lead a third attack wave toward the American task force. An unbelievably swift turn of the carrier threw off Gallaher's aim, and in endeavoring to throw his bomb rather than drop it, the pilot wrenched his back.[36] His missile dropped harmlessly off *Hiryu*'s stern, as did the next two.[37]

Shumway saw the near misses and instantly, without waiting for revocation of his earlier order, led his aircraft from the battleship and dived on the carrier. This was one more instance of the quick thinking and initiative of a junior officer so fortunate for the United States that day. Whether Shumway's VS-3, as he believed, or the remainder of VS-6 made the first hit on *Hiryu* is uncertain.[38]

Four bombs struck in rapid succession on the carrier's bow.[39] The first flung the forward elevator on end, blocking off the bridge from the bow. Fires spread throughout the ship, blocking passageways and hurtling debris from constant explosions. Kaku was caught in a squeeze. To avoid further bombs, he had to maneuver the carrier with all possible speed, but the wind whipped up thus fanned the flames and spread them over the entire ship. When Makajima opened his eyes, curiousity overcoming sensibility, *Hiryu* was burning from bow to stern, but still "running at high speed like a mad bull."[40]

Hashimoto, scheduled to lead the projected third wave off *Hiryu*, was snatching a nap while he awaited the call to action. Suddenly, "terrible sounds of explosions shook the vessel." Almost immediately, suffocating smoke enveloped him. The hatches had been closed and the passage was jammed with men who had scrambled up from below.

Another fearsome blast rocked the ship and the lights went out. Desperate for fresh air, Hashimoto ran toward a bright spot, which proved to be a hole made by an explosion. Everything outside the opening was on fire, but fortunately Hashimoto was wearing gloves, and he crawled out on all fours. Flakes of flame fell on his bare head, setting fire to his hair. A man nearby offered him a mask. It was half burned and full of dust, but Hashimoto accepted it gratefully.

At that moment, the executive officer ordered him, "Assistant Air

Officer, command the men around here and throw those hammock mantelets overboard before they catch fire." This task, and subsequent fire fighting, kept Hashimoto fully occupied until he was wounded in the left thigh and eventually evacuated.[41]

VB-6 was the last unit to charge the carrier, and Lieutenant Best, in command, believe that one of the hits could be credited to them.[42] It did not matter; they were all American airmen and glory for one was glory for all.

Two of Shumway's aircraft made a swipe at the battleship. This was *Haruna*, often shot at but never hit. The battlewagon seemed to bear a charmed life, for the best the attackers could do was what the Japanese reported as "very near misses," one at port and the other at starboard.[43]   In severe pain from his wrenched back, Gallaher was just pulling his planes out of the area with the loss of two SBDs from VB-3 and one from VB-6, when seven aircraft of VB-8 and eight from VS-8 came on the scene from *Hornet*. By this time, 1712, *Hiryu* was a mass of flames and no longer a worthwhile target, so the *Hornet* aircraft devoted their attention to *Tone* and *Chikuma*.[44] The former escaped with near misses at bow and stern, the closest being at fifty meters. *Chikuma* dodged a cluster 100 meters off her port bow.[45]

The *Hornet* planes were still diving on *Tone* when a group of B-17s, some from Midway, others from Molokai, tried their luck on the same targets. Although some of the participants were sure they had struck a carrier and a battleship or heavy cruiser, the big land-based bombers had no more success on this try than they had had earlier in the day.[46] Except for an equally abortive VMSB-241 sortie from Midway after sunset but before moonrise,[47] the battle of June 4 was over.

CHAPTER 33

"Don't Let Another Day Like This Come to Us Again!"

"Fires are raging aboard the *Kaga, Soryu,* and *Akagi* resulting from attacks carried out by enemy land-based and carrier-based attack planes. We plan to have the *Hiryu* engage the enemy carriers. In the meantime, we are temporarily retiring to the north, and assembling our forces . . ."

This radio to Yamamoto and Kondo from Abe, dispatched at 1050 during his brief period of command,[1] was, according to Ugaki, the first word of any importance to reach *Yamato* since picking up the *Tone* Number Four plane's message of 0855 advising Nagumo that ten torpedo planes were heading toward the Mobile Force. "This sad report immediately changed the prevailing atmosphere in the Operations Room into one of extreme gloom," Ugaki confided to his diary three days later, when he finally had a minute—and the heart—to return to his journal.[2]

Indeed, the shock was almost traumatic. Never since the war began had the Combined Fleet received ill tidings of the Nagumo force, and it struck at the very roots of their self-image. Furthermore, no shadow of doubt concerning a ringing victory at Midway had darkened *Yamato* for a single moment, and thus far that day all the news dribbling back to the flagship had been good. Now they must completely reorient themselves from an attitude of "How far-reaching will our victory be?" to "How much can we salvage?"[3]

These officers might have approached the Midway project with overconfidence and conceit, but they were not fools. Neither Yamamoto nor any of his staff expected the fleet to emerge unscathed from such a vast operation. One damaged carrier they could have taken in stride. Two, although a serious setback, could have been accepted, but three! This was an entirely unforeseen disaster.[4]

Therefore, Combined Fleet Headquarters was no calm, objective collection of cool heads and warm feet at this hour. Kuroshima exhibited a temperament which would have done credit to an Italian opera singer, pounding on tables in his impatience and fury, and occasionally breaking into tears.[5] But his ideas were still virile and sound, and he insisted that the Combined Fleet carry out the battle to its logical conclusion, even if three carriers were on fire. It was too early to throw in the towel yet, for *Hiryu* was as yet untouched and under her aggressive admiral might avenge her stricken sisters.[6]

Yamamoto counted heavily upon Yamaguchi's fighting qualities.[7] Ugaki, too, was very close to Yamaguchi, an Eta Jima classmate, particularly as both were less than enthusiastic about Nagumo. Although loyalty to one's chief and comrades has always stood high on the Japanese list of virtues, Yamaguchi complained to Ugaki about Nagumo's and Kusaka's lack of aggressiveness, as it appeared to him. Instead of pinning his ears back, Ugaki encouraged his classmate to go over Nagumo's head and bring his comments and suggestions direct to the high command.[8]

With this background, it is understandable that when Yamaguchi radioed Yamamoto somewhat as follows: "*Hiryu* attack group have completed takeoff. Expect to hit and sink enemy carrier," no one referred to the folly of counting unhatched chickens. The Commander in Chief and his staff fervidly clutched this straw. "*Kami yo Hiryu mamori tamse* (O God, please protect *Hiryu!*)" they murmured.[9]

Yamamoto sat in the Operations Room as stern and impassive as a judge while Kuroshima excitedly presented his first suggestions for salvage and reclamation.[10] His idea was to bring down the Aleutian force and throw it into the action. The carriers would be a blood transfusion for the First Air Fleet and the battleships would come in handy to tow the burning carriers, including any American flattop which fell to Yamaguchi, back to Japan. How the mighty had fallen! The best use Kuroshima could devise for the Northern Force's battlewagons was as seagoing tugs for the crippled carriers.

Kuroshima's second suggestion was to remove the submarine cordon from its position between Hawaii and Midway, as the horse was already out of the stable, and concentrate it in the battle area.[11]

Yamamoto bought at least a portion of this advice. Like Kurosh-

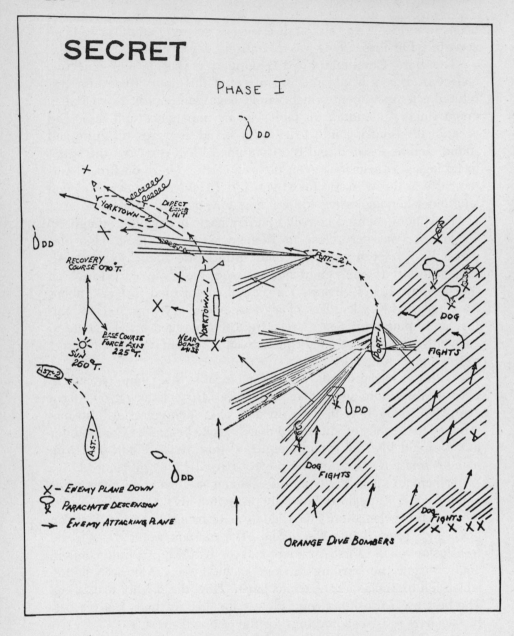

SECRET

PHASE I

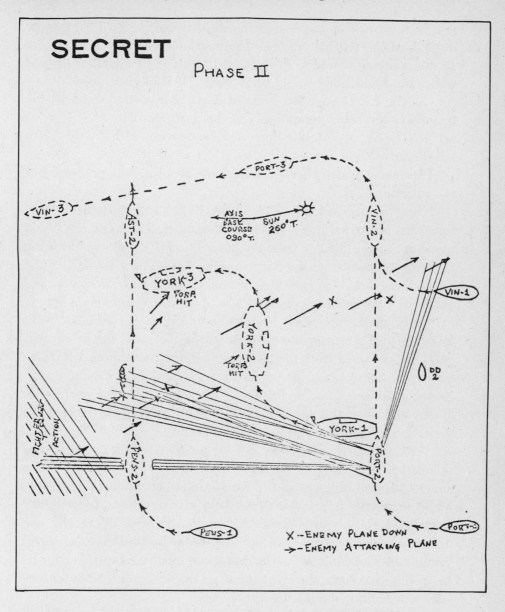

ima, he was by no means ready to hoist the white flag. At 1220 *Yamato* dispatched DesOpOrd Number 155 to all commanders in chief and all division commanders. In the first paragraph, Yamamoto advised where the Main Body would be located. Then he continued:

"2. The AF Occupation Force will assign a portion to escort the transports and retire temporarily to the northwest.

"3. The Second Mobile Force will rendezvous with the First Mobile Force as soon as possible. . . ."

This message also effected the change of submarine position. But no battleships!

Nagumo received this dispatch at 1300[12] and must have been somewhat heartened by its sensible implications. The transports would move out of the danger zone temporarily, and Kakuta would bring his carriers down from the Aleutian area to reinforce Nagumo.

In these hours of the duel between *Hiryu* and *Yorktown*, and Spruance's devastating counterattack, time and events pounded relentlessly against the First Mobile Force. With the familiar, well-loved deck of a cruiser beneath his sturdy feet, and the action, apparently, removed from the air to the surface, Nagumo revived like a parched house plant set out in the rich earth and healing rain.[13] Yamaguchi himself was no less full of plans for taking the fight to the enemy and retrieving the situation. As early as 1153 he signaled the entire force, "Plan to take to the attack now. Assemble."[14]

Throughout the afternoon and evening, however, Nagumo was inundated by a flood of messages from the various reconnaissance aircraft, all contradictory and all combining to give him a surrealistic, highly erroneous impression of the American position and strength.[15] In the midst of this Intelligence nightmare, Nagumo did receive two excellent reports which, had he used them as hard cores of truth, would have saved him as well as Yamamoto much confusion and heartburn. But, of course, the admiral had no magic touchstone to tell him what was truth and what was error.

The first of these realistic items was the previously mentioned radio of 1140 from the *Hiryu* bombers, which the fleet received at 1230 and which advised that the U.S. force had three carriers as its nucleus, with twenty-two support vessels. The second came from Captain Kosaku Ariga of Des Div 4, who at 1330 radioed Yamamoto,

Nagumo, Kondo, and Komatsu some information obtained from the prisoner from *Yorktown*:*

   1. Carriers involved are the *Yorktown, Enterprise*, and *Hornet*. In addition, 6 cruisers and about 10 destroyers.
   2. *Yorktown*, accompanied by 2 cruisers and 3 destroyers, acting independently of the others.
   3. Sortied from Pearl Harbor during the morning of 31 May arriving in the vicinity of Midway on 1 June. Patrolling along a north-south course ever since.
   4. There were no capital ships in Pearl Harbor up to 31 May. Prisoner had been training at base, and was not cognizant of capital ship movements.[16]

This was extremely important intelligence. The unfortunate ensign had short-counted the cruisers by two and the destroyers by four, but these were very minor errors. Anyone experienced in the evaluation of intelligence could have panned considerable gold from this shallow stream. In the first place, this told Nagumo exactly what carriers were opposing him. Furthermore, the captive indicated that no U.S. battleships were with the carriers or in the area, so the opposition, although formidable, was comparatively lightweight. The information that *Yorktown* was the center of an independent group should have cleared up any number of conflicting scout plane messages. The sortie date of May 31 explained, too, why the Japanese submarines had failed so miserably: The American ships had passed the cordon site before the subs were in position. This sortie date should also have given Yamamoto, Nagumo, et al a very good hint that a naval code had been broken, or at least that Japanese security had sprung a bad leak.

Nagumo had only a few minutes to digest this information when he received Yamamoto's DesOpOrd Number 156:
   "1. Employ Method C in attacking enemy fleet.
   "2. The Occupation Force will assign a portion of its force to shell and destroy enemy air bases on AF. The occupation of AF, and AO are temporarily postponed."[17]

Here was more fruit from Kuroshima's fertile brain. Method C called for a concentration of all forces to destroy the enemy fleet. As we have seen, AF represented Midway, while AO was the Aleutians.

_____

*See Chapter 28.

Thus it is apparent that Yamamoto had swung the original Japanese plan into reverse. First they must destroy the U.S. task force and knock out Midway's shore-based air power. Then and then only would they proceed with the occupation. Kuroshima visualized a night attack on the American ships to recoup the Japanese losses. Not only were night strikes a specialty of the Japanese Navy, but the distance between the opposing carrier forces was suitable for such an operation.[18]

Throughout these exchanges of information, the Main Body was hurrying through a pea-soup fog toward the scene of action as fast as its turbines could churn. From the bridge, Ugaki kept in touch with Yamamoto and the planners in the Operations Room, and supervised the voyage. As originally planned, the Main Body was to be 400 miles from the Nagumo force on M-Day and 200 miles after N-plus-1 day. However, as Ugaki explained in his long diary entry covering the events of June 4, "Contrary to plan, what had been entirely unexpected thus took place on N-minus-2 day." Due to the fact that refueling took less time than anticipated, the battleships were approximately a day ahead of schedule, so Ugaki hoped to be able to pull up the slack.

The fog was so thick that over an hour elapsed before *Nagato*, steaming in the rear of the formation, could receive orders and join the Main Body. During this time, as Ugaki noted sedately, "impatience prevailed."[19] We may spare a pang of imaginative pity for Captain Hideo Yano, *Nagato*'s skipper. Neither Yamamoto nor Ugaki were the type to suffer delays in silence. By the time the former flagship had joined her sisters, the Main Body was making twenty knots on a 120 degree course, not exactly a breakneck pace, but the best possible under the circumstances. A blanket of fog isolated each ship, fog beacons were useless, and the fleet had to resort to searchlights placed on the aft decks. Even with these guides, the ships became fearfully and wonderfully mixed up. During occasional breaks in the white gloom, Ugaki could see destroyers which should have been screening the starboard bow slipping along to port.[20]

Another type of fog prevailed throughout the Mobile Force. At 1345 Yamaguchi radioed a message received at 1405: "According to report from planes, the enemy's position at 0940 [1240 local time] is bearing 80 degrees, distance 90 miles from us. It is composed of 5 large cruisers and one carrier (burning fiercely.)" All well and good, but ten minutes later a message arrived from *Haruna*'s scout plane:

"At 0940 the enemy was in position bearing about 90 degrees to port. It is composed of 5 large cruisers and 5 carriers; the latter were burning."[21] By some strange alchemy, one American carrier had multiplied to five, all burning!

One flattop or five, this information meant the opportunity for a surface engagement was close at hand, and Nagumo did not shrink from the prospect. At 1420 he notified Kakuta, his own ships, and all others concerned of his grid position. Then he advised: "After destroying the enemy task force to the east, we plan to proceed northward. Second Mobile Force will rendezvous as soon as possible."[22] The last was for the benefit of Kakuta. But his carrier force was still operating near Dutch Harbor and could not join Nagumo until some time on June 7—three days too late.[23]

A blinker from Abe at 1535 altered Nagumo's plans perceptibly. "Enemy sighted to _Tone_'s Number 4 plane was in position bearing 114 degrees, distance 110 miles from us at 1230."[24] This looked to the admiral as though the enemy were withdrawing and, far from reassuring Nagumo, this information filled him with misgivings. With their air superiority, his opponents obviously were moving out of range of further Japanese air attacks, avoiding the risk of a torpedo and gunfire slugging match, and at the same time putting themselves in position to strike the Mobile Force at will. They were also wisely keeping in range of Midway's land-based aircraft and reconnaissance planes.

Actually, Spruance had not yet retired; he had turned into the wind to launch the _Enterprise_ and _Hornet_ attacks on _Hiryu_ and the support ships. But Nagumo did not know that. So he decided to abandon the idea of a daytime strike and to pin his hopes on a night engagement.[25] So at 1550 he shifted course from northeast to northwest.[26]

Yamamoto's staff were quite as confused as Nagumo over the actual enemy situation. According to Ugaki, their estimate at the time was "that the enemy force consisted of three _Enterprise_ type carriers, two or three converted carriers, five heavy cruisers, and fifteen destroyers spreading over a large area extending about 100 miles from north to south." The staff, too, were working on plans for the forthcoming battle under cover of darkness, but, again to quote Ugaki, "Whether this night engagement could be successful or not was considered to depend upon how much damage the first wave attack had inflicted upon the enemy base on the island."[27]

Accordingly, Ugaki sent out a radio over his own name to Kusaka rather than to Nagumo: "Report progress of attacks on Midway (particularly whether or not friendly units will be able to use shore bases on Midway tomorrow . . .)." Nagumo's chronology shows receipt of this message at 1655, but no record of a reply, and Ugaki indicates that "no reply was available."[28]

For some reason, perhaps his ingrained skepticism about Nagumo's effectiveness, Ugaki assumed that no news was bad news. "Judging that the base was not sufficiently destroyed in view of the prevailing circumstances, it was thought that unless it would be completely destroyed before dawn, enemy reinforcements would be sent to the island even tonight, not to speak of tomorrow, thus making our landing on the island more difficult." Ugaki "doubted the effectiveness of bombardment by 20-cm. shells on an air base." He also expected that to move ships close enough to hit the island would expose them to submarine attack. But the other staff officers so strongly urged a shelling that he ordered the Kondo fleet to bombard Midway. Even so, he had strong reservations.[29]

Kondo assigned the task to Kurita's Support Force, retaining the battleships *Kongo* and *Hiei* in his own Main Invasion Group. The ships to shell Midway would be the heavy cruisers *Kumano*, *Suzuya*, *Mikuma*, and *Mogami*, plus two destroyers. Kurita received his instructions at approximately 1500. Although his cruisers were the fastest ships in the Japanese Navy, he could not possibly reach Midway before dawn on the 5th. He would thus have to pull out after the bombardment in full daylight under continual menace from the air.[30] Ugaki had no faith in this "hopeless yet dangerous venture," so eventually he called it off.[31]

The Japanese seriously overestimated Midway's power, and almost certainly would have pressed on had they realized just how vulnerable the atoll was at this time. According to Major Warner, the afternoon of June 4 "was the most critical time of the whole engagement." He was in a sweat of anxiety lest the enemy return. Had the Japanese done so, they could have inflicted disastrous losses. For lack of bunkers, about seven or eight B-17s were dispersed along the runways, the most vulnerable location imaginable. Communication with Hawaii was so poor that Warner decided the best service he could render was fly back to Hickam and report the situation personally to General Hale.[32]

Ramsey was no less pessimistic. The lack of communication between land-based units and ships so unfortunate for Fletcher and Spruance was also a handicap for the Midway defenders. Ramsey had received word that *Yorktown* was hit, but he had little indication of damage to the Japanese carriers. Much of the information available to him was incorrect, especially land-based bombing claims, but this was how the situation looked to Ramsey:

> One Japanese carrier had been damaged by the Army. The losses of the Marine Air Group were so heavy that it appeared their attack had been broken up before reaching the enemy. The Yorktown had been hit. The battleships to the northwest, the four cruisers on 265°, the possible enemy carrier on 262°, and the large group to the west were all boring in. Three enemy carriers appeared to be left to deal with Task Force 16. . . . It appeared that it was quite possible we would be under heavy bombardment from surface vessels before sunset.

In line with Nimitz's orders to save the heavy aircraft, Ramsey prepared to evacuate all his patrol planes not actually necessary to the functioning of the Naval Air Station. As for danger to the Japanese from the air, only two fighters and very few bombers were undamaged.[33]

At 1730 Nagumo radioed Yamamoto and all commanders. "*Hiryu* burning as a result of bomb hits."[34] This was a fearful blow to Ugaki, in particular. "The only remaining carrier, upon which all hopes were placed, was finally damaged after inflicting damage upon two enemy carriers with a single-handed good fighting. Alas!" he lamented.[35] Yamaguchi was no more exempt than Nagumo from the fortunes of war.

Although not yet sure that *Hiryu* had sunk, Spruance found that knocking off the last Japanese carrier left him with a problem: *What do we do now?* he asked himself. *If we steam westward what will we run into during the night?* He had no use for futile heroics, and did not care to invite a night engagement with his carriers. The Japanese had far superior surface forces, they excelled in night operations, and Spruance did not have enough destroyers to screen and protect his flattops. Above all, his mission was not to chase a mortally wounded

Japanese task force. "I worried about Midway," he explained in retrospect, "because I thought the Japanese landing attack might be
going against Midway and my mission was to protect Midway." So
he turned due east and continued in that direction until midnight,
which put him in position to move in either quarter and be wherever
the action was. "I wanted to be within air striking distance of Midway
on June 5th in case the Japanese invaded it," he said.[36]

For a long time after the war, press room admirals and self-ap-
pointed critics took Spruance apart for sailing eastward for those few
hours. Actually, to have done otherwise would have been an act of
irresponsibility, even of criminal folly. This was not a matter of "failure to pursue," for the battle was not yet over. Had the Japanese
kept their heads and their nerve, it could have lasted much longer
and ended very differently.

In the first place, as Spruance said, his mission was to protect
Midway. This he could not do by leaving it to the tender mercies of
a Japanese invasion force while he went tilting at Nipponese wind-
mills. The possibility of Task Forces Sixteen and Seventeen annihi-
lating the enemy fleet had never crossed Nimitz's mind or anyone
else's. In cancelling out four Japanese carriers, Spruance and his men
had done all and infinitely more than was expected of them.

In the second place, Nimitz had specifically ordered Spruance and
Fletcher to abide by the principle of calculated risk and not jeopardize
the irreplaceable carriers and almost equally valuable surface ships.
One lost in exchange for four was an acceptable ratio, but the Japanese
had nothing left that was worth the loss of another carrier.

Third, the nature of the vessels involved on both sides precluded
any possibility that the Americans could take on the Japanese successfully at night. Had Spruance continued westward, he would have
run smack into the Nagumo support ships and the Kondo fleet. This
combination matched him cruiser for cruiser, outnumbered him in
destroyers nineteen to thirteen, and overwhelmed him four to zero
in battleships. *Haruno* and *Kirishima*, *Kongo* and *Hiei* were battlewagons of the same class, carrying eight 14-inch guns and sixteen 6-
inch guns each. Spruance had nothing larger than the 8-inchers on
his cruisers.

As for the carriers, at night they could be eliminated from consideration. A flattop is not geared for surface action at the best of
times, and at night is a distinct liability. In contrast to the low-slung

destroyers and cruisers, *Enterprise* and *Hornet* would loom against the soft Pacific night sky like floating skyscrapers. Lightly armored and with no heavy guns, they would be easy pickings. The darkness, too, clipped the fliers' wings. Under the most favorable of conditions, as Commander Leslie explained to Poco Smith, "It's not easy to score a direct hit on a fast-moving ship. It's like trying to drop a marble from eye-level on a scared mouse."[37] At night, that hopeful marble-dropper would be blindfolded. In the context of the time, aerial torpedoes, aimed for the "soft underbelly" of enemy ships, offered the best chance of real damage. But *Yorktown* had lost twelve of her thirteen TBDs, *Enterprise* eleven out of fourteen, and *Hornet* all of her fifteen.

What is more, as we have seen, the Japanese wanted nothing more than to lure the American task force westward in the dark hours of June 4, and Spruance must have known it.

Nagumo was no end annoyed to receive a message from *Chikuma*'s Number Two scout plane at 1733: "The enemy has commenced re-tiring to the east on course 70 degrees, speed 20 knots."[38] Oishi asked permission to continue hunting for the U.S. fleet, using the only night-scouting craft available, that of *Nagara*. Nagumo's staff officers were naturally skeptical of the single plane's chances of success, but the admiral agreed to try.[39] He badly wanted that night engagement, and it is difficult to see where Ugaki got his firmly fixed notion that Nagumo had lost his "fighting spirit."[40]

Looking back, the practical Kusaka realized that they were chasing rainbows. "Frankly speaking," he observed, "we were in a very difficult position from which we found ourselves unable to retreat for the sake of the Navy's honor. In retrospect, we were merely running, heading nowhere, hoping against hope in the hopeless night engagement."[41]

Kondo continued to make brisk preparations, radioing all concerned at 1750:

1. Engage the enemy in closed formation much in the manner of a daylight encounter by taking advantage of moonlight.

2. Depending on circumstances, CruDiv 5 and DesRon 2 (or DesRon 4) may be detached.

3. Torpedo depth setting will be 4 meters . . . [42]

Then *Chikuma's* Number Two plane added another weird ingredient to this unholy mess. The cruiser blinkered at 1830: "The Number Two plane of this ship sighted 4 enemy carriers, 6 cruisers, and 15 destroyers in position 30 miles east of the burning and listing enemy carrier at 1413. This enemy force was westward bound. Shortly after sighting it, our plane was pursued by enemy carrier-based fighters, and lost it."[43] At this point, Nagumo must have yearned to beat his skull against the bulkhead or strangle all reconnaissance pilots with his bare hands.

Six minutes later, Yamamoto and Ugaki received, not this latest report, but the earlier one advising that the enemy was retiring. By this time, confused messages plus a serious time lag in receipt and decoding aboard *Yamato* had produced such a royal mix-up between the respective headquarters of the Combined Fleet and Mobile Force that only a face-to-face meeting could have straightened them out.

Ugaki did some quick figuring. Sunset was just four minutes gone, and 100 miles separated the "retiring enemy force" and Kondo's "fast-advancing invasion force." All was not yet lost! Ugaki promptly issued "an order of fast-chasing the enemy, meaning a night engagement."[44] This directive was Combined Fleet DesOpOrd Number 158, radioed at 1915—a classic, horrible example of the problems of attempting remote control in a rapidly changing tactical situation:

1. The enemy fleet, which has practically been destroyed, is retiring to the east.
2. Combined Fleet units in the vicinity are preparing to pursue the remnants and at the same time, to occupy AF.
3. The Main Unit is scheduled to reach position FU ME RI 32 on course 90 degrees, speed 20 knots, by 0000, 6th.
4. The Mobile Force, Occupation Force (less CruDiv 7), and Advance Force will immediately contact and attack the enemy.[45]

Little imagination is required to picture a hundred brown, muscular hands reaching for a hundred bottles of aspirin. By the time *Nagara* decoded this masterpiece, *Soryu* and *Kaga* had sunk; those still aboard *Akagi* were preparing to abandon ship; *Hiryu*, although moving, was aflame; and four enemy carriers were reported heading westward. Reactions varied according to the recipient. Fuchida, his fractures set and fairly comfortable, was lying on a bunk below decks. Because Kusaka occupied a bunk in the same room, the airman heard all the information that came to the chief of staff. He could believe nothing ill of Yamamoto, and decided that the Commander in Chief was trying to shore up sagging morale before it collapsed in a heap. [46]

At the other extreme, Captain Hara, almost knocked off *Amatsukaze*'s bridge in his astonishment, thought that Yamamoto had lost his mind. The day had been one of particularly poignant suffering for Hara, because he was something of a protégé of Nagumo's and thought the world of the kindly admiral. He ached with sympathy for his patron. [47]

Nagumo himself charitably assumed that ". . . the above message was sent as a result of an erroneous estimate of the enemy." [48] From Ugaki's diary it appears that Nagumo was quite correct, although not exactly in the literal sense. The message originated with Ugaki, who was very much the doctrinaire. [49] He had almost reverent faith in the lessons taught in Naval General Staff College and in the concept of the Great All-Out Battle. According to this doctrine, an American fleet emerging from Pearl Harbor to engage a Japanese fleet was supposed to keep on sailing west into the reach of Japanese guns. Spruance's refusal to abide by the rules threw Ugaki for a total loss. He could not conceive that his opponent would turn his prows east unless he had no other choice.

Combined Fleet Headquarters began to come apart with the disabling of *Hiryu*, and Spruance's unconventional tactic completed the demoralization. The inflexible Midway plan had no leeway for so much of the unexpected, and blew up under the pressure.

That Yamamoto was not merely attempting to boost morale, but was quite serious in intending to continue with the Midway attack at this time, in accordance with DesOpOrd Number 158, is evidenced by his radio of 2030 to the submarine *I-168*. Lieutenant Commander Yahachi Tanabe's undersea craft had been lurking around the atoll since June 1 and was still very much on the job. "Submarine *I-168* will shell and destroy the enemy air base on AF until 2300. CruDiv 7 will carry on after 2300." [50]

An hour later, having had time to decode messages and estimate the situation, Nagumo decided that, between *Chikuma*'s 1830 blinker which convinced him of "the overwhelming superiority of the enemy's carrier strength" and his destroyers being tied up guarding the damaged carriers, the night attack was out. He would concentrate his efforts on saving *Hiryu*, still capable of a good 28 knots speed.

Therefore, he radioed Yamamoto to give him the true picture as he saw it and straighten out what he believed to be the Combined Fleet's misinterpretation. "The total strength of the enemy is 5 carriers, 6 cruisers, and 15 destroyers. These are steaming westward and were in the vicinity of position TO SU WA 15 at 1530. We are offering protection to the *Hiryu* and retiring to the northwest at 18 knots."[51]

Instead of causing the Combined Fleet Headquarters to re-evaluate the situation, this message only convinced them that Nagumo had lost his nerve.[52] Yamamoto countered with orders giving Kondo command of the Mobile Force, except for the damaged carriers and their escort ships. Five minutes before receipt of this message, Nagumo radioed an amplification of his previous explanation: "There still exist 4 enemy carriers (may include auxiliary carriers), 6 cruisers, and 16 destroyers. These are steaming westward. None of our carriers are operational. We plan to contact the enemy with float recco planes tomorrow morning."[53]

Before the Combined Fleet could react to this, Kondo, as the new commander, picked up the action. He radioed all concerned giving the Occupation Force position, and added,

> . . . Thereafter, it plans to search for the enemy to the east and participate as of midnight in a night engagement in accordance with Mobile Force Secret Dispatch #560.
>
> 2. The Mobile Force (less *Hiryu, Akagi*, and their escorts) will immediately turn about and participate in the Occupation Force's night engagement.[54]

The day's welter of confusion ended with Ugaki furious over Nagumo's latest message in which "no fighting spirit was observed." He burst out in his diary: "Don't let another day like this come to us again during the course of this war! Let this day be the only one of the greatest failure of my life."[55]

CHAPTER 34

"There Is No Hope"

By late afternoon of June 4, the warm Pacific sun shone down on a panorama of death and destruction such as Yamamoto and Ugaki had never dreamed possible. Messages between Japanese ships near the scene of desolation told the frightening story of confusion and chaos.

"Together with *Isokaze,* assume screening duties for the *Soryu* and at the same time retire to the northwest." Thus Nagumo ordered Commander Tsuneo Orita, skipper of the destroyer *Hamakaze,* at 1655. But it was Commander Shunuchi Toshima of *Isokaze* who radioed five minutes later to Captain Ariga, commanding DesDiv 4: "*Soryu* has become inoperational. What shall I do?"[1]

Half an hour elapsed before Ariga instructed Toshima: "Stand by in the vicinity of *Soryu* until otherwise ordered. Would she be inoperational if her fires were brought under control?"[2]

Having received no word by 1800, Ariga again flashed a message, this time to *Hamakaze* and also *Maikaze,* one of *Kaga's* escorts: "Advise whether there is any danger of the *Kaga* and *Soryu* sinking." Within two minutes, the faithful Toshima replied to Ariga's earlier query: "There is no hope of her navigating under her own power. All survivors have been taken aboard ship."[3]

Indeed, *Isokaze* was so heavy with approximately 600 survivors that Toshima had to order them not to move about, lest the ship capsize. The instruction was scarcely necessary, for almost every man from *Soryu* was wounded, and their heart-rending moans haunted the destroyer. Many had escaped *Soryu* only to die aboard *Isokaze.* As one after another perished, the bodies were picked up and removed to a separate room.[4]

At 1830, while Midway's bombers were attacking the Mobile Force's

cruisers, Nagumo received *Chikuma*'s blinker advising that four enemy
carriers with their escort were heading westward. Evidently because
of these unpleasant developments, Ariga sent a desperate message
to the destroyers shepherding *Akagi* and *Soryu:* "Each ship will stand
by the carrier assigned to her and screen her from enemy submarines
and task forces. Should the enemy task force approach, engage him
in hit-and-run tactics and destroy him."[5]

Here was a touching avowal of faith—ordering a brace of destroyers loaded to the gunwales with hundreds of survivors, many of them
wounded, to engage and destroy a full task force.

As the first soft pink of a beautiful sunset flushed the Pacific,
Soryu's escort destroyer circled slowly at a cautious distance. Aloft,
out of gun range, an American PBY hovered, shadowing the stricken
flattop, but making no attempt to attack. Fires eating away at the
carrier appeared to abate somewhat around 1900, and her ranking
survivor began rounding up fire fighters, intending to reboard *Soryu*
for another attempt to save her. But before the boarding party could
set out, a tremendous explosion from the carrier rocked the destroyer.
A spear of ruby flame shot high into the glowing sky, as if the gallant
soul of *Soryu* was leaping free of its tortured steel body. Someone
aboard the destroyer shouted an instinctive hail and farewell: "*Soryu*
banzai!" Every man within hearing echoed the cry, tears springing
to their eyes. The flattop slipped quietly beneath the surface. Some
ten minutes later, the survivors felt the shudder of a vast undersea
explosion. Then the waters settled and the sunset flamed over emp-
tiness.[6]

A few miles distant, the periscope of USS *Nautilus* knifed a line
of white bubbles through the blue water. At his post, Commander
Brockman watched with fascination as the Japanese carrier he had
been stalking for almost three hours slowed to a halt. The flattop was
on an even keel, its hull appeared undamaged, and the fire and smoke
which had first attracted Brockman's attention seemed to be under
control. He could see boats bobbing under the bow attempting to
pass a towing hawser. Visible, too, were many crewmen working on
the forecastle.

Brockman had three targets to choose from—the damaged carrier
or the two escort vessels, which he identified as "cruisers," some two
miles ahead of the flattop. As *Nautilus*'s battery might not hold up
under a long chase after two swift "cruisers," Brockman decided to

finish off the carrier before her crew put her back in shape or took her under tow. Cautiously he approached at periscope depth in a direction which would permit him to launch torpedoes against the ship's starboard side near the island. He and his officers repeatedly checked their silhouette charts of both American and Japanese carriers, and satisfied themselves that the carrier was "of the *Soryu* class."[7]

Actually, the submarine skipper's ship identification was 100 percent wrong. The two "cruisers" were the destroyers *Hagikaze* and *Maikaze*, and the carrier was *Kaga*, which, like *Soryu*, had its island on the starboard side. Although she was considerably larger than *Soryu*, *Kaga* from a periscope eyeview could be more readily mistaken for *Soryu* than could the latter's sister ship, *Hiryu*, which carried her island to port.[8]

At 1359 Brockman fired the first of three torpedoes for a 3,400-yard run, the other two at a somewhat closer range. He firmly believed that all three torpedoes hit, because at 1410 flames appeared the entire length of the ship.[9]

This was another very natural mistake, helped along by wishful thinking. In fact, two of the torpedoes missed their target altogether. Communications officer Mitoya saw the churning white wake as one of the steel fish sped directly toward *Kaga*. Certain that the carrier's hour had come, he held his breath and prayed.[10] His petition was answered, for the torpedo struck the hull and broke in half without exploding. The warhead sank, and the rear portion popped up to the surface like a huge cork. Some survivors treading water nearby swam over to this unexpected life raft and clutched it thankfully. One climbed aboard and straddled it. Those who saw their shipmate riding an American torpedo as if on horseback could not help laughing in spite of their many troubles.[11]

The flames Brockman saw may have been caused by the ship's heavy coat of paint, which began to burn sometime that afternoon, spreading fire throughout the vessel. *Nautilus* was thoroughly occupied for the next two hours avoiding a lengthy, uncomfortably close depth charge attack from *Hagikaze*. Commander Juichi Iwagami handled his destroyer very well, and had the depth charges been just a little deeper, the adventurous career of *Nautilus* would have ended then and there. As it was, the submarine sprang a few small leaks. At one point her crew heard a peculiar sound like a chain being dragged over her, and twice heavy objects thudded on the deck. The sound operator reported propeller noises all around the dial, and actually the destroyer passed directly over the submarine.

"Captain, I certainly got religion!" asserted a mess attendant fervently when *Nautilus* finally passed out of the danger zone. And for quite some time thereafter, he prepared a daily sermon, which he posted on the bulletin board.[12]

Meanwhile, Commander Amagai's fire fighters aboard *Kaga* waged incessant but increasingly futile war against the encroaching flames. The inflammable paint carried the fires throughout the ship, inducing explosions in ammunition magazines and among the bombs and torpedoes in the hangar. The heavy concussions blew men and even ship's plates overboard like matchwood.[13]

The sick bay, where medics under a young ensign worked like galley slaves, was cut off from the rest of the vessel. The ensign ordered an attendant named Okamoto to find a way to remove the patients to safety. Okamoto tried faithfully to carry out the order, but all passages were blocked. When he reported back, the officer said to him, "Many thanks for your good efforts," and closed his eyes resignedly.

But a veteran petty officer declared, "It is too early to give up, as we can get out of here through portholes." The ceiling had already started to burn as the medics began to push as many of the wounded as they could through the portholes, and then escaped themselves. But the valorous chief, whose quick thinking had saved so many, made no move. He was unusually stout, and knew he could not squeeze out. Okamoto was able to escape, however, and jumped into the sea, where a destroyer rescued him.[14]

Every passing moment brought Amagai nearer the inevitable time of decision, and a difficult decision it was. He was not a seaman, and all of his good common sense told him that he and his airmen were more hindrance than help to *Kaga*. They knew nothing of the complex business of handling a great ship, especially one in travail, and no one had the time to instruct them. Then, too, experienced naval aviators were at a premium and would be even more valuable in the days to come. The dictates of reason and practical patriotism urged Amagai to get himself and his airmen off *Kaga* to fight again.[15]

On the other hand, Japanese custom of the time placed an almost unbearable pressure and temptation on a man in Amagai's position to commit suicide. Airman or not, he was in command of *Kaga* by seniority, and the ancient tradition that a captain went down with his ship still lived in the Imperial Navy. The Japanese male's self-image as the chosen of the gods, superior by race and training to other men, was so deeply ingrained that almost anything was preferable to a situation which exposed him to public criticism. Neither Japanese religious, legal, nor social mores frowned on suicide—quite the contrary. By dying, something which he must do eventually, Amagai could relieve himself of all responsibility for *Kaga*, her crew, and his airmen. He would be enrolled at Yasakuni Shrine and worshipped by the Emperor himself as one of the guardian spirits of empire. All this would insure honor and preferential treatment for his family. To swim against this stream of tradition required a very special combination of good sense, clear thinking, and personal courage.

Amagai had these qualities in abundance. As it became increasingly apparent that *Kaga* was doomed, Amagai instructed as many fliers and aviation maintenance crewmen as possible to leave the carrier. After ordering "Abandon ship" at 1640, he jumped into the sea and swam to a destroyer. "Though we had been taught that Japanese seamen should never leave their ship even under the worst circumstances, I made such a decision believing that the skilled fliers, who could not be replaced, should be saved so that they could have another chance of fighting," he explained in retrospect. "I also believed that such would best serve the Emperor. At the same time, I thought that the fate of the ship would better be left to her skipper or the second command officer in case he was killed."[16]

At 1715 *Hagikaze* radioed Ariga, "The Emperor's portrait has been safely brought aboard. Since all hands were ordered to abandon ship, we have taken all personnel aboard."[17] This was not exactly an accurate report. Over 800 crewmen were already dead or hopelessly trapped below decks on the burning carrier.

The other escort destroyer, *Maikaze*, radioed Nagumo at 1750, "*Kaga* is inoperational. All survivors have been taken aboard." Immediately Nagumo relayed the sad news to Yamamoto aboard *Yamato* far to the westward.[18]

Ten minutes later, *Nautilus* raised periscope for another look at the scene of action. Heavy black smoke shrouded the carrier and billowed up to a 1,000-foot height. The officer making the observation compared the dense cloud of smoke to that which arose from *Arizona* at Pearl Harbor.[19] Survivors of *Kaga* watched with tearful heartbreak the boiling, churning smoke shot through with long tongues of licking flame.[20] Like *Lexington*, *Kaga* had been an unusually happy and beloved ship. Precisely at 1900 Mitoya saw her seem to leap out of the sea under the impact of two terrible explosions.[21] Then, still on an even keel, she slowly sank, disappearing forever at 1925.[22]

Sixteen minutes later, *Nautilus* surfaced, saw no trace of the carrier and so, her battery exhausted, the submarine returned to her patrol area. She had survived forty-two depth charges, and her crew jubilantly but erroneously credited themselves with sinking *Soryu*.[23]

Matters aboard *Hiryu* did not become really desperate until long after *Soryu* and *Kaga* had sunk. As late as 2100, the destroyer *Makigumo* was able to radio Nagumo, "*Hiryu* can attain 28 knots."[24] However, as the bridge was untenable and steering impossible, the carrier came to a halt. Fires burning along a hammock mantelet outside the bridge forced Yamaguchi, Kaku, and their staffs down to the flight deck, where they congregated on the port side aft of the bridge. The fore part of the flight deck was blazing so fiercely that steel rivets melted like snow and fire sparkled through the holes.[25]

Makigumo pulled in as closely as she could—too close, for *Hiryu*, listing about fifteen degrees to port, broke the destroyer's mast. In the rough sea, rescue work was extremely difficult. Among the wounded was Lieutenant Hiroshi Kadona, who had landed with a wounded leg after the morning attack on Midway. After the transfer, his injured limb had to come off, and was amputated in a bathroom of the destroyer.[26]

Kyuma worked feverishly to maintain contact with his engineering personnel below, but escape passages were blocked. He could only call encouragement to the men through a voice tube: "Hold on, hold on!" The last he heard was someone replying, "Nothing particular to be reported." Repeated attempts to restore contact failed, so Kyuma assumed that all had perished. At the time, however, they had moved to a nearby room which had no voice tube.

Meanwhile, survivors gathered on the port aft side of the flight deck, the only spot untouched by flame. Kyuma suggested to Senior Staff Officer Ito that they get Yamaguchi to safety, no matter how— drag him if necessary.

"Even if we take him off the ship by force now, I am sure the strong-willed admiral would kill himself later, as he has so firmly made up his mind to remain with the ship," replied Ito. "The thoughtful way would be to let him do as he wishes."[27]

Whereupon all the staff officers declared that they would stay with their admiral, and deputized Ito to so inform him. But Yamaguchi would have none of it. "I am very pleased and touched by your staff's desire to remain with me," he told Ito, "but you young men must leave the ship. This is my order."[28]

Kaku's "Abandon ship" came at 0230 on June 5. Twenty minutes later, Yamaguchi and Kaku delivered messages of farewell to all the survivors, numbering about 800. The gist of the admiral's remarks was that, as Commander in Chief of the Second Carrier Division, he assumed sole and full responsibility for the loss of *Hiryu* and *Soryu*. Therefore, he had decided to remain with the ship, but he commanded them all to leave and continue their loyal service to the Emperor. This speech was followed by "expressions of reverence and respect to the Emperor, the shouting of *Banzai*'s, the lowering of the battle flag and command flag."[29]

Following these ceremonies, Kyuma suggested to Ito that he ask the admiral for a parting gift. This Ito did. Yamaguchi took off his battle cap and handed it to his senior staff officer. Then Yamaguchi joined Kaku and his officers in a toast of eternal farewell, drunk in water from kegs handed up from the standby destroyer.[30]

At 0315, forty-five minutes after abandon ship was first announced, Kaku ordered all hands to leave.[31] It was none too soon, for the ship was virtually "a floating blast furnace." But evacuation was orderly and without panic.[32] Ito and Kyuma were the last over the side, climbing down a lifeline hung along the port side into a small boat. Kyuma could control his tears no longer. He had been with Yamaguchi since December 1940, longer than any other member of his staff, and he loathed leaving the ship while his beloved admiral remained. "I had admired him for a long time," said Kyuma, "and still believe he was the greatest man I have ever met in my whole life."[33]

By succumbing to the temptation which Amagai so courageously rejected, Yamaguchi became a national legend. For a Japanese to criticize Yamaguchi would be as shocking as to admit that he hates tea and is allergic to cherry blossoms. Yet the dispassionate eye cannot but observe that the admiral kept his staff and 800 crewman standing around for over half an hour on a flaming, badly listing carrier, while he indulged his taste for melodrama. Certainly he did the enemy a big favor. The loss to Japan of this aggressive, promising admiral was a large plus sign in the United States' column when Clio totaled the Midway score.

Evacuation was completed by 0430, and at 0510 *Makigumo* scuttled *Hiryu* by torpedo.[34] Commander Isamu Fujita, *Makigumo's* skipper, could not wait to confirm the sinking, for at the order of Captain Toshio Abe, commander of DesDiv 10, he hastened off to rejoin the Mobile Force.[35]

But *Hiryu's* story was not over. At 0730 Ugaki radioed Abe, "Has the *Hiryu* sunk? Advise of developments and position."[36] As soon as Nagumo heard this, he dispatched a plane from *Nagara* to return to the scene of the scuttling to determine the status of the abandoned carrier.[37] But at the site the observer saw only empty sea. In the meantime, however, a plane from the light carrier *Hosho* which *Yamato* had sent out to locate the Mobile Force found *Hiryu* still afloat and took several photographs. More important, the pilot reported men aboard the burned-out hulk.

Yamamoto relayed this information to Nagumo, who immediately ordered the destroyer *Tanikaze* to turn back, rescue the survivors, and destroy *Hiryu* if she still floated. However, as we shall see, *Tanikaze* ran into a blizzard of Spruance's dive bombers, and by the time Captain Motoi Katsumi shook them off, *Hiryu* had disappeared for good.[38]

But all those aboard her when she sank had not perished. On June 18, an American PBY on patrol reported to Midway the sighting of a lifeboat with survivors aboard. Simard promptly dispatched the seaplane tender *Ballard* to the spot. *Ballard* made a large and worthwhile catch—none other than the chief engineer of *Hiryu* and thirty-four others, mostly engineroom men, a few from the boiler room, and one electrician. At least two of the prisoners gave their captors false names, for *Hiryu's* chief engineer was Commander Kunize Aimune, and he appears in the American interrogation report as "Commander Eiso."[39]* A lieutenant calling himself "Kajishima" was almost certainly Fuchida's old friend Lieutenant Kazuo Kanegasaki, who later admitted to Fuchida that he had indeed used a nom-de-plume while in captivity.[40] Otherwise, all were remarkably candid in the course

---

*The difficulties of transliterating Japanese into English, rather than deceit, may account for the discrepancy. Walter Lord gives *Hiryu's* chief engineer as Kunizo Aiso. (*Incredible Victory*, p. 239).

of a two-day questioning on Midway, during which they were asked only about points "of immediate tactical value."

The information they gave the Americans was accurate and valuable, but possibly the most interesting was their own escape story. Evidently they did not know *Hiryu* had been scuttled and could not tell just what did sink her. They remained in the engineering space until the smoke became intolerable, then broke through a deck. Clambering topside, they found themselves the only men aboard, and very disgusted they were, particularly "Kajishima," to discover that their captain had abandoned them, as they thought. They saw nothing of either Kaku or Yamaguchi. They sighted *Hosho*'s plane, which buoyed up their spirits with hope of rescue. They jumped over the side and swam to a lifeboat just as *Hiryu* sank. Three of their wristwatches had stopped between 0607 and 0615 Japanese time, which set the hour of the carrier's sinking at about 0900, June 5.

The lifeboat contained hardtack, tallow, water, and beer. Apparently the chief engineer believed that "rank had its privileges" even in a lifeboat, for he "disposed of a little more than his share" of the supplies. Some of the prisoners hinted to their interrogators that in consequence they were considering throwing the officer overboard. The group originally numbered thirty-nine, but four died during their long ordeal at sea and one aboard *Ballard*. The remainder were flown to Pearl Harbor, thence to various prisoner of war camps on the mainland. None of the prisoners wanted to return to Japan, nor did they wish their government to be informed of their capture, preferring to be recorded as lost with their ship.[41]

CHAPTER 35

"I Will Apologize to the Emperor"

Of all the Japanese carriers, none was the object of more earnest attempts to save her, or of more soul-searching at high level, than *Akagi*. She was not just any carrier; she was the flagship, the queen of flattops, the symbol of Japanese naval air power.

From all accounts, Aoki handled the ship as well as possible under the terrible circumstances. At 1130 on June 4, just as Nagumo was resuming command from *Nagara*, Aoki ordered evacuation of all air personnel and the wounded. Five minutes later, a fearsome explosion in the torpedo and bomb storage room of the hangars renewed the fury of the flames. The boat deck, too, was a roaring furnace. Already driven from the bridge to the forward flight deck, Aoki and his staff then moved to the forward anchor deck.[1]

Below, crewmen were fighting the fires with the utmost valor but under crushing handicaps. As the ship's dynamo was inoperative, *Akagi* was not only completely without interior light, but the pressure pumps were out, so the firefighters had to use hand equipment. Some crewmen managed to struggle topside and force water from the sea through long hoses. But the attempt to control such a holocaust with manual equipment was like trying to put out a forest fire with a medicine dropper. As if to mock the crew's gallant efforts, the chemical fire extinguishers refused to work.[2]

At 1203, *Akagi* suddenly came to life and began turning to starboard. An ensign sent to investigate this spooky movement discovered that the entire engine room command had perished.[3]

Akagi's eerie circling undoubtedly saved Fujita's life. As he drifted, he had been killing time by trying to read his palm. But he was not really skilled in that esoteric art, and to his untutored eye his life-line looked altogether too short for comfort. So he abandoned this project and again scanned the seascape. To his joyous excitement, he saw that one of the columns of smoke was much larger and nearer. It soon resolved itself into a carrier moving in a circle and gradually closing in on him.

When the burning vessel reached no more than a mile from Fujita, he recognized *Akagi* and began swimming toward her and her escort destroyer. For one nasty moment, *Nowake* aimed a machine gun at him, but he hastily hand-signaled, "I am a flying officer from *Soryu*." At that instant, two of Fujita's Eta Jima classmates recognized him— Koichi Aoki and Toshio Kanai, respectively *Nowake*'s executive and navigation officers.

Hurriedly clad in one of Kanai's uniforms, and having eaten at last, Fujita climbed to the deck and saw *Akagi* burning in the distance. Men were jumping from her deck into the sea, and boats from *Nowake* were rushing to rescue survivors.

Fujita was too exhausted to form a reasoned, objective picture of the situation, but obviously Japan had lost the engagement. Dimly he heard discussions on the bridge—they must hurry the rescue operations and get out of this dangerous area where enemy subma-rines might be lurking. Some spoke of the destroyer's towing *Akagi*. But Fujita was too tired to take it all in and soon fell asleep.[4]

While these events were taking place, Captain Aoki of *Akagi* remained hopeful. Through *Nowake*, he radioed Nagumo at 1230, "All safe except on flight deck. Every effort being made to fight the fires." The first part of this message was, of course, far from the truth. Evacuation proceeded slowly and methodically, the Emperor's portrait being removed to *Nowake* at 1338. At 1345, the destroyer notified Yamamoto and Nagumo of this, adding that fires were still raging on *Akagi*. As if to emphasize this report, the carrier abruptly stopped her automatic, unnerving circling.[5]

About two hours later, an induced explosion in the hangar blew open the forward hangar bulkheads, and once more fires flared up, spreading to the forward and midship decks. Within the hour, Aoki completed his evacuation of the airmen, and the carrier remained in the sole company of her crew.[6]

Despite their valor and skill, the situation deteriorated steadily. All hope died when at 1915 the chief engineer, Commander K. Tampo, forced his way up from the engine room through the series of burning, fume-laden decks to inform Aoki that there was absolutely no hope of *Akagi* operating under her own power. Immediately, the captain ordered all of Tampo's engine crews topside, but the decision came too late. The orderly dispatched down with the message never returned, and the entire black gang was trapped.[7]

Aoki now requested Nagumo's permission to evacuate. It was granted at once. Accordingly, survivors of *Akagi*'s crew began leaving the ship at 2000, completing the evacuation two hours later. Five hundred evacuees, including Aoki, were squeezed aboard *Arashi* and 200 on *Nowake*.[8]

From the destroyer, Aoki radioed Nagumo, asking his authorization to scuttle the carrier. *Yamato* picked up this message. Shocked by its content, Yamamoto and Ugaki jumped to the conclusion that Aoki had given up too easily. The sun had set, and the Main Body was steaming east for a night engagement, so why abandon hope for the flagship? Yamamoto promptly radioed the Mobile Force to hold off scuttling *Akagi*.[9] Upon receipt of this order, Aoki returned alone to *Akagi* and lashed himself to the anchor chain lest he float away when the carrier sank.[10] This action gives eloquent testimony to just how *Akagi*'s skipper, on the spot, rated her chances.

At almost any other time, the Combined Fleet's Commander in Chief and staff might have accepted Aoki's decision that the flagship was no longer tenable, and acquiesced in his request to finish her off. After all, he was a seasoned captain, with a record sufficiently impressive to have earned him command of one of Japan's most prized carriers. He would never issue the agonizing order to sink his own vessel unless he believed it absolutely necessary.

But it so happened that Aoki's radio reached *Yamato* in the midst of the confusing, increasingly acrimonious exchanges between the Mobile Force and the Combined Fleet which convinced Ugaki, at least, that Nagumo had turned coward. In fact, about half an hour after postponing *Akagi*'s scuttling, Yamamoto relieved Nagumo of command of the Mobile Force.

As darkness crept inexorably across the Pacific, the prospect of a night engagement with the American task force and a successful bombardment of Midway waned with each passing hour. At 2330, with only four hours remaining until sunrise, Ugaki got on the voice tube from the bridge to the Operations Room: "Do not let the night engagement force go too far," he warned, "thus bringing about a pre-dawn situation beyond our control."[11]

Watanabe had another idea to put forward. Let the Main Body's battleships boldly advance on Midway the next day in full light, and bombard the island with their powerful guns. Watanabe put his plan to Kuroshima, who immediately agreed, and they carried it with great excitement to Yamamoto and Ugaki. Yamamoto listened calmly and silently to what Watanabe later called "my crazy explanation." Then the admiral said in a kindly tone, "I am sure you have studied in the Naval Staff College that Navy history teaches us not to fight against land forces with naval vessels."

"Yes, I know," replied Watanabe, abashed.

"Your proposal is against fundamental naval doctrine," continued Yamamoto, "and it is too late now for such an operation. This battle is almost coming to an end. In *shogi* too much fighting causes all-out defeat. One can lose everything."[12]

Ugaki expressed himself with much less restraint. That staunch doctrinaire was outraged. "You ought to know very well the absurdity of attacking a fortress with the guns of a fleet," he scolded. "Even powerful battleships would be defeated by enemy air forces and submarines before they could make an effective bombardment in a situation such as exists where there are quite strong land-based air forces operating from an undamaged base, as well as a still powerful carrier air force. We had better wait for the Second Carrier Striking Force, if the Invasion Force can stay long enough.

"Furthermore," he added, "we can have hopes for subsequent operations, because we will have eight carriers, including those expected to be completed soon, though we have lost four carriers in this operation. It is the plan of a fool without a brain," he continued acidly, "to challenge a hopeless game of *go* again and again out of desperation."[13]

Thoroughly squelched, Watanabe and Kuroshima retired to their Operations Room to restudy matters. It was evident to Watanabe, so sensitive always to Yamamoto's every mood, that the admiral already considered the situation beyond recovery. Nothing remained to be done but retire and make what Watanabe called a "turn-to-the-west escape." Therefore, he carefully worked out and prepared a message calling off the operation and arranging for a rendezvous.

Full of grief and regret, Yamamoto approved Watanabe's draft.[14]

At 0255 on June 5, *Yamato* radioed to all concerned Combined Fleet DesOpOrd No. 161:

1. The occupation of AF is cancelled.

2. The Main Unit will assemble the Occupation Force and the First Mobile Force (less the *Hiryu* and her escorts), and will carry out refueling operations during the morning of 7 June in position 33N, 170E.

3. The Screening Force, *Hiryu* and her escorts, and the *Nisshin* will proceed to the above position.

4. The Landing Force will proceed westward, out of Midway's air range.[15]

Thus perished on the altar of dogma the Japanese opportunity to pulverize Midway and land their invasion force. From having originally seriously underrated the enemy, the Combined Fleet top brass now fantastically overestimated their own difficulties.

Watanabe's message made no mention of *Akagi*. The decision to retreat had automatically posed the question of what to do about the flagship. In the Operations Room, Yamamoto presided over a gathering of his entire staff to thrash out the problem. Should they permit Aoki to scuttle her, rush in and take her under tow even at the risk of a further battle, or leave her? They were sure that, if they abandoned *Akagi*, "the Americans would come in and take her and she would become a museum piece in the Potomac River."

The atmosphere of this discussion was highly dramatic and emotional. Kuroshima in particular was "very passionately" excited. Ashamed to admit defeat, he fought for *Akagi* to the bitter end. In anger, grief, humiliation, and frustration, the senior staff officer wept. So did many others. "We cannot sink the Emperor's warships by the Emperor's own torpedoes!" Kuroshima cried in anguish.

His words seemed to suck the very air out of the room. "Virtually all the members of Yamamoto's staff choked and stopped breathing," Watanabe recalled.

"Yamamoto may have cried in his mind," he observed, "but there were no tears in his eyes." Perhaps the pain of this decision, which only he could make, cut too deep for tears.

Finally, he spoke up. "I was once the captain of *Akagi*," he said slowly and heavily, "and it is with heartfelt regret that I must now order that she be sunk." Then he added, "I will apologize to the Emperor for the sinking of *Akagi* by our own torpedoes."

With this final word, the meeting broke up. Watanabe "saw the battle turning and the world turning all by the decision of one man."[16]

Nagumo received Yamamoto's order at 0350 on June 5.[17] Dawn was close at hand, and fog lay low on the sea. *Akagi* seemed to have burnt herself out, and loomed against the mist like an ink stroke from the brush of a Japanese artist. A boat was sent with a deputation to persuade Aoki that he should not sacrifice himself. *Akagi*'s navigator, Commander Miura, pointed out that, as the carrier would sink beneath Japanese and not enemy torpedoes, her captain was under no obligation to go down with her. Next, Captain Ariga, who ranked Aoki, personally climbed aboard and gave the captain a direct order to leave the ship. Aoki had no choice but to obey.[18]

At 0500, three destroyers closed on the carrier and fired three torpedoes against her. Explosions blasted along the starboard side, and *Akagi* began to nose down. All aboard the destroyers shouted, "*Akagi* banzai, banzai, and banzai!" Within twenty minutes she had disappeared, leaving only huge bubbles to mark her passing.[19]

CHAPTER 36

"Why Should I Not Sleep Soundly?"

A young Marine on Midway tugged frantically at the mattress whereon his exhausted sergeant had tumbled, deep in slumber. "Hey, Sergeant, wake up, wake up, God damn it, we are being attacked!"

"Where, where, what is it?" mumbled the sleeper.

"A submarine," replied the Marine.

Whereupon his noncom uttered a disgusted, "Oh, pshaw!" and went back to sleep.[1]

And indeed the brief round of shots which Midway traded with the Japanese submarine *I-168* at about 0130 resulted in no damage to either side.[2]

But a danger to be taken seriously was bearing down on Midway. Kurita's four heavy cruisers, *Kumano*, *Suzuya*, *Mikuma*, and *Mogami*, with their escort destroyers *Asashio* and *Arashio*, were headed toward the atoll. Each cruiser carried ten 8-inch guns and could have inflicted fearful damage on Midway's defenses and installations. Kondo had detached them from his Invasion Force to carry out Yamamoto's orders for a night bombardment. Kurita's position when he received his orders—some 400 miles west of the target—virtually insured that he could not beat the sun to Midway. However, he would do his best. By 2300, his heavy cruisers, the speediest ships in the Japanese Navy, had outdistanced the destroyers.[3]

Bad luck had not finished with the Japanese. Deciding that Kurita could not possibly carry out the mission on schedule, at 0020 Yamamoto cancelled the bombardment. Although obviously intended for Kurita (ComCruDiv 7), somehow it was addressed to Abe (ComCruDiv 8) aboard *Tone* with the Mobile Force.[4] Receipt of this message at the intended time would have spared the Japanese another tragedy and correspondingly cut down on the American measure of victory.

The cruisers' officers and men had been keyed up in anticipation of "a dare-devil attack upon the island," so some experienced relief from tension. However, a few officers expressed regret at having to abandon the attempt after coming so far.[5]

By the time Kurita received his orders, he had continued to within ninety miles of Midway where, at 0215, the U.S. submarine *Tambor* "sighted the loom of four large ships on the horizon distributed across our bow." In the darkness, Lieutenant Commander John W. Murphy, *Tambor*'s skipper, could not tell whether these indeterminate shapes were friend or foe. He kept in sight of them, however, and shortly after 0238 radioed Admiral English at Pearl Harbor that he had spotted many unidentified ships, giving course, position, and speed. At this time the Pacific Fleet was so organized that submarine skippers were not under task force commanders, but reported directly to the Commander Submarine Forces, who in turn fed the information to Headquarters CinCPAC which coordinated the messages. By the time Murphy's report filtered through this roundabout channel, dawn was breaking, and Murphy could identify the ships as Japanese. He could also see an enemy destroyer heading directly for him, so he prudently crash dived.[6]

Meanwhile, Kurita had finally received Yamamoto's orders cancelling his mission. Scarcely had the cruisers altered course than *Kumano* spotted *Tambor*, and Kurita hastily ordered a 45° turn to port.[7] The signal "*Aka! Aka!* (Red! Red!)" flashed from *Kumano* to *Suzuya* and from *Suzuya* to *Mikuma*. The maneuver was a tricky one, and Kurita's heavy cruisers had no experience in this movement at night. When the crude signal from a dim lamp reached *Mogami*, last of the cruisers in line, *Mikuma* loomed directly ahead of her sister ship.

"Hard port rudder! Full astern!" screamed Lieutenant Commander Masaki Yamauchi, *Mogami*'s navigation officer. But it was too late. *Mikuma* crunched into *Mogami*'s port side aft of the bridge, crushing the victim's bow from the captain's cabin forward and bending it to port. The damage reduced her speed and seriously impeded steering.[8] *Mikuma*'s relatively slight damage did not significantly cut her speed, but the collision punctured one of the main fuel storage tanks on her port side. The resultant heavy leakage left a trail of oil, making the cruiser's course all too visible to any U.S. plane which might fly over the area.[9]

Lieutenant Commander Masayushi Saruwatari, *Mogami*'s damage control officer, sped forward and found his fore station crew at a loss what to do and how to do it. The sudden shock had completely disoriented them. Saruwatari commanded the men to patch up the holes and straighten out the compartment next to the damaged one. He also ordered all possible explosives and inflammables jettisoned, including depth charges. He even launched the torpedoes over the protest of Captain Akira Soji. These precautions were to pay off handsomely in the ensuing two days. When the damage control crew had finished their work, the ship went back to full power, but could limp westward at only twelve knots.[10]

As soon as Kurita aboard his flagship *Kumano* learned of the collision, he turned back to the rescue. Discovering that Soji was still coaxing some mileage from *Mogami*, Kurita left *Mikuma*, *Arashio*, and *Asashio* to escort the stricken vessel. Then he hustled *Kumano* and *Suzuya* westward to rendezvous with Yamamoto.[11]

Tambor's message to English reporting "many ships" set off a flurry of American action, for headquarters at Pearl Harbor knew that the ships sighted were not their own. Murphy's information seemed to indicate that the Japanese were continuing their landing attempts. Therefore, all submarines were ordered to close on Midway to attack the troop transports and supporting ships.[12]

At midnight, Spruance had been heading northward, planning to remain on that course for about an hour, then head west, so that by daylight he would be in a position either to defend Midway or take another crack at the Mobile Force. He was still not sure that he could count out *Hiryu*, and Intelligence had suggested that the Japanese might have a fifth carrier.[13] Then a radar contact, which he dispatched the destroyer *Ellet* to investigate, and which turned out to be false, sent Spruance back on his original course. He steamed east for about eighteen minutes, then south for roughly one hour. Not until nearly 0200 did he turn prows westward again.[14]

At dawn he received *Tambor*'s report, which must have been of particular interest to him, for his son, Edward D., was a lieutenant aboard *Tambor*. The admiral stepped up Task Force Sixteen's pace to some twenty-five knots and hastened southward to place himself near and directly north of Midway.[15] Spruance did not believe "that the enemy, after losing four carriers and all their planes, would remain in an offensive frame of mind . . ." But he could not afford to overlook the possibility, especially as a fifth Japanese flattop might be in the area.[16]

Murphy's report of "large enemy forces at 28-23N., 179-09 W." reached Midway's defenders at 0415. Within fifteen minutes, twelve B-17s were in the air to seek out and bomb the Japanese ships. The Army pilots, however, were unable to locate the enemy. But at 0630 a patrol plane reported, "Sighted 2 battleships bearing 264, distance 125 miles, course 268, speed 15." Two minutes later he added, "ships damaged, streaming oil."[17]

MAG-22 sent up the remaining airworthy planes of VMSB-241 at 0700 to attack the two "battleships" which, of course, were *Mogami* and *Mikuma*. This flight consisted of six Dauntlesses under Captain Marshall A. Tyler and six Vindicators under Captain Richard E. Fleming. After some forty-five minutes of flight, the pilots spotted a wide oil slick and followed it to its source. Tyler led his SBDs in a dive approach on *Mogami* from approximately 10,000 feet, twisting and turning to avoid the cruiser's heavy antiaircraft fire. This portion of the attack was a total loss on both sides. The Marines scored nothing better than a few near misses and the Japanese failed to hit any American aircraft.[18]

Fleming's Vindicators were a few minutes behind Tyler. About twenty miles west of Kure, Captain Leon M. Williamson noticed a ship below and called it to Fleming's attention. The flight swung off to investigate. Their discovery proved to be a submarine, which crash dived at their approach, so they returned to course. It was therefore around 0840 when Fleming led his flight into a glide from 4,000 feet, through heavy flack. Zooming out of the sun, Williamson saw Fleming's engine smoking throughout his dive. Then, as the leader started to pull out, his plane burst into flames.[19] It appears that, either by accident or design, Fleming crashed his fiery aircraft on *Mikuma*'s aft turret. According to Fuchida, the ensuing blaze was sucked into the air intake of the starboard engine room, where it ignited gas fumes and killed the crew.[20]

The Marines were just pulling out when Lieutenant Colonel Brooke Allen appeared on the scene, leading eight B-17s. Although claiming three near misses and an estimated two hits, the Flying Fortresses actually scored only one near miss which killed two men on *Mogami*.

For the time being, then, the two damaged cruisers were left to their own devices and continued to limp westward.[21]

Through the morning, Spruance was faced with an embarrassment of targets. If he wished, he could turn southwest toward the two "battleships." Yet he might prefer to veer in a more westerly direction to investigate a patrol plane report of 0700: "Two enemy cruisers bearing 286, distance 174, course 310, speed 20." Some alert-eyed pilot had seen *Kumano* and *Suzuya* and, moreover, recognized them as cruisers. But the report which made up Spruance's mind for him came at 0800: "Two battleships and one carrier afire, three heavy cruisers bearing 324, distance 240, course 310, speed 12."[22]

Here was a target really worth going after! Both Fletcher and Spruance knew that they had bagged three Japanese flattops and, as Fletcher remarked, "It was an indescribably wonderful feeling to know that we had destroyed three of their carriers. It was a tremendous relief."[23] But Spruance could not be truly satisfied until he knew the fourth carrier had followed her sisters into the deeps. A patrol plane report of 0821, "*Enterprise* on fire and sinking,"[24] must have caused a diversion on *Enterprise*'s bridge, but at least it indicated that somewhere some carrier was in bad straits. Accordingly, Spruance decided to head northwest after the remains of the Nagumo force. Although the more distant target, "it contained the crippled CV and 2 BBs, one of them reported damaged."[25]

At about 1100 Task Force Sixteen sighted a ditched PBY, so Spruance detached *Monaghan* to pick up the pilot and crew, with orders not to destroy the plane.[26] When the rescued pilot was hauled over *Monaghan*'s side, her skipper, Lieutenant Commander Bill Burford, took him down to the wardroom and asked, "What's going on?"

"There's a huge Japanese fleet out there," replied the pilot, and tried to convey to his unexpected host the number and types of enemy ships involved. Burford was frankly incredulous. "Hell, this pilot had so many Jap ships out there that they would have covered the whole ocean for miles in any direction," he said in retrospect.[27]

Later Burford discovered that the flier had indeed exaggerated. But oddly enough, sitting in *Monaghan*'s wardroom was the patrol pilot best qualified to have given Spruance an eyewitness account of the previous afternoon's action. For this man had flown sector I V 58, and it was his message of approximately 1558 on June 4 which gave the Midway Naval Air Station its first indication that the Japanese were taking a beating. At that time he reported "three burning ships," and at 1745 the glad tidings that "3 burning ships are Jap carriers, not damaged ships 2 enemy cruisers, 4 destroyers, bearing 320, distance 170." Fifteen minutes later, he had radioed "forces engaged in battle" and then, at 1815, "attacked by enemy planes."[28]

Here is a vivid indication of the strange nature of the battle of Midway. Bill Burford, an intelligent, experienced destroyer captain, had participated without having the faintest idea of what was going on, until a patrol pilot, dripping all over his wardroom floor, clued him in.

In the general excitement, the *Monaghan* rescue party failed to salvage the plane's Norden bombsight, a highly classified piece of equipment, and signaled *Enterprise* to that effect. Immediately Spruance directed the destroyer to return to the scene of rescue, rectify the error, and report to *Yorktown*. This whittled Spruance down to six destroyers. *Six destroyers to screen two carriers and six cruisers!* he said to himself grimly. *An impossible situation!* Impossible or not, he had to deal with the reality, and shortly after 1100 turned on course northwest by west to chase the Nagumo force.[29]

Throughout the morning, Yamamoto's Main Body continued to surge eastward to rendezvous with Nagumo and Kondo. The latter appeared on time, but Nagumo was not yet to be seen, so Yamamoto sent out a search plane from *Hosho* to hunt for the Mobile Force. Actually, Nagumo had been cruising almost parallel to Kondo's position, gradually pulling in, and by 1205 *Chikuma* had sighted the Main Body and Occupation Force some thirty-seven miles away.[30]

What a different meeting from the joyous get-together the fleets had anticipated! Four of Japan's finest carriers had gone forever, and with them a total of 332 aircraft—more even than the First Air Fleet's normal complement, for the flattops were carrying planes destined for the projected Japanese naval air station on Midway. Worst of all, a total of 2,155 skilled, experienced men had perished—221 from *Akagi*, 415 from *Hiryu*, 718 from *Soryu*, and approximately 800 from *Kaga*.[31] Small wonder that certain officers aboard Nagumo's new flagship felt that they could not endure the disgrace.

Kusaka sat stoically in *Nagara's* sick bay. A hospital corpsman was treating his burns when Senior Staff Officer Oishi approached him. "All of the staff have made up their minds to commit suicide to atone for Midway," he announced sorrowfully. "Please urge the Commander in Chief to make up his mind to do so as well."[32]

For a brief moment, when all the carriers were in flames, Kusaka had felt like his world had come to an end. How could he return to Japan and face her mountains and rivers, her Imperial family, her people? But once resting in *Nagara*'s sick bay, where the pain of his burns and injuries finally drove him, his natural strength reasserted itself. *I won't give up like this!* he swore to himself. Those still alive and the spirits of the valiant dead should stand up again to defend their country. The battle was not finished! So Oishi had arrived at an inopportune time to recruit Kusaka.

Anger darted from the admiral's eyes as he reproved Oishi roundly. Then he ordered him to fetch all the members of Nagumo's staff. When they had gathered, Kusaka sounded off loud and clear. "I am against suicide," he declared with all his determination. "You are just like hysterical women," he shouted at them contemptuously. "First you get excited over easy victories and now you are worked up to commit suicide because of a defeat. This is no time for Japan for you to say such a thing," he scolded. "Why not think of turning a misfortune into a blessing through your efforts? I am dead against committing suicide. I am going to advise the Commander in Chief of my opinion." That ended any talk of *hara-kiri* among the Mobile Force staff.[33]

After his wounds were bandaged, Kusaka went straight to Nagumo's cabin. He found his chief deeply troubled and sorely dejected. Kusaka repeated his sentiments that suicide would solve nothing. Japan needed them all to fight again.

Nagumo listened patiently. "I appreciate your advice very much," he replied, "but you must understand that everything a Commander in Chief does cannot be by reason."

Whereupon the realistic Kusaka rallied his despondent colleague. "Come on, Commander in Chief! What can you accomplish with a defeatist attitude?"

"Very well," answered Nagumo resignedly. "I will never commit a rash act."

Convinced that his message had fallen on fertile soil, Kusaka left his chief, well satisfied.[34]

Meanwhile, Fletcher's Task Force Seventeen concentrated on salvaging *Yorktown*, which hung through the night at her dangerous list. Immediately upon removing to *Astoria*, Fletcher had informed Nimitz of the situation. The CinCPAC dispatched to the scene the minesweeper *Vireo* from Hermes Reef and the fleet tug *Navajo* from French Frigate Shoals. He also diverted the destroyer *Gwin*, already a day out of Pearl Harbor en route to join Spruance, to augment *Yorktown*'s guard.[35]

Daylight had just gushed over the horizon when a rattle of machine-gun fire from *Yorktown* startled the nearby destroyermen. Lieutenant Commander Donald J. Ramsey, the skipper of *Hughes*, sent over a detachment to investigate. Much to their surprise, they found Seaman Second Class Norman M. Pichette, suffering from severe abdominal wounds resulting from shrapnel. Despite his painful injuries, Pichette had the raw courage to pull himself up three decks and the presence of mind to do the one thing sure to attract attention—fire a machine gun toward the destroyer.

The boarding party hurried him to *Hughes*, where he gasped out that another wounded seaman had been left for dead in *Yorktown*'s sick bay. Back went the search party and found Seaman First Class George K. Weise, unconscious from a fractured skull. Pichette's noble effort was his last, for he perished and was buried at sea on June 7, but he had saved his shipmate, who eventually recovered.[36]

The destroyer had another opportunity at rescue when Ensign Harry B. Gibbs, a fighter pilot shot down the day before, bobbed along in a rubber boat. His life raft had been punctured, but Gibbs kept it afloat all night by squeezing the holes shut with his knees. At dawn another raft, this one whole, floated by, and Gibbs swapped his leaky craft for this windfall. He had been afloat, all told, for sixteen hours when Ramsey welcomed him aboard.[37]

The boarding party had made another startling discovery aboard *Yorktown*—three mail sacks stuffed with code and cipher equipment. These highly secret items had been neatly and properly readied for removal, but for some unknown reason left adrift on the upper deck. Ramsey informed Nimitz of this important recovery. It also seemed to Ramsey that the carrier's list was not so heavy as to preclude salvage. Accordingly, he suggested to Nimitz that *Yorktown* might yet be saved. Encouraged by Ramsey's message, the CinCPAC directed that the flattop not be scuttled unless he personally ordered such action.[38]

The remaining ships of Task Force Seventeen had steamed parallel to Spruance through the night, then, at dawn, headed toward *Yorktown* at a slow ten knots to enable them to transfer men and material between vessels. The destroyers, dangerously top-heavy with *Yorktown* evacuees, began moving their passengers to the cruisers *Astoria* and *Portland*. The temporary flagship *Astoria* became a floating personnel office as soon as Buckmaster boarded her from *Hammann*. He was eager to take a salvage party back aboard *Yorktown,* and set to work listing exactly what men he needed—damage control, engineers, mechanics, and the like. As the destroyers in turn came alongside *Astoria*, the cruiser took on refugees over one side while out across the other moved a handpicked salvage group of twenty-four officers and 145 men. It was a slow process, for the men had been evacuated in no particular order and the key personnel Buckmaster wanted had to be carefully sorted out.[39]

Vireo joined the party by mid-morning and at 1436 began to pull *Yorktown* at a barely perceptible two knots toward Pearl Harbor.[40] About the same time, *Gwin* appeared, and her captain, Commander Harold R. Holcomb, assumed command of the salvage operations as senior officer present. With the *Hughes* boarding party augmented by a group from *Gwin*, the men worked rapidly, throwing overboard all loose gear and everything they could pry off the listing side in the attempt to lighten the ship. Burford brought his *Monaghan* into the area late that afternoon, but little more could be done as darkness approached, for *Yorktown* had neither power nor light.[41]

Midway sent out two B-17 flights that afternoon to seek two damaged enemy carriers, but of course all four flattops had disappeared and the rest of the Nagumo force had joined Yamamoto far to the northwest. The first group of Fortresses, still under Allen's command, found what they reported as a large cruiser, and claimed two hits and three near misses. Ten minutes later, the second group attacked a "heavy cruiser" reported as 20° and 125 miles away from the first target. This flight suffered heavily, for one of its aircraft, named "City of San Francisco" and donated to the government by the citizens of that metropolis, dropped its bomb bay tank and failed to return. Another aircraft ran out of gas and ditched fifteen miles from Midway, where all but one of the crew were rescued.[42]

It is generally believed that the two "cruisers" were actually the destroyer *Tanikaze*, returning to join the rest of the Japanese fleet after seeking *Hiryu*.[43] Discrepancies of time and place, however, leave a question mark. One hundred twenty-five miles in ten minutes is a good clip. Moreover, *Tanikaze* was under attack at that very time by Spruance's dive bombers.

At 1410 Yamamoto blinkered all his ships: "Planes have taken off of enemy carriers. (Communications Intelligence)." Again at 1435 he added, "The enemy is apparently overhead at high altitude (Communications Intelligence.)"[44] Evidently Japanese eavesdroppers picked up and misinterpreted a signal from Spruance to Allen's Flying Fortresses. As the flight droned over, the admiral advised them that he intended to launch within the hour. He received no reply, but heard them transmit his position to Midway.[45]

Plotting the distance to the target, Spruance's staff knew that the flight would be dangerously near the point of no return for the Dauntlesses. Nonetheless, their orders called for arming the planes with 1,000-pound bombs. Although grounded, McClusky regarded himself as responsible for his men. The previous day, he had lost valuable planes and good comrades for lack of fuel when inaccurate information on the enemy's position necessitated an extended search. So, after making his own calculations and confirming them with Short and Shumway, McClusky climbed the three decks to flag plot. There he asked Browning that the planes carry 500-pound bombs, and that their takeoff be delayed for an hour. The lighter bomb load would cut down on fuel consumption; the delay would permit a closer approach.

Despite the cogency of McClusky's arguments, Browning refused his request. McClusky persisted. The irresistible force of the air group commander's logic and sense of responsibility collided with the immovable object—Browning's obstinacy. The resultant friction heated up.

To one side, Spruance had been checking plots with other staff officers. Now he stepped up to the table where Browning and McClusky were having it out. He spoke directly to McClusky: "I'll do whatever you pilots want."[46] Browning retired to his cabin in a fit of the sulks. There he remained until Lieutenant Colonel Julian Brown, the task force's Marine officer,* persuaded him to return to his duty post.[47]

At 1500 *Enterprise* and *Hornet* swung back east into the wind,

---

*His official title was Fleet Marine, Aircraft, Battle Force. He was also detailed semi-officially as Intelligence Officer under Halsey.

and within forty-five minutes had launched a total of fifty-eight bombers. The aircraft flew an arc of 315 miles without success, but on their way back, some of the planes found what they believed to be a light cruiser of the *Katori* class. This time there is no doubt of the target: It was *Tanikaze*. Thanks to the superb handling of her skipper, Commander Motoi Katsumi, the little vessel dodged unscathed through a liberal peppering of "very near misses." One American plane fell to the destroyer's unusually heavy small caliber AA fire. By a strange twist of fate, the victim was the same Lieutenant Adams who had made such a fine sighting report on *Hiryu* the day before.[48]

Fuchida for one always believed that *Tanikaze*'s adventures of June 5 saved the Japanese Midway attack fleet from discovery and probably from another dose of the bitter medicine Nagumo had already swallowed.[49] Certainly the United States afternoon flights missed their objective—the fleeing Nagumo force—by a very narrow margin.

Dusk had already settled when *Hornet*'s planes began to return,* but there was still no sign of the *Enterprise* aircraft. Spruance was quite worried about his homing pigeons when darkness settled, because he knew that many of his pilots had received no training in night landings. Therefore he took another in his series of carefully calculated risks. Despite the obvious danger, he ordered the carrier's huge search lights turned on as beacons.[50] We doubt that any returning pilot, seeing those lights flooding out, would agree with the assessment of Spruance as cold and uncaring. His airmen did him proud, for only one accident occurred, and that was unavoidable. Lieutenant Ray Davis's plane ran out of gas just as it came in, and flopped into the wake of the ship. Fortunately, the quick, skillful work of the destroyer *Aylwin* saved all hands.[51]

Enterprise's landing signal officer, Lieutenant Robin Lindsey, knew that the carrier had launched thirty-two aircraft, and as they kept coming in by twos and threes, he wondered if he had miscounted. "How many planes have we to go before we get the complete group in?" he asked his assistant. "I'll be damned if I know," the latter replied. "We've got five more than we are supposed to have already!" Several *Hornet* planes had landed on *Enterprise*, and for good measure an *Enterprise* plane ended up on *Hornet*.

---

*Official records to the contrary, there is some evidence that a number of *Hornet*'s SBDs carried 1,000-lb bombs. This failure to obey orders provoked Spruance, who believed that, as a result, some of the *Hornet* aircraft had to return sooner than necessary. (Spruance/Barde interview.)

While the pilots were homing, Spruance had time to think over the situation. That fourth enemy carrier still haunted him, for he did not know that *Hiryu* could trouble him no more. He reflected that, if he were commanding that damaged carrier, he would head westward. Undoubtedly the skipper of the vessel his pilots had attacked would report the fact, then he, too, would turn to the west for two reasons: first, to take cover in the bad weather reported in that direction; second, to shake off the American pursuers.[52]

All things considered, "Go west, young man!" seemed like good advice. But, as always, Spruance moved prudently. His six destroyers were running low on fuel, and in the circumstances he was not eager to find himself tailgating any Japanese battleships in the dark, when his aircraft would be useless. So he slowed his pace to fifteen knots, and changed course from northwest to due west.[53]

Then he called it a day and retired to the sound sleep he enjoyed every night. "I had good officers with me; they knew their jobs; they would carry on. Why should I not sleep soundly?" he said matter-of-factly many years later. "Besides, a mind that suffers from lack of sleep is not likely to be clear and have good judgment. So I had to sleep soundly."[54]

In principle, who would not agree? But in practice, who but Raymond A. Spruance could drift into peaceful slumber while stalking the Japanese Mobile Force through the night with a pared-down task force?

CHAPTER 37

"I Trembled with Great Sorrow"

Yamamoto awoke early aboard *Yamato* on the morning of June 6, with the sickening realization that the battle of Midway had been lost. An upset stomach and a bad case of nervous exhaustion had resisted medical treatment for several days. Quite aside from the discomfort his ailment caused the Commander in Chief, it was one more source of worry to his loyal staff. For they knew the defeat tore at his heart, no matter how noble his efforts to hide his true feelings.[1] Indeed, the situation was enough to churn the insides of a wooden Indian.

"N Day, June 7 [Japanese dating], finally came," wrote Ugaki. "During the two months of April and May, planning and preparations were made with great efforts with this day as a goal. Before this target day came, however, the tables had been turned around entirely and we are now forced to do our utmost to cope with the worst. This should be kept in mind," he added sententiously, "as a lesson showing that a war is not predictive."[2]

One faint glimmer of northern lights flickered in the overall darkness. The Aleutian front had not been idle while all the dramatic events took place to the south. In the afternoon of June 4, Kakuta struck Dutch Harbor with an elite force of eleven dive bombers, six horizontal bombers and fifteen fighters. Once more the pilots enjoyed excellent weather over the target, and added to the damage score four fuel tanks, the barracks ship *Northwestern*, a hangar under construction and a hospital wing. On their way to rendezvous, *Junyo's* aircraft encountered eight P-40s over the Otter Point landing field. In the resulting dogfight, the Japanese lost one fighter and two bombers. Two other bombers were so badly mauled they crashed before reaching the carrier. While the Japanese were bombing Dutch Harbor, a group of B-26s and B-17s attacked Kakuta's ships, losing one of each type bomber with no hits to balance the losses.[3]

The off-again-on-again messages from Yamamoto to Hosogaya throughout the latter part of the fourth precluded any further action that day. No unusual keenness of intellect was needed to determine, as did Hosogaya's chief of staff, Captain Tasuku Nakazawa, that something had gone radically wrong. "Summing up the information received, got an impression that unexpectedly heavy damage was inflicted upon the 1st task force and couldn't help having grave worries."[4]

The next morning, having learned that all Nagumo's carriers had been destroyed, at 0800 Hosogaya recommended to Yamamoto that the Aleutian operation be suspended "at this time from an overall point of view . . ." He added that apparently neither the U.S. nor the U.S.S.R. had yet discovered the Northern Force, except for the Second Carrier Striking Force. Some hours later, the Northern Force received a message from Ugaki, "asking our view on carrying out the invasion operation" after certain ships had been added to the Northern Force. The Combined Fleet's intentions having thus been clarified, Hosogaya replied "that the invasion operation could be carried out after the reinforcement joined our force."[5]

Meanwhile, Hosogaya instructed Rear Admiral Sentaro Omori, whose Invasion Force was some 225 miles southwest of Adak, to turn around and occupy Attu. Determined to have Kiska and Attu, at 1259 Yamamoto radioed all concerned, "Second Mobile Force is returned to the Northern Force."[6]

"Seemingly encouraged by this move on our part," Ugaki recorded, "they decided soon after noon to launch the devil-may-care Aleutian Operation No. 5 on N-plus-1 Day. Under what circumstances they reached this decision we can only guess, but an explanation should be made later on." Yamamoto expected that, with the Midway operation called off, the Americans would intensify their efforts to defend and recapture the Aleutians. Accordingly at 2320 he transferred to Hosogaya the two battlewagons *Kondo* and *Hiei*, the heavy cruisers *Tone* and *Chikuma*, the light carrier *Zuiho*, the seaplane tender *Kamikawa Maru*, and fourteen submarines. All were to head northward as soon as refueling was completed. The Combined Fleet staff hoped that an opportunity would present itself to "pay off our scores at Midway," to use Ugaki's words.[7]

To anticipate a bit, the landings on Attu and Kiska proceeded according to schedule, not surprising as neither boasted an armed garrison.[8] The islands were of no strategic value to Japan with the key Midway link still under the Stars and Stripes, and two handfuls of fog and bog were a poor exchange for four aircraft carriers. Certainly Nakazawa had no illusions that anything his force could do would repay Japan for her losses at Midway. "The day of June 5 turned out to be the worst day for Imperial Japan, which must not be forgotten under any circumstances," he lamented. "It demands of us more extraordinary efforts than ever before, as the war has changed into a delaying war." Japan should thoroughly restudy "the overall operational policy and her war-guiding policy . . . ," while the Navy should "establish an emergency policy as rapidly as possible."[9]

During the afternoon of June 5, one by one Nagumo's carrier escort destroyers caught up with the retreat. As originally planned, survivors were to be transferred immediately to larger vessels so that the wounded men might receive the best possible care, but under the circumstances this was deemed impracticable. Ugaki allocated them to various battleships, with transfer to be made on June 6, at the scheduled refueling point beyond the 600-mile circle from Midway. As the evening wore on, with the ships running into bad weather and disquieting reports coming in of enemy aircraft nearby, the refueling rendezvous was shifted further west by one day's sailing. This made it possible to move the wounded immediately.[10]

The transfer was a nightmare, with the ships blacked out under a starless sky, while long, scudding rollers threatened to slam the destroyers into the battleships. Finally, the fleet had to halt long enough to permit small boats to finish their task of mercy. Many of the wounded were horribly burned and mangled.[11] Almost every carrier survivor experienced mysterious pains in the knees and wrists which the doctors eventually diagnosed as resulting from blast concussion.[12] Watanabe refused to permit any of the wounded aboard *Yamato*, lest the sight of their suffering impair Yamamoto's fighting spirit.[13]

Indeed, the admiral's morale needed all the boosting his staff could give him, for his troubles were by no means over with the dawning of June 6. At 0630 he received a report from *Mikuma:* "Two enemy carrier-borne planes in sight."[14] These were from a group of eighteen SBDs, each armed with one 500-pound bomb, which launched from *Enterprise* at 0502. No doubt one of them was 8-B-2, whose pilot, Ensign William D. Carter from *Hornet*, had spent the night aboard *Enterprise*. At 0645 he reported by voice radio that he had sighted a carrier and five destroyers.[15]

When Spruance heard that, he smiled and said, "That's what we are looking for." But his satisfaction did not live long. Carter had instructed his radiomen to report one BB, one CA, and three DDs. Either the radioman or radio central misunderstood, for "due to voice error, the expression 'BB' was heard as 'CV.' " *Hornet* advised *Enterprise* of the mistake by message drop.[16]

Spruance had already ordered *Hornet* to attack before the error was rectified, and at 0759 *Hornet* launched twenty-six Dauntlesses and eight Wildcats, the latter prudently "ordered along in case of previously undetected air opposition."[17]

Meanwhile, at 0730, another *Hornet* plane, 8-B-8, reported a sighting of two heavy cruisers and three destroyers.[18] A plot of the latitude and longitude of both contacts revealed a discrepancy of about fifty-two miles, enough to convince Spruance that he had to deal with two enemy groups. Oddly enough, neither the day's air actions nor cruiser-based scouting cleared up this matter. Of course, only one group of Japanese ships was in the area, the crippled *Mogami* and *Mikuma,* with their escorts *Arashio* and *Asashio.*[19]

These were but the first of a series of errors which make June 6, 1942, a classic study of just how easy it is to mistake one type of ship for another from the air.

Slightly less than two hours after takeoff, *Hornet*'s dive bombers found and attacked their targets. "All pilots of this attack insist that the principal target was definitely a BB (probably *Kirishima* class) and not a CA." However, not being able to tell the difference between a *Kirishima*-class battleship (slightly over 31,000-ton displacement) and a *Mogami*-class heavy cruiser (roughly 12,000-ton displacement) did not interfere appreciably with the pilots' aim.[20]

Hornet claimed to have hit one of the targets—probably *Mikuma*—with two 1,000-pound bombs and one 500-pound bomb. They also credited themselves with two hits on the second target—*Mogami*—and with a small bomb hit on a destroyer.[21]

We know of no Japanese records and damage charts for *Mogami* and *Mikuma* such as exist for the carrier action of June 4, so it is most difficult to pinpoint what happened aboard these cruisers. But according to survivors, *Mogami* did indeed take two hits, one of which killed everyone in Turret Number Five. The other struck amidships, "damaging the torpedo tubes and starting fires below decks."[22] Thanks to Saruwatari's forethought in jettisoning the torpedoes the previous day, no serious fires or explosions resulted.[23] Two or three bombs struck *Mikuma*, and a bomb on her stern damaged but did not disable *Asashio*. This damage, impressive as to hits but relatively minor as to results, cost *Hornet* one Dauntless shot down by antiaircraft fire.[24]

Next *Enterprise* tried her luck. Her thirty-one dive bombers and twelve fighters, under the overall command of the veteran Short, commenced launching at 1045. They had not been airborne long when they received voice radio orders to seek and attack a "battleship," believed to be some forty miles ahead of the previously assigned targets.[25]

To assist them, *Enterprise* was sending out three torpedo planes, made airworthy by strenuous maintenance work. Before these took off, Spruance gave Laub specific instructions not to attack if he encountered any opposition. The admiral thought that a more profitable target might yet present itself, for which he would need the TBDs. As it turned out, the screening destroyers shot off some quite accurate antiaircraft fire, and Laub was not sorry to obey orders.[26]

In pursuit of instructions, the group flew past the cruisers and destroyers, seeking the nonexistent battleship. After searching fruitlessly for some time, the fighters and one of the bomber squadrons turned back and hit the cruisers, one of which they accurately identified as of the *Mogami* class, the other of the *Atago* class. This was not a bad assessment, for the *Atago* class heavy cruisers only displaced about 1,000 tons less than *Mogami*.[27]

Laub described the dive bombing as the most accurate he had ever seen.[28] And Short claimed that the operation was relatively easy.[29] Indeed, with no deadly Zeros to contend with, the Americans had everything pretty much their own way.

Both the *Hornet* and *Enterprise* bridges tuned in on the voice attack frequency. Mitscher sedately reported that "interceptions . . . indicated a large measure of success."[30] Spruance listened with the liveliest appreciation to the pilots' interchanges. "The conversation was rare," he said, "and for the most part unprintable."[31]

"Look at that son-of-a-bitch burn! . . . Hit the son-of-a-bitch again! . . . Let's hit them all. . . . Your bomb really hit them on the fantail. Boy, that's swell! . . . Let's get a couple of those destroyers. . . . These Japs are easy as shooting ducks in a rainbarrel."

Then the comment struck a plaintive note: "Gee, I wish I had just one more bomb!" And another attacker, evidently having little trouble with the enemy's antiaircraft fire, observed scornfully, "These Japs couldn't hit you with a slingshot." Then an exultant shout. "Tojo, you son-of-a-bitch, send out the rest and we'll get those too!"

Spruance was so delighted that he sent a transcript to Nimitz, knowing how much the CinCPAC would enjoy it.[32]

The full transcript reveals beyond question that the *Enterprise* dive bombers believed that the last ship in the formation was a battleship.[33] This must have been *Mikuma,* for the attackers concentrated heavily upon her. Then, in another display of the individual initiative so fortunate for the United States throughout the battle of Midway, Ensign E. M. Isaman of VB-3 "dove on the *Atago*-class heavy cruiser* upon seeing it undamaged, and, through heavy antiaircraft fire directed at him alone, scored a direct hit aft."[34] He must have struck *Mogami,* although, according to some survivors, at this time she suffered only two hits, one amidships, the other "just forward of the bridge."[35]

Saruwatari claimed that the only hit to cause really serious damage plunged through the seaplane deck and fell below to start a raging fire. It made a hell out of the sickbay, for the medical officers and attendants were either killed or wounded, so that those patients not killed outright were left unattended. In spite of all the water Saruwatari's damage control men could pour on the conflagration, the flames threatened to spread out of control. At last, Saruwatari had to accept the terrible responsibility for ordering the entire damaged compartment sealed off. He feared some men might still be alive beyond the door, but had to take "this apparently unmerciful step" to save the ship.

Later when the fires were under control and the crew opened the compartment, the damage control officer found to his intense regret that a number of officers and men had indeed been trapped and killed.

*Why the Americans consistently mistook one cruiser for a battleship is a mystery, for *Mogami* and *Mikuma* were sister ships.

In fact, he saw an engineering sub-lieutenant in the act of committing *hara-kiri*. "I trembled with great sorrow toward them," Saruwatari recalled.[36]

The hapless *Mikuma* reeled under five direct hits which struck her fo'c's'le, amidships, and in the bridge area. The latter strike set off a number of antiaircraft shells on deck ready for firing and damaged the bridge structure. The amidships bomb exploded several torpedoes, while the fo'c's'le hit knocked out the forward guns.[37] *Mikuma*'s engineering division commander, Sub-Lieutenant Taketoshi Kawaguchi, has left a vivid word picture of the hit near the bridge:

> When a direct hit was made on No. 3 turret in front of the bridge (considered to be one of hits made by the enemy second wave attack at about 0930) [1230 local time], many men on the bridge were killed by fragments of the explosion. At that time, Capt. [Shakao] Sakiyama was commanding the ship with his head sticking out from a manhole at the top of the bridge, and he got wounded in his face and head and lost his consciousness immediately. Many officers were killed at this moment.
>
> The command of the ship was then taken over by Cmdr. [Hideo] Takashima, executive officer. Soon afterward, bombs hit on her starboard fore engine room and port after engine room, with a result that the ship became to be stopped. By an order of the executive officer, my men in charge of repairing made rafts with timbers at the ship's bow.
>
> On No. 1 raft Capt. Sakiyama and wounded men were lowered. On No. 2 raft boarded the paymaster, air officer bringing with them important documents and materials.[38]

Although severely damaged, *Mogami* assisted the two destroyers in rescuing about 300 men who had jumped or been blown off *Mikuma*. But they had to break off their work of mercy "due to the fierce enemy air raid," leaving about 100 to 150 men still adrift.[39]

At about this time, a little much-needed comic relief enlivened the action. Of course, Midway had received the morning's misleading reports indicating two groups of enemy ships had been sighted. Assuming that Task Force Sixteen would handle the northern target, at 1045 Simard dispatched all available B-17s—twenty-six—in search of the "cruiser group heading southwest." Midway also hoped that this group might rendezvous with the Japanese transports, thus producing a profitable target.

The B-17s were unable to locate their objective, but on the way home one section of six spotted what they took to be an enemy ship. They dropped twenty 1,000- and 1,100-pound bombs, and reported two hits on a cruiser, which "sank in 15 seconds."[40]

Amazing as the sight of a cruiser sinking in fifteen seconds would be, had the airmen lingered, they might have been treated to an even more startling scene—the same "cruiser" unsinking. With a mighty surge of water, USS *Grayling* surfaced. Her fuming skipper, Lieutenant Commander Eliot Olsen, flashed off an indignant report to headquarters. In essence, he wanted to know just why an American submarine should have to crash dive to avoid being plastered by the Army Air Force.[41]

Enterprise suffered no losses in her attack on the cruiser group. Obviously her planes had conducted a most successful strike, but Spruance did not do things by halves, and he had a worthwhile target in his sights. About an hour before *Enterprise* recovered her planes, he sent off a second attack group from *Hornet*, consisting of twenty-three dive bombers under Ring's command.* At 1445 Ring's men began pouncing on an already battered enemy, which Ring identified as consisting of one CA, probably of the *Kinugasa* class,** another CA or a CL, and two destroyers. This action was probably the closest American and Japanese ships came to each other in this strange sea battle, for the *Hornet* pilots could see simultaneously Task Force Sixteen behind them and the enemy ahead.[42]

After his group returned to *Hornet* with no losses, Ring claimed one hit on a CA, six on a CA or a CL, and one on a destroyer. "Very heavy explosions were seen in the CA, and it was left completely gutted by fire, personnel abandoning ship."[43] This seems to be as accurate a report as one could expect, although there is some evidence that *Mogami* escaped further damage at this time. The destroyers reported, ". . . *Mikuma* hit again and set on a big fire." But the report did not mention *Mogami*, which apparently evaded "repeated air attacks" during this third and last strike.

Under the *Hornet* pilots' rain of death, *Mikuma* broke out in fires so intense that it became obvious she was doomed. Her executive ordered abandon ship, although he himself remained aboard to share

*Twenty-four launched, but one had to return to *Hornet*.
**Kinugasa* displaced 9,380 tons. *Imperial Japanese Navy*, p. 140.

her fate.[44] Upon receipt of this directive, short, round-faced Lieutenant Masao Koyama requested his senior petty officer to witness his death, and committed *hara-kiri*. Koyama's position was commander of the main battery fire control center. As such, by no stretch of the imagination could he be assigned any responsibility whatsoever for *Mikuma*'s fate.[45] Needless to say, Koyama became a folk hero in Japan by thus assisting the U.S. Navy to kill off promising Japanese naval officers.

The hit on a destroyer which Ring chalked up struck *Arashio*'s third turret, and was particularly tragic from the Japanese standpoint. For a large number of refugees from *Mikuma* crowded the fantail, and the blast blew many of them into the sea, killed still others, and severely wounded the commander of DesRon 8, Commander Nobuki Ogawa. *Arashio* suffered some structural damage, but the tough little destroyer was still able to navigate on manual steering.[46]

As with *Hiryu*, chance gave the U.S. Navy eyewitness details about *Mikuma*'s last day. On June 9, the submarine *Trout* removed two Japanese enlisted men from a life raft and took them to Pearl Harbor. One of them, a chief radioman named Katsuichi Yoshida, was suffering from crushed ribs and taken to the Naval Hospital. The second man, Third Class Fireman Kenichi Ishikawa, was interrogated and not at all reticent. Only twenty-one years old, Ishikawa was "nonchalant and most content with his lot as a prisoner of war in the United States." Knowing that his family and friends would never forgive him for being so indiscreet as to be captured instead of killed, he indicated no particular desire to return to his homeland. In fact, questioned as to his preference, he frankly admitted that he would rather remain where he was.

Along with giving an eyewitness account of *Mikuma*'s sinking, Ishikawa told his captors much about her voyage out to Midway, and spoke freely about such Japanese ships as had come under his observation. He explained that he and Yoshida were the sole survivors of twenty men from *Mikuma* who climbed aboard a raft during the fight. They had been without food or water for three days when *Trout* picked them up.[47]

After the last attack group returned to Task Force Sixteen, Spruance remained unsure as to the exact nature of the target his men had been harassing. So he dispatched two scout planes on a photographic mission to settle the question.[48] Lieutenant (j.g.) Edwin J.

Kroeger of VB-6 flew Mr. A. D. Brick of Fox Movietone News, equipped to take movies. Lieutenant (j.g.) Cleo J. Dobson, assistant landing signal officer of *Enterprise*, veteran of many an aerial reconnaissance, piloted the second plane, carrying *Enterprise*'s senior photographer, charged with taking stills of the action results.[49]

Dobson flew in a bloodthirsty mood. A sensitive man, Dobson was unusually attached to his friends and shipmates, and suffered whenever they suffered. He told himself that if he saw any survivors in the water, he would strafe them as the Japanese had done to American sailors in similar circumstances. But when confronted with the actuality, he could not carry out his stern intent. "About 400 to 500 sailors were in the water, all around the ship. After flying over those poor devils in the water, I was chicken hearted and couldn't make myself open up on them." He could see "lots of bodies" lying on *Mikuma*'s deck, and five empty life boats floating about 300 yards from the cruiser. Some thirty miles to the west, two destroyers and one cruiser were trying to escape. The scouts flew over to photograph these ships, but could not get close as the fleeing vessels opened fire. The photographic mission headed back to the carrier, Dobson still brooding over the doomed Japanese sailors.

"Boy, I sure would hate to be in the shoes of those fellows in the water," he told his diary. "I shouldn't feel so sorry for them, because I might be in their shoes some day." Then he added with a touch of humor, "I'll enjoy reading this when I'm sitting by the fireside and haven't enough ambition to go out and repeat the performance."[50]

Spruance questioned the four men personally as to the nature of the target, and was annoyed when Dobson replied, "Sir, I don't know, but it was a hell of a big one." But one of the men insisted that one of the vessels was a heavy cruiser of the *Mogami* class. This was surprising news. "All through the day there had been no questions in our minds that a BB was involved," as Spruance reported to Nimitz. When the prints, excellent ones, were developed the next morning, Spruance examined them himself and found that the observant individual was correct. "My face was red," Spruance said ruefully, "because the afternoon of the attacks I had sent Admiral Nimitz a message that we had bombed a battleship."[51]

Had the photographic mission been delayed a little longer, they might have been able to confirm the end of *Mikuma*, for she went down soon after sunset.[52] Strangely enough, those who saw the two major Japanese vessels continued to insist that *Mikuma* was "definitely larger than the other cruiser accompanying her, which may have been a CL or DL. The smaller ship was last seen leaving a heavy oil streak about 15 miles away."[53]

One explanation for the error may have been her damaged bow. *Mogami* "was running at heavy bow trim causing larger bow waves . . . ," so the Japanese later speculated that this might have caused the Americans to mistake her speed, which was about fourteen knots. And she could still be steered, thanks to a strange circumstance not realized until she arrived at Truk. In the collision of June 5, *Mogami*'s anchor chain ran out to "its fullest extent." As Yamauchi explained, "The fact that the ship was pulling her chain along seemingly had much to do with giving her good steering ability in spite of her damaged bow." *Mogami* limped to Truk on her own steam. But she was out of action for nearly a year.[54]

If any one man could be credited with saving any one ship, that man was *Mogami*'s damage control officer, Saruwatari. He had the judgment to jettison her torpedoes after the collision left her vulnerable,* then during the attack had the courage to make that most difficult of all decisions—to sacrifice a few so that many might survive.

---

*In contrast, Lieutenant Commander Norio Abe, damage control officer of *Mikuma*, stated, "She sank due to explosions of her torpedoes caused by fires." (Sakamoto material.)

CHAPTER 38

"A Sober and Sickening Sight"

But the battle was not yet entirely over, and tragedy still hung over the victors. The United States had a further price to pay for mastery of the central Pacific.

Following *I-168*'s abortive bombardment of Midway early on the 5th, Tanabe received a message marked "Most Urgent": "As a result of our aerial attack, a large type carrier of *Enterprise* class has been severely damaged and is drifting at a point 150 miles northeast of Midway Island. The *I-168* submarine will immediately chase and sink her."[1]

Radio interceptions coming through his code officer had given Tanabe a fairly clear picture of the battle action. He understood well enough that Japan had lost the chance to take Midway, but prudently kept both the messages and his own conclusions from his crew. His orders now gave him a most welcome opportunity to avenge the lost Japanese carriers.[2]

Immediately he relayed the new instructions to the boat's officers and men. Some shouted with joy; others shook with tension and anticipation. Summoning his staff to the wardroom, Tanabe instructed them to prepare a detailed attack plan. Then he returned to the bridge. Sitting on a small, hard bench, Tanabe wondered very seriously whether he could locate and catch the carrier, and if he could, whether he could sink her. He anticipated a strong guard around the crippled ship, which might well prevent him from reaching a position for the kill.[3]

With his deep-set, intent eyes, slim body and graceful gestures, Tanabe bore a noticeable resemblance to Genda as he sat there on the bridge through the hours, pondering ways and means. He lacked the air officer's creative genius, but he had something even more valuable to a submarine skipper—the endless, surefooted, thinking patience of a cat stalking a squirrel.[4]

The problem occupying Tanabe's efficient mind was one of timing. He hoped and planned to obtain his first sight of the carrier just at dawn. As Japanese submarines were not equipped with radar at this time, Tanabe had to rely on his own good eyes and his excellent 12-cm. official binoculars. So he needed a certain amount of light to see the quarry while the sky was yet dark enough to hide his submarine from the destroyer escort and air patrols he was sure would ring the flattop.

At one point in his cogitations, his electronics officer came to the bridge and handed Tanabe an amulet from Suitengu Shrine. He explained that he had procured a number of them in Kure before departure, and intended to give one to each crew member.[5]

By the time his executive officer reported that attack preparations were completed and the crew released for a rest, night was coming on. Going below to look things over, Tanabe was surprised and proud to find some crew members already asleep, white *hachimakis* tied around their heads in anticipation of battle. Others, too keyed up for slumber, chatted together happily. The skipper took advantage of the darkness to bring the submarine up and skim along the surface toward his objective at a good sixteen knots.[6]

At precisely 0410, a lookout, who had been scanning eastward through his binoculars, suddenly cried out, "A black spot starboard ahead!" Tanabe took the lookout's place to see for himself. Peering intently into the gradually brightening horizon, he felt joy well up within him. There about 20,000 meters (approximately twelve miles) away lay his target, just when and where he wanted her. Coming in from the southwest, eyes into the rising sun, the submariners could see *Yorktown* clearly. But the enemy, looking toward the retreating night, would have trouble seeing the submarine unless Tanabe invited attention. This he had no intention of doing. With his target in sight, he cut speed from sixteen to twelve knots. At the former rate, his bow cut a wave through the sea which would be plainly visible to any patrol aircraft.[7]

At about 0600 Tanabe saw two destroyers guarding the carrier, so he submerged his craft and crept foward at a bare three knots.

Yeomen distributed battle rations to the crew and torpedomen put final touches on their deadly fish. With closer approach, Tanabe counted seven destroyers circling the carrier in two rows about 1,000 meters from the carrier. Actually, there were six destroyers, for Tanabe was not yet close enough to identify *Vireo* as a minesweeper.

In view of this heavy destroyer screen, and because his periscope would be clearly visible in the smooth sea, Tanabe brought the instrument down and navigated entirely by sound for a while. He had been lifting periscope about every ten minutes; from now on, he did so approximately once an hour.[8]

When he next ventured a look, he was about 15,000 meters from the target, and the destroyers seemed to be on a strict alert. He could hear noises indicating that they were using sound detection equipment. "Prepare for enemy depth charge attacks!" he ordered. As the crew waited, almost holding their breaths, Tanabe occasionally kept them posted concerning the enemy. By this time, a light east wind was blowing up a slight swell, which would work to *I-168*'s advantage.

However, his next few periscope sightings puzzled Tanabe profoundly. Although the carrier was almost at a standstill, her position did not match the calculations of the submarine's navigator. In spite of Tanabe's efforts, his relative position to the carrier had not improved; it had worsened. *What speed is she making? What is her average course? Is she drifting with the wind?* Tanabe asked himself these questions, and could reach no satisfactory answers.[9]

He had planned and prepared to attack from the carrier's port, but the flattop's movements decided him on hitting from starboard, so he moved accordingly. He also determined that further approach must depend entirely upon chart calculations. This meant he might miss the enemy altogether, but Tanabe felt he had to take the chance. He steered the submarine by chart and left the outcome on the knees of the war god. To increase Tanabe's uneasiness, the American destroyers crossed and recrossed directly over *I-168*, and sounds of their detection equipment reached the ears of the submariners.[10]

At 1237 Tanabe breathed a prayer and raised his periscope. Then he got the shock of his life, for the bulk of the carrier loomed over him like a mountain. He could clearly distinguish the faces of men aboard her. He had approached within 500 meters of *Yorktown*, far inside the circle of destroyers.

Tanabe dropped his periscope a lot faster than he had lifted it.

He was not only much too close for comfort; he was too close for a successful torpedo run. At such near range, the missiles would dart harmlessly under the carrier. Tanabe had a healthy respect for the American destroyer ring. In the face of such an intensive alert, he knew that he would have only one chance to attack; he must strike to kill on the first attempt. To do so, he had no choice but to run the gauntlet of destroyers once more, until he had at least doubled the distance between his submarine and the target.[11]

While Tanabe was cautiously easing into his turn, he discovered that suddenly all sounds of enemy detection activities had disappeared. Wondering what had happened, he remarked to his navigator, "It seems that their watchmen on sound detection have gone off to lunch." Whatever the reason for this unexpected reprieve, it gave Tanabe his chance. When he risked another look, he found himself about 1,500 meters from the carrier, a perfect distance. Moreover, the flattop was turning in his direction so that he faced her squarely amidships. *Yorktown*'s entire silhouette, bow to stern, was perfectly centered in his sights. He also caught a destroyer, but did not consider it any obstacle. *I have certainly been blessed by the war god*, thought Tanabe piously. *This is just what I wanted to insure a kill of the enemy.*[12]

I-168 carried eight torpedo tubes—four in her bow and four astern. Tanabe knew he would have to rely on the forward missiles; he would have no opportunity to maneuver the submarine into position to let off the aft tubes. So he determined to make every torpedo count. "Ready to fire!" he cried, and a few seconds later, "Fire!"

Two torpedoes sped off, with two more following two seconds later in the same direction. Ordinarily Tanabe would have fired the four on a more spreading course, each at an individual angle, so that one or two might hit if the others missed. This time Tanabe believed that he could not possibly miss, so he sent off both salvos toward the same point for maximum explosive power.[13]

At the time *I-168* launched her torpedoes, it looked very much like *Yorktown* was on the way to recovery. Throughout the morning, the salvage party under Buckmaster had labored mightily over the carrier, while *Hammann* provided the necessary power. One detachment was pumping water in and out of tanks to overcome the list, another worked to cut away heavy equipment on the heeling side. They had already disposed of the port anchor, five port-side 20-mm.

gun foundations, and one 5-inch gun. These measures had lessened *Yorktown*'s list by about two degrees. The long-smoldering fire in the rag compartment was at last extinguished; the water level on the third deck aft had been reduced three feet. One work party lowered aircraft from the forward hangar and dropped them overboard. Medical corpsmen completed the sad task of identifying the dead and preparing them for burial. Thirty-five bodies, all but ten identified, were consigned to the sea after Buckmaster conducted the appropriate services.[14]

At 1331—just six minutes short of an hour since Tanabe upped periscope practically in *Yorktown*'s shadow—Buckmaster saw the four torpedo streaks cutting through the smooth sea. One of the carrier's guns sounded the alarm and the word flashed out, "Torpedo Attack!" *Hammann* blazed away at the tracks on the chance of exploding the missiles before they reached the target. The first torpedo struck *Hammann* amidships, the next two passed under the destroyer to strike *Yorktown* at frame 85 starboard at the turn of the bilge, knocking a huge hole in the hull. The fourth torpedo was off target, passing the carrier just astern.

Yorktown's No. 3 auxiliary elevator pulled loose, various fixtures crashed to the hangar deck. "All rivets in the starboard leg of the foremast sheared." Men were thrown every which way, some overboard entirely, others incurring broken bones, cuts, and bruises.

Blasted nearly in half by a strike on her No. 2 fireroom, *Hammann* sank within three minutes.[15] "When those torpedoes struck they just broke *Hammann*'s back," recalled Burford. "The ship broke almost completely in two. It was a horrible sight. Many were blown right off her decks into the water and many died right there in their tracks."[16]

The explosion hurled the destroyer's skipper, Commander Arnold E. True, against a desk which caught him squarely in the solar plexus, breaking a rib and knocking him so completely breathless that he could not speak. So his executive officer had to give the order to abandon ship. But worse was yet to come. As *Hammann* plunged down, her depth charges exploded at three different levels, hurtling up water spouts a good fifteen feet high and killing nine of the ship's thirteen officers and seventy-two of her 228 crewmen.

Captain True believed *Hammann*'s depth charges had been placed on "safe"; in fact, in his report he warmly commended TM/1c B. M. Kimbrell, "who remained on the stern of the ship and made a final

check of depth charges to see that they were on 'Safe,' assisted several
men over the side who had been temporarily disabled by shock,
providing them with life jackets and then dived overboard himself
without a life jacket just as the stern was submerging. He was among
those missing. . . ."[17]

Despite the seaman's heroic efforts, the consensus is that these
violent explosions did indeed come from the destroyer's depth charges.
It is quite likely that True misinterpreted Kimbrell's actions, and the
seaman actually removed the charges from "Safe" when he saw the
torpedo tracks, believing that antisubmarine action was imminent.
When *Balch* rescued True, about four hours after the explosion, he
was closer to death than life, but still clutched a dead crewman under
each arm.[18]

The split second Tanabe's fourth torpedo got away, he submerged
about 100 meters, which was as deep as he could safely go, and boldly
headed straight back for *Yorktown*. He figured that the nearer the
scene the safer, for the destroyers would not explode their ashcans
near the carrier lest they kill any survivors floating in the area.

The seconds seemed to crawl while Tanabe and his crew awaited
the sound of the explosions. About forty seconds after firing, the
submarine vibrated with a fierce shock, then another, and another.
With each crash, sailors literally jumped with joy, flung their arms
around each other and shouted *"Banzai!"* at the top of their lungs.
Several petty officers ran to the conning tower to congratulate Tanabe.
A sailor brought him a cup of soft drink, and Tanabe was so moved
that he felt a lump in his throat. He had almost forgotten that he had
been in the conning tower with nothing to drink ever since spotting
Yorktown. Now he realized that, between tension and thirst, his
throat felt like a nutmeg grater, and he could scarcely speak.[19]

He knew that the fight was just starting for his men. It was easier
for a submarine to sneak up on a prey than to escape its area. So he
sent word throughout the ship: "A real battle will come from now on.
Request more attentiveness." Depth charges commenced within five
minutes of the torpedoing, but the destroyers seemed to be dashing
about in all directions and for the first hour, *I-168* had a relatively
easy time of it. But the scene drastically changed when one destroyer
passed directly overhead from starboard to port, dropping two depth
charges. The hunter had become the hunted.[20]

Tanabe took every evasive action in the book, but he could not avoid so many destroyers which seemed to pass over him in relays. Still, his luck was holding very well, and his executive officer reported that thus far they had evaded sixty depth charges. The words were no sooner out of his mouth than *I-168* bucked like a bronco and paint chips began to drop from overhead. The ship blacked out as the electric light failed, but the emergency lights worked promptly. An investigation of damage revealed the fore torpedo tube compartment and the aft steering rudder engine room both flooding, and the batteries were damaged. Quick crew work patched up the leaks, but the batteries were another matter. As time went on sulphuric acid leaked out of them, mixing with the ship's bilge water to form chlorine gas. Breathing became more and more difficult, and even the rats crawled out of the bilge to escape the suffocating fumes.[21]

Through it all, incessant depth charges shook *I-168* like a cocktail shaker. The submarine was at a dead standstill for lack of electric power; both horizontal and vertical rudders were out of commission. To keep the boat from bobbing to the surface, Tanabe had to distribute weight by sending crewmen chasing here and there and by alternately letting water in and pumping it out. The chief engineer and the electronics officer, wearing gas masks, made desperate efforts with their men to fix the deadly batteries. Poison gas overcame several men, who had to be carried away from the battery compartment. "Sunset will come in two hours," Tanabe rallied his men. "Stick it out till then!"

With the air pressure registering only forty kgs. the skipper knew his sub could not stay submerged another two hours. The air was almost unbreathable, the emergency light had failed, and the men were working by the dim glow of hand lanterns. At about 1640, *I-168* began to nose upward at thirty degrees, and Tanabe reached a last-ditch conclusion. Why not let her have her way, and surface? It would be better to die in a final, glorious fight under the sky than to skulk below any longer, choking to death. "Prepare the guns and machine guns for firing," he ordered. "Surface quickly to open fire."[22]

The hatch had scarcely cleared the surface when Tanabe bounded out on the bridge. To his amazement, nothing was in sight nearby. But as he peered into the distance, he saw three enemy destroyers about 10,000 meters away.[23] Undoubtedly these were *Benham, Monaghan*, and *Hughes* on the hunt for him.[24] What particularly interested Tanabe was the fact that there was no sign of the carrier. Concluding

that they had indeed sunk her, he hastened to share the good news
with his crew.[25]

Tanabe jumped the gun a bit, for at this time *Yorktown* was still
very much afloat. Curiously enough, *I-168*'s torpedoes had corrected
her list to seventeen degrees, and Buckmaster hoped to resume salvage operations in the morning. Much of the day's work had been
undone, including that of identifying the dead, for their effects and
the records, including fingerprints, had slid into the sea. With the
destroyers fully occupied in rescuing survivors, pulling bodies out of
the water, or hunting for *I-168*, Buckmaster decided to suspend operations until daylight, when he expected the fleet tug *Navajo*. He
and his salvage men therefore left the carrier and boarded *Balch*.[26]

Tanabe's pleasure was short-lived, for he soon saw the three destroyers reverse course and set off in his direction. He tried to run
for it, charging batteries as the submarine sped along, but he soon
realized that *I-168* was no match for the pursuers in surface speed.
One of the destroyers turned away, but the other two were rapidly
converging on him. Tanabe ordered his communications officer to
radio the Combined Fleet, "We sank *Yorktown*," and awaited the
showdown.

With repeated reports of "the enemy closing in" coming from
the lookouts, while the word, "the motor cannot be used yet," kept
coming with monotonous regularity from below, what to do? Submerge? Keep on running? Turn at bay and try to ram one of the
destroyers? Tanabe's own temperament tended toward the third course,
but he thought of his crewmen and their families. He glanced at his
watch. It lacked but thirty minutes to sunset, and the destroyers had
found the range, their shells bracketing the submarine. "How much
air have we so far?" Tanabe asked his executive officer. "We have
gone up to eighty kgs.," he replied.[27]

Immediately Tanabe ordered "urgent submerge to sixty meter
depth." Then came the welcome report from the chief engineer: "The
motor can be used." Moreover, the destroyers seemed to have lost
him, for their fire and depth charges came from farther and farther
away. Tanabe had won the fight for his ship and men.

At 1850 the submarine surfaced. Tanabe and his crew had been
without food for thirteen hours, and without drink except for the
victory cup. From the bottom of a grateful and proud heart, he thanked
his faithful officers and men for their unselfish devotion. After con-

firming that they had the sea to themselves, he ordered, "Open hatches to take fresh air," and they all breathed deeply of the clean, salty night breeze.

Tanabe was a little worried that they might not be able to make Kure with the remaining fuel. Before *I-168* set out, a fleet supply officer had informed Tanabe that he could refuel at Midway after its capture—the Japanese were just that sure of themselves!—but this happy solution was out. However, by skillful navigating on one engine instead of two, Tanabe brought his submarine into Kure with only 800 kgs. left in his fuel tanks, back to a hero's welcome for himself and his crew.[28]

The incredible *Yorktown* remained afloat throughout the night. Not until nearly dawn did her crew and escort really give her up. When Captain Edward P. Sauer, the destroyer squadron commander, saw that the great carrier was doomed, he arranged his destroyers around her for a final ceremony. It was particularly heart-breaking to see this ship in her death throes, for having made it through so much, it seemed that the grand old girl deserved to live.

Burford struggled with mixed emotions as, in the full glow of a splendid dawn, *Yorktown* gradually gathered momentum for her plunge to the bottom of the sea. "We all moved our destroyers in position and watched her go down," he recalled. "It was a sober and sickening sight to see that great ship go to her death. Our flags were at half mast, our heads were uncovered, and we all stood at attention while *Yorktown* went under. True, it was a fitting tribute to a gallant lady," he reflected, "but in a sense it was damn ridiculous. We should not have been wasting time and energy in such a ceremony; we should have been after the goddamn Japs!"[29]

With the end of *Yorktown* at 0458 June 7, Task Force Seventeen more or less broke up. Fletcher with *Astoria* and *Portland* returned to Pearl Harbor. *Balch*, *Hughes*, and *Monaghan* joined Task Force Sixteen at the refueling rendezvous. Buckmaster and his men moved from *Balch* to *Gwin* and also headed for home, accompanied by *Benham*, loaded with survivors from *Hammann*.[30] There he had the sad task of reporting *Yorktown*'s actions, which had caused him so much pride and so much grief. He ended his report:

> During all these actions and the many weeks at sea in preparation
> for them the fighting spirit of YORKTOWN was peerless; that fight-

ing spirit remains alive even though the ship herself has perished gloriously in battle. The wish closest to the hearts of all of us who were privileged to serve in that gallant ship is that she might be preserved not only in memory but by the crew's being kept together to man, commission, and return against the enemy a new aircraft carrier, preferably another YORKTOWN.[31]

CHAPTER 39

"Midway to Our Objective"

By 1900 on June 6, Spruance had completed his air operations and could take another overall look at his position. He had to send *Maury* and *Worden* back to *Cimarron* for refueling, leaving only four destroyers to screen two carriers and six cruisers. With his mission accomplished beyond the wildest dreams of the most light-headed optimist, Spruance sensibly concluded that he had reached the point beyond which courage becomes folly, and turned back east to rendezvous with his oilers.[1]

When the men of *Enterprise* realized that, for them, the battle was over, tempered rejoicing flooded the ship. As Lieutenant Lindsey remarked, "We'd lost lots of our good friends but there is a sense of elation after a battle that comes to one just to realize that he is still alive and that he'll still be around for a while and have a few drinks with the boys." This same reflection must have stirred the heart of the ship's head doctor, for during the voyage home he bore four gallons of bourbon in triumph right into the wardroom. "It was a welcome relief to see that in war time the old Naval Regulations go by the board in favor of a little human good sense," observed Lindsey.[2]

The United States had one final price to pay. On June 7, Emmons wrote to Marshall,

> The first phase of the battle of Midway is about over. I use the expression "first phase" because I think it is entirely possible that the Japanese will renew their attack. . . .
>
> I have felt for some time that we should make an attack on Wake Island for obvious reasons. We did not have ships of sufficient range until a few days ago when four LB-30s arrived from the mainland.

These airplanes are now at Midway and will, if conditions permit, attack Wake Island just before daylight tomorrow morning. We will flash you the results. Incidentally, I am glad to say that General Tinker will personally lead this flight. I am sorry that I cannot go along.[3]

Tinker's decision and Emmons's concurrence did more credit to their fighting spirit than to their good judgment. Tinker had broader responsibilities than accompanying a four-plane air raid to which his presence could add little or nothing. The four Liberators, equipped with extra gas tanks and four 500-pound bombs each, never found their target. Three made it back, but the bomber carrying Tinker disappeared without a trace.[4]

The defeated Japanese fleet retreated westward throughout the morning of June 6. Leaden clouds hung oppressively from the sky and fog swirled ghost-like from the waters, filtering through the masts of each ship. The sea itself seemed to reflect the mood of the hour, for it was rough with "considerable rolling and pitching."[5] In his cabin aboard his flagship, Yamamoto felt queasy and heartsick.[6] But he did not abandon without a final struggle his hope of luring Spruance into a surface fight.

When reports began to reach *Yamato* of the plight of *Mikuma* and *Mogami*, Yamamoto ordered Kondo to the rescue. No sooner had he done so than Ugaki began to worry about the wisdom of his decision. "The enemy force seems to consist of one or two carriers as a nucleus with accompanying cruisers," he explained to his diary. "Admittedly, *Mikuma* has already been doomed and furthermore other ships of the force might be wiped out. Not only that, if the worst comes to the worst, there is no guarantee that the Invasion Force itself won't be endangered."

With these possibilities in mind, Yamamoto decided to take the Main Body in full strength south "to prepare for the worst and at the same time seek an opportunity to destroy the enemy force within the air cover from Wake Island."

Yamamoto and Ugaki had no idea how small was the American unit which had shattered their grand design. They firmly believed that five or six enemy carriers were originally concentrated in the Midway area, and that they had sunk two of these. They also believed that a portion of this formidable strength, consisting of "at least one regular carrier, two converted carriers, and several destroyers and cruisers," was in hot pursuit. "It is considered that there is a great deal of possibility," Ugaki wrote nervously, "that this enemy force would tenaciously come after our Invasion Force tomorrow morning after it destroys the second half of the 7th CruDiv and 8th DesDiv and withdraw to the east for a while."

Ugaki thought that the best course for the Japanese was to force a night engagement with Kondo's ships. Otherwise, they would have no choice but to charge headlong into the Americans the next morning with the Main Body, scattering the enemy planes whenever they attacked. At the same time, the Japanese would try to destroy the enemy's carrier decks or lame their engines, using every available plane. Of course, they would have a much better chance if the Americans came within range of Wake Island, but Ugaki had little faith that his opponents would be so obliging.[7] In this he was dead right, for the wily Spruance firmly determined from the outset to keep out of the Wake circle.[8]

Yet Yamamoto decided to risk this last great engagement. "It needed an indescribable decision, as it was feared that all the Combined Fleet would be damaged if the operation went wrong," Ugaki recorded apprehensively. The necessary orders went out at 1500 on June 6, and the fleet followed the pattern until the next morning. At that time, air search failed to find any sign of the enemy, so the plan for an all-out battle risking the Main Body had to be abandoned.[9]

Unwilling to leave the field without one last effort to catch the U.S. task force, Yamamoto hastily devised a "Diversion Force," consisting of the cruisers *Haguro* and *Myoko*, plus the nine ships of DesRon 4, under Vice Admiral Takeo Takagi, commander of CruDiv 5. This force was to send out fake radio messages with the view to luring the Americans into an area northeast of Wake, within the range of the Base Air Force on the island, and where a number of submarines would be lurking.[10]

Both Takagi and his chief of staff, Captain Ko Nagasawa, took a dim view of this project, for they considered that the U.S. carrier planes probably would find the Diversion Force and attack before either the submarines or Wake's aircraft located the American flattops. In fact, the Takagi force never sighted the enemy and was dissolved on June 13.[11]

Even so, bad luck had not quite finished with the Japanese. At midnight on the 7th, the destroyer *Isonami*, in making a 60-degree turn to starboard in two 30-degree angles, rammed her starboard bow into the port amidships of *Uranami*. The damage to *Uranami*'s funnel restricted the use of her boilers, but she could still make twenty-four knots. However, *Isonami* lost several feet off her bow, reducing her speed to eleven knots. Ugaki was intensely irritated, for he had issued repeated warnings concerning just such destroyer movements.

One minor trouble cleared up that day. "It was learned that the C-in-C's stomache-ache after all came from roundworms," Ugaki recorded. "Taking medicine against them rid him of the trouble, with much joy to us."[12]

Acute embarrassment tinctured the joy, however. As Yamamoto came up on the bridge at about 0700 that morning, his staff shuffled around awkwardly, so ashamed that they could scarcely bear to look at him. They were not ashamed of the admiral; they were ashamed because the Combined Fleet had let him down.

For a tense moment no one spoke a word. Then Yamamoto broke the ice. He turned his direct, dark eyes upon his faithful Kuroshima, who carried the weight of the defeat heavily on his shoulders. "Kuroshima," he said reflectively, "it was a big mistake that the submarine sweep was not well done." This matter-of-fact comment, indicating that Midway was now a past issue from which lessons might be learned, cleared the air. Their beloved admiral was himself again.[13]

On the 9th, Yamamoto summoned *Nagara* to close with *Yamato* so that key staff officers of the First Air Fleet might come aboard for a conference. The representatives were to be Kusaka, Oishi, the fleet secretary and, inevitably, Genda, for the immediate problem facing Yamamoto was how to rehabilitate the carrier force.[14] Before the delegation arrived, Yamamoto summoned Ugaki, Kuroshima, Watanabe, Sasaki, and Arima. Yamamoto knew that *Yamato*'s voyage of retreat had been a floating inquest over the corpse of Operation MI. He also knew that the staff had reached certain conclusions not flattering to the First Air Fleet and its senior officers. So he ordered his staff to keep their criticisms to themselves. "Never tell anyone outside my staff that the Submarine Force and the First Air Fleet were responsible for the failure at Midway," he directed firmly. "The failure at Midway was mine."[15]

Kuroshima had been particularly critical of Kusaka, and Yamamoto now had a special word for his emotional henchman: "Do not accuse Nagumo and Kusaka. The failure is mine," he repeated.[16]

The quartet from *Nagara* came over the side, still wearing their heavy winter uniforms, and still looking exhausted from their long ordeal. Kusaka walked with the aid of a cane, and the fleet secretary's uniform was in tatters.[17] "I don't know what to say except to offer the utmost apologies." This was the essence of what Ugaki recalled as the delegation's first words. "Naturally, they should do so," he added unpleasantly.

The party moved to Yamamoto's cabin. Here Kusaka gave a lengthy report on what he considered the reasons for the disaster. He made six basic points: (1) The necessity to break radio silence on the eve of battle because of rendezvous difficulties; (2) the failure of the search planes to spot the enemy until the return leg of the arc; (3) the confusion caused by recovering aircraft while preparing the second wave; (4) the delay resulting from re-equipping the bombers; (5) another delay in awaiting the return of the first-wave fighters; and finally (6) the disadvantages of over-concentration of the carriers.

Ugaki carefully recorded these items in his diary, following each one by the lessons to be learned from it.[18] Actually, these men were much too close to the picture to see it in proper perspective. And it was characteristic of Kusaka that the list confined itself to the activities of the Nagumo force.

"All in all," Ugaki wrote, "we can't help concluding that the main cause for the defeat was that we had become conceited with past success and lacked studies of what to do in case an enemy air force appears on a flank while we are launching a concentrated attack—something which had worried me greatly, and to which I invited their attention repeatedly."[19]

Kusaka presented his report in his usual straightforward manner, with neither complaints nor excuses. Honest to the marrow of his bones, he also emphasized the wisdom of making the true facts known to the Japanese nation. Then he made a personal request of Yamamoto, as one fighting man to another.

"Commander in Chief Nagumo and I have a grave responsibility for this defeat," he said with massive dignity, "for which we do not hesitate to accept any punishment whatsoever. But I would like you to give us a special consideration, so that both of us may be able to have a chance to pay off old scores at the battle front as we used to do."

No man could have spoken more fairly and squarely. Tears welled up in Yamamoto's eyes, and he could only reply, "All right."[20]

A little later, Ugaki told Kusaka, "We of the Combined Fleet Headquarters realize our own fault, for which we extend our regrets to the First Air Fleet. But we are not made pessimistic at all by the present setback," he continued vigorously. "We still intend to try the Midway operation again and also to carry out the southern operation. Our immediate problem is to supplement sufficient strength to the north to prepare for an expected enemy move there, thus seeking an opportunity to pay off our scores. Above all," he stressed, "how to rehabilitate the fleet's air force is imperative at this moment, so we asked you to come aboard to talk over the matter with us."

A delicate matter still preyed on Kusaka's mind. He explained that when the First Air Fleet headquarters transferred from the burning *Akagi* to *Nagara*, Nagumo had been most unwilling to go. Kusaka had persuaded him by declaring that he, Nagumo, was responsible to fight on as long as a single First Air Fleet sailor remained alive. Even so, Nagumo's staff virtually had to drag him off *Akagi*. "I had a lot to think about myself," said Kusaka, "with all four carriers lost along with a division commander and three of the carrier skippers."

Ugaki listened intently and made comforting noises. At about 1600 he sent Kusaka and his officers back to *Nagara*. They left with small courtesy gifts to show that there were no hard feelings, and 2,000 yen for current expenses. That Ugaki understood exactly the real meaning of their little conversation is clearly revealed in his diary.

"Under such a severe blow, everyone feels deep grief," he wrote. "What to do with one's own life is naturally one's own concern, and especially so with those who have higher responsibilities. There is a great difference between those of a chief of staff and above and those of ordinary staff officers. I, as a man fighting at the battle front, have already made up my mind what to do in such a case," he continued somewhat smugly. "I can't help feeling sympathy for him, after thinking things over. The overall philosophic view and the Bushido view: one must not make a mistake in choosing between them."[21]

When the group returned to the cruiser, they looked less dejected than they had when departing that morning.[22] Genda sought out Fuchida and told him of the meeting aboard *Yamato*. With his customary dislike of circumlocution, Genda informed his colleague that Kusaka had asked Yamamoto if Nagumo should not, after all, commit suicide in atonement for the defeat. To this Yamamoto replied emphatically, "No, Nagumo is not to blame. I take full responsibility. If anyone is to commit *hara-kiri* because of Midway, it is I."[23]

As soon as Kusaka returned to *Nagara*, the cruiser increased speed and plunged ahead of *Yamato*, under orders to go direct to Kure, so that the First Air Fleet staff, in particular Genda, could set to work immediately on a reorganization plan.[24] Crew morale soared at the prospect of an early return to the homeland, but the men were doomed to disappointment. Upon arrival at Kure, they found themselves incommunicado. No shore leaves were granted and contact with anyone off ship was prohibited. Even the skipper fell under this ban, for only the Headquarters staff perforce were permitted to come and go. The crew had to stay aboard, wistfully gazing at the shore lights. Soon temporary headquarters for the First Air Fleet was established aboard *Kirishima*.[25]

Up in the Aleutians, Captain Nakazawa discovered that an official policy had been established to play down the Midway disaster as much as possible. On June 10, he received a message from the Vice Chief, Naval General Staff, and Vice Navy Minister "that it was decided to quote our damage in the Midway Sea Battle as one carrier lost, one carrier heavily damaged, one cruiser heavily damaged, and 35 planes failing to return."[26] Five days later, Ugaki reinforced this with a message reading: "Except for those made public by the General Staff, nothing should be revealed about Midway and the Aleutian operation inside of as well as outside the Navy. In the Navy it would be announced that *Kaga* was lost, while *Soryu* and *Mikuma* were seriously damaged, but their names would not be announced in public."[27]

Kusaka was disappointed and disgusted to find that his government was not following his excellent advice to tell the nation the truth about Midway. He could understand the need to keep up morale at home, but he considered that the whole nation must take this war seriously to bring about victory. And to that end, the people must know how the war was progressing, and share the armed forces' worries as well as their joys. Instead, the official press touted the engagement as a grand triumph, and preceded all radio reports by playing the "Battleship March," traditionally associated with victory.[28]

On June 11, the official *Japan Times and Advertiser* featured a fanciful painting of an American carrier being sunk by Japanese aircraft. Over the picture ran the caption: NAVY SCORES ANOTHER EPOCHAL VICTORY. Beneath it appeared a lyrical outburst, beginning:

> Blasting all American hopes of conducting guerilla warfare on Japan by means of planes from aircraft carriers, the mighty Imperial Navy has sunk two more of these monster warships. The epochal successes were scored in surprise attacks on Dutch Harbor, in the Aleutians, and on Midway Island between June 4 and 7. Incidentally, of the seven aircraft carriers America possessed at the outset of the war, only two remain . . .

An additional Imperial Headquarters communiqué released on June 15 added "one American A-Class cruiser of the *San Francisco* class and one American submarine to the war results of the surprise attack off Midway Island previously announced . . ." The "previously announced" claims were two *Enterprise* class carriers and one destroyer.[29]

Considering the notorious inaccuracy of contemporary estimates of battle results, the Japanese claims of damage to the American forces were not too badly out of line. As we have seen, Nagumo's battle report, intended only for Japanese eyes, and few Japanese eyes at that, reveals that he honestly believed his airmen had sunk two United States carriers. Changing a destroyer into a cruiser and tossing in a submarine was about par for the course.

Real deceit entered the picture, however, in the matter of Japanese losses. Naturally, the official communiqués stressed the successful northern actions, and referred to the dark side of the picture only obliquely. In a broadcast on June 11, quoted in the next day's Chicago *Daily Tribune,* civilian naval expert Masanori Ito observed that "in view of the great success" obtained in the Midway battle, "we should not be disappointed at the loss of two aircraft carriers, for the gain is far greater than the loss." Indeed, except for the participants and for certain key officers who could not be kept in ignorance, the Japanese Navy knew little more of the true facts than did Suzuki-san eagerly scanning his daily quota of propaganda.

To keep secret the extent of the casualties, the Japanese government went to amazing extremes. When *Nagara* left Kure and docked at Hashirajima on June 15, Fuchida and some 500 wounded were transferred to the hospital ship *Higawa Maru,* which sneaked into Yokosuka under cover of night. The wounded were landed at an inconspicuous pier and virtually smuggled to the base hospital along a road heavily guarded by Sea Police. At the hospital the men were segregated in two buildings. No visitors, not even wives, were permitted, nor were telephone calls or letters, incoming or outgoing. The Japanese Navy in effect had stamped these men "Top Secret" and secured them as such. *Just like we are in an internment camp!* thought Fuchida indignantly. Under this regimen, morale sunk to zero.

A complete extrovert, Fuchida suffered acutely from the isolation. His wounds, although painful and slow to heal, were localized, and from the knees up he felt quite well physically. The thoughts occupying his practical mind were not pleasant. The enemy knew the truth and would waste no time telling the world, so why try to hide it? Navy headquarters should admit the loss of the four carriers with their aircraft, and so prove that the government had confidence in the courage and determination of the people. Fuchida greatly feared that the Japanese navy was building a wall of distrust between itself and the people.[30]

Meanwhile, the United States suffered its own post-attack publicity crisis. "They Wanted To Know, 'Where's The U.S. Pacific Fleet?' Did They?" exulted the Honolulu *Star-Bulletin.* "Admiral Nimitz Had the Answer and It Has Been Delivered at Midway." Under big black headlines: MIDWAY BATTLE TOLL: JAPANESE SHIPS SUNK! appeared Nimitz's first battle communiqué, issued at 1245:

> Through the skill and devotion to duty of our armed forces of all branches in the Midway area, our citizens can now rejoice that a momentous victory is in the making.
>
> It was on a Sunday just six months ago that the Japanese made their peacetime attack on our fleet and army activities on Oahu . . .
>
> Pearl Harbor has now been partially avenged. Vengeance will not be complete until Japanese sea power has been reduced to impotence.
>
> We have made substantial progress in that direction.

Then, unable to resist a gentle pun, he continued, "Perhaps we will be forgiven if we claim we are about midway to our objective."[31]

Quite soon, however, misunderstanding and confusion arose, thanks to the premature claims of the jubilant Army airmen, who returned to Oahu before those of the Navy arrived in port and could place their version on the record. "Dope is out that the Army won the battle of Midway," remarked the VF-6 unofficial log economically.[32] Indeed, anyone reading the Honolulu press on June 12 could be forgiven for assuming that the Navy confined its part in the action to scouting. "We never once had to look for the enemy, because the Navy planes had located the task force perfectly," Colonel Sweeney told reporters. No doubt he meant the comment in a generous spirit, but it certainly was double-edged. According to reporter Bob Trumbull, "The Army pilots who actually dropped the eggs reported personally that they made hits on three Japanese carriers, one cruiser, and one other large vessel which may have been either a cruiser or a battle ship, one destroyer, and one large transport. These are still incomplete reports."[33]

A member of Emmons's staff later stated, "Emmons was just as proud of the Navy as Nimitz," and "raised holy hell about the Air Force claims."[34] No hint of any such irritation appears in his letter to Marshall summarizing the results of the battle to that date. He credited his airmen with:

2 Torpedo hits in carriers by B-26s.
1 Carrier badly damaged by bombs. There is a possibility that there
   was still another damaged by our bombs.
3 Battle ships damaged, one badly.
1 Cruiser sunk.
1 Heavy cruiser damaged.
1 Destroyer badly damaged, probably sunk.
2 Transports (1 described as being of the NORMANDIE class) damaged,—set on fire.
2 Hits on a carrier which was on fire.

Boasting that his combat crews "covered themselves with glory," Emmons added,

I offer the thought confidentially that I do not believe that the Navy would have risked their three carriers in this battle against the superior hostile force which had four or five carriers had not they been assured of the support of land-based aviation. Had the Navy not risked their carriers we might have suffered a defeat rather than an overwhelming victory.[35]

The New York Times editorialized on June 9, "So far as we can now learn, the main damage to the Japanese fleet off Midway was inflicted by our land-based airplanes. The battle shows what land-based air power can do to naval and air power attacking from the open sea when that land-based air power is alert, well-trained, courageous, and exists in sufficient quantity . . ."

Small wonder that an inflated idea of the Army Air Force's capability reached to a very high level in Washington. As early as June 5, Stimson recorded, "There is a great battle in the Pacific going on. Aparently the American forces, mainly land based air forces, have won a surprise on the Japanese. . . ."[36] And Assistant Secretary of State Adolf A. Berle noted, in a memorandum of recent events,

> . . . It is true that we smashed much of what was left of the Italian fleet; but fleets mean precisely nothing. The land-based aircraft do the trick.
>
> At or about the same time, the Japanese started in force for Midway Island and probably plan to come westward to tackle Hawaii. Our land-based craft caught both of their striking columns and so badly smashed them that I think the Pacific is clear between Hawaii and the Marshall Islands.[37]

On June 6, Stimson recorded with obvious satisfaction that matters in the Pacific seemed to be "sufficiently in hand . . . so that we could reverse our rush of reenforcements to the West Coast and send back the forces that we had diverted from BOLERO . . ." That was the code name for preliminary preparations for the projected main invasion of France, which later became the historic "Overlord." Willingness to rob Bolero to send reinforcements to the west coast testifies eloquently to the seriousness with which the War Department took the Japanese threat. Stimson added complacently,

> Our big bombers have played a decisive part in the battle and the facility with which they have hit and injured capital ships of the enemy marks a great change in the previous view of high altitude bombing. The Navy got into it also with its carriers. They had rather a hard time with the enemy carriers who outnumbered them. However they did the business . . . Emmons was able to keep pouring a heavy stream of these big bombers from Hawaii to Midway and then into the fight, until finally the enemy was driven off.[38]

When the Navy pilots reported in to Oahu, a more balanced picture emerged, but Nimitz, with his strong commitment to Army-Navy cooperation and good feeling, let the claims stand with only mild amendment. And so the popular impression that Midway was in large part an Army victory kept green until after the war, when Japanese interrogations and records became available.[39]

The inflated American claims were due to honest error rather than deliberate deceit, but when it came to U.S. losses, the government was not entirely candid with the American public, although on July 15 the Navy announced that *Hammann* had been lost and *Yorktown* was "out of action."[40] Not until September did the United States publicly admit her loss.[41]

Meanwhile, Americans seemed almost afraid to believe in good news, after such a long diet of ill tidings. As early as June 6, the West Coast seethed with the public's undefined sense that somewhere, something momentous was taking place:

> Fantastic, unfounded rumors swept San Francisco and apparently other parts of the Nation yesterday. They were whispered over lunch counters, repeated in taverns and gossiped about in offices.
>
> You could take your choice of the following:
> 1. Pearl Harbor is being bombed.
> 2. Washington, D.C. is being bombed.
> 3. Puget Sound is being bombed.
> 4. Seattle is being bombed.
>
> You could add to the list indefinitely, keeping the locations anywhere within 300 miles of either seacoast. The war jitters reached into Washington where Mass. Congressman McCormack told the House that he heard a radio report that "Pearl Harbor is being attacked." A Navy spokesman issued a flat denial. . . . The rumor factory was on wartime production basis in San Francisco. A report, started about noon that a downtown bank had received teletyped information from a Seattle branch that Seattle was under aerial attack. . . . [42]

As the locale and nature of the engagement became public, not all the press tossed hats in the air. "Experts Say Japs Still Have Means for Naval Offensive," warned a caption in the Washington *Post*. "This, in the opinion of Washington experts," the article continued, "boils down to saying that while the mid-Pacific triumph has advanced the United States far along the road to final victory, it has by no means clinched that victory."[43]

The well-known military analyst Hanson W. Baldwin was also cautious. "We have won a victory, but we have fallen short of a Manila

Bay or Tsushima," he wrote. He attributed the Japanese failure to achieve surprise to radio intelligence and "to land-based reconnaissance planes, probably in part Army bombers."[44]

The story which really threw the Navy into a most understandable tizzy appeared in the Chicago *Daily Tribune* on June 7. The headline alone was a blow to the solar plexus of security: NAVY HAD WORD OF JAP PLAN TO STRIKE AT SEA KNEW DUTCH HARBOR WAS A FEINT. The story continued,

> The strength of the Japanese forces with which the American navy is battling somewhere west of Midway Island in what is believed to be the greatest naval battle of the war, was well known in American naval circles several days before the battle began, reliable sources in the naval intelligence disclosed here tonight.
>
> The navy learned of the gathering of the powerful Japanese units soon after they put forth from their bases, it was said. Altho [sic] their purpose was not specifically known, the information in the hands of the navy department was so definite that a feint at some American base, to be accompanied by a serious effort to invade and occupy another base, was predicted. Guesses were even made that Dutch Harbor and Midway Island might be targets. . . .

The article continued with an amazingly accurate listing of the Japanese forces involved. Nowhere did the *Tribune* state in so many words that the United States had broken any Japanese code, but to anyone with even a slight knowledge of naval matters, the implication was fairly clear.

The author of this story was correspondent Stanley Johnston, who had been aboard *Lexington* at the Coral Sea. On the way back to San Diego aboard the cruiser *Chester,* a naval officer most unwisely showed Johnston Nimitz's dispatch giving the intelligence estimate of the Japanese destination and composition of forces. The leak generated an investigation but no public trial, and it is generally believed that the Japanese missed this tipoff. They continued to use JN25 with periodic changes, a major one occurring on August 1, 1942, which may or may not be coincidental.[45]

Largely thanks to the Japanese inclination to use codes beyond the point of safety, Yamamoto had less than a year to live. Intercepts allowed the Americans to pinpoint him on a flight out of Rabaul, and he was shot down over Bougainville on April 18, 1943.

He had kept his promise to Kusaka. Nagumo and his chief of staff remained on active duty and performed valuable service to Japan. Nagumo perished on Saipan, probably a suicide. Kusaka survived the war by many years. So did Genda who, upon the formation of Japan's Self Defense Air Force, once again donned his country's uniform, and rose to the rank of lieutenant general. Upon retirement, he won election to the upper house of the Diet. His good colleague, Fuchida, filled important air staff positions throughout the war, and some years later became a Christian evangelist. Among the American naval leaders he met during his travels in the United States were Nimitz and Spruance, for whom he entertained the liveliest respect.

It was typical of Nimitz that, after doing as much as any single American to win the Pacific war, he devoted much postwar energy to building friendship between the United States and Japan. He became "the guiding spirit" behind the restoration of Admiral Heihachiro Togo's flagship, *Mikawa*. As a tangible expression of thanks, the Japanese planted a "Nimitz" tree near the revered old battleship. [46]

One example of Nimitz's genius as a naval leader was his utilization of those two opposite personalities, Spruance and Halsey, as alternating commanders of the same fleet. When Halsey was in command, it was the Third Fleet, and Spruance was ashore, planning the next phase. Then Spruance took over, the organization became the Fifth Fleet, and Halsey went ashore to evaluate and plan. And so on until victory.

Midway did not touch everyone with gold. Less than three months later, two carriers under Fletcher's command suffered severely. *Enterprise* was seriously damaged in the Eastern Solomons on August 24, and on the 31st of that month *Saratoga* took her second torpedo of the year, although she made it back to Pearl Harbor for repairs. In this attack, Fletcher was slightly wounded and never again held a sea command. Whether he was a victim of chronic bad luck or of some basic unsuitability as a carrier commander remains a good question. Whatever the answer, he could say, "I was in command at Midway." It was enough for any sailor.

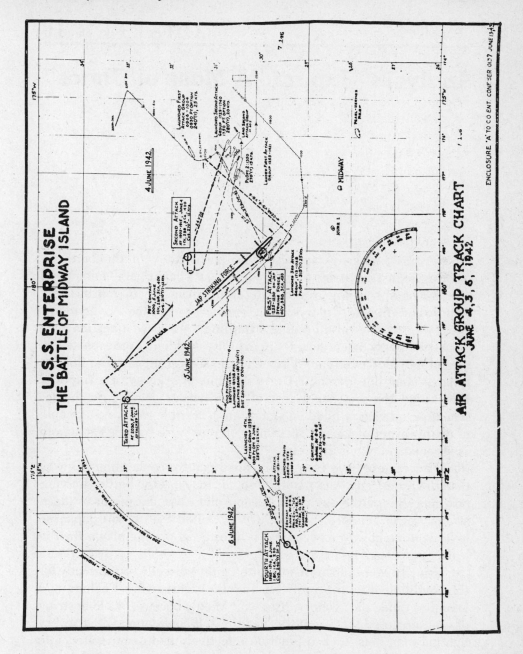

CHAPTER 40

Analysis—Japan: "A Mass of Chaos"

Many Japanese who participated in the battle of Midway soon saw their stunning defeat as a nightmare memory of crashing bombs, raging fires, sinking ships, struggling men in swirling waters, and dreams of glory fading irrevocably into the Pacific night. What went wrong? also became a burning, obsessive question.

A seemingly magnificent opportunity suddenly, unexpectedly, turned into a catastrophe. Why? Did the answer lie with the fleet or in Japan's naval leadership? Up to the time of Midway, the Imperial Navy sailed the seas like a pack of killer whales, leaving death, destruction and victory piled on victory in its terrible wake. And people in every corner of Japan's sprawling empire were hailing Yamamoto as an outstanding naval genius.

The Japanese have been more introspective concerning Midway than the Americans. And naturally so, for they lost the battle. Indeed, post-mortems on the operation became almost as ubiquitous in Japan as analyses of Pearl Harbor did in the United States. The Japanese investigators, however, were less interested in placing blame than in learning lessons.

Virtually every Japanese consulted either directly or indirectly for this study cited as the root cause of the defeat what Fuchida and Okumiya called the "victory disease."[1] Mainly because of a long string of uninterrupted victories, the healthy self-confidence which every fighting man must feel to function effectively had degenerated into overweening conceit and contempt for the enemy.

Some of the more spiritual-minded, such as Kusaka and Miwa, saw in the Midway disaster God's punishment for this sin of hubris.[2]

No one took the Japanese more sharply to task than Commander Masataka Chihaya, when in later days he evaluated the entire sweep of the Pacific War. To him, "there was nothing to wonder about" in the decisive defeat:

> We had as good as planned for it. If we had escaped that terrible disaster on that occasion, we should have met the same fate somewhere else on the Pacific theater perhaps in the course of 1942. . . . That defeat was . . . something pre-ordained. Why? Because it was visited on the Japanese navy to penalize its absurd self-conceit.[3]

Even those who did not credit direct heavenly intervention believed that smugness over past successes was the fundamental weakness from which all errors flowed.[4] The U.S. Naval War College agreed: "Vice Admiral Nagumo's errors were errors in judgment brought on by overconfidence and by improper analysis procedures."[5] Not only Nagumo's mistakes! As we shall see, the "victory disease" infected every aspect of Japanese planning and events at every level. One wonders if, in the days left him, Yamamoto, who read and studied the Bible,[6] did not wince when he came to Proverbs 16:18: "Pride goeth before destruction, and a haughty spirit before a fall."

Inevitably Nagumo, as the fleet commander on the spot, came in for the lion's share of criticism. Unlike Admiral Kimmel after Pearl Harbor, however, Nagumo retained his command and the Navy gave him the chance to rehabilitate his position. Perhaps Yamamoto's undoubtedly sincere generosity toward Nagumo and Kusaka struck a happy chord at the Naval General Staff. The Navy was playing up Midway as a significant victory, and firing a public hero like the Commander in Chief of the First Air Fleet might have posed a public relations problem. In any case, the Japanese Navy was able to do as it liked in this matter. The government was a collective military dictatorship at the time, so the Navy was under no pressure from an outraged electorate, an independent press howling for blood, and packs of maddened congressmen.

Today one of the complaints against Nagumo, and one for which he blamed himself, was breaking radio silence in order to effect a vital change of course.* Some of the young fliers, holding a post-

---

*This was in contrast to Pearl Harbor, when strict radio silence en route had been the task force's inflexible rule

mortem aboard *Kirishima* back in Japan after the battle, vowed that
this action "was tantamount to revealing our position to the enemy."[7]
And Ugaki noted in his diary, "Radio transmission at a short distance
from an enemy force is most risky business."[8] This principle is valid,
but so far as we know, the Americans did not pick up this transmission.
Moreover, Ugaki conveniently forgot to record that at the second
table maneuvers he himself had stressed the need to maintain contact,
"not hesitating to send out messages when necessary . . ."* .

A more serious charge is Nagumo's handling of his aerial reconnaissance. Genda considered "the incomplete search plan should be
said to be the initial cause for the Midway defeat."[9] A closer spread
dispatched earlier in the morning might have located the U.S. task
force and enabled the First Air Fleet to strike an initial and possibly
decisive blow. Certainly, as soon as Nagumo knew that the launching
of two scout planes would be delayed, he should have ordered sub-
stitutes up immediately, instead of waiting for the stragglers.** One
must point out, however, that had Nagumo covered the sky with
reconnaissance aircraft, not one would have had a better opportunity
than *Chikuma*'s Number Five plane, which apparently flew right over
the American ships without seeing them.[10]

The admiral's use of his aircraft against Midway is open to question. He used planes from all four carriers, which permitted swift
launching, but left all four carriers vulnerable at once. He got away
with that, but Fuchida and Okumiya believed that had he attacked
Midway with only two carriers, he would have had the other two
immediately available for any emergency, instead of having to land
planes on all four flattops at once.[11]

"Couldn't the second wave planes have been launched before the
enemy attack?" Ugaki asked his diary.[12] Indeed, one wonders why
Nagumo did not use the system employed at Pearl Harbor, when the
second wave was launched automatically, without waiting to hear from
the first wave leader that it was needed. Possibly the experiences in
the south Pacific and Indian Oceans, when Fuchida had led air strikes
much too potent for the target, influenced the pattern at Midway.
No doubt with memories of Pearl Harbor in mind, General Davidson
observed, "The enemy should have had a second wave of attackers

---

*See Chapter 8.
**See Chapter 20.

to destroy our aircraft on the ground during the slow servicing and refueling due to disrupted installations."[13]

Kuroshima thought that Nagumo erred in the utilization of his fighters. He believed that in this particular engagement it was more important to maintain as powerful as possible an air umbrella over the carriers than to escort the bombers over Midway. The dictum that fighters must protect bombers was an article of faith with Genda, and in most circumstances it was very sound. But Kuroshima thought that at Midway neither Nagumo nor Genda was fluid enough in his thinking to adjust dogma to the circumstances. "This overestimation of the value of fighters came first from the success at Pearl Harbor, from the initial difficulties the Japanese attack force experienced at Wake, from the Japanese raid on Darwin, and the attack against Ceylon," said Kuroshima. "The effectiveness of the fighters in these operations led to an overestimation of their capabilities at Midway."[14]

The reader has seen how the First Air Fleet's Zero pilots flew until exhausted, so it is possible that more fighters over the carriers could have permitted periodic short respites. And who knows? enough interceptors might have been available to take care of the U.S. dive bombers as well as the torpedo planes.

Ugaki criticized the fact that the carriers were "concentrated in one group offering many eggs in one basket." Such grouping had been the pattern since the outbreak of war and so far had been successful. Yamaguchi had opposed dispersion, which usually would have been enough to silence Ugaki. But Midway had revealed disadvantages in grouping.[15] It is certainly true that the Japanese flattops were so close together that the discovery of one had meant the discovery of all.

With remarkable unanimity, commentators agreed that Nagumo should have launched his aircraft against the U.S. ships as soon as he knew the reported task force contained a carrier, no matter whether armed with torpedoes or bombs, with or without interceptors. Considerable risks would have been involved, but as it happened, Nagumo's caution proved even more risky. Fuchida and Okumiya decided that Yamaguchi had been correct when he urged an immediate attack.[16] So did the critical fliers aboard *Kirishima*, who agreed that in the event of a prompt attack, "even if our carriers were attacked by enemy dive bombers our damage would have been far less than actually happened."[17] In other words, even if the Americans hit the carriers, the Japanese planes would have been airborne, not caught on deck.

Genda went even further; in his retrospective opinion, rearming of bombers should have been suspended immediately upon receipt of the first report from the *Tone* scout of the presence of American ships. At the time he had sanctioned waiting to recover Tomonaga's returning Midway flight rather than risk having them all ditch. "This was a very important lesson to me," he reflected. "Since the Midway sea battle I have tried hard to refrain from making operations inactive out of placing much importance on the lives of fliers."[18] This is one of the most difficult lessons for a conscientious officer to learn—that circumstances may demand sacrifice of a few to save many, and that misplaced sentiment may be the ultimate cruelty.

It may well be that Nagumo's first mistake occurred before he left the Inland Sea. In the days prior to sortie, one seeks in vain for the steady, realistic, not to say pessimistic, Pearl Harbor commander whose skeptical attitude had prodded such staff officers as Genda and flight leaders like Fuchida to give their best, to test every concept, examine every tactic, train their men to an edge of perfection—all in the expectation that they would be facing a worthy foe. Instead, before Midway Nagumo and his subordinates were just as cocky as their airmen and carrier crewmen, and seem to have let the reins go slack. Chihaya summed up the result:

> The crew of these four carriers . . . were in high spirits. They felt like a conqueror before making the test of strength, very encouraging sign indeed, but such an attitude and mentality is fatal in modern warfare for which no cautions can be too deep, no plans too minute and exact. Men full of hope and in high spirit are apt to be reckless. Such was fate. The final doom was there written on the wall. Only there were no eyes to read them. It could not be said of them "Everything was done that was humanly possible."[19]

Yet, having presented the case against Nagumo, one must point out that he and his carrier captains fought in the best tradition of seamanship. Thanks to those tactics, the performance of his gallant if too few Zero pilots, and atrocious American marksmanship, he smashed one attack after another. The final debacle was due to a stroke of good luck on the United States side—the uncoordinated coordination of the dive bombers hitting three carriers at once while the torpedo strikes were still in progress. Except for those six short minutes, Nagumo would have been the victor, and all his decisions would have been accounted to him for righteousness. Timidity would have become prudence, vacillation due deliberation, rigidity attention to the voice of experience.

Moreover, Nagumo had to operate within the framework of a strategic plan which almost guaranteed failure. Greatly to their credit, Combined Fleet staff officers never tried to evade their share of responsibility. Some indeed were almost morbidly eager to bring blame on themselves. Kuroshima and Watanabe always bitterly regretted not having insisted that Nagumo's instructions to keep half his bombers armed with torpedoes at all times be written into his orders. Yet, as Genda so sensibly pointed out in this connection, no field commander could be expected to operate under such rigid conditions.*

One exception was Ugaki. In his diary, quite probably written with an eye to future publication, he wrote on June 14: "Looking back, I think I have endured hardships well and have done what I should have done. These thoughts give me some consolation." Yet he was not quite so complacent as this entry indicates. In pre-Midway days, he wore his hair rather long; afterwards, he cut it short in token of humility.[20] Well he might, for not only was he a ringleader of the battleship coterie, but his high-handed conduct of the war games had precluded any possibility of a realistic evaluation of the Midway plan.**

Actually, efforts to evaluate so near the event were doomed to failure, for neither side had the necessary facts. Not until the records of a victorious United States and defeated Japan were available to each other did the Midway picture become clear. The real Japanese blind spot was Yamamoto. The effulgence of his personal glory dazzled everyone's eyes, and in the case of those who served under him, a real personal affection precluded objectivity. When Yamamoto told his staff, "The fault is mine," he was not merely accepting the responsibility of command, a concept somewhat foreign to Japanese military and naval tradition. He was speaking the exact truth. As far as any one Japanese was responsible for the Midway fiasco, that man was Isoroku Yamamoto. Just as he had done with his Pearl Harbor

---

*See Chapters, 4, 26.
**See Chapter 4.

plan, he had conceived the idea and forced it down the throats of the Naval General Staff. But the conditions which had made Pearl Harbor possible no longer applied. Moreover, Yamamoto seemed to have lost his touch. Had he deliberately set out to prove just how many of the principles of war one admiral could violate in one campaign, he would have come up with Operation MI.

These handy points of reference make a convenient framework to evaluate any military or naval battle. Let us see how the Japanese operation against Midway measured up to the formula O^2S^4MEC which U.S. Naval officers learn at the War College:

1. *Objective*. Of all the principles of war, this is the first and most basic. The planner must ask, "What is the point in fighting this battle? What do I hope to achieve? How will it forward the national interest of my country? Will it be worth the estimated cost in lives and treasure?"

This seems so elementary that one hesitates to bring it to the attention of the intelligent reader. Nevertheless, in none of the principles of war did the Combined Fleet fall so flat on its collective face as this one. From the very beginning, Operation MI was a monster with two heads, each arguing with the other. First, Yamamoto planned to attack and seize Midway atoll; second, he wanted to lure out and destroy the remains of the U.S. Pacific Fleet. The downiest of newly hatched ensigns could have seen that the twin objectives were fundamentally incompatible. To storm and occupy an island installation required a firm schedule tied to the immutables of nature. An engagement with a mobile enemy fleet called for the utmost flexibility.

To make matters worse, of the two objectives the Japanese stressed the wrong one. To the Combined Fleet, capture of Midway was the primary mission.* They should have concentrated on ridding the central Pacific of Nimitz's remaining capital ships. Then the Japanese could have taken Midway, at least temporarily, more or less at their leisure.

No wonder that Chihaya found "something fundamentally out of focus in our plan for this Midway battle." Why, for example, try to take the Aleutians? "To preclude these islands being used as air bases from which to attack Japan? Such a guess evinces only their ignorance of the topography, since the land features of these islands are not fit

---

*See Chapter 4.

as the base for the long range big bombers . . ." Was Midway intended as preparation for an attack on Hawaii? "But how could we hope to take Hawaii at this stage if we could not take it on the first occasion when the circumstances were far more favorable?" Was the campaign a preparation for the Great All-Out Battle? "But neither does this offer a satisfactory explanation. . . . If this had been meant as preparatory to the long cherished 'Great fleet battle,' why did they not wait two more months when the repairs should have been finished and the six carriers made all available?" And "why add such encumbrances as Midway and the Aleutians . . . ?" But in spite of all these incongruities, "the plan was forced and met the fate it deserved." He added with obvious disgust, "It called for superhuman abilities to extract a unified concentrated action out of such a mass of chaos."[21]

2. *Offensive.* At first glance, the idea of sailing with a gigantic fleet several thousand miles eastward and snatching Uncle Sam's mid-Pacific outpost from under the nose of his Navy, thus luring the latter out to fight a decisive battle, seems aggressive enough. And indeed one cannot fault Yamamoto for lack of daring. Yet boldness should not be confused with the spirit of the offensive. The thinking behind the project was essentially defensive—to secure an outer chain of bases to keep the enemy away from the Japanese homeland and home waters.

To be considered a successful offensive plan, it must give due consideration to such annoying "what ifs" as these: What if the Americans somehow gained advance warning of the Japanese approach? What if the enemy spotted the Tanaka fleet ahead of schedule? What if Nimitz had spotted a mobile force beyond Midway? What if the First Air Fleet suffered severe damage? These were all possibilities, and alternative offensive plans should have been ready and rehearsed. They were not, which is one reason why, at Midway, Japan's spirit of the offensive came apart under the pressure of the unexpected.

3. *Superiority at Point of Contact.* On no score did Yamamoto err more sorely than in the area of mass, where on paper he was so far ahead of the game. The Japanese had numerical superiority at Midway, but could have achieved true superiority if they arranged their forces differently. Having assembled the greatest array of naval strength ever seen on any ocean to that date, Yamamoto vitiated it by dispersal. Viewed on the map as a series of neat arrows, all pur-

posefully pointing in the right direction, the Midway strategy looks excellent—an application of the classic double-flank pincers movement.

But this was not Cannae and Yamamoto was not Hannibal. Each of the fleets converging on Midway was specialized and not truly self-sufficient. Apparently Yamamoto assumed that these groups could join forces if necessary, but events proved this impossible.[22] Meanwhile, these many avenues of approach practically invited American detection.

Worst, instead of massing all his ships against the primary objective, Yamamoto divided his strength by sending powerful fleet units against the Aleutians, far removed from the strategic scene of operation. And it was precisely there, where no decisive naval engagement could be fought at the time, that the Japanese enjoyed superiority. The forces wasted in that area might have tipped the scale at Midway. And the Aleutians, unlike the U.S. carrier task forces, would stay in position until later. Both Nimitz and Spruance, as well as Japanese experts, believe the failure to concentrate was Yamamoto's worst mistake.[23]

Not content with two major operations, Yamamoto misused the ships in the main sector. Survivors of the battle, in earnest if unofficial conclave aboard *Kirishima*, agreed emphatically that placing the battleships at the rear of the task force was unsound. "Had they been ahead of our force, the enemy attack would have been directed to them, thus saving our carriers that were the most important elements of a sea battle. Even if the Americans sank two or three battleships, this would have been far less of a loss to the Japanese Navy than a like number of carriers.[24] Instead, Yamamoto dilly-dallied 300 miles behind the Mobile Force. As matters went, he and his battlewagons might as well have remained in the Inland Sea.

4. *Surprise.* This was the cornerstone of Japan's war plans. Yamamoto counted heavily upon sneaking into the Midway area unsuspected, as Nagumo had at Pearl Harbor, until the atoll was actually under attack. He forgot what he of all men should have remembered: he was now up against a United States at war, its peacetime somnolence sunk at Pearl Harbor, and he faced a Pacific Fleet which, having been fooled once, was doubly alert.

Of course, it was not Yamamoto's fault that he no longer had the benefit of the local spy ring operating out of the Japanese consulate in Honolulu to keep him informed of American ship movements in and out of Pearl Harbor. Nor can one blame Yamamoto because the Japanese lost surprise the day Rochefort and his Hypo men penetrated the JN25 naval code. From that time onward, Nimitz received excellent information about the Japanese Navy.

To surprise a foe, it is not enough for the planner to try to put himself inside that opponent's mind and estimate his probable actions, although that helps if the planner guesses right. What he needs is a realistic idea of what the enemy can do. This was the point of elementary intelligence which Emmons annoyed Layton by stressing.* And this is precisely what Yamamoto did not do. The essence of his scheme was the supposition that Nimitz and his forces would behave exactly as the Japanese planned they should. This failure to weigh the enemy's capabilities was the basis for the tardiness of the planned submarine cordon and for the breakdown of the projected K operation to scout Oahu by large seaplanes.** Given a little less complacency, prompt and effective reconnaissance almost surely would have enabled the Japanese to pinpoint the American sorties, their strength, their course, and destination, hence be prepared to attack.[25]

5. *Security.* This principle always marches in step with "Surprise." A monumental underestimation of American brains and will to fight led the Japanese down the garden path of carelessness. Too many unnecessary people were in the know; preparations were not camouflaged; the care and precision which had made the Pearl Harbor attack a security classic were entirely missing.[26] Messages such as that of May 24 which enabled Nimitz to estimate the enemy strength so accurately*** should have gone in the top security flag officer's code—Safford's crack team in Washington was still striving unsuccessfully to break it—or have been confined to a courier's locked briefcase.

The Japanese took the precaution of changing their JN25 system toward the end of May, but once more the story was "too late." Hypo

---

*See Chapter 5.

**These were the type which the Japanese sent on March 3 to bomb the Pearl Harbor Navy Yard. Refueling from a submarine at French Frigate Shoals, they flew over Oahu and dropped a few bombs, but could not see their target due to thick clouds. (Ugaki Diary, June 10, 1942). See Chapter 4.

***See Chapter 8.

had already milked it of enough information to insure that both Nimitz and the Fleet were prepared and waiting.

6. *Simplicity*. This principle is closely allied with "Objective." Reduced to its lowest terms, it means that the fewer moving parts in any machine, the less chance there is of any one of them breaking down. But Operation MI was a "Rube Goldberg" monstrosity. As Miwa observed when by mid-June he had recovered his composure sufficiently to return to his diary, "Actually, there were many points in our operational plan that should be blamed and also that were not indispensable in carrying out the operation."[27]

The truly complicating factor was Yamamoto's inability to reconcile the battleship-carrier hassle, in spite of the spectacular record of Japan's naval airmen, both land- and carrier-based. As a result, he suffered from doctrinaire schizophrenia. Both schools went to extremes. The battleship coterie, of which Ugaki was a leading light, could not see the battlewagons in any capacity but as the central weapons in a surface slugging match. They could not visualize the "queens" as ladies-in-waiting.

The airminded were almost equally inflexible. To them the carrier was the heart of the new sea power, the battleship of little if any use at all, a parasite sucking men and material away from the real striking force. Yamamoto tried to reconcile both concepts in toto instead of extracting the best of each. Later in the war, Nimitz would demonstrate exactly how to do this as the Americans moved nearer and nearer to Japan. Then he used battleships to soften up Pacific islands and as screens for his carriers.[28]

Perhaps because of the Combined Fleet's battleship orientation, no Japanese carrier entered the battle equipped with radar. Two experimental sets became available two days before the Mobile Force sortied. However, they were installed aboard the battleships *Ise* and *Hyuga* which were with Takasu's Aleutian Screening Force. Had Nagumo possessed this vital equipment aboard his two flagship carriers, at least he could have had early warning of the U.S. attack planes, with what result who can say? Okumiya, for one, believed the battle might have gone the other way.[29]

7. *Movement-Mobility*. In battle, according to Naval War College dogma, the attacker should keep moving toward his objective. He must come to grips with the enemy. "As far as Midway was concerned," said Nimitz, "there was at least a partial violation of this

principle when the Japanese turned back westward after their carriers were hit so hard." Nimitz pointed out that this followed a pattern they had established at the onset of the war:

> They sailed in every direction at once. They took on too much and after their initial successes at Pearl Harbor, off Malaya in the Java Sea, they spread out to bomb Darwin and launched a large operation in the Indian Ocean when all the time the main enemy of Yamamoto's Combined Fleet was the U.S. Navy at Pearl Harbor which the Japanese left alone after their quick hit-and-run raid. The fact that the Japanese did not return to Pearl Harbor and complete the job was the greatest help for us, for they left their principal enemy with the time to catch his breath, restore his morale and rebuild his forces.[30]*

Furthermore, tying the objective of polishing off the U.S. Pacific Fleet with that of occupying Midway cancelled out the mobility and flexibility essential for a successful sea engagement. Yet one seeks in vain for any provision in their planning and preparations for maintaining this tactical offensive in the face of determined opposition. Instead, one finds war games rigged to make the enemy look incompetent, just as in planning for Pearl Harbor. And this time, their conceit was so overwhelming that they did not even take the elementary precaution of insisting that the aircraft carrier crews wear proper combat clothing. War experience had proved that any covering, even long-sleeved shirts and trousers, helped protect against fire. But serene in their conviction that the enemy could not touch them, the carrier crews worked in tropical shorts and short-sleeved shirts. In consequence, many suffered horribly and unnecessarily.[31]

Thus, when the unexpected American preparedness knocked the props from under the Japanese time schedule, the attackers lost their heads and their nerve. Yamamoto's forces still far outnumbered and outweighed Fletcher's in surface units. Even in carriers, from his own, Kondo's, and the Aleutian Force he could have summoned one carrier and three light carriers, with a total air strength of about fifty Zeros and sixty bombers. This was air power not to be shrugged off, especially as the Japanese believed they had sunk two out of three U.S. flattops. Instead, following the loss of Nagumo's carriers, Ya-

---

*See *At Dawn We Slept*, Chapter 65, for an exposition of Japan's failure to follow through at Pearl Harbor.

mamoto made a few tentative motions toward fighting on, then turned tail and scurried homeward with his massive force like a lumbering Saint Bernard dog pursued by a scrappy terrier.

8. *Economy of Force.* Correlating the principle of superiority at point of contact is that of economy—having enough to do the job but not too much. After committing himself to a double mission, Yamamoto brought along virtually everything but the fishing boats from the Inland Sea, wasting precious fuel, the lifeblood of an empire, tying up men and ships which could have been better occupied in preparing for the next scheduled thrust. The air strike on Midway was much too large for its objective. A lean, handpicked group such as Kakuta used at Dutch Harbor could have done the job as well, leaving forces aboard and surrounding the carriers in preparation for any American counteraction. Nimitz demonstrated the meaning of "Economy of Force" by deciding not to commit his battleships at Midway.

9. *Cooperation (Unity of Command).* Ironically, Yamamoto cancelled out this vital principle by tagging along personally in his flagship. Necessity for radio silence muzzled him and kept him from exercising the overall command, which he could have done easily and efficiently from the Inland Sea or from the center of communications at Tokyo. As a result of his taking his headquarters to sea, it was every man for himself with the individual fleets. The time lag between receipt of information on *Yamato* and actual events kept Yamamoto two jumps behind the action. In contrast, Nimitz at Pearl Harbor was right on top of events.

Had Nimitz, his various staffs, and sea commanders not taken positive, intelligent, and imaginative steps, the Japanese might have won the battle of Midway in spite of themselves.

CHAPTER 41

Analysis—United States: Brilliance "Shot with Luck"

Like so many Americans in assessing Pearl Harbor, most Japanese analysts of Midway erred in believing that the fault lay in their own nation's errors of omission or commission. Neither the United States after Pearl Harbor nor Japan after Midway could bring itself to admit that on those occasions they had not been masters of their fate. It would be just as wrong to assume that the Americans passively reaped a harvest of enemy mistakes at Midway as to credit Japan's victory at Pearl Harbor solely to American error. Midway was a positive American victory, not merely the avoidance of defeat.

The breaking of JN25 ranked high among the credits for the United States. Genda and his fellow officers had expected that some day the naval codes might be cracked, but they never dreamed that the Americans had broken JN25 as completely as they did. He credited their "earnest efforts to get Japanese information as much as possible" as one reason for their victory.[1] Ugaki suspected that somehow the United States had learned of the Japanese plans well before the sighting of the invasion force, but he never considered a code break, or at least never mentioned it in his diary.[2] Some of the junior officers were more perceptive, agreeing among themselves that the Americans must have broken the naval code, "otherwise, they could never have launched a concentrated attack upon our force from the flank with three carriers."[3]

Hypo's accomplishment was a tribute to the skill and dedication of Rochefort and his colleagues. While Rochefort seemed to regard as routine his tricking the Japanese into confirming that AF meant

Midway,* we believe he deserves full credit for a clever idea that worked.

Ironically, when Nimitz recommended to King that Rochefort be decorated for his brilliant contribution, King turned it down on the basis that no one person should be singled out for intelligence work in connection with Midway.[4] If this reasoning were carried to its logical end, no one would ever receive an award for anything, because human achievement is largely a cooperative matter. One is forced to the conclusion that, in King's eyes, intelligence was good enough to win battles, but not quite respectable.

Of course, all of Hypo's information would have been useless had Nimitz not accepted Rochefort's estimate of the situation and acted upon it. This, too, is the mark of a true leader—the ability to place faith and confidence in one's staff and to use one's experts effectively. Nimitz had long since shaken off the chains of the old "museum complex" which had driven so many intelligence experts up the walls—the squirreling away of data for their own sake without putting them to practical use. Nimitz's concept of intelligence was dynamic: Facts were high grade ore to be sifted carefully, the pure metal of knowledge extracted and forged into a weapon to defeat the enemy.

From this breakthrough stemmed all the successful American strategy. Once Nimitz knew that the Japanese were headed for Midway with the Nagumo carrier force in the lead, he knew not only where and approximately when he would have to fight, but how to fight. This would be an air battle, so he would leave his battleships on the west coast where they would not clutter up the action. He must have every available flattop, hence the drive and urgency behind his pressure to put the crippled *Yorktown* in fighting trim. This was a tremendous performance and a dramatic preliminary victory. In contrast, the Japanese dawdled over the repair of *Shokaku* and in replenishing *Zuikaku*, secure in their confidence that they could lick the hell out of the U.S. Pacific Fleet without the help of those two Pearl Harbor veterans.

But knowledge of when, where and how the enemy will strike is no guarantee of victory. Forewarning cannot produce ships, or multiply trained pilots and their aircraft like the miracle of the loaves and fishes. Victory at Midway resulted from American intelligence, civilian as well as military, from the wise use of what was available.

---

*See Chapter 5.

Nimitz did not allow himself to become paralyzed by the enormity of the enemy force headed his way. It would have been understandable had he looked at the comparative pictures of the Japanese fleet steaming toward him and the forces at his disposal, then tacitly admitted the situation was impossible. He could have decided to abandon Midway temporarily to its fate and move his precious carriers and cruisers to the west coast or keep them huddled in and around Pearl Harbor.

Instead, he acted promptly and aggressively, deliberately hurling his smaller force against a much stronger enemy. Knowing that he did not have the power for a head-on confrontation, he ordered Fletcher and Spruance to place their task forces on the flank of Nagumo's First Air Fleet. For he realized that if Midway were to be saved, his forces would have to come to grips with the enemy's aerial striking force at the earliest possible moment and from a position of strategic advantage. That the U.S. Navy had at Midway two commanders like Fletcher and Spruance with the will and the guts to hit the enemy first and with all their strength was a combination of fortune and Nimitz's good judgment.

Throughout his battle report, Nagumo bewailed the lack of time to prepare for Midway. Yet the best minds in the Japanese Navy had been planning Operation MI for months, and even so, virtually all of them regretted the haste. But what about Fletcher and Spruance? They had only a few days to prepare for the enormous challenge. Fletcher brought the badly damaged *Yorktown* into Pearl Harbor on the afternoon of May 27, and plunged absolutely cold into the Midway problem. Spruance sailed into Pearl Harbor just one day ahead of Fletcher, to discover that the Japanese were going to tackle Midway and that he was the new commander of Task Force Sixteen. After a few hurried conferences with Nimitz and Fletcher, Spruance went to sea on the morning of May 28. Two days later Fletcher was ready to sortie, his carrier battleworthy and his strategy worked out with Spruance.

Fletcher's decision to split his task force upon rendezvous with Spruance was a flash of inspiration. A good tactical commander not only knows the principles of war, he knows when and how to manipulate them. Fletcher's separating his numerically inferior force in the face of the enemy was a classic example of this flair. Had the three American carriers remained bunched, the tragedy of *Yorktown* could well have been multiplied by three, for no one could dispute the skill and daring of Nagumo's pilots. Once they were over a target, that target was virtually a dead duck. This chain reaction of destruction was precisely what happened to the First Air Fleet, whose carriers were within easy range of one another.

Later, Fletcher had to make another crucial decision. He knew well that the admiral who led his ships to the first major American sea victory of World War II would be a popular hero, assured of his place in history. Yet, when he realized that he could no longer command his air striking units at top efficiency, he turned the reins over to Spruance. This was an act of selfless integrity and patriotism in action. The reputations of Nimitz and Spruance have overshadowed Fletcher, but he was the link between the two, a man of talent who had the brains and character to give a free hand to a man of genius.

No command decison which Nimitz made in connection with Midway was more important, more far-reaching than his selection of Spruance to command Task Force Sixteen. He was almost unknown outside the small world of U.S. Navy brass, and he was not an airman. But Halsey recommended him and Nimitz gladly concurred. "It was a choice I never regretted," he said. "Spruance had excellent judgment; he was the type who thought things through very carefully after a thorough examination of all the facts, and then, when he decided to strike, struck hard. Spruance like Grant was the type who took the war to the enemy. I sorely needed commanders of that type," he emphasized. "Spruance was also bold but not to the point of being reckless. He had a certain caution, too, and a feeling for the battle."[5]

Nimitz's opinion of Spruance is that of a patron evaluating a protégé, one American admiral assessing another, a friend weighing the merits of a friend. It has been said that the best praise is an enemy's praise. Here is Watanabe's judgment: "Spruance personality was very high quality. He had air admiral's best character—strong, straight thinker, not impulse fluctuating thinker; he aims right at main point and go, no stop. That is good admiral."[6]

Spruance displayed those qualities from first to last at Midway. As soon as he knew where his target was, he hit with every available plane. He led his fleet with a sure hand, a delicate sense of timing. His turning east on the night of June 4 was exactly the right thing to do to avoid a Japanese night attack. By the same token, going west on June 5 was the correct decision, for it frightened the Japanese badly. Spruance displayed a nearly uncanny ability to read the enemy's mind. All along the line, he kept the Japanese guessing and off balance.

Spruance not only knew when to be aggressive, he knew when to stop. Very few admirals in his position could have resisted the temptation to go whooping after the retreating foe. But Spruance knew the exact point where courage becomes damn-foolishness. Furthermore, he knew his mission—to protect Midway—and stuck with it, despite the alluring will o'the wisps to westward. Second only to preserving Midway from invasion was the necessity of saving his carriers to fight again. Therefore he refused to be lured in reach of Wake Island's land-based bombers or beyond his own line of communications.

Naval historian Samuel Eliot Morison paid just tribute to Spruance:

> Fletcher did well, but Spruance's performance was superb. Calm, collected, decisive, yet receptive to advice; keeping in his mind the picture of widely disparate forces, yet boldly seizing every opening, Raymond A. Spruance emerged from this battle one of the greatest admirals in American naval history.[7]

At the lower level, the American fighting men were magnificent. Time and again in the Pacific War, the United States' junior officers proved their valor and good sense. Reid's decision to go beyond his sector enabled him to find the Invasion Force in advance of the Japanese schedule.* This discovery would not in itself have given the U.S. task forces time to reach the area, but it did give the garrison a chance to be armed and ready. Intelligence on Oahu had already done so, but Reid's sighting was a welcome confirmation that Rochefort's men were correct. Ady's spotting of the Nagumo force had no appreciable effect on the air raid on Midway, but it did pinpoint the enemy's location for Fletcher and Spruance.** Thereafter, Waldron, reaping the benefit of his study of Japanese tactics, used his initiative to find the enemy carriers when others, following a more rigid line of thought, missed the fight altogether.*** Most important, Mc-

---

*See Chapter 18.
**See Chapter 21.
***See Chapter 27.

Clusky's search in an unconventional pattern discovered the First Air
Fleet and enabled the dive bombers to make the attack which turned
almost certain defeat into triumph.*

Individual American fighting men demonstrated their bravery again
and again. In the attack on the carriers, they kept coming in the face
of Zeros, antiaircraft, and the sight of their comrades falling in flames.
Genda paid his opponents the true compliment of one warrior to
others: "Their fighting spirit, repeating attacks in spite of heavy losses
sustained, should also be credited for the victory."[8] Two Japanese
analysts likewise stated generously, "No one could have foreseen the
effectiveness of their courageous attacks; their tenacity brought the
Battle of Midway to a tragic end."[9]

Okumiya has observed, "It has been said from old times that a
battle is a succession of mistakes and that the party which blunders
less emerges victorious."[10] There is considerable truth in that somewhat cynical assessment, and it would be idle to deny that the United
States forces made mistakes at Midway, mistakes so serious that the
Japanese might well have won in spite of themselves. Spruance was
being more than modest when he remarked bluntly, "We were shot
with luck."[11]

Genda thought that the American "poor skill in torpedoing" was
the worst weakness on this side,[12] and Kusaka justly criticized "the
sporadic rather than concentrated nature of the attacks."[13]

Americans prided themselves upon their technology, yet in many
instances the quality of matériel was little short of miserable. The
500-lb. and 1,000-lb. bombs did not disable armored ships until the
target had been "knocked to pieces by many more hits than should
be necessary."[14] The United States had not yet gotten around to
having armored flight decks on its carriers, so they were quite inflammable.[15] It was indeed fortunate that if the Americans had to lose
any flattop, the Japanese concentrated on the already beat-up *Yorktown.*

"Action with Enemy" forms submitted by the B-17 pilots all too
frequently mention mechanical snafus which hampered them and in
some cases cancelled whatever effectiveness they might have had:
"On take off . . . the exhaust pipe on my number one engine ruptured . . ."; "Only 3 bombs dropped due to malfunction of racks";
"Did not drop bombs due to failure of interphone."[16]

---

*See Chapter 29.

Communications between the various forces involved left much to be desired. *Enterprise's* skipper pulled no punches in evaluating:

> Numerous contact reports initiated from the forces at Midway had a negative evaluation. The absence of amplifying reports after the initial contact report was made . . . might have been disastrous to our forces. Lack of amplification of contacts and failure of Midway based planes to provide continuous tactical scouting on June 4 and June 5 probably prevented complete destruction of enemy forces.[17]

Hornet's air report struck out even more sharply: "This failure to receive adequate information from our land based forces raises the question as to whether or not full dependence can be placed in units other than our own." The report reached this conclusion: "As the tactical situation was in our favor, it was only through errors on our part that we did not gain a more impressive victory."[18]

Kimes had a complaint of his own on behalf of his land-based troops: "We had no idea how they were faring as far as other forces in the vicinity were concerned, or what our forces afloat were doing. That seemed like a defect in communications planning."[19]

Some types of aircraft proved quite inadequate or unsuitable for the purpose to which they were put, none more so than the B-17. The United States would build bigger, faster, more destructive aircraft than the Flying Fortress, but never one quite so beloved. Grace and power in every line, readily responsive to the pilot's touch, the B-17 might be considered the answer of the Air Age to the Yankee clipper. It seemed impossible that this legendary machine could not do everything asked of it.

Midway provided an opportunity to prove once and for all that high altitude, land-based bombers could sink or seriously damage maneuvering surface vessels. But the B-17 struck out and so did the B-26. Later, some air enthusiasts insisted that the number of planes per target was far too small to call this experience a fair test.[20] Of course, if Emmons had been able to send up horizon-to-horizon B-17s, one or two might have scored a hit from sheer volume, but this would have done real violence to the principle of "Economy of Forces." Three Dauntless dive bombers, doing the job for which they were built, polished off *Akagi* to the point where the Japanese had to scuttle her.

One puzzle which persists is why the defenders of Midway failed

to obey Nimitz's instructions to leave the defense of Midway up to
its own antiaircraft guns, concentrating the fighter planes upon the
enemy flattops.* True, these fighters were hand-me-downs to the
Marines from the carriers, and, as events proved, no match for the
Zeros. But if they had accompanied the bombers and torpedo planes
from Midway against the First Air Fleet, they just might have dis-
tracted the Japanese fighter umbrella sufficiently to save some American lives or even to permit a hit or two. Near Midway, they suffered
terrible losses with no real results to show for it.

Perhaps one answer lay in the profound contempt many fighter
pilots felt for antiaircraft. During peacetime, major tactical emphasis
had been on how to avoid enemy AA. But in combat the pilots soon
found that the enemy fighter posed by far the greater danger. In an
official interview, Thach remarked,

> . . . I have done, roughly, two-thirds of my fighting in our own
> anti-aircraft fire and the other third in the Jap anti-aircraft fire, and
> I think that it is of little value in stopping a determined attack. They
> may shoot down a few planes but both the Japanese and our attacking
> pilots ignore it completely.[21]

But, as many and as grievous were the United States errors and
snafus, those of Japan were worse. Nimitz, Fletcher, and Spruance
emerged as winners, and military historians have placed the name of
Midway on that surprisingly small list of "decisive battles."

---

*See Chapter 8.

CHAPTER 42

The Meaning of Midway—
Forty Years Later

Now let us turn the calendar forward twenty years or so, to when Prange visited the three American victors at Midway, to see how the years had dealt with them and hear what they had to say about the crucial battle.

"Araby," the peaceful retirement home of Admiral and Mrs. Frank Jack Fletcher, rested in the rolling countryside of southern Maryland near the quaint old town of La Plata. After a warm welcome, the admiral led his visitor through several rooms richly furnished with Oriental art objects to his first-floor study.

Clad in slacks and shirt, Fletcher looked less like a war hero than a retired farmer of his native Iowa. He was modest and friendly, as plain and good as country bread. From some mysterious recess he produced bourbon and water, then lifted his glass in a toast to the men of the Fleet. He admitted frankly and with no hint of pathos that his memory was failing. But if the mists of time had blurred some of the background landscape, the forefront of the picture was still in sharp focus. As he spoke of those exciting days in June 1942, his eyes twinkled and his face split in a grin of satisfaction. His estimates were shrewd and he was in no doubt as to the meaning of the battle.

He agreed that the American forces had their share of luck at Midway, but, he declared, "It was not so much luck; it was the intelligent use of what information we had." Setting his highball to one side, he added, "We had better intelligence than the Japanese, and we were a better Navy. But the Japanese were a hell of a lot tougher than we thought they were going to be."

Fletcher recalled, too, that when he walked into Nimitz's office after the battle, the Commander in Chief, like himself, was greatly relieved that it was over and that they had won. "And he had reason to be," Fletcher emphasized, "because if the battle had gone the other way, things would really have been in a hell of a mess in the Pacific."[1]

Time had been kind to Admiral Raymond A. Spruance, paring every extra ounce from his always spare frame, changing his hair to steel color and lighting his sea-water eyes with gentle composure. As he sat in his spacious living room at Pebble Beach, California, amid the soft glow of Persian rugs and antique furniture, it was obvious that here was a man at home only with perfection. His tie matched his soft flannel shirt; his brown suit, donned for the first time that day, had the unmistakable texture and faint fragrance of Harris tweed.

As he spoke of Midway, he might have been a college professor, pleased to impart his knowledge and determined that his pupils should learn the facts thoroughly and accurately. Names, dates, places, remembered thoughts and reactions emerged exactly, as if his slim fingers had plucked each item from an invisible but neatly docketed file cabinet of memory.

"All operations are like a woman going to shop," he observed with a glint of humor, "for you must ask these two questions: 'What is it going to cost you and what is it worth to you?' " He was satisfied with his purchase at Midway for, as he pointed out, if the United States had lost, nothing would have stood between the West Coast and the Japanese Fleet. Yamamoto and his Imperial Navy would have gone on to greater triumphs. The admiral respected the fighting qualities of his opponents. "The Japanese put up an awful good war," he remarked simply.

Through the windows, flower beds burned with color and Monterey pines etched shadows over the velvety grass. At one precise tick of the clock, Spruance excused himself to go out and turn on the sprinkler system. When he returned, he carefully noted his action and the time on a sheet of paper.

He spoke frankly and with his own dry humor of certain criticisms leveled at him in the immediate post-Midway period for not chasing the Japanese farther west and for steaming east during the early night hours of June 4. He polished off these Monday morning quarterbacks with a brief "I considered my foresight at the time better than the hindsight of others later." But he insisted that the accolade for the Midway victory belonged to Nimitz, of whom he spoke with affectionate regard. "The credit must be given to Nimitz," he stated emphatically. "Not only did he accept the intelligence picture but he acted upon it at once."

A few evenings later at a Monterey restaurant, the admiral politely declined a cocktail. However, he operated on the principle of live and let live, so his vivacious wife sipped a champagne cocktail as sparkling as her own personality. Listening to the sea wash into Monterey Bay, Mrs. Spruance remarked suddenly, "The sea makes me restless, but I find the mountains quiet and peaceful." One could well imagine that after a lifetime of gambling with Neptune for her husband's life, she could find no peace in the sea. But the admiral merely smiled at her placidly. If ever a man was master of his environment, that man was Spruance.[2]

Although Fleet Admiral Chester W. Nimitz never invented the better mousetrap, to the end of his life the world beat a path to his door, as did Prange. The Nimitzes' guest book was filled with the names of the great and the small who came to pay him homage, to interview him, or just to visit. Among the many Japanese signatures were those of Kichisaburo Nomura, ambassador to the United States at the time of Pearl Harbor, and of Mitsuo Fuchida, leader of the air attack on December 7, 1941. This was just as it should be, for ever since Nimitz signed the instrument of Japan's surrender, he devoted much of his time and care to building a bridge between his country and the nation he did so much to defeat. "Japan was a very worthy and tenacious foe," he said, "and after we gave her a good drubbing there was no reason to rub salt into the old wound."

The years since Midway had touched the admiral with the mellow beauty of the old and the good, a beauty as warming as the vintage sherry he hospitably proffered. His blue eyes had not faded, and his hair was so white the visitor had to look twice to believe it. Here was not the mere absence of color, but the vigorous white of sunlit sails.

Nimitz recalled being very worried and tense during the preparations for the battle of Midway, but after the fight was under way he relaxed a bit. "Once Midway started it was something of a relief," he explained, "because the Japanese did what we thought they would.

At least we knew then that things were going according to plan. Once Midway started I had the greatest confidence in our people out there and I thought things would go well."

Mrs. Nimitz, leaning on two canes, entered the study to consult her husband. "Darling, do I have enough air mail stamps on this envelope?" she inquired. "Enough, my dear one!" exclaimed the admiral with an affectionate grin. "You have about two or three too many!"

As with so many couples who have lived a long and companionable married life, the Nimitzes resembled one another. The admiral's warmth, dignity, and charm were reflected in his wife's appealing face, and their delightful quarters gave evidence that she, like her husband, was a person of action. Many of the pictures hanging on the walls were from her own brush, and the *bonsai* trees on the wide, cool veranda testified to her skill with this exacting, sophisticated art.[3]

Nimitz always refused to write his memoirs, although any publisher in the United States would have paid a pretty penny for his autobiography. In speaking with him, Prange formed the impression that Nimitz had too much genuine humility and humor to relish writing a book of which he perforce would be the hero, too much gentleness and humanity to write harshly or even objectively of those who had made mistakes. If he could not praise he preferred not to speak at all. Many years later, Mrs. Nimitz confirmed this impression, telling an interviewer, "He didn't want to hurt anyone. He had to dismiss a couple of officers during the war, and they were bitter. If he had written his memoirs, written them honestly, he would have had to hurt them. Chester never hurt anyone."[4]

When he could praise, he did so with no misplaced economy, and one of his favorite topics was Spruance. "Admiral Spruance was responsible for the success of Midway," he declared. He brushed aside any tentative suggestion that perhaps Chester W. Nimitz had something to do with it. He returned to Spruance, his face alight with pride in his friend. "It was because of his judgment and wisdom that we won the battle," he insisted. "My judgment of Spruance was vindicated again and again in future operations in the Pacific. Spruance always understood his mission. The one supreme thing Spruance had was judgment—judgment based on intelligence and knowledge of his profession." Nimitz also warmly commended Rochefort for his intelligence breakthrough, which resulted in "as clear a picture as any command would want to have." In summary, he had this to say: "Midway was the most crucial battle of the Pacific War, the engagement that made everything else possible."[5]

Almost another twenty years have passed, and that judgment still stands. Midway was indeed what it has so often been called—the turning point. However, this became apparent only in the long view. At the time, very few Japanese realized the true import. One of those few was Miyo. He had opposed the operation to the point of tears, and he saw his judgment all too horribly vindicated. He lost all hope of eventual victory, for as an aviator he appreciated what it meant to lose so many carriers, planes, pilots, and technicians. Others at the Naval General Staff, still thinking in terms of surface warfare, could not or would not understand what had happened.[6]

Some young fliers took a gloomy view of the immediate future. They knew that Japan had to go on the defensive for the time being. Yet they themselves "had demonstrated to the world with their blood that offense was the best defensive way in the new era of the sea battle, in which air power played a major role, replacing the gun power centered around battleships."[7]

The result of the battle was a real shock to Genda, but he still had no idea that Japan had lost the ability to defeat the United States. Only retrospectively did he realize that Midway, coupled with the Japanese withdrawal from Guadalcanal, had been the turning point.[8] Nor did Kusaka think of Midway as a watershed, though it was "a terrible blow to the Japanese Navy." They still had strong carriers like *Shokaku* and *Zuikaku*, and more were in production.[9]

Nor did the responsible Americans assume that from now on, all seas would part for their passing. Spruance said that no one at Pearl Harbor had the idea at the time that Midway won the war then and there. "In the context of the time," he explained, "the idea was that we had not been set back. We had not been defeated by these superior Japanese forces. Midway to us at that time meant that here is where we start from, here is where we really jump off in a hard, bitter war against the Japanese."[10]

"With Midway things were just getting started," Nimitz emphasized. "The march across the Pacific had not begun. After Midway there was no feeling that we had won the war. No doubt it was the all-important turning point, but we still had a tenacious enemy to deal with and a difficult job to do."[11] Over three years of bitterly fought war proved both admirals to be correct.

What, then, did Midway mean? The most immediate fact, of course, appeared in the tangibles—men and matériel lost. The statistics leave no room for doubt as to who won this battle:[12]

	United States	Japan
Casualties	307	2,500
Carriers	1	4
Heavy cruiser	0	1
Destroyer	1	0
Aircraft	147	332

In addition, Japan suffered heavy damage to one cruiser, medium damage to two destroyers (not counting the two which collided), and slight damage to a battleship, a destroyer, and an oiler. The United States experienced extensive damage at Midway, moderate at Dutch Harbor, and lost Kiska and Attu.

One must also consider the intangibles—what might have happened but did not. Here we are on less firm ground, as all speculation must be debatable. But had Yamamoto fulfilled his projects of taking Midway and destroying Nimitz's carriers, the next program on his agenda was to turn to the Australian campaign. And with the aerial striking power of the U.S. Pacific Fleet out of the running, there would have been precious little to stop him. Had he succeeded in cutting the Australian lifeline, MacArthur's forces would have been isolated, and, in total command of the south Pacific and Indian Oceans, Japan would have held southeast Asia in fee for many a sad day. And in the meantime, possession of Midway would have given Japan the means to harass at least the Hawaiian Islands and even the West coast. One can readily imagine that public clamor to protect the United States might well have mounted to the point where the prime strategy—Hitler first—could have suffered a devastating setback. Perhaps the ultimate result of the war would have been the same, but the cost would have been more than one cares to think about.

But it did not happen. "At Midway the Japanese lost or left behind a naval air force that had been the terror of the Pacific—an élite force, an overwhelming force that would never again come back and spread destruction and fear as it had over the first six months of the war," said Layton. "This was the great meaning of Midway . . ."[13]

So it was, from the tactical point of view. A valuable study at the U.S. Naval War College takes us into deeper waters:

> . . . it had a stimulating effect on the morale of the American fighting forces; . . . it stopped the Japanese expansion to the east; it put an end to Japanese offensive action which had been all conquering for the first six months of war; it restored the balance of naval power in the Pacific which thereafter steadily shifted to favor the American side; and it removed the threat to Hawaii and to the west coast of the United States.
>
> . . . CinC Combined Fleet desired to fight a decisive naval action with the American fleet at the earliest possible moment and before American construction could overwhelm the Japanese fleet by sheer force of numbers. He now was forced to give up the idea of holding such a fleet engagement at an early date and in remote waters. He was instead forced to wait until the Americans took the offensive, and owing to the loss of his carriers he was restricted to waters much nearer the Empire. Thus it was that the Japanese were forced to a defensive role.[14]

This is the ultimate meaning. At Midway the United States laid aside the shield and picked up the sword, and through all the engagements to follow, never again yielded the strategic offensive.

APPENDIX

NOTES

CHAPTER 1
"A Breath of Fresh Air"

1. Diary of RADM Sadao Chigusa, December 23, 1941. Hereafter Chigusa diary.
2. Gordon W. Prange, *At Dawn We Slept*, New York, McGraw-Hill, 1981, pp. 578–579. Hereafter *At Dawn We Slept*.
3. Both December 8, 1942.
4. Meridian *Star*, December 8, 1942.
5. Treasury Department interoffice communication, December 26, 1941, Barth to Ferdinand Kuhn, Jr., Diary of Henry Morgenthau, Jr., Book 478, Franklin D. Roosevelt Library, Hyde Park, N.Y. Hereafter Morgenthau diary.
6. Winston S. Churchill, *The Hinge of Fate*, Boston, Houghton Mifflin, 1950, p. 109.
7. *Hearings before the Joint Committee on the Investigation of the Pearl Harbor Attack, Congress of the United States, Seventy-ninth Congress, First Session*, Part 26, p. 37. Hereafter *PHA*.
8. Interview with Col. William C. Farnum, October 15, 1963.
9. For an account of Knox's trip to Oahu and the sessions there of the Roberts Commission, see *At Dawn We Slept*, pp. 584–598.
10. For accounts of the Wake campaign, see the U.S. Marine Corps official monograph by Lt. Col. Robert D. Heinl, Jr., USMC, *The Defense of Wake*, Washington, D.C., 1947, and Samuel Eliot Morison, *The Rising Sun in the Pacific*, Boston, Little, Brown, 1950, pp. 223–254. Hereafter *Rising Sun in the Pacific*.
11. *Rising Sun in the Pacific*, pp. 235–254.
12. Interview with Admiral Raymond A. Spruance, September 5, 1964. Hereafter Spruance.
13. *PHA*, Part 23, pp. 1062–1064.
14. *Rising Sun in the Pacific*, p. 252.
15. Letter, RADM Frank E. Beatty to Harry Elmer Barnes, December 21, 1966. Papers of Charles C. Hiles, University of Wyoming, Laramie, WY., Box 13.
16. *Rising Sun in the Pacific*, p. 249.
17. VF-6 kept this log at the direction of its commander "for the private reference of its members." Lt. J. S. Gray, Jr., was the "historian," and all squadron members contributed. Cited hereafter as VF-6 unofficial log.
18. John Sabella, "Memories of Nimitz," *The Retired Officer*, June, 1976, p. 31. This article is primarily an interview with Catherine Nimitz. Hereafter "Memories of Nimitz."
19. E. B. Potter, *Nimitz*, Annapolis, Md., 1976, p. 17. Hereafter *Nimitz*.
20. Interview with Fleet Admiral Chester W. Nimitz, September 4, 1964. Hereafter Nimitz.
21. *Rising Sun in the Pacific*, p. 256.
22. Interview with Spruance, September 5, 1964.

23. Interview with Nimitz, September 4, 1964.

24. Interview with Admiral Arthur C. Davis, January 30, 1963.

25. *Nimitz*, p. 47.

26. *Rising Sun in the Pacific,* pp. 181, 198.

27. Ibid., pp. 258–260.

28. Ibid., pp. 289–291.

29. Ibid., pp. 263–264, 268.

30. Ibid., pp. 345–358, 362–363.

31. Ibid., p. 268.

32. Interview with Nimitz, September 4, 1964.

33. Treasury Department interoffice communication, January 16, 1942, Barth to Archibald MacLeish, Morgenthau diary, Box 486.

34. Diary of Henry L. Stimson, February 10, 1942, Yale University Library, New Haven, Conn. Hereafter Stimson diary.

35. *Rising Sun in the Pacific,* p. 256.

36. Interview with Spruance, September 5, 1964.

37. Washington *Evening Star,* January 4, 1942.

38. *Rising Sun in the Pacific,* p. 257.

39. Interview with Spruance, September 5, 1964.

CHAPTER 2

"We Should Occupy Midway"

1. Interview with Cmdr. Takayasu Arima, November 21, 1948.

2. Interview with Capt. Yasuji Watanabe, September 25, 1964. Hereafter Watanabe.

3. Interview with RADM Sadatoshi Tomioka, February 17, 1948. Hereafter Tomioka.

4. Interview with Watanabe, January 7, 1965. Watanabe brought to this interview a number of extracts from the Ugaki diary.

5. Interview which Barde held with Watanabe, 3–4 June, 1966. Hereafter Watanabe/Barde interview.

6. Interview with Watanabe, September 26, 1964.

7. Ibid., January 7, 1965.

8. Watanabe/Barde interview, 3–4 June, 1966.

9. Interview with Watanabe, January 7, 1965.

10. A. J. Watts and B. G. Gordon, *The Imperial Japanese Navy,* Garden City, N.Y., Doubleday, 1971, pp. 68–72. Hereafter *Imperial Japanese Navy.*

11. Interview with Capt. Mitsuo Fuchida, March 1, 1964. Hereafter Fuchida.

12. Interviews with Watanabe, September 25, 1964 and January 7, 1965; Watanabe/Barde interview, June 3–4, 1966.

13. Interview with Capt. Joseph Rochefort, August 26, 1964. Hereafter Rochefort.

14. Interview with Adm. Dundas P. Tucker, August 22, 1964. Hereafter Tucker.

15. Interview with Rochefort, September 1, 1964.

16. Ibid., August 25, 1964.

17. Ibid.

18. Interview with Adm. Edwin T. Layton, July 22, 1964. Hereafter Layton.

19. Interview with Rochefort, August 26, 1964.

20. *Nimitz,* p. 64; interview with Rochefort, September 1, 1964.

21. Interview with Tucker, August 22, 1964.

22. Interview with Rochefort, September 1, 1964.

23. Walter Lord, *Incredible Victory,* New York, Harper & Row 1967, pp. 22–23. Hereafter *Incredible Victory; Nimitz,* pp. 64–65.

24. Interview with Rochefort, August 26, 1964.

CHAPTER 3

"A Shiver over Japan"

1. Interviews with Watanabe, September 25, 1964 and January 7, 1965.

2. Interview which Barde held with Tomioka, May 6, 1966. Hereafter Tomioka/Barde interview.

3. Diary of Capt. Yoshitake Miwa, April 4, 1942. Hereafter Miwa diary; interviews with Watanabe, September 25, 1946, and RADM Kameto Kuroshima, November 28, 1964. Hereafter Kuroshima.
4. These descriptions are based on the author's long friendship with both Watanabe and Kuroshima.
5. Interviews with Watanabe, September 25, 1964 and Kuroshima, November 28, 1964.
6. Tomioka/Barde interview, May 6, 1966.
7. Ibid.; interview which Barde held with Capt. Tatsukichi Miyo, May 6, 1966. Hereafter Miyo/Barde interview.
8. Ibid. An excellent account of these discussions in the Naval General Staff is contained in an article by Masatake Okumiya, "The Battle of Midway," *Nippon Times*, May 3 and 4, 1950. Hereafter "Battle of Midway."
9. Interview with Kuroshima, November 28, 1964.
10. Mitsuo Fuchida and Masatake Okumiya, ed. Clarke H. Kawakami and Roger Pineau, *Midway: The Battle That Doomed Japan*, Annapolis, U.S. Naval Institute 1955, pp. 42–43. Hereafter *Midway*.
11. Interview with Kuroshima, November 28, 1964; Watanabe/Barde interview, February 3–4, 1966.
12. *Midway*, pp. 43–45.
13. Miwa diary, February 8, 1942.
14. Interview with Fuchida, August 24, 1967.
15. Miwa diary, April 18, 1942.
16. Interview with Fuchida, August 24, 1967.
17. Interview with Kuroshima, November 28, 1964.
18. Quoted in *Japan Times and Advertiser*, April 19, 1942.
19. Miwa diary, April 19, 1942.
20. Ibid., April 24, 1942.
21. Interview with Fuchida, April 24, 1967.
22. Watanabe/Barde interview, February 3–4, 1966.
23. Stimson diary, April 18, 1942.
24. Ibid., April 21, 1942.
25. "The Battle of the Coral Sea, May 1 to May 11, inclusive, 1942, Strategical and Tactical Analysis," U.S. Naval War College, 1947, p. 115. Hereafter Coral Sea Analysis.
26. Undated questionnaire completed by VADM Ryunosuke Kusaka. Hereafter Kusaka statement. See also *Midway*, p. 93.
27. Undated questionnaire completed by Lt. Gen. Minoru Genda. Hereafter Genda statement.
28. Interview with Fuchida, February 14, 1964.
29. Kusaka statement.
30. Ibid.
31. Miwa diary, April 28, 1942.
32. *Midway*, pp. 98–99.
33. Miwa diary, April 29, 1942.
34. Papers of Franklin D. Roosevelt, Franklin D. Roosevelt Library, Hyde Park, N.Y., Map File, Box 40. Hereafter Roosevelt Papers.

CHAPTER 4
"One Touch of an Armored Sleeve"

1. *Midway*, pp. 93–94.
2. Ibid., p. 95.
3. Ibid., p. 96.
4. Ibid., pp. 79, 84.
5. Ibid., p. 89; interview with Watanabe, September 26, 1964.
6. *Midway*, p. 88; Miyo/Barde interview, May 6, 1966.
7. Interviews with Watanabe, September 26, and October 6, 1964.
8. *Midway*, pp. 82–83.
9. Ibid., pp. 80–81, 85, 106.
10. Ibid., pp. 85–86.
11. Interview with Watanabe, September 26, 1964.
12. *Midway*, pp. 81–82, 86.
13. Ibid., pp. 80, 85.
14. Ibid., p. 86.
15. Interview with Watanabe, September 26, 1964.
16. *Midway*, p. 99.
17. Ibid., p. 96.
18. Interview with Watanabe, September 26, 1964.

19. Teuchi Makajima, "Middoue no Higeki" (The Tragic Sea Battle of Midway), *Shosetsu fan*, 1956. Hereafter "Tragic Battle."
20. *Midway*, pp. 117–118.
21. Interview with Watanabe, September 26, 1964.
22. *Midway*, pp. 96–97. Similar cheating occurred during the war games for Pearl Harbor. See *At Dawn We Slept*, Chapters 28–29.
23. Genda and Kusaka statements.
24. Interview with Watanabe, October 6, 1964.
25. Ibid.
26. Genda statement.
27. "Tragic Battle."
28. Interview with Nimitz, September 4, 1964.
29. Letter, Lt. Col. Robert C. McGlashan, USMC, to Director, Division of Public Information (Historical Section), August 12, 1947, located in Headquarters, U.S. Marine Corps, Washington, D.C. Hereafter McGlashan letter.
30. Ibid. See also Lt. Col. Robert D. Heinl, Jr., USMC, *Marines at Midway*, Division of Public Information, Washington, D.C., 1948, p. 23. Hereafter *Marines at Midway*.
31. Samuel Eliot Morison, *Coral Sea, Midway and Submarine Actions, May 1942-August 1942*, Boston, Little, Brown, 1949, p. 80. Hereafter *Coral Sea, Midway and Submarine Actions*.
32. Interview with Brig. Gen. James A. Mollison, December 19, 1966. Hereafter Mollison.
33. Interview with Nimitz, September 4, 1964.
34. Honolulu *Advertiser*, May 4, 1942.
35. *Coral Sea, Midway and Submarine Actions*, p. 75.

CHAPTER 5
"The Expected and Constant Threat"

1. Miwa diary, May 7, 1942.
2. Coral Sea Analysis, p. 82. For concise, interesting accounts of the Coral Sea battle, see *Coral Sea, Midway and Submarine Actions*, pp. 21–68, and *Midway*, pp. 100–107.
3. Miwa diary, May 8, 1942.
4. *Midway*, p. 79n.
5. U.S.S. Yorktown (CV5) Bomb Damage, Coral Sea, 8 May, 1942, War Damage Report No. 23, BuShips, Navy Department, 28 November 1942, pp. 7–8, 13. Hereafter Yorktown Coral Sea Damage Report; Coral Sea Analysis, pp. 96–97.
6. Coral Sea Analysis, pp. 94–95, 102; *Coral Sea, Midway and Submarine Actions*, p. 59.
7. *Coral Sea, Midway and Submarine Actions*, pp. 14, 59.
8. Ibid., pp. 59–60.
9. Ibid., p. 52; Coral Sea Analysis, pp. 107–108; Miwa diary, May 10, 1942.
10. *Coral Sea, Midway and Submarine Actions*, p. 39.
11. Miwa diary, May 8, 1942.
12. Ibid.
13. *Coral Sea, Midway and Submarine Actions*, pp. 61–63.
14. Smith, VADM William Ward, USN (Ret), *Midway: Turning Point of the Pacific*, New York, Thomas Y. Crowell 1966, pp. 54–55. Hereafter *Turning Point; Midway*, p. 109n; *Coral Sea, Midway and Submarine Actions*, p. 60.
15. *Japan Times and Advertiser*, May 9, 1942.
16. *Coral Sea, Midway and Submarine Actions*, p. 62.
17. Replies to a questionnaire submitted to Cmdr. Takashi Hashiguchi. This document is undated, but was undoubtedly completed in the autumn of 1964 when Prange was in Japan researching for this study. Hereafter Hashiguchi statement.
18. Interviews with Nimitz, September 4, 1964 and Rochefort, September 1, 1964; *Incredible Victory*, p. 23.
19. Interview with Rochefort, September 1, 1964.
20. Interview with Layton, July 22, 1964. See *At Dawn We Slept*, pp. 469–471, 511.

21. Honolulu *Star-Bulletin*, May 15, 1942.
22. *Incredible Victory*, pp. 24–25; *Nimitz*, pp. 79–80.
23. *PHA*, Part 3, p. 1158.
24. Fleet Admiral William F. Halsey, USN and Lt. Cmdr. J. Bryan III, USNR, *Admiral Halsey's Story*, New York, Mc-Graw-Hill 1947, pp. 105–106. Hereafter *Admiral Halsey's Story*.

CHAPTER 6
"Required to Aim at Two Hares"

1. The Japanese Story of the Battle of Midway (A Translation), OPNAV P32-1002, U. S. Office of Naval Intelligence, Washington, D.C., June 1947, p.6. Hereafter Japanese Story.
2. Genda statement.
3. Hashiguchi statement.
4. Japanese Story, p. 5.
5. Ibid., pp. 5–6.
6. Ibid., p. 5.
7. Hara, Capt. Tameichi, IJN, with Fred Saito and Roger Pineau, *Japanese Destroyer Captain*, New York, Ballantine 1961, p. 103. Hereafter *Destroyer Captain*.
8. Kusaka statement. See also Kusaka, VADM Ryunosuke, *Rengo Kantai* (Combined Fleet), Tokyo, 1952, pp. 73–74. Hereafter *Rengo Kantai*.
9. *Midway*, pp. 6–8.
10. Japanese Story, p. 6.
11. *Rengo Kantai*, p. 75.
12. Genda Statement.
13. Interview with VADM Mitsumi Shimizu, January 16, 1965.
14. Genda statement.
15. Miwa diary, May 15–16, 1942.
16. Ibid., May 17, 1942.
17. *Coral Sea, Midway and Submarine Actions*, p. 202.
18. *Midway*, p. 106.
19. *Coral Sea, Midway and Submarine Actions*, p. 191.
20. Ibid., pp. 188, 202.
21. Midway Analysis, p. 26; *Midway*, p. 259.
22. Diary of VADM Matome Ugaki, May 17,

1942. Hereafter Ugaki diary. Ugaki's diary has been published under the title *Senso Roku* (War Records), Tokyo, 1953. However, the extracts used in this study are taken from a translation which was prepared for Prange, who owned the English-language rights.
23. Miwa diary, May 18, 1942.
24. Japanese Story, p. 5.
25. Ugaki diary, May 17, 1942.
26. Ibid.
27. Ibid., May 19, 1942.
28. Miwa diary, May 19, 1942.
29. Japanese Story, p. 2; *Midway*, pp. 108–109.
30. Midway Analysis, p. 13.
31. Japanese Story, pp. 2–3; Midway Analysis, p. 13.
32. Japanese Story, pp. 2–3; Midway Analysis, p. 14.

CHAPTER 7
"There Was No Rest"

1. Interview with Nimitz, September 4, 1964.
2. *Coral Sea, Midway and Submarine Actions*, p. 83.
3. Midway Analysis, p. 70.
4. Letter, CinCPAC to Cominch, June 28, 1942, Subject: Battle of Midway. Hereafter Nimitz report.
5. Midway Analysis, p. 66; *Coral Sea, Midway and Submarine Actions*, pp. 82–83.
6. Interview with Adm. James M. Shoemaker, January 31, 1963.
7. Letter, Hq 7th AF to CG, AAF, June 13, 1942, Subject: Air Employment at Midway. Hereafter Davidson report.
8. *Midway*, pp. 110, 255–256.
9. Ibid., p. 256.
10. *Imperial Japanese Navy*, pp. 280–281, 283–284.
11. *Destroyer Captain*, p. 97.
12. Interview with RADM Sadao Chigusa, December 15, 1964. Hereafter Chigusa.
13. Official interview with Lt. Col. Ira L. Kimes, USMC, in Bureau of Aeronautics, Navy Dept., Washington, D.C.,

August 31, 1942. Hereafter Kimes interview.

14. Letter, Executive Officer, MAG-22, to CO, MAG-22, June 7, 1942, Subject: Marine Aircraft Group Twenty-two, Second Marine Aircraft Wing, Midway Island T. H., Executive Officer's Report of The Battle of Midway, June 3, 4, 5, 6, 1942, with preliminary phase from May 22, l942. Hereafter McCaul report.

15. Nimitz report, June 28, 1942.

16. Stimson diary, May 21–22, 1942.

17. Miwa diary, May 21, 1942.

18. *Midway*, p. 84.

19. Miwa diary, May 22, 1942; *Midway*, p. 110.

20. McCaul report.

21. Ugaki diary, May 24, 1942.

22. Miwa diary, May 24, 1942.

CHAPTER 8
"Can You Hold Midway?"

1. Ugaki and Miwa diaries, May 25, 1942.

2. This account of the war game of May 25, 1942, is based upon a memorandum of VADM Tasuki Nakazawa. According to Capt. Sakamoto, a researcher for the Japanese Self-Defense Agency's historical department, this memorandum is the only material remaining today covering this important tabletop exercise. This was included in material furnished Prange by Capt. Sakamoto through Cmdr. Chihaya. Hereafter Sakamoto material.

3. Ugaki diary, June 8, 1942.

4. Sakamoto material.

5. Ibid.

6. Miwa diary, May 25, 1942.

7. *Japan Times and Advertiser*, May 26, 1942.

8. Miwa diary, May 26, 1942.

9. McCaul report.

10. *Incredible Victory*, p. 27; *Nimitz*, pp. 81–82.

11. Unpublished study, The Battle of Midway, Including the Aleutian Phase, June 3–14, 1942, Strategical and Tactical

Analysis, U.S. Naval War College, 1948, p. 41. Hereafter Midway Analysis.

12. *Incredible Victory*, p. 27; *Nimitz*, pp. 82–83.

13. *Incredible Victory*, p. 28; *Nimitz*, p. 82.

14. *Marines at Midway*, p. 23.

15. McGlashan letter.

16. *Marines at Midway*, p. 19.

17. *Coral Sea, Midway and Submarine Actions*, pp. 86, 93; J. Bryan III, "Never a Battle Like Midway," *Saturday Evening Post*, March 26, 1949, p. 52. Hereafter "Never a Battle Like Midway."

18. *Marines at Midway*, p. 9.

19. Ibid., p. 22; *Coral Sea, Midway and Submarine Actions*, p. 85.

20. Interview which Barde held with Col. John F. Carey, USN (Ret), July 1, 1966. Hereafter Carey/Barde interview.

21. Interview which Barde held with Col. Verne J. McCaul, USMC, June 1, 1966. Hereafter McCaul/Barde interview.

22. *At Dawn We Slept*, p. 501.

23. *Marines at Midway*, p. 22; *Incredible Victory*, p. 50.

24. "Never a Battle Like Midway," p. 52.

25. For a technical discussion of the Buffalo, see Joe Mizrahi, "Farewell to the Fleet's Forgotten Fighter: Brewster F2A," *Air Power*, March 1972.

26. McCaul/Barde interview, June 1, 1966.

27. Midway Analysis, p. 49.

28. "Never a Battle Like Midway," p. 52.

29. McCaul/Barde interview, June 1, 1966.

30. Undated memorandum to Capt. Arthur C. Davis, the CinCPAC air officer, quoted in *Marines at Midway*, p. 23.

31. McGlashan letter.

32. Interview which Barde held with Ens. A. K. Earnest, USN, April 28, 1966. Hereafter Earnest/Barde interview.

33. Kusaka statement; *Rengo Kantai*, p. 74.

34. Interview with Watanabe, November 24, 1964.

35. *Marines at Midway*, p. 23; McGlashan letter.

36. *Incredible Victory*, p. 50; *Marines at Midway*, p. 23.

37. Commentary on draft of Marine Historical Monograph "Marines at Midway," by

Maj. John Apergis, USMCR. Apergis's comments are undated; however, Hq. USMC had requested replies by February 1, 1948, so presumably this document was written somewhat earlier.

38. McCaul report.
39. Davidson report.

CHAPTER 9
"An Admiral's Admiral"

1. For a personalized account of Halsey's career, see *Admiral Halsey's Story*.
2. Logs of *Enterprise* and *Hornet*, May 26, 1942.
3. *Admiral Halsey's Story*, pp. 106–107.
4. Ibid., pp. 106, 97.
5. Interview with Barde held with Fleet Admiral Chester W. Nimitz, October 14, 1965. Hereafter Nimitz/Barde interview.
6. Interview with Nimitz, September 4, 1964.
7. *Admiral Halsey's Story*, p. 107; *Turning Point*, p. 56.
8. Interview with Spruance, September 5, 1964.
9. VADM. E. P. Forrestel, USN (Ret), *Admiral Raymond A. Spruance, USN: A Study in Command*, Washington, D. C., 1966, p. 35. Hereafter *Spruance*.
10. Interview with Spruance, September 5, 1964; replies by Spruance, November 4, 1966, to a questionnaire which Prange submitted to him. Hereafter Spruance questionnaire.
11. Interview with Spruance, September 5, 1964; *Spruance*, pp. 35, 59.
12. Interview with Spruance, September 5, 1964; *Spruance*, p. 35.
13. Fletcher Pratt, "Spruance: Picture of the Admiral," *Harper's Magazine*, August 1946, p. 146. Hereafter "Spruance: Picture of the Admiral."
14. *Turning Point*, p. 62.
15. Interview with Nimitz, September 4, 1964. In the course of his interviews, correspondence, and research, Prange

came to share Nimitz's opinion of Spruance to the fullest.
16. Interview with Spruance, September 14, 1964.
17. Interview with Nimitz, September 4, 1964.
18. Interview with Watanabe, October 4, 1964.
19. Log of *Enterprise*, May 27, 1942.
20. Logs of *Enterprise* and *Hornet*, May 26 and 27, 1942.
21. Pearl Harbor Navy Yard Diary, May 25 and 27, 1942.
22. Interview with Mollison, December 19, 1966.
23. Interview with Maj. Gen. Howard C. Davidson, December 13, 1966. Hereafter Davidson.
24. Log of *Enterprise*, May 27, 1942.
25. Honolulu *Star-Bulletin*, May 27, 1942; *Admiral Halsey's Story*, p. 96.
26. Honolulu *Star-Bulletin*, May 27, 1942; *Incredible Victory*, p. 33.
27. Diary of Cmdr. Cleo J. Dobson, May 27, 1942. Hereafter Dobson diary. Dobson kept his journal for his family, and they never released it until they permitted Barde to examine and quote from it.
28. Ibid., May 20, 21, 26 and 27, 1942.
29. Honolulu *Star-Bulletin*, May 27, 1942. See *At Dawn We Slept*, pp. 514–515.

CHAPTER 10
"The Moment of Fulfillment"

1. *Midway*, p. 4.
2. "Tragic Battle."
3. *Japan Times and Advertiser*, May 27–28, 1942.
4. Ibid. May 27, 1942.
5. *Nichi Nichi*, quoted in *Japan Times and Advertiser*, May 27, 1942.
6. Ibid. May 27, 1942.
7. Ibid.
8. *Japan Times and Advertiser*, May 27, 1942.
9. Ibid., May 27–28, 1942.
10. For an excellent study of Tojo, see Rob-

ert J. C. Butow, *Tojo and the Coming of the War*, Princeton, Princeton University Press 1961.

11. *Japan Times and Advertiser*, May 28, 1942.
12. Ibid.
13. Ibid.
14. Ibid.
15. Japanese Story, p. 6.
16. *At Dawn We Slept*, p. 310.
17. Japanese Story, p. 6.
18. *Japan Times and Advertiser*, May 27, 1942.
19. *Rengo Kantai*, p. 78.
20. "Tragic Battle"; interview with Fuchida, February 14, 1964.
21. Interview with Fuchida, February 14, 1964.
22. "Tragic Battle."
23. Genda statement.
24. Stimson diary, May 27, 1942.

CHAPTER 11
"The Principle of Calculated Risk"

1. Understandably, the officer who delivered this judgment asked to remain anonymous.
2. *Rising Sun in the Pacific*, p. 237.
3. Interview with Admiral Frank Jack Fletcher, September 17, 1966. Hereafter Fletcher.
4. Interview with Spruance, September 5, 1964.
5. Log of *Enterprise*, May 27, 1942; interview with Fletcher, September 17, 1966.
6. Interview with Fletcher, September 17, 1966.
7. *Nimitz*, p. 86.
8. Interview with Fletcher, September 17, 1966.
9. Ibid.; *Turning Point*, p. 55.
10. *Coral Sea, Midway and Submarine Actions*, p. 84; Midway Analysis, pp. 71–72.
11. Interview with Fletcher, September 17, 1966.

12. *Yorktown* Damage Report, pp. 5–6.
13. Ibid., p. 7.
14. *Coral Sea, Midway and Submarine Actions*, p. 81.
15. *Turning Point*, pp. 56, 58–59.
16. Interview with Layton, July 22, 1964. During this interview, Layton recalled that this exchange took place at about 0730 on June 4, 1942. However, in his biography of Nimitz, Potter, who also interviewed Layton, placed this conversation in late May, which seems more logical. *Nimitz*, p. 83.
17. Interview with Spruance, September 5, 1964.
18. Nimitz report, June 28, 1942.
19. *Incredible Victory*, p. 39; *Coral Sea, Midway and Submarine Actions*, p. 97.
20. Nimitz report, June 28, 1942.
21. Interview with Spruance, September 5, 1964.
22. Nimitz report, June 28, 1942.
23. The fact that the Main Body was not included in Nimitz's estimate is proof that he did not have the information. Moreover, in his Foreword to *Midway*, Spruance wrote, "The fact that Admiral Yamamoto with seven battleships, one carrier, cruisers, and destroyers was operating to the northwestward of Midway was not known to us for several months after the battle." (p.v.)
24. Interview with Spruance, September 5, 1964.
25. Ibid.
26. Insert to VF-6 unofficial log, May 27, 1942.
27. Interview with Fletcher, September 17, 1966.

CHAPTER 12
"On a Major Mission"

1. Midway Analysis, p. 22; *Midway*, p. 112.
2. Interview with Chigusa, December 15, 1964.
3. *Midway*, pp. 185–186, 256.

4. Ibid., pp. 112, 228; 255; *Imperial Japanese Navy*, p. 154.
5. *Midway*, p. 112; *Coral Sea, Midway and Submarine Actions*, pp. 169, 173.
6. *Midway*, pp. 111, 139; *Coral Sea, Midway and Submarine Actions*, p. 172.
7. *Midway*, p. 113.
8. Ugaki diary, May 28, 1942.
9. Miwa diary, May 28, 1942.
10. McCaul report.
11. Journal of VII Bomber Command Liaison Officer at Midway, Battle of Midway Supplementary Report R.S. No. 7-529. Hereafter Warner report.
12. Log of *Enterprise*, May 28, 1942.
13. Pearl Harbor Navy Yard War Diary; *Coral Sea, Midway and Submarine Actions*, p. 81.
14. Logs of *Hornet* and *Enterprise*, May 28, 1942.
15. Log of *Enterprise*, May 28, 1942.
16. Log of *Hornet*, May 28, 1942.
17. Midway Analysis, p. 69; interview with Burford. For an account of the adventures of *Aylwin* and *Monaghan* at Pearl Harbor, see *At Dawn We Slept*, pp. 528–529, 531.
18. Interview with Spruance, September 5, 1964.
19. *Midway*, pp. 113, 254; *Imperial Japanese Navy*, pp. 148–151.
20. *Midway*, pp. 93–94.
21. *Destroyer Captain*, p. 157.

CHAPTER 13

"Constant Vigilance Has to Be Maintained"

1. Ugaki diary, May 29, 1942; *Midway*, p. 113.
2. *Midway*, p. 113; *Imperial Japanese Navy*, pp. 128–131, 134.
3. *Imperial Japanese Navy*, pp. 68–72.
4. Ibid., pp. 56–58.
5. Ibid., pp. 48–54; *Midway*, p. 113.
6. *Midway*, p. 113; *Imperial Japanese Navy*, pp. 169–170.

7. *Midway*, pp. 85, 135, 252.
8. Miwa diary, May 30, 1942.
9. Ugaki diary, May 29, 1942; *Midway*, p. 115.
10. Interview which Barde held with RADM Logan C. Ramsey, July 1, 1966. Hereafter Ramsey/Barde interview.
11. Pearl Harbor War Diary, p. 518; *Coral Sea, Midway and Submarine Actions*, p. 81.
12. *Yorktown* Coral Sea Damage Report, p. 12.
13. Ibid.
14. Frank, Pat and Harrington, Joseph D., *Rendezvous at Midway: USS Yorktown and the Japanese Carrier Fleet*, New York, John Day, 1967, pp. 143–146. Hereafter *Rendezvous at Midway*.
15. Interview which Barde held with RADM Wallace C. Short, May 24, 1966. Hereafter Short/Barde interview.
16. Log of *Hornet*, May 28, 1942.
17. Log of *Enterprise*, May 28, 1942.
18. Logs of *Hornet* and *Enterprise*, May 28, 1942.
19. Interview with Spruance, September 5, 1964.
20. Ramsey/Barde interview, July 1, 1966.
21. McCaul report.
22. Warner report.
23. Nimitz report, June 28, 1942; Midway Analysis, pp. 66–67; *Coral Sea, Midway and Submarine Actions*, p. 97.
24. Ugaki diary, May 30, 1942; *Midway*, p. 119.
25. Ugaki diary, May 30, 1942.
26. Miwa diary, May 30, 1942.
27. *Midway*, pp. 120–121.

CHAPTER 14

"Not the Least Doubt About a Victory"

1. May 30, 1942.
2. Ibid.
3. Interview of Lt. Cmdr. C. C. Ray, USN, Communications Officer, USS *Yorktown*, in the Bureau of Aeronautics, July

15, 1942. Hereafter Official Ray interview.

4. *Coral Sea, Midway and Submarine Actions*, pp. 90, 97.

5. *Turning Point*, p. 69.

6. Interview with Fletcher, September 17,
1966.

7. *Nimitz*, p. 81n; *Coral Sea, Midway and
Submarine Actions*, pp. 80, 84.

8. Interview with Nimitz, September 4,
1964.

9. Interview with Kuroshima, December
13, 1964.

10. *Incredible Victory*, p. 35.

11. Miwa diary, June 21, 1942.

12. Ibid., May 31, 1942.

13. Ugaki diary, May 31, 1942.

14. Comparative figures used in this chapter
are taken from *Coral Sea, Midway and
Submarine Actions*, pp. 87–93, and *Midway*, Appendix 2, pp. 251–260.

15. Ibid.

16. *Incredible Victory*, p. 84.

17. June 3, 1942.

CHAPTER 15
"The Clock Was Running Ever Faster"

1. Logs of *Hornet* and *Enterprise*, May 30,
1942.

2. Letter, Cmdr. Logan C. Ramsey, USN
to CinCPAC, June 15, 1942, Subject: Air
Operations of Midway Defense Forces
during Battle of Midway May 30, 1942,
to June 6, 1942. Hereafter Ramsey report.

3. Encl. B, Contact Reports for period May
30–June 6, 1942, to letter, CO, U. S.
Naval Air Station, Midway Island, to
CinCPAC, 18 June 1942, Subject: Report of Engagement with Enemy, Battle
of Midway, May 30–June 7, 1942. Hereafter Report of Contacts.

4. Ramsey report; McCaul report;*Coral Sea,
Midway and Submarine Actions*, p. 96n.

5. Ramsey report.

6. McCaul report.

7. Ramsey report; Letter, CG 7th AF to

CinCPAC, July 17, 1942, Subject: Operational Report of Air Force Employment at Midway. Hereafter 7th AF
Report.

8. McCaul report.

9. "Never a Battle Like Midway," p. 52;
Marines at Midway, p. 24; McCall report.

10. Interview with Nimitz, September 4,
1964.

11. *Coral Sea, Midway and Submarine Actions*, pp. 86–87.

12. Logs of *Hornet* and *Enterprise*, May 31,
1942.

13. Japanese story, p. 6.

14. Genda statement.

15. For a thorough study of Genda's part in
the Pearl Harbor attack, see *At Dawn
We Slept*.

16. Genda statement.

17. Ugaki diary, June 1–3, 1942.

18. Miwa diary, June 1, 1942.

19. Ugaki diary, June 1, 1942.

20. *Coral Sea, Midway and Submarine Actions*, p. 97.

21. Miwa diary, June 1, 1942.

22. Ugaki diary, June 1, 1942.

23. For a full account of this operation, see
*Coral Sea, Midway and Submarine Ac-
tions*, pp. 65–68.

24. June 1, 1942.

25. VF-6 unofficial log.

26. Report of contacts.

27. Ramsey and McCaul reports.

28. *Midway*, p. 122.

29. Stimson diary, June 1, 1942.

CHAPTER 16
"In High Spirits and Full of Confidence"

1. Interview with Watanabe, October 6,
1964.

2. The following account of a typical day for
Yamamoto is based upon an interview
with Watanabe, September 30, 1964.

3. Interview with Nimitz, September 4,
1964.

4. Ugaki diary, June 2, 1942.

5. Ugaki and Miwa diaries, June 2, 1942.
6. Ugaki diary, June 2, 1942.
7. Japanese Story, p. 6.
8. Japanese Monograph No. 110, Submarine Operations in Second Phase Operations, Part I: April–August 1942, compiled by Capt. Tatsuwaka Shibuya, General Hq, FEC, Military History Division, Japanese Research Division; *Midway*, p. 123.
9. *Midway*, pp. 123–124.
10. Interview with Kuroshima, November 28, 1964.
11. Interview with Spruance, September 5, 1965; *Spruance*, p. 39.
12. Midway Analysis, p. 63; *Coral Sea, Midway and Submarine Actions,* pp. 156–157; logs of *Hornet* and *Enterprise*, June 1, 1942.
13. VF-6 unofficial log, June 2, 1942.
14. *Midway*, pp. 123–124.
15. Ibid., p. 126; Japanese Story, p. 6.
16. *Midway*, p. 127.
17. Ibid., pp. 127–128; Japanese Story, p. 6.
18. Japanese Story, pp. 6, 42; *Midway*, p. 128n.
19. "Tragic Battle."
20. Ugaki diary, June 3, 1942.
21. Ibid.
22. Ibid.
23. *Coral Sea, Midway and Submarine Actions*, p. 98.
24. Midway Analysis. pp. 62–63.

CHAPTER 17
"Take Off for Attack!"

1. *Midway*, pp. 137–139.
2. Ibid., p. 138.
3. Ibid., p. 139.
4. Ibid., pp. 139–140.
5. Ibid., p. 140; Midway Analysis, p. 24.
6. Diary of Capt. Tasuka Nakazawa, June 4, 1942. Courtesy of Chihaya. Hereafter Nakazawa diary.
7. Midway Analysis, p. 9.
8. *Midway*, p. 142.
9. Okumiya, Masatake and Horikoshi, Jiro, with Martin Caidin, *Zero!*, New York,

E.P. Dutton, 1956, p. 115. Hereafter *Zero!*
10. Ibid., pp. 115–116.
11. Ibid., p. 116.
12. Mizraki, Joe, "Samurai," *Wings,* December 1977, pp. 26–28.
13. *Zero!*, pp. 116–117. See also Editor's Note to "Samurai," op. cit., pp. 22, 25; Potter, John Deane, *Yamamoto: The Man Who Menaced America*, New York, Viking, 1965, pp. 241–242. Hereafter *Yamamoto*.
14. *Coral Sea, Midway and Submarine Actions*, p. 166n.
15. Ibid., pp. 173–174.
16. Ibid., p. 166.
17. Ibid., pp. 167, 170.
18. Ibid., p. 164; Midway Analysis, p. 44.
19. Midway Analysis, p. 44.
20. *Coral Sea, Midway and Submarine Actions*, pp. 172–174.
21. Ibid., p. 170.
22. Midway Analysis, p. 36.
23. *Coral Sea, Midway and Submarine Actions*, pp. 168–170.
24. Ibid., p. 168.
25. Ibid., pp. 171–172.
26. *Midway*, p. 141; Midway Analysis, p. 24.
27. Midway Analysis, pp. 15, 24; *Midway*, p. 141; Col. C. V. Glines, USAF, "The Forgotten War in the Aleutians," *Air Force Magazine*, March 1968, p. 77.
28. *Coral Sea, Midway and Submarine Actions*, pp. 176–177.
29. Stimson diary, June 3, 1942.
30. June 4, 1942.
31. Morgenthau diary, June 16, 1942.

CHAPTER 18
"Extra Luck Riding with Us"

1. Letter, Captain Jack Reid to Prange, December 10, 1966. Hereafter Reid letter.
2. Ibid.
3. Ibid.
4. Statement by Robert Swan which he prepared for Reid, who enclosed it with his letter of December 10, 1966. Hereafter Swan statement.

5. Ibid.
6. Reid letter.
7. Swan statement.
8. Reid letter.
9. Diary of U.S. Naval Air Station, Midway Island. Hereafter NAS diary.
10. Report of Contacts.
11. Reid letter.
12. Sweeney report. (See Chap. 19 n. 15.)
13. NAS diary; Ramsey report; Midway Analysis, p. 55; War Diary, Patrol Squadron 24.
14. Midway Analysis, p. 55; *Midway*, pp. 256–257.
15. Report of Contacts; NAS diary.
16. Swan statement; NAS diary; Report of Contacts.
17. NAS diary; Report of Contacts.
18. Reid letter.
19. Ibid.
20. NAS diary; Reid letter; Report of Contacts. Strangely enough, neither the NAS diary nor the Report of Contacts lists the important amplification of types of vessels. They record only the 8V55 report of eleven ships, their course and speed.
21. Swan statement.
22. Reid letter; Report of Contacts.
23. Reid letter.
24. Ugaki diary, June 4, 1942.
25. Reid letter.
26. *Destroyer Captain*, p. 99.
27. NAS diary.
28. Midway Analysis, p. 76; *Midway*, p. 135.
29. Interview with Watanabe, October 6, 1964.
30. Ugaki diary, June 4, 1942.
31. NAS diary; Report of Contacts; Ramsey report.
32. Letter, Capt. Cecil F. Faulkner, AC, to CG, VII Bomber Command, Hickam Field, TH, June 6, 1942, Subject: Special Mission. Hereafter Faulkner report.
33. Midway Mission Report, June 12, 1942, by Lt. W. A. Smith. This was a supplement to his original report of June 6. Hereafter Smith supplemental report; Ramsey report.
34. Ramsey report.
35. NAS diary; Report of Contacts; Smith supplemental report.

36. Narrative by Cmdr. John Ford, USNR, Photographic Experiences from Pearl Harbor, December 7, 1941–August 17, 1943. Office of Naval Records, Washington, D.C. Hereafter Ford narrative.

CHAPTER 19
"Even the Midst of the Pacific Is Small"

1. Log of *Hornet*, June 3, 1942.
2. Log of *Enterprise*, June 3, 1942.
3. *Nimitz*, pp. 91–92.
4. *Coral Sea, Midway and Submarine Actions*, p. 102.
5. *Midway*, p. 142.
6. Japanese Story, p. 12.
7. Ibid., p. 13.
8. Ibid.
9. *Midway*, p. 142.
10. Japanese Story, p. 13.
11. Miwa diary, June 4, 1942.
12. Ugaki diary, June 4, 1942.
13. NAS diary; Report of Contacts; Midway Analysis, pp. 76–77.
14. *Destroyer Captain*, pp. 99–100.
15. Letter, CO, 431st Bombardment Squadron (H), to CO, 11th Bombardment Group (H), Hickam Field, T. H., Subject: Combat Operations, Midway Area, June 3–4, 1942. Hereafter Sweeney report; NAS diary; Report of Contacts.
16. Faulkner report.
17. Letter, 1st Lt. Edward A. Steedman, to CG, 7th Bomber Command, Hickam Field, T.H., June 6, 1942, Subject: Special Mission. Hereafter Steedman report.
18. Sweeney report.
19. 7th AF report.
20. Midway Analysis, p. 80.
21. Ramsey report.
22. Ugaki diary, June 4, 1942.
23. Miwa diary, June 4, 1942.
24. Reid letter.
25. Swan statement.
26. Pratt, Fletcher, "The Mysteries of Midway," *Harper's*, July 1943, p. 13. Hereafter "Mysteries of Midway"; NAS diary.
27. U.S. Pacific Fleet and Pacific Ocean

Areas, Press Release No. 56, June 16, 1942, covering a broadcast over NBC at 1100–1114, June 16, 1942, over station KGU. Hereafter Press Release No. 56.

28. Letter, W. L. Richards, June 18, 1942, Subject: Night Torpedo Attack 3–4 June, report of.

29. Press release No. 56.

30. Ibid.; Richards report, op. cit.

31. Ibid.

32. Richards report, op. cit.

33. USSBS No. 252, Interrogation of Capt. Yasumi Toyama, IJN, chief of staff, DesRon 2, who was aboard *Jintsu* at the time: *Coral Sea, Midway and Submarine Actions*, pp. 99–100.

34. *Rengo Kantai*, pp. 80–81.

CHAPTER 20
"This Was to Be a Day of Days"

1. *Midway*, pp. 143–144.
2. Interviews with Fuchida, February 14, 1964, and September 1, 1967.
3. Ibid.
4. *Rengo Kantai*, p. 81.
5. Interview with Fuchida, September 1, 1967.
6. *Midway*, pp. 146, 153–154.
7. Interview with Fuchida, September 1, 1967.
8. Japanese Story, pp. 7, 11–13.
9. *Midway*, pp. 147–148.
10. Ibid. See also *Rengo Kantai*, p. 82.
11. *Rengo Kantai*, p. 82.
12. *Midway*, p. 149.
13. Genda statement.
14. Japanese Story, p. 3.
15. Ibid.
16. *Midway*, p. 150.
17. NAS diary.
18. *Midway*, p. 150; "Tragic Battle."
19. Interview with Fuchida, February 14, 1964.
20. *Midway*, p. 151; Japanese Story, p. 7.
21. Ibid; *Rengo Kantai*, p. 81.
22. *Midway*, p. 152; Genda Statement.
23. Japanese Story, pp. 42–43; *Rengo Kantai*, p. 81; *Midway*, p. 152.

24. Japanese Story, p. 7; Sakamoto material, Part 2.
25. Midway Analysis, p. 86.
26. Japanese Story, p. 13; Sakamoto material, Part 2.
27. Sakamoto Material, Part 2.
28. *Midway*, p. 148.
29. Sakamoto material, Part 2; undated questionnaire completed by Chuichi Yoshioka. Hereafter Yoshioka statement.
30. Genda statement.
31. *Midway*, p. 148.
32. Interview with Watanabe, October 6, 1964.

CHAPTER 21
"Hawks at Angels Twelve"

1. Ramsey report; Letter, Executive Officer, Motor Torpedo Boat Squadron One to Commander, Motor Torpedo Boat Squadron One, June 7, 1942, Subject: Report of Incidents in connection with participation of Motor Torpedo Boat Squadron One in battle of Midway, June 4–6, 1942. Hereafter PT Executive report.

2. Unpublished doctoral dissertation, "Midway: A Study in Command," which Barde prepared under Prange's direction, pp. 134–135. Hereafter "Study in Command."

3. Kimes interview.

4. Letter, CO, Marine Aircraft Group Twenty-Two to CinCPAC, June 7, 1942, Subject: Battle of Midway Islands, report of. Hereafter MAG-22 report.

5. "Study in Command."

6. Statements of 2d Lts. J. C. Musselman, Jr., and H. Phillips, June 6, 1942. Hereafter Musselman statement and Phillips statement, respectively.

7. Statement of 2d Lt. Elmer P. Thompson, USMCR (V), June 7, 1942. Hereafter Thompson statement.

8. Kimes interview.

9. Ibid.

10. NAS diary; "Study in Command."

11. Memorandum, CO Marine Aircraft

Group Twenty-Two to Senior Naval
Aviation Second Marine Aircraft Wing,
Present in Hawaiian Area, June 8, 1942,
Preliminary Report of Marine Aircraft
Group Twenty-Two of Battle of Mid-
way, June 4, 5, 6, 1942. Hereafter Kimes
report; Carey/Barde interview, July 1,
1966.

12. Report of Contacts; Midway Analysis; NAS
diary; Honolulu *Advertiser*, June 17, 1942.
13. Report of Contacts.
14. Thompson statement.
15. Letter, CO, 6th Defense Bn, Fleet Marine Force, to CO, NAS, June 13, 1942,
Subject: Report of Actions on morning
of June 4, 1942 and nights of June 4–6,
1942. Hereafter Shannon report.
16. McCaul report; Nimitz report, June 28,
1942.
17. Ramsey report; NAS diary; Honolulu
Advertiser, June 17, 1942.
18. Press Release No. 56.
19. NAS diary.
20. Japanese Story, p. 13.
21. Shannon report.
22. Thompson statement.
23. Statement of 2d Lt. C. M. Canfield,
USMCR, June 6, 1942. Hereafter Canfield statement.
24. McCaul report.
25. Statement of Capt. K. Armistead, USMC,
June 4, 1942. Hereafter Armistead statement; McCaul report.
26. Kimes interview.
27. Armistead statement; Kimes report.
28. Canfield Statement; "Never a Battle Like
Midway," p. 56.
29. Japanese Story, pp. 4, 42.
30. Carey/Barde interview, July 1, 1966.
31. Canfield statement.
32. Carey/Barde interview, July 1, 1966.
33. Statement of Capt. M. E. Carl, USMC,
June 6, 1942. Hereafter Carl statement.
34. Japanese Story, p. 43.
35. Statement of 2d Lt. Charles S. Hughes,
USMCR, June 4, 1942. Hereafter Hughes
statement.
36. Statement of 2d Lt. D. D. Irwin,
USMCR, June 6, 1942. Hereafter Irwin
statement.

37. Japanese Story, p. 43.
38. Irwin statement.
39. Statement of Capt. P. H. White, USMC,
June 6, 1942. Hereafter White statement.
40. Japanese Story, p. 14.
41. White statement.
42. Carey/Barde interview, July 1, 1966.
43. White Statement.
44. Armistead statement.
45. Statement of Capt. W. B. Humberd,
USMC, June 4, 1942.
46. Statement of 2d Lt. C. M. Kunz, USMCR,
June 4, 1942.
47. Statement of 2d Lt. W. V. Brooks,
USMCR, June 4, 1942.
48. Musselman statement.
49. Statement of 2d Lt. R. A. Corry, USMCR,
June 6, 1942.

CHAPTER 22
"There Is Need for a Second
Attack"

1. Shannon report.
2. Kimes interview.
3. Thompson statement.
4. Letter, CO Motor Torpedo Boat Squadron One to CinCPAC, June 9, 1942,
Subject: Report of Battle with Enemy
Forces at Midway Island on June 4 and
5, 1942. Hereafter MTB Sqdn One report.
5. Ford narrative.
6. Armistead statement; Carey/Barde interview, July 1, 1966.
7. Japanese Story, pp. 42–43, 68.
8. Thompson statement.
9. *Midway*, pp. 164–165.
10. "Never a Battle Like Midway," p. 56.
11. PT Executive report.
12. Japanese Story, p. 43.
13. Ibid., pp. 44–45.
14. Statement of 2d. Lt. Robert W. Vaupell,
USMCR (V), June 7, 1942. Hereafter
Vaupell statement.
15. Ford narrative.
16. "Never a Battle Like Midway," p. 56.
17. Ford narrative.

18. Japanese Story, p. 43; Kimes report.
19. Ford narrative.
20. Kimes interview; *Marines at Midway*, pp. 32, 38–39.
21. Ford narrative.
22. "Mysteries of Midway," p. 142.
23. "Never a Battle Like Midway," p. 56; Shannon report.
24. Japanese Story, pp. 43, 45; "Never a Battle Like Midway," p. 56.
25. Hughes statement.
26. Irwin statement.
27. Vaupell statement.
28. Thompson statement.
29. Warner report.
30. PT Executive report.
31. Japanese Story, p. 14.
32. Shannon report.
33. Kimes report.
34. "Never a Battle Like Midway," p. 56.
35. Japanese Story, p. 66.
36. NAS diary; Letter, CO Midway NAS to CinCPAC, June 18, 1942, Subject: Report of Engagement with Enemy, Battle of Midway, May 30–June 7, 1942. Hereafter Simard report; *Marines at Midway*, p. 32.
37. Japanese Story, pp. 7, 43–45, 67.
38. Ibid., p. 14.
39. Kimes report.
40. McCaul report.
41. Answers to Lt. Toshio Hashimoto to questionnaire. Hereafter Hashimoto statement.
42. Japanese Story, p. 14.

CHAPTER 23
"A Complete Failure"

1. Interview which Barde held with Ens. Albert K. Earnest, USN, April 28, 1966. Hereafter Earnest/Barde interview.
2. Ibid.; Lt. Harold H. Ferrier, USN, "Torpedo Squadron Eight, The Other Chapter," *United States Naval Institute Proceedings*, October, 1964, p. 75. Hereafter "The Other Chapter."
3. *Marines at Midway*, p. 23.
4. Earnest/Barde interview, April 28, 1966.
5. Ibid.; "The Other Chapter," pp. 74–75.
6. Earnest/Barde interview, April 28, 1966.
7. Ibid.; Kimes report.
8. Nimitz report, June 28, 1942.
9. Earnest/Barde interview, April 28, 1966.
10. Japanese Story, p. 14.
11. Earnest/Barde interview, April 28, 1966.
12. "The Other Chapter," p. 76.
13. Earnest/Barde interview, April 28, 1966.; "The Other Chapter," p. 76.
14. Nimitz report, June 28, 1942.
15. Letter, Capt. James F. Collins, Jr. to CG, VII Bomber Command, June 6, 1942, Subject: B-26 in Battle of Midway. Hereafter Collins report.
16. Japanese Story, p. 14.
17. Collins report.
18. Letter, 1st Lt. James P. Muri to CG, VII Bomber Command, June 6, 1942, Subject: Report of Combat: B26 Airplane A. P. #42-1394. Hereafter Muri report.
19. Interview with Iyozo Fujita, December 29, 1964. Hereafter Fujita.
20. Collins report.
21. Japanese Story, p. 14.
22. "Tragic Battle."
23. Interview with Fuchida, February 14, 1964.
24. "Tragic Battle."
25. Collins report.
26. Muri report.
27. Collins and Muri reports.
28. Craven, Wesley Frank and Cate, James Lea, ed., *The Army Air Forces in World War II, Vol. I, Plans and Early Operations, January 1939 to August 1942*, Chicago, University of Chicago Press, 1948, p. 459. Hereafter *AAF in WWII*.
29. Japanese Story, pp. 47–49; 64–65. Exact Japanese claims are difficult if not impossible to figure out, as Nagumo's statistics are not consistent.
30. Ibid., p. 14.
31. Genda statement.
32. *Midway*, p. 161; Japanese Story, p. 7; *Rengo Kantai*, p. 83; *Coral Sea, Midway and Submarine Actions*, pp. 106–107.
33. Genda statement; Japanese Story, p. 14.
34. Genda statement.

35. Kusaka statement.
36. Genda statement.

                 CHAPTER 24
               "There They Are!"

 1. Japanese Story, p. 13.
 2. "Study in Command," p. 206.
 3. Japanese Story, p. 13; Midway, p. 159.
 4. Japanese Story, p. 15.
 5. Kusaka statement.
 6. Genda Statement.
 7. Midway, pp. 167–168.
 8. Kusaka statement.
 9. Japanese Story, p. 15.
10. Ibid., p. 7; Rengo Kantai, p. 84; Genda statement.
11. Japanese Story, pp. 13–14.
12. Midway, pp. 168–169.
13. Japanese Story, p. 15.
14. Letter, CO Marine Scout-Bombing Squadron Two Forty-One to CO, Marine Aircraft Group 22, June 12, 1942, Subject: Report of Activities of VMSB-241 during June 4 and June 5, 1942. Hereafter VMSB-241 report.
15. Statement of 2d Lt. Thomas F. Moore, Jr., USMCR (V), June 4, 1942. Hereafter Moore statement.
16. Kimes report.
17. Statement of 2d Lt. Harold G. Schlendering, June 4, 1942. Hereafter Schlendering statement.
18. Statement of Capt. Elmer G. Glidden, Jr., USMCR (V), June 4, 1942. Hereafter Glidden statement.
19. Interview with Fujita, December 29, 1964.
20. Glidden statement.
21. Japanese Story, p. 54.
22. Midway, pp. 162–163.
23. Statement of 1st Lt. Daniel Iverson, Jr., USMCR (V), June 7, 1942. Hereafter Iverson statement.
24. Japanese Story, p. 53.
25. Iverson statement.
26. VMSB-241 report.
27. Moore statement.

28. Statement of Capt. R. L. Blain, USMC. Hereafter Blain statement.
29. Schlendering statement.
30. VMSB-241 report.
31. Interview with Fujita, December 29, 1964.
32. VMSB-241 report.

                 CHAPTER 25
          "The Japanese Were Not As Yet
                    Checked"

 1. Japanese Story, p. 15; Midway, p. 168.
 2. Turning Point, p. 86.
 3. Japanese Story, p. 15.
 4. Rengo Kantai, pp. 83–84; Kusaka statement.
 5. Japanese Story, p. 15.
 6. Ramsey report.
 7. Sweeney report.
 8. Japanese Story, p. 15.
 9. Midway, p. 168.
10. Kusaka statement.
11. Genda statement.
12. Kusaka statement.
13. Midway, p. 163.
14. Ibid., p. 162.
15. "Action with Enemy" form, Capt. C. E. Wuerterle.
16. "Action with Enemy" form, Lt. H. S. Grundman.
17. "Action with Enemy" form, Lt. Col. B. E. Allen.
18. Japanese Story, p. 53.
19. Faulkner report.
20. Steedman report.
21. Andrews report.
22. Faulkner and Steedman reports.
23. Sweeney report; Sweeney's "Action with Enemy" form; Japanese Story, p. 16.
24. "Action with Enemy" form, Capt. Charles E. Gregory.
25. Midway, p. 162.
26. Warner report.
27. Letter, CinCPAC to Cominch, July 25, 1942, Subject: Battle of Midway—Supplementary Report. Hereafter Nimitz Supplementary Report.

28. Log of *Nautilus*, June 4, 1942; CO, USS *Nautilus* patrol report to Commander, Submarine Division 41, June 7, 1942, Narrative of June 4, 1942. Hereafter *Nautilus* narrative.
29. VMSB-241 report.
30. Statement of 2d Lt. George E. Koutelas, USMCR (V), June 7, 1942. Hereafter Koutelas statement.
31. *Marines at Midway*, p. 22.
32. Japanese Story, p. 16; VMSB-241 report.
33. Kusaka statement.
34. *Midway*, p. 176.
35. State of 2d Lt. Sumner H. Whitten, USMCR (V), June 7, 1942.
36. Statement of 2d Lt. Daniel L. Cummings, USMCR (V), June 7, 1942.
37. VMSB-241 report.
38. Japanese Story, p. 16; *Coral Sea, Midway and Submarine Actions*, p. 111.
39. Statement of Capt. Leon M. Williamson, USMCR (V), June 7, 1942. Hereafter Williamson statement.
40. Koutelas statement.
41. Cummings statement, op. cit.: PT Executive report.
42. Statement of 2d Lt. Allan H. Ringblom, USMCR (V), June 7, 1942, Hereafter Ringblom statement: PT Executive report.
43. VMSB-241 report.
44. Japanese Story, p. 16.
45. Kimes interview.
46. Nimitz report.

CHAPTER 26
"What the Hell Is Headquarters Doing?"

1. Japanese Story, p. 7.
2. Kusaka statement; *Rengo Kantai*, p. 85.
3. Kusaka statement.
4. Japanese Story, p. 7.
5. "Tragic Battle."
6. Japanese Story, p. 6.
7. Genda statement.
8. Genda and Kusaka statements; "Tragic Battle"; *Midway*, pp. 169–170. This message does not appear in Nagumo's log in Japanese Story.
9. Ugaki diary, June 8, 1942.
10. Genda statement.
11. Kusaka statement.
12. Genda statement.
13. Japanese Story, p. 16.
14. *Midway*, pp. 170–171.
15. "Tragic Battle."
16. *Midway*, p. 164.
17. Hashimoto statement.
18. "Tragic Battle."
19. Japanese Story, pp. 16–17.
20. Kusaka statement.
21. *Midway*, p. 171.
22. Japanese Story, p. 7.
23. Ibid., p. 8.
24. Ibid., p. 16.
25. Ibid., p. 17.
26. Ugaki diary, June 8, 1942.
27. Interview with Kuroshima, November 28, 1964.
28. Japanese Story, p. 17.
29. Ibid.

CHAPTER 27
"At Last They Have Come"

1. Interview with Spruance, September 5, 1964.
2. Log of *Enterprise*, June 4, 1942.
3. Interview with Spruance, September 5, 1964.
4. Ibid.
5. Interview with Fletcher, September 17, 1966.
6. Midway Analysis, p. 121.
7. Letter, CO, USS *Enterprise*, to CinCPAC, June 8, 1942, Subject: Battle of Midway Island, June 4–6, 1942—Report of. Hereafter *Enterprise* report; interview with Fletcher, September 17, 1966; Midway Analysis, p. 125.
8. *Coral Sea, Midway and Submarine Actions*, p. 113.
9. Interview with Spruance, September 5, 1964.
10. Letter, Commander Task Force Sixteen

to CinCPAC, June 16, 1942, Subject: Battle of Midway; forwarding of reports. Hereafter Spruance report.

11. Midway Analysis, pp. 122–123.

12. George Gay, *Sole Survivor*, Naples, Fla., 1979, p. 108. Hereafter *Sole Survivor*.

13. Ibid., p. 95.

14. Narrative by Lt. George Gay, Torpedo Squadron 8, Midway, Solomons, Munda, October 12, 1943. Hereafter Gay narrative.

15. *Incredible Victory*, p. 142.

16. Interview which Barde conducted with RADM Clarence Wade McClusky, USN (Ret), June 30, 1966. Hereafter McClusky/Barde interview.

17. Midway Analysis, p. 123; Spruance report.

18. Letter, Commander Cruisers, Task Force Sixteen, to Commander Task Force Sixteen, June 11, 1942, Subject: Report of Action, June 4, 1942. Hereafter TF 16 Cruisers report.

19. *Coral Sea, Midway and Submarine Actions*, p. 114.

20. Logs of *Enterprise* and *Hornet*, June 4, 1942; *Enterprise* report; Letter, CO, USS *Hornet* to CinCPAC, June 13, 1942, Subject: Report of Action—June 4–6, 1942. Hereafter *Hornet* report; Midway Analysis, p. 124.

21. Japanese Story, p. 17.

22. Letter, Air Operations Officer, USS *Hornet* to CO, *Hornet*, June 12, 1942, Subject: Defects Observed During the Action Off Midway on June 4, 1942. Hereafter *Hornet* Air Operations report.

23. Letter, CO, USS *Enterprise* to CinCPAC, June 13, 1942, Subject: Air Battle of the Pacific, June 4–6, 1942, report of. Hereafter *Enterprise* supplementary report.

24. Log of *Nautilus*, June 4, 1942; *Nautilus* narrative.

25. Midway Analysis, p. 126.

26. Letter, Capt. James E. Vose, USN (Ret), to Barde, January 9, 1967; Midway Analysis, pp. 129–130.

27. Letter, RADM W. F. Rodee, USN (Ret), to Barde, October 18. 1966.

28. *Incredible Victory*, p. 151.

29. Interview which Barde conducted with Capt. Edgar E. Stebbins, May 25, 1966. Hereafter Stebbins/Barde interview. Also interview which Barde conducted with Capt. A. J. Brassfield, USN, November 6, 1966. Hereafter Brassfield/Barde interview.

30. Vose letter; Ramsey/Barde interview.

31. Letter from Capt. T. N. Guillory, USN (Ret), to Barde, April 27, 1967.

32. *Incredible Victory*, p. 179; *Hornet* report.

33. Spruance report.

34. *Hornet* report.

35. *Coral Sea, Midway and Submarine Actions*, p. 122n.

36. Interview which Barde held with Capt. S. E. Ruehlow, USN (Ret), May 25, 1966.

37. Gay narrative.

38. Griffin, Alexander R., *A Ship to Remember: The Saga of the Hornet*, New York, Howell Soskin 1943, pp. 37–39.

39. Gay narrative.

40. Japanese Story, p. 17.

41. Genda statement.

42. Gay narrative; Memorandum from R. A. Ofstie to CinCPAC, June 7, 1942, Subject: Report of Action, 4 June 1942, by Ensign G. H. Gay, USNR.

43. Kusaka statement.

44. Gay narrative.

45. Enclosure H to *Hornet* report.

46. Gay narrative.

47. Interview with Fujita, December 29, 1964.

48. Gay narrative.

49. Enclosure C to *Hornet* report.

50. Interview which Barde conducted with Robert E. Laub, May 13, 1966. Hereafter Laub/Barde interview.

CHAPTER 28
"They Were Almost Wiped Out"

1. Midway Analysis, pp. 127–128; Encl. A to TF 16 Cruisers report; *Hornet* Air Op-

erations report; Letter, Commander, Fighting Squadron SIX to Commander ENTERPRISE Air Group, June 8, 1942, Subject: Narrative of Events 4–6, June 1942. Hereafter VF-6 action report.

2. *Coral Sea, Midway and Submarine Actions,* p. 122; *Incredible Victory,* p. 190.
3. "Spruance: Picture of the Admiral," p. 147.
4. Midway Analysis, pp. 127–128; Encl A to TF 16 Cruisers report.
5. Laub/Barde interview.
6. Japanese Story, p. 18.
7. Letter, Lt. Cmdr. Stephen B. Smith, USN (Ret), to Barde, February 3, 1967.
8. Japanese Story, p. 19.
9. Genda statement.
10. Japanese Story, p. 19.
11. Ibid., p. 18.
12. *Nautilus* narrative.
13. Genda statement.
14. *Enterprise* supplementary report; Laub/Barde interview.
15. *Midway,* p. 176.
16. Genda statement.
17. *Midway,* p. 176.
18. Laub/Barde interview.
19. Letter, Douglas M. Cossett to Barde, July 20, 1966.
20. Letters, Capt. Shigeo Hirayama, JMSDF, June 6 and 10, 1966, to Barde.
21. United States Strategic Bombing Survey (USSBS) *Interrogation of Japanese Officials,* 2 vol, Washington, 1947. Interrogations of Lt. Taneyo Namba, October 23, 1947 and of Ens. Koju Kanechiku, October 29, 1947.
22. USSBS interrogation of Petty Officer 1/c Takeshiko Suzuki, September 5, 1947.
23. USSBS interrogations of Namba, op. cit., and of Machinist Mate Yoshio Saito.
24. Nearly all the interrogees agreed upon the means of execution. The exact date is unknown.
25. Hirayama letter, June 6, 1966.
26. Interview which Barde held with RADM Murr E. Arnold, USN (Ret), May 6, 1966. Hereafter Arnold/Barde interview.
27. *Rendezvous at Midway,* pp. 167–168.
28. Interview which Barde conducted with

Capt. Harry B. Gibbs, USN, March 1967. Hereafter Gibbs/Barde interview.
29. Letter, Admiral J. S. Thach, USN, November 26, 1965 to Barde. Hereafter Thach letter.
30. Japanese Story, p. 19.
31. Interviews with Fujita, December 29, 1946 and January 4, 1965.
32. Letter, The Commanding Officer, USS *Yorktown* to CinCPAC, June 18, 1942, Subject: Report of Action for June 4, 1942 and June 6, 1942. Hereafter *Yorktown* report; *Hornet* log, June 4, 1942; *Rendezvous at Midway,* p. 170.
33. Interview with Fujita, January 4, 1965.
34. Letter, Cmdr. W. G. Esders, USN (Ret) to Barde, October 10, 1966.
35. *Midway,* p. 175.
36. Esders letter, op. cit.
37. USSBS interrogations of Lt. Kiyosumi Tanikawa, December 15, 1947, and April 12, 1948, and of Petty Officer 2d Class Shigetoshi Kuramochi, February 26 and June 10, 1948. The identity of the prisoner is a matter of record, but Prange believed that publication would only cause needless pain. According to a survivor of VT-3, the ensign was "very highly thought of and admired by all." Esders letter, op. cit.
38. See for example Midway Analysis, p. 131; *Coral Sea, Midway and Submarine Actions,* p. 121; "Never a Battle Like Midway," p. 61.
39. *Rendezvous at Midway,* p. 170.
40. Japanese Story, pp. 18–19.
41. Ibid., p. 19.

CHAPTER 29
"A Burning Hell"

1. McClusky/Barde interview, June 30, 1966; Midway Analysis, p. 131.
2. Interview which Barde held with Lt. Comdr. Richard H. Best, USN (Ret), May 15, 1966. Hereafter Best/Barde interview.

3. McClusky/Barde interview, June 30, 1966.

4. Interview with Spruance, September 5, 1964.

5. McClusky/Barde interview, June 30, 1966.

6. *Enterprise* report, June 13, 1942; Nimitz report, June 28, 1942.

7. McClusky/Barde interview, June 30, 1966.

8. *Coral Sea, Midway and Submarine Actions,* p. 122.

9. VB-6 Action Report; letter, Captain T. F. Schneider to Barde, May 31, 1966.

10. Schneider letter, op. cit.

11. Best/Barde interview, May 15, 1966.

12. Ibid.; McClusky/Barde interview, June 30, 1966; interview which Barde held with RADM W. Earl Gallaher, USN (Ret), June 29, 1966. Hereafter Gallaher/Barde interview.

13. Barde/Best interview, May 15, 1966; VB-6 Action Report.

14. Genda statement; *Incredible Victory,* p. 291. Lord questioned Kusaka and Lt. Comdr. Otojiro Sasabe, Nagumo's Navigation Officer, closely on this point.

15. Barde/Best interview, May 15, 1966.

16. Genda statement.

17. Japanese Story, p. 19.

18. Genda statement.

19. Replies by Capt. Takahisa Amagai to questionnaire. Hereafter Amagai statement; Lt. Comdr Sesu Mitoya, "I Fought the Americans at Midway," contained in Major Howard Oleck's compilation, *Heroic Battles of World War II,* New York, Belmont Books 1962, p. 154. Hereafter "I Fought the Americans."

20. "I Fought the Americans," p. 154.

21. Japanese Story, pp. 9, 19, 53.

22. Ibid., p. 9; Gallaher/Barde interview, June 29, 1966.

23. "I Fought the Americans," p. 154.

24. Ibid., pp. 154–155; Japanese Story, pp. 9, 53.

25. Japanese Story, pp. 9, 53.

26. Amagai statement.

27. Japanese Story, p. 9.

28. Amagai statement.

29. Japanese Story, p. 53.

30. Ibid., p. 9; Interviews with Fuchida, February 14, 1964 and September 1, 1967; *Midway,* p. 177.

31. Best/Barde interview, May 15, 1966.

32. *Midway,* p. 177.

33. Interview with Fuchida, September 3, 1967.

34. Japanese Story, p. 52.

35. Genda statement.

36. Japanese Story, pp. 9, 52; "Tragic Battle."

37. Interviews with Fuchida, February 14, 1964 and September 1, 1967.

38. Japanese Story, p. 52.

39. "Tragic Battle"; *Midway,* p. 177.

40. Genda statement.

41. Kusaka statement.

42. Genda statement.

43. "Tragic Battle."

44. *Midway,* pp. 178–179; interview with Fuchida, September 1, 1967.

45. Interview with Fuchida, September 1, 1967.

46. Kusaka statement; Japanese Story, p. 9.

47. Japanese Story, p. 20.

48. Kusaka statement.

49. Ibid., *Rengo Kantai,* p. 86.

50. Japanese Story, pp. 4, 20.

51. Kusaka statement; *Rengo Kantai,* pp. 86–87; "Tragic Battle."

52. Interview with Fuchida, September 1, 1967.

53. Genda statement.

CHAPTER 30
"A Calamity Like This"

1. *Incredible Victory,* p. 290.

2. Arnold/Barde interview.

3. Letter, June 7, 1942, from Commander, Bombing Squadron Three to Commander, *Yorktown* Air Group, Subject: Attack conducted 4 June 1942 on Japanese carriers located 156 miles NW Midway Island; narrative concerning. Hereafter Leslie VB-3 Action Report.

4. Letter, June 10, 1942, Commander Bombing Squadron Three to Command-

ing Officer, USS *Enterprise,* Subject: Report of Actions—period 4 June 1942 to 6 June 1942, inclusive. Hereafter Shumway VB-3 Action Report. Leslie and Shumway had become separated during the action, and Shumway submitted a report as acting commander.

5. Interview which Barde held with RADM Paul A. Holmberg, June 3, 1966. Hereafter Holmberg/Barde interview.
6. Leslie and Shumway VB-3 Action Reports; Holmberg/Barde interview.
7. Leslie and Shumway VB-3 Action Reports.
8. Leslie VB-3 Action Report.
9. Ibid.
10. *Imperial Japanese Navy,* pp. 175, 179.
11. Letter, Leslie to Admiral W. W. Smith, December 15, 1964. Courtesy of Barde.
12. *Imperial Japanese Navy,* p. 181.
13. Leslie VB-3 Action Report; interview which Barde held with RADM Maxwell F. Leslie, USN (Ret), July 25, 1965. Hereafter Leslie/Barde interview.
14. Leslie VB-3 Action Report.
15. Holmberg/Barde interview, June 3, 1966.
16. Shumway VB-3 Action Report.
17. Japanese Story, pp. 10, 53.
18. Holmberg/Barde interview, June 3, 1966.
19. USSBS No. 165, Interrogation of Capt. Hisashi Ohara.
20. Japanese Story, p. 10.
21. "Tragic Battle."
22. "Study in Command," pp. 270–271; Japanese Story, p. 10.
23. Japanese Story, p. 10; *Midway,* p. 188.
24. *Midway,* pp. 188–189.
25. Shumway VB-3 report.
26. *Incredible Victory,* p. 173.
27. Shumway VB-3 report.
28. Official Ray interview.
29. Holmberg/Barde interview, June 3, 1966; Leslie VB-3 Action Report.
30. Midway Analysis, p. 133.
31. McClusky/Barde interview, June 30, 1966; VF-6 unofficial log.
32. Clarence E. Dickinson, *The Flying Guns,* New York, Charles Scribner's Sons, 1942, pp. 155–157. Hereafter *Flying Guns.*
33. Ibid., pp. 162–166.
34. Interview which Barde held with Capt.

35. Joe E. Penland, USN (Ret), May 18, 1966.
35. Honolulu *Advertiser,* June 17, 1942.
36. Best/Barde interview, May 16, 1966.
37. VF-6 unofficial log; *Incredible Victory,* p. 176; *Flying Guns,* p. 159.
38. Interview with Fujita, January 4, 1965.
39. "Tragic Battle"; *Incredible Victory,* p. 185.

CHAPTER 31
"We, with *Hiryu* Alone"

1. Japanese Story, p. 21.
2. Hashimoto statement.
3. Letter, CinCPAC to CNO, June 28, 1942, Subject: Interrogation of Japanese Prisoners rescued at Sea off Midway on 19 June 1942. Hereafter Interrogation of Japanese Prisoners.
4. Replies which Lt. Cmdr. Takeo Kyuma submitted to a questionnaire. Hereafter Kyuma statement.
5. Japanese Story, p. 8; Hashimoto statement; *Incredible Victory,* p. 94.
6. Japanese Story, p. 21.
7. Ibid., p. 22.
8. *Rengo Kantai,* pp. 87–88.
9. Japanese Story, p. 22.
10. *Yorktown* report; log of *Astoria,* June 4, 1942; Letter, CO *Hammann* to CinCPAC, June 16, 1942, Subject: Action Report 4–6 June 1942. Hereafter *Hammann* report. All this destroyer's records were lost when she sank, so her captain prepared this report from memory.
11. *Yorktown* report; *Rendezvous at Midway,* p. 182.
12. *Rendezvous at Midway,* p. 183.
13. *Yorktown* report.
14. Brassfield/Barde interview, October 30, 1966; *Morning News,* Enid, Okla., July 19, 1942.
15. A. J. Brassfield, USN, VF-42 Report of Action, June 4, 1942. Although the report does not so indicate, it was submitted to the CO, VF-3. Capt. Brassfield gave a copy to Barde. Hereafter Brassfield report.
16. Japanese Story, pp. 22–23.

17. *Yorktown* report.
18. Ibid.
19. Ibid.; interview which Barde held with Capt. C. N. Conaster, USN, May 11, 1966.
20. *Yorktown* report; Letter, USS *Yorktown*, The Executive Officer to the Commanding Officer, June 16, 1942, Subject: Executive Officer's Report of Action for Period of June 4–June 7, 1942. Hereafter *Yorktown* Executive report.
21. *Yorktown* report.
22. Ibid.; *Yorktown* Executive report; *Turning Point*, p. 118.
23. Interview with Fletcher, September 17, 1966.
24. Letter, CO, *Astoria* to CinCPAC, June 11, 1942, Subject: Action Report—Sea area North of Midway Island June 4, 1942. Hereafter *Astoria* report; Tuleja, Thaddeus V., *Climax at Midway*, New York, W.W. Norton p. 159. Hereafter *Climax at Midway*.
25. *Astoria* report.
26. Log of *Enterprise*, June 4, 1942.
27. Logs of *Balch*, *Vincennes*, and *Enterprise*, June 4, 1942.
28. Log of *Hornet*, June 4, 1942.
29. Comments written for Prange by VADM William R. Smedberg, III, July 27, 1977, concerning certain admirals at the time of Pearl Harbor. At that time Ingersoll was Assistant CNO.

CHAPTER 32
"Determined to Sink an Enemy Ship"

1. "Study in Command," pp. 301–302.
2. *Rengo Kantai*, p. 88.
3. Hashimoto statement.
4. Hashiguchi statement.
5. Hashimoto statement.
6. Japanese Story, p. 8; Hashiguchi statement.
7. Hashiguchi statement.
8. Hashimoto statement.
9. Japanese Story, p. 25.
10. Hashimoto statement.
11. *Yorktown* report.

12. Letter, Milton Tootle, IV. to Barde, November 9, 1966; Honolulu *Advertiser*, June 13, 1942; Letter, CO *Anderson* to CinCPAC, June 5, 1942, Subject: Report Required by U.S. Navy Regulations, Art. 712, concerning engagement with Japanese carrier based planes, near Midway Island, on June 4, 1942. Hereafter *Anderson* report.
13. *Coral Sea, Midway and Submarine Actions*, p. 135.
14. Japanese Story, p. 26.
15. Hashimoto statement.
16. Japanese Story, p. 26.
17. Hashimoto statement.
18. *Yorktown* report; Letter, The Commanding Officer, *Yorktown* to Chief, Bureau of Ships, Subject: War Damage Reports. Hereafter *Yorktown* Damage Report.
19. Ibid.
20. *Yorktown* report.
21. Log of *Balch*, June 4, 1942.
22. Interview with Fletcher, September 17, 1966.
23. *Yorktown* report.
24. Interview which Barde conducted with VADM Elliott Buckmaster, March 14, 1966. Hereafter Buckmaster/Barde interview; *Incredible Victory*, p. 227.
25. *Yorktown* report; *Rendezvous at Midway*, p. 213.
26. Midway Analysis, p. 140; *Coral Sea, Midway and Submarine Actions*, p. 136n.
27. Shumway VB-3 report; CO, VS-6 report of action, June 4–6, 1942 to CO, USS *Enterprise*, 21 June 1942. Hereafter VS-6 Action report; Midway Analysis, p. 140.
28. *Coral Sea, Midway and Submarine Actions*, p. 141n; *Turning Point*, pp. 125–126; *Spruance*, p. 49; *Incredible Victory*, pp. 231–232. Various sources give slightly different terminology and timing of this exchange. For example, Midway Analysis, p. 142, gives 1816 as time of receipt. This would be well after the attack on *Hiryu* was over. (Smith states the exchange happened during launching.)
29. Hashimoto statement.
30. "Tragic Battle."

31. Japanese Story, p. 27.
32. Commander, Bombing Squadron Six, report of action during 4–6 June 1942 to CO, USS *Enterprise*, June 10, 1942. Hereafter VB-6 Action Report.
33. Japanese Story, p. 29.
34. Midway Analysis, p. 141.
35. "Tragic Battle."
36. Gallaher/Barde interview.
37. Japanese Story, p. 54.
38. "Study in Command," p. 317.
39. Japanese Story, p. 54.
40. "Tragic Battle"; statements of Hyuma and Hashimoto.
41. Hashimoto statement.
42. VB-6 Action Report.
43. Leslie VB-3 Action Report; Japanese Story, p. 58.
44. War diary, Bombing Squadron Eight, June 1942; Midway Analysis, p. 142.
45. Japanese Story, pp. 56–57.
46. See for example Wuerterle's "Action with Enemy" form and letter, 1st. Lt. Robert B. Andrews, to CG, VII Bomber Command, Hickam Field, TH, June 6, 1942, Subject: Special Mission. Hereafter Andrews report.
47. VMSB-241 report.

CHAPTER 33
"Don't Let Another Day Like This Come to Us Again!"

1. Japanese Story, pp. 20–21.
2. Ugaki diary, June 8, 1942.
3. Interview with Kuroshima, December 5, 1964.
4. Interview with Watanabe, October 6, 1964.
5. Ibid., October 8, 1964.
6. Interview with Kuroshima, December 5, 1964.
7. Interview with Watanabe, October 8, 1964.
8. Ugaki diary, June 8, 1942.
9. Interview with Watanabe, October 8, 1964.
10. Ibid.
11. Interview with Kuroshima, December 5, 1964.
12. Japanese Story, p. 23.
13. "Tragic Battle"; Kusaka statement.
14. Japanese Story, p. 22.
15. Ibid., pp. 23–37.
16. Ibid., p. 24.
17. Ibid.
18. Interview with Kuroshima, December 5, 1964.
19. Ugaki diary, June 8, 1964.
20. Ibid.
21. Japanese Story, p. 25.
22. Ibid.
23. Ugaki diary, June 8, 1942.
24. Japanese Story, p. 27.
25. *Rengo Kantai*, p. 89.
26. Japanese Story, p. 11.
27. Ugaki diary, June 8, 1942.
28. Japanese Story, p. 29; Ugaki diary, June 8, 1942.
29. Ugaki diary, June 8, 1942.
30. *Midway*, p. 219.
31. Ugaki diary, June 8, 1942.
32. Warner report.
33. Ramsey report.
34. Japanese Story, p. 30.
35. Ugaki diary, June 8, 1942.
36. Interview with Spruance, September 5, 1964.
37. *Turning Point*, p. 59.
38. Japanese Story, p. 30.
39. *Midway*, pp. 202–203.
40. Japanese Story, p. 10; Ugaki diary, June 8, 1942.
41. Kusaka statement; *Rengo Kantai*, p. 89.
42. Japanese Story, p. 31.
43. Ibid., p. 34.
44. Ugaki diary, June 8, 1942.
45. Japanese Story, p. 34.
46. *Midway*, p. 213.
47. *Destroyer Captain*, p. 101. Throughout his book, Hara made a number of affectionate, respectful references to Nagumo.
48. Japanese Story, p. 11.
49. Ugaki diary, June 8, 1942.
50. Japanese Story, p. 35.
51. Ibid., pp. 11, 35–36.
52. Ugaki diary, June 8, 1942.

53. Japanese Story, p. 36.
54. Ibid.
55. Ugaki diary, June 8, 1942.

CHAPTER 34
"There Is No Hope"

1. Japanese Story, p. 29.
2. Ibid., p. 30.
3. Ibid., p. 31.
4. "Tragic Battle."
5. Japanese Story, p. 34.
6. "Tragic Battle"; Japanese Story, p. 10.
7. Nautilus narrative.
8. Midway, p. 186. Imperial Japanese Navy, pp. 179, 181.
9. Log of Nautilus, June 4, 1942; Nautilus narrative.
10. "I Fought the Americans," p. 155.
11. Ibid.; "Tragic Battle".
12. Log of Nautilus, June 4, 1942; Nautilus narrative; Coral Sea, Midway and Submarine Actions, p. 129n.
13. Amagai statement.
14. "Tragic Battle."
15. Amagai statement.
16. Ibid.; Japanese Story, p. 9.
17. Japanese Story, p. 29.
18. Ibid., p. 30.
19. Nautilus narrative.
20. "Tragic Battle."
21. "I Fought the Americans," p. 155.
22. Japanese Story, p. 9.
23. Nautilus narrative.
24. Japanese Story, p. 35.
25. Kyuma statement.
26. Ibid.
27. Ibid.
28. Ibid.; Hashiguchi statement.
29. Japanese Story, p. 9; Midway, pp. 197–198.
30. Kyuma statement.
31. Japanese Story, p. 9.
32. "Tragic Battle."
33. Kyuma statement.
34. Japanese Story, pp. 9–10.
35. Incredible Victory, p. 251.
36. Japanese Story, p. 39.

37. Ibid., p. 11.
38. Ibid.; Midway, pp. 199, 225.
39. "Interrogation of Japanese Prisoners."
40. Interviews with Fuchida, April 19 and 21, 1964.
41. "Interrogation of Japanese Prisoners."

CHAPTER 35
"I Will Apologize to the Emperor"

1. Japanese Story, pp. 21–22.
2. Ibid., p. 9; Midway, pp. 181–182.
3. Japanese Story, p. 23; Incredible Victory, p. 183.
4. Interview with Fujita, January 4, 1965.
5. Japanese Story, pp. 9, 25.
6. Ibid., pp. 26–27.
7. Ibid., p. 34; Midway, p. 182.
8. Japanese Story, pp. 9, 35–36.
9. Ibid., p. 36; Ugaki diary, June 8, 1942.
10. "Tragic Battle"; Midway, pp. 182–183.
11. Japanese Story, p. 38; Ugaki diary, June 8, 1942.
12. Interview with Watanabe, November 24, 1964.
13. Ugaki diary, June 8, 1942.
14. Interview with Watanabe, November 24, 1964.
15. Japanese Story, p. 36.
16. Interview with Watanabe, November 24, 1964; Ugaki diary, June 8, 1942.
17. Japanese Story, p. 60.
18. "Tragic Battle"; Midway, pp. 182–184.
19. Japanese Story, p. 38; "Tragic Battle."

CHAPTER 36
"Why Should I Not Sleep Soundly?"

1. Ford narrative.
2. Written statement which Lt. Cmdr. Yahachi Tanabe gave to Prange upon the occasion of their interview of November 30, 1964. Hereafter Tanabe statement; Ramsey report.
3. Midway, pp. 219–220.
4. Japanese Story, p. 37.

5. Sakamoto material, part 2.
6. War Diary, Third War Patrol (USS *Tambor*), June, 1942.
7. Sakamoto material, part 2.
8. Undated statement of Masaki Yamauchi, courtesy of Chihaya. Hereafter Yamauchi statement; USSBS No. 46, Interrogation of Cmdr. H. Sekino, Communications Officer, Sixth Fleet.
9. Midway Analysis, p. 154.
10. Undated statement of Masayuki Saruwatari, courtesy of Chihaya. Hereafter Saruwatari statement.
11. *Midway*, p. 221.
12. Nimitz report, June 28, 1942.
13. Interview which Barde conducted with Admiral Raymond A. Spruance, May 25, 1966. Hereafter Spruance/Barde interview.
14. Midway Analysis, pp. 156–157.
15. Log of *Enterprise*, June 5, 1942; *Climax at Midway*, p. 185; interview with Spruance, September 5, 1964.
16. Spruance report, June 16, 1942.
17. NAS Diary; Report of contacts.
18. VMSB-241 report.
19. Reports of Williamson and Ringblom, June 7, 1942.
20. This is one of the Midway incidents which raises questions. According to Kimes's report of June 8, "Captain Richard B. Fleming's plane was hit and set afire by AA during his dive, but in spite of this, continued the dive and scored a direct hit. His plane continued on into the sea . . ." To the best of our knowledge, no one else on the American side questioned that Fleming crashed into *Mikuma*, and he received the Medal of Honor posthumously—the first Marine aviator to be so honored in WW II. (*Marines at Midway*, p. 41n). Morison quotes Capt. Akira Soji of *Mogami:* "I saw a dive bomber dive into the last turret and start fires. He was very brave." Morison also directed attention to the supposed wreckage of Fleming's plane in a famous photograph of the damaged *Mikuma*. (*Coral Sea, Midway and Submarine Actions,* p. 145). However, in 1961 Soji de-

nied the statement which Morison quoted "and said that he thought there was no damage inflicted upon the force at this moment." (Sakamoto material, part 2). And Saruwatari did not think that the plane "seen amidships the *Mikuma*" in the picture "was an enemy plane." (Saruwatari statement). Ugaki's diary entry of June 8, 1942, covering the entire battle, also claims that no damage was inflicted in this attack. However, although Saruwatari did not recall the hit, he remembered hearing "such a story after the battle." But Fuchida's account not only confirms Fleming's act, it credits him with doing appreciable damage. (*Midway*, p. 226).
21. "Action with Enemy" form, Lt. Col. B.E. Allen; *Midway*, p. 226.
22. NAS Diary; Report of Contacts.
23. Interview with Fletcher, September 17, 1966.
24. NAS Diary.
25. Spruance report, June 16, 1942.
26. Ibid.; *Enterprise* log, June 5, 1942.
27. Interview with Burford, August 18, 1964.
28. Ibid.; NAS Diary, Report of contacts.
29. Spruance report, June 16, 1942; interview with Spruance, September 5, 1964.
30. Japanese Story, p. 39; Midway Analysis, pp. 147–150.
31. *Midway*, p. 250.
32. Kusaka statement.
33. *Rengo Kantai*, p. 90.
34. Ibid., pp. 90–91; Kusaka statement.
35. Nimitz report, June 28, 1942; Midway Analysis, pp. 161, 162.
36. Letter, CO *Hughes* to CinCPAC, June 11, 1942, Subject: Report of Battle with Japanese Aircraft on June 4, 1942. Hereafter *Hughes* report.
37. Gibbs/Barde interview, March 1, 1967.
38. *Hughes* report; Midway Analysis, p. 161.
39. *Yorktown* report; Midway Analysis, p. 161.
40. Log of *Vireo* , June 5, 1942.
41. *Coral Sea, Midway and Submarine Actions*, pp. 154–155.
42. "Action with Enemy" form, Lt. Col. Allen, op. cit.; 7th AF report.

43. Midway Analysis, p. 164.
44. Japanese Story, p. 39.
45. Spruance report, June 16, 1942.
46. McClusky/Barde interview, June 30, 1966.
47. Interview which Barde conducted with Brig. Gen. Julian P. Brown, USMC (Ret), June 27, 1966.
48. *Enterprise* report; *Hornet* report; Action reports of VB-3 and VS-6; Midway Analysis, p. 160.
49. *Midway*, p. 225.
50. Interview with Spruance, September 14, 1964; log of *Hornet*, June 5, 1942.
51. Letter, Capt. Ray Davis, USN (Ret), to Barde, January 5, 1967.
52. Narrative by Lt. Robin M. Lindsey, USN, recorded on 17 September 1943. Hereafter Lindsey narrative; *Enterprise* Supplemental Action report, June 13, 1942.
53. Interview with Spruance, September 5, 1964; Spruance report, June 16, 1942.
54. Interview with Spruance, September 5, 1964.

CHAPTER 37
"I Trembled with Great Sorrow"

1. Interview with Watanabe, September 26, 1964; Ugaki diary, June 8, 1942.
2. Ugaki diary, June 8, 1942.
3. *Coral Sea, Midway and Submarine Actions*, pp. 177–178; Midway Analysis, pp. 190–191. Fuchida gave a figure of nine fighters (*Midway*, p. 218).
4. Diary of Capt. Tasuku Nakazawa, June 5, 1942. Courtesy of Chihaya. Hereafter Nakazawa diary.
5. Ibid., June 6, 1942.
6. *Coral Sea, Midway and Submarine Actions*, pp. 180–181; Japanese Story, p. 39.
7. Ugaki diary, June 8, 1942.
8. Midway Analysis, pp. 193–194; *Coral Sea, Midway and Submarine Actions*, pp. 180–182.
9. Nakazawa diary, June 7, 1942.
10. Ugaki diary, June 8, 1942.
11. *Midway*, p. 225.
12. Amagai statement; "Tragic Battle"
13. Interview with Watanabe, November 25, 1964.
14. Ugaki diary, June 8, 1942.
15. Spruance report, June 16, 1942; VB-8 War Diary June 1942; *Enterprise* report, June 8, 1942.
16. Interview with Spruance; *Hornet* report, June 13, 1942.
17. *Hornet* report, June 13, 1942.
18. *Enterprise* report, June 8, 1942.
19. Midway Analysis, p. 174.
20. *Hornet* report, June 13, 1942; *Imperial Japanese Navy*, pp. 47, 155.
21. *Hornet* report, June 13, 1942; Nimitz report, June 28, 1942.
22. Midway Analysis, p. 169.
23. Saruwatari statement.
24. Midway Analysis, p. 169; *Hornet* Report, June 13, 1942.
25. *Enterprise* supplementary report, June 13, 1942.
26. Laub/Barde interview; May 13, 1966; Shumway VB-3 report.
27. *Enterprise* supplementary report, June 13, 1942; Shumway VB-3 report; *Imperial Japanese Navy*, pp. 151, 155.
28. Laub/Barde interview, May 13, 1966.
29. Short/Barde interview, June 5, 1966.
30. *Hornet* report, June 13, 1942.
31. Interview with Spruance, September 5, 1964.
32. Personal letter, Spruance to Nimitz, June 8, 1942, with enclosure.
33. Enclosure to Spruance letter, op. cit.
34. Shumway VB-3 report.
35. Midway Analysis, p. 169; Ugaki diary, June 8, 1942; Sakamoto material.
36. Saruwatari statement; Sakamoto material.
37. Letter, June 21, 1942, CinCPAC to CNO (Director of Naval Intelligence), Subject: Interrogation of Japanese Prisoners taken after Midway Action, June 9, 1942.
38. Sakamoto material. Capt. Sakiyama's fate is an example of how difficult it has been to be precise about action in this engagement of June 6. According to Fuchida, "Captain Sakiyama was wounded in the third attack of the day but he continued in command until *Mikuma* went down. He was thrown clear of the sinking

ship and picked up by a destroyer. However, death overtook this valiant officer on 13 June in the sickbay of cruiser *Suzuya.*" (*Midway*, p. 229) Lord tells us, "The very first attack knocked out her bridge, fatally wounding Captain Sakiyama, yet the exec Commander Takagi took over and fought on." (*Incredible Victory*, p. 273).

39. Sakamoto material.
40. NAS Diary; Report of Contacts; Ramsey report; Nimitz report, June 28, 1942.
41. Nimitz report, June 28, 1942; *Turning Point*, p. 146.
42. *Hornet* report, June 13, 1942; Midway Analysis, p. 176.
43. *Hornet* report, June 13, 1942.
44. Sakamoto material.
45. Yoshioka statement.
46. Sakamoto material; USSBS No. 295, interrogation of Cdr. Otakichi Shibata, navigator of *Suzuya.*
47. Letter, June 21, 1942, CinCPAC to CNO, op. cit.
48. Interview with Spruance, September 5, 1964.
49. VB-6 Action report, June 10, 1942; Dobson/Barde interview, May 12, 1966.
50. Dobson diary, June 6, 1942.
51. Interview with Spruance, September 5, 1964; Dobson/Barde interview, May 12, 1966; Spruance report, June 16, 1942.
52. Sakamoto material.
53. Spruance report, June 16, 1942.
54. Sakamoto material; Yamauchi statement.

CHAPTER 38
"A Sober and Sickening Sight"

1. Tanabe statement. Tanabe's statement follows closely the article which he wrote with Joseph D. Harrington, "I Sank the *Yorktown* at Midway, *United States Naval Institute Proceedings,* May 1963, pp. 58–65.
2. Interview with Tanabe, November 30, 1964.
3. Tanabe statement.
4. This is the appraisal of Prange and Chi-

haya during their interview with Tanabe, November 30, 1964.
5. Interview with Tanabe, November 30, 1964.
6. Ibid.; Tanabe statement.
7. Tanabe statement.
8. Interview with Tanabe, November 30, 1964.
9. Tanabe statement.
10. Ibid.
11. Ibid.; interview with Tanabe, November 30, 1964.
12. Ibid.
13. Tanabe statement.
14. *Yorktown* report; *Hammann* report.
15. Ibid.
16. Interview with Burford, August 18, 1964.
17. Log of *Balch*, June 6, 1942; *Hammann* report.
18. Log of *Balch*, June 6, 1942.
19. Tanabe statement.
20. Ibid.
21. Ibid.
22. Ibid.
23. Ibid.; interview with Tanabe, November 30, 1964.
24. Logs of *Benham, Monaghan,* and *Hughes,* June 6, 1942.
25. Tanabe statement; interview with Tanabe, November 30, 1964.
26. Log of *Balch*, June 6, 1942; *Yorktown* report.
27. Tanabe statement.
28. Ibid.
29. Interview with Burford, August 18, 1964.
30. Logs of *Balch* and *Monaghan*, June 6, 1942.
31. *Yorktown* report.

CHAPTER 39
"Midway to Our Objective"

1. Spruance report, June 16, 1942; interview with Spruance, September 5, 1964.
2. Lindsey narrative.
3. Letter, Emmons to Marshall, June 7, 1942, PSF 86, Roosevelt Papers.
4. *Coral Sea, Midway and Submarine Actions,* p. 151; *Incredible Victory*, p. 279.

See also Chicago *Daily Tribune*, June 13, 1942.

5. Ugaki diary, June 8, 1942.

6. Interview with Watanabe, September 26, 1964.

7. Ugaki diary, June 8, 1942.

8. Interview with Spruance, September 1964.

9. Ugaki diary, June 8, 1942.

10. Midway Analysis, p. 183; Ugaki Diary, June 8, 1942.

11. Barde interview with RADM Ko Nagasawa, JMSDF (Ret), February 4, 1966.

12. Ugaki diary, June 9, 1942.

13. Interview with Watanabe, September 26, 1964.

14. Ugaki diary, June 9, 1942.

15. Interview with Watanabe, October 6, 1964.

16. Interview with Kuroshima, December 5, 1964.

17. "Tragic Battle."

18. Ugaki diary, June 10, 1942.

19. Ibid.

20. Kusaka statement; *Rengo Kantai*, p. 91; Ugaki diary, June 10, 1942; interview with Kuroshima, December 5, 1964. In both his book and his statement, Kusaka stated that he went to *Yamato* alone. However, Ugaki's diary and other sources make it clear that others were present.

21. Ugaki diary, June 10, 1942.

22. "Tragic Battle."

23. Interview with Fuchida, February 16, 1964.

24. "Tragic Battle"; Genda statement.

25. Interview with Fuchida, February 16, 1964; "Tragic Battle."

26. Nakazawa diary, June 10, 1964.

27. Ibid., June 15, 1964.

28. Kusaka statement; *Rengo Kantai*, p. 91.

29. *Japan Times and Advertiser*, June 15, 1942.

30. Interview with Fuchida, February 16, 1964.

31. Evening edition, June 6, 1942.

32. June 11, 1942.

33. Honolulu *Advertiser*, June 12, 1942.

34. Interview with Maj. Gen. Robert J.

Fleming, Jr., June 24, 1977. Fleming was a lieutenant colonel at the time of Midway, and an informal liaison channel between Emmons and Nimitz.

35. Emmons letter.

36. Stimson diary, June 5, 1942.

37. Memorandum, June 20, 1942, Diary of Adolf A. Berle, Jr., Box 214, Franklin D. Roosevelt Library, Hyde Park, N.Y.

38. Stimson diary, June 6, 1942.

39. *Nimitz*, pp. 104–105.

40. Chicago *Daily Tribune*, July 15, 1942.

41. *Time*, September 28, 1942.

42. San Francisco *Chronicle*, June 6, 1942.

43. June 8, 1942.

44. *The New York Times*, June 9, 1942.

45. *Nimitz*, pp. 82, 103, 179.

46. Interview with Nimitz, September 4, 1964.

CHAPTER 40
Analysis—Japan:
"A Mass of Chaos"

1. *Midway*, p. 245.

2. Miwa diary, June 18, 1942; *Rengo Kantai*, p. 92.

3. Masataka Chihaya, manuscript of a book about the Pacific War in the Prange files, p. 70.

4. Ugaki diary, June 10, 1942; "The Battle of Midway."

5. Midway Analysis, p. 227.

6. *Yamamoto*, p. 6.

7. "Tragic Battle."

8. Ugaki diary, June 10, 1942.

9. Genda statement.

10. *Midway*, p. 236; Ugaki diary, June 10, 1942.

11. *Midway*, p. 237. See also Ugaki diary, June 10, 1942.

12. Ugaki diary, June 10, 1942.

13. Davidson report, June 13, 1942.

14. Interview with Kuroshima, December 13, 1964.

15. Ugaki diary, June 10, 1942.

16. *Midway*, p. 237.

17. "Tragic Battle."

18. Genda statement.
19. Chihaya mss, p. 73.
20. Interview with Watanabe, November 25, 1964.
21. Chihaya mss, pp. 71–72, 103.
22. *Midway*, p. 246.
23. Interviews with Nimitz, September 4, 1966, and Spruance, September 5, 1966; *Midway*, p. 234.
24. "Tragic Battle." See also *Midway*, p. 234.
25. Ugaki diary, June 10, 1942.
26. See for example *Midway*, pp. 8, 107.
27. Miwa diary, June 14, 1942.
28. See for example *Midway*, p. 241.
29. "The Battle of Midway"; *Midway*, pp. 243–244.
30. Interview with Nimitz, September 4, 1964.
31. *Midway*, pp. 246–247.

CHAPTER 41
Analysis—United States:
Brilliance "Shot with Luck"

1. Genda statement.
2. Ugaki diary, June 8, 1942.
3. "Tragic Battle."
4. Interview with Nimitz, September 4, 1964.
5. Ibid.
6. Interview with Watanabe, November 24, 1964.
7. "Six Minutes," p. 103.
8. Genda statement.
9. *Zero!*, p. 114.
10. "The Battle of Midway."
11. Interview with Spruance, September 14, 1964.
12. Genda statement.

13. Kusaka statement.
14. Spruance report, June 16, 1942.
15. Interview with Spruance, September 5, 1964.
16. Action with Enemy forms, June 5, 1942, Capt. O. H. Rigley, Jr.; 1st Lt. H. S. Grundman; 1st Lt. Paul I. Williams respectively.
17. *Enterprise* report.
18. *Hornet* air operations report.
19. Kimes official interview.
20. *AAF in WWII*, pp. 459–460.
21. Official interview with Lt. Cmdr. John S. Thach, USN, in Bureau of Aeronautics, August 26, 1942.

CHAPTER 42
The Meaning of Midway—Forty Years
Later

1. Interview with Fletcher, September 17, 1966.
2. Interviews with Spruance, September 5 and 14, 1964.
3. Interview with Nimitz, September 4, 1964.
4. "Memories of Nimitz," p. 31.
5. Interview with Nimitz, September 4, 1964.
6. Miyo/Barde interview.
7. "Tragic Battle."
8. Genda statement.
9. *Rengo Kantai*, p. 92.
10. Interview with Spruance, September 5, 1964.
11. See n. 5 above.
12. These figures come from *Midway*, p. 249 and *Nimitz*, p. 107.
13. Interview with Layton, July 22, 1964.
14. Midway Analysis, p. 210.

A	(as part of aircraft designation) Brewster Aeronautical Corp. (See **Note 1**, following)
AA	antiaircraft
AAF	Army Air Forces
BB	battleship
BatDiv	battleship division
B-17	"Flying Fortress" 4-engine bomber
B-26	"Marauder" 2- engine bomber
C	(as part of aircraft designation) Curtiss-Wright Corp.
CA	heavy cruiser
CarDiv	carrier division
CinC	Commander in Chief
CinCPAC	Commander in Chief, U.S. Pacific Fleet
CL	light cruiser
CO	Commander officer
Com	(as part of a title) commander, i.e. ComCruDiv 6 = Commander, Cruiser Division 6.
Cominch	Commander in Chief, United States Fleet
CruDiv	cruiser division
CV	aircraft carrier
CVL	light carrier
CVS	seaplane tender
D	(as part of aircraft designation) Douglass Aircraft Company
DD	destroyer
DesDiv	destroyer division
DesRon	destroyer squadron
F	fighter
F	(as part of aircraft designation) Grummann Aircraft Engineering Corp.
F2A-2	Buffalo (Brewster) fighter
F4F-3	Wildcat fighter with fixed wings
F4F-4	Wildcat fighter with folding wings
MAG-22	Marine Aircraft Group Twenty-two
N	(as part of aircraft designation) Naval Aircraft Factory
NAS	Naval Air Station

OS	observation scout plane
pgc	per gyro compass
PT	motor torpedo boat
SB	scout bomber
SBD	single engine scout bomber "Dauntless"
SB2U	single engine scout bomber "Vindicator"
SO	scout observation plane
SubDiv	submarine division
SubRon	submarine squadron
TB	torpedo bomber
TBD	single-engine torpedo bomber "Devastator"
TBF	single-engine torpedo bomber "Avenger"
TF	Task Force
TG	Task Group
U	(as part of aircraft designation) United Aircraft Corp. (i.e. Vought-Sikorsky)
V	heavier than air (See **Note 2**, following)
VB	bomber or bomber squadron
VF	fighter or fighter squadron
VMB	Marine bomber squadron
VMF	Marine fighter squadron
VP	patrol plane or squadron
VS	scouting plane or squadron
YP	patrol vessel

Note 1. U.S. naval aircraft were designated to follow a pattern: The first initial or initials represented the type of aircraft. The number following showed that type plane's position in a series. The next initial was that of the manufacturer. There might or might not appear another number following a hyphen. This represented modifications. Example: the F4F-4, Wildcat, was a fighter plane, the fourth type of its series (in this case a midwing monoplane), manufactured by Grumman Aircraft Engineering Corporation, and had been modified—in this instance to have folding wings.

Note 2. U.S. naval carrier-based squadrons were designated first with the initial V, signifying that the aircraft assigned were heavier than air; second, by the initial of the type aircraft; then by the hull number of the home carrier. The numbers involved at Midway were 5 (*Yorktown*), 6 (*Enterprise*), 8 (*Hornet*), and 3 (*Saratoga*). The latter was not at Midway, but some of her aircraft participated.

ORDER OF BATTLE

Japanese*
COMBINED FLEET
Adm. Isoroku Yamamoto, Commander in Chief

MAIN BODY—Admiral Yamamoto
  BatDiv 1—*Yamato* (flagship), *Nagato, Mutsu*
  Carrier Group—*Hosho* (CVL) with eight bombers; 1 DD.
  Special Force—*Chiyoda, Nisshin* (seaplane carriers serving as tender)
  Screen (DesRon 3)—RADM Shintaro Hashimoto
    Sendai (CL, flagship)
    DesDiv 11—4 DDs
    DesDiv 19—4 DDs
    1st Supply Unit—2 oilers
  GUARD (Aleutians Screening) FORCE—VADM Shiro Takasu
    BatDiv 2—*Hyuga* (flagship), *Ise, Fuso, Yamashiro*
      Screen—RADM Fukuji Kishi
        CruDiv 9—*Kitakami* (CL, flagship, *Oi* (CL)
        DesDiv 20—4 DDs
        DesDiv 24—4 DDs
        DesDiv 27—4 DDs
        2d Supply unit—2 oilers

FIRST CARRIER STRIKING FORCE (1st Air Fleet)—VADM Chuichi Nagumo
  Carrier Group—VADM Nagumo
    CarDiv 1
      Akagi (CV, flagship)
        21 Zero fighters, 21 dive bombers, 21 torpedo bombers
      Kaga (CV)
        21 Zero fighters, 21 dive bombers, 30 torpedo bombers
    CarDiv 2—RADM Tamon Yamaguchi
      Hiryu (CV, flagship)
        21 Zero fighters, 21 dive bombers, 21 torpedo bombers
      Soryu (CV)
        21 Zero fighters, 21 dive bombers, 21 torpedo bombers

---

*Data taken from *Midway*, pp. 251–260.

432

Support Group—RADM Hiroaki Abe
  CruDiv 8—*Tone* (CA, flagship), *Chikuma* (CA)
  2d Section, BatDiv 3—*Haruna, Kirishima*
Screen (DesRon 10)—RADM Susumu Kimura
  Nagara (CL), flagship
  DesDiv 4—4 DDs
  DesDiv 10—3 DDs
  DesDiv 17—4 DDs
Supply Group—5 oilers, 1 DD

MIDWAY INVASION FORCE (2d Fleet)—VADM Nobutake Kondo
  Invasion Force Main Body
    CruDiv 4 (less 2d section)
      Atago (CA, flagship), *Chokai* (CA)
    CruDiv 5—*Myoko* (CA), *Haguro* (CA)
    BatDiv 3 (less 2d section)—*Kongo, Hiei*
  Screen (DesRon 4)—RADM Shoji Nishimura
    Yura (CL, flagship)
    DesDiv 2—4 DDs
    DesDiv 9—3 DDs
  Carrier Group
    Zuiho (CVL)—12 Zero fighters, 12 torpedo bombers; 1 DD
  Supply Group—4 oilers, 1 repair ship
  Close Support Group—VADM Takeo Kurita
    CruDiv 7
      Kumano (CA, flagship); *Suzuya* (CA), *Mikuma* (CA), *Mogami* (CA)
    DesDiv 8—2 DDs
    1 oiler
  Transport Group—RADM Raizo Tanaka
    12 transports carrying troops
    3 patrol boats carrying troops
    1 oiler
  Escort (DesRon 2)—RADM Tanaka
    Jintsu (CL, flagship)
    DesDiv 15—2 DD
    DesDiv 16—4 DD
    DesDiv 18—4 DD
  Seaplane Tender Group—RADM Riutaro Fujita
    Seaplane Tender Div 11
      Chitose (CVS)—16 fighter seaplanes, 4 scout seaplanes
      Kamikawa Maru (AV)—8 fighter seaplanes, 4 scout planes
      1 DD; 1 patrol boat carrying troops
  Minesweeper Group
    4 minesweepers
    3 submarine chasers
    1 supply ship
    2 cargo ships

NORTHERN (Aleutians) FORCE (5th Fleet)—VADM Moshiro Hosogaya
  Northern Force Main Body

Nachi (CA, flagship)
Screen—2 DDs
Supply Group—2 oilers, 3 cargo ships

Second Carrier Striking Force—RADM Kakuji Kakuta
Carrier Group (CarDiv 4)
Ryujo (CVL, flagship)—16 Zero fighters, 21 torpedo bombers.
Junyo (CV)—24 Zero fighters, 21 dive bombers
Support Group (2d section, CruDiv 4)—*Maya* (CA), *Takao* (CA)
Screen (DesDiv 7)—3 DDs, 1 oiler

Attu Invasion Force—RADM Sentaro Omori
Abukuma (CL, flagship)
DesDiv 21—4 DDs
1 minelayer; 1 transport carrying troops

Kiska Invasion Force—Capt. Takeji Ono
CruDiv 21—*Kiso* (CL), *Tama* (CL), *Asaka Maru* (auxiliary cruiser)
Screen (DesDiv 6)—3 DDs
2 transports carrying troops
Minesweeper Div. 13—3 minesweepers
Submarine Detachment—RADM Shigeshi Yamazaki
SubRon 1—*I-9* (flagship)
SubDiv 2— 3 submarines
SubDiv 4—2 submarines

ADVANCE (Submarine) FORCE (6th Fleet)—VADM Teruhisu Komatsu
Katori (CL, flagship) at Kwajalein
SubRon 3—RADM Chimaki Kono
Rio de Janeiro Maru (submarine tender, flagship) at Kwajalein
SubDiv 19—4 submarines
SubDiv 30—3 submarines
SubDiv 13—3 submarines

SHORE-BASED AIR PATROL (11th Air Fleet)—VADM Nishizo Tsukahara at Tinian
Midway Expeditionary Force—Capt. Chisato Morita
36 Zero fighters (aboard Nagumo's carriers)
10 land-based bombers at Wake; 6 flying boats at Jaluit
24th Air Flotilla—RADM Minoru Maeda at Kwajalein
Chitose Air Group—36 Zero fighters, 36 torpedo bombers at Kwajalein
1st Air Group—36 Zero fighters, 36 torpedo bombers at Aur and Wotje
14th Air Group—18 flying boats at Jaluit and Wotje

United States*
U.S. PACIFIC FLEET AND PACIFIC OCEAN AREAS
Adm. Chester W. Nimitz, Commander in Chief

CARRIER STRIKING FORCE—RADM Frank Jack Fletcher
Task Force 17—Admiral Fletcher
TG 17.5 Carrier Group—Capt. Elliott Buckmaster

---

*Data taken from *Coral Sea, Midway and Submarine Actions*, pp. 90–93, 173–174.

    Yorktown (CV)—Captain Buckmaster
        VF-3—25 F4F-4
        VB-3—18 SBD-3
        VS-3—19 SBD-3
        VT-3—13 TBD-1
TG 17.2 Cruiser Group—RADM William W. Smith
    Astoria (CA), *Portland* (CA)
TG 17.4 Destroyer Squadron—Capt. Gilbert C. Hoover (ComDesRon 2)
    6 DDs (1 joined on June 5)
Task Force 16—RADM Raymond A. Spruance
    TG 16.5 Carrier Group—Capt. George D. Murray
      Enterprise—Captain Murray
        VF-6—27 F4F-4
        VB-6—19 SBD-2 and -3
        VS-6—19 SBD-2 and -3
        VT-6—14 TBD-1
      Hornet—Capt. Marc. A. Mitscher*
        VF-8—27 F4F-4
        VB-8—19 SBD-2 and -3
        VS-8—18 SBD-1, -2, -3
        VT-8—15 TBD
    TG 16.2 Cruiser Group—RADM Thomas C. Kinkaid (ComCruDiv 6)
      New Orleans (CA)
      Minneapolis (CA)
      Vincennes (CA)
      Northampton (CA)
      Pensacola (CA)
      Atlanta (CL)
    TG 16.4 Destroyer Screen—Capt. Alexander R. Early (ComDesRon 1)
      9 DDs
      Oiler Group— 2 oilers, 2 DDs

SUBMARINES—RADM Robert H. English, Commander, Submarine Force, Pacific Fleet, at Pearl Harbor (operational control)
    TG 7.1 Midway Patrol Group—12 submarines
    TG 7.2 On roving assignment—3 submarines
    TG 7.3 North of Oahu Patrol—4 submarines

MIDWAY SHORE-BASED AIR—Capt. Cyril T. Simard
    Detachments of PatWing 1 and 2
      32 PBY-5 and PBY-5A Catalinas
    VT-8 Detachment - 6 TBF
    Marine Aircraft Group 22, 2d Marine Air Wing—Lt. Col. Ira L. Kimes
      VMF-221—20 F2A-3; 7 F4F-3
      VMSB-241—11 SB2U-3; 16 SBD-2
    Detachment of 7th Army Air Force—Maj. Gen. Willis P. Hale
      4 B-26; 19 B-17

---

*Promoted to Rear Admiral en route to Midway.

MIDWAY LOCAL DEFENSES—Captain Simard
    6th Marine Defense Bn (reinforced), Fleet Marine Force, Col. Harold D. Shannon
    Motor Torpedo Squadron 1
        8 PT Boats at Midway; 2 at Kure; 4 small patrol craft
    (Deployed in area)
        2 tenders, 1 DD at French Frigate Shoals
        1 oiler, 1 converted yacht, 1 minesweeper at Pearl and Hermes Reef
        2 converted tuna boats at Lisianski, Gardner Pinnacles, Laysan and Necker
    Midway Relief Fueling Unit—1 oiler, 2 DDs

FORCES IN THE ALEUTIAN CAMPAIGN
    Task Force 8—RADM Robert A. Theobald (in *Nashville*)
        TG 8.6 Main Body— 2 CA, 3 CL
          DesDiv 11—4 DDs
        TG 8.1 Air Search Group
          3 tenders with 20 PBY of Pat Wing 4; 1 B-17
        TG 8.2 Surface Search or Scouting Group
          1 gunboat, 1 oiler, 14 YP, 5 Coast Guard cutters
        TG 8.3 Air Striking Group—Brig. Gen. William O. Butler, USA*
          Ft. Randall—21 fighters, 14 bombers
          Ft. Glenn, Umnak—12 fighters
          Kodiak—32 fighters, 5 bombers, 2 light bombers
          Anchorage—44 fighters, 24 bombers, 2 light bombers
        TG 8.4 Destroyer Striking Group—9 DD
        TG 8.5 Submarine Group—6 submarines
        TG 8.9 Tanker Group—2 oilers, SS *Comet*

---

*Initial deployment.

CHRONOLOGY*

1941

December 7	Nagumo carrier force attacks Pearl Harbor.
December 10	Guam falls.
December 16	VADM William S. Pye assumes temporary command of U.S. Pacific Fleet.
December 23	Wake Island falls. Pye calls off attempted rescue.
December 31	Adm. Chester W. Nimitz assumes command of U.S. Pacific Fleet.

1942

January 11	*Saratoga* torpedoed and goes to Bremerton for repairs.
January 1–14	Ugaki writes sketch of future operations, including the occupation of Midway.
January 20–22	Nagumo force covers Japanese landings at Rabaul.
January 25	Ugaki turns project over to Kuroshima, who recommends instead a strategy centered on India and Burma.
February 15	Singapore surrenders.
February 19	Nagumo force hits Darwin.
February 20–25	Table maneuvers aboard *Yamato* where Army turns down India project.
March (mid-month)	Japanese plans now center on Midway.
March 28	Kuroshima and Combined Fleet staff begin work on Midway operation.
April 2–5	Watanabe and Kuroshima discuss Midway at Naval General Staff and obtain reluctant approval.
April 5	Nagumo force strikes Colombo and sinks two British cruisers.
April 9	Nagumo force strikes Trincomalee and sinks British carrier *Hermes* and destroyer *Vampire*.
April 18	Doolittle raid on Japan.
April 21	Stimson warns Marshall and Arnold of possible attack on West Coast.
April 22	Nagumo's carriers return to Japan. Shortly thereafter he and his staff learn of the Midway project.
April 28–29	Yamamoto holds critique aboard *Yamato*.

*Japanese events are given in Japanese time until June 3, after which times are local.

April 29	Nimitz advises King Midway could hold off a moderate attack but would need fleet support against a major one.
May 1–4	Preliminary war games for Midway.
May 2	Nimitz flies to Midway to inspect defenses.
May 5	Nagano orders Midway and Aleutians operations.
May 6	Corregidor surrenders.
May 7–11	Battle of the Coral Sea. *Lexington* sunk and *Yorktown* damaged; *Shoho* sunk and *Shokaku* damaged.
May 10 (approx.)	Midway at Hypo's arrangement sends trap message that they are short of water.
May 12 (approx.)	Hypo intercepts a Japanese message that "AF" is short of water.
Mid-May	Simmons warns Nimitz to estimate enemy capabilities.
May 15	Nimitz orders Halsey's task force to Pearl Harbor.
May 17	*Triton* sinks *I-164*.
May 17	Nimitz forms a North Pacific Force to send to Aleutians.
May 18	7th Air Force placed on special alert, and new B-17s begin to arrive from mainland.
May 20	Yamamoto issues official order of forces to participate and estimate of U.S. strength.
May 20	Midway Transport Group and Seaplane Tender Group sortie from Japan for rendezvous at Saipan.
May 21	Midway begins its alert phase.
May 22	Yamamoto's Main Body exercises at sea.
May 22	Marshall flies to West Coast because War Department fears attack there.
May 22	Demolition charge tripped and blows up Midway's gasoline dump.
May 22	Midway initiates search and reconnaissance phase.
May 22	Part of VP-44 arrives on Midway.
May 23	Rest of VP-44 reaches Midway.
May 24	Final table maneuvers aboard *Yamato*.
May 25	Midway receives more reinforcements for VP-44.
May 25	Rochefort brings Nimitz his intercept of Japanese order of battle. (Shortly thereafter Japanese change JN25 system).
May 25	Nimitz advises Midway D-Day has been changed to June 3.
May 25	Reinforcements reach Midway—Marine 3d Defense Battalion AA battery, and Companies C and D of 2d Raider Battalion.
May 26	General Tinker, CG 7th AF visits Midway, brings with him Maj. Warner as AF Liaison Officer.
May 26	More personnel and aircraft of MAG-22 arrive at Midway.
May 26	*Enterprise* and *Hornet* reach Pearl Harbor. Halsey too ill to command the operation. He recommends Spruance.
May 27	Navy Day in Japan.
May 27	Nagumo Force sorties; Fuchida stricken with appendicitis.
May 27	Midway Transport Group and Seaplane Tender Group sortie from Saipan.
May 27	Close Support Group sorties from Guam.
May 27	Nimitz meets with Spruance and gives him his instructions.
May 27	*Enterprise* and *Hornet* refurbishing and remanning.
May 27	*Yorktown* enters Pearl Harbor and repairs begin immediately.
May 28	Northern Forces sortie from Japan.
May 28	Fletcher named commander of U.S. task forces.

May 28	Nimitz briefs Fletcher and Spruance.
May 28	Nimitz briefs Ramsey and sends him to Midway to take charge of air operations.
May 28	Task Force 16 sorties from Pearl Harbor.
May 29	Main Body of Midway Invasion Force sorties.
May 29	Yamamoto's Main Body sorties.
May 29	Midway receives another B-17, 4 B-26s and their crews.
May 30	*I-123* finds 2 U.S. ships at French Frigate Shoals; Operation K postponed.
May 30	Task Force 17 sorties.
May 30	Midway initiates air search.
May 30	2 PBYs encounter 2 Japanese land-based bombers from Wake.
May 30	The Japanese damage the PBYs.
May 30	Seven more B-17s arrive at Midway with crews.
May 31	*I-123* reports two U.S. flying boats at French Frigate Shoals: Operation K canceled.
May 31	Nine more B-17s reach Midway, including the B-17 commander, Lt. Col. Walter C. Sweeney, Jr.
May 31	B-17s scouting from Midway.
May 31	Last cargo of drummed aviation gasoline reaches Midway.
May 31	Mitscher, captain of *Hornet*, is promoted to Rear Admiral.
May 31–June 1	Two Japanese midget submarines attack Sydney harbor.
June 1	Genda ill, ordered to sick bay.
June 1	Japanese land-based aircraft report U.S. submarines and hear U.S. dispatching many "urgent" messages.
June 1	2 PBYs on patrol again are attacked by 2 Japanese bombers.
June 1	Fuchida decides this means U.S. search arc has been extended, and Tanaka's Transport Group may be sighted prematurely.
June 1	RADM Theobald, commanding Task Force 8, leaves Kodiak in *Nashville* to rendezvous with his Main Body.
June 1	Spruance orders radio silence after a freak TBS interception.
June 1	*Saratoga* sorties San Diego in attempt to reach Midway in time to participate in the battle.
June 2	Fog hampers Japanese refueling.
June 2	Nagumo breaks radio silence to insure change of course.
June 2	Spruance signals all ships of the expected battle.
June 2	Task Forces 16 and 17 meet at Point Luck.
June 3	
Time unknown	Japanese submarine cordons arrive on station two days late.
0415	Ramsey sends up B-17s on reconnaissance.
0600	Nagumo's oilers drop away.
0700	2d Carrier Striking Force attacks Dutch Harbor.
0800	Aleutian Guard Force breaks from Yamamoto's Main Body.
0820	The B-17s return to Midway from scouting.
0825	Abe orders next day's antisubmarine patrols.
0900	Escort Force spots a U.S. plane.
0904	Ens. Eaton advises Midway of sighting (part of Minesweeper Gp.).
0925	Midway receives Ens. Reid's message of "Sighting Main Body."
1130	PBY 7V55 reports "two cargo vessels . . ."
1158	B-17 OV 58 (Lt. Smith) up on reconnaissance.
1200	2d Carrier Striking Force begins to withdraw toward Adak.

1228	Nine B-17s under Sweeney take off to hit Invasion Force.
1325	Nagumo signals fleet movements to be taken on June 4.
1611	Smith reports two transports and two destroyers.
1640	B-17s begin attack on Transport Group. No hits.
1830	Abe signals changes in the antisubmarine patrols.
1950	Fletcher changes *Yorktown*'s course toward launching point.
2115	4 PBYs equipped with torpedoes take off.

June 4

(Times in parentheses are approximate)

0130	Catalinas begin attack on Transport Group.
0245	Catalinas report attack completed.
0245	*Akagi* air crews awakened.
0300	Reveille on Midway.
0400	Nagumo orders all hands to stations.
0400	6 F4Fs of VMF 221 take off from Midway on cover patrol.
0400	11 Catalinas of VP-44 take off from Midway on search sector.
0405	16 B-17s take off for second strike on transport group.
0430	Nagumo begins launching Midway attack force.
0430	*Akagi, Kaga,* and *Haruna* launch reconnaissance planes.
0430	*Yorktown* launches 10 SBDs to cover northern arc.
(0430)	Midway aircraft begin to warm up.
0435	*Chikuma* launches No. 5 reconnaissance plane.
0437	Dawn.
0438	*Chikuma* launches No. 6 reconnaissance plane.
0442	*Tone* launches No. 3 reconnaissance plane.
0500	*Tone* launches No. 4 reconnaissance plane.
(0500)	On Midway, aircraft engines off, pilots return to flight shacks.
(0505)	Kimes calls in the six patrol fighters.
0510	*Tone* No. 4 plane reports "two enemy surfaced submarines . . ."
0520	Ady reports an unidentified aircraft.
0530	Ady reports an enemy carrier.
0530	Air crews alerted on Midway.
0534	*Enterprise* receives report of a carrier.
0545	Chase reports "Many planes heading Midway . . ."
0552	Ady reports "Two carriers and main body ships . . ."
0553	*Enterprise* receives "many planes" report.
0553	Sand Island radar reports incoming Japanese.
0555	*Tone* No. 4 plane reports "15 enemy planes are heading toward you."
0556	Air raid alarm on Midway; Brewsters and Wildcats up.
0600	B-17s ordered to divert to carriers.
0600	A messenger advised B-26s and TBFs to "attack enemy carriers."
0603	*Enterprise* receives word of "two enemy carriers . . ."
0607	Fletcher orders Spruance to proceed westerly and attack.
(0610)	VMSB 241 bombers take off.
0610	Japanese planes 47 miles out of Midway.
0612	Wildcats make initial contact: "Hawks at Angels Twelve."
0615	TBFs take off from Midway.
0615	B-17s take off from Midway.
0615	Japanese planes at 30 miles out.
0616	Midway fighters engage attackers.

0620	Enemy now 22 miles out.
0630	Battalion Headquarters orders AA to open fire.
0632	"One plane in formation of 20 is on fire."
0632	"Hangar and runways have been hit several times."
0633	"Eastern Island has been hit several times."
0635	An enemy plane downed. Laundry hit; hospital on fire.
0638	Power house hit, electricity out.
0638	Eastern Island being dive bombed.
0641	Hangar on fire. One Japanese plane crashed on ramp.
0643	Nagumo receives radio from Tomonaga—attack completed.
0658	Tomonaga reports that he has been hit.
0700	*Hornet* begins to launch.
0705	Tomonaga radios "There is need for a second attack wave."
0706	*Enterprise* commences launching.
0707	Air officer of *Kaga* reports "Sand Island bombed and great results obtained."
0708	*Akagi* and *Tone* begin firing at U.S. planes.
0709	10 Zeros head off U.S. planes.
0710	Kimes orders Maj. Norris's SB2U-3s to attack enemy carrier.
0710	*Nautilus* sighted smoke and AA fire and investigated.
0710	The U.S. planes "divide into 2 groups." Actually the TBFs and B-26s were attacking independently.
0712	*Akagi* made a full turn, evaded torpedo to starboard and another to port.
0714	U.S. level bomber attack on carriers, no hits.
0715	"All Clear" sounded on Midway.
0715	Nagumo ordered planes to stand by for a second wave, and to re-equip with bombs.
0720	Spruance split his command to assist operations.
0728	*Tone* No. 4 plane reported "what appears to be 10 enemy surface ships."
0732	Sweeney (B-17) sighted the enemy but no carrier in sight.
0745	Nagumo prepared to attack and ordered torpedoes left on those planes not yet switched to bombs.
0748	*Soryu* sighted "6 to 9 enemy planes." These probably VMSB-241.
0755	*Hornet* completed launch.
0755	*Nautilus* strafed.
0755	*Soryu* under attack, no hits.
0755	*Soryu* reported 14 "twin-engine planes" coming in. This was Sweeney and his B-17s.
0756	*Akagi* and *Hiryu* under attack.
0758	*Tone* No. 4 plane reports enemy change of course.
0800	Nagumo orders *Tone* No. 4 to advise ship types.
0800	*Akagi* sights 16 enemy planes and assumes battle speed.
0806	*Chikuma* reported what they thought were carrier-based planes. Probably Tomonaga coming in or the SB2U-3s.
0809	*Tone* No. 4 reports enemy fleet consists of 5 cruisers, 5 destroyers.
0810	*Nautilus* depth bombed.
0810	*Akagi* and *Hiryu* under attack.
0812	Miss astern *Kaga*.
0819	"Many bombs" near *Soryu*.

0820	SB2U-3s reach outskirts of Mobile Force.
0820	*Tone* No. 4 advised the enemy ships include "what appears to be a carrier." Yamamoto asks if he should order Nagumo to attack at once. Kuroshima does not think necessary.
0820	Miss astern *Akagi*.
0821	*Akagi* assumes maximum battle speed.
0822	*Akagi* heads into torpedo planes.
0824	*Soryu* under attack.
0827	*Haruna* under attack.
0830	Ten enemy planes dive on *Haruna*.
0837	*Akagi* commences landing Tomonaga's planes.
0838	*Yorktown* launches.
0839	*Akagi* sights U.S. torpedo planes and stops landing.
0840	*Akagi* resumes the recovery.
0855	Nagumo orders force to proceed northward after completing homing.
0859	Homing of bombers completed.
0905	*Akagi* receives *Tone* No. 4 report that 10 enemy torpedo planes are heading for the task force.
0905	Leslie's VB-3 launches off *Yorktown*.
0910	*Nautilus* attacked by *Arashi*.
0917	*Akagi* changes course to 70°, away from Midway to close U.S. task force.
0918	1st Air Fleet completed homing of all attack units.
0918	*Chikuma* sights VT-8 and opens fire; *Akagi* evades.
0925	*Akagi* maneuvers to bring VT-8 astern.
0930	*Arashi* advises of *Nautilus* attack.
0945	Leslie flies over VT-3 and 6 VF-3 fighters, follows VT-3.
0952	Gray wires Task Force 16 he is over target.
0955	McClusky sees *Arashi*'s wake and follows.
0958	*Akagi* sights 14 enemy planes in 2 groups (Ely and Lindsey had split forces); *Kaga* under fire.
(1005)	McClusky sights the Mobile Force.
1005	Leslie's gunner spots the Mobile Force about 35 miles off.
1014	*Akagi* under attack; no hits.
1015	*Akagi* spots torpedo planes (VT-3).
(1015– 1020)	Torpedo drops; no hits.
1020	Dive bombers spotted over *Kaga*; *Akagi* goes into maximum turn.
1022	*Kaga* being dive bombed (Best—VB-6).
1024	*Akagi* maneuvers to avoid torpedo; sees dive bombers and makes maximum reverse turn.
1024	Fires break out on *Kaga*.
(1025)	Leslie and Holmberg (VB-3) start dive on *Soryu*.
1025– 1028	*Soryu* hit twice.
1026	Three dive bombers attack *Akagi*; 1 near miss, 2 hits.
1033	*Akagi* goes into maximum turn to avoid 4 torpedo planes.
1036	*Akagi* can still proceed at cruising speed.
1042	*Akagi*'s steering gear damaged and her engines stop.
1043	Fighter planes aboard *Akagi* catch fire.

1046	Nagumo and his staff abandon bridge and commence transfer to *Nagara*.
1050	*Chikuma* sees 5 torpedo bombers.
1050	Nagumo radios Yamamoto that fires are raging on *Kaga, Soryu*, and *Akagi*.
1050	Yamaguchi wires Abe that planes are taking off to destroy enemy.
1054	First wave off *Hiryu*.
1055	Yanagimoto orders abandon ship on *Soryu*.
1058	Takeoff from *Hiryu* completed.
1100	*Hornet* dive bombers jettison bombs off Midway.
1127	*Akagi* stopped.
1130	*Akagi* air personnel and wounded ordered transferred to destroyers.
1140	*Hiryu* bombers report U.S. force of 3 carriers and "22 destroyers."
1145	Nagumo's flag hoisted aboard *Nagara*.
1200	*Hiryu* attacks *Yorktown*.
1201	*Hiryu* reports fires breaking out on *Yorktown*.
1203	*Akagi* starts turning on her own.
1220	Yamamoto orders Main Body, Occupation Force and 2d Mobile Force to rendezvous.
1235	Spruance detaches 2 cruisers and 2 destroyers to *Yorktown*.
1237	*Enterprise* begins to recover VB-3.
1310	Yamamoto temporarily postpones Operations AF and AO.
1310	Nagumo hears U.S. task force of 5 large cruisers and 1 carrier, the latter "burning fiercely."
1313	Fletcher transfers to *Astoria*.
(1320)	*Hiryu* launches second attack wave.
1350	*Akagi* stopped.
1355	Nagumo now hears U.S. force of 5 cruisers and 5 carriers, the latter all burning fiercely.
1359	*Nautilus* fires 3 torpedoes at *Kaga*. All miss.
1434	Tomonaga orders his planes to attack.
1437	*Yorktown* able to make 19 knots.
1445	Adams message locating *Hiryu* and her support ships. Spruance immediately arranged to attack.
1454	*Hiryu* reports two certain hits in *Yorktown*, which is believed to be a second U.S. carrier.
1455	Buckmaster orders abandon ship on *Yorktown*.
1531	Yamaguchi plans a dusk attack.
1550	Nagumo shifts course from northeast to northwest.
1550	All dive bombers (from VS-6, VB-6 and VB-3) clear *Enterprise*.
1600	Yamaguchi advises he has hit two carriers.
1600	All air personnel off *Akagi*.
1640	Amagai orders abandon ship on *Kaga*.
1645	Gallaher sights *Hiryu*.
1701	*Chikuma* sights U.S. planes. They dive on *Hiryu*.
1705	*Hiryu* on fire from several hits.
1707	*Haruna* under attack.
1712	VB-8 and VS-8 come from *Hornet*. They attack *Tone* and *Chikuma*. No hits.
1715	*Isokaze* taking *Kaga* survivors aboard.

1730	Yamamoto reinstated occupation of Aleutians.
1745–	B-17s attack *Tone* and *Chikuma*. No hits.
(1815)	
1750	All *Kaga* survivors aboard *Maikaze*.
1800	*Nautilus* sees *Kaga* burning.
1915	*Soryu* sinks.
1915	SB2U-3s and SBD-2 take off from Midway for night attack.
1925	*Kaga* sinks.
2000	All hands abandoning *Akagi*.
2030	*I-168* ordered to "shell and destroy" air base on Midway.
2200	SBD-2 returns safely to Midway. They did not sight the objective.
2340	Nagumo ordered to turn around and back up Occupation Force's night engagement.

June 5

0020	Yamamoto cancels bombardment of Midway by Kurita's cruisers.
0130	*I-168* fires on Midway. No damage. Shortly thereafter he is ordered to sink a U.S. carrier some 150 miles away.
0200	Following various movements since midnight, Spruance turns west.
0215	*Tambor* sights 4 large ships.
0230	Kaku ordered "abandon ship" aboard *Hiryu*.
0238	*Tambor* reports many unidentified ships.
0255	Yamamoto cancels Midway operation.
(0300)	*Mikuma* crashes into *Mogami*.
0315	Kaku orders all hands to leave *Hiryu* after farewell ceremonies.
0350	Nagumo receives orders to scuttle *Akagi*.
0415	*Tambor* report reaches Midway.
0430	12 B-17s seeking the enemy ships.
0430	Evacuation of *Hiryu* completed.
0500	*Akagi* scuttled.
0510	*Makigumo* torpedoes *Hiryu*.
0630	Patrol planes report 2 Japanese "battleships."
0700	MAG-22 sends up Dauntlesses and Vindicators to find above.
0700	Patrol plane reports 2 enemy cruisers.
0800	Patrol plane reports 2 BBS, 1 CV and 3 CAs.
0800	Hosogaya recommends suspension of Aleutians operation.
0840	Vindicators attack *Mikuma*.
0900	*Hiryu* sinks.
1100	TF 16 detaches *Monaghan*. Turns northwest by west to seek Nagumo force.
1205	*Chikuma* sights Main Body and Occupation Force (Japanese forces rendezvousing for retreat homeward).
1259	Yamamoto returns 2d Carrier Force to Northern Force.
1430	*Vireo* begins to tow *Yorktown* to Pearl Harbor. Boarding party working to lighten the ship.
1435	B-17s attack "a heavy cruiser."
1545	*Enterprise* and *Hornet* begin launching 58 bombers. Find only *Tanikaze*. No hits.
after dark	*Enterprise* and *Hornet* recover planes and Spruance heads due west.
2320	Yamamoto transfers a large body of surface ships to the Northern Force.

At night	Nagumo's destroyers transfer wounded to the battleships.

June 6

0410	*I-168* lookout spots *Yorktown* in distance.
0502	*Enterprise* launches 18 SBDs.
0600	*I-168* sees destroyers on guard near *Yorktown.*
0630	*Mikuma* reports two U.S. planes sighted.
0645	Plane 8B2 reports sighting a carrier and 5 DDs (erroneous).
0730	Plane 8B8 reports two CAs and 3 DDs.
0759	*Hornet* launches 26 dive bombers and 8 fighters.
(0945)	*Hornet* planes attack, hits on *Mogami, Mikuma,* and *Asashio.* Minor damage.
1045	*Enterprise* launches 31 dive bombers and 12 fighters. Midway sends out 26 B-17s after the cruisers. Bomb *Grayling* in mistake for cruiser.
1230	*Enterprise* planes score hits on both cruisers.
1237	*I-168* within 500 meters of *Yorktown;* moves back.
1245	In Honolulu *Star-Bulletin,* Nimitz announces "midway to our objective."
1331	*I-168* torpedoes *Yorktown,* but she still does not sink. One of the torpedoes hits *Hammann,* which sinks immediately.
(1336)	Depth charges begin on *I-168* and continue several hours.
1445	Second *Hornet* group of 23 dive bombers hits *Mikuma.*
1500	Yamamoto orders all-out battle risking Main Body, but air search fails to find U.S. fleet so plan is abandoned.
(after sunset)	*Mikuma* sinks.
1850	*I-168* has evaded all depth charges.
1900	Spruance has completed air operations, turns east to rendezvous with oilers.

June 7	*Yorktown* sinks at 0458.
	Task Force 17 breaks up. 3 DDs join Task Force 16, the other ships return to Pearl Harbor.
	General Tinker lost in an abortive air expedition against Wake.
	Destroyer *Isonami* collides with destroyer *Uranami.* Slowed but not sunk.
	Article in Chicago *Tribune* strongly implies the JN25 break.
June 9	Conference aboard *Yamato* with representatives of the Nagumo force to discuss reasons for the defeat. Yamamoto promises Nagumo and Kusaka another chance. He accepts full responsibility for the defeat.
June 11	Japan claims a great victory.
June 12	AAF claims most of the credit for the victory.
June 13	Task Force 16 returns to Pearl Harbor.
June 15	Fuchida and about 500 wounded taken aboard hospital ship, thence to Yokosuka where they are kept incommunicado.
June 18	USS *Ballard* saves 35 survivors of *Hiryu.*

SELECTED BIBLIOGRAPHY

Unpublished Sources Located in the Prange Files:
Official Reports and Correspondence

USS *Yorktown* (CV5) Bomb Damage, Coral Sea, 8 May 1942, War Damage Report No. 23, Buships, Navy Department, 28 November 1942.

Letter, CinCPAC to Cominch, June 28, 1942, Subject: Battle of Midway.

Letter, Cmdr. Logan C. Ramsey, USN to CinCPAC, June 15, 1942, Subject: Air Operations of Midway Defense Forces during Battle of Midway, May 30, 1942 to June 6, 1942.

Encl B. Contact Reports for period 30 May to 6 June, 1942, to letter, U.S. Naval Air Station, Midway Island, to CinCPAC, 18 June 1942, Subject: Report on Engagement with Enemy, Battle of Midway, 30 May to 7 June, 1942.

Letter, Executive Officer, Motor Torpedo Boat Squadron One to Commander, Motor Torpedo Boat Squadron One, June 7, 1942, Subject: Report of Incident in connection with participation of Motor Torpedo Boat Squadron One in battle of Midway, June 4–6, 1942.

Letter, CO, Motor Torpedo Boat Squadron One to CinCPAC, June 9, 1942, Subject: "Report of Battle with Enemy Forces, Midway Island on June 4 and 5, 1942.

Letter, CO Midway NAS to CinCPAC, June 18, 1942, Subject: Report of Engagement with Enemy, Battle of Midway, 30 May to 7 June, 1942.

CO, USS *Nautilus* patrol report to Commander, Submarine Division 4, 7 June, 1942, Narrative of 4 June 1942.

Letter, CO, USS *Enterprise*, to CinCPAC, June 8, 1942, Subject: Battle of Midway Island, June 4–6, 1942—Report of.

Letter, Commander Cruisers, Task Force Sixteen, to Commander Task Force Sixteen, June 11, 1942, Subject: Report of Action, June 4, 1942.

Letter, Commander Task Force Sixteen to CinCPAC, June 16, 1942, Subject: Battle of Midway: forwarding of reports.

Letter, CO, USS *Hornet* to CinCPAC, June 13, 1942, Subject: Report of Action—4–6 June, 1942.

Letter, Air Operations Officer, USS *Hornet* to CO, *Hornet*, June 12, 1942, Subject: Defects Observed During the Action Off Midway on June 4, 1942.

Letter, CO, USS *Enterprise* to CinCPAC, June 13, 1942, Subject: Air Battle of the Pacific, June 4–6, 1942, report of.

Letter, Commander, Fighting Squadron SIX to Commander *Enterprise* Air Group. June 8, 1942, Subject: Narrative of Events 4–6 June 1942.

Letter, The Commanding Officer, USS *Yorktown* to CinCPAC, June 18, 1942, Subject: Report of Action for June 4, 1942 and June 6, 1942.

Letter, Commander, Bombing Squadron THREE to Commander, *Yorktown* Air Group, June 7, 1942, Subject: Attack conducted June 4, 1942 on Japanese carriers located 156 miles NW Midway Island; narrative concerning.

Letter, Commander Bombing Squadron THREE to Commanding Officer, USS *Enterprise*, June 10, 1942, Subject: Report of Actions—period June 4–6, 1942, inclusive.

Letter, CinCPAC to CNO, June 28, 1942, Subject: Interrogation of Japanese Prisoners rescued at Sea off Midway on 19 June 1942.

Letter CO *Hammann* to CinCPAC, June 16, 1942, Subject: Action Report, June 4–6, 1942.

Report, A. J. Brassfield, USN to CO, VF-3, VF-42 Report of Action, June 4, 1942.

Letter, CO *Anderson* to CinCPAC, June 5, 1942, Subject: Report Required by U.S. Navy Regulations, Art. 712, concerning engagement with Japanese carrier-based planes, near Midway Island, on June 4, 1942.

Letter, The Commanding Officer, *Yorktown*, to Chief, Bureau of Ships, Subject: War Damage Reports.

CO, VS-6 report of action, June 4–6, to CO, USS *Enterprise*, June 21, 1942.

Commander, Bombing Squadron Six, report of action during June 4–6, 1942 to CO, USS *Enterprise*, June 10, 1942.

Letter, CO *Hughes* to CinCPAC, June 11, 1942, Subject: Report of Battle with Japanese Aircraft on June 4, 1942.

Letter, June 21, 1942, CinCPAC to CNO (Director of Naval Intelligence), Subject: Interrogation of Japanese Prisoners taken after Midway Action 9 June 1942.

Letter, Executive Officer, MAG 22, to CO, MAG 22, June 7, 1942, Subject: Marine Aircraft Group Twenty-two, Second Marine Aircraft Wing, Midway Island T. H., Executive Officer's Report of The Battle of Midway, June 3, 4, 5, 6, 1942, with preliminary phase from May 22, 1942.

Letter, CO, Marine Aircraft Group Twenty-Two to CinCPAC, June 7, 1942, Subject: Battle of Midway Islands, report of.

Memorandum, CO Marine Aircraft Group Twenty-Two to Senior Naval Aviator, Second Marine Aircraft Wing, Present in Hawaiian Area, June 8, 1942, Preliminary Report of Marine Aircraft Group Twenty-Two of Battle of Midway. June 4, 5, 6, 1942.

Letter, CO, 6th Defense Bn, Fleet Marine Force, to CO, NAS, June 13, 1942, Subject: Report of Actions on morning of June 4, 1942 and nights of June 4–6, 1942.

Undated commentary on draft of Marine Historical Monograph "Marines at Mi   vay," by Maj. John Apergis, USMCR.

Letter, Lt. Col. Robert C. McGlashan, USMC, to Director, Division of Public Information (Historical Section), August 12, 1947, located in Headquarters U.S. Marine Corps, Washington, D.C.

Letter, CO, Marine Scout-Bombing Squadron Two-Forty-One to CO, Marine Aircraft Group 22, June 12, 1942, Subject: Report of Activities of VMSB-241 during June 4 and June 5, 1942.

Letter, Capt. Cecil F. Faulkner, AC to CG, VII Bomber Command, Hickam Field, TH, June 6, 1942, Subject: Special Mission.

Midway Mission Report, June 12, 1942, by Lt. W. A. Smith.

Letter, CO, 431st Bombardment Squadron (H) to CO, 11th Bombardment Group (H), Hickam Field, TH, Subject: Combat Operations, Midway Area, 3–4 June 1942.

Letter, 1st Lt. Edward A. Steedman, to CG, 7th Bomber Command, Hickam Field, TH, June 6, 1942, Subject: Special Mission.

Letter, Lt. Gen. Delos C. Emmons to General George C. Marshall, June 7, 1942, Papers of Franklin D. Roosevelt, Franklin D. Roosevelt Library, Hyde Park, N. Y.

Letter, Hq 7th AF to CG AAF, June 13, 1942, Subject: Air Employment at Midway.

Letter, 1st Lt. Robert B. Andrews, to CG, VII Bomber Command, Hickam Field, TH, June 6, 1942, Subject: Special Mission.

Official Statements

Capt. K. Armistead, USMC, June 4, 1942

Capt. R. L. Blain, USMC, June 4, 1942

2d Lt. W. V. Brooks, USMCR, June 4, 1942

2d Lt. C. M. Canfield, USMCR, 6 June 1942.

Capt. M. E. Carl, USMC, June 6, 1942

2d Lt. R. A. Corry, USMCR, June 6, 1942

2d Lt. Daniel L. Cummings, USMCR (V), June 7, 1942

Capt. Elmer G. Glidden, Jr., USMCR (V), June 4, 1942

2d Lt. Charles S. Hughes, USMCR, June 4, 1942

Capt. W. B. Humberd, USMC, June 4, 1942

2d Lt. D. D. Irwin, USMCR, June 6, 1942

1st Lt. Daniel Iverson, Jr., USMCR (V), June 7, 1942

2d Lt. George E. Koutelas, USMCR (V), June 7, 1942

2d Lt. C. M. Kunz, USMCR, June 4, 1942

2d Lt. Thomas F. Moore, Jr., USMCR (V), June 4, 1942

2d Lt. J. C. Musselman, Jr., June 6, 1942

2d Lt. H. Phillips, June 6, 1942

2d Lt. Allen H. Ringblom, USMCR (V)

2d Lt. Harold G. Schlendering, June 4, 1942

2d Lt. Elmer F. Thompson, USMCR (V), June 7, 1942

2d Lt. Robert W. Vaupell, USMCR (V), June 7, 1942

Capt. P. H. White, USMC, June 6, 1942

2d Lt. Sumner H. Whitten, USMCR (V), June 7, 1942

Capt. Leon M. Williamson, USMCR (V), June 7, 1942

AAF "Action with Enemy" Forms

Lt. Col. B. E. Allen

Capt. Charles E. Gregory

Lt. H. S. Grundman

Capt. O. H. Rigley, Jr.

Lt. Col. Walter C. Sweeney, Jr.

1st Lt. Paul I. Williams

Capt. C. E. Wuerterle

Logs of Ships

Balch

Benham

Enterprise

Hornet

Hughes

Lexington

Monaghan

Nautilus

Pensacola

Tambor

Vincennes

Vireo

Official Diaries

Pearl Harbor Navy Yard

U.S. Naval Air Station, Midway Island

Patrol Squadron 24

Bombing Squadron Eight, June 1942

Journal of VII Bomber Command Liaison Officer at Midway, Battle of

Midway Supplementary Report R. S. No. 7-529.

Official Narratives and Interviews

Narrative by Lt. George Gay, Torpedo Squadron 8, Midway, Solomons, Munda, October 12, 1942

Narrative by Lt. Robin M. Lindsey, USN, recorded on 17 September 1943.

Interview with Lt. Col. Ira L. Kimes, USMC, in Bureau of Areonautics, Navy Department, Washington, D. C., August 31, 1942

Interview with Lt. Cmdr. C. C. Ray, Communications Officer, USS *Yorktown,* in the Bureau of Aeronautics, Navy Department, 15 July 1942

Interview with Lt. Cmdr. John S. Thach, USN, in Bureau of Aeronautics, August 26, 1942.

Miscellaneous Official Sources

Japanese Monograph No. 110, Submarine Operations in Second Phase Operations Part I: April–August 1942, compiled by Capt. Tatsuwaka Shibuya, General Hq, FEC, Military History Division, Japanese Research Division.

"The Battle of the Coral Sea, May 1 to May 11, inclusive, 1942, Strategical and Tactical Analysis," U.S. Naval War College, 1947.

"The Battle of Midway, including The Aleutian Phase, June 3 to June 14, 1942, Stragetical and Tactical Analysis," U.S. Naval War College, 1948.

U.S. Pacific Fleet and Pacific Ocean Areas, Press Release No. 56, June 16, 1942, covering broadcast over NBC at 1100–1114, June 16, 1942, over station KGU.

Unofficial Diaries

Adolf A. Berle, Jr., located in Franklin D. Roosevelt Library, Hyde Park, New York

RADM Sadao Chigusa

Cmdr. Cleo J. Dobson

Capt. Yoshitake Miwa

Henry Morgenthau, Jr., located in Franklin D. Roosevelt Library, Hyde Park, New York

Capt. Tasuka Nakazawa

Henry L. Stimson, located in Yale University Library, New Haven, Conn.

VADM Matome Ugaki. (The Ugaki diary has been published in Japan under the title *Senso Rohu* (War Records), by Nippon Shupan Kyodo, Tokyo, 1953. However, the extracts used in this study are taken from a translation prepared for Prange, who owned the English-language rights.

VF-6 unofficial log. A diary kept for the reference of the members.

Letters

Capt. Ray Davis, USN (Ret) to Barde, January 5, 1967.

Cmdr. W. G. Esders, USN (Ret) to Barde, October 10, 1966.

Capt. Shigeo Hirayama, JMSDF, to Barde, June 6 and 10, 1966.

Capt. Jack Reid to Prange, December 10, 1966. This letter included a statement by Robert Swan.

RADM W. F. Rodee, USN (Ret) to Barde, October 18, 1966.

Lt. Cmdr. Stephen B. Smith, USN (Ret) to Barde, February 3, 1967.

RADM Raymond A. Spruance to Admiral Chester W. Nimitz, June 8, 1942, with enclosure. (Copy in Prange files)

Admiral J. S. Thach, USN, to Barde, November 26, 1965.
Milton Tootle, IV, to Barde, November 9, 1966.

Miscellaneous Unofficial Sources

Unpublished doctoral dissertation, "Midway: A Study in Command," which Barde prepared under Prange's direction.

Masataka Chihaya, book manuscript concerning the Pacific War.

Material furnished Prange by Capt. Sakamoto of the Japan Self-Defense Agency's historical department, through Masataka Chihaya. Part 1 pertains to the war games of May 25, 1942. Part 2 pertains to various battle actions.

Written statement, Lt. Cmdr. Yahachi Tanabe to Prange, November 30, 1964.

Undated statement of Masaki Yamauchi.

Undated statement of Masayuki Saruwatari
Replies to questionnaires submitted by Prange from the following:
Admiral Raymond A. Spruance
Lt. Gen. Minoru Genda
VADM Ryunosuke Kusaka
Chuichi Yoshioka

Published Sources:
Books

Barker, A., *Midway: The Turning Point*, New York: Ballantine Books, 1971.

Buell, Thomas B., *The Quiet Warrior: A Biography of Admiral Raymond A. Spruance*, Boston: Little, Brown & Co., 1974.

Butow, Robert J. C., *Tojo and the Coming of the War*, Princeton, N.J.: Princeton University Press, 1961.

Churchill, Winston S., *The Hinge of Fate*, Boston: Houghton Mifflin Co., 1950.

Coale, Lt. Cmdr. Griffith B., USNR, *Victory at Midway*, New York: Farrar and Rinehart, 1944.

Craven, Wesley Frank and Cate, James (eds.), *The Army Air Forces in World War II*, Chicago: University of Chicago Press, 1948.

Dickinson, Lt. Clarence E., *The Flying Guns*, New York: Charles Scribner's Sons, 1942.

Forrestel, VADM Edmund P., *Admiral Raymond A. Spruance, USN: A Study in Command*, Washington: U.S. Government Printing Office, 1966.

Frank, Pat and Harrison, Joe., *Rendezvous at Midway*, New York: John Day Co., 1967.

Fuchida, Mitsuo and Okumiya, Masatake, *Midway: The Battle That Doomed Japan*, Annapolis, Md.: U.S. Naval Institute, 1955.

Gay, George H., *Sole Survivor*, Naples, Fla: Naples Ad/Graphics Services, 1979.

Griffin, Alexander R., *A Ship to Remember: The Saga of the HORNET*, New York: Howell Soskin, 1943.

Halsey, Fleet Admiral William F., USN and Lt. Cmdr. J. Bryan III, USNR, *Admiral Halsey's Story*, New York: McGraw-Hill Book Co., 1947.

Hara, Capt. Tameichi, *Japanese Destroyer Captain*, New York: Ballantine Books, Inc., 1961.

Hashimoto, Mochitsura, *Sunk*, New York: Henry Holt & Co., 1954.

Haugland, Vern, *The AAF against Japan*, New York: Harper & Brothers, 1948.

Heinl, Lt. Col. Robert D., Jr., USMC, *The Defense of Wake*, Washington; Historical Section, Division of Public Information, Hq. USMC, 1947.

————., *Marines at Midway*, Washington: Historical Section, Division of Public Information, Hq, USMC, 1948.

Hough, Frank, Ludwig, Verle E., and Shaw, Henry I., Jr., *History of U.S. Marine Corps Operations in World War II, Vol. I: Pearl Harbor to Guadalcanal*, Washington: U.S. Government Printing Office, 1958.

Hough, Richard A., *The Battle of Midway*, New York: Macmillan Co., 1970.

Hoyt, Edwin T., *How They Won the War in the Pacific: Nimitz and His Admirals*, New York: Weybright-Tully, 1970.

————., *The Japanese Story of the Battle of Midway* (a translation), Washington: U.S. Government Printing Office, 1947.

Kojima, Noboru, *Higeki no teitoku* (Tragic Admiral), Tokyo: Chuokoron, 1967.

Kusaka, Ryunosuke, *Rengo Kantai* (Combined Fleet), Tokyo: Mainichi Newspaper Co., 1952.

Lord, Walter, *Incredible Victory*, New York: Harper & Row, Inc., 1967.

Matsushima, Keizo, *Higeki no Nagumo Chujo* (Tragic Vice Admiral Nagumo), Tokyo: Tokuma, 1967.

Morison, Samuel Eliot, *History of United States Naval Operations in World War II, Vol. III, The Rising Sun in the Pacific*, Boston: Little, Brown & Co., 1950.

————., *History of United States Naval Operations in World War II, Vol. IV, Coral Sea, Midway and Submarine Actions*, Boston: Little, Brown & Co., 1949.

Okumiya, Masatake and Horikoshi, Jiro., *Zero!* New York: E. P. Dutton & Co., Inc., 1956.

Potter, E. B., *Nimitz*, Annapolis: Naval Institute Press, 1976.

Potter, John Dean, *Yamamoto, The Man Who Menaced America*, New York: The Viking Press, 1965.

Prange, Gordon W., *At Dawn We Slept*, New York: McGraw-Hill Book Co., 1981.

Pratt, Fletcher, *Battles That Changed History*, Garden City, N.Y.: Hanover House, 1956.

Sherman, Frederick C., *Combat Command*, New York: E. P. Dutton & Co., 1950.

Sherrod, Robert, *History of Marine Corps Aviation in World War II*, Washington: Combat Forces Press, 1952.

Smith, Chester Leo, *Midway: 4 June 1942*, Los Angeles, Bede Press, 1967.

Smith, Peter Charles, *The Battle of Midway*, London: New English Library, 1976.

Smith, VADM William Ward, USN (Ret)., *Midway: Turning Point of the Pacific*, New York: Thomas Y. Crowell Co., 1966.

Tuleja, Thaddeus V., *Climax at Midway*, New York: W. W. Norton & Co., Inc., 1960.

————., *United States Strategic Bombing Survey, Interrogation of Japanese Officials*, 2 vols., Washington: U.S. Government Printing Office, 1947.

Watts, A. J., and Gordon, B. G., *The Imperial Japanese Navy*, Garden City, N.Y.: Doubleday, 1971.

Werstein, Irving, *The Battle of Midway*, New York: Crowell, 1961.

Wolfert, Ira, *Torpedo 8*, New York: Literary Classics, Inc., 1943.

————. *Hearings Before the Joint Committee on the Investigation of the Pearl Harbor Attack, Congress of the United States, Seventy-ninth Congress First Session*, Washington: Government Printing Office, 1946.

Articles and Newspapers

Anzai, Jiro, "The IJN, or the Ill-omened Navy," *Bungei Shunjyui*, September 1966.

"Battle of Midway," *Flying* (February 1943).

Birmingham, Alabama, *News*

Bryan, J. III, "Never a Battle Like Midway," *The Saturday Evening Post* (March 26, 1949).

Burke, Admiral Arleigh, "Admiral Marc Mitscher: A naval aviator," *U.S. Naval Institute Proceedings* (April, 1975).

Chicago *Daily-Tribune*.

Collett, Lt. Cmdr. John A., "The Aircraft Carrier—The Backbone of Aero-Sea Warfare," *U.S. Naval Institute Proceedings* (December 1942).

Critchfield, John Sherman, "The Halsey-Doolittle Tokyo Raid," *Sea Power* (December 1971).

Dickinson, Clarence E., "I Fly For Vengeance," *The Saturday Evening Post* (October 24 and 31, 1942).

Eller, E. M., "The Battle of Midway," *Ordnance* (September–October, 1955).

Ferrier, Lt. Harold H., "Torpedo Squadron Eight, The Other Chapter," *U.S. Naval Institute Proceedings* (October 1964).

Fields, James A., Jr., "Admiral Yamamoto," *U.S. Naval Institute Proceedings* (October 1949).

"Fightingest Ship, Carrier *Yorktown*, Sunk Near Midway," *Time* (September 28, 1942).

Glines, Col. C. V. USAF, "The Day Doolittle Hit Tokyo," *AF and Space Digest* (April 1967).

————., "The Forgotten War in the Aleutians," *Air Force Magazine* (March 1968).

Gray, James S., "Development of Naval Fighters in World War II," *U.S. Navy Institute Proceedings* (July 1948).

Honolulu *Advertiser*.

Honolulu *Star-Bulletin*.

James, Sidney L., "Torpedo Squadron 8," *Life* (August 31, 1942).

Japan Times and Advertiser.

"The Japanese Story of the Battle of Midway," *ONI Review* (May 1947).

Lord, Walter, "Midway," *Look* (August 8 and 22, 1967).

Los Angeles *Times*.

Makajima, Teuchi, "Middoue no Higeki" (The Tragic Battle of Midway), *Shosetsu fan*, 1956. This series later appeared in book form.

Meridian, Mississippi *Star*.

Mitoya, Lt. Cmdr. Sesu, "I Fought the Americans at Midway," in Major Howard Oleck's compilation, *Heroic Battles of World War II*, New York: Belmont Books, 1962.

Mizrahi, Joe, "Farewell to the Fleet's Forgotten Fighter: Brewster F2A," *Air Power* (March 1972).

———., "Samurai," *Wings* (December 1977).

"Moment at Midway: McClusky's Decision," *U.S. Naval Institute Proceedings* (April 1975).

Moore, Tom, "I Divebombed a Jap Carrier," *Collier's* (April 10, 1943).

Morison, Samuel Eliot, "Six Minutes That Changed the World," *American Heritage* (February 1963).

———., "Two Minutes That Changed the Pacific War," *Illustrated New York Times Magazine* (June 1, 1942).

Morris, Frank D., "Four Fliers from Midway," *Collier's* (July 25, 1942).

The New York Times.

Nippon Times.

Okumiya, Masatake, "The Battle of Midway," *Nippon Times* (May 3 and 4, 1950).

Potter, E. B., "Admiral Nimitz and the Battle of Midway," *U.S. Naval Institute Proceedings* (July 1976).

———., "Chester William Nimitz, 1885–1966," *U.S. Naval Institute Proceedings* (July 1966).

Powers, Lt. Cmdr. Thomas E., "Incredible Midway," *U.S. Naval Institute Proceedings* (June 1967).

Pratt, Fletcher, "Nimitz and His Admirals," *Harper's* (February 1945).

———., "Spruance: Picture of the Admiral," *Harper's* (August 1946).

———., "The Mysteries of Midway," *Harper's* (July 1943).

Robinson, Walter, "AKAGI, Famous Japanese Carrier," *U.S. Naval Institute Proceedings* (May 1948).

Slonim, Capt. Gilven M., "A Flagship View of Command Decisions," *U.S. Naval Institute Proceedings* (April 1958).

Smith, Lt. Cmdr. Roy C., Jr., "Seapower and the Japanese Empire," *U.S. Naval Institute Proceedings* (November 1946).

Tanabe, Lt. Cmdr. Yahachi, "I Sank the YORKTOWN," *U.S. Naval Institute Proceedings* (May 1962).

Thach, John S., "Red Rain of Battle: Story of Fighting Squadron 3," *Collier's* (December 12, 1942).

Tillman, Barret, "Dauntless over Midway," *American Aviation Historical Society Journal* (Fall 1976).

"U.S.S. *Yorktown*—Sunk at Sea," *Life* (September 28, 1942).

Vogel, Bertram, "Japan's Navy and the Battle of Midway," *Marine Corps Gazette* (December 1947).

Washington *Evening Star*.

Interviews Conducted by Prange

Arima, Cmdr. Takayasu
Burford, RADM William P.
Chigusa, RADM Sadao
Davidson, Maj. Gen. Howard C.
Davis, Admiral Arthur C.
Farnum, Col. William C.
Fleming, Maj. Gen. Robert J.
Fletcher, Admiral Frank Jack
Fuchida, Capt. Mitsuo
Fujita, Iyozo
Kuroshima, RADM Kameto

Layton, Admiral Edwin T.
Mollison, Brig. Gen. James A.
Nimitz, Fleet Admiral Chester W.
Rochefort, Capt. Joseph
Shimizu, VADM Mitsumi
Shoemaker, Admiral James M.
Spruance, Admiral Raymond A.
Tanabe, Lt. Cmdr. Yahachi
Tomioka, RADM Sadatoshi
Tucker, Admiral Dundas P.
Watanabe, Capt. Yasuji

Interviews Conducted by Barde

Arnold, RADM Murr E.
Best, Lt. Cmdr. Richard H.
Brassfield, Capt. A. J.
Brown, Brig. Gen. Julian P., USMC
Buckmaster, VADM Elliott
Carey, Col. John M., USMC
Conaster, Capt. C. N.
Dobson, Cmdr. Cleo J.
Earnest, Capt. A. K., USN
Gallaher, RADM W. Earl
Gibbs, Capt. Harry B.
Holmberg, RADM Paul A.
Laub, Robert E.
Leslie, RADM Maxwell F.

McCaul, Col. Verne J., USMC
McClusky, RADM Clarence Wade
Miyo, Capt. Tatsukichi
Nagasawa, RADM Ko
Nimitz, Fleet Admiral Chester W.
Penland, Capt. Joe E.
Ramsey, RADM Logan C.
Ruehlow, Capt. S. E.
Short, RADM Wallace C.
Spruance, Admiral Raymond A.
Stebbins, Capt. Edgar E.
Tomioka, RADM Sadatoshi
Watanabe, Capt. Yasuji

INDEX